D1540592

# Training Systems Management

Southern Illinois University
Department of Workforce Education
and Development

Randy L. DeSimone
Rhode Island College

Jeffrey S. Hornsby
Ball State University

Peter Dowling
University of Tasmania

M. Eugene Hall (Editor)
Southern Illinois University

SOUTH-WESTERN

TM

THOMSON LEARNING

COPYRIGHT © 2003 by South-Western College Publishing, a division of Thomson Learning Inc. Thomson Learning™ is a trademark used herein under license.

Printed in the United States of America

**South-Western College Publishing**
**5191 Natorp Boulevard**
**Mason, OH 45040**
**USA**

For information about our products, contact us:
**Thomson Learning Academic Resource Center**
**1-800-423-0563**
http://www.swcollege.com

**International Headquarters**
Thomson Learning
International Division
290 Harbor Drive, 2nd Floor
Stamford, CT 06902-7477
USA

**UK/Europe/Middle East/South Africa**
Thomson Learning
Berkshire House
168-173 High Holborn
London WCIV 7AA

**Asia**
Thomson Learning
60 Albert Street, #15-01
Albert Complex
Singapore 189969

**Canada**
Nelson Thomson Learning
1120 Birchmount Road
Toronto, Ontario MIK 5G4
Canada
United Kingdom

ALL RIGHTS RESERVED. No part of this work covered by the copyright hereon may be reproduced or used in any form or by any means—graphic, electronic, or mechanical, including photocopying, recording, taping, Web distribution, or information storage and retrieval systems—without the written permission of the publisher.

ISBN 0-324-27632-X

The Adaptable Courseware Program consists of products and additions to existing South-Western College Publishing products that are produced from camera-ready copy. Peer review, class testing, and accuracy are primarily the responsibility of the author(s).

# CUSTOM CONTENTS

# 1

# INTRODUCTION TO HUMAN RESOURCE DEVELOPMENT

## LEARNING OBJECTIVES

*After reading this chapter, you should be able to:*

1. Define human resource development (HRD).

2. Relate the major historical events leading up to the establishment of HRD as a profession.

3. Distinguish between HRD and human resource management (HRM).

4. Identify and describe each of the major HRD functions.

5. Describe how HRD can be linked to the goals and strategies of the organization.

6. Recognize the various roles of an HRD professional.

7. Cite some of the contemporary challenges facing HRD professionals.

8. Identify the major phases of the training and HRD process.

**OPENING CASE**

TRW Inc. is a large manufacturer of automotive and aerospace products. Air bags, antilock brakes, and seat belt systems are among their leading products. TRW's headquarters is in Cleveland, Ohio. In 2000, it had over 100,000 employees in thirty-five countries. Over half of their employees were not U.S. employees. Their sales exceeded $17 billion in 2000, with over 40 percent of their revenues coming from international operations. Their mission statement reads:

**TRW is a global technology, manufacturing and service company, strategically focused on supplying advanced technology products and services to the automotive, space, defense and information systems markets.**

One of the challenges that TRW faced in the mid-1990s was the need for more leaders with global expertise. They wanted executives with expertise concerning issues in more than one country. They also wanted leaders who could help promote a seamless organization, that is, an organization that had fewer boundaries between functions, business units—and countries.

TRW had already established an executive development program that it called the Business Leadership Program (BLP). This was aimed at developing the top one percent of "promotable" employees. The BLP addressed issues such as global strategy, leadership style and behavior, culture, and organization capabilities. The program used various techniques during the formal training portion, including lectures, discussion, individual projects, case studies, and team-building interaction. There was also an "action learning" module, where trainees worked on individual or team projects based on actual issues that the company was currently facing. Approximately thirty-five people at a time went through the BLP process.

An assessment made by TRW senior managers was that, in general, TRW management did not have the level of global competency that was required to manage their increasingly global corporation. In particular, the company's succession planning process had identified a sufficient gap between the global skills required and those possessed by their top managers. This led them to refocus their leadership program, which they renamed the Global Leadership Program (GLP).

*Questions: If you were part of the leadership development team at TRW, what types of global or international issues would you like to see emphasized in the new GLP? What types of training methods do you think might be appropriate for training top managers and executives? Why? Are there other things that you would include besides formal training (e.g., projects, mentoring, overseas assignments)? Finally, do you think it is necessary for a global leader to have the capacity to work outside of his or her normal comfort zone? Why or why not?*

SOURCE: Neary, D. B., & O'Grady, D. A. (2000). The role of training in developing global leaders: A case study at TRW Inc. *Human Resource Management* 39(2/3), 185–193.

# INTRODUCTION

Have you ever:

- ■ *trained a new employee to do his or her job (either formally or informally)?*
- ■ *taught another person how to use a new technology, for example, how to conduct an effective PowerPoint presentation?*
- ■ *attended an orientation session for new employees?*
- ■ *taken part in a company-sponsored training program, for example, diversity training, sexual harassment awareness and prevention, or career development?*

- *gone through an experiential training experience, such as a ropes course or other outdoor learning experience?*
- *completed some type of career planning project or assessment, for example, a vocational interest inventory?*
- *participated in an organization-wide change effort, for example, your organization was seeking to change its culture and move toward a flatter, more team-oriented structure?*

If you said yes to any of the above questions, you've been involved in some form of human resource development. It is often said that an organization is only as good as its people. Organizations of all types and sizes, including schools, retail stores, government agencies, restaurants, and manufacturers, have at least one thing in common: they must employ competent and motivated workers. This need has become even stronger as organizations grapple with the challenges presented by a fast-paced, highly dynamic, and increasingly global economy. To compete and thrive, many organizations are including employee education, training, and development as an important and effective part of their organizational strategy. It has been estimated that education and training programs accounted for as much as 26 percent of the increase in U.S. production capacity between 1929 and 1982.[1] In 1995, Alan Greenspan, chairman of the U.S. Federal Reserve Board, stated, "It has become quite apparent that many firms have concluded that it makes more sense to invest in worker training than to bid up wage scales in a zero-sum competition for the existing limited pool of well-qualified workers."[2] A 2000 survey of human resource managers in large organizations ranked training and development as the most important functional area these managers had to deal with. This was followed in descending order by recruiting and selection, productivity and quality, succession planning, employee job satisfaction, compensation, globalization, and diversity.[3]

**Human resource development (HRD)** can be defined as a set of systematic and planned activities designed by an organization to provide its members with the opportunities to learn necessary skills to meet current and future job demands. *Learning* is at the core of all HRD efforts (and will be the central focus of Chapter 3). HRD activities should begin when an employee joins an organization and continue throughout his or her career, regardless of whether that employee is an executive or a worker on an assembly line. HRD programs must respond to job changes and integrate the long-term plans and strategies of the organization to ensure the efficient and effective use of resources.

This chapter provides a brief history of the significant events contributing to contemporary thought within the HRD field. We briefly discuss human resource management and HRD structure, functions, roles, and process. We also discuss certification and education for HRD professionals. We then describe several critical challenges facing HRD professionals. Finally, we present a systems or process framework that can guide our HRD efforts.

## THE EVOLUTION OF HUMAN RESOURCE DEVELOPMENT

While the term **"human resource development"** has only been in common use since the 1980s, the concept has been around a lot longer than that. To understand its modern definition, it is helpful to briefly recount the history of this field.

### EARLY APPRENTICESHIP TRAINING PROGRAMS

The origins of HRD can be traced to apprenticeship training programs in the eighteenth century. During this time, small shops operated by skilled artisans produced virtually all household goods, such as furniture, clothing, and shoes. To meet a growing demand for their products, craft shop owners had to employ additional workers. Without vocational or technical schools, the shopkeepers had to educate and train their own workers. For little or no wages, these trainees, or apprentices, learned the craft of their master, usually working in the shop for several years until they became proficient in their trade. Not limited to the skilled trades, the apprenticeship model was also followed in the training of physicians, educators, and attorneys. Even as late as the 1920s, a person apprenticing in a law office could practice law after passing a state-supervised exam.[4]

Apprentices who mastered all the necessary skills were considered "yeomen," and could leave their masters and establish their own craft shops; however, most remained with their masters because they could not afford to buy the tools and equipment needed to start their own craft shops. To address a growing number of yeomen, master craftsmen formed a network of private "franchises" so they could regulate such things as product quality, wages, hours, and apprentice testing procedures.[5] These craft guilds grew to become powerful political and social forces within their communities, making it even more difficult for yeomen to establish independent craft shops. By forming separate guilds called yeomanries, the yeomen counterbalanced the powerful craft guilds and created a collective voice in negotiating higher wages and better working conditions.[6] Yeomanries were the forerunners of modern labor unions.

### EARLY VOCATIONAL EDUCATION PROGRAMS

In 1809, a man named DeWitt Clinton founded the first recognized privately funded vocational school, also referred to as a manual school, in New York City.[7] The purpose of the manual school was to provide occupational training to unskilled young people who were unemployed or had criminal records. Manual schools grew in popularity, particularly in the midwestern states, because they were a public solution to a social problem: what to do with "misdirected" youths. Regardless of their intent, these early forms of occupational training established a prototype for vocational education.

In 1917, Congress passed the Smith-Hughes Act, which recognized the value of vocational education by granting funds (initially $7 million annually) targeted for state programs in agricultural trades, home economics, industry, and teacher training.[8] Today, vocational instruction is an important part of each state's public education system. In fact, given the current concerns about a "skills gap" (especially for technical skills), vocational education has become even more critical.

## EARLY FACTORY SCHOOLS

With the advent of the Industrial Revolution during the late 1800s, machines began to replace the hand tools of the artisans. "Scientific" management principles recognized the significant role of machines in better and more efficient production systems. Specifically, semiskilled workers using machines could produce more than the skilled workers in small craft shops could. This marked the beginning of factories as we know them today.

Factories made it possible to increase production by using machines and unskilled workers, but they also created a significant demand for the engineers, machinists, and skilled mechanics needed to design, build, and repair the machines. Fueled by the rapid increase in the number of factories, the demand for skilled workers soon outstripped the supply of vocational school graduates. In order to meet this demand, factories created mechanical and machinist training programs, which were referred to as "factory schools."[9]

The first documented factory school, in 1872, was located at Hoe and Company, a New York manufacturer of printing presses. This was soon followed by Westinghouse in 1888, General Electric and Baldwin Locomotive in 1901, International Harvester in 1907, and then Ford, Western Electric, Goodyear, and National Cash Register.[10] Factory school programs differed from early apprenticeship programs in that they tended to be shorter in duration and had a narrower focus on the skills needed to do a particular job.

## EARLY TRAINING PROGRAMS FOR SEMISKILLED AND UNSKILLED WORKERS

Although both apprenticeship programs and factory schools provided training for skilled workers, very few companies during this time offered training programs for the unskilled or semiskilled worker. This changed with the advent of two significant historical events. The first was the introduction of the Model T by Ford in 1913. The Model T was the first car to be mass-produced using an assembly line, in which production required only the training of semiskilled workers to perform several tasks.

The new assembly lines cut production costs significantly, and Ford lowered its prices, making the Model T affordable to a much larger segment of the public. With the increased demand for the Model T, Ford had to design more assembly lines, and this provided more training opportunities. Most of the other automobile manufacturers who entered the market used assembly line processes, resulting in a proliferation of semiskilled training programs.

Another significant historical event was the outbreak of World War I. To meet the huge demand for military equipment, many factories that produced nonmilitary goods had to retool their machinery and retrain their workers, including the semi-skilled. For instance, the U.S. Shipping Board was responsible for coordinating the training of shipbuilders to build warships. To facilitate the training process, Charles Allen, director of training, instituted a four-step instructional method referred to as "show, tell, do, check" for all of the training programs offered by the Shipping Board.[11] This technique was later named job instruction training (JIT) and is still in use today for training workers on the job.

### THE HUMAN RELATIONS MOVEMENT

One of the by-products of the factory system was the frequent abuse of unskilled workers, including children, who were often subjected to unhealthy working conditions, long hours, and low pay. The appalling conditions spurred a national anti-factory campaign. Led by Mary Parker Follett and Lillian Gilbreth, the campaign gave rise to the "human relations" movement advocating more humane working conditions. Among other things, the human relations movement provided a more complex and realistic understanding of workers as people instead of merely "cogs" in a factory machine.

The human relations movement highlighted the importance of human behavior on the job. This was also addressed by Chester Barnard, the president of New Jersey Bell Telephone, in his influential 1938 book titled *The Functions of the Executive*.[12] Barnard described the organization as a social structure integrating traditional management and behavioral science applications.

The movement continued into the 1940s, with World War II as a backdrop. Abraham Maslow published his theory on human needs, stating that people can be motivated by noneconomic incentives.[13] He proposed that human needs are arranged in terms of lesser to greater potency (strength), and distinguished between lower order (basic survival) and higher order (psychological) needs. Theories like Maslow's serve to reinforce the notion that the varied needs and desires of workers can become important sources of motivation in the workplace.

### THE ESTABLISHMENT OF THE TRAINING PROFESSION

With the outbreak of World War II, the industrial sector was once again asked to retool its factories to support the war effort. As had happened in World War I, this initiative led to the establishment of new training programs within larger organizations and unions. The federal government established the Training Within Industry (TWI) Service to coordinate training programs across defense-related industries. TWI also trained company instructors to teach their programs at each plant. By the end of the war, the TWI had trained over 23,000 instructors, awarding over 2 million certificates to supervisors from 16,000 plants, unions, and services.[14]

Many defense-related companies established their own training departments with instructors trained by TWI. These departments designed, organized, and coordinated training across the organization. In 1942, the American Society for Training Directors (ASTD) was formed to establish some standards within this emerging profession.[15] At the time, the requirements for full membership in ASTD included a college or university degree plus two years of experience in training or a related field, or five years of experience in training. A person working in a training function or attending college qualified for associate membership.

### EMERGENCE OF HUMAN RESOURCE DEVELOPMENT

During the 1960s and 1970s, professional trainers realized that their role extended beyond the training classroom. The move toward employee involvement in many organizations required trainers to coach and counsel employees. Training and development (T&D) competencies therefore expanded to include interpersonal skills such as coaching, group process facilitation, and problem solving. This additional emphasis on employee development inspired the ASTD to rename itself as the **American Society for Training and Development (ASTD).**

The 1980s saw even greater changes affecting the T&D field. At several ASTD national conferences held in the late 1970s and early 1980s, discussions centered on this rapidly expanding profession. As a result, the ASTD approved the term **human resource development** to encompass this growth and change. In the 1990s, efforts were made to strengthen the *strategic* role of HRD, that is, how HRD links to and supports the goals and objectives of the organization. There was also an emphasis within ASTD (and elsewhere) on **performance improvement** as the particular goal of most training and HRD efforts, and on viewing organizations as **high performance work systems.**[16] These will be discussed more fully below, but first it would be helpful to discuss the relationship between human resource management and HRD.

## THE RELATIONSHIP BETWEEN HUMAN RESOURCE MANAGEMENT AND HRD/TRAINING

In some organizations, training is a stand-alone function or department. In most organizations, however, training or human resource development is part of a larger human resource management department. **Human resource management (HRM)** can be defined as the effective selection and utilization of employees to best achieve the goals and strategies of the organization, as well as the goals and needs of employees. An important point to stress is that the responsibility for HRM is (or, at least, should be) *shared* by human resource specialists and line management. How the HRM function is carried out varies from organization to organization. Some organizations have a centralized HRM department with highly specialized staff, but in other organizations, the HRM function is decentralized and conducted throughout the organization.

The most comprehensive way to present the HRM function is to examine the activities carried out by a larger department, such as the HRM division headed by a vice president depicted in Figure 1–1. HRM can be divided into primary and secondary functions. **Primary functions** are directly involved with obtaining, maintaining, and developing employees. **Secondary functions** either provide support

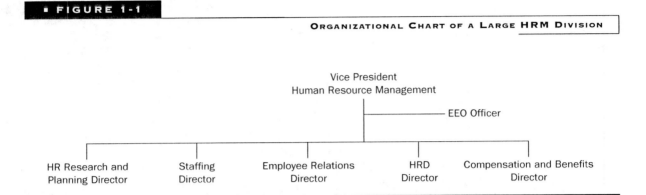

**■ FIGURE 1-1**

ORGANIZATIONAL CHART OF A LARGE **HRM** DIVISION

Vice President
Human Resource Management

— EEO Officer

| HR Research and Planning Director | Staffing Director | Employee Relations Director | HRD Director | Compensation and Benefits Director |

for general management activities or are involved in determining or changing the structure of the organization. These functions are detailed below.

### PRIMARY HRM FUNCTIONS

■ **Human resource planning** activities are used to predict how changes in management strategy will affect future human resource needs. These activities are becoming increasingly important with the rapid changes in external market demands. HR planners must continually chart the course of the organization and its plans, programs, and actions.

■ **Equal employment opportunity** activities are intended to satisfy both the legal and moral responsibilities of the organization through the prevention of discriminatory policies, procedures, and practices. This includes decisions affecting hiring, training, appraising, and compensating employees.

■ **Staffing (recruitment and selection)** activities are designed for the timely identification of potential applicants for current and future openings and for assessing and evaluating applicants in order to make a selection and placement decision.

■ **Compensation and benefits** administration is responsible for establishing and maintaining an equitable internal wage structure, a competitive benefits package, as well as incentives tied to individual, team, or organizational performance.

■ **Employee (labor) relations** activities include developing a communications system through which employees can address their problems and grievances. In a unionized organization, labor relations will include the development of working relations with each labor union, as well as contract negotiations and administration.

■ **Health, safety, and security** activities seek to promote a safe and healthy work environment. This can include actions such as safety training, employee assistance programs, and health and wellness programs.

■ **Human resource development** activities are intended to ensure that organizational members have the skills or competencies to meet current and future job demands. This, quite obviously, is the focus of this book.

### SECONDARY HRM FUNCTIONS

Other functions that may be shared by HRM units include the following:

■ **Organization/job design** activities are concerned with interdepartmental relations and the organization and definition of jobs.

■ **Performance management and performance appraisal systems** are used for establishing and maintaining accountability throughout the organization.

■ **Research and information systems** (including Human Resource Information Systems) are necessary to make enlightened human resource decisions.

### LINE VERSUS STAFF AUTHORITY

One of the primary components of an organization's structure is the authority delegated to a manager or unit to make decisions and utilize resources. **Line authority** is given to managers and organizational units that are directly responsible for the production of goods and services. **Staff authority** is given to organizational units that advise and consult line units. Traditionally, HRM functional units, including HRD, have *staff* authority. In general, line authority supersedes staff authority in matters pertaining to the production of goods and services. For example, suppose several trainees miss training sessions because their supervisor assigned them to duties away from the job site. Can the HRD manager or trainer intervene and force the supervisor to reassign these employees so that they can meet their training responsibilities? The short answer is no. The long answer is that HRD managers and staff must exert as much influence as possible to ensure that organizational members have the competencies to meet current and future job demands. At times this may require some type of intervention (such as organization development) to achieve a greater amount of understanding across the organization of the values and goals of HRD programs and processes.

## HUMAN RESOURCE DEVELOPMENT FUNCTIONS

Human resource development, as we discussed, can be a stand-alone function, or it can be one of the primary functions within the HRM department. The structure of the HRD function and its scope have been shaped by the trends faced by organizations. An ASTD-sponsored study by Pat McLagan sought to identify the HRD roles and competencies needed for an effective HRD function. The study identified four trends affecting modern HRD:

1. Greater diversity in the workforce.
2. More people involved in knowledge work, which requires judgment, flexibility, and personal commitment rather than submission to procedures.
3. Greater expectations of meaningful work and employee involvement.
4. A shift in the nature of the contract between organizations and their employees.[17]

The ASTD study documented a shift from the more traditional training and development topics to a function that included career development and organization development issues as well. The study depicted the relationship between HRM and HRD functions as a "human resource wheel" (see Figure 1-2). The HR wheel identifies three primary HRD functions: 1) training and development, 2) organization development, and 3) career development. We will now discuss these functions in greater detail.

### TRAINING AND DEVELOPMENT (T&D)

Training and development (T&D) focus on changing or improving the knowledge, skills, and attitudes of individuals. **Training** typically involves providing employees the knowledge and skills needed to do a particular task or job, though attitude change may also be attempted (e.g., in sexual harassment training). **Developmental** activities, in contrast, have a longer-term focus on preparing for future work responsibilities, while also increasing the capacities of employees to perform their current jobs.

T&D activities begin when a new employee enters the organization, usually in the form of employee orientation and skills training. **Employee orientation** is the process by which new employees learn important organizational values and norms, establish working relationships, and learn how to function within their jobs. The HRD staff and the hiring supervisor generally share the responsibility for designing the orientation process, conducting general orientation sessions, and beginning the initial skills training. **Skills and technical training programs** then narrow in scope to teach the new employee a particular skill or area of knowledge.

Once new employees have become proficient in their jobs, HRD activities should focus more on developmental activities—specifically, coaching and counseling. In the **coaching** process, individuals are encouraged to accept responsibility for their actions, to address any work-related problems, and to achieve and to sustain superior performance. Coaching involves treating employees as partners in achieving both personal and organizational goals. **Counseling** techniques are used to help employees deal with personal problems that may interfere with the achievement of these goals. Counseling programs may address such issues as substance abuse, stress management, smoking cessation, or fitness, nutrition, and weight control.

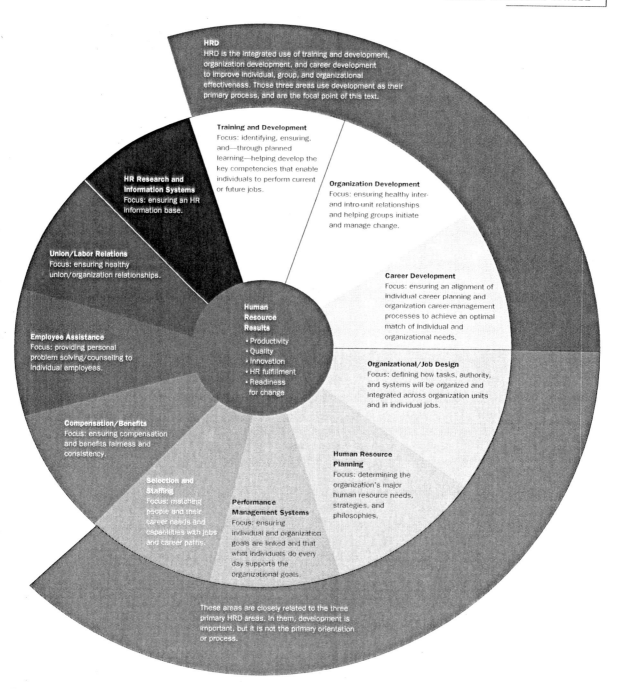

SOURCE: From P. A. McLagan (1989). Models for HRD practice, *Training and Development Journal*, 41:53.

HRD professionals are also responsible for coordinating **management training and development programs** to ensure that managers and supervisors have the knowledge and skills necessary to be effective in their positions. These programs may include supervisory training, job rotation, one-day seminars, or college and university courses.

## ORGANIZATION DEVELOPMENT

Organization development (OD) is defined as the process of enhancing the effectiveness of an organization and the well-being of its members through planned interventions that apply behavioral science concepts.[18] OD emphasizes both macro and micro organizational changes: macro changes are intended to ultimately improve the effectiveness of the organization, whereas micro changes are directed at individuals, small groups, and teams. For example, many organizations have sought to improve organizational effectiveness by introducing employee involvement programs that require fundamental changes in work expectations, reward systems, and reporting procedures.

The role of the HRD professional involved in an OD intervention is to function as a *change agent*. Facilitating change often requires consulting with and advising line managers on strategies that can be used to effect the desired change. The HRD professional may also become directly involved in carrying out the intervention strategy, such as facilitating a meeting of the employees responsible for planning and implementing the actual change process.

## CAREER DEVELOPMENT

**Career development** is "an ongoing process by which individuals progress through a series of stages, each of which is characterized by a relatively unique set of issues, themes, and tasks."[19] Career development involves two distinct processes: career planning and career management. Career planning involves activities performed by an individual, often with the assistance of counselors and others, to assess his or her skills and abilities in order to establish a realistic career plan. Career management involves taking the necessary steps to achieve that plan, and generally focuses more on what the organization can do to foster employee career development.

There is a strong relationship between career development and T&D activities. Career plans can be implemented, at least in part, through an organization's training programs.

## STRATEGIC MANAGEMENT AND HRD

Strategic management involves a set of managerial decisions and actions that are intended to provide a competitively superior fit with the external environment and enhance the long-run performance of the organization.[20] It involves several distinct processes, including strategy formulation, strategy implementation, and control. At the formulation level, top management must first assess the viability of the current mission, objectives, strategies, policies, programs, technology, workforce, and other resources. Then, they must monitor and assess different external environments that may pose a threat or offer potential opportunities. Finally, in light of these assessments, management must identify strategic factors (for example, mission, technology, or product mix) that need to be changed or updated.

The past decade has seen increasing interest, research, and action concerning strategic human resource management.[21] The emphasis has been on more fully integrating HRM with the strategic needs of the organization. To do this, two types of fit or alignment are necessary. First, as just described, *external alignment* is necessary between the strategic plans of the organization and the external environment that it faces. Second, *internal alignment* is necessary within the organization. That is, the strategy of the organization must be aligned with the mission, goals, beliefs, and values that characterize the organization.[22] Further, there needs to be alignment among the various sub-systems that make up the organization. Some areas that need to be addressed include:

- management practices—how employees are managed and treated (e.g., how much do employees participate in decision making?)
- organizational structure—how the organization is structured (e.g., how "flat" is the organization's managerial hierarchy?)
- human resource systems—how employees are selected, trained, compensated, appraised, and so on (e.g., how closely is pay linked to individual, team, or organizational performance measures?)
- other work practices and systems (e.g., to what extent is technology or information systems used to facilitate the work process?)

The value of this approach lies in looking at the organization as an entire system. All of the parts of an organization must work together as a whole to reach the goals of the organization. Some of the desired outcomes of such a **high performance work system** are increased productivity, quality, flexibility, and shorter cycle times, as well as increased customer and employee satisfaction and quality of work life.[23] As one example, Federal Express uses several different practices that foster high performance. Much of their employee training is conducted via interactive video instruction. A pay-for-knowledge system has been implemented that rewards employees who have completed the video training and passed job knowledge tests. A performance management system is in place that allows employees to track service performance, and an elaborate information system is used to monitor the progress of each item in the FedEx system. All of this is complemented by a survey feedback process that allows employees to "grade" their manager's leadership skills and suggest solutions for any problems they encounter. As you can see, it is the effective synergy of everything working together that defines high performance work systems.[24]

A current challenge (or opportunity) for HRD professionals is to play a more strategic role in the functioning of their organization. Progress has been made in moving toward a more "strategically integrated HRD."[25] In particular, HRD executives and professionals should demonstrate the strategic capability of HRD in three primary ways: 1) directly participating in their organization's strategic management process, 2) providing education and training to line managers in the concepts and methods of strategic management and planning, and 3) providing training to all employees that is aligned with the goals and strategies of the organization.[26]

First, HRD executives should contribute information, ideas, and recommendations during strategy formulation and ensure that the organization's HRD strategy is consistent with the overall strategy. The HRD strategy should offer answers to the following questions: Are the organization's HRD objectives, strategies, policies, and programs clearly stated, or merely implied from performance or budgets? Are all HRD activities consistent with the organization's mission, objectives, policies, and internal and external environment? How well is the HRD function performing in terms of improving the fit between the individual employee and the job? Are appropriate concepts and techniques being used to evaluate and improve corporate performance? Tom Kelly, director of worldwide training for Cisco Systems in San Jose, California, states that there have been dramatic changes in the HRD field since 1999. He adds, "This is our chance to actually achieve strategic partnerships within the organization."[27]

Second, HRD professionals should provide education and training programs that support effective strategic management. Training in strategic management concepts and methods can help line managers to develop a global perspective that is essential for managing in today's highly competitive environment. These issues are offered as part of the organization's management development program. According to a 1996 survey of HRD professionals by *Training* magazine, approximately 50 percent of organizations provide training in strategic planning.[28] Management education efforts (such as university programs, discussed in Chapter 13) also place a heavy emphasis on strategic management issues. Increasingly, separate courses (or portions of courses) are emphasizing strategic HR issues and how these relate to organizational strategies and outcomes.

Finally, HRD professionals must ensure that all training efforts are clearly linked to the goals and strategies of the organization. While this may seem obvious, unfortunately, it is not uncommon for the link between training programs and organizational strategy to be far from clear. As an extreme example, a medical products manufacturer, Becton-Dickinson, went through a major restructuring in 1983, in response to a downturn in its business. Before that they had offered a large number of training and education opportunities, particularly to their managers. After restructuring, these education and training programs were completely eliminated.[29] Some have argued that the reason training is frequently the first thing to be cut or reduced in times of financial stress is that top executives fail to see a link between training and the bottom line.[30] In contrast, IBM has set up a Human Resource Service Center in Raleigh, North Carolina. The goal was to provide information and high quality service to over 500,000 active and retired IBM employees. An array of technology was put in place to assist Service Center employees. This included Lotus Suite, a Web site within the organization's intranet (called HR INFO), a call tracking system, and an HR Information System, which employees and managers could use to view and retrieve HR-related information, as well as process certain HR transactions (salary changes, address changes, etc.). However, the key factor in the success of this effort was training. According to Bob Gonzales and colleagues,

"Training Customer Service Representatives well [was] critical to the Center's success because they are the initial point of contact with the customer."[31] Service representatives are carefully selected, and then put through three weeks of intensive training, including lectures, role playing, and partnering with an experienced employee. Refresher training is provided throughout the employee's career, as well as additional training whenever new programs are offered. This example suggests how training can be linked to the strategic goals and strategies of the organization (in this case, a shift to a centralized HR Service Center). As we will discuss in Chapter 7, HRD professionals are increasingly expected to demonstrate that their efforts are contributing to the viability and financial success of their organizations. The growing emphasis on strategic HRD is part of this movement to build a stronger business case for HRD programs and interventions.[32]

## THE SUPERVISOR'S ROLE IN HRD

Supervisors play a critical role in implementing many HRD programs and processes. As we will emphasize throughout this book, many organizations rely on line supervisors to implement HRD programs and processes such as orientation, training, coaching, and career development. Especially in smaller organizations, there may be no "training department" (or even an HR department), so most HRD effort falls upon supervisors and managers.

## ORGANIZATIONAL STRUCTURE OF THE HRD FUNCTION

The HRD function, like HRM, should be designed to support the organization's strategy. Using the chart from Figure 1–1, Figure 1–3 further delineates how the HRD function might be organized within an HRM department. Alternatively,

■ FIGURE 1-3

ORGANIZATIONAL CHART OF A LARGE HRD DEPARTMENT

Figure 1–4 depicts how the HRD function might be organized in a multiregional sales organization. In this example, the training activities, except for management/executive development, are decentralized, and other HRD activities are centralized.

## ROLES OF AN HRD PROFESSIONAL

An HRD professional must perform a wide variety of functional roles. A functional role is a specific set of tasks and expected outputs for a particular job. We will briefly discuss the roles played by two types of HRD professionals: the HRD executive/manager and the HRD practitioner.

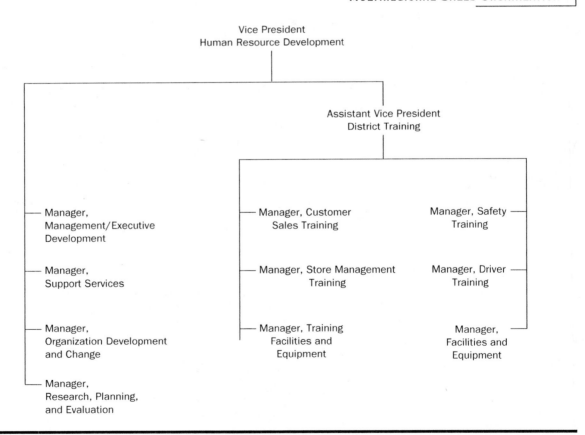

■ **FIGURE 1-4**

ORGANIZATIONAL CHART OF AN **HRD** DEPARTMENT IN A MULTIREGIONAL SALES ORGANIZATION

## The HRD Executive/Manager

The HRD executive/manager has primary responsibility for all HRD activities. This person must integrate the HRD programs with the goals and strategies of the organization, and normally assumes a leadership role in the executive development program, if one exists. If the organization has both an HRM and an HRD executive, the HRD executive must work closely with the HRM executive. The HRD executive often serves as an adviser to the chief executive officer and other executives. The outputs of this role include long-range plans and strategies, policies, and budget allocation schedules.

One of the important tasks of the HRD executive is to promote the value of HRD as a means of ensuring that organizational members have the competencies to meet current and future job demands. If senior managers do not understand the value of HRD, it will be difficult for the HRD executive to get their commitment to HRD efforts and to justify the expenditure of funds during tough times. Historically, during financial difficulties, HRD programs (and HRM, in general) have been a major target of cost-cutting efforts. Unless the HRD executive establishes a clear relationship between HRD expenditures and organizational effectiveness (including profits), HRD programs will not receive the support they need. But how does an HRD executive who wants to offer a program on stress management, for example, compete with a line manager who wants to purchase a new piece of equipment? The answer is clear: the executive must demonstrate the benefit the organization receives by offering such a program. Evaluation data are vital to the HRD executive when presenting a case.

The role of the HRD executive has become more important and visible as organizations make the necessary transition to a global economy. The immediate challenge to HRD executives is to redefine a new role for HRD during this period of unprecedented change. According to Jack Bowsher, former director of education for IBM, when HRD executives "delve deeply into reengineering, quality improvement, and strategic planning, they grasp the link between workforce learning and performance on the one hand, and company performance and profitability on the other."[33] The HRD executive is in an excellent position to establish the credibility of HRD programs and processes as tools for managing in today's challenging business environment. A 1999 *Training* magazine survey found that the average salary for U.S. HRD executives was $82,448.[34]

## Other HRD Roles and Outputs for HRD Professionals

As organizations have adjusted to environmental challenges, the roles played by HRD professionals have changed. Based on the ASTD study results, Pat McLagan states that contemporary HRD professionals perform nine distinct roles, which are described below.[35]

The **HR strategic adviser** consults strategic decision makers on HRD issues that directly affect the articulation of organization strategies and performance goals. Outputs include HR strategic plans and strategic planning education and training programs.

The **HR systems designer and developer** assists HR management in the design and development of HR systems that affect organization performance. Outputs include HR program designs, intervention strategies, and implementation of HR programs.

The **organization change agent** advises management in the design and implementation of change strategies used in transforming organizations. The outputs include more efficient work teams, quality management, intervention strategies, implementation, and change reports.

The **organization design consultant** advises management on work systems design and the efficient use of human resources. Outputs include intervention strategies, alternative work designs, and implementation.

The **learning program specialist (or instructional designer)** identifies needs of the learner, develops and designs appropriate learning programs, and prepares materials and other learning aids. Outputs include program objectives, lesson plans, and intervention strategies.

The **instructor/facilitator** presents materials and leads and facilitates structured learning experiences. Outputs include the selection of appropriate instructional methods and techniques and the actual HRD program itself.

The **individual development and career counselor** assists individual employees in assessing their competencies and goals in order to develop a realistic career plan. Outputs include individual assessment sessions, workshop facilitation, and career guidance.

The **performance consultant (or coach)** advises line management on appropriate interventions designed to improve individual and group performance. Outputs include intervention strategies, coaching design, and implementation.

The **researcher** assesses HRD practices and programs using appropriate statistical procedures to determine their overall effectiveness and communicates the results to the organization. Outputs include research designs, research findings, and recommendations and reports.

A 1999 article on "hot jobs" in HRD focused on employees in four jobs where there was a high demand for HRD professionals.[36] Three of those jobs are found in the list above: instructional designer (for consulting firm Arthur Andersen), change agent (for the city of Carlsbad, California), and executive coach (working as a consultant to teach "soft" skills to executives). The fourth job, multimedia master, is held by an individual trained in instructional technology and graphic design and involved in designing online learning courses for an information technology firm in Arlington, Virginia. For more information on this particular position and individual, see the nearby box, "Master of Multimedia."

### CERTIFICATION AND EDUCATION FOR HRD PROFESSIONALS

One indication of the growth of the HRD field is the push for professional certification. According to a survey of over 1,500 trainers, approximately 60 percent expressed a preference for some form of certification.[37] This response was probably based on an increasing desire to enhance the credibility of the broadening HRD

## MASTER OF MULTIMEDIA

Consider the following want ad: "Creator of award-winning training programs has immediate opening for dynamic individual in multimedia development department. Must have instructional design background and knowledge of Authorware or Dreamweaver. General business knowledge a plus." While this may not have been exactly how this appeared in a newspaper, this captures the type of person that Centech Group in Arlington, Virginia, was seeking to hire. Centech designs training programs for other organizations, and makes extensive use of the Internet and CD-ROMs for their programs. Therefore, they were looking for people with strong computer skills, especially knowledge of HTML and graphic design.

In 1999, Kevin Schmohl earned a master's degree in instructional technology from Bloomsburg University in Bloomsburg, Penn-

sylvania. Prior to that, he had worked in public relations and advertising. He was considered a hot commodity because of his knowledge of HTML, as well as software programs such as Tool-Book, Quest, Designer's Edge, Authorware, and Director. However, what really set him apart was his ability to know when to use Web-based training and when not to. "Until we get a totally computerized generation, we will always need some form of stand-up training," he says. As Kim Kiser writes, "Just because a company can put training on the Web doesn't mean employees will find those courses interesting or, for that matter, learn anything from them." What is most critical is to find course designers who understand training and instructional design issues, as well as the technological issues involved. Such people must "speak the language of both the training and informa-

tion systems departments," says Kiser.

David Brinkerhoff, a recruiter of HRD professionals, finds that some of his most difficult searches have been for people like Schmohl who possess the necessary computer skills, and also understand how to get their message across to various audiences. "It's a very unique combination," Brinkerhoff says. "Those people are worth their weight in gold, if they can deliver what they say."

When Schmohl interviewed at Centech after graduation, he was offered a position as an instructional technologist for $46,500. When he got home later that day, there was a message from Centech saying they wanted him so badly, they were increasing their offer by $2,000.

SOURCE: Adapted from Kiser, Kim (1999). Hot jobs, *Training*, 32.

field. For human resource management in general, two certification exams are offered by the **Human Resource Certification Institute** (in conjunction with the Society for Human Resource Management). They are called the Professional in Human Resources (PHR) and Senior Professional in Human Resources (SPHR) exams. Both exams consist of 225 multiple-choice items that cover various HRM topics.[38] Eleven percent of the PHR, and 12 percent of the SPHR exam covers human resource development. To be certified, individuals must pass the test and have two years of HR exempt-level work experience. Students who pass the test, but lack the work experience, are certified once they have obtained the relevant work experience. To date, over 43,000 HR professionals have been certified with either the PHR or SPHR designations.[39]

Over the past decade or more, the HRD profession has become better connected to and involved with the academic community. Three developments illustrate this relationship: 1) since 1990, the ASTD has co-published the *Human Resource Development Quarterly*, an academic research journal focusing on HRD issues; 2) the ASTD changed its governance structure to include a Professors' Network and an Academic Relations Committee; and 3) a new organization has been formed, the **Academy of Human Resource Development,** to further advance scholarly research concerning human resource development issues (see its Web address at the end of this chapter).

HRD programs at colleges and universities are most often found in one of three academic departments: business/management, psychology, and education. The Academy of Human Resource Development lists HRD programs (and links) on its Web site.[40] The content and philosophy of these programs tend to reflect the founding professors.[41] Certain schools of business (or management) offer majors or minors in HRD, with courses in training and development, organization development, and career development. The SHRM Foundation has recently published a directory of graduate HR programs, and placed this on the SHRM Web site.[42] Some psychology departments offer degree programs and courses in industrial and organizational psychology and personnel psychology with specific courses in HRD. In addition to HRD classes, schools of education may offer degrees and courses in fields related to HRD, such as educational technology, curriculum development, adult education, and organization development.

Another way HRD professionals can keep current is to examine the practices of leading organizations. The ASTD has established a Benchmarking Forum for the purpose of identifying and learning about the so-called best practices among member organizations so that they can be adopted by other organizations. The benchmarking process involves a questionnaire that "helps to define the focus, criteria, and context for practices, and provides information about the incidents that led to adopting the practices."[43] The best-practices organizations are selected at a biannual meeting of the ASTD and members of the Benchmarking Forum. These organizations and a description of their practices are published in ASTD reports and highlighted in the professional journal *Training & Development*.

## CHALLENGES TO ORGANIZATIONS AND TO HRD PROFESSIONALS

Many challenges face organizations as a new century unfolds before us. Michael Hitt and his colleagues have identified increasing globalization and the technological revolution (in particular, the Internet) as two primary factors that make for a new competitive landscape.[44] They suggest a number of actions that organizations can take to address the uncertainty and turbulence in the external environment. These actions include developing employee skills, effectively using new technology, developing new organizational structures, and building cultures that foster learning and innovation. These obviously have a great deal to do with human resource development. We will add to and build upon their list to present five challenges currently facing the field of HRD. These challenges include: 1) changing workforce demographics, 2) competing in a global economy, 3) eliminating the skills gap, 4) meeting the need for lifelong individual learning, and 5) facilitating organizational learning. Each of these challenges and their potential impact on HRD will be briefly discussed below and further amplified in later chapters.

## CHANGING WORKFORCE DEMOGRAPHICS

The workforce has become increasingly more diverse, and this trend toward diversity will continue. According to a report by Judy and D'Amico titled *Workforce 2020*, the following changes are predicted to occur by the year 2020:

- African Americans will make up about 11 percent of the U.S. workforce—the same as in 1995.
- Hispanics will increase to 14 percent of the workforce—up from 9 percent in 1995.
- Asians will increase to 6 percent of the workforce—up from 4 percent in 1995.
- Whites will decrease to 68 percent—down from 76 percent in 1995.[45]

The racial/ethnic shift will not happen uniformly across the country, but is predicted to occur most significantly in the West and the South. Women are predicted to increase from 46 percent of the workforce in 1995 to about 50 percent in 2020. The biggest shift will be in the age composition of the workforce. Overall, older Americans will make up a greater percentage of the workforce. People aged 55 to 64 are predicted to increase from about 10 percent of the workforce to about 20 percent in 2019, and people aged 65 and older are predicted to increase to over 5 percent of the workforce during the same period.[46]

These trends have several implications for HRD professionals. First, organizations need to address racial and ethnic prejudices that may persist, as well as cultural insensitivity and language differences (this will be discussed in more detail in Chapter 15). Second, with the increasing numbers of women in the workforce, organizations should continue to provide developmental opportunities that will prepare women for advancement into the senior ranks and provide safeguards against sexual harassment. Third, the aging of the workforce highlights the importance of creating HRD programs that recognize and address the learning-related needs of older workers (this will be discussed in Chapter 3).

## COMPETING IN A GLOBAL ECONOMY

As U.S. companies prepare to compete in a global economy, many are introducing new technologies that require more educated and trained workers. In fact, in the United States today, over one-half of all jobs require education beyond high school. Thus, successful organizations must hire employees with the knowledge to compete in an increasingly sophisticated market.

Competing in the global economy will require more than educating and training workers to meet new challenges. In addition to retraining the workforce, successful companies will institute quality improvement processes and introduce change efforts (e.g., high involvement programs). The workforce must learn to be culturally sensitive to communicate and conduct business among different cultures and in other countries. Developing managers to be global leaders has been identified as a major challenge for organizations in this decade.[47] Developing globally competent managers will be discussed in more detail in Chapter 13. Additionally, employers are learning and implementing new ways of managing their employees. Approaches to managing change will be discussed in Chapter 14.

### ELIMINATING THE SKILLS GAP

As we discussed, for companies to compete successfully in a global economy, they must hire *educated* workers; however, portions of the U.S. public education system are in need of considerable reform. Almost 30 percent of today's high school students fail to graduate, and employers must confront the fact that many young adults entering the workforce are unable to meet current job requirements. Even though the United States has one of the highest standards of living in the world, the Upjohn Institute for Employment Research reports that between 25 and 40 percent of hourly employees have some basic skills deficiency.[48]

This skills gap poses serious consequences for American companies. For example, how can trainees learn how to operate new equipment if they cannot read and comprehend operating manuals? Furthermore, how can new employees be taught to manipulate computer-controlled machines if they do not understand basic math? Obviously, the business community has a vested interest in education reform. There are some encouraging signs, however. For example, the Los Angeles public school system is offering a guarantee to employers, stating that if any high school graduate is found to be deficient in basic skills, such as computation and writing, the school system will retrain the graduate at no cost to the employer.

Other industrialized nations have made systematic changes in order to bridge the skills gap. For example, Japan and Germany, two of the United States' biggest competitors, have educational systems that do a better job of teaching students the basic skills needed by most employers. Among other things, Germany emphasizes vocational education and school-to-work transition programs, so that school-age children can begin apprenticeship programs as part of their formal education. These and other approaches will be discussed in more detail in Chapter 9.

### THE NEED FOR LIFELONG LEARNING

Given the rapid changes that all organizations face, it is clear that employees must continue the learning process throughout their careers in order to meet these challenges. This need for lifelong learning will require organizations to make an ongoing investment in HRD.

Lifelong learning can mean different things to different employees. For example, for semiskilled workers, it may involve more rudimentary skills training to help them to build their competencies. To professional employees, this learning may mean taking advantage of continuing education opportunities. This is particularly important for certified professionals who are required to complete a certain number of continuing education courses to maintain their certificates. To managers, lifelong learning may include attending management seminars that address new management approaches.

The challenge to HRD professionals is to provide a full range of learning opportunities for all kinds of employees. One way that some organizations are meeting this challenge is by establishing multimedia learning centers (sometimes on the organization's intranet). These centers offer a variety of instructional technologies that can be matched to each trainee's unique learning needs. Individual assessments can determine academic deficiencies or gaps in employees' performance capabilities, while also pointing out their preferred learning styles. For instance, self-motivated employees found to be deficient in arithmetic might be trained in an interactive video program allowing them to set their own pace. A multimedia learning center could also provide teleconferencing facilities for technical and professional employees to participate in a seminar that is being conducted thousands of miles away. These and other different approaches to learning will be discussed in future chapters. What is clear, however, is that whether they use multimedia or other training approaches, organizations must find a way to provide lifelong learning opportunities to all of their employees.

### FACILITATING ORGANIZATIONAL LEARNING

Organization development scholars such as Chris Argyris, Richard Beckhard, and more recently Peter Senge, author of the best-selling book *The Fifth Discipline*, have recognized that if organizations are going to make a fundamental change, they must be able to learn, adapt, and change. Senge advocates that a learning organization must embrace the following five principles: systems thinking, person mastery, mental models, building shared vision, and team learning.[49] In recent years, there has been tremendous interest in the concept of a learning organization. For example, a 1995 survey of HRD executives reported that 94 percent of the respondents felt that it is important for an organization to become a learning organization.[50] Chapter 14 includes a discussion of how macrolevel organization transformation approaches can be used to help an organization adopt the principles of a learning organization.

Although such principles emphasize the organizational level, they also have implications at the group and individual levels. One challenge to HRD professionals is to facilitate the transition of traditional training programs to an emphasis on learning principles and tactics, on how learning relates to performance, and more importantly, on the relationship between learning and fundamental change.[51] To do this, HRD professionals must develop a solid understanding of learning theory and be able to devise learning tools that enhance individual development. These concepts and tools will be discussed in more detail in Chapters 3, 9, and 12.

## A FRAMEWORK FOR THE HRD PROCESS

HRD programs and interventions can be used to address a wide range of issues and problems in an organization. They are used to orient and socialize new employees into the organization, provide skills and knowledge, and help individuals and groups become more effective. To ensure that these goals are achieved, care must be taken when designing and delivering HRD programs.

Designing HRD interventions involves a process, which includes a four-step sequence: needs assessment, design, implementation, and evaluation. For ease of memory, this can be referred to as the "A DImE" framework (assess, design, implement, and evaluate). In this book, we will use this four-phase process approach to describe HRD efforts: **needs assessment, design, implementation,** and **evaluation** (see Figure 1–5).[52]

### NEEDS ASSESSMENT PHASE

HRD interventions are used to address some need or "gap" within the organization. A need can either be a current deficiency, such as poor employee performance, or a new challenge that demands a change in the way the organization operates (new legislation or increased competition). For example, in 1997, when the extent of sexual harassment and sexist behavior in the U.S. Army became clear, the

**■ FIGURE 1-5**

TRAINING AND **HRD** PROCESS MODEL

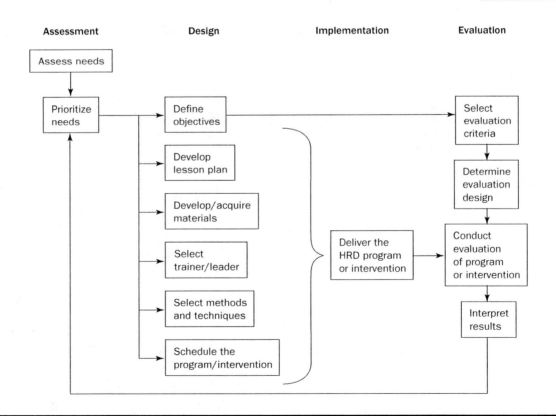

Army added one week to its eight-week basic training for new recruits to provide training in the values that the Army felt were necessary to end this behavior and ensure that its mission will be fulfilled. Similarly, in the 1980s, it became obvious to the Ford Motor Company that the poor quality of its cars and trucks was a major reason the company was losing market share to foreign competitors. In response, Ford boosted spending on HRD programs to train employees in quality improvement and problem-solving techniques.

Identifying needs involves examining the organization, its environment, job tasks, and employee performance. This information can be used to:

- establish priorities for expending HRD efforts
- define specific training and HRD objectives
- establish evaluation criteria

## DESIGN PHASE

The second phase of the training and HRD process involves designing the HRD program or intervention. If the intervention involves some type of training or development program, the following activities are typically carried out during this phase:

- selecting the specific objectives of the program
- developing an appropriate lesson plan for the program
- developing or acquiring the appropriate materials for the trainees to use
- determining who will deliver the program
- selecting the most appropriate method or methods to conduct the program
- scheduling the program

Once the assessment phase has been completed, it is important to translate the issues identified in that phase into clear objectives for HRD programs. This should also facilitate the development of clear lesson plans concerning what should be done in the HRD program. Selecting the proper person to deliver the HRD program is also an important decision, and it can be difficult, depending on the resources available. If the organization employs a group of full-time HRD professionals, the choice will depend largely on the expertise and work schedules of those professionals. However, if the organization does not have an HRD staff, it will have to rely on other people, including managers, supervisors, coworkers, or outside consultants. Using such individuals raises a host of issues, including their willingness, ability, and availability to train, as well as cost issues.

The design phase also involves selecting and developing the content of the program. This means choosing the most appropriate setting for the program (on the job, in a classroom, online, etc.), the techniques used to facilitate learning (such as lecture, discussion, role play, simulation), and the materials to be used in delivering the program (workbooks, job aids, Web-based or Web-enhanced materials, films, videos, PowerPoint presentations, etc.). Inherent in these decisions is the issue of whether to develop the program in-house or purchase it (or parts of it) from an outside vendor.

Scheduling the program may not be as easy as it appears. Issues to be resolved include lead time to notify potential participants, program length and location, covering participants' regular job duties, and potential conflicts (such as vacations, busy periods, and facility availability).

The needs assessment may also reveal that training is not the ideal solution for the issues or problems facing the organization. It may be that some management practice needs to be changed, or that changes need to be made in another human resource practice (such as selection or compensation). It may also be the case that a different type of HRD intervention is called for besides training, for example, a change in the organization of work, or a change in the focus on total quality or process reengineering. Such HRD interventions would not require a "lesson plan." However, other design issues occur with career management and organizational development interventions (and these will be discussed in later chapters of the text).

### IMPLEMENTATION PHASE

The goal of the assessment and design phases is to implement effective HRD programs or interventions. This means that the program or intervention must be delivered or implemented, using the most appropriate means or methods (as determined in the design phase). Delivering any HRD program generally presents numerous challenges, such as executing the program as planned, creating an environment that enhances learning, and resolving problems that may arise (missing equipment, conflicts between participants, etc.).

### EVALUATION PHASE

Program evaluation is the final phase in the training and HRD process. This is where the effectiveness of the HRD intervention is measured. This is an important but often ignored activity. Careful evaluation provides information on participants' reaction to the program, how much they learned, whether they use what they learned back on the job, and whether the program improved the organization's effectiveness. HRD professionals are increasingly being asked to provide evidence of the success of their efforts using a variety of "hard" and "soft" measures, that is, both bottom line impact, as well as employee reaction.[53] This information allows managers to make better decisions about various aspects of the HRD effort, such as:

- continuing to use a particular technique or vendor in future programs
- offering a particular program in the future
- budgeting and resource allocation
- using some other HR or managerial approach (like employee selection or changing work rules) to solve the problem

It is important that HRD professionals provide evidence that HRD programs improve individual and organizational effectiveness. Armed with this information, HRD managers can better compete with managers from other areas of the organization when discussing the effectiveness of their actions and competing for resources.

## ORGANIZATION OF THE TEXT

The text is organized to ensure the reader builds a base of *foundational* concepts before exploring the HRD process and the various ways that HRD is practiced in organizations. Chapters 1 through 3 present foundational material. As you have just seen, Chapter 1 presents an overview of HRD, including its three major areas of emphasis: training and development, career development, and organizational development. Because all HRD efforts involve trying to bring about changes in learning and behavior, it is important for you to understand why people in the workplace behave the way they do and how people learn. These issues are the focus of Chapters 2 and 3. Chapter 2 explores the major factors that affect workplace behavior, while Chapter 3 focuses on how people learn, the factors that affect learning, and ways to maximize learning.

Chapters 4 through 7 describe the HRD and training process, focusing on the activities described above, namely needs assessment, design, implementation, and evaluation. These chapters are anchored in the *framework* shown in Figure 1-5, and really provide the heart or main story line of the book. Chapter 4 details the importance of assessing the need for HRD and the approaches that can be used to perform a needs assessment. Chapter 5 focuses on designing HRD interventions based on the information obtained from the needs assessment. Activities discussed in this chapter include establishing program objectives and content, selecting the trainer, HRD methods and media, and the practical issues involved in delivering the program. Chapter 6 emphasizes implementation issues, and highlights the different types of training methods that are available to deliver training content, especially the increasing use of technology to deliver HRD programs. Chapter 7 completes our discussion of the HRD process by explaining the importance of evaluating HRD efforts and ways that evaluation can be done to ensure that decisions made about HRD programs are based on meaningful and accurate information.

The remainder of the book focuses on particular topic areas within human resource development, that is, HRD *applications*. Chapters 8 through 12 focus more on individual-level employee development issues, from orientation to career development. Chapter 8 discusses the socialization process, its importance to employee and organizational effectiveness, and how orientation programs can be used to facilitate successful socialization. Chapter 9 describes skills training programs, including ways to ensure that employees possess the specific skills (such as literacy and technological and interpersonal skills) that they need to perform effectively and contribute to the organization's success. Chapter 10 discusses the importance of supervision and coaching as an employee development process and explains how supervisors and line managers can successfully fulfill their critical coaching responsibilities. Chapter 11 provides an overview of employee counseling as a way to help employees overcome personal and other problems (such as substance abuse or stress) to remain effective in the workplace. Finally, Chapter 12 focuses on career development as a way to ensure organization members can be prepared to meet their own and the organization's needs over the course of their working lives.

The final three chapters in the book focus on more macro issues in HRD. Chapter 13 discusses how individuals can be developed to fulfill the multifaceted challenge of becoming effective managers. Chapter 14 explores how HRD can be used to prepare organizations for change, including ways to diagnose organizational problems and how to create and implement intervention strategies to improve individual, group, and organizational effectiveness. Chapter 15 closes the book with a discussion of the challenges organizations face as the workforce becomes increasingly diverse, and the role HRD can play in meeting these challenges and achieving the goal of full participation by all members of the organization.

We think you will find this to be an exciting and dynamic field. Everyone working in an organization of any size is impacted by human resource development. Whether you currently work in the field, some day hope to do so, or simply want to learn more about HRD, you will be affected by the topics discussed in this book. Our hope is that you will study and learn the content of this book, enjoy the process (really!), and then apply what you learn to your own work experiences. The concepts and models in this book can make you a more effective employee, manager, or trainer/HRD professional. The text before you (along with the materials on the Harcourt Web site) are our part. Your professor or instructor will add her or his part. But the last piece of the equation is yours—what will you put into and get out of your study of the field of human resource development?

## SUMMARY

This chapter traced several historical events that contributed to the establishment of human resource development. Most early training programs (such as apprenticeship) focused on skills training. At the turn of the century, more emphasis was placed on training semiskilled workers in response to the Industrial Revolution. It was during World War II that training departments as we know them today were introduced in many large companies. The establishment of the professional trainer led to the formation of a professional society (the ASTD). This culminated in the 1980s when the ASTD, in partnership with the academic community, officially recognized the professional designation of human resource development.

HRD, as part of a larger human resource management system, includes training and development, career development, and organization development pro-

## RETURN TO OPENING CASE

TRW faced a number of challenging issues as it restructured its leadership training to form the Global Leadership Program. | Many of the issues the company faced have been mentioned in this chapter. Your instructor has additional information concern- | ing what was done at TRW to develop greater global competence among their top managers.

grams and processes. HRD managers and staff must establish working relationships with line managers in order to coordinate HRD programs and processes throughout the organization. To be effective, HRD professionals must be able to serve in a number of roles. These roles will help the HRD professional to meet the challenges facing organizations in this new century. These challenges include changing workforce demographics, competing in a global economy, eliminating the skills gap, meeting the need for lifelong learning, and becoming a learning organization. The systems framework (assess, design, implement, evaluate) was presented as the major framework for promoting effective HRD efforts. The remainder of the book will expand upon the concepts introduced in this chapter.

## WEB SITES WORTH CLICKING ON

**American Society for Training and Development:** http://www.astd.org

**Society for Human Resource Management:** http://www.shrm.org

**Academy of Human Resource Development:** http://www.ahrd.org

*Training Magazine:* http://www.trainingsupersite.com

**Harcourt site for this textbook:**

> http://www.harcourtcollege.com/management/humresources.html

**Big Dog's Human Resource Development page:**
http://www.nwlink.com/~donclark/hrd.html

## KEY TERMS AND CONCEPTS

| | |
|---|---|
| apprenticeship training | human resource management (HRM) |
| ASTD | individual development |
| career development | instructor/facilitator |
| career management | learning organization |
| career planning | management development |
| coaching | multicultural environment |
| competencies | needs analyst |
| craft guilds | organization change agent |
| employee counseling | organization development |
| evaluator | orientation programs |
| high performance work system | professional development |
| HRD/training process model | researcher |
| human relations | roles |
| Human Resource Certification | skills training |
| Institute (HRCI) | technological change |
| human resource development (HRD) | training and development (T&D) |

## QUESTIONS FOR DISCUSSION

1. Do supervisors have HRD responsibilities? If so, how do they coordinate these with HRD professionals?

2. In your opinion, what competencies does an HRD manager need? How are these competencies learned?

3. What qualities do you think an HRD professional must possess to be effective in an organization of approximately 1,000 employees? How might your answer be different for an organization with 10,000 employees? Support your answers.

4. Briefly describe an HRD effort in an organization that you are familiar with. Was it successful? If so, why? If not, what contributed to its failure?

5. A manager states that "HRD must become more strategic." What does this statement mean, and what can HRD professionals do to practice "strategic HRD"?

6. Which challenges to HRD professionals discussed in this chapter will directly affect your present or future working environment? What additional challenges do you foresee affecting HRD?

## EXERCISE: INTERVIEW AN HRD PROFESSIONAL

Conduct an informational interview with an HRD professional. This could be someone working in the areas of training and development, career development, or organizational development. Some of the questions you might ask include 1) what do they do in their job? 2) what has changed in their job over the past five to ten years? and 3) where do they see the HRD field going in the next five to ten years? Your instructor will give you guidelines as to the appropriate length and format for the written document you turn in for this assignment.

## REFERENCES

1. Carnevale, A. P., & Gainer, L. J. (1989). *The learning enterprise.* Alexandria, VA: American Society for Training and Development (ASTD) and Washington DC: Government Printing Office.

2. Greenspan, A. Quips and quotes. *BNA's Employee Relations Weekly,* 13, December 4, 1995, 1315.

3. Langbert, M. (2000). Professors, managers, and human resource education. *Human Resource Management,* 39, 65–78.

4. Steinmetz, C. S. (1976). The history of training. In R. L. Craig (ed.), *Training and development handbook* (1–14). New York: McGraw-Hill.

5. Hodges, H. G., & Ziegler, R. J. (1963). *Managing the industrial concern.* Boston: Houghton Mifflin. Miller, V. A. (1987). The history of training. In R. L. Craig (ed.), *Training and development handbook* (3–18). New York: McGraw-Hill.

6. Miller (1987), *supra* note 5.

7. Nadler, L., & Nadler, Z. (1989). *Developing human resources.* San Francisco: Jossey-Bass.

8. Steinmetz (1976), *supra* note 4.

9. Pace, R. W., Smith, P. C., & Mills, G. E. (1991). *Human resource development*. Englewood Cliffs, NJ: Prentice-Hall.

10. Steinmetz (1976), *supra* note 4.

11. Miller (1987), *supra* note 5.

12. Barnard, C. (1938). *The functions of the executive*. Cambridge, MA: Harvard University.

13. Maslow, A. H. (1943). A theory of human behavior. *Psychological Review, 50*, 370–396.

14. Miller (1987), *supra* note 5.

15. Nadler & Nadler (1989), *supra* note 7.

16. Parry, S. B. (2000). *Training for results: Key tools and techniques to sharpen trainers' skills*. Alexandria, VA: ASTD; Van Buren, M. E., & Werner, J. M. (1996). High performance work systems. *Business and Economic Review, 43*(1), 15–23.

17. McLagan, P. A. (1989). Models for HRD practice. *Training and Development Journal, 41*(9), 49–59.

18. Beckhard, R. (1969). *Organization development: Strategies and models*. Reading, MA: Addison-Wesley; Alderfer, C. P. (1977). Organization development. *Annual Review of Psychology, 28*, 197–223; Beer, M., & Walton, E. (1990). Developing the competitive organization: Interventions and strategies. *American Psychologist, 45*, 154–161.

19. Greenhaus, J. H. (1987). *Career management*. Hinsdale, IL: Dryden Press, 9.

20. Wheelen, T. L., & Hunger, J. D. (1986). *Strategic management and business policy* (2nd ed.). Reading, MA: Addison-Wesley; Daft, R. L. (1995). *Understanding Management*. Fort Worth, TX: Dryden Press.

21. Schuler, R. S. (1992). Strategic human resources management: Linking the people with the strategic needs of the business. *Organizational Dynamics, 21*, 18–32; Ulrich, D. (1997). *Human resource champions*. Boston: Harvard Business School Press.

22. Van Buren & Werner (1996), *supra* note 16.

23. *Ibid*.

24. *Ibid*.

25. Gilley, J. W., & Maycunich, A. (1998). *Strategically integrated HRD: Partnering to maximize organizational performance*. Reading, MA: Perseus Books; Littlefield, D., & Welch, J. (1996). Trainers focus on a more strategic role. *People Management, 2*, April 4, 1996, 11–12.

26. Torraco, R. J., & Swanson R. A. (1995). The strategic roles of human resource development. *Human Resource Planning, 18*(4), 10–29.

27. Ellis, K., & Gale, S. F. (2001). A seat at the table. *Training, 38*(3), March, 90-97.

28. Industry Report. (1996). Who's learning what? *Training, 33*(10), 55–66.

29. Williamson, A. D. (1995). *Becton-Dickinson (C): Human resource function*. Boston: Harvard Business School, Case 9–491–154.

30. Watad, M., & Ospina, S. (1999). Integrated managerial training: A program for strategic management development. *Public Personnel Management, 28*, 185–196.

31. Gonzales, B., Ellis, Y. M., Riffel, P. J., & Yager, D. (1999). Training at IBM's human resource center: Linking people, technology, and HR processes. *Human Resource Management, 38*, 135–142.

32. Phillips, J. J. (1996). How much is the training worth? *Training and Development, 50*(4), 20–24.

33. Sorohan, E. G. (1995). Basic skills training on the rise. *Training and Development, 49*(5), 12–13; Gonzales et al. (1999), *supra* note 31.

34. Dobbs, K. (1999). Trainers' salaries 1999. *Training, 36*(11), November, 26–38.

35. McLagan, P. (1996). Great ideas revisited. *Training & Development, 50*(1), 60–65.

36. Kiser, K. (1999). Hot jobs. *Training, 36*(8), August, 28–35.

37. Lee, C. (1986). Certification for trainers: Thumbs up. *Training, 23*(11), 56–64.

38. http://hrci.proexam.org/hrci hand.pdf.

39. http://www.shrm.org/hrci/

40. http://www.ahrd.org/about/about __ main.html.

41. Gerber, B. (1987). HRD degrees. *Training, 24*(7), 49.

42. http://my.shrm.org/foundation/directory/

43. Overmeyer-Day, L., and Benson, G. (1996). Training success stories. *Training & Development, 50*(6), 24–29.

44. Hitt, M. A., Keats, B. W., & DeMarie, S. M. (1998). Navigating in the new competitive landscape: Building strategic flexibility and competitive advantage in the 21st century. *Academy of Management Executive, 12,* 22–42.

45. Judy, R. W., & D'Amico, C. (1997). *Workforce 2020: Work and workers in the 21st century.* Indianapolis: Hudson Institute.

46. *Ibid.*

47. Black, J. S., & Gregersen, H. B. (2000). High impact training: Forging leaders for the global frontier. *Human Resource Management, 39*(2/3), 173–184; Dotlich, D. L., & Noel, J. L. (1998). *Action learning: How the world's top companies are re-creating their leaders and themselves.* San Francisco: Jossey-Bass.

48. Sorohan, E. G. (1995). High performance skill survey. *Training & Development, 49*(5), 9–10.

49. Senge, P. M. (1990). *The fifth discipline: The art and practice of the learning organization.* New York: Doubleday.

50. Gephart, M. A., Marsick, V. J., Van Buren, M. E., & Spiro, M. S. (1996). Learning organizations come alive. *Training and Development, 50*(12), 35–45.

51. Argyris, C. (1994). The future of workplace learning and performance. *Training & Development, 48*(5), S36–S47.

52. Goldstein, I. L. (1974). *Training: Program development and evaluation.* Monterey, CA: Brooks/Cole.

53. Goldwasser, D. (2001). Beyond ROI. *Training, 38*(1), January, 82–87.

# 2

# THE HUMAN RESOURCE FUNCTION AND EMERGING FIRMS

## QUESTIONS TO CONSIDER WHILE READING THIS CHAPTER

1. Why is human resource management so important to smaller and emerging businesses?

2. What role should functional managers play in the human resource process?

3. What are the important human resource functions? Which functions should involve extensive managerial input?

4. What historical developments have helped the human resource function reach its current level of maturity and complexity?

5. What new challenges face those who practice human resource management?

## THE EMERGING ISSUE

Approximately 99.7 percent of all businesses in the United States have fewer than 500 employees and 78.8 percent have fewer than 10 employees.[1] However, most of the research and literature in human resource management has tended to focus on larger, more established companies. Most human resource management books assume that a firm has at least one human resource professional in place who has the expertise and competence to understand and carry out the practices they describe in their publications. Most smaller firms aspire to grow into larger firms. However, focus is needed to provide guidance on effectively dealing with human resource issues as a smaller firm emerges from a fledgling company to one that must deal with the challenges presented by larger employee groups. In support of this argument, a recent study of young entrepreneurs found that human resource (HR) topics ranked highest among areas for needed learning.[2]

## CHAPTER OVERVIEW

According to Abraham Zaleznik, "The work of human resources is to identify and develop people who have the talents and imagination companies need to compete in a changing, complex, competitive environment. That means that HRM [human resource management] ought to be the most important job in every business."[3]

Zaleznik's comments pinpoint the critical importance of human resource activities in organizations. However, the responsibility for identifying and developing key personnel does not rest solely in the human resource department. Managers play a crucial role in these and other human resource activities. In fact, managers actually implement most functions while human resource representatives administer and coordinate these activities. Specifically, managers are usually responsible for interviewing, training, appraising, and disciplining their subordinates. In addition, managers play important roles in compensation, safety, job analysis, and planning. Therefore, managers will serve as the first-line human resource managers for the company. This is especially the case in smaller firms and growing firms where the existence of a human resource department is less likely.

Events of the last decade have led managers to become more involved in human resource management. There are numerous pressures that have caused the "emergence" of human resource management as a general management responsibility. Listed below are eight critical managerial issues impacting emerging firms.[1]

1. *Increasing international competition.* Global competition from areas such as the Far East causes a need for higher employee commitment and more skilled employees.

2. *Increasing complexity and size of organizations.* Companies have been challenged by the need to reduce bureaucracy while at the same time dealing with a more geographically distant workforce. Employment laws and customs vary from country to country and managers must be aware of these differences.

3. *Organizational downsizing.* An organization's ability to offer career advancement opportunities has become limited.

4. *Greater government involvement in human resource activities.* Equal employment practices, especially the recent Americans with Disabilities Act and the Family and Medical Leave Act, place great responsibility on functional managers for compliance.

5. *Increasing education of the workforce.* Managers must now be concerned with the level of responsibility desired by employees.

6. *Changing values of the workforce.* Employees are demanding more involvement in the management of the organization. Managers need to develop mechanisms for more employee participation.

7. *More concern with career and life satisfaction.* Traditional assumptions about career paths do not hold true anymore. Lifestyle choices will continue to force companies to investigate alternative career paths to keep key personnel.

8. *Workforce diversity.* The increased numbers of females and members of minority groups in the workforce have forced companies to reexamine their employment policies and practices.

These eight issues, coupled with the other issues involved with growing firms, will continue to provide challenges for management in the future, especially in smaller organizations. The changing dynamics of the workforce, as cited above, coupled with the decreased supply of labor found in most communities, have made it very hard for smaller firms to develop a productive workforce.

## HUMAN RESOURCE MANAGEMENT IN THE EMERGING FIRM

The human resource management challenges facing organizations today are as relevant or probably even more relevant to the emerging company or organization. The

■ **EXHIBIT 1.1**

| HRM Practice | 1–50 Employees 1990 Use (%) | Current | 51–100 Employees 1990 Use (%) | Current | 101–150 Employees 1990 Use (%) | Current |
|---|---|---|---|---|---|---|
| Job analysis | | | | | | |
| Observation | 50 | 33 | 63 | 52 | 69 | 60 |
| Questionnaires | 10 | 9 | 21 | 14 | 46 | 27 |
| Interviews | 31 | 23 | 42 | 34 | 50 | 51 |
| Recruitment | | | | | | |
| Newspaper | 50 | 44 | 62 | 65 | 63 | 64 |
| Government Employment Agency | 27 | 18 | 38 | 25 | 50 | 28 |
| Private Employment Agency | 23 | 23 | 38 | 34 | 25 | 62 |
| Referrals | 67 | 73 | 75 | 73 | 69 | 71 |
| Walk-ins | 58 | 57 | 67 | 64 | 66 | 69 |
| Radio | 2 | 6 | 0 | 11 | 0 | 14 |
| Selection | | | | | | |
| Application blanks | 88 | 73 | 100 | 90 | 100 | 93 |
| Reference checks | 90 | 80 | 100 | 88 | 98 | 90 |
| Interviews | 100 | 90 | 100 | 97 | 100 | 93 |
| Drug tests | 2 | 27 | 9 | 34 | 24 | 48 |
| Psychological tests | 25 | 16 | 25 | 31 | 43 | 35 |
| Aptitude tests | 25 | 30 | 23 | 37 | 43 | 35 |
| Compensation | | | | | | |
| Market rate | 30 | 36 | 40 | 38 | 44 | 46 |
| Performance appraisal | 18 | 17 | 22 | 20 | 18 | 29 |
| Job requirements | 21 | 10 | 38 | 8 | 12 | 15 |
| Experience/Seniority | 34 | 27 | 33 | 32 | 28 | 22 |
| Minimum wage | 19 | 5 | 20 | 3 | 5 | 5 |
| Union contract | 2 | 2 | 6 | 2 | 12 | 7 |
| Incentives | 9 | 9 | 2 | 6 | 10 | 4 |

emerging firm is one that has grown in employee size and/or complexity, causing increased attention to employee attraction and retention and legal issues. Too many times, smaller but growing firms wait until there is an employee crisis such as a sexual harassment suit, an Occupational Safety and Health Administration (OSHA) penalty, or an inability to retain key talent before they start to focus on the human resource function. Recently, the need to investigate the types of human resource management issues for emerging firms has received heightened attention.

It has been recommended that the emerging firms develop an HR strategy similar to that of more recognized firms to be able to more effectively recruit key talent.[5] Also, it was found that venture capitalists are more likely to back firms that have vice presidents of human resource than firms that do not. It seems that they

| | **USE OF CURRENT HUMAN RESOURCE PRACTICES IN SMALL VENTURES** | | | | | |
|---|---|---|---|---|---|---|
| | **1–50 Employees** | | **51–100 Employees** | | **101–150 Employees** | |
| **HRM Practice** | **1990 Use (%)** | **Current** | **1990 Use (%)** | **Current** | **1990 Use (%)** | **Current** |
| Benefits | | | | | | |
| Health insurance | 68 | 66 | 95 | 89 | 100 | 100 |
| Dental insurance | 15 | 21 | 33 | 49 | 34 | 60 |
| Vision insurance | 5 | 16 | 22 | 18 | 9 | 31 |
| Life insurance | 54 | 41 | 85 | 66 | 97 | 66 |
| Disability | 37 | 28 | 73 | 59 | 87 | 66 |
| Pension | 19 | 24 | 53 | 51 | 67 | 63 |
| Sick leave | 27 | 37 | 55 | 67 | 70 | 76 |
| Vacation plan | 72 | 76 | 98 | 91 | 100 | 93 |
| Incentive plans | | | | | | |
| Commissions | 31 | 38 | 36 | 34 | 39 | 40 |
| Bonuses | 48 | 50 | 55 | 68 | 54 | 63 |
| Profit sharing | 17 | 13 | 31 | 28 | 26 | 31 |
| ESOP | 3 | 2 | 9 | 6 | 6 | 9 |
| Piecework | 4 | 1 | 16 | 6 | 5 | 0 |
| Standard hour | 3 | 5 | 16 | 10 | 15 | 6 |
| Gain sharing | 12 | 1 | 12 | 1 | 13 | 3 |
| Performance appraisal | | | | | | |
| Rating scale | 35 | 26 | 49 | 59 | 59 | 49 |
| Narrative essay | 29 | 33 | 49 | 48 | 59 | 37 |
| Goal setting | 32 | 31 | 49 | 48 | 59 | 37 |
| Training | | | | | | |
| On-the-job | 96 | 93 | 100 | 96 | 100 | 97 |
| Apprenticeships | 24 | 17 | 43 | 42 | 33 | 31 |
| Coaching | 79 | 67 | 85 | 70 | 69 | 69 |
| Seminars | 50 | 34 | 60 | 46 | 59 | 45 |
| Computer-aided instruction | 16 | 21 | 25 | 27 | 21 | 41 |

SOURCE: Hornsby, J. S., and Kuratko, D. F. (2000). "Human resource management in U.S. small businesses: Critical issues for the new millennium." *Proceedings: United States Association of Small Business and Entrepreneurship.*

prefer to invest in companies that have a senior management team member dedicated to people-related issues.[6]

These findings seem to imply that smaller, emerging firms are rushing to formalize many of the critical HR functions such as planning, recruitment, staffing, and compensation. However, another recent study suggests that many smaller firms may be lagging behind in terms of formalizing HR functions. As an example, two parallel studies were conducted over the last decade.[7] The results of these studies suggest that human resource practices in smaller ventures of all sizes have generally stagnated over the past decade. (See Exhibit 1.1 for a detailed description of the findings.) Important legislation and the changing dynamics of the U.S. workforce have not put enough pressure on small firms to increase their emphasis on human resource issues. It appears that the issues of concern in HRM by owners of smaller ventures have not changed significantly over the last 10 years. Attraction and retention of quality workers, benefits, wages, and government regulations are still recognized as critical HRM issues regardless of the venture's size. This finding may be the most valuable result of the research because it reveals that owners of small ventures have been concerned about the same human resource issues regardless of their size. In other words, although the sophistication of the current practices utilized by small ventures is affected by size, the perceived concern over the most important future human resource issues and trends has not been affected by size throughout the last 10 years. Regardless of size or ability to actually implement the procedures, small venture owners recognize and agree upon the same issues of concern for the new millennium.

It has also been suggested that the appropriate mix of human resource activities may assist a company that is pursuing an entrepreneurial-based strategy.[8] Schuler identified the following organizational characteristics as being associated with entrepreneurial efforts: creative and innovative behavior, risk taking, long-term thinking, focus on results, flexibility, cooperation, independent behavior, and a willingness to take on responsibility.[9] Others have also suggested that entrepreneurial activities in emerging firms require a culture that promotes emotional commitment, autonomy, empowerment, respect, and a strong work ethic. Thus, for an emerging firm to remain entrepreneurial, it should focus its recruitment, selection, and reward systems on the type of entrepreneurial behaviors that are critical to a growing firm.

The purpose of this book is to provide managers in and owners of emerging and growing businesses with an understanding of the important human resource functions as well as the practical tools necessary to carry them out. Very few research articles or books address this very important segment of business enterprise. The goal of this chapter is to introduce the human resource function to the reader by providing an overview of the different functional areas of human resources, briefly reviewing the historical development of the human resource function, discussing the role of human resource management activities in implementing total quality management, examining the HR focus in light of the entrepreneurial challenge facing organizations, and making suggestions for the future practice of human resource management.

## THE MAJOR HUMAN RESOURCE FUNCTIONS

The preceding discussion emphasized the importance of the manager in the human resource function. With this focus in mind, the specific human resource functions can be described. Exhibit 1.2 provides a model of how the various human resource activities fit together in light of the critical managerial issues discussed earlier. Examination of the model reveals two types of human resource

■ **EXHIBIT 1.2**

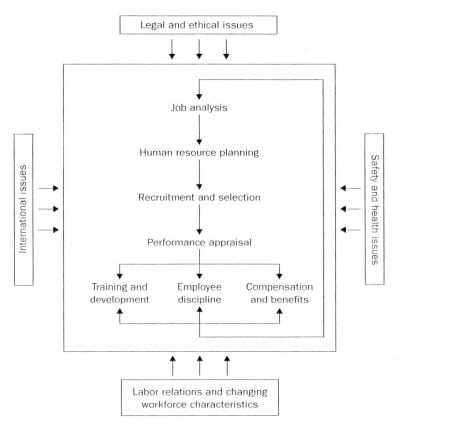

THE HUMAN RESOURCE PROCESS

activities. The first type of activities is core human resource duties. We refer to these as internal challenges and they include the following:

- Job analysis
- Human resource planning
- Recruitment and selection
- Performance appraisal
- Training and development
- Discipline
- Compensation

The second type involves external factors that influence the practice of the core activities. These challenges include the following:

- Legal and ethical issues
- Global challenges
- Labor relations and changing workforce characteristics
- Health and safety requirements

Let's examine types of human resource activities that are internal or external.

### INTERNAL FACTORS

**Job analysis** is the most fundamental human resource activity. The identification of the required tasks or duties to be performed provides the foundation for all other human resource activities. For example, conducting a job-related selection interview requires extensive knowledge of job responsibilities and requirements. Job analysis information is summarized into a job description and is used in recruiting, selecting, training, appraising, and compensating employees. Job analysis information also plays a major role in compliance with most Equal Employment Opportunity Act requirements. Although viewed as a tedious activity by many managers, documenting job-related information will help alleviate many future employment issues.

**Human resource planning** serves as a link between corporate strategy and human resource practice. Activities such as determining staffing levels, defining job requirements, and identifying training needs must be correlated with the goals and objectives of the company. In addition, the organization's ability to deal effectively with environmental changes related to the economy and technology is directly related to the success of the human resource planning effort.

**Human resource information systems** (HRIS) are important for effective human resource planning. Included in such an information system are job requirements and data concerning employees' knowledge, skills, abilities, and interests. This type of information, if readily accessible, can accelerate the hiring process and aid in succession planning activities. The success of the human resource planning process relies on top management viewing the human resource management function as a strategic function necessary for organizational goal accomplishment.

The attraction and retention of quality personnel have been consistent problems for organizations over the last decade, especially for smaller firms wanting to grow. As mentioned earlier, in two parallel studies conducted 10 years apart, this issue had not changed as the number one priority for firms with fewer than 150 employees.[10] Employee recruitment and selection are activities in which the general manager plays a critical role. With the assistance of accurate job analysis information, the manager must identify the job specifications required when recruiting potential employees. The **recruitment** process involves activities such as determining the appropriate sources of applicants, managing recruitment operations, and evaluating recruiting effectiveness. The success of any recruitment effort is its ability to develop a large pool of qualified applicants from whom to choose. The larger the pool of applicants, the more likely the firm is to make a successful selection decision.

The **selection** process involves using procedures such as application blanks, interviews, reference and background checks, aptitude tests, and drug testing. The selection procedures used for any position must be related to job content to meet Equal Employment Opportunity Act requirements. In most instances, managers over-rely on interviews as their main selection procedure. It is important to utilize other selection devices when appropriate. This will increase the likelihood of a successful selection decision.

**Performance appraisal** involves the evaluation of how well employees perform their jobs. Performance appraisal is a direct responsibility of the manager and often determines employee training needs, pay increases, and sometimes discipline. It is important that the standards utilized for appraisal be related to job content. If job relatedness can be substantiated, performance appraisal data can be utilized to defend employment decisions.

**Training and development** activities include providing employee orientation, training employees to perform their current jobs, and developing new employee skills and abilities as jobs change or employees are promoted. The specific activities involved in developing a training program include needs assessment, selection of appropriate methods, and evaluation. Training should be a critical concern for emerging firms as they attempt to develop a staff to meet increasing demands.

If an employee violates a company policy or is unable to perform his or her job at an acceptable level, disciplinary action should be expected. Organizations should identify the types of employee actions that necessitate disciplinary actions and create a formal step-by-step procedure for carrying out them out. **Discipline** usually includes one of three actions. These actions are incremental/progressive discipline (i.e., verbal warning, written warning, probation, etc.), suspension, and termination. It is important that documentation be maintained at every step in the discipline process in case an employment decision needs to be justified in court.

**Employee compensation** is usually divided into two categories: direct monetary compensation and benefits such as health insurance and retirement plans. Organizations should develop compensation systems that are competitive with those of other organizations and that are fair to employees based on various inputs each employee brings to the job (i.e., education, skill, and effort). Activities such as job evaluation, market pricing, and pay for performance programs are used to determine direct compensation.

The development of an effective benefits package is one of the most complex human resource functions. Rising insurance costs coupled with the changing lifestyles of employees have created a demand for organizations to scrutinize their benefits packages. One such response to these changes is the use of some type of flexible benefits plan.

## EXTERNAL CHALLENGES

As seen in Exhibit 1.2, the environmental factors described below influence the human resource function. An understanding of these factors is critical to human resource management.

There are a host of **legal** and **ethical** issues involved with human resource activities. Most human resource activities have gained importance because of one of several pieces of equal employment legislation or Supreme Court decisions. This fact was especially evident in the 1990s with the passage of the Americans with Disabilities Act and the Family and Medical Leave Act. These more recent acts required organizations to reevaluate their selection and benefit practices. All employment decisions must be made in light of the legislation and court decisions that exist to protect the rights of employees, especially those in "protected classes" identified in discrimination legislation. Other legal issues have been defined by the courts, not by Congress. The two most common of these are employment-at-will and negligent hiring or retention.

The geographic boundaries for businesses are rapidly expanding and the **global market** is easily accessible. For most professional employees, the likelihood of having at least one international assignment during their careers has increased greatly. Also, employees from sites located in other countries may be transferred to the United States. The exporting and importing of employees raises important recruitment, selection, training, and compensation issues. In addition, cultural differences as well as cost-of-living adjustments must be addressed for a successful international assignment.

**Labor relations** and **workforce diversity** will continue to challenge firms. While union membership may be on the decline, the involvement of unions in key industries such as auto manufacturing and transportation requires some understanding of labor relations. A basic understanding of legal requirements, contract negotiation tactics, and contract administration issues can help improve labor-management relationships. In addition, the use of employee grievance procedures has become an important employee relations tool in non-unionized firms.

In addition, managing a diverse workforce (e.g., increasing numbers of female, physically challenged, ethnically diverse, and aging employees) provides new challenges in recruitment, selection, training, and performance appraisal.

**Health and safety issues** have always been a concern, especially in manufacturing environments. The Occupation Safety and Health Act of 1970 legally requires companies to maintain a safe and healthy work environment. Regulations established by OSHA have as their goal the reduction of workplace accidents and illness. Some of the most common regulations center on the handling and use of hazardous chemicals, lock-out/tag-out of dangerous equipment, confined space entry, and air quality. OSHA has also established investigation and enforcement activities to ensure adherence to the Act. Emerging firms in the manufacturing and medical sectors must attend to OSHA regulations as they grow and expand with additional equipment and untrained employees.

## THE HISTORICAL DEVELOPMENT OF THE HUMAN RESOURCE FUNCTION

Essentially, human resource management originated as a very rigid discipline, emphasizing record keeping and payroll systems; however, it has grown into a very complex set of responsibilities involving employee motivation, total quality management, and strategic planning. With the evolution of the complexity of human resource activities also came an increasing demand for expertise in human resource practitioners. The historical development of the human resource function can be divided into at least five major periods. Each period and the activities that promoted it are described below.

### PRE-1910: PRODUCTION CENTERED

The first period, which is considered to be before 1910, emphasized a production mentality in which the major concern was producing products as cheaply as possible. There was almost no need for any human resource function. The work was of the unskilled variety, and laborers were asked to work long hours for very low wages. Those employees who could not keep up were simply replaced. Employers also took somewhat of a paternalistic approach toward their employees. In some cases, they provided the employees with housing and other services to ensure a steady workforce.

### 1910–1930: THE BIRTH OF THE HR FUNCTION

During this period, the human resource function started to include some of the more traditional activities of employee selection and training. The skills required for jobs grew in complexity, and employees started expressing a desire for work that suited their individual needs. Several activities spurred these changes. These included the Psychological Reform Movement that occurred in the 1920s and 1930s, the implementation of scientific management principles, and World War I. These changes caused an increased demand for efficiency and work specialization.

### 1930–1960: HR'S CHILDHOOD — A TIME OF EXPANDING RESPONSIBILITIES

Three major historical changes greatly affected the growth and importance of human resource activities. First, several fundamental pieces of legislation that dictated how organizations treat their employees were passed. The legislation enacted during this period gave unions the right to exist, established ground rules for union-management relations, specified a minimum wage, outlined child labor requirements, and set overtime pay guidelines. Second, employee values changed dramatically. Experiences with World Wars I and II coupled with increasing levels of skill and education brought employees an overall awareness of what they valued in terms of their jobs. Third, as a response to legislation and changing employee values, there was a shift in personnel philosophy. Companies became more human relations oriented, focusing on employee morale and job satisfaction.

### 1960–1980: HR's Teenage Years — An Increasing Awareness of the Value of Employees

As an outgrowth of the changes that occurred from 1930 to 1960, employers worked to increase employee participation and redesign jobs to make them more challenging and interesting. During this time employees were beginning to be viewed as a valuable resource to a firm. This new outlook prompted a change in the name of the field from "Personnel Management" to "Human Resource Management." Also during this time, most of the currently existing discrimination legislation was passed by the U.S. Congress. Organizations were then legally responsible for prevention of discrimination in their employment decisions.

### 1980–Present: The Maturing of the HR Function — Dealing with Crisis Management

The current period presents many new challenges to the human resource function. Employee displacement through downsizing has brought about a renewed emphasis on training so that these displaced workers can gain skills, which will make them employable in the marketplace. Also, legislation such as the Americans with Disabilities Act and the Family and Medical Leave Act is forcing employers to take another look at their hiring and benefits policies.

## HUMAN RESOURCE MANAGEMENT'S ROLE IN TOTAL QUALITY MANAGEMENT

Improving quality has become a key objective for most managers. Traditionally the quality movement has focused on technical system improvements. According to Bowen and Lawler[11] this emphasis is necessary but may not be the "key variable" in enhancing quality. They cite a recent Gallup survey of senior managers concerning total quality management, which found that managers most frequently cited productivity and quality as the top competitive issues facing their firms. Furthermore, senior managers were asked to rank the most effective approaches to improving quality. The top eight approaches were the following:

1. Employee motivation
2. Change in corporate culture
3. Employee education
4. Process control
5. Expenditures on capital equipment
6. More control of supplies
7. More inspections
8. Improved administrative support

While some of these approaches to quality enhancement involve technical improvements, it is obvious that the majority of the most effective approaches to improving quality center on the effective management of human resources. Bowen and Lawler add further evidence for the importance of human resource management in the quality process by citing the fact that utilization of human resources is one of the seven categories evaluated for determining the Malcolm Baldridge National Quality Awards.

A survey of 184 small firms in the United States was conducted using a classification scheme for quality systems consistent with the Malcolm Baldridge National Quality Award (MBNQA) performance criteria. These criteria include leadership, strategic planning, customer and market focus, information and analysis, human resource focus, process management, and business results.[12] Overall, the results support the proposition that small firms tend to employ quality practices that enable change and position the firm to pursue flexibility as a competitive priority.

In particular, the importance of a human resource focus was highlighted. The survey findings suggest that quality strategies focusing on training programs, employee involvement, employee/team recognition programs, and formal education programs were rated as moderately to highly valuable. However, except for training programs, less than half of the respondents used these quality strategies.

How can human resource activities be utilized to enhance quality? It is recommended that the same principles of total quality management (TQM) that are applied elsewhere in the organization be applied to human resources. The five most common principles of total quality management[13] are (1) quality work the first time, (2) focus on the customer, (3) strategic, holistic approach to improvement, (4) continuous improvements as a way of life, and (5) mutual respect and teamwork. Additionally, a recent study of small to medium-sized manufacturing firms found that a TQM strategy was most effective when it was supported by significant training and group-based compensation. The study found that goal setting and incentive compensation systems yielded positive TQM results and did not have a dysfunctional effect on the implementation of TQM.[14]

Human resource employees as well as the managers who perform human resource activities should approach their work in human resources with the same quality emphasis that they place on other functions. Quick fixes or quick decisions should be avoided and the decision-maker should be given the time and resources necessary to make quality decisions. For example, managers often view performance appraisal as a painful, time-consuming process that is somewhat unrelated to the rest of their activities. Top management should emphasize the importance of appraisals by integrating them into corporate decision making and provide managers with the time to effectively conduct their appraisals. Also, to accomplish this, managers need to be given training to both write the appraisal and conduct the appraisal interview. At the managerial level this applies to other human resource activities including job analysis, selection, training, and compensation. If the firm has a human resource department, its staff should take the time to evaluate their programs on a regular basis instead of repeating an activity without knowing how effective it is in terms of achieving company objectives. Furthermore, human resource departments need to be more sensitive to employees' needs instead of focusing on their own special projects.

## HUMAN RESOURCE MANAGEMENT AND THE ENTREPRENEURIAL CHALLENGE

It is important for owners and managers of emerging organizations to establish a firm that remains flexible during the growth stages. Kuratko and Hodgetts emphasize the need for the development of an "adaptive firm," which provides continued opportunity for employees to be innovative and entrepreneurial.[15] However, entrepreneurial activities require employees to act and think in ways not normally associated with bureaucratic organizations. Thus, the challenge for emerging companies is to recognize and implement the particular human resource practices that will enhance the levels of entrepreneurial activity by employees.

One of the few studies that attempted to determine if HRM practices actually affect entrepreneurial performance in companies was conducted by Morris and Jones.[16] They conducted a cross-sectional survey of multiple managers in companies representing a wide range of industries. They focused on human resource management practices as they were being applied to midlevel operational managers. A total of 36 practices in the five categories presented in Exhibit 1.3 (planning and job design, selection and staffing, training and development, appraisal, and compensation) were evaluated. The research attempted to capture the dimensionality reflected in the HRM practices. For instance, respondents were asked to characterize the extent to which selection and staffing practices rely primarily on internal versus external sources for job candidates and are based on implicit selection criteria. In addition, levels of entrepreneurship in the companies were measured using a scale developed for the purpose of assessing the degree and amount of entrepreneurial activity.[17]

Using the median scores produced from the survey, firms were split into two groups: those with a stronger entrepreneurial orientation and those with a weaker entrepreneurial orientation. Statistical analysis was then used to determine whether firms that were more entrepreneurial differed from their less entrepreneurial counterparts with regard to the 36 HRM practices. Those firms demonstrating stronger entrepreneurial orientations were more likely to have selection and staffing procedures designed around multiple career paths and extensive socialization and orientation of new employees.

Training and development programs in more entrepreneurial firms were more likely to include high employee participation and active trainee involvement, be group oriented, assume a longer-term career perspective, be systematic and planned, and be continuous or ongoing. The performance appraisals in these organizations included higher employee involvement and participation in the process, a greater emphasis on individual performance criteria, assessments based more on outcomes or end results, a longer-term performance focus, and explicit

■ **EXHIBIT 1.3**

**HRM POLICIES CONSISTENT WITH
ENTREPRENEURIAL BEHAVIOR**

| General Area | Practices Encouraging Entrepreneurship |
|---|---|
| Planning/Overall Job Design | Reliance on formal planning<br>Long-term orientation in planning and job design<br>Implicit job analysis<br>Jobs that are broad in scope<br>Jobs with significant structure<br>Integrated job design<br>Results-orientated job design<br>High employee involvement |
| Recruitment and Selection | Reliance on external and internal sources for candidates<br>Broad career paths<br>Multiple career ladders<br>General, implicit, less formalized selection criteria<br>Extensive job socialization<br>Open recruitment and selection procedures |
| Training and Development | Long-term career orientation<br>Training with broad applications<br>Individualized training<br>High employee participation<br>Unsystematic training<br>Emphasis on managerial skills<br>Continuous/ongoing training |
| Performance Appraisal | High employee involvement<br>Balanced individual-group orientation<br>Emphasis on effectiveness over efficiency<br>Result oriented (vs. process)<br>Based on subjective criteria<br>Emphasis on long-term performance<br>Includes innovation and risk criteria<br>Reflects tolerance of failure<br>Appraisals done based on project life cycle |
| Compensation/Rewards | Emphasizes long-term performance<br>Decentralized/customized at division or department levels<br>Tailored to individuals<br>Emphasizes individuals' performance with incentives for group efforts<br>Merit and incentive based<br>Significant financial reward<br>Based on external equity |

SOURCE: Morris, M. H., and Kuratko, D. F. (2002). *Corporate Entrepreneurship*. (Ft. Worth, TX: Harcourt College Publishers).

encouragement of innovative and risk-taking behaviors. Their compensation practices were more likely to include bonuses and incentives based on long-term performance, an emphasis on job security over high pay, and greater stress on individual rather than group performance.

Further examination of the practices associated with a stronger entrepreneurial orientation suggests that the performance appraisal and training/development areas generated the highest numbers of practices that distinguished more entrepreneurial from less entrepreneurial organizations. Next in order was compensation, followed by selection and staffing and, last, planning and job design.

It becomes apparent that human resource management is a vital link to the entrepreneurial activities needed to keep emerging companies dynamic and successful. Once the HRM functions are understood, owners and managers of emerging firms can apply the variations to each function that enhance the levels of entrepreneurship within the firms.

## THE FUTURE OF THE HUMAN RESOURCE FUNCTION

Over the next decade, the practice of human resource management faces many challenges and offers many opportunities. The integration of human resource management and total quality management is one such example. However, Jain and Murray[18] claim that the human resource function in most companies has had very little impact on company performance. They state:

> In spite of the strenuous efforts of many wise practitioners, teachers, and researchers over the years, the personnel function has failed to have any significant impact of its own. Rather it has been, and remains today, a reactive function, only responding to problems once they arise. Furthermore, it is heavily constrained by forces that effectively work against the adoption of many of the policies that have been advocated by leading personnel experts for decades. (p. 25)

These authors cite several facts to support their contention. These facts include the following:

- Job analysis is seldom done or if performed, it is not done accurately.
- Human resource planning is rarely integrated into company strategic planning.
- Almost all companies rely heavily on interviews despite evidence of their unreliability and invalidity.
- Formal training programs are utilized in less than 20 percent of organizations and are seldom integrated into company strategic objectives.
- Performance appraisal policies are seldom carried out and if performance appraisals are completed, their results are seldom used in organizational decision making.
- Although open pay systems have been recommended for a long time, most companies fight to keep this information confidential.
- Very few companies have employee representation on their board of directors.
- Research and evaluation of human resource efforts are seldom conducted.

## THE HR INVESTMENT

Recently, the success of companies in almost every industry has, in part, been determined by the companies' willingness to invest money in the human resource side of the business. Many of these expenditures, unfortunately, have been for *reactive* responses to problems such as competitive pressures and tight labor markets instead of for the creation of strategically executed *proactive* strategies. Companies are finally beginning to realize that these increasing HR costs are not going away and need to be used for adopting proactive strategies.

A survey was conduced by Best Software in McLean, VA, and used the responses of 150 HR professionals who gave their opinions about the importance of human resources today. This survey supported the fact that although many companies are making progress in attempts to fully understand and implement HR practices, many are still having difficulty "walking the walk." Of those surveyed 73 percent reported that they are spending more on wages and that the salary increases are increasing faster than increases in the cost of living. Also, 66 percent are spending more on recruiting, and many expect these costs to continue to increase in the next year. The finding supports the current national trends because the Bureau of Labor Statistics predicts that unemployment will continue to be low for the near future. This will probably keep pressure on companies to continue raising employees' wages.

Many of those surveyed reported that, while company budgets for technology are increasing, little of the allocated money is being earmarked for HR departments. Also, more than 40 percent of the respondents who reported that their companies did have HR budgets indicated that they were not permitted to spend any of the money without prior approval, and 36 percent reported that they felt like they "always" had to compete with other departments to be allocated capital.

The survey showed that companies that are not investing in HR technologies might also undervalue the human aspects of the company. Interestingly, 52 percent of those who reported using a manual or paper-based HR system as opposed to a computer-based system also reported various concerned attitudes about how employees within their corporations are valued. Even more interesting, 31 percent of these HR professionals indicated that a select group of employees are valued but, "most are just seen as a necessary expense."

As companies move into this new millennium, they will be required to put a great deal of emphasis on issues relating to people. Companies will have to focus attention on creating a long-term commitment to the human aspect of business. It will be an organization's performance, capabilities, and talents that are its primary competitive tools, and it will be the decisions about investments in these areas that determine how the company fares in the competitive environment and also how the company is perceived by others.

SOURCE: Adapted from Linda Davidson. *Who's Investing in HR?*, December 1, 1999. Available at www.workforce.com.

Their contention is that the implementation of recommended human resource practices has been unsuccessful. They recommend that the human resource function take a more strategic position within the firm so that its activities are taken seriously. Brown[19] supported such a recommendation when she claimed that human resources was an important piece of the "puzzle" for organization survival. She stated that the competitiveness of U.S. companies depends on top management's understanding that human resource activities are important for survival. She cited the fact that increasing numbers of top human resource managers are reporting directly to the chief executive officer (CEO). Thirty-three of the

**FREQUENTLY ASKED QUESTIONS**

**In setting up an HR record-keeping system, what should, and should not, be included in the personnel file?**

*Include the following items in a personnel file:*

- Employment application and resume
- Reference/recommendation checks
- Educational transcripts
- Job descriptions
- Hiring, promotion, demotion, transfer, and layoff records
- Rates of pay and other forms of compensation
- Training and development records
- Letters of recognition
- Disciplinary documentation and reports
- Performance appraisals
- Career development forms
- Tests used by employer during employment process
- Exit interviews
- Termination records

*The following items should not be included in a personnel file:*

- Medical/insurance records
- Equal employment opportunity records
- Immigration forms (I-9)
- Safety training records
- Garnishments
- Litigation documents
- Workers' compensation claims

**What is the typical ratio of HR people to employees in an organization?**

According to the Society for Human Resource Management (SHRM), employers have an average of 1.0 full-time HR professionals for every 100 employees in the workforce. Also, organizations that have highly technical jobs usually find it helpful to have a full-time HR person when they grow to 50 to 75 employees. The ratio of HR personnel to total employees depends on the following factors:

- The individual company's structure
- Actual size of the company
- Complexity of jobs in the organization
- The company's reliance on in-house staff versus outside HR consultants or outsourcing firms

*continued*

top 50 U.S. firms have their top human resource official reporting to the CEO. Also, more human resource managers are becoming CEOs themselves. This claim has been more recently supported by research in the area of entrepreneurship and human resource management.[20]

## CHAPTER SUMMARY

This new millennium does represent a challenging time for the human resource function. Schuler sums up the challenge when he states, "they [HR departments] can continue in their functional specialists mode or they can reorient themselves and see HR issues as business issues and help line managers solve them."[21] Owners and senior executives of emerging and growing firms need to empower their managers to perform human resource functions in such a way that the firm achieves a sustainable competitive advantage. And that is the major goal of today's emerging firms.

**WEB ADDRESSES**

**www.shrm.org**
The Society for Human Resource Management (SHRM) offers a very robust web site for the HR professional. The site contains a nearly exhaustive list of helpful links and an examination of countless topical issues. In addition, the site has current news stories that are relevant to the field and links to web sites focusing on various topics. It also gives information on the magazine published by SHRM, organization membership, contests, and regional chapters of SHRM. The site also has special members-only sections. It is an excellent resource and a great place to start for all HR professionals, regardless of company size or industry.

**www.workforce.com**
Workforce.com is a first-class web site for HR professionals. It has great news resources, as well as informational and how-to articles. The site offers information in a variety of HR areas.

**www.hrnext.com**
Another great informational web site for the HR professional, hrnext.com has information in many topical areas. HR professionals should find the current and archived topical articles and discussion pieces very helpful for managing their own issues. This site requires a membership to see many of the articles, but appears to be well worth it.

**www.dol.gov**
The United States Department of Labor web site, along with other government labor-related web sites, provides HR professionals with valuable information about rule and law changes. It also well provides the user with information on government programs and current issues, and articles for examination.

**www.bizmove.com/personnel.htm**
This site, the Small Business Knowledge Base, is specifically designed for the small business owner and/or HR professional. Its site offers many articles on various topics related to small business and personnel relations.

**www.hrvillage.com**
hrVillage.com is a powerful web site for the HR professional. The site is full of resources, including sample policies and procedures, legal guides, administrative forms, and job descriptions. The site also offers an HR bookstore, a course finder, a list of HR events, HR news, and an HR web search tool, as well as other valuable tools and features.

**NOTES**

1. United States Small Business Administration Office of Advocacy. (1997). "Characteristics of small employers and owners." Available at http://www.sba.gov.

2. Heneman, R. L., Tansky, J. W., and Camp, S. M. (2000). "Human resource management practices in small and medium-sized enterprises: Unanswered questions and future research perspectives." *Entrepreneurship Theory and Practice* 25: 11–26.

3. Zaleznik, A. (1988). "What's wrong with HRM." *The Harvard Business Review* 66: 170–171.

4. Adapted from Beer, M., Spector, B., Lawrence, P. R., Mills, D. Q., and Walton, R. E. (1985). *Human Resource Management: A General Manager's Perspective* (New York: The Free Press).

5. Williamson, I. O. (2000). "Employer legitimacy and recruitment success in small businesses." *Entrepreneurship Theory and Practice* 25: 27–42.

6. Cyr, L. A., Johnson, D. C., and Wilbourne, T. M. (2000). "Human resources in initial public offering firms: Do venture capitalists make a difference?" *Entrepreneurship Theory and Practice,* 25: 77–92.

7. Hornsby, J. S., and Kuratko, D. F. (1990). "Human resource management: Critical issues for the 1990s." *Journal of Small Business Management,* 28: 9–18; Hornsby, J. S., and Kuratko, D. F.

(2000). "Human resource management in U.S. small businesses: Critical issues for the new millennium." *Proceedings: United States Association of Small Business and Entrepreneurship.*

8. Morris, M. H., and Jones, F. F. (1993). "Human resource management practices and corporate entrepreneurship: An empirical assessment from the USA." *The International Journal of Human Resource Management* 4: 873–896; Schuler, R. S. (1986). "Entrepreneurship in organizations." *Human Resource Management* Winter: 614–629; Olian, J. D., and Rynes, S. L. (1984). "Organizational staffing: Integrating practice with strategy." *Industrial Relations* 23: 170–183.

9. Schuler, R. S. (1986). "Entrepreneurship in organizations." *Human Resource Management* Winter: 614–629.

10. Hornsby, J. S., and Kuratko, D. F. (2000). "Human resource management in U.S. small businesses: Critical issues for the new millennium." *Proceedings: United States Association of Small Business and Entrepreneurship.*

11. Bowen, D. E., and Lawler, E. E. (1992). "Total quality-oriented human resources management." *Organizational Dynamics* Spring: 29–41.

12. Kuratko, D. F., Hornsby, J. S., and Goodale, J. C. (2001). "Quality practices for a competitive advantage in smaller firms." *Journal of Small Business Management* October: 293–311. See also Hodgetts, R. M., Kuratko, D. F., and Hornsby, J. S. (1999). "Quality implementation in small business: Perspectives from the Baldridge award winners." *SAM Advanced Management Journal* 64(1): 37–47.

13. Bowen and Lawler (1992).

14. Chandler, G. N., and McEvoy, G. M. (2000). "Human resource management, TQM, and firm performance in small and medium-size enterprises." *Entrepreneurship Theory and Practice* 25: 43–57.

15. Kuratko, D. F., and Hodgetts, R. M. (2001). *Entrepreneurship: A Contemporary Approach*, 5th ed. (Ft. Worth, TX: Harcourt College Publishers).

16. Morris, M. H., and Jones, F. F. (1993). "Human Resource Management Practices and Corporate Entrepreneurship: An Empirical Assessment from the USA," *International Journal of Human Resource Management* 4: 873–896.

17. Morris, M. H., and Kuratko, D. F. (2002). *Corporate Entrepreneurship.* (Ft. Worth, TX: Harcourt College Publishers).

18. Jain, H., and Murray, V. (1990). "Why the human resources management function fails." In *Human Resource Management: Perspectives and Issues*, 2nd ed., Ed. G. R. Ferris, K. M. Rowland, and M. R. Buckley (Needham Heights, MA: Allyn & Bacon), 25–36.

19. Brown, Donna (1991). "HR is the key to survival in the '90s." *Personnel* March: 5–6.

20. Katz, J. A., Aldrich, H. E., Welbourne, T. M., and Williams, P. M. (2000). "Human resource management and the SME: Toward a new synthesis." *Entrepreneurship Theory and Practice*, Special Issue, 25: 7–10. See also Williamson, I. O. (2000). "Employer legitimacy and recruitment success in small businesses." *Entrepreneurship Theory and Practice* 25: 27–42; and Cyr, L. A., Johnson, D. C., and Wilbourne, T. M. (2000). "Human resources in initial public offering firms: Do venture capitalists make a difference? *Entrepreneurship Theory and Practice* 25: 77–92.

21. Schuler, R. S. (1990). "Repositioning the HR function; Transformation or demise?" *Academy of Management Executive* 4: 49–60.

# 3

# RECRUITING AND SELECTING QUALIFIED EMPLOYEES

## QUESTIONS TO CONSIDER WHILE READING THIS CHAPTER

1. What are the typical components of a recruiting procedure?
2. What are the typical components of a selection procedure?
3. How do you show that your selection procedures are job related?
4. How viable are newer selection methods such as honesty and drug testing?

## THE EMERGING ISSUE

The "care and feeding" (otherwise known as attraction and retention) of quality personnel is the number one priority human resource issue for managers of emerging firms.[1] Employers, especially smaller ones with limited resources, are forced to compete for talent in a tight labor market. To deal with this competition, growing enterprises must formalize their recruitment and selection efforts and also seek ways to attract people away from larger organizations. Along with the human resource planning effort described in the previous chapter, recruitment and selection activities must be carefully planned and carried out by competent managers and not haphazardly performed on the spur of the moment. Highly skilled individuals who might be attracted to a smaller firm will probably be turned off if procedures lack professionalism.

## CHAPTER OVERVIEW

There are numerous social, legal, economic, and ethical issues to consider in the selection of qualified employees. Understanding this process is important for both job applicants and employers. Whether or not one will become an active participant in the process of searching for qualified employees, it is particularly important to have a thorough understanding of this human resource activity. It has also become increasingly important for organizations to develop sound selection programs to ensure organizational competitiveness and survival.

This chapter will provide familiarity with the events many job applicants experience during the selection process as well as with legal rights of employers. For example, is it legal for employers to discriminate against pregnant women, human immunodeficiency virus (HIV)-positive individuals, unmarried applicants, or job applicants with disabilities when making selection decisions? Also, how an organization can develop the best possible program for selecting qualified individuals will be addressed.

## THE INTEGRATIVE NATURE OF SELECTION SYSTEMS

It is becoming increasingly important to understand the integrative relationship between the functions of recruitment and selection and other human resource activities. Among the human resource activities related to the selection system are job analysis, planning, performance appraisal, and compensation.

**Job analysis** (covered in Chapter 3) is the foundation of all selection systems.[2] For example, how would a manager select an individual for a job if the knowledge, skills, and abilities (KSAs) associated with that job were unknown? Such a procedure would probably result in a mismatch between individual and organizational needs.

**Planning** for future staffing needs, given the continuously changing technological aspects of jobs today, is an important consideration. For example, managers must decide whether it is more economical to select individuals with the required skills for a particular job or to train individuals once hired.

**Appraising** employees' performance levels is an extremely important component of evaluating the success of any selection system. Performance appraisal ratings become the criterion used to assess the success of selection procedures through a process of establishing test validity.

**Compensation** is a very important component for any selection program. Without the ability to develop a competitive and attractive compensation package, organizations are not in a position to recruit highly competent and motivated individuals from which to make selection decisions.

Besides the related human resource functions already described, the individuals available for selection are only as qualified as those job applicants in the applicant pool. Currently, organizations are becoming extremely creative in developing a diverse applicant pool, which is important in a competitive business environment. As a result, the recruitment process becomes particularly important for attracting highly talented individuals because managers make their selection choice from the applicant pool. Therefore, we now turn our attention to the recruitment process.

## THE RECRUITMENT PROCESS

The first step in staffing an organization is developing an applicant pool of qualified job applicants. This process is achieved by actively implementing an aggressive recruitment strategy.[3] Given the global competition facing many organizations today as well as the changing demographic characteristics of the workforce, it is becoming imperative from a survival perspective that organizations actively recruit individuals from a variety of ethnic backgrounds and differing work experiences. This strategy requires active planning on the part of all managers. Several methods, including both internal and external, exist for developing a pool of qualified job applicants.[4]

## INTERNAL METHODS

Internal methods of recruitment generally obtain potential job candidates from a pool of employees currently working for the organization. Internal methods of recruitment include practices such as job posting, promotion, and personal referrals. Job posting refers to employers notifying employees about a position opening via newsletters, company bulletin boards, or e-mail or an Intranet. Promotion from within simply involves offering an employee who has excelled in his or her current job (as evidenced by an accurate performance appraisal) a new position. The last method of internal recruitment involves current employees providing the company with names of qualified individuals to consider for possible hire.

There are several advantages to working with current employees to fill job openings within the company. First, since the employee has been with the company a while, the organization knows more about the employee's skills, aptitudes, and interests. Similarly, the individual is familiar with the position and the culture of the organization. Second, job applicants referred by an employee tend to have a more realistic understanding of the job and organization than do walk-in applicants. Therefore, these situations are more likely to facilitate a match between organization and employee needs. Finally, internal recruitment methods serve as a potential motivator for employees to excel in their current job since they have an opportunity to advance within the company.

There are also several disadvantages associated with promoting from within an organization. First, the policy of promoting from within can create a homogeneous workforce. This type of workforce may produce an inbreeding of ideas and hinder organizational growth, innovativeness, and progress. Thus, creativity may be stifled. Another disadvantage of internal recruitment methods is that such practices may perpetuate the demographic characteristics of the current workforce, thus excluding women and minority groups. Such an occurrence may decrease the competitiveness of the organization in a global business market and result in illegal discrimination. Finally, subordinates may have a problem adjusting to a new supervisor who was once a peer or even a friend. The supervisor may have problems enforcing work rules, and the subordinates may have problems respecting the supervisor's authority. Furthermore, some passed-over employees may be jealous and actually set out to make life miserable for the new supervisor.

## EXTERNAL METHODS

External methods of recruitment obtain new employees from outside the organization. External sources include applicants who "walk in," colleges, and advertising via newspapers, trade journals, professional conferences, radio, television, and the Internet. These external sources all require some type of written advertisement. Exhibit 5.1 provides an example of a typical advertisement. A good advertisement is constructed to include information such as a clear identification of the company (i.e., name, location, contact name, and phone number), a concise description of job responsibilities, and clear job specifications. A well-written advertisement should help facilitate the matching process that occurs between the

**A TYPICAL RECRUITING ADVERTISEMENT**

*Memorial Hospital*
1000 University Avenue
Anywhere, USA 00000

### Employment Representative

Immediate opportunity for a dynamic human resources professional as full-time Health Care Recruiter. Responsibilities include all phases of recruitment, interviewing, and screening of nursing and other health care professionals; travel to conventions, college career events, and other recruitment activities; and planning, organizing and hosting recruitment events, presentations, and hospital tours.

This fast-paced, highly visible position is an excellent opportunity for a recruiter with the right blend of organizational, marketing, and communication talents to play a key role in our continuing success. Requires BS in human resources or related field with minimum 1 year related experience.

Memorial Hospital is a 550+ bed teaching hospital and medical referral center for the East Central Region, employing over 2,300. Excellent salary and benefit package.

To apply, send resume and salary history in complete confidence to
Andrea Smith, Manager of Employment.

company and the applicant. Applicants should be motivated to apply only if they have an interest in the company and/or job as well as the required knowledge, skills, and abilities.

Companies of all sizes are increasing their use of the Internet as a tool for external recruitment. A company Internet site can help enlarge the pool of prospective employees and serve as a source for effective public relations. The web's interactivity allows the creation of highly personalized and responsive web pages that deliver results for both the applicant and the company. Some of the interactive tools used in the recruitment process include web-site search engines, interactive job application forms, and e-mail autoresponders.[5]

Obtaining new employees from outside the organization may result in several advantages for the organization. First, such recruiting efforts are more likely to result in development of a diverse work environment. Second, external recruitment is more likely to bring in individuals with new and varying ideas, which may stimulate company growth and innovation. One disadvantage of external recruitment is poor morale among current employees that may result in decreased motivation levels. Another disadvantage is that it is more difficult to assess the person-organization fit with an outside job applicant.

## REALISTIC JOB PREVIEW

One method of ensuring that an appropriate match will be made in selecting an outside job applicant is to use a realistic job preview (RJP). An RJP involves informing potential employees about all aspects of the job, both positive and negative. As a result, job applicants are more capable of assessing the match between their personal needs and the organization's needs and making an informed selection decision. Providing realistic expectations has been associated with higher levels of employee satisfaction and job involvement, enhanced communication, and lower levels of turnover.[6] It is important that information included in the RJP be obtained directly from the job analysis.

## AFFIRMATIVE ACTION

Managers need to be aware of several legal issues when recruiting employees (these were discussed in detail in Chapter 2). In an attempt to obtain diversity throughout the organization, many organizations are voluntarily implementing affirmative action programs. Affirmative action programs are concerned with developing a recruitment strategy that has the goal of hiring the best possible candidate for a job. Such a strategy includes actively seeking out and recruiting minority group individuals and women to fill open positions.

There are two strategies that an organization can implement to uphold the requirements of affirmative action. First, the organization must develop a comprehensive recruitment plan. This plan must include a "good faith" effort for recruiting individuals from diverse backgrounds. Second, selection decisions must be made by utilizing selection methods with proven validity. It is important to keep in mind that affirmative action is not synonymous with quotas or the hiring of incompetent individuals. If fact, the worst solution to solving the problem of discrimination in the workplace is to hire an incompetent person from a minority group because such situations tend to perpetuate the negative stereotypes traditionally held by many individuals.

## PREEMPLOYMENT INQUIRIES

Several different types of applicant information are collected during the recruitment phase. Often the first piece of information collected from job applicants is information contained in the application blank. Today there is legislation that limits the types of information an organization can obtain from a job applicant. Although application blanks appear to be nonthreatening, traditionally most application forms have required job applicants to provide information that could be interpreted as being potentially illegal or discriminatory. Exhibit 5.2 lists some important questions to be asked when the appropriateness of application blank items is examined.

There are numerous questions that signal to a regulatory agency that an organization may be participating in a discriminatory practice. Therefore, it is important for an organization to solicit only job-relevant information on an application

**■ EXHIBIT 5.2**

QUESTIONS TO BE ASKED WHEN APPROPRIATENESS
OF APPLICATION BLANK ITEMS IS EXAMINED

| Yes | No | |
|-----|-----|-----|
| ____ | ____ | 1. Will the answers to this question, if used in making a selection decision, have an adverse impact in screening out minorities and/or members of one sex? |
| ____ | ____ | 2. Is this information really needed to judge an applicant's competence or qualifications for the job in question? |
| ____ | ____ | 3. Does the question conflict with the EEOC guidelines or recent court decisions? |
| ____ | ____ | 4. Does the question conflict with the spirit and intent of the Civil Rights Act or other federal and state statutes? |
| ____ | ____ | 5. Is the question an invasion of privacy? |
| ____ | ____ | 6. Is there information available that could be used to show that responses to a question are associated with success or failure on a specific job? |

SOURCE: Adapted from Gatewood, R. D., and Feild, H. S. (1998). *Human Resource Selection,* 4th ed. (Fort Worth, TX: Dryden Press).

blank. The following are some guidelines to follow in the development of an application blank and examples of potentially illegal questions.[7]

*Gender.*   It is not recommended that an application blank solicit information regarding applicant gender unless it can be proved that gender is a bona fide occupational qualification (BFOQ) for the position. Typically gender is not a BFOQ except for certain entertainment positions (e.g., model or dancer) or for public morality reasons (e.g., a female for an attendant in a female locker room).

*National Origin.*   It is not permissible to ask questions regarding an applicant's ancestry or the ancestry of his or her parents or grandparents unless a BFOQ exists (see Section 703 of the 1964 Civil Rights Act).

*U.S. Citizenship.*   Although it is not recommended that employers ask applicants if they are U.S. citizens, it is strongly recommended that organizations ask applicants if they have permission to work in the United States. However, the form of this legal permission should not be taken into account when an employee is hired. After the selection decision, new employees are required to provide evidence of their legal status in the United States.

*Age.* It is potentially illegal to ask questions regarding an individual's age or birth date. In fact, the Age Discrimination in Employment Act prohibits organizations from discriminating against individuals who are 40 years old or older. Only under certain specific instances is it permissible to inquire about an applicant's age. One is when age has been proven to be a legitimate BFOQ. However, based on the child labor provision of the Fair Labor Standards Act, it is permissible to ask individuals if they are old enough to hold the position under question. After the individual is hired, it is an acceptable practice for an employer to collect information regarding an applicant's age because many jobs have age restrictions (e.g., pilot) or for administrative purposes.

*Race.* An applicant's race should only be asked in the collection of equal employment data. When this information is requested on an application blank, it should be set apart (many times on a separate perforated sheet) so that it can be separated before hiring decision-makers see it. Such information has a great potential to be used in a discriminatory fashion during the recruitment and selection process. It is always important to emphasize the skills relevant to the position regardless of personal demographic characteristics.

*Disabilities/Illnesses.* Because the Americans with Disabilities Act requires reasonable accommodation, it is not acceptable to require applicants to list all the disabilities or illnesses they have had or that their relatives may have had in the past. Therefore, disability information should be used only for making placement decisions and not selection choices.

*Marital Status.* It is not recommended that organizations ask for information regarding an applicant's marital status because many decision-makers may use this information in an illegal manner, usually in the form of sex discrimination. Rather, a safe question to ask applicants regarding this issue is, "Do you have any personal obligations that would in any way hinder your job performance?" However, it is important to remember to ask both males and females this question if it is deemed absolutely necessary for the job.

*Organizational Memberships.* Only professional organization membership information that is related to the job should be solicited on an application blank. Under no circumstances should information be required about organizations that have discriminatory membership policies in terms of gender, race, religion, etc.

*Height and Weight.* Only in rare circumstances is height or weight an important job-related work qualification. Even in those rare instances when a job requires a certain height or weight, applicants should not be required to provide specific numbers but rather indicate whether or not their measurements fall within the acceptable range.

## SELECTION METHODS

After an appropriate applicant pool has been established, the actual selection process begins. During this process, managers use many different methods of determining who is best qualified for the position as well as whose personal needs match those of the organization. Techniques commonly used during the selection process include interviews, personality tests, ability tests, honesty tests, and drug testing.

### INTERVIEW

Currently, employers utilize numerous selection methods in making their staffing decisions. Perhaps the most commonly used method for selecting qualified employees is the interview. During the 1970s many companies primarily used paper-and-pencil tests for selection purposes. Because the courts and legal agencies extensively scrutinized these measures, many organizations have begun to rely solely on the employment interview. However, as we shall see shortly, the courts view the interview as a "test" and thus it must also exhibit certain psychometric characteristics (e.g., reliability and validity) just as traditional paper-and-pencil tests.[8]

Interviews can be either structured or unstructured (free form), conducted individually or in groups, and/or administered by one or more than one interviewer. Whereas it is generally recommended that organizations use a structured format (as described in the following section), the group or board interviews may be appropriate, depending on the types of jobs being filled.

*Problems.*    Although the interview can be a rich source of information regarding a job applicant's motivation, interpersonal skills, and job enthusiasm, many problems exist.[9] A major problem with the interview process is that the interviewers are often not knowledgeable about the job position being filled. In this situation, the interview is spent discussing issues that are unrelated to the job. This creates a situation in which the interviewer has no relevant information about the job applicant to make an informed selection decision. Equally important, job applicants may find themselves working for an organization that does not meet their personal needs. Therefore, the best candidate to fill the job may not be selected, leading to a mismatch between applicant and organization needs and a low validity coefficient.

A second problem with the interview process is that interviewers tend to make a decision about the interviewee's potential within a few minutes after meeting the individual.[10] Such snap judgments can lead to serious errors in selection. Thus, interviewers need to be properly trained in interviewing techniques.

A third problem with the interview is that interviewers may commit one of several judgment errors. Research shows that interviewers tend to remember events that transpired either early (primacy effect) or late (recency effect) in the interview while they tend to forget events occurring during the middle of the interview period. Therefore, as an interviewee it is extremely important to make a good "first impression" and also to summarize your strengths and interest in the position at the conclusion of the interview period.

Interviewers are also prone to making the "halo error." A halo error occurs when the interviewer bases a selection decision on only one positive or negative aspect of the interviewee. For example, the interviewer may falsely believe that the candidate has exceptional all-important characteristics required for the job because he or she was impressed with the candidate's style of dress. However, as we know, many other qualifications are more important for making selection decisions than clothing style.

Conversely, a job applicant may be rejected solely on the basis of attire. This would be an example of the halo error and may result in the organization's passing up a highly qualified individual. In this situation, the candidate may not be able to afford to buy new clothes for interviewing purposes. Therefore, it is extremely important for managers to base their hiring decisions on job-related and not superficial issues.

The solution to most of the problems cited above is to develop and conduct a structured interview. A structured interview is a set of job-related interview questions, based on a job analysis, that are consistently asked of each applicant for a specific job.[11] In addition, interviewers should have a predetermined set of criteria on which to base their judgments of each candidate's performance so that they refrain from comparing job applicants with each other and use the "contrast effect." With the contrast effect candidates are judged on the basis of prior candidates. For example, if the first individuals who were interviewed were excellent, the next applicants may not be rated as highly by the interviewer as their performance would objectively indicate. Conversely, if the individuals interviewed first were absolutely unacceptable, the next applicants would more likely be rated higher than their objective performance level.

A final problem with the interview situation is that it represents what researchers call a "strong situation." A strong situation is characterized by a set protocol of desired behaviors. For example, we all know that we should have eye contact with the interviewer, sit erect during the interview, and greet the interviewer with a strong handshake. Because almost everyone is familiar with this etiquette, it becomes increasingly difficult for the interviewer to determine whether candidates are behaving in accordance with their "true personality" or acting according to what they know is correct interview behavior. Several books have been written and programs are offered by University Placement Offices covering the topic of appropriate interview etiquette. For this reason, organizations are reluctant to make a selection decision solely on interview performance.

*Recommendations.*   Numerous recommendations can be provided to help managers overcome many of the problems associated with the interview. First, if the supervisor is not the person conducting the interview, it is imperative that the interviewer have a thorough understanding of important tasks associated with the job. Such information can be obtained from an updated job description. Second, interviewers should be instructed during a training program to delay making any judgments about the interviewee until the conclusion of the interview. Third, to prevent the interviewer from making judgments based on non-job-related issues, the interviewer should ask situational questions. Again, the situational questions should be derived directly from a recent job analysis.[12] In addition, these questions should be evaluated by using a predetermined scoring procedure.[13] Such a procedure is more likely to ensure that all interviewees, regardless of their age, sex, or nationality, are treated in a similar manner. Finally, for legal reasons the interview should always be checked for adverse impact.

*Legal Questions.*   Several general job-related interview questions may be used to better understand the candidate.[14] It is always important to keep in mind that each question must be job related. This type of questions gives the candidate ample opportunity to divulge important information necessary for making an informed choice as to whether there is a match between the individual's and organization's needs. For example, the interviewer may start the interview by asking "What can you tell me about the position you are interested in or the company?" Later in the interview, the interviewer may ask, "Do you think that you would accept an offer if one was offered to you today? Why or why not?" Both of these questions allow the interviewer to gauge the candidate's interest in and enthusiasm for the position and to learn whether the candidate did any research regarding the company or position before the interview. To maximize the chances of being selected, it is imperative that the candidate be an active participant during the interview process. Therefore, the interview should be a two-way communication process.

Another question that may be asked during the interview is, "Why do you think you are qualified for this position?" or, "Is there anything else you can tell me about yourself that would help me make a selection decision regarding this position?" Again, these questions allow the interviewer to assess the candidate's knowledge about the job and thoughts about his or her "fit" with the company. It also gives the candidate an opportunity to discuss past accomplishments and how those experiences may benefit the organization. In addition, it gives the interviewer a better understanding of who the candidate is, what he or she has done in the past, and what future goals he or she has.

## PERSONALITY ASSESSMENT

Numerous organizations are currently using personality measures as a way of identifying qualified job applicants. Such measures usually require job applicants to answer questions regarding their own personal characteristics. Although personality measures can provide reliable and valid information for making selection decisions, managers need to be aware of several potential limitations. First, research has shown that off-the-shelf personality measures often have less potential use in organizational settings than measures specifically designed for a particular position.[15] Second, because the information is collected from the potential employee, the responses may be biased toward providing information the job applicant feels the employer wants to obtain.[16] Although such a method of completing a measure benefits neither the individual nor the organization because a mismatch may occur, many applicants in search of a job resort to such a strategy when completing selection measures of this nature.

When should personality measures be used for making selection decisions? First, the validity of the personality measure for a particular situation must be established to justify its use as a selection device. Second, personality measures have been suggested to be a valuable selection tool in weak rather than strong situations, such as an interview.[17] A strong situation occurs when the repertoire of appropriate behaviors is highly defined or structured in terms of identifying acceptable behaviors. Under these circumstances, an individual's behavior is probably more a result of past learning than "true" personality since these situations are clearly defined in terms of what behaviors are considered "right" for the occasion. An example of a strong situation would be the interview session. Several books have been written as well as programs offered by University Placement Offices covering the topic of appropriate interview etiquette. Therefore, a manager would be well advised to not rely solely on personality tests and observe the potential employee's behavior in a multitude of situations before making any selection decision.

## ABILITY TESTS

Since enactment of the Americans with Disabilities Act of 1990 (discussed in Chapter 2), which indicates that organizations must accommodate individuals with various disabilities, it has become extremely important for organizations to identify the minimum ability requirements necessary for a job and not discriminate against job applicants who meet the minimum job requirements. In addition, given the potential problems associated with personality measures, many organizations are using ability tests to directly assess the relationship between various skills and qualifications necessary for the job and job performance. Examples of commonly used ability tests include mental, mechanical, clerical, and sensory (i.e., hearing and vision acuity).

Although the validity of these measures has received extensive support, it is strongly suggested that managers conduct their own reliability and validity studies because certain ability tests are more appropriate for some positions than others. Despite the evidence indicating the minimization of adverse impact for ability tests, it is important that participants in the validity study represent the diversity present in the organization.

## HONESTY TESTING

Because the Polygraph Act of 1988 prohibited most organizations from using the polygraph as a selection device, many organizations have turned to paper-and-pencil honesty tests. It is purported that honesty tests are essential for curbing employee theft. However, recently the validity of these tests has been highly criticized.[18] For example, many items on these tests inquire about applicants' personal habits that are unrelated to job performance. It is questionable whether such information is important for the job and whether job applicants' privacy is invaded by soliciting such information. As a result, many items on these types of tests may have to be revised and additional research conducted to investigate the psychometric characteristics of honesty tests.

## PHYSICAL EXAMINATIONS

No matter what the circumstances, an employer cannot require a preemployment physical examination because of perceived disability. However, a medical exam is permitted during the period between the job offer and the start of work, but only if this is the standard practice for all applicants for that particular job category.[19]

Generally the employer pays for the entire costs of the exams, provides the applicant with a copy of the results, and maintains confidentiality of the results. Depending on the test results, accommodation for those with physical or other impairments may be required, barring undue hardship to the employer. It is important to note that physically challenged individuals cannot be singled out for physical exams. It is recommended that this be one of the final steps in the selection process because of its high costs.

## DRUG TESTING

It has been estimated that alcohol and drug abuse by employees is costing employers at least 75 billion dollars each year.[20] Given the high incidence of drug use in our society, many organizations are testing job applicants as well as employees for potential drug use as a means to improve productivity. Usually a drug test requires the job applicant or employee to provide a medical specialist with a urine, blood, or hair sample. As you can probably imagine, there are several potential problems associated with drug testing. First, many of the procedures used for testing are unreliable and may result in adverse impact. A second concern with drug testing is the potential violation of an individual's right to privacy.

Several issues must be considered before a legally defensible drug-testing program can be implemented. First, drug testing should be reserved for those jobs that could endanger the lives of either the employee, coworkers, or customers (e.g., bus driver, truck driver, etc.). Second, it is more legally defensible to test job applicants than current employees. Under such conditions, employers should always obtain written consent from the participants before testing them for drugs. Implementing a drug-testing program with current employees is more controversial. In most instances, drug testing of current employees should be reserved for those situations in which it is warranted by some external factor such as poor job performance or an accident on the job. Most importantly, a drug-testing program for current employees should be consistently implemented and equitably enforced for all employees. Third, given the low reliability of many screening procedures, any positive findings should be confirmed with a more comprehensive and elaborate testing procedure. Such a policy would increase the validity of the results. Fourth, drug-testing procedures should be analyzed for possible adverse impact. Fifth, results from drug-tests must be considered confidential material. Any results and disciplinary action should only be available on a need-to-know basis. Finally, organizations should adopt a policy of rehabilitation involving counseling rather than punitive procedures when dealing with an employee with a drug problem. This approach is more likely to identify the origin of the problem rather than only treat the symptoms of the problem. Exhibit 5.3 describes some of the most commonly asked questions concerning the use of drug testing in the workplace.

## ESTABLISHING TEST RELIABILITY AND VALIDITY

Several concepts that need to be considered in the development of a valid and legally defensible selection system need to be discussed. Among these concepts are reliability and validity.[21] Both reliability and validity are usually measured using a correlation coefficient. Establishing "test" reliability and validity is the appropriate defense to a claim of illegal discrimination.

### CORRELATION COEFFICIENT

A correlation coefficient is the linear relationship between two variables.[22] The relationship can be either positive or negative and ranges from $-1$ to $+1$. In the selection situation, a manager would hope to find a strong relationship between a selection test and subsequent job performance. A high positive correlation ($r = +1$) would mean that individuals who scored higher on the selection test also performed job activities better than individuals who scored lower on the selection test. Such a relationship ensures that the best-qualified individual will be hired.

Can you think of a situation in which a manager might also be interested in a strong negative correlation ($r = -0.9$) between a selection test and job performance? Often job applicants are given a battery of tests to assess psychological stability (e.g., applicants for police officer). In this situation, a manager would hope to find a negative correlation between the selection test and job performance. That is, research has shown that job applicants who score low on tests assessing tendencies associated with psychological pathological conditions such as schizophrenia or depression perform better on the job.[23]

Is there a situation in which a manager might be interested in a selection test that has no relationship ($r = 0$) with job performance? The answer is probably not,

**EXHIBIT 5.3**

## COMMONLY ASKED QUESTIONS ABOUT DRUG TESTING

### 1. Do I have to test?

There is no legislation that makes drug testing mandatory in all organizations; however, the federal government requires drug testing in three areas. Employers must utilize drug testing if:

(1) they are involved in a contract with the federal government;
(2) they are in the transportation industry; or
(3) they are involved in the construction or operation of nuclear power plants.

### 2. If I have to test, what kind of testing should be utilized?

The options of when and whom to test include the following:

(1) *Job Applicant Testing:* Pre-employment drug screening is the most common substance abuse testing practice.
(2) *Incident-Driven Substance Abuse Testing:* Specific incidents such as a medical emergency that appears to be drug related, may warrant drug testing.
(3) *Postaccident Investigation Testing:* On-the-job accidents that may have involved human error may warrant drug testing.
(4) *Retesting Employees After Drug Rehabilitation Programs:* It is common to test employees who participated in some form of drug rehabilitation program.

(5) *Periodic Testing with Advanced Notice:* Tests are scheduled in advance and usually made a part of regular employee physical examinations.
(6) *Random, Unannounced Tests:* Testing without prenotification is probably the most likely to catch drug abusers. It is also the most likely to cause morale problems and increase employee grievances.

### 3. Can I test even if I am not required to do it?

Yes, you can utilize drug testing. There is no federal law that prohibits drug screening. Also, drug testing is not a legal exception to at-will employment so it may be implemented.

### 4. What problems may arise when a drug testing program is used?

There are several potential problem areas including the following:

(1) Violation of Title VII requirements
(2) Compliance with the Americans with Disabilities Act (ADA)
(3) Criminal and civil suits involving defamation, false imprisonment, assault and battery, invasion of privacy, negligence, and intentional infliction of emotional distress

### 5. Are there any special problems regarding alcohol testing?

Yes, because the ADA considers alcohol tests to be medical examinations and employers should treat them that way. To utilize alcohol testing a conditional job offer must be made. If the offer is rescinded the employer must show business necessity and that no reasonable accommodation can be made.

### 6. How are public employers affected?

The Fourth Amendment prohibits unlawful search and seizure by the government and the courts have found that drug testing may violate this amendment. A balancing test should be applied to determine whether there is a potential violation of the Fourth Amendment. Specifically, it is all right to test if the interest of the government outweighs the interest of the employee or applicant.

### 7. What effect does a unionized environment have on implementing drug testing?

According to the National Labor Relations Board (NLRB), drug testing is a mandatory bargaining issue and the unilateral implementation of drug testing may cause an unfair labor practice.

---

because a job applicant's selection test score would not predict subsequent job performance. That is, an individual who scored high on the selection test could either perform extremely well or poorly on the job if hired. Therefore, such a test would be unimportant for making selection decisions and add unnecessary costs to the selection process.

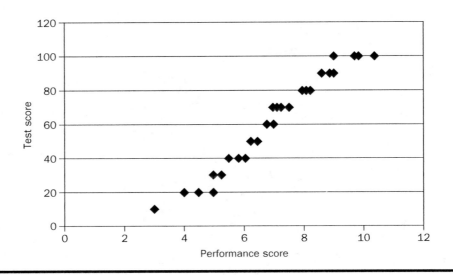

The relationship between two variables can be graphically depicted using a scattergram or scatterplot.[24] The scattergram diagram graphically depicts the relationship between two variables. For example, the scattergram can show the relationship between a selection test and job performance. See Exhibit 5.4 for an example of such a scattergram. In this situation, each dot on the scattergram would represent the intersection of an individual's selection test score before hire and his or her on-the-job performance. This linear relationship between two variables can best be explained using the straight-line equation:

$$Y = ax + b$$

where $Y$ = criterion variable, $a$ = slope, $x$ = predictor score, and $b$ = y-axis intercept.

The straight-line equation can be very useful in selecting human resources. For example, once the slope and intercept values are known, a manager can predict how well the applicant would perform on the job by placing his or her selection test score in the equation. Although this equation does not represent an exact relationship between a test score and job performance due to error, it does represent a good estimate. Selection tests must also be reliable and valid to withstand pressure from the courts and disgruntled employees. These two concepts will be discussed in the following sections.

## RELIABILITY

Reliability refers to the consistency or stability of test scores over time. It also refers to the extent to which a measure is free from random error. Managers need to have a thorough understanding of at least four different types of reliability. These include: (a) test-retest, (b) parallel forms, (c) internal consistency, and (d) inter-rater. Each method investigates the reliability issue from a slightly different perspective.

*Test-Retest Reliability.* Test-retest reliability refers to the consistency or stability of an individual's test score over time. That is, you would expect an individual's test score to be similar each time the test was administered even though the test was taken at different times.

The procedure for determining test-retest reliability is to administer a test to a group of individuals. Next, at a later date the same test would be administered to the same group of individuals. A test is thought to have high test-retest reliability to the extent that the test scores in each testing situation are highly correlated. In this instance the correlation coefficient involving the two test scores is called the coefficient of stability.

Several potential problems may plague a test-retest reliability study. The main source of error associated with this type of study is due to time sampling. For example, if the tests are administered too close together in time, the scores for the second administration may be higher due to practice or memory effects (prior knowledge of questions on the test). Conversely, if the tests are taken at vastly different time periods, the scores for the second administration may be higher due to different events that may have occurred during the time interval (e.g., training or maturation). Therefore, when a test-retest reliability study is evaluated, one must always pay special attention to the time interval used in the study.

*Parallel Forms Reliability.* Parallel forms reliability refers to the consistency of an individual's test score across two "equivalent" tests. That is, you would expect an individual to perform similarly on two different tests designed to test similar content issues.

The procedure for determining parallel forms reliability is to develop two different tests covering the same content domain of items. Next, administer both tests to the same group of individuals and determine the correlation coefficient between the two test scores. Again, the test is thought to be reliable to the extent that the two test scores are highly correlated. The correlation coefficient between the two test scores in this case is referred to as the coefficient of equivalence.

The primary source of error for this type of reliability is sampling error. It is imperative that each test have the same type and number of items, as well as similar difficulty levels. It is also important that both tests have similar mean and standard deviation scores.

*Internal Consistency (Split-Half Reliability).* Internal consistency refers to the extent to which items thought to measure the same thing actually correlate with each other. An advantage to this type of reliability is that it requires only one test administration. A manager splits a test in half and correlates each half to determine the reliability coefficient.

An important question to consider with this type of reliability is, How should the manager split the test? For example, would it be wise to compare the first half with the second half? Probably not, for several reasons: First, individuals may perform better on the first half due to fatigue effects. Second, because many tests are designed according to item difficulty, with the most difficult items reserved for the latter part of the test, individuals may perform better on the first half of the test. Therefore, it is advisable to split the test in terms of odd-even items or to match each half according to item difficulty.

*Inter-Rater Reliability.*   Inter-rater reliability is concerned with the agreement of ratings of an individual's performance across several different managers or raters. For example, if several managers simultaneously interview a job applicant, one would expect high consistency with the managers' performance ratings. If there were a lack of consistency or a low correlation across managers' ratings, one would conclude that the interview process was unreliable. As a result, the managers would need to agree upon and more clearly define the criteria upon which to base their evaluations when they are rating an individual's interview performance.

## VALIDITY

Validity refers to how well a test measures what it purports to measure or whether it is related to other measures as predicted by theory. There are several types of validity that are important for all managers to understand.[25] These include content and criterion-related validity.

*Content Validity.*   Content validity refers to whether a test measures what it is suppose to measure. For example, does a selection test actually assess the most important aspects of the job under consideration? The best way to ensure content validity for selection measures is to develop your measure by incorporating information obtained in a thorough job analysis.

The process of determining content validity is a judgmental process whereby several subject matter experts determine the relevancy of test items for the situation under investigation.

*Criterion-Related Validity.*   Criterion-related validity is concerned with the relationship or correlation between a predictor (i.e., selection test score) and a criterion (i.e., job performance). In contrast to content validity, criterion-related validity is objective or empirical in nature. The process of conducting a criterion-related validity study would be to statistically assess the relationship between a predictor and criterion variable. There are two different types of criterion-related validation strategies: (a) concurrent and (b) predictive. The time perspective is the main difference between these two validation strategies.

The concurrent validation study measures the relationship between a predictor and criterion at the same time. Another unique characteristic of this validation strategy is that current employees are typically used in the study. For example, a manager might be interested in answering the research question, Does age predict job performance? To conduct this study, the manager would first simultaneously collect information about employee age (predictor) and job performance (criterion). Next, the manager would perform a correlation analysis between the predictor and criterion. Of course, the study would have to control for variables such as job experience and type.

The major advantage to a concurrent validation strategy is the short time period required to complete the study. Conversely, the major disadvantage to this strategy is that only current employees are utilized in the study. This may create some bias, especially if the test under investigation is going to be used for selection purposes. That is, current employees may perform differently on a test than job applicants because they are more knowledgeable about the job and culture of the organization and may be under less stress to perform well. In addition, the applicant pool may be more representative of minority groups and females than the current workforce. For this situation, it is recommended that a manager conduct a predictive validity study for selection purposes when feasible.

A predictive validity study uses job applicants and collects predictor and criterion information at two different times. For example, if a manager wanted to assess the relationship between a selection test and job performance a predictive validation study would be used. During this procedure the manager would administer the selection test to all job applicants and place the scores in a locked file drawer where no manager would have access to the scores. Next, the manager would select the most qualified individuals using past selection methods with proven validity.

Once the selected job applicants had an opportunity to perform the tasks of the job, criterion or job performance information would be collected and correlated with the earlier selection test score. If the correlation is high, the selection test may be used in making future selection decisions, provided the test had no adverse impact. Conversely, if the correlation is low or zero, the selection test would not give the manager any useful information for making future selection decisions.

The major advantage to the predictive validity study is that job applicants are used. However, the major limitation to this validation strategy is the length of time required to complete the study. In addition, it is imperative that managers not have access to the selection test scores before providing performance evaluations. Criterion contamination exists when the manager responsible for providing criterion or job performance information is also familiar with the predictor information. If the manager was not aware of the employee's job performance, he or she may rely on the selection test score as an indicator of current job performance and thus bias the evaluation process.

## RELATIONSHIP BETWEEN RELIABILITY AND VALIDITY

What is the relationship between reliability and validity? The reliability coefficient is thought to set the upper limit for what could be expected in terms of the validity coefficient. Remember that a reliability coefficient represents the correlation between a test score with itself. In contrast, a validity coefficient represents the correlation between a test score and something else, often job performance. Therefore, one would not expect a test to correlate better with "something else" than it correlates with itself.

## CHAPTER SUMMARY

In summary, many issues need to be taken into consideration in development of a selection program. As mentioned earlier, the first step in the development of any selection procedure is to conduct a job analysis. In fact, this is the first piece of evidence courts investigate when an individual sues an organization. As discussed in Chapter 3, there are two aspects to any job analysis. The first outcome of a job analysis is the job description that describes all the tasks and job duties associated with the job. This information is used to develop our criterion or job performance measure. It is important to conduct a content validity study for the performance appraisal measure to ensure that it is representative of the important job responsibilities. In addition, it is important to establish the reliability of the performance measure. One method of establishing the reliability of a performance evaluation would be to use multiple raters. That is, an individual's job performance evaluation should remain fairly consistent regardless of who is providing the rating. Finally, the performance measure should be assessed for potential adverse impact.

The second aspect of the job analysis is to identify employee specifications or the KSAs (knowledge, skills, abilities) associated with a job. This information is then utilized in identifying important predictors for a job. Examples of selection predictors include personality measures, honesty tests, and interviews. As with the criterion, the reliability and validity of predictors must be established. In addition, predictors must also be investigated for potential adverse impact for an organization to protect itself from a legal challenge.

Once the predictor and criterion measures have been identified, developed, and evaluated we are in a position to test our selection procedure. This task is accomplished using the variety of validation strategies presented earlier in the chapter. For example, the ideal selection evaluation program would involve conducting a predictive validity study to establish that a relationship does exist between the selection test or predictor and job performance or criterion variable. Among the potential benefits of implementing a valid selection procedure are increased employee satisfaction, decreased turnover and absenteeism, and increased proficiency on the job.

The *Uniform Guidelines for Selecting Employees* is an important document to consult when any selection procedure is developed. This document was prepared by several different groups of selection experts and articulates the important social, ethical, empirical, and legal issues to consider when any selection program is developed and implemented.

## THE POWER OF INTERNET HIRING

The Internet is now allowing companies to recruit employees more easily than ever before. Human resource personnel are using the Internet to find qualified job applicants for jobs ranging from entry level to chief executive officer positions. It seems that there are actually no jobs that are not within the reach of the Internet. This is particularly significant because emerging firms may become particularly susceptible to recruiting problems while simultaneously trying to maintain control of the numerous unpredictable variables that are inherent in new businesses.

The worsening labor shortage in the United States has created a fierce competitive rivalry among businesses. The Internet, however, has given emerging firms an extremely effective tool to help them arrange successful job placements. The only drawback to the Internet that emerging firms recognize is how complicated it can be to sort though all of the information.

Job boards and career-related sites are often frequented by employers because they allow easy access to the resumes of on-line job searchers. When employers are willing to spend more time searching online, they can access numerous helpful web sites and use various techniques to narrow their search for potential employees. Sometimes these search tricks can even make it possible for employers to follow potential job candidates who are not actively looking for a job.

It is estimated that 75 percent of *Fortune* 500 companies are posting the jobs that are available within their firms on their own companies' web sites. Large firms are not alone as all types of companies are now posting job openings on their own sites. This new strategy has made it substantially easier for interested applicants to view the advertised positions and pursue those in which they are interested.

Each of the recruiters and consultants who was interviewed for this article felt that posting job openings on the most popular job boards is very effective since the resume databases contained in some of these sites work extremely well. Many experts believe, however, that it is essential for people to check web sites themselves and not be attracted by sites' claims of having "the largest resume database on the web" or "the most visited job site on the web," because these claims can be misleading.

A 1998 study by J. Walter Thompson found that 70 percent of the 550 human resource professionals who were polled used the Internet as a tool for recruiting. A similar study in 1996 showed that only 21 percent used the Internet for recruiting. According to Gerry Crispin, a recruiting expert who co-authored the book *CareerXroads 2000: Where Talent and Opportunity Connect on the Internet,* Internet recruiting is as high as 80 percent. According to Crispin, there are at least 30,000 web sites that are trying to grasp a piece of this market.

SOURCE: Leonard, L. (2000). "Online and Overwhelmed." *Society for Human Resource Management* 45(8): 36–42.

## HR TOOL KIT

### FREQUENTLY ASKED QUESTIONS

**What direct and indirect costs should be included in a cost per hire calculation?**

*Direct costs include (but are not limited to):*

- Advertising
- Employment agency fees
- Job fairs
- Employee referrals
- Credit and reference checking costs
- Examination and testing costs during the selection process
- Signing bonuses
- Relocation costs
- Human resources overhead costs
- College recruiting costs
- Internet costs
- Training and communication costs

*Indirect costs include (but are not limited to):*

- Lower productivity
- Costs of turnover
- Morale impacts
- Safety
- Disruption of regular business functions
- Hiring to maintain production

**What are the legal issues related to reference checking?**

Reference checks are an important aspect of the selection process. Failure to conduct reference checks can result in a negligent hiring claim against an employer. Negligent hiring exists when the organization hired a person it should have known would cause harm to other employees or customers.

Use the following steps when conducting reference checks:

1. Gather as much information as possible directly from the applicant.

2. Obtain written authorization from the applicant to check references.

3. Specify the type of information being requested and obtain the information in writing.

4. Check relevant state laws about permissible reference check practices.

**What questions should I avoid asking during an interview?**

The interviewer should avoid asking a candidate discriminatory questions. Title VII of the Civil Rights Act prohibits employers from asking information about applicant's race, religion, creed, sex, national origin, or ancestry in making an employment decision. Other laws prohibit asking questions regarding an applicant's

## NOTES

1. Hornsby, J. S., and Kuratko, D. F. (2000). "Human resource management in U.S. small businesses: Critical issues for the new millennium." *Proceedings of the United States Association of Small Business and Entrepreneurship;* Heneman, R. L., Tansky, J. W., and Camp, S. M. (2000). "Human resource management practices in small and medium-sized enterprises: Unanswered questions and future research perspectives." *Entrepreneurship Theory and Practice* 25: 11–26.

2. Wernimont, P. F. (1988). "Uses for job analysis results in human resource management: Recruitment, selection, and placement." In *Job Analysis Handbook for Business, Industry, and Government* (New York: Wiley).

3. Rynes, S. L., and Barber, A. E. (1990). "Applicant attraction strategies: An organizational perspective." *Academy of Management Review* 15: 286–310.

4. Breaugh, J. A. (1992). *Recruitment: Science and Practice* (Boston: PWS-Kent).

5. Dysart, J. (1999). "HR Recruiters Build Interactivity into Web Sites." *HRMagazine*, March.

age, disability, military history, union membership, or sexual orientation. If a question is not related to actual job behaviors (as identified by a job analysis), it probably should not be asked.

**Our company is interested in conducting drug testing as part of our selection process. What issues should we be concerned with?**

- Check state and federal laws regarding drug tests before using them.
- Obtain consent of applicant before test.
- Maintain confidentiality of all records.
- Establish procedures for confirming test results and investigating possible false-positive results.

**What are some innovative ways to retain high-tech employees?**

- Make employees feel that they make a difference in the company.
- Make employees feel that their work is meaningful to the company.
- Make employees feel that they have a balance between life and work.
- Set up good communication channels.
- Consider alternative work schedules such as flex time, compressed workweeks, and telecommuting.
- Empower people to make decisions.
- Offer an innovative benefit plan such as signing bonuses, stock options, and on-site fitness facilities.

**WEB ADDRESSES**

**www.interviewedge.com**
Interviewedge.com offers a quiz to evaluate the HR professional's skills, a section on quick tips, and several news stories related to interviewing and selection. Management Team Consultants, Inc. sponsors this site.

**www.interbiznet.com/hrstart.html**
This site offers several good news stories regarding recruitment.

**www.recruitersnetwork.com**
Recruiters Network is an excellent resource for HR professionals who currently recruit on-line or would like to. It offers a free membership and several "tools." The site also offers a guide to free job posting sites, *Recruiting on the Web Newsletter*, a resource center for HR and recruiting professionals, and free HR and recruiting calculators.

**www.careerbuilder.com/sales/index.html**
This site offers an extensive on-line job-posting system. It also offers new hiring tips and an events calendar.

6. Bretz, R. D., and Judge, T. A. (1998). "Realistic job previews: A test of self-selection hypothesis." *Journal of Applied Psychology* 83: 330–337; Wanous, J. P. (1989). "Installing a realistic job preview: Ten tough choices." *Personnel Psychology* 42: 117–133.

7. Arvey, R. D., and Faley, R. H. (1988). *Fairness in Selecting Employees* (New York: Addison-Wesley).

8. Latham, G. P. (1988). "The reliability, validity, and practicality of the situational interview." In *The Employment Interview: Theory, Research and Practice* Ed. R. W. Eder and G. R. Ferris (Newbury Park, CA: Sage).

9. Gatewood, R. D., and Feild, H. S. (1998). *Human Resource Selection*, 4th ed. (Fort Worth, TX: Dryden Press).

10. Bolster, B., and Springbett, B. (1961). "The reaction of interviewers to favorable and unfavorable information." *Journal of Applied Psychology* 45: 97–103.

11. Pursell, E. D., Campion, M. A., and Gaylord, S. R. (1980). "Structured interviewing: Avoiding selection problems." *Personnel Journal* 59: 908.

12. Feild, H. S., and Gatewood, R. D. (1988). "Development of a selection interview: A job content strategy." In *The Employment Interview: Theory, Research and Practice* Ed. R. W. Eder and G. R. Ferris (Newbury Park, CA: Sage).

13. Campion, M. A., Pursell, E. D., and Brown, B. K. (1988). "Structured interviewing: Raising the psychometric properties of the employment interview." *Personnel Psychology* 41: 25–42.

14. Goodale, J. G. (1988). "Effective employment interviewing." In *The Employment Interview: Theory, Research and Practice* Ed. R. W. Eder and G. R. Ferris (Newbury Park, CA: Sage).

15. Day, D. V., and Silverman, S. B. (1989). "Personality and job performance: Evidence of incremental validity." *Personnel Psychology* 42: 25–36.

16. Hough, L. M., Eaton, N. K., Dunnette, M. D., Kamp, J. D., and McCloy, R. A. (1990). "Criterion-related validities of personality constructs and the effect of response distortion on those validities." *Journal of Applied Psychology* 75: 581–595.

17. Gatewood and Feild (1998).

18. Sackett, P. R., Burris, L. R., and Callahan, C. (1989). "Integrity testing for personnel selection: An update." *Personnel Psychology* 42: 491–529.

19. Hans, M. (1992). "Question of the month." *Safety and Health*, February: 61–62.

20. Bell, A. H. (1992). *Extraviewing* (Homewood, IL: Business One Irwin).

21. Gatewood and Feild (1998).

22. Anastasi, A. (1982). *Psychological Testing* (New York: McGraw-Hill).

23. Arvey and Faley (1988).

24. Gatewood and Feild (1998).

25. Schneider, B., and Schmitt, N. (1992). *Staffing Organizations* (Prospect Heights, IL: Waveland Press).

# 4

# TRAINING AND DEVELOPMENT: INVESTING IN YOUR EMPLOYEES

## QUESTIONS TO CONSIDER WHILE READING THIS CHAPTER

1. What steps should be followed to increase the probability that training will achieve stated objectives?
2. What steps should be taken to evaluate the training program's effectiveness?
3. What criteria would you suggest to assess a training program's effectiveness?
4. When training programs fail, what problems will growing firms have with implementing future training programs?

## THE EMERGING ISSUE

Training is time-consuming and expensive. Employees are taken from their regular work, consultants/trainers may be hired to develop and deliver training programs, and internal staff may be used to administer the training. However, even if the direct and indirect costs of training are high, it is also necessary for the viability of any growing organization. Why is this true? Recently, U.S. companies have been confronted with a workforce that has a very low supply of trained workers, and changing technology has forced most employees to enhance their computer-related skills. Also, for emerging firms, compensation budgets may be too low to attract highly trained individuals, so individuals are hired who can learn on the job. Therefore, the cost-effectiveness of training must be addressed. Companies should not adopt the latest fad but assess their own needs, develop programs that are understood by their employees, and evaluate training to determine that objectives have been achieved. Training is an investment that will pay dividends if training dollars are spent on the right programs.

## CHAPTER OVERVIEW

Employee training and development activities are key tools corporations can utilize to gain the proper combination of skills and motivation needed to be competitive. Training and development activities are directly related to a corporation's ability to remain flexible and to adapt quickly to changes in the environment. Thus, employee training and development are vital for ensuring organizational survival and growth. Unfortunately, the approach to training and development programs in many corporations is uncoordinated and inconsistent even though more than $60 billion is spent annually on such programs.[1] These programs are usually not designed to fit the needs of individual employees, and as a result, are not geared toward the strategic needs of the corporation.

When the terms training and development are used, they represent three different types of activities. These activities include orientation of employees, training to develop new skills, and development of existing skills. **Orientation** refers to the training that provides the introductory information a new employee needs to get started on the job. Orientation activities include an overview of the organization, a description of policies and procedures, an outline of the compensation and benefits program, a description of relevant safety information, and a tour of the plant or office's physical facilities.[2] **Training** refers to a systematic effort by an organization to facilitate the learning of job-related knowledge, skills, and abilities. **Development** refers to the acquisition of knowledge, skills, and abilities that enhance an employee's performance of his or her current job.

In 1999, U.S. organizations spent approximately $62.5 billion on all forms of training activities.[3] This amount confirms the importance placed on training and development activities by corporations. However, very few organizations approach their training effort systematically to more effectively utilize their training dollars. This chapter will discuss the major components of training and development programs by presenting a diagnostic tool that helps organizations systematically develop training programs.

## A DIAGNOSTIC APPROACH TO TRAINING

The Goldstein Model is a well-known diagnostic approach to establishing a training and development program.[4] There are three phases in this model. The first phase is needs assessment and it consists of two stages: needs assessment and deriving training program objectives. The second phase is the training and development phase, which is also made up of two stages. These stages include instructional design and conducting the training. The final phase of the Goldstein Model is the evaluation phase. There are five stages to this phase: (1) developing criteria; (2) pretesting trainees; (3) monitoring training; (4) evaluating training; and (5) evaluating transfer of training. These three phases of the Goldstein Model (see Exhibit 6.1) will be discussed in detail in the following section.

### NEEDS ASSESSMENT PHASE

The needs assessment phase consists of two major activities: needs assessment and deriving instructional objectives. These activities and the functions required to successfully complete them are described below.

*Needs Assessment.*    Whereas the organization is responsible for providing an environment that encourages change, it is the employee's responsibility to take advantage of the learning opportunities that are provided to him or her. No matter how reliable the selection and placement procedures are, there will be changes inside and outside of the organization that create a need for improvement. This

■ **EXHIBIT 6.1**

GOLDSTEIN SYSTEMATIC TRAINING MODEL

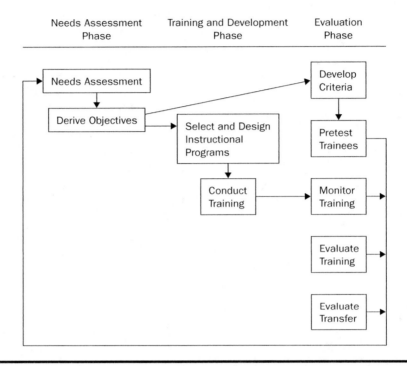

SOURCE: Adapted from Goldstein, I. L. (1974). *Training : Program Development and Evaluation* (Wadsworth Publishing Co.) and Goldstein, I. L. (1993). *Training in Organizations*, 3rd ed. (Pacific Grove, CA: Brooks/Cole Publishing Co.).

improvement can be acquired through training and development. The needs assessment phase is the foundation of training and development. The following are five steps that may help in conduction of a needs assessment:

1. Establish development objectives.
2. Analyze the existing climate for change.
3. Feed results back to management.
4. Secure top management commitment to development objectives and to improve organizational practices that conflict with development.
5. Secure top management participation in program design.

If no training and development program exists, the first step is to conduct a needs analysis. This is necessary to discover what areas have deficiencies and need training programs. If there is a current training and development program,

**EXHIBIT 6.2**

**QUESTIONS TO ASK WHEN AN ORGANIZATIONAL ANALYSIS IS CONDUCTED**

1. Are there unspecified organizational goals that should be translated into training objectives or criteria?

2. Are the various levels in the organization committed to the training objectives?

3. Have the various levels and/or interacting units in the organization participated in the development of the program, beginning at the end of assessment?

4. Are key personnel ready both to accept the behavior of the trainees and to serve as models of the appropriate behavior?

5. Will trainees be rewarded on the job for the appropriate learned behavior?

6. Is training being utilized as a way of overcoming organi-zational problems or organiza-tional conflicts that require other types of solutions?

7. Is top management willing to commit the necessary resources to maintain work organizations while individ-uals are being trained?

Goldstein, I. L. (1993). *Training in Organizations*, 3rd ed. (Pacific Grove, CA: Brooks/Cole Publishing Co.).

then the first step is to analyze the current program to assess whether or not orga-nizational goals are being met. This analysis should include looking at how the program interacts with other organizational systems. After the analysis, training needs should be developed by clearly stating the training objectives. The assess-ment of instructional need is the foundation for training and development. The training and development phase and the evaluation phase depend on the results of the assessment phase. The following is a discussion of the three types of analy-ses: organizational, task, and person.

The first step is an **organizational analysis,** which should look at the goals (both long and short term) of the organization. This analysis should include the structure, strategy, systems, work to be done, and norms and values that guide the individual's behavior in the organization.[5] If an organizational analysis is not completed or if it is improperly completed, the company will face many problems in the future. Exhibit 6.2 outlines seven questions to be considered when an orga-nizational analysis is conducted.

The second step of the assessment is to conduct a **task analysis** to determine the job requirements on which the training will be based. A job description is required, and this should focus on the individual's duties and any conditions spe-cific to the job.[6] Task specifications are also required and should focus on the tasks required to perform the job. Task specification should consist of a complete list of tasks, providing information about what the worker does, how the worker does it, to whom or what, and why. It is also important to decide what knowledge, skills, and abilities are essential to perform the tasks. In some instances, it would be beneficial to interview the job incumbent or his or her supervisor to gain insight into the knowledge, skills, and abilities for that particular job. (See Chap-ter 3 for a complete description of the job analysis interview process.)

When conducting a job or task analysis, the training professional should con-sider the following questions:

1. What are the characteristics of good and poor employees on the particular task(s)?
2. Think of someone you know who is better than anyone else at the particular task(s). What is the reason he or she does so well?
3. What does a person need to know to perform the particular task(s)?
4. Ask a panel to recall concrete examples of effective or ineffective performance. Then ask, "What caused the performance to be effective or ineffective?"
5. If you are going to hire a person to perform the particular task(s), what kind of knowledge, skills, and abilities (KSAs) would you want the person to have?
6. What do you expect persons to learn in training that would make them perform the particular task(s) effectively?[7]

All of the information gathered from these questions is vital to ensure that training programs are job specific and useful.

The last assessment, a **person analysis,** can be conducted in two different ways. An employee's performance discrepancies can be analyzed by (1) comparing an evaluation of employee proficiency on each required skill dimension with the proficiency level required for each skill or (2) comparing actual performance with the minimum acceptable standards of performance. The first method can be used to identify development needs for future jobs. The second method can be used to determine training needs for current jobs because it is based on the actual job performance of the employee.

Some other methods used to evaluate a person's needs include a **self-assessment** and an **attitude survey.** Self-assessment is based on the theory that the employee is more aware of his or her own weaknesses. This means that the employee is best suited to decide if there is a need for training or not. Self-assessment can be the posting of a list of activities where sign-up is optional or it can be the completion of a survey to see who has training needs. An example of a supervisory needs assessment survey can be found in the "Survey on Supervisory Training Needs" in the HR Tool Kit at the end of this chapter.

An attitude survey provides management with information about services and reveals deficiencies of employees. This survey is usually completed by the employees or by customers. Attitude surveys help point out problems, but they give no solutions. An example of a survey is the Satisfaction with Supervisor Scale[8] (Exhibit 6.3). This scale assesses three necessary supervisory skills: technical, human relations, and administrative.

Trainers have noticed that their trainees may be able to learn, but they are not motivated to learn. One way to encourage trainees to learn is to have trainees participate in the assessment of the training process. Although there is little evidence to support this, some adult learning theorists believe that people will only learn what they want to learn. This leads to the conclusion that involvement in the selection of training programs can be a motivator for learning.[9]

**EXHIBIT 6.3**

## SATISFACTION WITH SUPERVISOR SCALE

Please indicate how satisfied you are with your supervisor. Use the following scale, and next to each item write the number that best represents your degree of satisfaction with that particular aspect of supervisory behavior.

**Very Dissatisfied**                                                                                    **Very Satisfied**
  1                          2                          3                          4                          5

_____ 1. The way supervisor listens when I have something important to say.
_____ 2. The way my supervisor sets clear work goals.
_____ 3. The way my supervisor treats me when I make a mistake.
_____ 4. My supervisor's fairness in appraising my job performance.
_____ 5. The way my supervisor is consistent in his/her behavior toward subordinates.
_____ 6. The way my supervisor helps me to get the job done.
_____ 7. The way my supervisor gives me credit for my ideas.
_____ 8. The way my supervisor gives me clear instructions.
_____ 9. The way my supervisor informs me about work changes ahead of time.
_____ 10. The way my supervisor follows through to get problems solved.
_____ 11. The way my supervisor understands the problems I might run into doing the job.
_____ 12. The way my supervisor shows concern for my career progress.
_____ 13. The way my supervisor backs me up with other management.
_____ 14. The frequency with which I get a pat on the back for doing a good job.
_____ 15. The technical competence of my supervisor.

SOURCE: Adapted from Ledvinka, J., and Scarpello, V. G. (1991). _Federal Regulation of Personnel and Human Resource Management_ (Boston: PWS-Kent Publishing Co.)

_Derive Objectives._   Once the training and development needs have been established, specific objectives can be determined. Training objectives can be stated in terms of behaviors or operations. Behavioral objectives are actions, movements, or behaviors that are observable and measurable. Operational objectives refer to specific results such as "lower the cost of producing widgets by 5 percent by May 1, 2002." These instructional objectives are based upon the tasks the trainee will be able to perform and the KSAs that the trainee will have upon completion of the training. The more precise these objectives are, the more likely it is that a successful contribution will be made to the organization.

## TRAINING AND DEVELOPMENT PHASE

The training and development phase focuses on the selection and design of instructional programs and conducting the actual training. Instructional design activities include selecting learning principles and using appropriate training media.

The section on learning principles will focus on behavioral modeling, meaningfulness of material, practice, feedback, individual differences, and transfer of training to the job. The selection of training media will be classified into two types of techniques: on-the-job training and off-the-job training. This approach will help the trainer determine the appropriate training method. At the conclusion of this section, attention will be focused on conducting training in the environment best suited for different types of teaching techniques.

### Selection and Design of Instructional Programs

*Learning principles.*   The main objectives of the learning process are efficient learning, long-term retention, and the ability to apply and transfer skills or factual information learned in training back to the job situation. These objectives can be attained by using traditional principles of learning. To ensure skill learning, one should include goal setting, behavior modeling, practice, and feedback. To learn facts, goal setting, meaningfulness of material, practice, and feedback should be utilized.

For learning to take place, one must want to learn; therefore, motivation plays a part in training.[10] **Goal setting** plays a very important part in this process. The theory of goal setting is founded on the assumption that an individual's conscious goals or intentions govern his behavior. To achieve a desired behavior, objectives must be set that are clear and concise and specified to occur within a specific time frame.[11] For example, in 2 weeks you should be able to assemble a gadget using correct step-by-step procedures within a 2-hour time frame, providing the environmental tools — such as machinery and electricity — are available and working properly to meet the standards of the department. For an individual to achieve personal satisfaction, goals should be challenging and difficult, but obtainable. Difficult yet obtainable goals result in higher levels of performance. Research on goal setting suggests that people will accept and work hard to attain difficult goals, until they reach the limits of their capabilities. However, as goals become too difficult, they may be rejected and performance will suffer.[12] During training, informal checkpoints such as quizzes and evaluations should be used to let the employee feel successful or enable him or her to see areas that need improvement to reach the final goal. Also, to increase motivation in the trainee, the trainer must have expectations and want the employees to perform better. If a trainee is encouraged to perform better by the trainer, the trainee may work harder to improve.

Many employees learn by observing others through the use of **behavior modeling** because it focuses on specific successful behaviors. During training, the trainer should use a reward system to increase the desired behavior he or she wishes to reinforce. Training should move from simple to complex tasks using repetition to encourage retention. Also, the use of several models versus one specific model helps trainees to learn because they may understand one technique better than another. Employees should rehearse what has been demonstrated to improve learning. Trainees should be given a question and answer time for feedback and rewards.[13]

If the material is meaningful to the trainee, he or she will remember the information more easily. To maximize the learning process by using meaningful material, the instructor must start with an overview of the content to orient the trainee. Next, the material should be presented using examples, terms, and concepts that are familiar to the trainee. Reinforcement should be on key learning points and start with simple skills moving to complex skills. In the training design itself, the essential components of a task needed to achieve the final desirable behavior are identified.[14] Also, the trainer should ensure that the tasks are accomplished in their entirety and use a logical connection from one component to another.

**Practice** is an essential component of any program designed to teach a new skill.[15] The training specialist should observe trainee practice sessions and make recommendations to improve trainee behavior. Because of the amount of time required to observe trainee behavior, the use of a low instructor-trainee ratio is recommended. If the task becomes "second nature," it is said to be overlearned, which has several advantages: the length of time the training material will be retained is increased; the task becomes automatic even under stressful situations; and transfer of training to on-the-job situations is facilitated.[16] Also, the length one practices is better when practice is distributed rather than massed because continuous practice causes fatigue that leads to poorer performance.[17] Breaks should be scheduled throughout the day and the day should not last more than 8 hours.

**Feedback** is essential in the learning process and increases trainee motivation. The trainer should emphasize when and how the trainee performs correctly. Feedback provides direct information so the trainee can make correct adjustments and helps reinforce accurate behavior.[18] This should be done immediately after the trainee's action. Success in achieving a desired behavior, as stated by a trainer, increases the willingness of the trainee to learn. Also, specific goal setting will maintain performance.[19]

People learn at different speeds, depending on their ability and motivation. However, the learning curve is an S-shaped curve that indicates remarkable similarities in the overall pattern of how trainees learn.[20] See Exhibit 6.4 for an illustration of the S-shaped learning curve.

Learning rises at the beginning, hits a plateau, and then rises again. The increase at the beginning can be attributed to beginner's luck. The plateau is normal and could be caused by discouragement of the trainee, use of a different training method or technique that the person does not comprehend, or fatigue. Trainers should encourage and support trainees when this occurs and may want to offer more frequent breaks during training sessions to increase learning.

The impact of training on job performance can be positive, negative, or neutral. Trainers must use long-term techniques and emphasize retraining periodically to retain information learned from previous sessions. To transfer training in a positive manner, trainers should maximize similarity between the training situation and job performance, provide time for practice for the trainee to become experienced, provide examples, ensure that principles are understood, design the training so that applicability is easily seen by the trainee, set goals that are established by both trainer and trainee, and, lastly, reward the trainee when transferred behavior has taken place on the job. Supervisors and top management should aid in the reinforcement process.

■ **EXHIBIT 6.4**

THE LEARNING CURVE

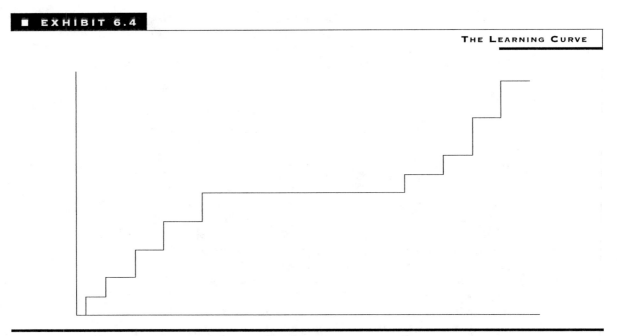

SOURCE: Baron, R. A., and Greenberg, J. (1990). *Behavior in Organizations—Understanding and Managing the Human Side of Work*, 3rd ed. (Needham Heights, MA: Allyn & Bacon). 53.

*Selecting training media.*    To select a training or "learning" method, one must consider individual learning objectives, the educational and experience level of the audience, the personal style of the instructor, and how the learning principles will be incorporated to achieve the objectives of the organization, time, and cost.[21] A trainer should never choose a method solely because it is available and has been used in the past. A trainer may choose a method or combination of methods from a well-founded learning theory or use a more advanced, updated, technological approach.

Employee training can take many forms, some very simple and others quite complex. The techniques may be differentiated with respect to whether the training takes place on the job or off the job. On-the-job methods of training give the trainee hands-on experience and are at least as effective as more formal approaches. In some instances they are even more effective because transfer of knowledge and experience to the job is immediate. Off-the-job methods are used to support on-the-job training. See Exhibit 6.5 for a breakdown of on-the-job and off-the-job training methods.

A needs analysis can be an effective tool when a decision is made to use specific on-the-job and off-the-job training methods. Once the needs analysis is completed, what needs to be taught can be defined. The method or methods chosen should accomplish the following:

**■ EXHIBIT 6.5**

| Training Method | Description |
|---|---|
| **On-the-job methods** | |
| Orientation | A clear understanding of the specific obligations of the company and employee is established. Employees are introduced to company policies and to the people they will work with. |
| Apprenticeship programs | An inexperienced trainee works alongside a senior coworker for a certain number of years. Often formal classroom training is also used. This method is used to train skilled trade workers (e.g., carpenters, electricians). |
| Job instruction training | Trainees are told about the job, instructed on how to do it, allowed to try out the job, given feedback, and then permitted to work on their own (with someone nearby to help, if needed). |
| Coaching | The supervisor provides a periodic review of performance to improve communication and provide a framework for job improvement. |
| Mentoring | A senior employee teaches the new employee the "ropes" of the organization. |
| Job Aids | Instructional material is located on the job to assist in recalling important information presented during training. |
| **Off-the-job methods** | |
| Lectures | Information is communicated in a one-way channel from the expert to the receiver. Problems occur in transfer of training to the job. |
| Programmed Instruction | A self-instructional method in which the trainee gets evaluation of success at specific intervals. The trainee is provided with feedback about the accuracy of responses and moves through the information at his or her own pace. |
| Films/video presentations | Complex procedures not easily demonstrated in person may be shown on film or video tape. Because questions cannot be asked, presentations are often used in conjunction with a live lecture by a knowledgeable trainer. |
| Teleconferencing | Learners participate in remote classrooms hooked up via satellite or telephone technology. Organizations no longer have to pay to develop in-house training programs. |
| Simulations | Simulations may range from the most simple procedures, such as cases and role-playing exercises used to train managers in interpersonal skills, to the most complex computer-assisted simulations used to train astronauts for space flights. |

- Motivate the trainee to improve or change to the desired performance.
- Clearly illustrate desired skills needed.
- Provide adequate participation and practice for the trainee.

**EXHIBIT 6.6**

**DEVELOPING A CONDUCIVE TRAINING ENVIRONMENT**

1. Flexibility is important because the room or rooms chosen should be able to accommodate all types of instructional techniques and materials for each day of the training period.

2. The room should be large enough to hold the number of people in the program, taking into consideration things such as how far a screen or chalkboard is from where the students are sitting.

3. Check the dimensions of the room, the acoustics, and the ceiling height in the planning process before the actual training takes place.

4. Make sure the room is well ventilated with adequate heat or air conditioning.

5. Training should take place in an isolated area so that disruptions are limited.

6. Lighting control should be adequate for visual presentations yet be able to block out light for special types of media. Try to eliminate glare.

7. Make sure equipment is ordered early so it will be available and in good working condition for the training program.

SOURCE: Adapted from Laird, D. (1990). *Approaches to Training and Development,* 2nd ed. (Reading, MA: Addison-Wesley), 202.

- Provide feedback and reinforcement when the desired behaviors are exhibited.
- Show how to adapt to change and handle problems as they arise.
- Be structured to go from simple to complex tasks or behaviors.
- Encourage the trainee so that positive transfer from training to the job situation occurs.

*Conduct Training.*    The type of learning and training materials that have been selected will determine the specific environment in which the training will take place. Some organizations have designated training rooms while others must find space within the organization's building, which will take much planning. Others must go outside of the organization to train employees. The trainer must ensure that the setting is similar to the work environment so that the trainee will transfer the skills learned to the job. An extravagant room is not always necessary for training, but general conditions of the room and media selected should be considered. See Exhibit 6.6 for specific points to follow for selection of a training room. Exhibit 6.7 provides an example of a checklist that a trainer should go through before conducting the actual training. After consideration of the assessment and training and development phases of the Goldstein Model, it is now time to conduct the actual training.

**EVALUATION PHASE**

The previous two phases of the Goldstein model explain the actual steps of training and development; however, to maintain these phases in an on-going and effective

EXHIBIT 6.7

## INSTRUCTOR PREPARATION AND PLANNING CHECKLIST

Have you:

1. Publicized the program or activity?

2. Informed everyone about the time, place, location and other meeting arrangements?

3. Arranged all details of the meeting room?

4. Checked the physical requirements for conducting the session?

   a. Seating arrangement

   b. Podium

   c. Ashtrays

   d. Drinking water

   e. Coat racks

   f. Ventilation, heat, light, class comfort

   g. Projectors, screens

   h. Blackboard, chart pad, easel

   i. Chalk, crayon, eraser

   j. Papers, pencils

5. Secured necessary aids and equipment:

   a. Charts

   b. Handouts

   c. Demonstration materials

   d. Record-keeping items

   e. Films

   f. Slides

6. Checked to be certain equipment is in working order and familiarized yourself with it?

7. Established the objective for the session?

8. Carefully studied the lesson plan?

   a. Determined important points to be emphasized?

   b. Considered anticipated responses and group reactions?

   c. Considered experiences, examples and stories to be used?

   d. Built in a reasonable amount of flexibility?

9. Developed enthusiasm for the program?

10. Arranged for breaks and/or mealtime when appropriate?

SOURCE: Adapted from Randall, J. S. (1978). "You and effective training." *Training and Development Journal* 32, 10–19. Copyright 1978 by the American Society for Training and Development, Inc. Reprinted by permission.

manner, evaluation is necessary at every step in training and development. Evaluation is defined as a process of appraising something carefully to determine its value.[22]

During the actual training and development phase, selection of content, methods of training, instructional supplements, and environment are taken into consideration to aid in the completion of company goals. Nevertheless, it does not matter how much consideration, planning, and attentiveness to detail are used there must be some method to evaluate training that is currently in practice. Procedures and attitudes change as time passes and to adequately maintain a viable training and development program, updating is imperative.

There are four levels of evaluation. These levels are reactions, learning, behavior, and results. Participant reactions are the simplest and easiest form of evaluation. Reactions evaluations usually involve some type of survey assessing feelings about important elements of the training program itself. Learning evaluations include an assessment of whether or not the participant has learned the ideas, facts, and/or processes taught in the training program. Behavior evaluations assess whether or not the participant has incorporated learned facts and processes in performing the job and represent the first step in assessing transfer of training. Finally, results evaluations involve the measurement of bottom-line results such as increased sales, decreased mistakes, etc. Results evaluations are most effective for evaluating transfer of training to actual job behaviors. In a recent report to the American Society for Training and Development,[23] criticism was directed at the lack of results-driven training evaluations. Managers are under increasing pressure to move away from simply measuring reactions (if they even do that) to tying training results to company performance. Given the costs of training programs, it simply is not enough to say that the participants liked the training or learned a lot. The real question is whether the information provided or skills learned are transferred to the job and cause a desired improvement in performance.

There are at least eight important questions to be considered in the evaluation of training programs[24]:

1. Was the needs assessment correctly accomplished?
2. Did the needs assessment correctly identify the training needs?
3. Are the objectives of the program correct?
4. Is the choice of trainees for the program on target?
5. Is the training content being delivered and received as intended?
6. Do the trainees actually apply the skills during the training?
7. Do the trainees transfer to the workplace the skills learned at the program?
8. Are the trainees achieving the performance goals they have established?

In the evaluation phase there are six important steps to follow in evaluating training. These evaluation steps are (1) develop criteria, (2) pretest trainees, (3) monitor training, (4) evaluate training, (5) evaluate transfer of learning, and (6) give feedback.

*Develop Criteria.*    Instructional designers and instructors have continuously been involved in the preceding phases of the Goldstein Model. Consequently, it is just as important to involve these same personnel in identifying the criteria for evaluation. Participation in criteria planning will enable the designers to look at the training from the participants' point of view and what is important to them.

Another important area of criteria is the ability to identify problems with language, clarity, difficulty, design, and interest level in reference to the training objectives.[25] It is important to determine if the desired training has credibility in the "real world." If participants perceive no real application benefits within the program, their interest level, and thus their maintenance level, will be low.

Several factors may lead to a weak training result. These factors include the design and delivery of the training, motivation and background of the trainees, and organizational environment within which trainees work.[26] Consequently, if the previous phases have been accomplished competently, evaluation should be fairly easy to complete and utilize. Specific criteria should be developed at the same time training program objectives are set.

*Pretest Trainees.*　　Pretesting trainees will enable the designers and instructors to understand the areas in which a lack of training is causing the employee to not perform his or her job adequately. The intention of pretesting is to evaluate the necessity for further training and the acceptance of the employee of new ideas and methods.

To better evaluate results of the pretest, an objective method of testing is preferred to a subjective method. In determining content of the pretest, the program will benefit as descriptions of tasks become more specific and are tested in regard to knowledge, skills, and abilities. Competency examinations before actual training are gaining acceptance due to the increase in the participants' motivation level because of the perception that a "testing hurdle" is required at the end of training. Potential trainees could complete questionnaires at their desks sometime before the actual training is implemented to reduce the anxiety of a test environment. This allocation of time would also enable the trainee to become familiar with the type of training that will be offered and perceive its value before the actual training takes place.

A case study done by Ban and Faerman for the New York State's Advanced Human Resources Development Program shows that variables in potential trainees such as age, sex, education, years of service, years in current position, bargaining unit, grade level, previous training courses attended, and span of control had a significant relationship to the level of change. Another discovery in the case study was that respondents scoring lower on the pretest showed more improvement after training and those scoring higher lost retention of material at a much faster rate after training.[27]

Individual supervisors should be consulted about participation of employees. A pretraining questionnaire could also be completed by the supervisor to get a better idea of the needs of the participant. Participants should meet with supervisors to ascertain what areas are needed for further training and discuss potential areas of training that would accomplish advancement within the organization. Jointly, the participant and supervisor should be able to determine an appropriate area of training that meets the abilities, motivation, and determination of the trainee to complete the training satisfactorily.

The difference between desired performance and actual performance will be indicated by the employee's training needs. It is not advisable to train an employee who is already performing adequately and does not desire additional knowledge to achieve a change in position.

*Monitor Training.*　　It is important to monitor training to determine any changes or deficiencies within the training program. To offer quality, pertinent information within the training program, trainers should establish a systematic procedure for collecting and documenting feedback from designers and subject matter experts (SMEs) periodically for the duration of the program. A checklist of definite areas will require designers and SMEs to focus on each area and comment on specific aspects during the training period.

Trainers can also monitor whether participants are acquiring the knowledge, skills, and abilities by testing at periodic times during the program. The number of times tests should be administered is based on the length of the program. Areas to be addressed in monitoring training include trainee's perceived need of subject; trainer's ability to convey information to the trainees; reasonable organization and sequence of subject material; adequate time allocated to absorb information; quality of training materials, equipment, and strategies; type of facilities and logistics; ease of transportation to the training site; and the administration and management of the training program.[28]

Midcourse evaluations assist the instructor in determining if the class is meeting specified needs. If not, midcourse corrections can be made. Also, instructors will be able to elicit information on comprehension of material presented to the participants. If a particular trainee is experiencing a problem, then the instructor will be able to place him or her back on track by meeting individually with the employee. This method also conveys the instructor's commitment to making the class work for the participant.

*Evaluate Training.*   Goal setting assures a direction for the training program and clearly affects the employee's motivation to accomplish the expectations of the trainer. The higher the participant's expectations, the more likely he or she will perform better during the training course. Of course, the reason for attending a training course is to attain better performance on the job; therefore, goal setting must be reasonable and attainable in regard to the job expectations. Participants and supervisors should work together to ascertain what goals to establish for the present and near future.

Many evaluators emphasize the necessity of objective behavioral measures of training; however, many organizations do not have the resources to measure behavior through direct observation. Surveys utilizing detailed and specific items that are descriptive of a wide range of actual job behaviors will allow the observer to draw more definitive conclusions reflecting behavior. Instructors should collect data by using two types of questionnaires: *closed* and *open-ended*. By collecting the data at the end of the course, instructors can assess the participants' reactions to the program, such as the following:

- Importance and relevance of content
- Value of exercises
- Pace and length of the program
- Quality of materials
- Quality of instruction

Multiple sources of data are critical; therefore, after questionnaires are completed by the participant, an in-depth interview with the employee and supervisor reports should be used to verify the information. End-of-course questionnaires may be subjective also. Although they are viewed as a weak evaluation tool, they can be used as an initial measurement of the reactions of the participants to training. The rule of thumb is to keep questionnaires short and simple.[29]

Training must be evaluated by systematically documenting the outcomes of the training in terms of how trainees actually behave when they are back on their jobs and the relevance of the trainees' behavior to the objectives of the organization. To assess the value of the training program, at least four questions need to be answered:

1. Did change occur?
2. Is the change due to training?
3. Is the change positively related to the achievements of organizational goals?
4. Will similar changes occur with new participants in the same training program?

Evaluating change is difficult when an attempt is made to determine if the change is temporary or lasting. Although there are different behavior patterns followed by participants once training has been completed, some of the more common are a continual improvement over time and a noticeable early increase in improvement followed by a sharp drop-off, almost to the pretraining level.

In some instances, participants do not acquire the knowledge and skills to perform their job once the course is completed; retraining is a viable solution and may improve the employee's performance. Both designers of training programs and instructors must recognize that there may be instances in which an employee is not trainable, and in that situation, further training efforts are a waste of the organization's resources.

*Evaluate Transfer of Training.*    Evaluation should take place from 3 to 12 months after a training course and should take the form of evaluating the learning retention, application on the job, and organizational impact.

Observation of on-the-job application can be made by the supervisor through reports and performance appraisals. If the exercises have been closely related to on-the-job expectations, performance appraisals should show an increase in ability. The instructor may occasionally visit to ascertain the successful transfer of information by assisting with any clarification the employee may need and thereby reinforcing the learning process.

It the trainee fails to transfer training to the workplace, the trainer must ascertain whether the proper instruction was given. If the failure is not within the program, an examination of the work environment is necessary to determine whether circumstances beyond the employee's control are present. To achieve successful transfer of training the employee must be motivated to apply new knowledge and skills to the actual job, and the organizational environment must be flexible to institute the change. If the employee is returning to a hostile, nonreceptive atmosphere, he or she may institute the change initially, but will not continue the practice. Therefore, posttraining evaluation will show no real change in performance after a period of time.

Another incentive for successful transfer of training is the knowledge that an evaluation will be conducted at a specified time after course completion. Employees are motivated to continue to apply knowledge and skills learned when they are aware that they will be asked to complete a questionnaire or be observed doing the job. This technique could be used effectively to encourage employees to take their training opportunities more seriously.

*Give Feedback.* Evaluation not only takes place after learning, but before, during, and after instruction. It is a continuous flow of information, occurring from the initial steps through return to on-the-job activity. Constantly collecting data at various stages of training and development enables designers and instructors to continually update and perfect their curriculum, materials, equipment, and methods and set the stage for the next employee training program.

To obtain truly useful feedback, participants in training should be given adequate time to complete questionnaires so that adequate consideration can be given to answers. Although numerical scales on questionnaires simplify summarizing data with the use of a computer, providing an area for additional comments on the questionnaire allows participants an opportunity to express more clearly what was rated.

If the training program is not meeting the organizational performance goals, feedback from questionnaires and in-depth interviews will be one of the first indicators. Employees will express dissatisfaction with methods, materials, or exercises that are perceived as nonessential to job performance.

It is necessary to examine the results of questionnaires thoroughly to determine strengths and weaknesses within the training program. The quality of future training programs will be assessed through results gathered from questionnaires. Although it is difficult to link results from training to measurable organizational factors such as rejection rates, profits, turnover, and attendance, training does present a strong link to achieving organizational goals. Training and development programs, which can be offered during, before, or after work, should be accepted by the employees with the anticipation of gaining better working conditions, better quality of living, and better attitudes toward one's ability to improve. As a result, employees who are more challenged and feel good about their environment perform better in the workplace.

Very few organizations emphasize assessing outcomes from training, but to continue a training and development program that fails to produce results is a waste of organizational resources. Not only will the organization as a whole benefit from feedback, but supervisors and managers also gain invaluable information about employees and their attitudes regarding training and motivation.

## FUTURE TRENDS IN TRAINING AND DEVELOPMENT PRACTICES

More than 10 years ago, in their article "Training Issues in the Year 2000," Goldstein and Gilliam suggested that training must be able to adapt to four major activities. These activities are changes in demographics of entry-level persons in the workforce, increased technology in the world of work, shifts from manufacturing to service-oriented jobs, and increased influence of international markets.[30]

The implications of these changes include an increase in the number of skilled persons for entry-level jobs, increased sophistication of technological systems, and the additional training that jobs, which utilize this technology, will require.

In light of the implications cited above, Goldstein and Gilliam suggested five training areas that needed to be addressed. First, the United States has a problem with unskilled youth. Individuals are not graduating from high school with the math, computer, and reading skills necessary for successful performance in technical manufacturing environments. Second, jobs are increasing in "cognitive complexity." Employees are being required to work in teams, to troubleshoot problems, and to keep complex charts. Third, there is a growing need to maximize individual worker potential. As companies continue to drastically downsize, they will have to effectively utilize all of their human resources. Fourth, the impact of the Equal Employment Opportunity Act on training programs needs to be investigated. Any discussion of training after the year 2000 needs to address employment discrimination. Any technique used to make an employment decision (this includes training) must be demonstrated to be job related. Finally, managers should be trained to better deal with working in a competitive environment. Managers need to be trained on how to maximize the use of employee skills and abilities and be able to demonstrate program effectiveness through evaluation activities.

Although great strides have been made, it appears that those issues cited over 10 years ago are just as critical today. Advances in distance or Internet training have increased the availability of training media to many who otherwise would not be able to receive training. The use of teams has increased dramatically, bringing about even more demand for team-based training. Organizations continue to struggle to provide communication, problem-solving, decision-making training to these teams.[31] Also, front-line supervision still remains an area of great concern for training professionals. Too often, individuals are thrown into management positions and are expected to learn on the job. This lack of formal preparation can cause employee morale problems, increased turnover, and legal problems such as discrimination and harassment.[32]

In addition to the issues described above, several other changes should be considered as we now are in the "next century." Some of the major changes or challenges that need to be addressed are summarized below:

- Job requirements will demand more than basic skills. Jobs will require more complex cognitive and interpersonal skills but pay less than the average manufacturing job. Advanced technology jobs will go unfilled because there will not be enough qualified people to fill them.

- More emphasis will be placed on increasing the skills of managers by making provisions to continuously conduct on-the-job training and integrate younger workers and workers from different cultures into the workforce.

- The number of team-based and empowered organizations will increase, causing additional pressures to develop a workforce with interpersonal and

### THE EXPANSION OF IN-HOUSE TRAINING FOR PROFIT

National Catastrophe Adjustors Group (NCA Group) is a mid-sized company based in Indianapolis, IN, that does damage assessment work (adjusting) for many of the largest insurance companies in the United States. Until the early 1980s adjustors who worked for companies like NCA learned their trade in a classroom-type setting. Subsequently, however, the most common type of adjustor training took place in the form of a "ride along." For this training an apprentice adjustor rode along with one who was more experienced. Although this worked fine for some companies, major insurance carriers became concerned that adjustors had lost their technical forte. Indeed, insurance adjusters now offer more of a service-oriented profession.

Having hands-on technical training is important to insurance carriers because this assures that the adjustor will assess damage as accurately as possible. Until now, NCA and other midwestern adjusting firms had been required to send their adjustors to distant and costly training centers in Pennsylvania, Texas, or California.

David Ross, NCA Group CEO, and his executive team determined that some of the excess capacity within their new Indianapolis headquarters could be used to do something revolutionary within the adjusting industry: they created an in-house training center. NCA soon realized that this undertaking would not only allow the company to train its adjustors at one-quarter of the cost required to send them to outside training centers, but it would also have a number of benefits for its adjustors.

The outside training courses that NCA's adjustors have histor-ically been required to complete have been extremely time-consuming. Not only have adjustors had to travel long distances, but the generic format of the courses also required NCA's adjustors to sit through hours or even days of training that was not helpful in their work at NCA. NCA decided to offer training programs that met the needs of their adjustors while weeding out all of the unneeded information that was taught in the outside centers. This streamlining cut the time that adjustors had to spend in training by 50 percent.

While eliminating all of the unnecessary information from the training program, NCA experienced benefits that exceeded the company's expectations. NCA has developed its training center into a dynamic adjustor learning center where adjustors at all skill levels and from companies all over

decision-making skills. Managers will have to learn to adapt to new roles as their traditional function continues to disappear.

- The issues summarized above present major challenges to those involved in the training process. Perhaps a major implication of this challenge is that emerging organizations and those empowered to manage training will require more training to develop training programs that address these issues.

## CHAPTER SUMMARY

Training and development are vital for ensuring organizational survival and growth. Guidelines have been established by federal and state governments to the country can come and receive custom tailored training that meets the needs of their individual companies. This allows companies who wish to have their adjusters trained by NCA to have their adjustors back in half the time. They also benefit from the lower costs that are associated with training an adjuster in Indianapolis because such costs are lower in many parts of the Midwest than in the other cities where training is currently available. In addition, NCA's instructors can go on site anywhere in the country and provide firms with customized adjustor training.

While NCA's new training center helps the company to reduce the costs that are associated with training its employees, it also generates a substantial amount of revenue. By offering training to adjustors who work at firms that are located throughout the country and having a team of instructors who can provide custom tailored training anywhere in the country, NCA has truly found that giving its employees world-class training can also be quite profitable.

Many of the states, such as Texas, that require adjustors to receive a certain number of in-state training hours per year, have accredited NCA to train their adjustors. There are also states that grant automatic reciprocity to adjustors accredited in other states. So Michigan, for example, may automatically recognize the accreditation of an adjustor who is licensed in Texas. That adjustor in Texas may have been trained at NCA in Indiana.

By using a bit of ingenuity, NCA has been able to utilize its resources to create a training center that keeps its employees happy while generating revenue at the same time. Many companies generate revenue from their training programs *indirectly* through higher sales levels achieved by better-trained employees. NCA has been able to make money *directly* by providing to others the same training that benefits its own employees. So, they profit in two ways: they profit from the service they offer, and they profit from the training they offer to their own and other adjusters. Training is not an essential profit strategy for every company; however, for a growing company like NCA Group, the revenue that is generated from the employee-training program may translate into the resources needed to secure a competitive advantage in the adjusting business.

SOURCE: Personal Interview with David Ross.

guarantee protection of employees in regard to employment, including training and development programs. The Goldstein Model is a well-known approach to establishing a training and development program. Included within this model are three phases. The needs assessment phase consists of determining the instructional need of employees and deriving objectives. The training and development phase focuses on instructional design and conducting training. The environment plays a major part in how trainees absorb information during a training program. The evaluation phase is many times excluded from training and development programs; however, this is actually the most important aspect of the program due to constant input from participants. The ability to continually update and define these programs contributes to an innovative and aggressive organizational strategy. Finally, over the next decade, training specialists face many challenges due to the increasing complexity of the workforce and the jobs performed.

**FREQUENTLY ASKED QUESTIONS**

### What are the major issues in training of adult learners?

The employee as adult learner is much different from a college or high school student. Older learners differ from younger students in the following ways:

- They are usually more goal or purpose driven.
- They like to work in a self-directed manner.
- They need to relate training material to their own experiences.

In designing a training program, it is critical to consider the type of audience. In particular, what are the average age, educational level, and types of occupations of the trainees? Training usually should be targeted to the common denominator of the group so that the information exchange is most effective.

### What is a needs assessment and why should my company conduct one?

A needs assessment determines the types of training an organization needs to overcome performance weaknesses or adapt to changes in work process or in the work environment. Remember the old adage: "Give a person a hammer and everything needs hammering." Too many firms offer training without determining whether there really is a specific need for that particular training. Managers and human resource specialists are prone to follow the latest training fads, often spending thousands of dollars on something that will not enhance performance. Some of the most often utilized sources of training needs information include the following:

- Performance appraisal data
- Surveys of supervisors and employees
- The company strategic plan

### Why is it important to evaluate a training program's accomplishments?

In 1999, employers spent an estimated $62.5 billion on training. During the 1990s, spending on training increased more than in any other decade. Although training is a necessary component in a dynamic workplace, it is critical to assess the success of all training programs. In many cases, those in charge of the training program are cautious about evaluating program success because if the training is proven to be a failure or is not successful enough, they feel that their job or reputation may be threatened. However, to constantly repeat a flawed training program is also problematic and a waste of resources. Consistent evaluation of training allows for continuous improvement of the programs and enables the company to truly reach its performance goals.

**WEB ADDRESSES**

**www.trainingsupersite.com/ tss_link/trainset.htm**
*Training* magazine on-line offers the latest news and information about training and employee development. The magazine offers many of its stories and topical discussions on-line.

**http://homepage.tinet.ie/ ~mjcollins/**
The web site of Michael J. Collins and Associates, a training consultant, offers a great selection of articles and links related to training and development.

**www.trainingsupersite.com/**
The "Training SuperSite" is also an excellent resource for training needs. The site offers an on-line magazine, links, and educational programs and helps the HR professional find the best resources for training and development.

**SURVEY ON SUPERVISORY TRAINING NEEDS**

Think about what a supervisor does in terms of interactions with people. Some of these behaviors are listed below in the left column.

a. For each item in the left column, circle one response code in the center column to indicate your feeling about how important that behavior is for first-line supervisors generally.

Use the following scale:
0 represents neither importance nor unimportance
1 represents a very low degree of importance
2 represents a low degree of importance
3 represents a high degree of importance
4 represents a very high degree of importance

b. For each item in the left column, circle one response code in the right column to indicate how much need for training there is on the subject.

Use the following scale:
0 represents neither little nor much need for training
1 represents very little need for training
2 represents little need for training
3 represents much need for training
4 represents very much need for training

| Supervisory Behavior | Importance of the Behavior Very Low → Very High | | | | | Need for Training Very Low → Very High | | | | |
|---|---|---|---|---|---|---|---|---|---|---|
| 1. Applying motivation theory, taking individual differences into account. | 0 | 1 | 2 | 3 | 4 | 0 | 1 | 2 | 3 | 4 |
| 2. Checking to make sure subordinates understand orders. | 0 | 1 | 2 | 3 | 4 | 0 | 1 | 2 | 3 | 4 |
| 3. Establishing clear goals at the beginning of a task/ assignment. | 0 | 1 | 2 | 3 | 4 | 0 | 1 | 2 | 3 | 4 |
| 4. Establishing clearly understood deadlines. | 0 | 1 | 2 | 3 | 4 | 0 | 1 | 2 | 3 | 4 |
| 5. Exciting enthusiasm among others about a job task. | 0 | 1 | 2 | 3 | 4 | 0 | 1 | 2 | 3 | 4 |
| 6. Explaining clearly to others how to perform a task. | 0 | 1 | 2 | 3 | 4 | 0 | 1 | 2 | 3 | 4 |
| 7. Facilitating information sharing across a team. | 0 | 1 | 2 | 3 | 4 | 0 | 1 | 2 | 3 | 4 |
| 8. Following up with subordinates during a task to see how things are going. | 0 | 1 | 2 | 3 | 4 | 0 | 1 | 2 | 3 | 4 |
| 9. Giving praise to individuals when it is due. | 0 | 1 | 2 | 3 | 4 | 0 | 1 | 2 | 3 | 4 |

SOURCE: Sredl, H. J., and Rothwell, W. J. (1987). *The ASTD Reference Guide to Professional Training Roles and Competencies*, Vol. II (Amherst, MA: HRD Press, Inc.).

| Supervisory Behavior | Importance of the Behavior<br>Very Low        Very High | | | | | Need for Training<br>Very Low        Very High | | | | |
|---|---|---|---|---|---|---|---|---|---|---|
| 10. Identifying what motivates different people. | 0 | 1 | 2 | 3 | 4 | 0 | 1 | 2 | 3 | 4 |
| 11. Issuing clear orders. | 0 | 1 | 2 | 3 | 4 | 0 | 1 | 2 | 3 | 4 |
| 12. Maintaining good feelings in a group. | 0 | 1 | 2 | 3 | 4 | 0 | 1 | 2 | 3 | 4 |
| 13. Providing corrective counseling to individuals when necessary. | 0 | 1 | 2 | 3 | 4 | 0 | 1 | 2 | 3 | 4 |
| 14. Providing clear, specific feedback on individual performance. | 0 | 1 | 2 | 3 | 4 | 0 | 1 | 2 | 3 | 4 |
| 15. Providing regular feedback on individual performance. | 0 | 1 | 2 | 3 | 4 | 0 | 1 | 2 | 3 | 4 |
| 16. Resolving conflicts between individuals. | 0 | 1 | 2 | 3 | 4 | 0 | 1 | 2 | 3 | 4 |
| 17. Setting a good example for others to follow. | 0 | 1 | 2 | 3 | 4 | 0 | 1 | 2 | 3 | 4 |
| 18. Setting priorities among competing interests. | 0 | 1 | 2 | 3 | 4 | 0 | 1 | 2 | 3 | 4 |
| 19. Other (specify) _____ _____ | 0 | 1 | 2 | 3 | 4 | 0 | 1 | 2 | 3 | 4 |
| 20. Other (specify) _____ _____ | 0 | 1 | 2 | 3 | 4 | 0 | 1 | 2 | 3 | 4 |
| 21. Other (specify) _____ _____ | 0 | 1 | 2 | 3 | 4 | 0 | 1 | 2 | 3 | 4 |

Describe briefly, in your own words, what would be the single most useful skill in dealing with other people that a participant in this course could learn (or improve).

There are various ways to present a course of this kind. Assume that this one will be application-oriented, with very little lecture but with many exercises. What kind of exercises would be most useful in building effective interpersonal skills? Answer this question by responding to the questions in the box below.

| Kind of Exercise | Brief Description | Usefulness | | | |
|---|---|---|---|---|---|
| | | None | Not Much | Some | Great |
| 1. Cases | 2–3 page discussion of a problem in dealing with people faced by a first-line supervisor. | 0 | 1 | 2 | 3 |
| 2. Critical incidents | 1–3 sentence scenario in dealing with people faced by first-line supervisors. | 0 | 1 | 2 | 3 |
| 3. Roleplay | Dramatic illustration of a common scene in dealing with people. | 0 | 1 | 2 | 3 |
| 4. Other _____ | | 0 | 1 | 2 | 3 |
| (Specify) _____ | | 0 | 1 | 2 | 3 |
| _____ | | 0 | 1 | 2 | 3 |
| 5. Other _____ | | 0 | 1 | 2 | 3 |
| (Specify) _____ | | 0 | 1 | 2 | 3 |
| _____ | | 0 | 1 | 2 | 3 |

6. Please add any other comments you wish.

## NOTES

1. "Industry Report." (1998). *Training* 35: 43–45.

2. Wexley, K. M., and Latham, G. P. (1997). *Developing and Training Human Resources in Organizations*, 2nd ed. (Reading, MA: Addison-Wesley).

3. "Industry Report 1999." (1999) *Training* October: 37–81.

4. Goldstein, I. L. (1993). *Training in Organizations*, 3rd ed. (Pacific Grove, CA: Brooks/Cole Publishing Company). Goldstein, I. L. (1974). *Training: Program Development and Evaluation* (Belmont, CA: Wadsworth Publishing Company, Inc.); Goldstein, I. L., and Ford, K. (2000). *Training in Organizations*, 4th ed. (Boston: Course Technology, Inc).

5. Mailick, S., Hoberman, S. J., and Wall, S. (1988). *The Practice of Management Development* (Brooklyn, NY: Praeger Publishers).

6. *Ibid.*

7. *Ibid.*

8. Carpello, V. G., Ledvinka, J., and Bergmann, T. J. (1995). *Human Resource Management, Environments and Functions*, 2nd ed. (Cincinnati: South-Western Publishing Co.); Ledvinka, J., and Scarpello, V. G. (1991). *Federal Regulation of Personnel and Human Resource Management* (Boston: PWS-Kent Publishing Co.).

9. Baldwin, T. T., Magjuka, R. J., and Loher, B. T. (1991). "The perils of participation: Effects of choice training on trainee motivation and learning." *Personnel Psychology* 51–65.

10. Baron, R. A., and Greenberg, J. (1999). *Behavior In Organizations — Understanding and Managing the Human Side of Work*, 7th. ed. (Upper Saddle River, NJ: Prentice Hall).

11. Mirabile, R. J.(1991). "Pinpointing development needs." *Training & Development* 45(12): 19–25.

12. Locke, E. A., and Latham, G. P. (1984). *Goal Setting for Individuals, Groups, and Organizations* (Chicago: Science Research Association).

13. Baron and Greenberg (1999).

14. *Ibid.*

15. Schendel, J. D., and Hagman, J. D. (1982). "On sustaining procedural skills over a prolonged retention interval." *Journal of Applied Psychology*, 605–610.

16. Baron and Greenberg (1999).

17. Rothenberg, R. G., and Drye, T. R. (1991). "Train 700 people in quality? No problem." *Training & Development* 45(12): 43–46.

18. Mirabile (1991).

19. Rothenberg and Drye (1991).

20. Baron and Greenberg (1999).

21. Laird, D. (1990). *Approaches to Training and Development*, 2nd ed. (Reading, MA: Addison-Wesley).

22. Sredl, H. J., and Rothwell, W. J. (1987). *The ASTD Reference Guide to Professional Training Roles and Competencies*, Vols. I and II (Amherst, MA: HRD Press, Inc.).

23. Bassi, L. J., and VanBuren, M. E. "The 1999 ASTD state of the industry report." *Training & Development*, (Supplement) 1–26.

24. Bienbrauer, H. (1987). "Trouble-shooting your training program." *Training & Development* September: 18–20

25. Connolly, S. M. (1988). "Integrating evaluation, design and implementation." *Training & Development* February: 20–23.

26. Ban, C., and Faerman, S. R. (1990). "Issues in the evaluation of management training." *Public Productivity and Management Review* Spring: 271–285.

27. *Ibid.*

28. Connolly (1988).

29. *Ibid.*

30. Goldstein, I. L., and Gilliam, P. (1990). "Training issues in the year 2000." *American Psychologist* 45: 134–142.

31. Johnson, C. (1999). "Teams at work: Getting the best from teams requires work on the teams themselves." *HRMagazine* May: 30–37.

32. Segal, J. A. (1996). "Sexual harassment: Where are we now?" *HRMagazine* October: 68–73.

# 5

## INFLUENCES ON EMPLOYEE BEHAVIOR

### LEARNING OBJECTIVES

1. Identify the major external and internal factors that influence employee behavior.

2. Describe two primary types of outcomes that may result from behavior and tell how they may influence future behavior.

3. State how a supervisor's leadership and expectations for employees can affect their behavior.

4. Recognize the impact that coworkers and the organization itself have on employee behavior.

5. Define motivation and describe the main approaches to understanding motivation at work.

6. Discuss how knowledge, skill, ability, and attitudes influence employee behavior.

**OPENING CASE**

United Technologies Corporation (UTC) is a conglomerate with headquarters in Hartford, Connecticut. Worldwide, it has a workforce of over 148,000 employees. Some of its major subsidiaries include: Pratt & Whitney (jet engines), Carrier (air conditioning systems), Otis (elevators), Hamilton Sundstrand (aerospace and industrial equipment), and Sikorsky (helicopters). Since 1990, it has undergone a major downsizing of its workforce in the United States, with a substantial increase in its workforce outside the U.S. George David, CEO of UTC, said in a 1995 speech, "We and others create jobs overseas fundamentally for market access, to extend our global market leadership and thereby to make our company stronger and to assure employment at home." Later, he stated that "we cannot guarantee anyone a job, but we are nonethe-less obliged to provide employees reasonable opportunities to reestablish themselves, ideally on more favorable conditions, in the event of job loss." One of the commitments made by UTC was to provide tuition reimbursement for undergraduate or graduate courses taken by their employees. By 1995, approximately 6 percent of eligible UTC employees had taken advantage of this opportunity.[1]

The Pratt & Whitney subsidiary has been hit hard by the overall decline in the world aerospace markets. It has 31,000 employees worldwide, with approximately 13,000 working in Connecticut. In January 2000, Pratt & Whitney announced the elimination of up to 1,700 jobs, primarily in Connecticut. This is in addition to the 3,500 jobs cut since 1998 as part of their major restructuring.[2]

An obvious challenge in the midst of such changes is the maintenance of employee skills and morale. What happens to employee training and development efforts during a downsizing of this magnitude? Will employees take advantage of such a tuition reimbursement program during restructuring? What happens to employees who are laid off at the time they are taking college classes? Can Pratt & Whitney (and UTC) maintain their commitment to tuition reimbursement in such an environment?

[1] SOURCE: George David (1995). Remarks on restructuring. National Press Club, December 14, 1995, http://www.utc.com/company/ARCHIVE/gdavid2.htm.

[2] Pratt and Whitney to reduce manufacturing workforce, http://www.prattwhitney.com/news/2000/0121.html.

# INTRODUCTION

Have you ever wondered:

- *why a coworker behaves the way he or she does?*
- *why people so often live up (or down) to the expectations that others have of them?*
- *why managers seem to develop relationships of different quality with different subordinates?*
- *why some work teams develop more trust and cohesiveness than others?*
- *how motivation influences employee behavior?*
- *whether there are some general frameworks or models that can help in understanding the various influences on employee behavior?*

The overarching goal of Human Resource Development interventions is to provide activities and other mechanisms that assist employees *and* organizations in attaining their goals. HRD professionals can help employees meet their personal goals by providing programs and interventions that promote individual development, for example, career development activities, mentoring, and formal training and educational opportunities. Concerning organizational goals, the ultimate objective of most, if not all, HRD programs is to *improve organizational performance*. HRD efforts are not the only contributors to organizational performance; however, they are increasingly recognized as a critical component of organizational success.[1] Further, a major focus of most HRD interventions is an effort to *change employee behavior*. That is, the hope is that providing employees with the skills and behaviors they need to perform successfully should lead to the greatest accomplishment of both employee and organizational goals. Thus, the field of HRD has had (and continues to have) a strong focus on employee behavior. In order to change any behavior, we must first understand the factors that cause employees to behave the way that they do. Armed with this knowledge, we can more accurately diagnose performance problems, understand what makes effective performance possible, and design HRD programs to create the behavior we want.

Identifying the causes of employee behavior is no easy task. The factors contributing to any behavior are numerous, complex, and difficult to ascertain. Yet a thorough understanding of employee behavior and its causes is critical for any HRD program to be effective. The purpose of this chapter is to introduce readers to the major factors influencing employee behavior and their implications for HRD. Students with backgrounds in organizational behavior or applied psychology will find that this chapter provides an important review and an opportunity to relate these issues to topics within HRD.

## MODEL OF EMPLOYEE BEHAVIOR

The model of employee behavior shown in Figure 2-1 presents what we consider to be the key factors affecting employee behavior and their corresponding relationships. It includes two main categories: 1) **external forces**—that is, those found in the *external environment* (outside the organization) and in the *work environment* (inside the organization), including leadership/supervision, aspects of the organization itself, coworkers, and the outcomes of performance (such as praise); and 2) **internal forces**—that is, those within the employee, including motivation, attitudes, and KSAs (knowledge, skills, and abilities). The model assumes that external and internal forces interact or combine to produce a given behavior, and that employee behavior has a direct relationship to the personal and organizational outcomes that are obtained. Although it may be possible in some cases to trace the cause of a behavior to one or two dominant forces, we believe that overall patterns of behavior can best be explained by the combination of many factors.

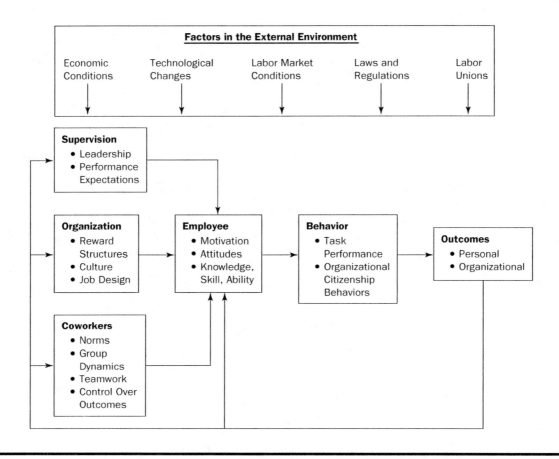

The model is relatively simple for purposes of clarity and relevance to HRD. Our goal is not to cover all of the possible causes for employee behavior, but to include only those most critical to designing, delivering, and using HRD programs. Additional relevant concepts will be presented in later chapters. The remainder of this chapter will focus on the elements contained within the model.

### MAJOR CATEGORIES OF EMPLOYEE BEHAVIOR

If HRD efforts are primarily intended to change employee behavior, then it is useful to first ask what types of behavior they are intended to change. Recent research and writing strongly suggests that individual performance is multidimensional.[2] While many different aspects or dimensions of individual performance have been identified, one vital distinction is between those behaviors that are central to performing one's job (often called **task performance**), and other behaviors that are less central yet still valuable for the effective functioning of the team, department, or organization as a whole.[3] Many training efforts have focused on the first group of behaviors, namely those relating to performing the critical tasks associated with a given job. But the second category of behaviors is also important. Behaviors in this category have been given different labels (such as organizational citizenship behaviors, discretionary behaviors, or contextual performance).[4] A central aspect of such behaviors (we will call them **organizational citizenship behaviors**) is that in the aggregate, they also contribute to organizational effectiveness.[5] For example, HRD efforts to inculcate a culture of innovation and initiative taking would be focusing more on this second category of behaviors. Similarly, team-building efforts that seek to promote cooperation and teamwork emphasize such citizenship behaviors. Alternately, coaching or mentoring efforts often seek to promote behaviors that are helpful to the organization as a whole, yet are not "enforceable requirements" of a given job.[6] The motivational issues discussed later in this chapter are particularly critical in determining the extent to which employees engage in behaviors that are "above and beyond" their formal job requirements. As Daniel Katz wrote many years ago, "An organization which depends solely upon its blueprints of prescribed behavior is a very fragile social system."[7] As we seek to present you with a "systems" perspective on human resource development, we think it is necessary to begin our discussion by highlighting these two critical aspects of individual employee behavior. Next, we will describe the major factors that influence such behavior.

## EXTERNAL INFLUENCES ON EMPLOYEE BEHAVIOR

### FACTORS IN THE EXTERNAL ENVIRONMENT

Influences from outside the organization, that is, the external environment, clearly influence employee behavior. Further, factors within the work environment also play a strong role in determining employee behavior. Factors from the *external environment* include the general state of the economy (e.g., the rate of inflation and the level of unemployment), the various governmental laws and regulations, what other organizations or competitors are doing, plus the many global and technological issues mentioned in Chapter 1. Our model in Figure 2–1 depicts these as general forces that influence the organization and all parts within it.[8] Even organizations with strong internal work environments and high levels of employee behaviors can be negatively impacted by external factors such as a downturn in the economy or a sudden technological change. Two factors that have their roots in the external environment deserve special mention, namely downsizing and mergers and acquisitions. These are labeled as external factors primarily because the forces that lead organizations to consider either one are generally outside of the organization (such as global competition or technological advancement).

**Downsizing** refers to voluntary actions on the part of organizations to reduce the overall size of their workforce, generally to reduce costs.[9] A huge number of companies have reduced their workforce over the past two decades, including AT&T, Boeing, DuPont, IBM, Xerox, and United Technologies (the organization highlighted in the Opening Case). Despite the widespread nature of downsizing over the past twenty years, there is in fact little solid evidence concerning its effectiveness as a business practice.[10] For example, a survey conducted by Watson Wyatt Worldwide found that 46 percent of the companies surveyed met their expense-reduction goals after downsizing, fewer than 33 percent met their profit objectives, and only 21 percent increased their return on investment for shareholders.[11] A study by Wayne Cascio of companies that downsized more than 3 percent in a given year between 1980-1990 found no improvement in financial or stock performance as a result of downsizing.[12] An ASTD survey found that downsized organizations reported lower organizational performance, lower quality products or services, and lower employee satisfaction compared to organizations that had not downsized.[13]

In order for organizations to ensure their future success, they must maintain their investment in their workforce, even when they are restructuring or downsizing.[14] This includes training the "survivors" of downsizing on how to carry out their responsibilities after downsizing has occurred,[15] but can also include decisions to retrain rather than lay off employees. For example, Digital Equipment, Eastman Kodak, Hallmark, Pacific Bell, and Raychem have all been cited for their efforts to retrain workers who would otherwise be laid off.[16] Similarly, amid all the layoffs at AT&T since its court-ordered breakup in 1984, AT&T developed a Safe Landing program to assist their employees in obtaining other positions, either within AT&T or elsewhere.[17]

The ASTD study cited above found that organizations did best when they emphasized both organizational and individual performance. In particular, three individual-level practices were more common in companies designated as high performance work systems, namely coaching and mentoring, individual development, and multirater feedback. Further, companies with the most extensive high performance work systems were nearly three times less likely to cut their workforces than were companies with less extensive usage of such practices.[18] It should be clear from this brief discussion that downsizing has enormous implications for human resource development, and conversely, that HRD efforts can have a significant impact on the effectiveness of organizational downsizing. A leading HRD scholar, Warner Burke, has argued that HRD professionals should play a more active role in challenging or redirecting corporate downsizing efforts.[19]

**Mergers and acquisitions** (M&As) are increasingly reshaping modern organizations. The argument for one organization to acquire another, or for two firms to merge into one is that such efforts "create value when they enhance the strategic capabilities of both firms, improving the competitive position of either or both, resulting in improved financial operating results."[20] Unfortunately, in the majority of cases, mergers and acquisitions fail to live up to expectations, or worse, can be classified as "outright failures."[21] While changes in the economy can contribute to some of this, the consensus seems to be that merger failures (and disappointments) are most often the result of the mismanagement of people issues.[22] Problems can occur in communications (before, during, and after the merger), in retaining key employees, and in managing the integration of the two organizations (including the respective cultures of each). HRD professionals, especially those with expertise in organizational development and change (see Chapter 14) should be actively involved in such integration efforts. Sadly, a 1999 survey found that only 19 percent of human resource executives felt that they had sufficient technical expertise to properly assist top management in the merger and acquisition process. According to Clemente and Greenspan, "This lack of knowledge and experience is ostensibly the reason HR is not being brought in by senior management to directly support acquisition strategy and target company evaluations."[23] HR professionals need greater competency in the area of strategic management. Further, HRD professionals can be actively involved in the communications and training needed to carry out a successful merger or acquisition. For example, employees and managers at all levels of the organization need information on what to expect at each phase of the M&A process.[24] With the skills and competencies described in this book, HRD professionals should be in a prime position to facilitate the successful completion of a merger or acquisition.

### FACTORS IN THE WORK ENVIRONMENT

In addition to factors in the external environment, there are also factors within the organization that influence employee behavior. We will emphasize four sets of forces within the *work environment* that affect employee behavior: outcomes, the supervisor, characteristics of the organization itself, and coworkers. Table 2-1 presents a list of these forces and some of the issues found in each.

*OUTCOMES.* **Outcomes** occur as a result of a given employee behavior. Outcomes can be personal or organizational. *Personal outcomes* are those that have value to the individual, such as pay, recognition, and emotions. *Organizational outcomes* are things valued by the organization, such as teamwork, productivity, and product quality. These outcomes are what the organization would ultimately hope to achieve by the collective efforts of all organizational members. The word *value* in this context should not imply that outcomes are always positive or desirable. Behavior can also result in outcomes that employees fear or dislike. Embarrassment, disciplinary actions, transfers, loss of pay or privileges, and ostracism are all possible unpleasant outcomes of employee behavior.

Figure 2–1 presents these outcomes as following from employee behaviors. That is, though clearly other factors influence individual and organizational outcomes,

■ **TABLE 2-1**

INFLUENCES ON EMPLOYEE BEHAVIOR FROM THE WORK ENVIRONMENT

| Factor | Issues |
|---|---|
| Outcomes | Types |
| | Effect on motivation |
| Supervision | Leadership |
| | Performance Expectations |
| Organization | Reward Structure |
| | Organizational Culture |
| | Job Design |
| Coworkers | Norms |
| | Group dynamics |
| | Teamwork |
| | Control of outcomes |

we have limited our discussion to those things that influence employee behaviors, and the subsequent influence that these behaviors have on personal and organizational outcomes. However, it is also important to note the likely influence that organizational outcomes have on employee behaviors (this is actually the reverse of the ordering presented in Figure 2-1). For example, several of the motivation theories that we present later in the chapter propose that *employee perceptions* of outcomes are important determinants of behavior. Consider two examples:

1. **Expectancy theory** states that people will perform behaviors that they perceive will bring valued outcomes. If employees fulfill certain obligations to the organization but do not receive promised outcomes (such as promotions or pay raises), they may reduce their expectations about the link between their performance and the desired outcomes and thus choose to behave differently. Further, if outcomes are not as rewarding as anticipated, the employees may revise their judgments about the value of that outcome and perform different behaviors.[25]

2. **Equity theory** states that outcomes are evaluated by comparing them to the outcomes received by others. If employees perceive an inequity, they may change their performance or cognitions, or both, to reduce the inequity. In addition, outcomes can serve as a form of feedback to employees. Bonuses and recognition, for example, let employees know if they have performed appropriately and if their performance is valued by the organization.[26]

Outcomes and outcome perceptions are important to HRD. If employees do not believe that attending a training program will lead to valued outcomes, they may choose not to attend the program, or they may devote little effort to learning and using the skills being taught. If an employee perceives that company training will require increased individual effort with no greater personal outcomes than what other employees receive, the training may be seen as unfair. As a result, the employee may resist participating in the program.

It is often the outcomes of performance (such as embarrassment or a poor evaluation) that serve as attention getters, convincing an employee that training or development is needed. For example, if a nurse who treats patients rudely never experiences any unpleasant outcomes as a result (such as complaints to the supervisor or disciplinary actions), it is unlikely that the nurse will perceive any need to change this behavior. Similarly, if college professors who have not kept current in their field continue to receive support and recognition for their work in the classroom, they may perceive that their behavior is acceptable and see no reason to attend professional seminars or engage in other developmental actions.

Thus, it is important that supervisors and managers remain aware of the outcomes of their subordinates' performance, as well as how their subordinates view these outcomes. This knowledge can be useful in detecting needs for training, motivating employees to participate in training, and in ensuring that what employees learn in training is applied to their jobs.

*SUPERVISION AND LEADERSHIP.* The immediate supervisor plays an important role in the employee's work life, delegating tasks and responsibilities, setting expectations, evaluating performance, and providing (or failing to provide) feedback, rewards, and discipline. Even with the shift toward greater use of teams, including more self-directed work teams, supervisors continue to play a critical role in the success of most organizations.[27] Although the influences supervisors have on subordinates are numerous and sometimes complex, two factors deserve comment: self-fulfilling prophecy and leadership.

Research on **self-fulfilling prophecy,** or the Pygmalion effect, has shown how the expectations a supervisor establishes can influence a subordinate's behavior. First demonstrated in classroom settings, self-fulfilling prophecy states that expectations of performance can become reality because people strive to behave consistently with their perceptions of reality. If supervisors (or trainers) expect good performance, their behavior may aid and encourage their subordinates (or trainees) to raise their own self-expectations, increase their efforts, and ultimately perform well. The opposite would happen if supervisors or trainers expected poor performance.[28]

Dov Eden and his colleagues have demonstrated in a variety of work settings that raising managers' performance expectations results in higher levels of performance in their employees.[29] Interestingly, research to date has failed to demonstrate that self-fulfilling prophecy occurs when females are leaders; confirmatory evidence has only been obtained when males are leaders.[30] The implications for supervisors and HRD professionals who conduct training programs are clear: All must be aware of their own expectations and what they communicate to others, while taking advantage of the benefits resulting from high but realistic expectations. In addition, supervisory expectations play a key role in the coaching process, which will be discussed in greater detail in Chapter 10.

The supervisor's approach to leadership can influence employee performance as well. **Leadership** is the use of noncoercive influence to direct and coordinate the activities of a group toward accomplishing a goal.[31] There are almost as many definitions of leadership and theories about it as there are leadership researchers! Two examples serve to demonstrate the effect a supervisor's or manager's leadership may have on employee behavior.

First, Robert House argued in his path-goal theory that a leader's role is to identify goals and clarify the paths employees may take to reach these goals.[32] If this is done effectively (according to the theory, by applying one of four possible leader styles, depending on employee characteristics and environmental factors), then motivation, job satisfaction, and employee performance are all predicted to increase. Subsequent research has provided support for the theory's predictions regarding job satisfaction.[33]

Second, George Graen's Leader-Member-Exchange (or LMX) model of leadership (earlier called the vertical-dyad linkage approach) observes that supervisors tend to develop different quality relationships with different subordinates.[34] In early research, this was depicted in terms of two extremes, that is, those employees with high quality relationships with the supervisor (the "in-group"), and those with low quality relationships (the less favored "out-group"). In-group members have relationships with their supervisors characterized by respect, liking, mutual trust, and influence; the opposite is true of relationships for out-group members. In-group members tend to have higher performance and satisfaction than out-group members, lower turnover, and more positive career outcomes.[35] More recent writing on LMX has focused on improving the leadership exchange relationship with *all* employees. As Graen and Uhl-Bien write, the emphasis is now placed "not on how managers discriminate among their people but rather on how they may work with each person on a one-on-one basis to develop a partnership with each of them."[36] Supervisors should work to develop effective dyadic relationships with each employee under their supervision.

These and other leadership theories highlight the effect the immediate supervisor can have on employee behavior. Subordinates look to their managers and supervisors for cues about appropriate and inappropriate behavior. If a manager or supervisor speaks and behaves in ways that indicate training and development are unimportant, employees will likely have little enthusiasm for these activities. Alternatively, if managers and supervisors take these activities seriously and reward employees for learning and using new skills, techniques, and attitudes, HRD efforts will be more effective, and ultimately the employee, manager, and organization will benefit. Leadership is also a key aspect of management development. Many organizations use management development programs (discussed in Chapter 13) as a way to improve the leadership skills of managerial employees.

In organizations that use teams as the primary way to accomplish tasks, some of the influences supervisors ordinarily control can be controlled by team members or the team leader (if one exists), or by both. There is evidence that the differential quality of exchange relationship among team members can influence team cohesiveness, satisfaction with coworkers, and general job satisfaction.[37] Although the dynamics of a self-managed team are more complex than the traditional supervisor-subordinate relationship, the impact of expectations and leadership will likely be similar. More will be said about teams and teamwork in Chapter 14.

*THE ORGANIZATION.* The organization itself can influence employee behavior through its reward structure, culture, and job design. **Reward structure** focuses on

- the **types** of rewards an organization uses (material, social);
- how rewards are **distributed** (equally to all, relative to each individual's contribution, or on the basis of need); and
- the **criteria** for reward distribution (results, behavior, or nonperformance issues, such as seniority or tenure).[38]

Further, rewards include not only tangible things, such as financial bonuses and plaques, but also intangible things, such as recognition and acceptance.

Reward systems should ideally provide the outcomes desired by members of the organization. Similar to our discussion of "outcomes" above, motivation theories can serve as the foundation for organizational reward systems as well. That is, motivation theories can help to explain why reward systems sometimes fail. As expectancy theory and reinforcement theory predict, employees tend to do what they are rewarded for. If management does not carefully design and implement the reward system, then it may unintentionally reinforce undesirable behavior in employees (such as lack of initiative, acceptance of the status quo, and low participation rates in HRD programs). Also, when reward systems are perceived too strongly as "control mechanisms," this can serve to reduce employee motivation and performance.[39]

Therefore, it is important for supervisors and HRD professionals to understand what the organization's reward system is intended to do, how it is put into practice, and how employees respond to it. Some performance problems may be solved simply by adjusting the reward system. It must also be understood that a major reason why many employees become involved in HRD programs is to obtain valued rewards, such as promotions, pay increases, and more desirable assignments. As mentioned earlier, some organizations choose to highlight the linkages between desired rewards and HRD as a way to pique employee interest in them. Rewards and their effective distribution can also be a topic of training, particularly in supervisory and management development programs. And in some instances, access to HRD programs can be used as a reward, or access may be perceived to be a reward.

An organization's culture also can have a strong effect on individual behavior. **Organizational culture** is a set of values, beliefs, norms, and patterns of behavior that are shared by organization members and that guide their behavior.[40] Individuals who understand an organization's culture are better able to accurately interpret organizational events, know what is expected of them, and behave in appropriate ways in novel or unfamiliar situations. Organizations that have a strong culture try to perpetuate that culture by selecting individuals who already share the culture (as Southwest Airlines does in its efforts to recruit people who have a "fun," team-oriented attitude) and by socializing new members so that they accept these norms and values.

Two examples can illustrate the impact of organizational culture on individual behavior. If an organization firmly embraces the idea of continuous improvement as the way to ensure high levels of quality (as is done in total quality management efforts), employees should be motivated to find ways to improve quality, engage in HRD programs to improve their knowledge and skills, and focus their efforts on trying to satisfy customer needs and expectations. Similarly, in organizations committed to diversity (where individuals from all cultural backgrounds are viewed and treated as full organizational members and participate fully within the organization), employees will strive to appreciate one anothers' differences and behave in ways that encourage active participation and acceptance of all members in achieving the organization's goals.

One clear implication of organizational culture for HRD is that HRD can be a means through which an organization's culture is perpetuated or changed, and HRD can also be influenced by the organization's culture (in terms of HRD content, importance, and acceptance).

**Job design** is the development and alteration of the components of a job (such as the tasks one performs and the scope of one's responsibilities) to improve productivity and the quality of the employee's work life. As proposed by Richard Hackman and Greg Oldham, when jobs contain factors that satisfy employees' personal growth needs or provide elements that generate feelings of responsibility, meaningfulness, and knowledge of results, employees will be more satisfied and more productive. Job design has received considerable attention and research support.[41]

The implication of job design for HRD is twofold. First, the way an organization chooses to construct its jobs can affect an employee's behavior and attitudes. Second, to improve an employee's performance and attitudes (or reduce excessive stress), the focus can be on altering the job rather than the employee. Job design will receive more attention in our discussion of organizational development in Chapter 14.

*COWORKERS AND TEAMS.* Coworkers, and especially team members, can exert a strong influence on an employee's behavior in at least three ways. First, coworkers control some of the outcomes valued by an employee, and may use those outcomes to influence the employee's behavior. For example, if an employee behaves in a way coworkers value, they may reward or reinforce that behavior by offering friendship and recognition. Similarly, coworkers may choose to react to behavior they disapprove of by withholding desired outcomes or punishing the employee through insults, ostracism, or threats. This is especially true in team situations, where members hold one another accountable for behaviors and performance, and where access to rewards is based on team performance.

Second, **norms,** or informal rules for appropriate behavior established within work groups, can serve as guidelines for appropriate behavior, if the employee chooses to comply.[42] Norms send a clear message about what behavior is expected and may lead employees to behave in ways that differ from typical patterns.

Third, because HRD programs are often administered to groups of employees and employees must perform newly learned behaviors in group settings, HRD professionals need to understand the effect of group dynamics on behavior. **Group dynamics** influence the way an employee may behave when interacting in a group. Dynamics such as groupthink and social loafing show that the performance of individuals within groups can differ from their behavior alone.[43] **Groupthink** occurs when group members are primarily concerned with unanimity, making poor decisions by failing to realistically assess alternatives. **Social loafing** is the tendency for group members to reduce their effort as the size of the group increases. The implication of dynamics such as social loafing and groupthink is that consideration must be given to how employees will behave when they are in group settings. Care should be taken when designing and implementing HRD programs to ensure that group dynamics do not undermine the learning process. **Teamwork** both amplifies the importance of coworkers' influences on individual behavior and brings other dynamics to the forefront. Two teamwork issues are trust and cohesiveness. **Trust** has to do with expectations that another person (or group of people) will act benevolently toward you. There is a certain vulnerability or riskiness to trust, in that the other party may not fulfill your expectations. Yet, research has demonstrated strong links between interpersonal trust and employee performance (including citizenship behaviors), problem solving, and cooperation.[44] **Cohesiveness** is the members' sense of togetherness and willingness to remain as part of the group. Given team members' high level of interdependence, they must trust one another and feel a sense of cohesiveness if the team is to work together and be successful.

Similarly, group and team dynamics should be taken into account when planning actions designed to ensure that what is learned is transferred back to the job. Supervisors, managers, and team leaders can monitor potentially destructive dynamics, as well as the level of trust and cohesiveness, and act to address them to maximize the chances that what employees learn in training and development activities will be used. Involving coworkers and team members in the learning process, as participants or trainers, can increase their acceptance of newly learned skills and the likelihood that they'll use them on the job. Likewise, managers and supervisors should pay attention to employee attitudes toward training and toward using new methods and skills.

## MOTIVATION: A FUNDAMENTAL INTERNAL INFLUENCE ON EMPLOYEE BEHAVIOR

**Motivation** is one of the most basic elements of human behavior. Motivational theories attempt to explain how effort is generated and channeled. Terry Mitchell synthesized many definitions of work motivation as "the psychological processes that cause the arousal, direction, and persistence of voluntary actions that are goal directed."[45]

This definition makes several important points. First, work motivation pertains to the causes of **voluntary** behavior—the nature of nearly all behaviors performed in the workplace. Even in situations where employees feel they do not have a choice, their behavior reflects their consideration of the perceived consequences of their actions.

Second, motivation focuses on several **processes** affecting behavior:

- **Arousal or energizing**—The generation or mobilization of effort
- **Direction**—Applying effort to one behavior over another
- **Persistence**—Continuing (or ceasing) to perform a behavior

Third, motivation at work is usually seen as an individual phenomenon because all people have unique needs, desires, attitudes, and goals.[46] Most motivational theories recognize these differences, and often include components that describe how they affect the motivational process.

Understanding motivation is critical to HRD. The success of many HRD programs and processes depends in part on whether the individual is motivated to participate, learn, and use what is learned to improve performance. The reason a person chooses to attend a training class but then fails to use the skills learned in training back on the job may be rooted in motivation. Programs designed with an eye toward motivation can explicitly address these issues. In addition, motivation theories are useful in diagnosing the cause of performance problems and often serve as the basis for designing or choosing HRD programs to remedy those problems.

There are an abundance of theories of work motivation available. Although some theories share common processes and constructs,[47] there is still no single, inclusive, and widely accepted explanation of work motivation.[48] In general, approaches to explaining motivation can be grouped into the three categories displayed in Table 2-2: need-based, cognitive, and noncognitive. After we present various prominent motivational theories, we will use a diagnostic model of motivation to synthesize these various theories.[49]

### NEED-BASED THEORIES OF MOTIVATION

Several motivational theories are rooted in the concept of needs. **Needs** are deficiency states or imbalances, either physiological or psychological, that energize and direct behavior. Henry Murray proposed that humans experience a large number of needs, such as aggression, affiliation, autonomy, and achievement.[50] Although needs are internal states, they can be influenced by forces in the environment. The opening case, for example, suggests that forces in the global economy and the potential for layoffs within an organization may heighten an employee's need for security, thereby reducing motivation to learn or engage in educational opportunities.

**■ TABLE 2-2**

| Approach | Theories |
| --- | --- |
| **Need-Based** | |
| Underlying needs, such as the needs for safety or power, drive motivation. | Maslow's Need Hierarchy Theory |
| | Alderfer's Existence, Relatedness, and Growth (ERG) Theory |
| | Herzberg's Two-Factor Theory |
| **Cognitive Process** | |
| Motivation is a process controlled by conscious thoughts, beliefs, and judgments. | Expectancy Theory |
| | Goal-Setting Theory |
| | Social Learning Theory |
| | Equity Theory |
| **Noncognitive** | |
| Motivation is explained as an interaction between behavior and external events without appealing to internal thoughts or needs. | Reinforcement Theory |

Needs are said to drive behavior through the combination of need activation and need satisfaction, a process depicted in Figure 2–2. A need becomes activated when a person lacks something necessary for maintaining psychological or physiological equilibrium. The activated need is felt as tension. The tension may be a recognizable feeling such as loneliness, or it may be more general, such as anxiety. Because tension is unpleasant, the person will look for ways (i.e., he or she will perform behaviors) to reduce the tension by eliminating the deficiency that is causing it. That person will continue to perform different behaviors until one is found that effectively reduces the tension and, thus, satisfies that need. Only activated needs can be motivational, because only an activated need produces the tension the person is motivated to eliminate. Once the need is satisfied, the tension is gone and the need is no longer felt.

Two widely cited need-based theories of motivation, **Maslow's need hierarchy theory**[51] and **Alderfer's existence, relatedness, and growth (ERG) theory,**[52] suggest that needs are arranged in a hierarchy. They propose that needs emerge in a particular pattern, in which certain groups of needs (those important to physical survival) emerge first and must be satisfied before other needs (psychological and social needs like affiliation and esteem) can emerge and affect behavior. Once the currently activated needs are satisfied, the next most powerful group of needs are felt and thus will drive behavior.

Maslow's need hierarchy lists five categories or levels of needs: physiological, safety and security, love, status and esteem, and self-actualization. Alderfer's ERG theory reduces Maslow's hierarchy to only three levels of needs: existence, relatedness, and growth. More important, ERG theory proposes that if a person

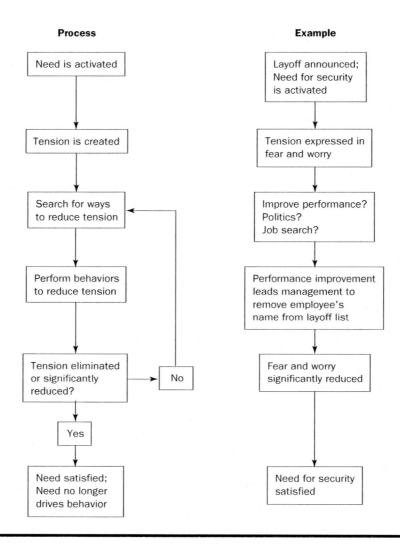

**■ FIGURE 2-2**

THE NEED ACTIVATION-NEED SATISFACTION PROCESS

becomes frustrated trying to satisfy the currently activated needs, this frustration will cause previously satisfied needs to be activated and drive behavior.

Another widely discussed need-based theory is Herzberg's **two-factor theory.**[53] Herzberg claimed that people have two sets of basic needs, one focusing on survival and another focusing on personal growth. He argued that factors in the workplace that satisfy survival needs, or hygiene factors, cannot of themselves provide job satisfaction—they only prevent dissatisfaction. Alternatively, **motivator** factors, which satisfy the growth needs, can create feelings of job satisfaction, but their absence will not necessarily lead to dissatisfaction. Following the two-factor theory, workers can be motivated by ensuring that hygiene factors are present, thereby preventing dissatisfaction, and then adding motivator factors to create job satisfaction. This strategy is referred to as **job enrichment.**

Need-hierarchy theories have been popular with managers and students in part because they are easy to understand and are intuitively appealing. They seem to make sense. But it is unclear whether these theories are valid explanations of motivation. Need-hierarchy theories are difficult to rigorously test, in that they require measuring internal states that people find difficult to accurately identify and explain. While most of the studies of Maslow's theory have failed to support it, much of this research has not been conducted properly.[54] Although some research has been conducted to test the ERG theory, there is insufficient evidence to support or reject the theory.[55] Needs exist, but a generalizable hierarchy explaining the relationships among them is not yet available.

Similar problems exist with two-factor theory. Herzberg's initial studies supported the notion that there are two separate sets of factors that affect job satisfaction differently.[56] But other researchers could not replicate these results using other methods. The theory became embroiled in controversy.[57] While there is some support for job enrichment as a way to motivate employees, the validity of the two-factor theory remains unclear.

So while need-based theories of motivation provide some insight into one category of possible forces that drive behavior, they have proven difficult to test and apply and are insufficient as an explanation of motivation. Even so, HRD programs based on need-based theories, such as job enrichment and achievement motivation training, have been used in organizations with some success.

## COGNITIVE PROCESS THEORIES OF MOTIVATION

Few of us would deny that our conscious thoughts play a role in how we behave. A second group of motivation theories, called cognitive process theories, recognizes this and argues that motivation is based on a person's thoughts and beliefs (or cognitions). These theories are sometimes referred to as process theories because they attempt to explain the sequence of thoughts and decisions that energize, direct, and control behavior.

Cognitive motivation theories have direct relevance to HRD. Most HRD programs include attempts to change employee behavior by influencing their thoughts, beliefs, and attitudes. Learning, which lies at the heart of HRD, is often seen as a cognitive process (learning will be discussed in Chapter 3). We can do a better job of designing and implementing HRD programs if we understand how employees' thoughts and beliefs affect their behavior.

In the section below, we will briefly review four cognitive theories of motivation: expectancy theory, goal-setting theory, social learning theory, and equity theory. Each theory has relevance for the practice of HRD.

*EXPECTANCY THEORY.* **Expectancy theory** was first proposed by Victor Vroom and assumes that motivation is a conscious choice process.[58] According to this theory, people choose to put their effort into activities that they believe they can perform and that will produce desired outcomes. Expectancy theory argues that decisions about which activities to engage in are based on the combination of three sets of beliefs: expectancy, instrumentality, and valence.

**Expectancy** beliefs represent the individual's judgment about whether applying (or increasing) effort to a task will result in its successful accomplishment. Stated another way, people with high expectancy believe that increased effort will lead to better performance, but people with low expectancy do not believe that their efforts, no matter how great, will affect their performance. All other things being equal, people should engage in tasks for which they have high expectancy beliefs.

The second belief, called **instrumentality,** is a judgment about the connection the individual perceives (if any) between task performance and possible outcomes. Making instrumentality judgments is like asking the question, "If I perform this task successfully, is it likely to get me something I want (or something I don't want)?" Instrumentality ranges from strongly positive (the individual is certain that performing a task will lead to a particular outcome), through zero (the individual is certain there is no relationship between performing the task and the occurrence of a particular outcome), to strongly negative (the individual is certain that performing a certain task will prevent a particular outcome from occurring).

The third belief important to expectancy theory is called **valence.** Valence refers to the value the person places on a particular outcome. Valence judgments range from strongly positive (for highly valued outcomes), through zero (for outcomes the person doesn't care about), to strongly negative (for outcomes the person finds aversive).

Expectancy theory states that employees will make these three sets of judgments when deciding which behaviors and tasks to engage in. Specifically, the theory predicts that employees will choose to put effort into behaviors they

- believe they can perform successfully (high expectancy) and
- believe are connected (high instrumentality) to outcomes they desire (high valence) or
- believe will prevent (negative instrumentality) outcomes they want to avoid (negative valence).

Figure 2–3 graphically depicts this process. For example, suppose the manager of a bus company tries to motivate bus drivers to drive more safely by offering safe drivers additional vacation days. Whether this will motivate a driver to drive more safely depends on whether

1. the driver thinks he or she can improve his or her safety record to the level desired by the manager (expectancy),
2. the driver believes the manager will give more vacation days if his or her safety record is improved to the desired level (instrumentality), and
3. the driver values having more vacation days (valence).

**FIGURE 2-3**

A GRAPHIC REPRESENTATION OF EXPECTANCY THEORY

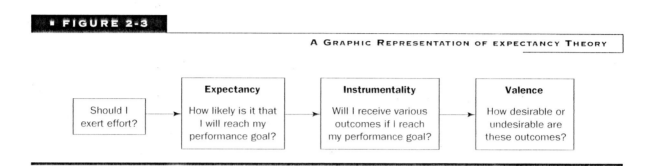

Do people behave in the way expectancy theory predicts? Empirical studies testing the theory have shown some support for its predictions.[59] However, several writers have pointed out that methodological problems in some of these studies may have led to underestimates of the theory's predictive ability.[60]

Expectancy theory may seem complex, and more research is needed to understand whether the theory accurately represents the behavioral choices we make.[61] Expectancy theory is, however, clearly relevant to HRD. It offers a way to diagnose performance problems and then suggests how these problems can be overcome. In addition, expectancy theory has implications for the design and effectiveness of HRD programs. For example, according to expectancy theory, employees will not be motivated to attend HRD programs and try to learn from them unless they believe

1. their efforts will result in learning the new skills or information presented in the program,

2. attending the program and learning new skills will increase their job performance, and

3. doing so will help them obtain desired outcomes or prevent unwanted outcomes.

Viewing employee behavior from an expectancy theory perspective, supervisors and HRD professionals can design and market programs in ways to ensure that employees make the appropriate judgments and as a result will be motivated to attend, learn, and apply what they have learned back on the job. Some ways to do this include offering incentives such as holding HRD programs in attractive locations (e.g., such as resorts), offering paid time off from work to attend, designing a program that is interesting and enjoyable, providing proof that the program is effective, and making success in the program a prerequisite for promotion and other desirable outcomes.

*GOAL-SETTING THEORY.* A second cognitive theory of motivation that has relevance to HRD is **goal-setting theory.** Goal-setting theory states that performance goals play a key role in motivation. The theory proposes that the presence of performance goals can mobilize employees' efforts, direct their attention, increase their persistence, and affect the strategies they will use to accomplish a task.[62] Goals influence the individual's **intentions,** which are defined as the "cognitive representations of goals to which the person is committed."[63] This commitment will continue to direct employee behavior until the goal is achieved, or until a decision is made to change or reject the goal.

Writers on motivation generally agree that goal setting is the best-supported theory of work motivation and one of the best-supported theories in management overall.[64] Research convincingly shows that goals that are specific, difficult, and accepted by employees will lead to higher levels of performance than easy, vague goals (e.g., "do your best") or no goals at all. This research also demonstrates that the presence of feedback enhances the effectiveness of goal setting.[65] Further research is needed to understand how and under what conditions goal setting works best.[66] For example, a study on the effectiveness of assertiveness training gave "assigned" goals to half the trainees at the end of the training program. These trainees were told to use the key points taught in training in two settings per week for four weeks. Checklists were provided to assist these trainees in tracking their goal attainment. Interestingly, trainees who had been assigned goals liked the training significantly less right after training than those in the no goal-setting condition. However, in a follow-up session four weeks later, reactions from trainees in the goal-setting condition had improved. More importantly, they could reproduce from memory a significantly larger portion of the training content than could the trainees without assigned goals, and they also demonstrated more assertive behaviors in a role-playing experience than could the no goal trainees. A basic point of this research is that adding a goal-setting condition to an already effective training program made it even more effective.[67]

Goal setting has become an integral part of many HRD programs, particularly in helping participants understand the desired result of each program and to motivate them to achieve these results. Goals can then be discussed with their supervisors back on the job to ensure that the employees use what they have learned during the HRD program to improve their performance. For example, a key component of the career development process (and many career development programs) is setting career goals.[68] According to goal-setting theory, an employee who establishes career goals is more likely to advance his or her career, especially if the goals are specific, challenging, and accompanied by regular feedback on progress toward the goals. The career development program should ensure that employees set such goals and help employees and the organization establish mechanisms for regular feedback.

*SOCIAL LEARNING THEORY.* Albert Bandura has developed a third cognitive theory of motivation, which is **social learning theory.**[69] Bandura proposes that outcome and self-efficacy expectations affect individual performance. An **outcome expectation** (similar to instrumentality in expectancy theory) is a person's belief that performing a given behavior will lead to a given outcome. **Self-efficacy** can be defined as "people's judgments of their capabilities to organize and execute courses of action required to attain designated types of performances. It is concerned not with the skills one has but with judgments of what one can do with whatever skills one possesses."[70] A shorthand way of looking at self-efficacy is that it is a person's judgment of the likelihood that he or she can successfully perform a particular task or activity. Self-efficacy beliefs are malleable and can be influenced by one's accomplishments, observations of others, verbal persuasion, and physiological states.[71]

The major prediction of the social learning theory is that a person's self-efficacy expectations will determine

1. whether a behavior will be performed,
2. how much effort will be spent, and
3. how long the person will continue to perform the behavior.

Bandura argues that people who have high self-efficacy for a particular task will focus their attention on the challenges of the situation and use greater effort in mastering them, thus increasing the chances of successful task performance. Conversely, people who have low self-efficacy for a particular task will focus their thoughts on obstacles and shortcomings, and as a result, reduce their chances of successful task performance. A model depicting the influence of self-efficacy on performance is shown in Figure 2–4.

Research conducted by Bandura and others shows that self-efficacy is strongly related to task performance.[72] Furthermore, research has also shown that self-efficacy can predict performance in training programs.[73] Clearly, self-efficacy has direct relevance for success in HRD. If employees have low self-efficacy

■ **FIGURE 2-4**

A MODEL OF THE RELATIONSHIP BETWEEN
SELF-EFFICACY AND PERFORMANCE

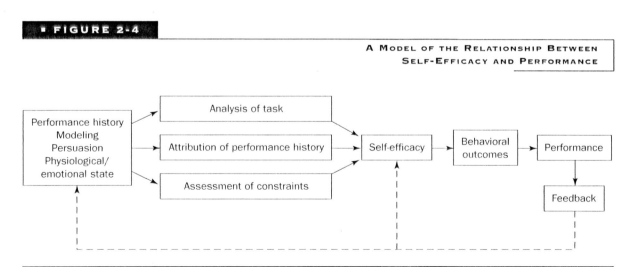

SOURCE: Adapted with permission from M. E. Gist, & T. R. Mitchell (1992). Self-efficacy: A theoretical analysis of its determinants and malleability, *Academy of Management Review, 17*,189.

expectations, it is unlikely that they will attempt to improve performance. If they do try to improve performance, they will not put forth the same effort as persons with high self-efficacy. Therefore, trainers and supervisors should behave in ways that increase the trainees' judgments of their self-efficacy.

Of particular relevance to HRD, social learning theory also proposes that most behavior is learned by observing others, a process called **modeling.** Research suggests that through observing a behavior and its consequences in others, individuals can learn new behaviors and make decisions about whether to perform a particular behavior themselves. Modeling is a key component of mentoring, a developmental technique we will discuss in Chapter 12.

Modeling has also been applied to HRD with great success in a training approach known as **behavior modeling.**[74] In behavior modeling training, the trainee is told the components of the behavior to be learned (e.g., firing a poor performer) and shown a film or videotape in which an actor (the model) demonstrates how to perform the behavior. Then the trainee practices the behavior with feedback from others and finally receives social reinforcement for performing the behavior.

*EQUITY THEORY.* A fourth cognitive theory of motivation, called **equity theory,** suggests that motivation is strongly influenced by the desire to be treated fairly and by people's perceptions about whether they have been treated fairly. As a theory of work motivation, it is based on the following three assumptions:

1. People develop beliefs about what is fair for them to receive in exchange for the contributions that they make to the organization.
2. People determine fairness by comparing their relevant returns and contributions to those of others.
3. People who believe they have been treated unfairly (called inequity) will experience tension, and they will be motivated to find ways to reduce it.[75]

Equity theory predicts that employees who believe they are being treated fairly (a judgment called equity) will be motivated to continue their present performance and behavior patterns, whereas employees who believe they are victims of inequity will search for ways to reduce their feelings of unfairness. There are at least five ways in which individuals reduce their feelings of inequity:

1. cognitively **distorting** views of contributions or rewards ("She must be smarter than I thought")
2. **influencing the perceived rival to change** his or her contributions or rewards (e.g., convincing the person to be less productive)
3. **changing** one's own contributions or rewards (either working harder or contributing less)
4. **comparing** one's self to a different person
5. **leaving** the situation (requesting a transfer or quitting)[76]

Typically, people choose the way to reduce inequity that appears to be the least costly to them.[77] Figure 2–5 depicts this process.

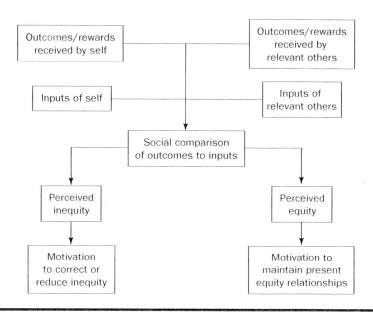

■ **FIGURE 2-5**

A GRAPHIC REPRESENTATION OF EQUITY THEORY

Are the predictions made by equity theory supported by research? In general, there is support for the predictions made about what people do when they believe they are underrewarded.[78] There is less support for predictions about what people do when they believe they are overrewarded.[79]

Equity theory has clear implications for HRD, particularly in understanding how employees perceive HRD programs and their response to them. In some organizations, participation in HRD programs is used (or perceived) as a reward for good performance or punishment for poor performance. Also, the decisions concerning which employees will be included in HRD programs are not without consequences. Equity theory suggests, for example, that employees who consider themselves unjustly left out of an HRD program (e.g., a management development seminar) will experience inequity. As a result, those employees may attempt to reduce the inequity by lowering their job performance or becoming less committed to the organization. Employees may even leave the organization for someplace where they feel their talents will be more appreciated. To prevent this from occurring, managers should make the selection criteria for attending HRD programs clear and provide employees with feedback so they can see that participation judgments are made fairly.

Equity theory can also help us determine whether employees will use the skills or knowledge they have learned in an HRD program back on the job. For example, if the employees view the application of their new skills or knowledge as an input in their exchange with the employer, they may expect the organization to provide them with certain outcomes in return. If the employees see other employees who lack the newly acquired skills receiving the same outcomes as themselves, they may choose not to use the new skills on the job as a way to restore a feeling of equity.

### REINFORCEMENT THEORY: A NONCOGNITIVE THEORY OF MOTIVATION

The last motivation theory we will discuss, **reinforcement theory,** is rooted in behaviorism, which attempts to explain behavior without referring to unobservable internal forces such as needs or thoughts.[80] Behaviorists seek to explain behavior by focusing only on things that can be directly observed: the behavior itself and environmental events that precede and follow the behavior. In short, reinforcement theory argues that behavior is a function of its consequences. This is based on the **law of effect,** which states that behavior that is followed by a pleasurable consequence will occur more frequently (a process called reinforcement), and behavior that is followed by an aversive consequence will occur less frequently.[81] According to reinforcement theory, a manager or trainer can control an employee's behavior by controlling the consequences that follow the employee's behavior.

Reinforcement theory can be applied by using a set of techniques known as **behavior modification.** Behavior modification suggests four choices for controlling an employee's behavior:

1. **Positive reinforcement** refers to increasing the frequency of a behavior by following the behavior with a pleasurable consequence.
2. **Negative reinforcement** increases the frequency of a behavior by removing something aversive after the behavior is performed.
3. **Extinction** seeks to decrease the frequency of a behavior by removing the consequence that is reinforcing it.
4. **Punishment** seeks to decrease the frequency of a behavior by introducing an aversive consequence immediately after the behavior.

In addition to the type of consequence that follows a behavior, the way that consequences are paired with behaviors, called a schedule of reinforcement, is an important part of how behavior modification can be effectively applied.

Reinforcement theory and behavior modification have received strong support in a large body of research and have helped increase our understanding of work-related behavior.[82] Reinforcement theory has also had a strong influence on HRD. Methods of instruction, such as programmed instruction and some approaches to computer-based training, draw heavily from reinforcement theory (we will discuss this more in Chapter 6). Trainers and managers can also motivate employees to learn and use what they have learned back on the job by using behavior modification techniques.[83] While a strict behaviorist would reject any emphasis on thoughts or needs (i.e., all the methods covered above), we feel that such an approach is too narrow, and that an effective HRD professional should consider a more holistic or integrated approach to motivation.

### SUMMARY OF MOTIVATION

As we have seen, there are many approaches to explaining and understanding motivation. Each theory we have discussed enhances our understanding of employee behavior and has at least some research support (with the strongest support going to goal setting, reinforcement theory, social learning theory, and expectancy theory). In addition, each approach offers valuable insight into the design and implementation of HRD programs.

This brief discussion of different approaches to work motivation is not exhaustive and does not explain the complexity and interrelationships among the theories. Some theories, such as expectancy theory and reinforcement theory, make many similar predictions.[84] In addition, researchers have attempted to integrate several theories into a larger, more inclusive model (for example, the Porter-Lawler model, which combines expectancy and equity theories). One recent attempt to synthesize multiple motivational models was proposed by John Wagner and John Hollenbeck.[85] Their model can be seen in Figure 2–6. In this model, four employee outcomes are of particular interest (these are the rectangles in the center of the model): employee desire to perform, the effort they put forth, their performance, and their satisfaction. Expectancy theory is used as the overarching framework to depict influences on employee motivation and performance. However, the other theories described above are also used to increase our understanding of how this process unfolds.

For example, valence, instrumentality, and expectancy were described above in our discussion of expectancy theory. However, the various need theories can assist us in understanding *valences*, that is, what it is that people value or want. Similarly, both reinforcement theory and social learning theory can provide guidance in understanding what employees believe will lead to the attainment of what they want, that is, their *instrumentality* beliefs. The various forms of reinforcement, as well as the vicarious learning via modeling (suggested by social learning theory) lead to such instrumentality beliefs. These then combine to produce a given desire to perform on the part of employees. As suggested by expectancy theory, this then interacts with *expectancy* (the judgment that one's efforts will lead to a successful outcome) to produce a high level of effort. Effort, in turn, must be accompanied by a sufficient level of ability (described below), as well as accurate role perceptions. Goal-setting theory is useful here in providing guidance to employees concerning what needs to be done, at what performance level, and who has responsibility for doing it. When effort, ability, and accurate role perceptions are all present, then high levels of individual performance are predicted to occur. The final outcome variable in this model, satisfaction, is predicted to follow from performance, as well as from a perception that rewards have been given out fairly. Equity theory provides a helpful framework for understanding employees' perceptions of the equity of rewards. Finally, the model portrays return arrows back to valence, instrumentality, and expectancy. This is meant to

■ **FIGURE 2-6**

THE WAGNER-HOLLENBECK MODEL OF
MOTIVATION AND PERFORMANCE

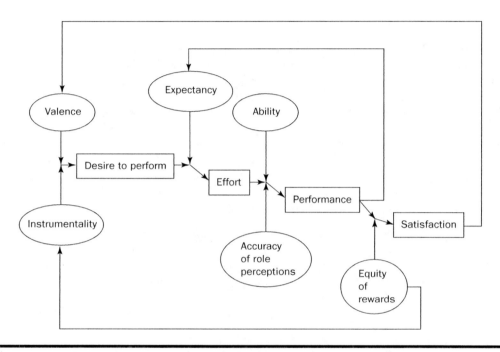

SOURCE: Wagner, J. A., III, and Hollenbeck, J. R. (1995). *Management of organizational behavior* (2nd ed.). Englewood Cliffs, NJ: Prentice-Hall.

portray the dynamic nature of employee motivation and performance, that is, motivation and performance can change over time. A highly motivated person can lose motivation when valence, instrumentality, or expectancy decline. On the other hand, when one of the aspects of this model is improved or increased, then higher levels of motivation, performance, and satisfaction are predicted to occur. We view this model as a useful diagnostic tool to understand employee motivation, as it very effectively synthesizes and summarizes our discussion of the various motivational theories.

We hope that this discussion encourages the reader to appreciate both the importance of motivation in determining employee behavior as well as the richness of potential applications that motivation theories have for HRD. For an interesting motivational challenge faced by corporate trainers many years ago, see the box nearby, "An HRD Classic: 'On the effectiveness of not holding a formal training course.'"

## AN HRD CLASSIC: "ON THE EFFECTIVENESS OF NOT HOLDING A FORMAL TRAINING COURSE"

Have you ever wondered if maybe training *isn't* the answer to an organization's performance problems? Industrial psychologists Paul Thayer and William McGehee faced this question many years ago when they worked for Fieldcrest Mills in North Carolina. The plants were unionized, and the managers were urging McGehee, the training director at the time, to hold training courses for the supervisors on the contents of the company's contract with the union. It seems that the union stewards (who spoke on behalf of the employees in the various plants) knew the contract in great detail, and were frequently challenging the authority of the supervisors to assign jobs, discipline employees, or conduct other supervisory responsibilities. Thayer and McGehee write that a supervisor's request "that a loom fixer fill in for an operator for a brief time, for example, might be challenged by an unsupported reference to certain clauses in the union contract. Stewards capitalized on [supervisor] ignorance. Many managers suspected that stewards frequently ran bluffs just for sport" (p. 455).

While these trainers felt they could provide competent instruction, they were concerned that a course on the contract would not be well received by the supervi-

sors. Their concern was that the stewards' actions were more frustrating to the managers than they were to the supervisors, and that an "essential condition for learning was missing," namely motivation. Their suggestion was that before conducting training, some baseline data should be collected to see what the supervisors already knew and avoid covering unnecessary materials. Since each supervisor could make use of a pocket edition of the contract on the job, the test should be open book.

As an incentive, the president of the company agreed to host a steak dinner for the supervisor with the best score on the test. That individual's manager would also be invited. While preparations were being made for the supervisors to take the test, suggestions were made among the managers that certain supervisors would do better than others. This led quickly to bets "being placed at all levels among plants, from [supervisor] to manager" (p. 456). A very difficult, "hair-splitting" exam was prepared, and then delivered to all mills on the same morning. Supervisors began taking the exam "before work, during breaks, at lunch, after work, at home, etc." (p. 456). Thayer and McGehee comment that Thayer's phone did not stop ringing for a week, with supervisors claiming

that there were two, three, or even four correct answers to various questions.

Within a week, all exams were turned in, and all were perfect or near perfect. Two weeks later, the president hosted a steak dinner for 75 supervisors and their managers. Thayer and McGehee raise the question of whether supervisors learned something from this "nontraining course." Throughout the course of the dinner, "Thayer was surrounded by indignant [supervisors] who quoted sections of the contract verbatim to support contentions as to the unfairness of certain exam questions" (p. 456). Perhaps just as interesting was that the pressure from the mill managers to provide such a training course for supervisors "disappeared." They ask, "Essential learning conditions must exist. Do we look at those conditions first before—or instead of—building a course?" (p. 456). In the context of this chapter, it is evident that proper motivation for training was lacking among the supervisors. However, a rather ingenious manipulation of incentives (an informal part of the reward system) led to significant changes in how the supervisors treated the union contract. Despite the passage of almost fifty years, there is a lesson in this classic note for current HRD professionals.

SOURCE: Thayer, P. W., & McGehee, W. (1977). Comments: On the effectiveness of not holding a formal training course. *Personnel Psychology, 30*, 455-456

## OTHER INTERNAL FACTORS THAT INFLUENCE EMPLOYEE BEHAVIOR

Internal factors, in addition to motivation, that influence employee behavior include attitudes and knowledge, skills, and abilities (KSAs). Each of these factors is discussed below.

### ATTITUDES

Attitudes are the second major internal influence depicted in our model of work behavior (refer again to Figure 2–1 on page 36). Attitudes add to our understanding of employee behavior by showing another way thoughts can influence behavior. Many HRD programs and processes, including training evaluation, management development, and organizational development, either focus on modifying employee attitudes or use attitudes as a central component. For example, one common way HRD programs are evaluated is by means of assessing employee attitudes toward the program and its content.

What is an attitude? An attitude "represents a person's general feeling of favorableness or unfavorableness toward some stimulus object."[86] Attitudes are always held with respect to a particular object—whether the object is a person, place, event, or idea—and indicate one's feelings or affect toward that object. Attitudes also tend to be stable over time and are difficult to change.[87]

Of particular interest to HRD is the nature of the relationship between attitudes and behavior. Although common sense tells us that attitudes often cause behavior, the reality is often more complex. If attitudes did directly affect our behavior, without any other intervening factors, our behavior should be consistent with those attitudes. Unfortunately, this is not always the case. Attitudes can be used to predict behavior, but the predictions are at best only moderately accurate. Researchers attempting to prove a direct relationship between attitudes and behavior have experienced considerable frustration.

Research conducted over the past thirty years suggests that the relationship between attitudes and behavior is not simple or direct. One widely discussed model that explains this relationship is the behavioral intentions model.[88] This model states that it is the combination of attitudes with perceived social pressure to behave in a given way (called subjective norms) that influences an individual's intentions. These intentions, in turn, more directly influence behavior (see Figure 2–7). When attitudes and subjective norms conflict, the stronger of the two plays the dominant role in determining what the individual's intentions will be. According to the behavioral intentions model, then, attitudes appear to affect behavior only to the extent that they influence one's intentions.

One example of how the behavioral intentions model of attitudes can inform HRD practice is when measuring a program's effectiveness (see Chapter 7). Relying solely on measuring attitudes to determine whether employees will apply what they have learned in an HRD program will likely produce only moderately accurate results. The behavioral intentions model suggests that it may be more useful to measure trainees' **intentions** to use what they have learned, because

**■ FIGURE 2-7**

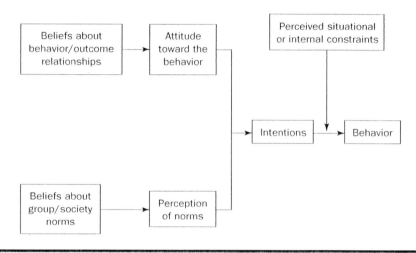

A GRAPHIC REPRESENTATION OF THE BEHAVIORAL
INTENTIONS MODEL

SOURCE: Adapted with permission from D. Hellriegel, J. W. Slocum, Jr., & R. W. Woodman (1989). *Organizational behavior* (5th ed.), St. Paul, MN: West, 51.

intentions incorporate attitudes and more directly influence behavior. While this is no substitute for assessing an actual change in job behavior, the behavioral intentions model implies that intentions, rather than attitudes alone, may be a better indicator of program effectiveness.

Attitudes are an important factor in HRD programs. Ray Noe proposed that two types of attitudes—reaction to skills assessment feedback and career/job attitudes—can have a direct effect on the motivation to learn.[89] An empirical test of the model suggested that these factors do in fact influence motivation and learning in a training program.[90] Based on these results, a modifed model was proposed. This model (shown in Figure 2–8) suggests that job involvement and career planning can have a significant impact on pretraining motivation and motivation to learn. We believe that explicitly considering and understanding the effects that trainees' attitudes can have on training effectiveness, as suggested here, is a promising avenue of research—one that will likely yield new insights into ways HRD programs can be made more effective.

## KNOWLEDGE, SKILLS, AND ABILITIES (KSAS)

The third and final internal factor included in our model of employee behavior (Figure 2–1) is the employee's knowledge, skills, and abilities (KSAs). It is clear that KSAs have a significant impact on employee performance. All other things

■ **FIGURE 2-8**

A MODEL OF MOTIVATIONAL AND ATTITUDINAL INFLUENCES
ON TRAINING EFFECTIVENESS

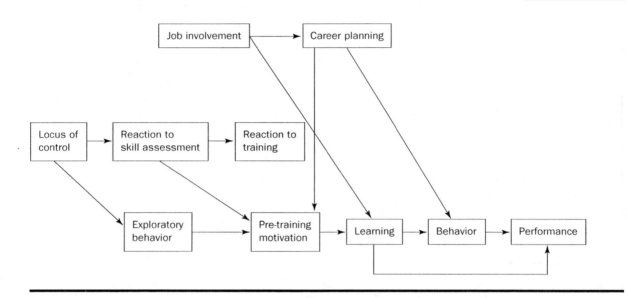

SOURCE: From R. A. Noe, & N. Schmitt (1986). The influence of trainee attitudes on training effectiveness, *Personnel Psychology, 39,* 515.

being equal, if employees lack the KSAs to perform a task or behavior, they will likely fail. Almost all HRD programs focus on improving or renewing the KSAs of employees.

Despite the ubiquitous nature of KSAs in HRD, these factors can be difficult to define with precision. Definitions differ according to the person defining them. Edwin Fleishman, a leading researcher of human abilities, defines **abilities** as general capacities related to the performance of a set of tasks.[91] Abilities develop over time through the interaction of heredity and experience, and are long-lasting. **Skills** are similar to abilities, but differ in that they combine abilities with capabilities that are developed as a result of training and experience.[92] Skills are often categorized as psychomotor activities (while abilities tend to be more cognitive) and are typically measured in terms of the ease and precision evident in the performance of some task.[93] Finally, **knowledge** is defined as an understanding of factors or principles related to a particular subject.

Over 100 different types of abilities have been identified, including general intelligence, verbal comprehension, numerical ability, and inductive reasoning.[94] Some types of abilities, like general strength, have even been partitioned into subcategories (including explosive, dynamic, and static abilities).[95]

## RETURN TO OPENING CASE

Pratt & Whitney and UTC have established an Employee Scholars Program that pays 100 percent of the costs of tuition and books for employees pursuing college courses at any accredited educational institution. According to the UTC Web site, "Employees can enroll in classes and obtain a degree in any field, whether or not it is related to their jobs. Students receive up to half of their classroom time as paid time off for studying, up to three hours per week. UTC further rewards its employee scholars when they graduate. Employees who attain a bachelor's or graduate degree receive 200 shares of UTC stock. Those who attain an associate's degree receive 100 shares, and another 100 shares if they go on to get their bachelor's."[1]

As of 1998, approximately 14 percent of UTC's worldwide workforce was enrolled in this program. Your instructor has additional information about what happened to Pratt & Whitney, UTC, and their Employee Scholars Program after the restructuring in 2000.

[1]Empoyee Scholars Program, http://www.utc.com/opportun/benefit_scholar.htm

Researchers have attempted to develop taxonomies to describe the abilities needed to perform particular tasks. Taxonomies help HRD professionals to select and assign employees to training, choose appropriate learning strategies for individuals of differing skill levels, and specify training needs and content when designing training programs. Fleishman and his colleagues have developed one such taxonomy that has been applied to HRD.[96] We will discuss needs assessment in Chapter 4.

It should be clear from the preceding discussion that motivation, attitudes, and ability are critical to explaining employee behavior and to understanding and applying HRD. It is the combination of these influences with the external influences described earlier that affect employee behavior.

### SUMMARY

Because HRD programs are generally attempts to change employee behavior, it is important to understand the factors that influence employee behavior. This chapter presented a number of such factors that have direct relevance to HRD, using a simple model of employee behavior to guide the discussion. The model contains two sets of factors that interact to influence employee behavior: 1) external factors, which include factors in the external environment (economic, governmental, and competitive issues), as well as those in the work environment (e.g., outcomes, the supervisor, the organization, and coworkers) and 2) internal factors, which include motivation, ability, and attitudes.

Outcomes—the results of performing a behavior in a particular way—are an external influence on employee behavior. Both personal outcomes (relevant to the individual, like pay or recognition) and organizational outcomes (relevant to the organization, like productivity or profits) can be used to diagnose and motivate employees to attend, learn, and apply what they have learned in HRD programs. Theories of motivation, such as equity theory, expectancy theory, and reinforcement theory, attempt to explain whether and how outcomes affect employee behavior.

Supervisors, through their leadership and expectations, also influence employee behavior. A supervisor can use leadership (noncoercive influence) to affect a subordinate's performance, attitudes, and motivation. According to the leader-member-exchange theory, employees who are treated by their supervisor with trust, respect, and friendship are more satisfied and perform better than those who are not. Research on self-fulfilling prophecy has shown that a supervisor's expectations of an employee can affect the way the supervisor interacts with the employee, with the employee's performance tending to live up or down to those expectations.

Two additional factors in the work environment that influence employee behavior are coworkers and the organization itself. Coworkers provide influence through group norms, group dynamics, and teamwork, and by controlling valued outcomes. The organization can also affect employee behavior in several ways, including its culture, reward structure, and the way it designs the employee's job.

One of the key internal factors that influence employee behavior is motivation. Motivation is defined as the psychological processes that energize, direct, and lead to the persistence of voluntary behavior. Theories of motivation use different sources to explain behavior, including needs (Maslow's need hierarchy, Alderfer's ERG theory, and Herzberg's two-factor theory), cognitions (expectancy theory, goal-setting theory, social learning theory, and equity theory), and the consequences of behavior (reinforcement theory). Each of these theories has implications for developing and conducting HRD programs. The Wagner-Hollenbeck model of motivation and performance was put forward as a useful means of combining the various theories to diagnose motivational and performance issues.

Attitudes and the employee's knowledge, skills, and abilities (KSAs) are also important internal factors of behavior. Without ability (the capability one has to perform a set of tasks) a person will be unable to perform a given behavior, regardless of motivation. Attitudes, which are made up of beliefs, feelings, and behavioral tendencies, affect behavior indirectly through intentions. According to the behavior intentions model, attitudes combine with the perception of social pressure to form intentions, which in turn directly affect behavior. Research has shown that both employee attitudes and ability play a role in the effectiveness of HRD programs.

HRD professionals, as well as supervisors and managers, are in the business of understanding and influencing employee behavior. As the sampling of concepts and theories in this chapter shows, there are many possible explanations though fewer unequivocal facts. The techniques we discuss in the chapters that follow draw upon the foundations laid by researchers of work motivation and behavior. Obviously, applying these theories to a given situation requires judgment and modifications. In this sense, designing and delivering HRD programs is an art as well as a science.

## KEY TERMS AND CONCEPTS

abilities

attitudes

behavioral intentions model

cohesiveness

equity theory

expectancy

expectancy theory

goal-setting theory

group dynamics

instrumentality

job design

job enrichment

job satisfaction

law of effect

leadership

motivation

needs

norms

outcomes

reinforcement theory

rewards

self-efficacy

self-fulfilling prophecy

social learning theory

teamwork

trust

valence

## QUESTIONS FOR DISCUSSION

1. Describe at least three ways that factors in the external environment influence employee behavior. If you were an HRD professional involved with an action team that was charged with evaluating the likely success of a proposed merger of your organization with another organization, what factors would you want to consider in making this recommendation? That is, based on what you know of HRD to this point, how can HRD professionals impact the likely success or failure of a merger or acquisition?

2. Select a familiar problem that you have encountered in the workplace. Use the model of employee behavior presented in this chapter to seek to explain why this problem exists. Be specific.

3. Suppose that you are the recruitment manager for a medium-sized bank. One of your best recruiters appears to be unmotivated lately. The number of recruits the recruiter brings in is normally above the average for effective performance but has fallen below the standard for the past two weeks. What might expectancy theory suggest is causing the drop in the employee's performance? What might equity theory suggest? Based on your knowledge of equity and expectancy theories, develop two recommendations for helping to improve the recruiter's performance.

4. Suppose you are the HRD manager for a large electric utility company. The quarterly report shows a 25 percent decrease in participation in management development programs over the same quarter last year. The number of managers employed by the company has not changed, and the company's profits have remained stable. You already hold these programs in desirable locations off-site (local hotels and conference centers) and participating in these programs counts toward the employees' annual performance evaluation. Using your knowledge of motivation theory, suggest three possible reasons that could explain why participation rates are down. If, after investigation, those reasons turned out to be the true causes, what might you be able to do to improve participation rates?

5. Compare and contrast the need-based and cognitive-based approaches to understanding motivation.

6. The HRD manager for a chicken processing plant has come to you for advice. Even though all of the employees in the plant recently completed a safety training program, the accident rate has not improved. In particular, the manager has found that employees are not wearing safety gear (goggles, shoes with nonskid soles) consistently and are not following safe procedures. Using your knowledge of attitudes and supervisory expectations, develop two possible reasons to explain the employees' behavior. If your hypotheses are true, how could the HRD manager improve the situation?

7. Why do people with low self-efficacy perform more poorly in training programs than those with high self-efficacy?

8. Briefly describe three ways that coworkers can affect an employee's behavior at work.

9. Recall a time at work or school when you found it difficult to motivate yourself to complete a required task (like start a report or study for an exam). Using two different motivation theories, explain why this lack of motivation may have occurred.

**EXERCISE**

Assume that you have been asked to design a portion of the orientation program that your organization is using for new employees. How might the three concepts from expectancy theory (expectancies, instrumentality, and valence; see Figure 2-3) be used to increase the motivation of new employees? That is, what activities or discussions might be conducted that would increase the liklihood that employees will exert high levels of effort toward achieving work-related goals?

**REFERENCES**

1. Ellis, K., and Gale, S. F. (2001). A seat at the table. *Training, 38*(3), March, 90-97.

2. Campbell, J. P., McCloy, R. A., Oppler, S. H., and Sager, C. E. (1993). A theory of performance. In N. Schmitt and W. C. Borman (eds.), *Personnel selection in organizations* (35–70). San Francisco:

Jossey-Bass; Werner, J. M. (2000). Implications of OCB and contextual performance for human resource management. *Human Resource Management Review, 10*, 3–24.

3. Murphy, K. R., & Shiarella, A. H. (1997). Implications of the multidimensional nature of job performance for the validity of selection tests: Multivariate frameworks for studying test validity. *Personnel Psychology, 50*, 823–854.

4. Organ, D. W. (1988). *Organizational citizenship behavior: The good soldier syndrome.* Lexington, MA: Lexington Books; Tompson, H. B., and Werner, J. M. (1997). The impact of role conflict/facilitation on core and discretionary behaviors: Testing a mediated model. *Journal of Management, 23*, 583–601; Borman, W. C., and Motowidlo, S. J. (1993). Expanding the criterion domain to include elements of contextual performance. In N. Schmitt and W. C. Borman (eds.), *Personnel selection in organizations* (71–98). San Francisco: Jossey-Bass.

5. Organ, D. W. (1997). Organizational citizenship behavior: It's construct clean-up time, *Human Performance, 10(2)*, 85–97.

6. *Ibid.*, Werner (2000), *supra* note 2.

7. Katz, D. (1964). The motivational basis of organizational behavior. *Behavioral Science, 9*, 131–133.

8. Heneman, H. G., III, Schwab, D., Fossum, J., & Dyer, L. (1989). *Personnel/human resource management* (4th ed.). Homewood, IL: Irwin.

9. Nelson, D. L., & Burke, R. J. (1998). Lessons learned. *Canadian Journal of Administrative Sciences, 15*, 372–381.

10. Mishra, K. E., Spreitzer, G. M., & Mishra, A. K. (1998). Preserving employee morale during downsizing. *Sloan Management Review, 39*, Winter, 83–95.

11. Cited by Nelson, B. (1998). The care of the un-downsized. *Public Management, 80*, April, 20–22.

12. Cascio, W. F. (1998). Learning from outcomes: Financial experiences of 311 firms that have downsized. In M. K. Gowing, J. D. Kraft, and J. C. Quick (eds.), *The new organizational reality: Downsizing, restructuring, and revitalization* (55–70). Washington, DC: American Psychological Association.

13. Bassi, L. J., & Van Buren, M. E. (1997). Sustaining high performance in bad times. *Training and Development, 51*, June, 32–41.

14. Nelson & Burke (1998), *supra* note 9.

15. Mishra et al. (1998), *supra* note 10.

16. Allan, P. (1997). Minimizing employee layoffs while downsizing: Employer practices that work. *International Journal of Manpower, 18*, 576–596.

17. Barkley, W. J., Jr., & Green, T. B. (1992). Safe landings for outplaced employees at AT&T. *Personnel Journal, 71(6)*, June, 144–147.

18. Bassi & Van Buren (1997), *supra* note 13.

19. Burke, W. W. (1997). The new agenda for organization development. *Organizational Dynamics, 26*, Summer, 7–20.

20. Graaff, S. K., & Case, W. N. (2000). Mergers and human resources. In E. E. Kossek and R. N. Block (eds.), *Managing human resources for the 21st century: From core concepts to strategic choice.* Cincinnati: South-Western College Publishing, 5.1–5.25.

21. *Ibid.*

22. Overman, S. (1999). Learning your M&ABC's, *HR Focus, 76*, August, 7–8.

23. Clemente, M., & Greenspan, D., cited in Overman (1999), *ibid.*, 7.

24. Graaff & Case (2000), *supra* note 20.

25. Mitchell, T. R. (1974). Expectancy models of satisfaction, occupational preference, and effort: A theoretical, methodological, and empirical appraisal. *Psychological Bulletin, 81,* 1053–1077.

26. Campbell, J. P., & Pritchard, R. D. (1976). Motivation theory in industrial and organizational psychology. In M. D. Dunnette (ed.), *Handbook of industrial and organizational psychology* (63130). Chicago: Rand McNally.

27. Mohrman, S. A., Cohen, S. G., & Mohrman, A. M., Jr. (1995). *Designing team-based organizations: New forms for knowledge work.* San Francisco: Jossey-Bass.

28. Eden, D. (1984). Self-fulfilling prophecy as a management tool: Harnessing Pygmalion. *Academy of Management Review, 9,* 64–73.

29. Eden, D., & Ravid, G. (1982). Pygmalion versus self-expectancy: Effects of instructor and self-expectancy on trainee performance. *Organizational Behavior and Human Performance, 30,* 351–364; Eden, D., & Shani, A. B. (1982). Pygmalion goes to boot camp: Expectancy, leadership, and trainee performance. *Journal of Applied Psychology, 67,* 194–199.

30. Divr, T., Eden, D., & Banjo, M. L. (1995). Self-fulfilling prophecy and gender: Can women be Pygmalion and Galatea? *Journal of Applied Psychology, 80,* 253–270.

31. Jago, A. G. (1982). Leadership: Perspectives in theory and research. *Management Science, 22,* 315–336.

32. House, R. J. (1971). A path-goal theory of leader effectiveness. *Administrative Science Quarterly, 16,* 321–338.

33. Al-Gattan, A. A. (1985). Test of the path-goal theory of leadership in the multinational domain. *Group and Organizational Studies, 10,* 425–429; Schriesheim, C., and DeNisi, A. (1981). Task dimensions as moderators of the effects of instrumental leadership: A two-sample replicated test of path goal leadership theory. *Journal of Applied Psychology, 66,* 587–589.

34. Graen, G. B., & Uhl-Bien, M. (1995). Relationship-based approach to leadership: Development of leader-member exchange (LMX) theory of leadership over 25 years: Applying a multi-level multi-domain perspective. *Leadership Quarterly, 6,* 219–247; Dansereau, F., Graen, G. B., & Haga, W. (1975). A vertical dyad linkage approach to leadership in formal organizations. *Organizational Behavior and Human Performance, 13,* 46–78.

35. Vecchio, R. P., & Godbell, B. C. (1984). The vertical dyad linkage model of leadership: Problems and prospects. *Organizational Behavior and Human Performance, 34,* 5–20; Ferris, G. R. (1985). Role of leadership in the employee withdrawal process: A constructive replication. *Journal of Applied Psychology, 70,* 777–781; Wakabayashi, M., & Graen, G. B. (1984). The Japanese career progress study: A seven-year follow-up. *Journal of Applied Psychology, 69,* 603–614.

36. Graen and Uhl-Bien (1995), *supra* note 34, 229.

37. Seers, A., Petty, M. M., & Cashman, J. F. (1995). Team-member exchange under team and traditional management: A naturally occurring quasi-experiment. *Group and Organization Management, 20,* 18–38.

38. Pearce, J. L., & Peters, R. H. (1985). A contradictory norms view of employer-employee exchange. *Journal of Management, 11,* 19–30; Von Glinow, M. A. (1985). Reward strategies for attracting, evaluating, and retaining professionals. *Human Resource Management, 24*(2), 191–206.

39. Deci, E. L., & Porac, J. (1978). Cognitive evaluation theory and the study of human motivation. In M. R. Lepper and D. Greene (eds.), *The hidden costs of rewards.* Hillsdale, NJ: Lawrence Erlbaum Associates.

40. Schein, E. H. (1985). *Organizational Culture and leadership.* San Francisco: Jossey-Bass.

41. Hackman, J. R., & Oldham, G. R. (1980). *Work redesign.* Reading, MA: Addison-Wesley; Loher, B. T., Noe, R. A., Moeller, N. L., & Fitzgerald, M. P. (1985). A meta-analysis of the relation of job characteristics to job satisfaction. *Journal of Applied Psychology, 70,* 280–289.

42. Feldman, D. C. (1984). The development and enforcement of norms. *Academy of Management Review, 9*, 47–53.

43. Janis, I. (1982). *Groupthink* (2nd ed.). Boston: Houghton Mifflin; Latane, B., Williams, K., & Harkins, S. (1979). Many hands make light the work: The causes and consequences of social loafing. *Journal of Personality and Social Psychology, 37*, 822–832.

44. For a review, see Whitener, E. M., Brodt, S. E., Korsgaard, M. A., & Werner, J. M. (1998). Managers as initiators of trust: An exchange relationship framework for understanding managerial trustworthy behavior. *Academy of Management Review, 23*, 513–530.

45. Mitchell, T. R. (1982). Motivation: New directions for theory, research, and practice. *Academy of Management Review, 7*, 80–88, p. 81.

46. *Ibid.*

47. Evans, M. G. (1986). Organizational behavior: The central role of motivation. *Journal of Management, 12*, 203–222; Ilgen, D. R., & Klein, H. J. (1988). Individual motivation and performance: Cognitive influences on effort and choice. In J. P. Campbell & R. J. Campbell (eds.), *Productivity in organizations*. San Francisco: Jossey-Bass.

48. Katzell, R. A., and Thompson, D. E. (1990). Work motivation: Theory and practice. *American Psychologist, 45*, 144–153; Pinder, C. C. (1984). *Work motivation: Theory, issues, and applications*. Glenview, IL: Scott, Foresman.

49. Wagner, J. A., III, & Hollenbeck, J. R. (1995). *Management of organizational behavior* (2nd ed.). Englewood Cliffs, NJ: Prentice-Hall.

50. Murray, H. (1938). *Explorations in personality*. New York: Oxford University Press.

51. Maslow, A. H. (1943). A theory of human behavior. *Psychological Review, 50*, 370–396; Maslow, A. H. (1954). *Motivation and personality*. New York: Harper and Row; Maslow, A. H. (1968). *Toward a psychology of being* (2nd ed.). New York: Van Nostrand Reinhold.

52. Alderfer, C. P. (1969). An empirical test of a new theory of human needs. *Organizational Behavior and Human Performance, 4*, 143–175; Alderfer, C. P. (1972). *Existence, relatedness, and growth*. New York: Free Press.

53. Herzberg, F. H. (1966). *Work and the nature of man*. Cleveland: World Publishing Co.

54. Wahba, M. A., & Bridwell, L. G. (1976). Maslow reconsidered: A review of research on the need hierarchy. *Organizational Behavior and Human Performance, 15*, 121–140; Mitchell, V. F., & Moudgill, P. (1976). Measurement of Maslow's need hierarchy. *Organizational Behavior and Human Performance, 16*, 334–349.

55. Alderfer (1972), *supra* note 52.

56. Herzberg, F. H., Mausner, B., & Snyderman, B. B. (1959). *The motivation to work*. New York: Wiley.

57. See Pinder, C. C. (1984). *Work motivation: Theory, issues, and applications*. Glenview, IL: Scott, Foresman, and Caston, R. J., & Braito, R. (1985). A specification issue in job satisfaction research. *Sociological Perspectives*, April, 175–197.

58. Vroom, V. H. (1964). *Work and motivation*. New York: Wiley.

59. Mitchell (1974), *supra* note 25; Wanous, J. P., Keon, T. L., & Latack, J. C. (1983). Expectancy theory and occupational/organizational choice: A review and test. *Organizational Behavior and Human Performance, 32*, 66–86.

60. Behling, O., & Starke, F. A. (1973). The postulates of expectancy theory. *Academy of Management Journal, 16*, 373–388; Mitchell (1974), *supra* note 25; Van Eerde, W., & Thierry, H. (1996). Vroom's expectancy models and work-related criteria: A meta-analysis. *Journal of Applied Psychology, 81*, 575–586.

61. For a summary, see Landy, F. J., & Becker, L. J. (1987). Motivational theory reconsidered. In L. Cummings & B. Staw (eds.), *Research in organizational behavior* (vol. 9). Greenwich, CT: JAI Press. Also see Kanfer, R. (1990). Motivation theory and industrial and organizational psychology. In M. D. Dunnette & L. M. Hough (eds.), *Handbook of industrial and organizational psychology* (2nd ed., vol. 1) (75170). Palo Alto, CA: Consulting Psychologists Press.

62. Locke, E. A. (1968). Toward a theory of task motivation and incentives. *Organizational Behavior and Human Performance, 3,* 157–189; Locke, E. A., Shaw, K. N., Saari, L. M., and Latham, G. P. (1981). Goal setting and task performance: 1969–1980. *Psychological Bulletin, 90,* 125–152.

63. Katzell, R. A., & Thompson, D. E. (1990). Work motivation: Theory and practice. *American Psychologist, 45,* 144–153, p. 145.

64. Pinder, C. C. (1984) *supra* note 57; Miner, J. B. (1984). The validity and usefulness of theories in an emerging organizational science. *Academy of Management Review, 9,* 296–306.

65. Locke et al. (1981), *supra* note 62; Mento, A. J., Steel, R. P., & Karren, R. J. (1987). A meta-analytic study of the effects of goal setting on task performance: 1966–1984. *Organizational Behavior and Human Performance, 39,* 52–83.

66. Wexley, K. N., & Baldwin, T. T. (1986). Posttraining strategies for facilitating positive transfer: An empirical exploration. *Academy of Management Journal, 29,* 503–520.

67. Werner, J. M., O'Leary-Kelly, A. M., Baldwin, T. T., & Wexley, K. N. (1994). Augmenting behavior-modeling training: Testing the effects of pre- and post-training interventions. *Human Resource Development Quarterly, 5,* 169–183. See also Wexley and Baldwin (1986), *supra* note 66.

68. Greenhaus, J. H. (1987). *Career management.* Hinsdale, IL: Dryden Press.

69. Bandura, A. (1977). *Social learning theory.* Englewood Cliffs, NJ: Prentice-Hall.

70. Bandura, A. (1986). *Social foundations of thought and action.* Englewood Cliffs, NJ: Prentice-Hall, 391.

71. Bandura, A. (1977). Self-efficacy: Toward a unifying theory of behavior change. *Psychological Bulletin, 84,* 122–147.

72. Bandura, A., & Cervone, D. (1983). Self-evaluation and self-efficacy mechanisms governing the motivational effects of goal systems. *Journal of Personality and Social Psychology, 45,* 1017–1028; Bandura, A., & Cervone, D. (1987). Differential engagement of self-reactive influences in cognitive motivation. *Organizational Behavior and Human Decision Processes, 38,* 92–113; Brief, A. P., & Hollenbeck, J. R. (1985). An exploratory study of self-regulating activities and their effects on job performance. *Journal of Occupational Behavior, 6,* 197–208; Frayne, C. A., & Latham, G. P. (1987). The application of social learning theory to employee self-management of attendance. *Journal of Applied Psychology, 72,* 387–392; Locke, E. A., Frederick, E., Lee, C., & Bobko, P. (1984). Effects of self-efficacy, goals, and task strategies on task performance. *Journal of Applied Psychology, 69,* 241–251. A more detailed discussion of the implications of self-efficacy for work behavior is provided by Gist, M. E. (1987). Self-efficacy: Implications for organizational behavior and human resource management. *Academy of Management Review, 12,* 472–485 and Gist, M. E., & Mitchell, T. R. (1992). Self-efficacy: A theoretical analysis of its determinants and malleability. *Academy of Management Journal, 17,* 183–211.

73. Gist, M. E., Schwoerer, C., & Rosen, B. (1989). Effects of alternative training methods on self-efficacy and performance in computer software training. *Journal of Applied Psychology, 74,* 884–891; Gist, M. E., Stevens, C. K., & Bavetta, A. G. (1991). Effects of self-efficacy and post-training interventions, on the acquisition and maintenance of complex interpersonal skills. *Personnel Psychology, 44,* 884–891; Mathieu, J. E., Martineau, J. W., and Tannenbaum, S. I.

(1993). Individual and situational influences on the development of self-efficacy: Implications for training effectiveness. *Personnel Psychology, 46,* 125–147; Tannenbaum, S. I., Mathieu, J., Salas, E., and Cannon-Bowers, J. (1991). Meeting trainees' expectations: The influence of training fulfillment on the development of commitment, self-efficacy, and motivation. *Journal of Applied Psychology, 76,* 759–769.

74. Baldwin, T. T. (1992). Effects of alternative modeling strategies on outcomes of interpersonal-skills training. *Journal of Applied Psychology, 77,* 147–154; Decker, P. J., & Nathan, B. R. (1985). *Behavior modeling training: Principles and applications.* New York: Praeger; Goldstein, A. P., & Sorcher, M. (1974). *Changing supervisor behavior.* Elmsford, NY: Pergamon Press.

75. Adams, J. S. (1963). Toward an understanding of inequity. *Journal of Abnormal and Social Psychology, 67,* 422–436; Carrell, M. R., & Dittrich, J. E. (1978). Equity theory: The recent literature, methodological considerations, and new directions. *Academy of Management Review, 3,* 202–210.

76. Campbell, J. P., & Pritchard, R. D. (1976). Motivation theory in industrial and organizational psychology. In M. D. Dunnette (ed.), *Handbook of industrial and organizational psychology* (63130). Chicago: Rand McNally.

77. *Ibid.*

78. *Ibid.*; Pinder (1984), *supra* note 57.

79. Mowday, R. T. (1979). Equity theory predictions of behavior in organizations. In R. D. Steers & L. W. Porter (eds.), *Motivation and work behavior* (2nd ed.). New York: McGraw-Hill; Huseman, R. C., Hatfield, J. D., & Miles, E. W. (1987). A new perspective on equity theory: The equity sensitivity construct. *Academy of Management Review, 12,* 222–234.

80. Skinner, B. F. (1953). *Science and human behavior.* New York: Macmillan; Skinner, B. F. (1974). *About behaviorism.* New York: Knopf; Watson, J. B. (1913). Psychology as the behaviorist views it. *Psychology Review, 20,* 158–177.

81. Thorndike, E. L. (1913). *The psychology of learning: Educational psychology* (vol. 2). New York: Teachers College Press.

82. See Campbell, J. P. (1971). Personnel training and development. *Annual Review of Psychology, 22,* 565–602.

83. A more complete discussion of how reinforcement theory has been applied to HRD can be found in Latham, G. P. (1989). Behavioral approaches to the training and learning process. In I. L. Goldstein & associates (eds.), *Training and development in organizations* (256295). San Francisco: Jossey-Bass.

84. Vecchio, R. P. (1991). *Organizational behavior* (2nd ed.). Hinsdale, IL: Dryden Press.

85. Wagner & Hollenbeck (1995), *supra* note 49, 172.

86. Fishbein, M., & Ajzen, I. (1975). *Belief attitude, intention, and behavior.* Reading, MA: Addison-Wesley, 216.

87. Staw, B. M., and Ross, J. (1985). Stability in the midst of change: A dispositional approach to job attitudes. *Journal of Applied Psychology, 70,* 469–480.

88. Ajzen, I., & Fishbein, M. (1977). Attitude-behavior relations: A theoretical analysis and review of empirical research. *Psychological Bulletin, 84,* 888–918; Ajzen, I., & Fishbein, M. (1980). *Understanding attitudes and predicting social behavior.* Englewood Cliffs, NJ: Prentice-Hall; Fishbein, M., and Ajzen, I. (1975). *Belief attitude, intention, and behavior.* Reading, MA: Addison-Wesley.

89. Noe, R. A. (1986). Trainee's attributes and attitudes: Neglected influences on training effectiveness. *Academy of Management Review, 11,* 736–749.

90. Noe, R. A., & Schmitt, N. (1986). The influence of trainee attitudes on training effectiveness: Test of a model. *Personnel Psychology, 39,* 497–523.

91. Fleishman, E. A. (1972). On the relation between abilities, learning, and human performance. *American Psychologist, 27,* 1017–1032.

92. Dunnette, M. D. (1976). Aptitudes, abilities, and skills. In M. D. Dunnette (ed.), *The handbook of industrial and organizational psychology* (473520). Chicago: Rand McNally.

93. Goldstein, I. L. (1991). Training in work organizations. In M. D. Dunnette & L. M. Hough (eds.), *The handbook of industrial and organizational psychology* (2nd ed., vol. 2) (507619). Palo Alto, CA: Consulting Psychologists Press.

94. See Guilford, J. P. (1967). *The nature of human intelligence.* New York: McGraw-Hill; Dunnette (1976), *supra* note 92; Fleishman, E. A. (1975). Toward a taxonomy of human performance. *American Psychologist, 30,* 1127–1149.

95. Fleishman, E. A., & Mumford, M. D. (1988). The ability requirement scales. In S. Gael (ed.), *The job analysts handbook for business, government, and industry.* New York: Wiley.

96. *Ibid.*; see also Fleishman, E. A. (1967). Development of a behavior taxonomy for describing human tasks: A correlational-experimental approach. *Journal of Applied Psychology, 51,* 1–10; Fleishman, E. A. (1972). On the relation between abilities, learning, and human performance. *American Psychologist, 27,* 1017–1032; Fleishman, E. A., & Quaintance, M. K. (1984). *Taxonomies of human performance: The description of human tasks.* Orlando, FL: Academic Press.

# 6

# PERFORMANCE APPRAISAL: MEASURING SUCCESS

**The Emerging Issue**

**Chapter Overview**

**A Systems Perspective of Performance Appraisal**

**Chapter Summary**

**HR Tool Kit**

## QUESTIONS TO CONSIDER WHILE READING THIS CHAPTER

1. What are the typical problems with performance appraisal systems?
2. What are the legal and business reasons for conducting performance appraisals?
3. What are the elements of an effective appraisal system?
4. What role do other human resource functions have in the performance appraisal process?
5. What impact do poor appraisal programs have on other areas of human resource management?

## THE EMERGING ISSUE

Performance appraisal is probably the most difficult function for growing firms to implement. Managers in emerging firms often find themselves with little or no time to systematically evaluate the behavior of their employees. Also, new managers and supervisors who were promoted up the "ranks" may find it difficult to provide critical feedback to an employee who was once a coworker and maybe even a friend. Finally, the need for consistency among managers makes performance appraisal hard to implement. Many managers want to do things their own way and in their own time, so getting managers to agree on a positive approach to performance appraisal is not an easy task. For these and probably many other reasons, many firms fail to evaluate or appraise employee performance. This lack of assessment, however, hinders quality, productivity, communication, and legal compliance. Motivation research consistently emphasizes the importance of performance feedback. The development of performance standards is essential for achieving high levels of quality. In addition, documentation of performance deficiencies over time provides the organization with the necessary evidence for a negative employment decision.

## CHAPTER OVERVIEW

A systematic approach to performance appraisal is necessary for all types of organizations. Today, employees are much more likely to bring legal action against their employer for discrimination or wrongful discharge situations. These can be minimized or prevented with a well-formulated performance appraisal system. This system can also be an effective tool in helping the business enterprise prosper. The identification of key talent (and the early identification of poor

■ **EXHIBIT 7.1**

SYSTEMS MODEL OF PERFORMANCE APPRAISAL

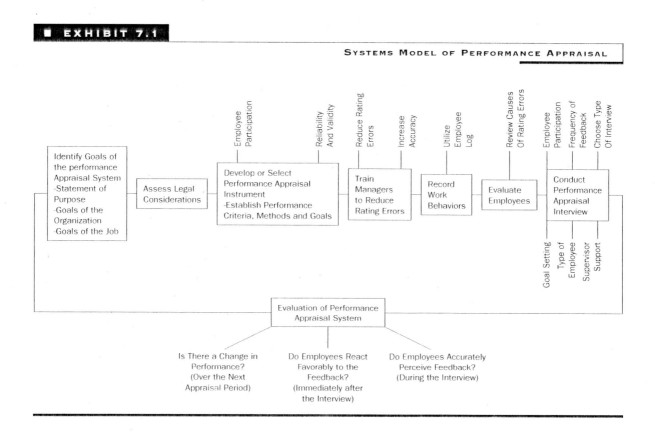

performers) promotes the most efficient use of human resources. Furthermore, a performance appraisal system helps identify future company training needs (especially as the business grows) that will also lead to increased company effectiveness. Finally, basing pay decisions on a systematic appraisal system should reduce turnover and increase employee satisfaction and morale. Exhibit 7.1 shows a systems model of performance appraisal for organizations. Components of this model include determining performance appraisal goals, assessing legal considerations, selecting or developing an instrument, training evaluators, preparing to rate employees, conducting a performance appraisal interview, and evaluating the system. Adherence to such a model will result in a sense of procedural equity or fairness that is seldom realized in many areas of human resource management. This model emphasizes the concept of *performance appraisal* which is viewed as an ongoing and continuous process, and managers and subordinates manage performance on a year-round basis. Based on this model, the following discussion describes the essential steps in developing a useful performance appraisal program.

## A SYSTEMS PERSPECTIVE OF PERFORMANCE APPRAISAL

### IDENTIFY GOALS OF THE PERFORMANCE APPRAISAL SYSTEM

A systematic model of performance appraisal begins with an identification of the system's goals. Identifying the goals of the performance appraisal system requires consideration of a statement of purpose, organizational goals, and job goals.

*Statement of Purpose.*   As seen in Exhibit 7.1, the first step in developing a performance appraisal system is constructing a "Statement of Purpose," which helps ensure full participation, understanding, and support for the program. Many companies have a tendency to implement or develop appraisal systems that do not meet the specific needs and goals of their enterprises. A clear specification of the intended purpose of an employee appraisal system can prevent the implementation of an appraisal system that does not produce the desired effects and further erodes employee trust and commitment to such human resource management systems. Furthermore, a clear statement of the goals and objectives of the appraisal system that is supported by upper management relieves the tension and ambiguity felt by employees when any new program that directly affects their career is implemented. This is especially the case for companies establishing human resource management programs for the first time. Ambiguity and confusion concerning human resource management practices set a tone that is hard to erase when future programs are implemented.

Performance appraisal systems suffer from many problems related to a misdirected or unidentified purpose. These problems are poor definition, poor communication, inappropriateness, lack of support, and a failure to monitor the system. A clear statement of purpose should help solve these problems.[1] The statement of purpose should answer the following questions:

- How does the appraisal system relate to the corporate strategy?
- What are the reasons for and goals of developing the program?
- Who will be evaluated?
- Who conducts the performance appraisal?
- When the appraisal will be conducted?
- How will the appraisal information be used?

*Identifying Goals of the Organization.*   When the goals of the performance appraisal system are identified, both the goals of the company and the job must be considered. The evaluation process allows an opportunity for the manager to discuss with the employee what he or she should be doing, answer any questions that the employee may have, recommend further training and/or development, and respond to complaints and problems. On the other hand, the employee is able to use the evaluation process to specify what his or her duties are and both give and receive feedback.

To identify the goals of the organization, the company must consider the uses of the performance appraisal information. There are four general uses of performance appraisal information.[2]

First, performance appraisal information allows the manager to make equitable or fair distinctions among individuals. Appraisal information allows the manager to recommend the right employee(s) for a pay raise and thus correlate pay and performance in the employee's mind. Research in the area of worker motivation suggests that if pay is to be a motivator, employees must see a clear correlation or relationship with performance.[3] Furthermore, performance appraisal information provides a basis for placement and promotion decisions. A "promotion from within" policy helps decrease turnover, increase motivation, and attract good applicants. In addition, performance appraisal information can be used to identify positions that a troubled employee or borderline performer can be transferred into to better utilize his or her specific talents.

Second, performance appraisal information assists in the assessment of future human resource development needs. Many human resource management professionals[1] consider this to be the most productive aspect of performance appraisal. Specifically, performance appraisal information can help achieve the following development objectives:

*Managerial Feedback.*   Employees find out where they stand with their manager. The lack of any systematic assessment of employee performance and formal feedback of that assessment increases employee skepticism about their relationship with their manager and standing in the company. An uninformed employee is one who is surprised or even shocked when it becomes necessary to pass the employee over for promotion or pay raises.

*Increased Security.*   Employees may not know what areas of their performance need improvement. The feedback provided through performance appraisal relieves employee fears about their employment situation and increases acceptance of management decisions.

*Improved Manager/Employee Relations.*   The manager-subordinate relationship is strengthened because the process encourages mutual agreement on performance expectations. As will be discussed later, the key to developing an acceptable performance appraisal system is to encourage employee involvement at all stages of the program.

*Identify Training Needs.*   Future training and development needs are identified. This includes the knowledge and skills necessary to improve employees' productivity in their present job and those they need to be considered for promotion.

*Improved Communication.*   The performance appraisal interview phase of the program provides an opportunity for the manager and/or the subordinate to express themselves on a variety of work-related issues. A key benefit of any successful performance appraisal system should be increased communication in all aspects of the working relationship. A fair system increases employee morale and trust, and this often leads to more effective communication.

Third, performance appraisal data can be used in the validation process. Title VII of the 1964 Civil Rights Act and its amendments have required that selection procedures be job related. According to the *Uniform Guidelines on Employee Selection Procedures,* a selection procedure includes anything used to make an employment decision. When performance appraisal results are used in test validation, the goal is to show a correlation or relationship between a selection procedure and job performance. The higher this relationship is, the higher or more predictive the selection procedure is of job performance. This process is called "criterion-related validity" and is the most accurate way to assess validity according to the *Uniform Guidelines.* However, companies with fewer than 15 employees are exempted from Title VII and the requirements of the *Uniform Guidelines on Employee Selection Procedures.*

Fourth, performance appraisal information can be used as documentation for taking disciplinary actions against employees. Managers often claim that the process of dealing with problem employees is one of the most troublesome aspects of their jobs. By focusing on job behaviors, performance appraisal data can help relieve the stress of discipline as well as reduce the incidence of reprisals against management because of disciplinary actions taken. A performance appraisal system that identifies employee problems through frequent observation and feedback provides both reasonable and legal justification for taking actions such as denial of pay raises, demotion, or termination.

Although any of the four reasons just discussed are valid uses of performance appraisal information, top management support is essential to the performance appraisal program. Without this support the process may be administered haphazardly or simply viewed as unwelcome paperwork and ignored. A firm commitment helps to ensure that the results of these reviews are utilized when making promotion, dismissal, and disciplinary decisions.

Top executives can show commitment to the appraisal process by budgeting resources (both money and time) to develop and implement the system, utilizing appraisal results to make employment decisions, and including a performance standard for effective performance appraisal on each manager's own appraisal form.

*Identifying Goals of the Job.*   According to the Supreme Court ruling in *Albermarle v. Moody,*[5] job expectations should be based on an accurate job analysis. More specifically, job analysis must objectively assess the critical job behaviors that will be evaluated in the performance appraisal process. (See Chapter 3 for a description of the job analysis process.) Job analysis information ensures objective and valid performance criteria and reduces the likelihood of subjective appraisals by managers based on employee personality traits.

## ASSESS LEGAL CONSIDERATIONS

The next step in the performance appraisal model is to assess the legal considerations related to conducting performance appraisals. It is important for a manager to realize that performance appraisal becomes a legal issue whenever it is used as the basis for an employment decision,[6] including promotions, pay raises, selection for training programs, etc. Many laws exist to enforce the requirement that the evaluation of work behavior be based on objective, job-related criteria so that an individual's employment situation is not unjustly affected because of the manager's stereotypes or biases. For a more in depth discussion of employment discrimination, see Chapter 2. The remainder of this section will discuss the implications of these laws for performance appraisal by identifying the important court decisions that affect the use of performance appraisal and some prescriptions for legally defensible appraisal systems that will help companies new to the use of performance appraisal systems comply with the many laws and court decisions.

The important court cases that directly influence the use of performance appraisals center around the issue of validity, i.e., the evaluation of employee performance based on dimensions directly related to the job. There are four court decisions that have directly influenced the use of performance appraisal.

*Griggs v. Duke Power (1971).*     *Griggs v. Duke Power*[7] was the first Supreme Court decision to involve Title VII of the 1964 Civil Rights Act. The case centered on the fact that the Duke Power Company employed blacks in only one department and whites in three other higher paying departments. To get a job in the departments where the whites worked, applicants had to have a high school diploma or a satisfactory score on two standardized aptitude tests. According to the Supreme Court, this employment practice constituted adverse impact against blacks, a protected group under Title VII of the 1964 Civil Rights Act. As a result of this decision, employers must demonstrate that all criteria used to make an employment decision are valid or job related. Because performance appraisals are criteria used in many employment decisions, they too must be validated.

*Brito v. Zia Company (1973).*     The Zia Company was found guilty of violating Title VII when it laid off a disproportionate number of Hispanics on the basis of low performance appraisal scores. The court ruled that this was illegal because the performance appraisal instrument used to make these decisions was not related to important elements of work behavior, but was only based on "the best judgments and opinions of supervisors."[8]

*Wade v. Mississippi Cooperative Extension Service (1974).*     In this case, the Mississippi Cooperative Extension Service was found guilty of discriminating against blacks. The Extension Service used a performance appraisal instrument based on supervisory ratings of traits such as leadership, public acceptance, attitude, grooming, resourcefulness, and outlook on life. The Court ruled that this method was not an "objective appraisal of job performance" and unfairly froze blacks in nonsupervisory positions.[9]

*Albermarle Paper Company v. Moody (1975).*     In this case, the Court ruled that the Albermarle Paper Company wrongly relied on subjective supervisory

**EXHIBIT 7.2**

**PRESCRIPTIONS FOR LEGALLY DEFENSIBLE APPRAISAL SYSTEMS**

1. Ensure that procedures for personnel decisions do not vary as a function of the race, sex, national origin, religion, or age of those affected by such decisions.

2. Use objective and unbiased data whenever they are available.

3. Provide a formal system of review or appeal to resolve disagreements regarding appraisals.

4. Use more than one independent measure to evaluate performance.

5. Use a formal, standardized system for personnel decisions.

6. Ensure that evaluators have ample opportunity to observe employee performance before they rate their subordinates.

7. Avoid rating on traits such as dependability, drive, aptitude, or attitude.

8. Provide documented performance counseling before performance-based termination decisions.

9. Communicate specific performance standards to employees.

10. Provide raters with written instructions on how to complete performance evaluations.

11. Evaluate employees on specific work dimensions, rather than on a single overall or global measure.

12. Require documentation in terms of specific behaviors (e.g., critical incidents) for extreme ratings.

13. Base the content of the appraisal form on a job analysis.

14. Provide employees with an opportunity to review their appraisals.

15. Educate personnel decision-makers on discrimination laws.

SOURCE: Adapted from Bernardin, H. J., and Cascio, W. F. (1987). "Performance appraisal and the law." In *Readings in Personnel and Human Resource Management*, 3rd ed., Ed. R. S. Schuler, S. A. Youngblood, and V. Huber (St. Paul: West Publishing Co.).

rankings as the criterion on which they validated their selection procedures. More specifically, the court stated that the company failed to conduct a job analysis that could identify the critical requirements of the job.[10] The implication of this case is that a job analysis must be the basis of a performance appraisal instrument that is used in the validation of selection procedures.

*Legal Prescriptions.* Based on many court decisions and laws that affect human resource management practices, several characteristics of legally defensible performance appraisal systems can be suggested.[11] These legal prescriptions are listed in Exhibit 7.2 and could be utilized to train supervisors and managers before they conduct actual employee appraisals.

The U.S. Congress and the U.S. Supreme Court have outlined the essential components of a legally defensible performance appraisal system: essentially, a performance appraisal system that is based on a job analysis which identifies critical job duties is defensible in court. In development of a performance appraisal system, legal considerations such as those proposed in Exhibit 7.2 should be followed but should not be the driving force of the project. Instead, the main objective should be to increase company productivity and morale by identifying the most talented personnel and rewarding them with pay raises, promotions, and additional training. The only way to accomplish this objective is to base employment decisions on objective performance criteria. The next section of this chapter describes a process for accomplishing this objective.

## DEVELOP OR SELECT THE PERFORMANCE APPRAISAL INSTRUMENT: ESTABLISH PERFORMANCE CRITERIA, METHODS, AND GOALS

After assessment of the legal considerations, the next phase suggested in Exhibit 7.1 is development of the performance appraisal instrument. This typically is accomplished by first establishing criteria, selecting a method, and setting goals. Each aspect of instrument development is described below.

*Performance Appraisal Criteria.* As we already demonstrated, a valid performance appraisal system must be job related.[12] As stated in the *Uniform Guidelines*, validity can be defined as the evaluation of employee performance on criteria (job duties) identified in the job analysis (discussed in Chapter 2) and the achievement of preestablished performance goals. This process of establishing validity is what differentiates an objective appraisal (one based on the supervisor's evaluation of actual job duties) from a subjective one (general evaluations of personality, likeability, etc.). Employees should be evaluated on how they perform the required duties of their job; therefore, personality traits such as disposition, sense of humor, and enthusiasm should not be evaluated unless they are directly related to job requirements.

Performance criteria should be multidimensional in nature. This means that a company should rely on more than just one overall measure of job performance. Organizations should not rely on an overall or global rating of employees; instead, each employee should be evaluated on all the important job duties to achieve the most accurate assessment of job performance.

Finally, employee participation in establishing performance criteria adds to the accuracy and acceptance of the performance appraisal results. Anytime someone is critical of his or her performance, an employee usually feels defensive and questions the fairness of the criticism. However, employee representation in the development of appraisal criteria can help increase the acceptance of the results of the performance appraisal program.

## SELECT A PERFORMANCE APPRAISAL METHOD

Once the criteria for performance have been established, a method of appraisal is needed that differentiates good performers from bad performers. There are two categories of performance appraisal methods, comparative and absolute.

**Comparative methods** compare one employee to another. The most commonly used comparative method is straight ranking where the evaluator develops a list of subordinates in order of best to worst. The criteria for the ranking are usually some overall measure of job performance. The weaknesses of using the comparative method center on its subjectivity. Because a global criterion (where individual aspects of the job are ignored) is used and particular areas of job performance are ignored, this process can by influenced by personal biases and stereotypes that may invite charges of illegal discrimination. Furthermore, subjective standards drastically reduce the usefulness of the performance appraisal information. For example, if pay cannot be tied directly to performance, the motivating potential of the pay increase will decrease.

In contrast to the comparative method, the use of an **absolute method** enables an evaluator to assess an employee's performance without making reference to other employees. Also, employees can be evaluated on several dimensions of job performance instead of one global measure. Five of the most popular absolute methods include narrative essays, critical incidents, weighted checklists, graphic rating scales, and goal setting.

A *narrative essay* is the simplest form of absolute method in which the supervisor is asked to describe a subordinate's strengths, weaknesses, and potential as well as to make suggestions for improvement. Although narrative essays are useful for providing feedback to employees, comparisons across employees are virtually impossible, especially if different supervisors are doing the appraising. The information is only qualitative in nature; therefore, no quantitative decisions among employees can be made (i.e., pay and promotion).

The *critical incident approach* is based on observations made by managers concerning particularly effective or ineffective performance. Included is the description of the critical incident that led to the good or bad performance and the situation in which it occurred. This method provides specific feedback to employees concerning their performance. Also, it has been suggested that this approach is ideal for smaller organizations that have few employees in the same or similar jobs, for situations in which objective measures of performance are unavailable, and for companies in which budgetary limitations prohibit the development of a system unique to the company.[13]

Although critical incidents may be useful, the drawbacks of their use reduce their viability as a sole means of measuring work performance. There are three basic drawbacks to the use of critical incidents.[14] First they are nonquantitative in nature. This prohibits the comparisons across employees needed to make pay and promotion decisions. Second, the record-keeping aspect of the task is extremely time consuming. Managers often grow weary of keeping track of these incidents and decrease the amount of record keeping as the appraisal period grows longer. Also, as the number of employees supervised increases, the ability to observe and record critical incidents of performance decrease. Third, the critical incidents are often not weighted in importance to their contributions to successful job performance, and they only assess performance on a small percentage of the job.

Even though the critical incident approach should not be the sole performance appraisal method, it is a good way to identify important job duties that should be evaluated and incorporated into the appraisal system. It is not true that smaller companies, either in size, revenues, or scope of human resource management programs, are limited in the type of performance appraisal system that they can offer. The

**EXHIBIT 7.3**

**A TRADITIONAL GRAPHIC RATING SCALE**

Please rate your subordinate on the following job duties. Use the following rating scale to make your ratings:

1 = very poor

2 = poor

3 = average

4 = above average

5 = excellent

**Job Duties**

| | | | | | | |
|---|---|---|---|---|---|---|
| 1. Defines instruction to subordinates. | 1 | 2 | 3 | 4 | 5 |
| 2. Completes paperwork by designated dates. | 1 | 2 | 3 | 4 | 5 |

quantitative performance appraisal model recommended in this chapter is inexpensive to develop and is only limited by the amount of work that is put into it.

A *weighted checklist* utilizes qualitative and quantitative data in the appraisal process. Using the critical incident technique as its foundation, this method eliminates some of its drawbacks by assigning weights or values to each incident. In the checklist, the evaluator simply checks the incidents that the job incumbent performs, and the values are totaled to achieve a final performance score. The major drawback of this approach is the difficulty of developing a checklist that is representative of a job, especially given the fact that it is centered on the critical incidents of the job and leaves out behaviors that are most frequently performed on the job. Also, the creation of weights is difficult for newer and smaller companies that do not have the sample size necessary to calculate a reliable set of critical incident values.

The *graphic rating* scale is the most widely used approach for assessing performance. The goal of this approach is to identify important dimensions of job performance and then rate them on a continuum from excellent to poor. These scales generally range from 1 to 5 or 1 to 7. Research shows that scales longer than seven points add little to rating accuracy while they make the rating task much more confusing and difficult.[15]

Traditional graphic rating scales vary in the number of job dimensions measured, the specificity of these job dimensions, and the extent to which each scale point is defined.[16] The indicators of performance vary from personality traits to specific job behaviors or duties. To achieve the highest level of job relatedness or validity, it is usually recommended that the performance dimensions be as specific and closely related to the job as possible and avoid measuring personality traits (See "Assess Legal Considerations" in the previous section). It is also recommended that the performance dimensions be taken from the important job duties identified in the job analysis. A simple 1 to 5 or 1 to 7 scale anchored as seen in Exhibit 7.3 can be effective, easy to use, and more accurate than other absolute methods.

A specific type of graphic rating scale is the behaviorally anchored rating scale (BARS). The BARS builds on the critical incident approach and defines performance dimensions by developing anchors corresponding to different levels of performance.[17] Each performance dimension is described by a number of incidents associated with different levels of behavior. The development of the BARS includes the following steps.

Step 1: Collect critical incidents.

Step 2: Sort incidents into behavioral or performance dimensions.

Step 3: For each performance dimension, use incidents with high agreement as anchors for the rating scale.

Although BARSs are easy to use, the major disadvantage of this method is that it is very time consuming to develop. Therefore, organizations with many jobs or jobs that are rapidly changing may find BARS too cumbersome to implement. Also, BARSs do not appear to add anything to traditional trait scales that are less time consuming to develop.[18]

The main advantage of graphic rating scales is that they allow a quantitative score to be calculated, which accurately represents a job incumbent's performance. Furthermore, if all important job duties are rated using the same graphic rating scale, one employee's average score can be compared to that of others in the company.

Although the graphic rating scale provides the most advantages for appraising employee performance, it lacks the feedback potential that methods such as critical incidents or narrative essays provide. Therefore, when a company constructs a performance appraisal system, the use of more than one method is useful. For example, the quantifiable score provided by the graphic rating scale would allow pay and promotion decisions to be made and the narrative essay would help explain to the employee how the supervisor arrived at his or her ratings.

*Setting Goals.*    A performance appraisal program should not be limited to simply evaluating past performance of employees. To achieve goals such as increased productivity or quality of work, the performance appraisal system must also deal with future job performance as well. This can be accomplished through *goal setting*. During the formal performance appraisal interview, the manager and subordinate can set mutually agreed upon goals that will guide the employee toward improved job performance and greater success on the job. The appraisal, if performed correctly, will identify areas of weakness and then through mutual goal setting, objectives that are reasonable and challenging can be set to correct these weaknesses in performance.

The most common method for incorporating mutual goal setting into performance appraisal is **management by objectives (MBO).**[19] MBO consists of the following five basic steps:

1. Goals are established for the new venture and its specific areas. These goals are performance related and are based on a 1- to 3-year time span.

2. The manager and subordinate mutually agree on several objectives that are congruent with the goals identified in step 1. The time span for goal attainment is usually 1 year.

3. Performance requirements consisting of accomplishments, results, and timetables are established. These are the standards for measuring goal accomplishment.

4. The manager and subordinate meet for interim progress reviews. This allows corrective actions to be undertaken as necessary. For example, if changes occur that are out of the employee's control, the goals can be adjusted to make them more realistic.

5. At the end of the appraisal period, employee accomplishments are measured against performance objectives. Based on the degree of goal accomplishment attained, objectives are then set for the next appraisal period.

Two reasons help explain the popularity of MBO.[20] First, it is based on the commonly held value that people should be rewarded for their accomplishments. Second, MBO helps achieve greater "individual-organizational goal congruence." In other words, MBO puts the manager and the employee on the same team with the same goals. MBO is also attractive because, if constructed properly, the goals can be very objectively formulated.

However, like the other appraisal systems discussed previously, MBO has some problems. First, MBO, if not developed properly, may not cover all the important dimensions of the job. As jobs increase in complexity, important dimensions of these jobs cannot always be measured in terms of their output. Second, MBO may cause a "results-at-all-costs" attitude among employees where the ends may not be justified by their means. For example, a salesperson who steals a client from a coworker to reach a performance goal may cause dissension among the sales force and give the client a bad image of the company. Third, performance outcomes, by themselves, do not tell the employee what he or she needs to do to increase productivity. For example, a cable TV sales manager who is told that he failed to sign 500 new accounts in a year's time knows that he fell short of his goal. What is needed is a clear explanation of what areas of job performance need improvement and the particular training he needs to achieve this improvement. Lastly, many objective-based systems emphasize the need to develop several objectives instead of dealing with one or two meaningful objectives at a time.

Based on these problems, MBO should be combined with other performance appraisal methods to provide a more detailed description and evaluation of an employee's job behavior. In fact, there is no one best performance appraisal method. Appraisal systems are developed to serve a wide variety of purposes. To meet the many needs of the enterprise, the company may choose to rely on a variety of different performance appraisal methods. On the other hand, the developer of a performance appraisal system should not rely on methods such as ranking and trait rating scales that are based on subjective criteria and allow for personal stereotypes and biases to enter into the evaluation process. Moreover, an employer that wishes to use nonquantitative techniques such as the narrative essay or critical incident approaches may also want to include graphic rating scales that measure job performance. This will allow comparisons between employees to determine promotions, pay increases, etc. The suggested performance appraisal program and form in the HR Tool Kit of this chapter incorporate many of these appraisal methods.

### TRAIN MANAGERS TO REDUCE RATING ERRORS

Once the appraisal criteria and method(s) are selected, managers should be trained on how to conduct effective appraisals. Training is necessary to reduce rating errors and increase evaluation accuracy. Ratings become inflated because of leniency, halo error, and failure to take the necessary time to complete the appraisal. There are many types of errors that can occur during the rating of an employee's performance. A supervisor can be too lenient or too strict, can rate everyone average, or can be swayed by situational factors such as the order in which he or she conducts the evaluations. In the following sections we describe four of the most detrimental errors and illustrate ways of preventing or minimizing them.

**Central tendency errors** occur when managers consistently rate all their employees as average. Computing the mean and standard deviation of a supervisor's ratings can identify this error. Specifically, a mean rating close to the center of the scale and a low standard deviation are ways of identifying the occurrence of central tendency. This error can be avoided in two ways. First, the rater should rank his or her employees before rating them. In this way, it is easier to differentiate good, average, and poor employees. Second, the manager should justify ratings in writing.

**Leniency and severity errors** occur when a manager consistently gives all employees favorable (leniency) or unfavorable (severity) ratings. These errors occur when an evaluator uses only one end of the rating scale and can be identified by computing the average of the ratings across all subordinates. If the average is close to either end of the rating scale, leniency or severity errors may have occurred. Leniency can be avoided by reducing ambiguity in the rating scales through clearer definitions of each of the points on the rating scale. This way a manager may be better able to assess the different levels of employee behavior. Another way to avoid leniency is to enforce a company policy that requires managerial justification of ratings.

**Halo errors** occur when a rater gives a rating of good or bad performance on one dimension of job performance and then applies the same rating to other dimensions of job performance. This error is difficult to correct because its occurrence may not be consistent for all subordinates. The best way to avoid the error is to consider each performance dimension independently and base each rating on specific examples of worker performance.

**Contrast effects** occur when a rater lets extremely bad or extremely good employee evaluations color subsequent evaluations of other employees. Again, this is a difficult error to detect and can best be controlled by not rating all subordinates in one sitting. An evaluator should allow some time between each rating so that the "glow" of the previous evaluation is forgotten and does not adversely affect the next evaluation.

In general, having written justification for all ratings can control the rating errors described above. If the evaluator can provide specific examples of work behavior and the manager reviews these comments before the appraisal is completed, a more accurate performance appraisal can be achieved. According to the research, the use of extensive training to reduce rating errors is unnecessary.[21] The simple process of requiring raters to review the descriptions of the different types of errors that can occur and how to correct them before they rate **each** employee provides the same results at much less costs both in terms of time and money. However, some form of decision-making and observation training is still necessary to increase rater accuracy.[22]

## RECORD WORK BEHAVIORS

The next step in the performance appraisal process (see Exhibit 7.1) is to record work behaviors. Valid appraisals are often time consuming, but this time can be useful later in preparing evaluations. It may help the supervisor to document employee behavior on a regular basis (e.g., once a week). This documentation will increase the accuracy of employee appraisals and make them more defensible in court. When recording both good and bad employee behaviors, the supervisor should include the time and date of such behaviors.

## EVALUATE EMPLOYEES

After work behaviors have been observed and documented, the manager is now ready to begin the evaluation process. It is critical that the manager take time to prepare to rate each employee. Appraisal preparation includes the following:

- Review each employee's job description and pay close attention to what duties the employee performs. If a particular job duty is no longer appropriate, the subordinate(s) should be consulted and the necessary changes should be made.

- Gather and organize all notes about the employee's performance during the past appraisal period. Any previous performance appraisal report should also be reviewed.

- Meet with top level executives to discuss company goals and objectives, as well as how employees will be rated, before conducting the formal review with employees.

- Clear dates and times of reviews with human resources or the manager who is coordinating this activity. Consistent application of the appraisal process across all departments is important.

As cited above, record keeping or performance monitoring is critical to making accurate ratings, especially as the number of employees directly supervised increases. The supervisor should take time out of his or her workweek to keep a log of important employee behaviors. This is similar to the critical incident method but is not limited to "critical behaviors." In addition to increasing the accuracy of the ratings given, these notes provide a good tool for feedback and legal defense of the ratings.

An effective appraisal system emphasizes performance monitoring on a year-round basis. Managers should keep records of employee behaviors on a daily basis. Information should be dated and reviewed for employee evaluation and feedback. This documentation may also be useful when employee actions such as dismissal need to be defended. Also, performance monitoring has a positive independent effect on employee performance[23]; it can "cue" or "signal" the employees about the relative importance of the various tasks they perform.

### CONDUCT PERFORMANCE APPRAISAL INTERVIEW

The next element in the performance appraisal process is the feedback interview. The appraisal feedback interview is a key link in the success of any performance appraisal system. In fact, all the work involved in developing and selecting accurate performance appraisal criteria, goals, and methods can be wasted if the interview is not taken seriously. It is the link between the evaluation of past employee performance and the improvement of future performance.

As part of a performance appraisal system, the evaluation of an employee's performance should be a daily occurrence. The manager should point out to the employee when he or she is performing well or poorly. It has been suggested that the formal performance review be conducted on a quarterly basis to coincide with other required quarterly reports.[24] The quarterly review would allow for more frequent problem solving and goal adjustment; however, it could also be too time consuming and result in short-term planning and goal setting. It is usually recommended that managers conduct a formal performance review of every employee on an annual basis. This will allow for formal record keeping and discussion of the employee's strengths and weaknesses.

The appraisal interview should be conducted by the manager (the immediate supervisor) and should occur soon after the evaluation form is completed. It is recommended that the manager complete his or her ratings before the interview so that personal interactions and pressures that occur during the performance appraisal interview do not bias the evaluations. Also, on some occasions it may be necessary to conduct a special performance appraisal and interview. A special evaluation may be conducted if an employee has an unsatisfactory rating or if an employee is being recommended for a special pay raise or promotion that is based on previous work or experience.

The interview should also take place at a predetermined time and place. It should not be a spur-of-the-moment event that causes the supervisor and subordinate to be unprepared. More specifically, the interview should take place during regular working hours in a place that is nonthreatening, comfortable, and free from distractions.

**EXHIBIT 7.4**

## CRITICAL CONCEPTS FOR A PERFORMANCE REVIEW

1. Notify employees of the time and place of their review at least a week in advance to allow them time to prepare.

2. Be sure to locate a quiet place in which to conduct the formal reviews to minimize interruptions.

3. Allow employees a chance to rate themselves before the formal review. Give a copy of the performance appraisal form to each employee for completion before the review.

4. Set aside an adequate amount of time to evaluate each employee.

5. Explain to the employee the reason for the annual review and what the results will be used for. Try to clear up any misunderstandings about the review and your role in the process.

6. Be sure that the atmosphere is relaxed, making it easier to discuss an employee's performance. The employee should feel free to make comments and ask questions. However, a relationship such as this cannot be developed overnight; the process of building a climate of trust and mutual respect should be an ongoing priority for managers.

7. Listen to the employee and indicate to him or her that you are concerned about performance or lack of performance.

8. Be sure that all decisions concerning the employee's performance are based on the duties performed and not personal biases.

9. Explain to the employee what chance he or she has to advance in the company.

10. Allow time for the employee to ask questions and make comments.

11. Set up a follow-up time to discuss the employee's salary increase. Discussion of salary will interfere with the developmental aspects of the performance appraisal review. Schedule a follow-up session for salary discussions.

12. Sign the performance appraisal form and ask the employee to sign it. These signatures indicate that the manager has reviewed the performance ratings with the employee.

The annual review or performance appraisal interview can be difficult for managers because they are placed in a position of judging their employees. It is equally disturbing to the employees because they realize that their work is being evaluated. The research in the area of performance appraisal interviews also suggests the following three problems[25]: (1) Employees were more concerned about where they stood after the interview than before. In fact, some subordinates never realized that a performance appraisal interview took place. (2) Employees rated their supervisors less favorably after the interview than before. (3) Subordinates generally felt that supervisors act in an autocratic manner, and few cases of improvement were cited after the interview had taken place.

To overcome these problems, Exhibit 7.4 presents 12 critical concepts that need to be considered when an annual performance review are conducted.

## EVALUATION OF PERFORMANCE APPRAISAL SYSTEM

The evaluation of a performance appraisal program is essential. A program that is not accomplishing its goals and objectives should be discontinued or changed

## THE "AVERAGE" WORKER: THE BACKBONE OF THE COMPANY

Managers have been required to conduct performance evaluations of their subordinates for many years. This has not always been a manager's favorite task because doing so requires him or her to tell subordinates the way that they have performed with respect to the company's expectations. While many of those who are evaluated hope to be given high marks and maybe even a promotion, the reality is that the majority of employees are told that they are average. How can this be? And how can a manager tell his or her subordinates that they are doing an average job and not cause them to lose the motivation needed to improve performance and damage the manager-subordinate relationship? The answer often lies in the expected method of performance appraisal required of managers.

One of the more common types of performance appraisals that managers are expected to conduct uses a simple 1 to 5 rating scale with 1 being "outstanding" and 5 being "serious deficiency." With this type of performance appraisal, it is important for managers to understand the percentage of employees that should fall into each of the five categories. Companies often require that 5 to 10 percent of the employees fall into the "outstanding" category. In this category, managers place their top performers so that these employees are given sufficient compensation to ensure that they stay at the company, while also making sure that they receive the proper training for future advancement. In category number two, also known as "above standard," managers are expected to place 20 to 25 percent of all employees evaluated. These employees will receive above average compensation to entice them to stay at the firm. Companies rarely set percentage targets for category four (needs improvement) because evaluators often are hesitant to rate employees poorly. On rare occasions, 5 percent targets are set for this category but are rarely achieved. Companies typically reserve category five (serious deficiency) for rare circumstances under which superiors have requested that an employee be evaluated so that a case for termination can be made.

Companies often require that 60 to 75 percent of remaining employees be placed in category number three. These employees are neither above the company's standard nor are they having problems with performance. Category three employees hold up the company's structure, and it is these people who carry the company to achieve its goals. For this group, performance appraisals normally do not yield positive results because they often include the message that the employee is just average. Although this message might not be spoken in direct words, those placed in category three often interpret their evaluations as, "You are an average employee and although we appreciate you, we will not take any significant measures to retain you." Once employees receive this message they tend to disregard the other parts of their evaluations, including ways of improving performance and goal setting for the following year. This is one of the downfalls of performance appraisals that are conducted mainly to recognize the high achievers and those who are having problems performing at the level that the company requires of its employees.

People work hard to avoid telling their friends and family that they are just average. For example, when a friend gets an "A" on an exam at a university class we congratulate the person for the exam grade and do not emphasize the fact that he or she received mediocre grades in the

to save the company's resources. On the other hand, even if the program is determined to be successful, it may need fine-tuning periodically. Therefore, every systematic model of performance appraisal should have an evaluation component. The evaluation component should include cognitive, affective, behavioral, and strategic elements. These evaluation questions include the following:

other course work. This is common behavior in the friends-and-family environment; however, managers are often not afforded the luxury of highlighting only the positive aspects of an employee's performance while leaving out the overall assessment that the person is an average performer. There are a few different creative ways that managers deal with this situation so that the manager's relationship with his or her employees does not suffer.

There are certain managers who refuse to put any employee into category number three. They make the claim that "all of my employees are above average." This is a common technique that is utilized by managers who find it too painful to tell employees that they are average. Companies often spend a lot of money to secure systems that help to make it difficult for managers to use this strategy.

Other managers will put all of their employees into category number three, making the claim that "all of my employees are fantastic performers, and therefore, they are all standard." This technique eliminates the attached meaning of category number three (meets standard), and although employees may not be happy to receive this evaluation, their motivation may not be damaged because they are not being directly told that they are average. Another strategy that managers use to avoid hurting the ego of employees who are put into category number three is to tell them that they really are a three plus. This gives the employees the false hope that in the next year or two they will be a category two employee. Finally, a manager may tell employees that they have been put into category three because their evaluation was result of an evaluation of the entire group. This makes it easier for those evaluated to blame the rest of the group for the average evaluation and not feel that it was the result their own individual performance.

When a manager is confronted with the task of telling his or her employees that they are "average," it can be beneficial to discuss the overall performance assessment and the strategies for future improvement in two separate meetings. This will minimize the chance that a discouraged employee will tune out the strategies for future improvement that were discussed in the same meeting. Furthermore, it is not necessary for a company to formally rate employees who are repeatedly average performers, as doing so will only make their unhappiness within the firm a certainty. For a category three employee, frequent formal evaluations are only necessary in the event that the employee requests it. In this case, managers often find it easier to give employees truthful evaluations.

It is critical that the management of a new firm receive accurate evaluations of employees' performance. While distorted performance appraisals may go unnoticed in a larger firm for some time, a small emerging firm may suffer greatly if managers base their decisions upon incorrect data regarding employee productivity. Management in these firms may also want to develop programs that are geared toward employee appreciation. If managers can communicate to the average (most common) employees within the firm that they are appreciated, the level of employee retention and productivity can be much higher.

SOURCE: Adapted from Flynn, P. (2001). "You are simply average." *Across the Board* March/April: 51–55.

- Do employees accurately perceive feedback during the performance appraisal interview? (Cognitive component)

- Do employees react favorably to the feedback immediately following the interview? (Affective component)

- Is there a change in performance over the next performance appraisal period? (Behavioral component)
- Are organizational goals being fulfilled? (Strategic component)

Acceptance of feedback about job performance is an essential component of any performance appraisal system that has employee development and change as a goal. In many cases, however, employees report that no feedback was given in the interview or that the feedback was inaccurate.[26] These problems may be a result of the supervisor's authoritarian style,[27] the inability of the supervisor to convey the feedback, the importance of the feedback given to the employee, or the lack of attention paid by the subordinate. Whatever the cause, its correction is essential to the success of the program. Several procedures can be implemented to evaluate the success of the performance appraisal program, including the following:

- The manager should review all appraisals.
- A formal grievance and review procedure to process complaints about any part of the performance appraisal system should be implemented. The number of grievances received is a good indicator of employee acceptance of the program.
- Employees should be surveyed concerning their perceptions of the performance appraisal system. Specifically, the survey should attempt to measure rating accuracy and fairness, quality of feedback, and overall satisfaction with the appraisal. Suggestions provided by employees could help improve the system for the next appraisal period.
- Overall employee performance changes should be assessed. If performance appraisal results are effectively linked to rewards, improvement should result. If not, then there is a defect in the system.
- Improvements in quality and quantity of output should be sought.

The nature of the systematic model presented in this chapter is that performance appraisal is an ongoing process which needs to be fine-tuned from year to year. A company that implements a performance appraisal program and does not evaluate its effectiveness runs the risk of alienating employees instead of motivating them. Trust in the program is essential. Employee participation in all steps of the process helps build and sustain that trust and results in a more productive enterprise.

## CHAPTER SUMMARY

Whether informal or formal, the primary goal of performance appraisal is to provide feedback to the employee regarding his or her job performance. The feedback should motivate the employee to continue to do a good job or to take corrective action to improve performance. However, regardless of a system's specific components, employee perceptions concerning the overall appraisal system will determine the system's effectiveness.[28] The process described in this chapter should have a positive influence on these perceptions.

The process of appraisal has motivation and change as its central themes. The supervisor or rater seeks to motivate employees to perform at their highest level, and also develop and guide them toward this performance level. Performance appraisal is an on-going process, not an isolated occurrence. Informal performance appraisal occurs on a daily or weekly basis as the supervisor observes employee job behavior and performance. If the process is working effectively, informal evaluation, in the form of comments, constructive criticism, praise, and suggestions will provide the basis for more formal evaluations.

Performance appraisal is based on the fact that all employees are accountable for performing their jobs in accordance with specific job duty standards and criteria. The desired level of performance must be clearly understood by the manager and the employee before performance appraisals can be effective. It is critical to the success of any performance appraisal system that employees and supervisors understand what will be measured and evaluated, who will evaluate, when formal appraisal will occur, what assistance will be provided to improve performance, what the employee's role is, and what rewards exist for exceptional performance.

## NOTES

1. Lee, C. (1989). "Poor performance appraisals do more harm than good." *Personnel Journal* September: 91–99.

2. Cleveland, J., Murphy, K. R., and Williams, R. E. (1989). "Multiple uses of performance appraisal: Prevalence and correlates." *Journal of Applied Psychology* 74: 130–135.

3. Schuster, J. R., and Zingheim, P. K. (1996). *The New Pay: Linking Pay and Organizational Performance* (San Francisco: Jossey Bass); Lawler, E. E. (1981). *Pay and Organizational Development* (Reading, MA: Addison-Wesley).

4. Shaw, D., Beatty, R. W., Baird, L. S., and Schneier, C. E. (1995). *The Performance Measurement, Management, and Appraisal Sourcebook* (Amherst, MA: Human Resource Development Press); Bernardin, H. J., and Beatty, R. W. (1984). *Performance Appraisal: Assessing Human Behaviors at Work* (Boston: Kent Publishing Co); Henderson, R. I. (1984). *Performance Appraisal*, 2nd ed. (Reston, VA.: Reston Publishing Co.); Latham, G. P., and Wexley, K. N. (1988). *Increasing Productivity through Performance Appraisal*, 2nd ed. (Reading, MA: Addison-Wesley).

5. *Albermarle Paper Company v. Moody*, U.S. Supreme Court, 10 FEP Cases 1181 (1975).

6. Bernardin and Beatty (1984). Latham and Wexley (1988).

7. *Griggs v. Duke Power Company*, 401 U.S., 3 EPD 8137 (1971).

8. *Brito v. Zia Company*, 478 f.2d. 1200 (1973).

9. *Wade v. Mississippi Cooperative Extension Service*, 372 F. Supp. 126,7 EPD 9186 (1974).

10. *Albermarle Paper Company v. Moody*.

11. Bernardin, H. J., and Cascio, W. F. (1987). "Performance appraisal and the law." In *Readings in Personnel and Human Resource Management*, 3rd ed. Ed. R. S. Schuler, S. A. Youngblood, and V. Huber (St. Paul: West Publishing Co.).

12. Uniform Guidelines on Employee Selection Procedures (1978). *Federal Register* 43: 39290–8315.

13. McEvoy, G. M. (1984). "Small business personnel practices." *Journal of Small Business Management* October: 1–8.

14. Jackson, S. E., and Schuler, R. S. (1999). *Managing Human Resources: A Partnership Perspective,* 7th ed. (Cincinnati: South-Western Publishing Co.).

15. Lissitz, R. W., and Green, S. B. (1975). "Effects of the number of scale points on reliability: A Monte Carlo approach." *Journal of Applied Psychology* 60: 10–13.

16. Cascio, W. F. (1997). *Applied Psychology in Human Resource Management*, 5th ed. (Englewood Cliffs, NJ: Prentice-Hall).

17. Smith, P., and Kendall, L. (1963). "Retranslation of expectations: An approach to the construction of unambiguous anchors for rating scales." *Journal of Applied Psychology* 47: 149–155.

18. Wiersma, U., and Latham, G. (1986). "The practicality of behavioral observation scales, behavior expectation scales, and trait scales." *Personnel Psychology* 38: 619–628.

19. Drucker, P. F. (1954). *The Practice of Management* (New York: Harper).

20. Jackson and Schuler (1999); Schuler, R. S. (1991). *Personnel and Human Resource Management*, 4th ed. (St. Paul: West Publishing Co).

21. Landy, F. J., and Farr, J. L. (1983). *The Measurement of Work Performance: Methods, Theory, and Applications* (New York: Academic Press).

22. Hedge, J. W., and Kavanagh, M. J. (1988). "Improving the accuracy of performance evaluations: Comparison of three methods of performance appraiser training." *Journal of Applied Psychology* 73: 68–73.

23. Larson, J. R., and Callahan, C. (1990). "Performance monitoring: How it affects work productivity." *Journal of Applied Psychology* 75: 530–538.

24. Odiorne, G. S. (1990). "The trend toward the quarterly performance review." *Business Horizons* July-August: 38–41.

25. Cederblom, D. (1982). "The performance appraisal interview: Review, implications, and suggestions." *Academy of Management Review* 7: 219–227.

26. French, J. R. P., Jr., Kay, E., and Meyer, H. H. (1966). "Participation and the appraisal system." *Human Relations* 19: 3–20.

27. Maier, N. (1976). *The Appraisal Interview: Three Basic Approaches* (La Jolla, CA: University Associates).

28. Mohrman, A. M., and Lawler, E. E. (1981). "Improving the contextual fit of appraisal systems." Paper presented at the 89th Annual Convention of the American Psychological Association, Los Angeles.

## HR Tool Kit

### Frequently Asked Questions

**How much should employees be involved in their own appraisals?**

Employees who are allowed to self-evaluate, set goals, and engage in a feedback session as part of the appraisal process usually take more ownership of the performance appraisal process. Employee participation builds trust and communication between the employee and the manager. Some specific activities include the following:

- Provide the employee with an appraisal form, and allow him or her to self-evaluate. Give the employee the form before the appraisal so that he or she has enough time to complete the evaluation.

- During the appraisal feedback session, tell the employee how you rated him or her on each performance standard and then ask the employee to discuss his or her rating. If there is a gap between the ratings, take time to explain why.

- Engage in mutual goal setting for the next appraisal period. Based on the appraisal just completed, set reasonable but challenging goals that will motivate the employee.

**Why should line managers take the time to conduct accurate appraisals?**

Performance appraisal information, if based on job-related dimensions, can provide the necessary documentation for job decisions. Whether the person is being considered for a promotion, transfer, demotion, or termination, performance documentation will enhance the accuracy of the decisions made. Job-related documentation is especially useful when negative job actions such as demotions and terminations must be defended. Employers who can document that performance counseling has taken place have a better chance of fending off the lawsuit or accusation.

**What is a 360-degree appraisal, and when should we use it?**

For a 360-degree appraisal, performance appraisal information is collected from all directions: subordinates, peers, manager/supervisor, self, clients/customers, and vendors. This type of feedback helps managers understand how others perceive them and serves as a diagnostic tool for employee development. A 360-degree appraisal should be used as organizations become flatter and utilize team-based management structures.

Steps of the 360-degree feedback system are as follows:

- Establish feedback criteria.
- Select and train evaluators.
- Conduct evaluations.
- Analyze results.
- Provide feedback to the employee being evaluated.
- Develop a performance action plan for the employee.

**What is management by objectives? How is this technique different from standard performance appraisals?**

Management by objectives (MBO) is a goal-setting approach that uses attainment of objectives to indicate the level and quality of performance. The supervisor and employee work together to develop objectives and determine how to meet those objectives. The MBO process allows employees to actively participate in setting goals. It defines expectations and evaluative standards in advance and concentrates on results achieved, not on subjective personality traits. It is important to set realistic goals and coordinate the individual's goals with the goals of the organization.

### Web Addresses

**www.shrm.org/performance-review/index.html**
The Society for Human Resource Management (SHRM) offers this on-line software package to ease the performance appraisal process. SHRM members receive a discount on the software cost.

**www.ipmaac.org**
The International Personnel Management Association Assessment Council web site is an excellent tool for the HR professional needing information about performance appraisal issues. The site offers training sessions and an on-line library.

**www.p-management.com**
The Performance Appraisal platform focuses on positive reinforcement. This web site offers

*continued*

articles, current news, free testing, and performance models. In addition, the site offers a free electronic newsletter to HR professionals.

### ELEMENTS OF A SUGGESTED PERFORMANCE APPRAISAL PROGRAM

An effective formal performance appraisal program includes the completion of an evaluation form. The form should be completed before the performance appraisal meeting because the completion of the form in the presence of the employee may bias the outcome of the appraisal. A complete form can be found below. The following describes the critical elements of the performance appraisal form:

*Part I: Identification.* Fill in this section completely. It is important to give an accurate number of months the rater has directly observed job performance.

*Part II: Rating Scales.* In this section, you are to appraise how well the person carried out the duties and responsibilities of the job. Read carefully and understand the description of each job duty as identified in the job analysis. Disregard the general impression of the person being rated and concentrate on one job duty at a time. Then rate the person on his or her typical performance during the entire rating period, using the scale below:

1 2   Is <u>not</u> reasonable and consistent with normal expectations of job proficiency.

3 4 5   Is reasonable and consistent with normal expectations of job proficiency.

6 7   <u>Exceeds</u> normal expectations of job proficiency.

In rating each standard, it is important to observe the following rules:

1. Rating must be based on facts.

2. Previous ratings should carry no weight.

3. Although several duties might be related, each duty must be rated independently.

4. Remember that the best employee has weaknesses, while the poorest employee has strong points.

5. Raters can appraise performance *only* on those duties the rater has regularly and directly observed.

Make comments in the blank space provided at the right of each set of duties. For duties rated 3-4-5 comments are optional; however, explain any rating below 3 or above 6.

*Part III: Goal Accomplishment.* In this section, appraise performance on achieving specified goals during the rating period. Both supervisor and employee should agree upon goals. The blank space entitled "Goal" should indicate the agreed-upon goals from the last appraisal review. The space entitled "Measure" indicates how the goal was measured. Use the same 1 to 7 rating scale to assess the level of goal achievement over the past appraisal period. Space is provided for four organizational goals and two personal goals.

As part of the appraisal process, the supervisor and subordinate must hold periodic conferences to review progress, overcome obstacles, and possibly modify goals in light of changed conditions. The final appraisal must also specify those factors beyond the control of the subordinate that influenced performance.

*Part IV: Development Appraisal Summary.* Review the analysis of the employee in attaining acceptable levels of performance. Consider the employee's strengths and weaknesses in terms of overall job requirements. Determine whether the employee's knowledge, skills, and abilities are adequate, less than adequate, or more than adequate for the job. In the comments include the following:

1. A statement of overall job performance.

2. Employee's strengths and weaknesses.

3. Areas that need improvement.

4. Specific actions needed for growth and development.

*Part V: Goals Setting (for the Next Review Period).* These work sheets are designed to help manager and subordinate reach mutual agreement on goals to be accomplished during the next rating period and to provide a basis for appraising the results achieved. Space is provided for four organizational goals and two personal goals.

Goals should be specific and stated in measurable terms. Use indicators such as man-hours, dollars, dates, percentages, etc., wherever possible. They must support the overall mission of the department. They may fall within one major work area of the job, such as planning, or they may cut across several areas. They may be related to new or innovative efforts or to the improvement of normal work output. Identify only those goals that can be reasonably accomplished during the rating period without causing normal work output to suffer as a consequence of the attention they receive. Do not set standards either unrealistically high or unrealistically low.

*Part VI: Employee Career Goals (Optional).* The supervisor, especially in a growing company, should ask the employee what goals the employee has concerning his or her career with the company. This information will help the company in its human resource planning and training and development efforts. This discussion should include the following:

1. Whether or not the employee is satisfied with his or her current position

2. Whether or not there are any other jobs in the company that the employee desires

3. A projected time schedule for attaining the desired job(s)

The manager should then comment on the employee's career goals by making suggestions and outlining some appropriate steps for the employee to take in order to obtain the desired position.

*Part VII: Job Description Review.* During the performance appraisal review, the manager and employee should discuss the accuracy of the job description. It is essential that this document be kept up to date to ensure the validity of the performance appraisal outcome. Enter any changes or corrections in the space allotted. These changes will then become part of the updated performance appraisal instrument to be used during the next appraisal period.

*Part VIII: Signatures.* Both the employee and the manager should sign the completed appraisal form. The employee's signature does not indicate agreement with the rating but is evidence that the employee has seen and reviewed the ratings. (This should be made explicit to the employee!). The employee should carefully study the ratings given and may ask the rater for more information and clarification. When the employee has reviewed the ratings and comments, he or she should sign the appraisal form.

*continued*

**PERFORMANCE APPRAISAL FORM**

## PART I IDENTIFICATION

Name _____     Position _____

Rating Period From _____     To _____

Rater Name _____     Title _____

Number of months rater has directly observed job performance _____

## PART II RATING SCALES

| Job Duties | Rating | Comments |
|---|---|---|
| 1. | 1  2  3  4  5  6  7 | |
| 2. | 1  2  3  4  5  6  7 | |
| 3. | 1  2  3  4  5  6  7 | |
| 4. | 1  2  3  4  5  6  7 | |
| 5. | 1  2  3  4  5  6  7 | |
| 6. | 1  2  3  4  5  6  7 | |

7.        1  2  3  4  5  6  7

8.        1  2  3  4  5  6  7

9.        1  2  3  4  5  6  7

10.       1  2  3  4  5  6  7

11.       1  2  3  4  5  6  7

12.       1  2  3  4  5  6  7

---

## PART III  GOAL ACCOMPLISHMENT

*Organizational Goals*

Goal #1                                    Measure:

Performance Assessment      1   2   3   4   5   6   7

Goal #2                                    Measure:

Performance Assessment      1   2   3   4   5   6   7

Goal #3                                        Measure:


Performance Assessment      1  2  3  4  5  6  7 _____

Goal #4                                        Measure:


Performance Assessment      1  2  3  4  5  6  7 _____


*Personal Goals*

Goal #5                                        Measure:


Performance Assessment      1  2  3  4  5  6  7 _____

Goal #6                                        Measure:


Performance Assessment      1  2  3  4  5  6  7 _____


## PART IV DEVELOPMENTAL APPRAISAL SUMMARY

_____
_____
_____
_____
_____
_____
_____
_____
_____

## *PART V  GOAL SETTING*
(for the next review period)

### *Organizational Goals*

Goal #1                          Measure:

Goal #2                          Measure:

Goal #3                          Measure:

Goal #4                          Measure:

### *Personal Goals*

Goal #5                          Measure:

Goal #6                          Measure:

███████████████████████████████████████████████

---

## *PART VI  EMPLOYEE CAREER GOALS*

Are you satisfied with your current position?

Is there another job that you would like to have in this company?

What are your ultimate career goals with this company?

*Supervisor Comments and Recommendations for career goals:*

_____

_____

_____

_____

_____

_____

_____

_____

_____

_____

_____

## PART VII  JOB DESCRIPTION REVIEW

List any changes or corrections to be made for the next review period.

_____

_____

_____

_____

_____

_____

_____

_____

_____

_____

_____

_____

_____

## PART VIII  SIGNATURES

This report is based on my observation and knowledge. My signature indicates that I have reviewed this appraisal of both employee and the job. It does not mean that I agree with the results.

_____          _____
Supervisor                    Date          Employee                      Date

The above performance appraisal
appears to be accurate and
complete.

_____
Human Resources Representative    Date

# DESIGNING EFFECTIVE HRD PROGRAMS

## LEARNING OBJECTIVES

*After careful study of this chapter, the learner will be able to:*

1. Write training objectives for a specific program or HRD intervention that contain all three qualities for useful objectives (described by Robert Mager).

2. Identify several sources outside one's own organization where HRD programs could be obtained.

3. Compare the relative merits of developing an HRD program in-house versus purchasing it from an outside source.

4. List the activities involved in employer-designed HRD programs.

5. Compare various types of training materials and describe how they are prepared.

6. Point out some of the constraints to scheduling HRD programs, and suggest ways of dealing with them.

Rockwell is a large manufacturer of electronic controls and communications devices. Their two primary business units are Rockwell Automation and Rockwell Collins. The Rockwell Collins unit is headquartered in Cedar Rapids, Iowa, and employs over 14,000 employees. Approximately half of these employees work in Cedar Rapids, with other large operations in California, Florida, Texas, and Mexico. It also has subsidiaries in Europe and Australia, as well as service locations around the world.

Rockwell has long maintained a strong commitment to employee training and development. How-ever, in 1998, all Rockwell Collins training was being conducted via classroom instruction. Twelve in-house trainers provided much of this training. One difficulty was that most of the employees who worked outside of Cedar Rapids had very limited access to train-ing. In that same year, 28 percent of those who signed up for train-ing within the company did not attend that training, citing work demands in a majority of the cases as the reason for cancel-ing. In an effort to provide more training to a greater number of employees, the Learning and Development group at Rockwell Collins considered making in-creased use of outside training vendors, as well as changing the types of methods used to deliver training.

*Questions: If you were manager of learning and development at Rock-well Collins, where would you start in your efforts to improve the avail-ability and effectiveness of company-sponsored training? What sugges-tions would you have concerning how training is designed and pro-vided? Further, what suggestions do you have concerning who should pro-vide the training (i.e., in-house train-ers versus outside vendors)? Finally, how would you seek to "sell" your rec-ommendations to top management?*

## INTRODUCTION

Once needs assessment has been done, an HRD professional faces a number of important questions, such as:

- *Is this an issue that can and should be addressed by a training or HRD intervention?*
- *If so, how do I translate the results of the needs assessment into a specific training or HRD intervention?*
- *If training is necessary, how do we handle the "make" or "buy" decision, that is, do we create the training program in-house, or purchase it from an outside vendor?*
- *Who will be an effective trainer (or trainers) for this particular training or development project?*
- *What is the best way to organize the program or intervention?*
- *How should training methods and materials be selected or prepared?*
- *Are there particular scheduling issues that should be considered in preparing for training?*

The purpose of this chapter is to discuss the second phase of the HRD process: designing training and HRD interventions. At this point, an organization following effective HRD practices will have completed Phase I of the training and HRD process — needs assessment — and will have data that indicate:

1. where the training or HRD program is needed
2. what kind of training or HRD program is needed
3. who needs to be trained
4. the conditions under which training will occur

In addition, the needs identified will have been prioritized so that senior management and the HRD staff know which programs or issues require attention and resources.

We recognize that in some cases the availability of needs assessment data may be limited. Although HRD practitioners may feel that it will be difficult to design effective training programs, sometimes they must improvise and make the best of such suboptimal situations. At the same time, every effort should be made to persuade management of the importance of conducting needs analysis and prioritizing HRD needs, as time and resources allow.

Armed with needs assessment data, the focus now turns to designing an effective HRD program. The key activities involved in designing an HRD program are:

1. setting objectives
2. selecting the trainer or vendor
3. developing a lesson plan
4. selecting program methods and techniques
5. preparing materials
6. scheduling the program

Figure 5-1 shows where these activities fit within the training and HRD process model. It is important to stress at the outset that program design can be a lengthy process. HRD professionals must simultaneously accomplish several other critical tasks throughout the design process. These responsibilities are presented in the boxed insert nearby. While the focus of this chapter is on more pragmatic concerns relating to the six points mentioned above (and described in more detail below), the "big picture" responsibilities described by Ronald Sims are vital to the success of any program that results from such design efforts. Readers are well advised to keep these overarching responsibilities in mind as they design new HRD initiatives.

Assuming that an important need for training has been identified, the manager or HRD professional must begin by translating that need into a set of objectives. Objectives define what participants will be expected to learn or do as a result of participating in the HRD program or intervention. However, some managers and HRD professionals may be tempted to make a decision about whether to design the program internally or purchase the program or its key parts, that is, contract a consultant to serve as a trainer, buy program materials, and so on, *before* establish-

■ **FIGURE 5-1**

TRAINING AND **HRD** PROCESS MODEL

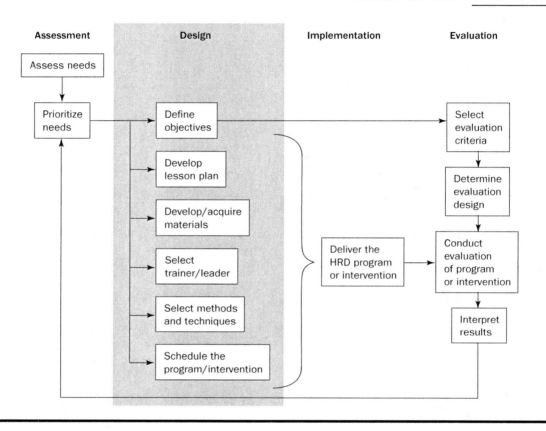

ing objectives. In outside purchases, the organization typically uses the objectives developed by the vendor rather than defining its own. The chances of success are far greater if the organization identifies the HRD objectives first, before deciding whether to design or purchase the program. How can HRD professionals or top managers know what to buy when they haven't clearly defined what they want the program to accomplish?

Statements of HRD needs are often not detailed enough to be used as specific program outcomes. Rather, they state the problem at hand, and ideally, include a diagnosis of the problem's causes. Objectives, in contrast, should state the *outcome* the program is intended to produce, including the specific performance expected, the conditions under which it will be performed, and the criteria to be used to judge whether the objective has been achieved.

## SEVEN OVERARCHING RESPONSIBILITIES OF HRD PROFESSIONALS WHEN DESIGNING HRD PROGRAMS

Management professor Ronald Sims wrote in a recent book that training and development initiatives must emphasize "pivotal" employee competencies (or KSAOs, as we've described them in Chapter 4). To do this, HRD professionals must engage in a number of significant actions, including the following:

1. Identify the kinds and levels of KSAOs that employees need to attain high levels of performance and to achieve organizational results.

2. Develop and maintain organizational structures, conditions, and climates that are conducive to learning.

3. Generate and provide the necessary resources to conduct a program design.

4. Identify and provide access to off-the-job as well as on-the-job learning resources.

5. Provide individual assistance and feedback on various dimensions of individual performance.

6. Serve as role models and mentors to trainees and the organization in the pursuit of mastery of "pivotal" KSAOs.

7. Develop efficient learning processes that take into account individual learning styles, abilities, and work and life circumstances.

These types of responsibilities (especially those in points 2 and 3) cannot be completed without active support and involvement from top management. However, with the increasing focus on high performance from all organizations and employees, HRD professionals must ensure that every HRD initiative serves to help the organization meet its strategic goals and objectives. The above activities must be carried out at the same time that other design issues are being addressed.

SOURCE: From Ronald R. Sims (1998). *Reinventing training and development.* Westport, CT: Quorum Books. Reprinted by permission

## DEFINING THE OBJECTIVES OF THE HRD INTERVENTION

One of the first things an HRD professional should do (after the needs assessment) is to define the objectives for the training or HRD program. Robert Mager defines an objective as a "description of a performance you want learners to be able to exhibit before you consider them competent."[1] As such, HRD or **training program objectives** describe the intent and the desired result of the HRD program. The results can be achieved in many ways (such as lecturing, role playing, and coaching), but this is not specified in the objective. Rather, objectives are used as the *basis* for determining which methods should be used to achieve the specified outcome.

As we have stated, objectives are essential to a successful training or HRD program. In addition to forming the basis for selecting the program content and methods, objectives are used by the organization to evaluate the program's success, and they also help participants to focus their own attention and efforts during the program.[2] In short, objectives tell you where the program is going and how to know when you have reached your desired target. The measurement and

■ **TABLE 5-1**

| | |
|---|---|
| **Performance** | An objective always says what a learner is expected to be able to do and/or produce to be considered competent; the objective sometimes describes the product or result of the doing. Example: "Write a product profile for a proposed new product." |
| **Conditions** | An objective describes the important conditions (if any) under which the performance is to occur. Example, "Given all available engineering data regarding a proposed product, trainee will write a product profile." |
| **Criteria** | Wherever possible, an objective identifies the criteria of acceptable performance by describing how well the learner must perform in order to be considered acceptable. Example: "The product profile must describe all of the commercial characteristics of the product that are appropriate for its introduction to the market, including descriptions of at least three major product uses." |

SOURCE: From R. F. Mager (1997). *Preparing instructional objectives* (3rd ed.) Atlanta: Center for Effective Performance, 21. Reprinted by permission.

evaluation issues that we will cover in Chapter 7 are predicated on defining clear objectives in the design phase; without these, learning is less likely to occur, and evaluation less likely to succeed.

Needs assessment data are useful for defining program objectives because they identify the deficiencies or challenges to be addressed. For example, suppose the needs analysis data for a brokerage firm showed that many brokers were insensitive to clients' fears and concerns about the future. A training program could be designed that would increase the brokers' sensitivity to and support for their clients. The objectives of this program will be determined by the specific deficiencies, client preferences, concerns, and other factors identified in the needs analysis.

Mager states that useful objectives describe the **performance** the learners (trainees) should be able to do, the **conditions** under which they must do it, and the **criteria** (how well they must do it) used in judging its success (see Table 5-1).[3] Some examples of program objectives include the following:

- Given a packing list, the trainee will correctly identify (by circling) all items on the list that have not been included in the shipment.
- Given standard hospital equipment, the trainee will draw 10 cc of blood from a patient's arm in not more than two tries (using any member of the class).
- Using the information found on a completed loan application, identify (in writing) whether a client meets the bank's criteria for an acceptable auto loan candidate.
- After completion of training, trainee will **accurately** identify and describe all major points in the organization's antidiscrimination policy.

**■ TABLE 5·2**

GUIDELINES FOR DEVELOPING USEFUL OBJECTIVES

1. An objective is a collection of words, symbols, pictures, and/or diagrams describing what you intend for trainees to achieve.
2. An objective will communicate your intent to the degree that you describe what the learner will be **doing** when demonstrating achievement or mastery of the objective, the important conditions of the doing, and the criteria by which achievement will be judged.
3. To prepare a useful objective, continue to modify a draft until these questions are answered:

   ■ What do I want trainees to be able to do?
   ■ What are the important conditions or constraints under which I want them to perform?
   ■ How well must trainees perform for me to be satisfied?

4. Write a separate statement for each important outcome or intent; write as many as you need to communicate your intents.
5. If you give your written objectives to your trainees, you may not have to do much else. Why? Because often employees are already able to do what you are asking them to do and will be happy to demonstrate their ability, now that they know what is expected of them.

SOURCE: From R. F. Mager (1997). *Preparing instructional objectives* (3rd ed.) Atlanta: Center for Effective Performance, 136.

Program objectives that lack the performance, conditions, and criteria are often ambiguous and can cause those who interpret the objectives differently to feel frustrated and come into conflict with one another. Two ways to ensure that objectives are clear are to choose words carefully and have the objectives reviewed by others (such as managers and potential participants). If a reviewer is confused, the objectives should be revised.

Writing objectives for behaviors that can be directly observed by others (like giving a patient an injection or performing the Heimlich maneuver to aid a choking victim) can be easier than writing objectives for behaviors that are unobservable (like judging whether a painting is of high quality or determining whether the use of deadly force is warranted). When dealing with broad or "unobservable" objectives, it is necessary to specify observable behaviors that indicate whether an unobservable outcome has been achieved.[4] Thus, an objective for judging whether a painting is of high quality can be written as "to be able to judge whether a painting is of high quality by orally listing the characteristics the painting possesses that indicate its quality."

Mager notes that, in many cases, simply presenting trainees with objectives for learning or performance may be enough to elicit the desired behavior.[5] That is, sometimes people do not meet performance expectations because they were never clearly told what the expectations were or how they were supposed to meet them. Clear objectives provide this information and represent the organization's expectations, which can play a key role in shaping employee performance.

Writing objectives is a challenging but essential aspect of effective HRD. Table 5-2 provides a list of the main issues that are essential to consider when writing useful program objectives. Some useful questions to ask when writing objectives include:

■ Is your main intent stated (concerning what you want the trainee to do)?

■ Have you described all of the conditions that will influence trainee performance?

■ Have you described how well the trainee must perform for his or her performance to be considered acceptable?[6]

It is remarkably easy to write objectives for training or educational courses that contain phrases with little or no meaning (Mager calls these "gibberish" objectives).[7] For example, after reading this textbook, we might wish for you to "demonstrate a thorough comprehension of the systems or process model of training" (presented in Figure 5-1, among other places). While this may be fine as an overarching goal, can you see the weaknesses here if this is presented as an objective? (Hint: if not, go back to Tables 5-1 and 5-2 for guidance.) An effective behavioral objective will spell out clearly what is expected of the learner or trainee. In the above example, what does it mean to "demonstrate a thorough comprehension of . . ."? This fuzzy statement needs to be clarified to be of real value as a learning objective.

As another example, of the following two statements, which do you think is the better (as in more specific) objective?

1. In at least two computer languages, be able to write and test a program to calculate arithmetic means.

2. Discuss and illustrate principles and techniques of computer programming.[8]

Our choice (and Mager's) is Statement 1, as it describes an intended outcome, that is, something the learner is expected to be able to do. The second statement is more like a training program or course description. It is not clear concerning precisely what the learner would do to demonstrate competence in this area.

EXERCISE 1: Evaluate the following statement as a program objective for a diversity-training program. Individually or in small groups, rewrite this objective to conform more closely to the principles spelled out above concerning effective program objectives.

"Develop a thorough understanding of the corporate culture of our organization, including our policies on harassment, ethnic and gender diversity, and equal access to individual counseling and promotion opportunities."[9]

EXERCISE 2: Individually or in small groups, write your own program objective(s) for a training program of your choice. Critique your objectives by comparing them to the principles described in Tables 5-1 and 5-2.

Several comments are in order before leaving this topic. First, behavioral objectives have served HRD professionals extremely well for the past four decades, as they put the focus squarely on what the trainee is expected to *do* at the completion of training. Without this, it is very easy to get lost in muddled or "mushy" training that doesn't end up producing much in the way of tangible results. As noted in Chapter 4, an increasing number of HRD interventions deal with changing attitudes and emotions, for example, managing diversity or increasing the "emotional intelligence" of employees. As Leonard and Zeace Nadler remind us, efforts to change attitudes are often the most controversial of all training or learning endeavors.[10] While not impossible, it is much harder to write specific behavioral objectives for interventions dealing with attitudes or emotions. The reader is advised that writing good objectives becomes more difficult as one moves from knowledge- and skill-based training to training intended to change attitudes and emotions.

Further, Danny Langdon has recently promoted the idea of moving beyond objectives to what he terms developing "proformas."[11] A key point Langdon makes is that objectives can fail to make clear all of the issues going on *in the organization* that can influence individual performance. His approach suggests six issues that should be emphasized: inputs, process, outputs, consequences, conditions, and feedback. Langdon highlights issues taking place during the process of training, as well as the ongoing feedback that is received from various parties interested in training. This approach emphasizes that training and trainee behaviors must be seen as taking place within a dynamic organizational context. Further work along these lines is encouraged. Developing a proforma does not take the place of writing objectives, yet it does provide considerably more detail about how training and issues within the organization *interact* to produce (or fail to produce) desired organizational outcomes.

## THE "MAKE VERSUS BUY" DECISION: CREATING OR PURCHASING HRD PROGRAMS

After a manager or HRD professional has identified the program objectives, a series of decisions must be made regarding the development and delivery of the program. One of those decisions is whether to design the program internally, purchase it (or portions of it) from an outside vendor, or use some combination of the two.[12] Many services are available through outside vendors or consultants, including:

- assisting with conducting needs analysis
- guiding internal staff to design or implement a program
- designing a program specifically for the organization
- providing supplemental training materials (exercises, workbooks, computer software, videos)
- presenting a previously designed program
- conducting a train-the-trainer program to build the instructional skills of internal content experts.[13]

There are many sources of HRD programs, materials, and advice, and their number continues to grow. Many consulting firms, educational institutions, professional societies, trade unions, publishing houses, governmental agencies,

■ **TABLE 5-3**

FACTORS TO CONSIDER BEFORE PURCHASING
AN **HRD** PROGRAM

| | |
|---|---|
| Expertise | When an organization lacks specialized KSAOs needed to design and implement an HRD program. |
| Timeliness | When it is timelier to hire an outside agency to facilitate the process. |
| Number of Trainees | Generally, the larger the number of trainees the greater the likelihood the organization would be willing to design the program itself. Thus, for just a few trainees the HRD department would send them to an outside training agency. |
| Subject Matter | If the subject matter is sensitive or proprietary the HRD department would conduct the program in-house using employees as trainers. |
| Cost | The HRD department always considers cost, but only in concert with other factors. |
| Size of HRD | The size of the HRD department is important for assessing the capacity to design, conduct, and/or implement skills training as opposed to using an outside agency. |
| "X" Factor | Some other extraneous conditions that would make it preferable that an outside agency be used to conduct the skills training. |

SOURCE: From A. P. Carnevale, L. J. Gainer, J. Villet, & S. L. Holland (1990). *Training partnerships: Linking employers and providers.* Alexandria, VA: American Society for Training and Development, 6.

and nonprofit community-based organizations offer training programs and information to interested organizations. The American Society for Training and Development, as well as *Training & Development* (now T&D) and *Training* magazines, are useful places to begin a search for external training providers.

Table 5-3 lists a number of factors that should be considered when making a purchase decision. For example, suppose a small manufacturer plans to computerize its billing operation. Given the nature of the training needed, it is likely that the firm's management would contract with an outside vendor because: 1) the firm would probably not have the expertise to design the program in-house, 2) management would not likely have the time to design the training program, and 3) it is not likely that the firm has an HRD department. In general, when the number of people needing the HRD intervention is small, it is more likely that the project will be outsourced. That is, those needing the intervention may be sent outside the organization for the program. This could come in the form of the organization providing the resources for professional development or tuition reimbursement.

Other factors that may influence an organization's decisions include personal contacts or past experience with an outside vendor, geographical proximity to the vendor, local economic conditions, and the presence of government incentives to conduct training.[14]

Once an organization decides to purchase a program or part of a program from an outside source, a vendor must be chosen. One rational way to do this is to determine the match between the vendor's product or capability with the organization's needs and objectives. The criteria for these decisions vary among organizations, but in general they include:

1. **cost:** price relative to program content and quality
2. **credentials:** including certificates, degrees, and other documentation of the vendor's expertise
3. **background:** number of years in business and experience in the particular content area
4. **experience:** vendor's prior clients, success with those clients, references
5. **philosophy:** comparison of the vendor's philosophy to that of the organization
6. **delivery method:** training methods and techniques used
7. **content:** topics included in program or materials
8. **actual product:** including appearance, samples, or whether a pilot program is available
9. **results:** expected outcomes
10. **support:** especially in terms of implementation and follow-up
11. **request for proposal:** the match between a vendor's offer and the requirement spelled out in the organization's request for a proposal (RFP).[15]

Some of these factors will carry greater weight with particular managers. For example, some managers want to work only with the "best" providers, so they may weigh the vendor's experience and client list more heavily. Other managers may be swayed by "star power," as evidenced by the vendor's identity as a leading expert (such as management professor Dave Ulrich for training concerning strategic human resource management) or the presence of a movie or TV star in the vendor's films and videos (actor and former Monty Python member John Cleese appears in a series of widely used training films).

In summary, outside training vendors offer organizations a wide choice of options in designing and developing training and HRD programs. These programs represent viable options when organizations have a small HRD function and a small number of trainees and when program content has no proprietary value. Even large organizations that have well-respected training functions make regular use of outside vendors for a variety of HRD programs. When organizations, large or small, elect to go outside to purchase training services and programs, they should, of course, first conduct a needs assessment so that they can make an informed decision.

## SELECTING THE TRAINER

Once the organization has made a decision to design its own training program, or has purchased a program that it will run, a trainer must be selected, provided that the instructional format will include one. Selecting a trainer can be a fairly easy process when an organization has a large, multifaceted training staff with the competencies and subject-matter expertise to train in high demand areas. **Training competency** involves the knowledge and varied skills needed to design and implement a training program. Effective trainers must be able to communicate their knowledge clearly, use various instructional techniques, have good interpersonal skills, and have the ability to motivate others to learn.

**Subject-matter expertise** refers to the mastery of the subject matter. However, subject-matter expertise alone does not guarantee that an individual will be an effective trainer — many experts (including some college professors, we are sad to say) make poor trainers. Ideally, then, a subject-matter expert (SME) should have the ability to train others. Individuals who lack the ability to design and implement effective training programs may rely too heavily on a single method of instruction that may be inappropriate to the subject matter (such as using a lecture format to train employees in CPR and other first-aid techniques), or they may lack the interpersonal skills to effectively interact with or motivate participants. For example, a study by Pat McLagan indicated that trainers needed to possess an advanced level of expertise as instructors and facilitators in order for training to be most effective.[16] However, in a recent survey, 165 technical trainers (and ASTD members) rated their proficiency in various instructor/facilitator competencies as "intermediate," on average.[17]

Alternately, trainers who lack subject-matter expertise may rely too heavily on a textbook or other training materials and not be able to explain important concepts and/or how these are applied to the job. Besides contracting with an outside vendor, less qualified trainers can be aided through:

1. **teaming** skilled trainers with in-house subject-matter experts to form an instructional team.[18]

2. **using a training technique that does not require a human trainer,** such as programmed instruction or computer-aided instruction programs (these options will be discussed in the next chapter).

3. **train-the-trainer programs,** which involve identifying in-house content experts who lack training skills and training them to become effective trainers.

### TRAIN-THE-TRAINER PROGRAMS

The purpose of train-the-trainer programs is to provide subject-matter experts (SMEs) with the necessary knowledge and skills to design and implement a training program. Train-the-trainer programs are available through local professional associations, colleges, and consultants. These programs range from instruction in a single training technique (e.g., behavior modeling) to a comprehensive program on how to design a training program. The latter would present several training methods and techniques with an emphasis on how each can be used to maximize learning in different situations. Some training providers, such as Development Dimensions International (DDI), conduct train-the-trainer programs in which their client's employees become certified by the consulting firm to present their programs to the organization.

Some organizations elect to design their own train-the-trainer programs, which can be desirable when there is a constant demand for skilled or technical trainers or when employers want to emphasize some training technique. These programs should focus on many of the issues discussed in this chapter, including:

1. developing trainee objectives and lesson plans

2. selecting and preparing training materials

3. selecting and using training aids (e.g., PowerPoint slide presentations, videos, overhead projectors)

4. selecting and using different training methods and techniques

When it is not possible to design a train-the-trainer program, some organizations have developed training manuals that include these various components of the design and implementation process. Manuals can be valuable when there are insufficient numbers of SMEs to warrant a train-the-trainer program or when the potential trainers are in different geographical areas. For example, in the early 1990s, the Training Center of Alexander Consulting Group in Massachusetts relied on subject-matter experts to provide the majority of their technical and financial training. These individuals had the expertise to teach the necessary courses, but were often lacking in the skills necessary to design and implement effective training courses. What this organization did was to create a self-directed Instructor's Guide. This guide provided information and techniques to conduct needs assessment, translate this information into course objectives and course content, and then select appropriate instructional techniques and visual aids. After the SME trainers completed this self-directed training, trainee reactions were very positive. Further, 90 percent of all SMEs indicated that they found the Instructor's Guide to have been invaluable in preparing them to be a trainer.[19]

Overall, then, the selection of the trainer is an important decision for any HRD effort. Obviously, even a competently designed program that has the potential to address a significant organizational need can be a failure if an incompetent, unmotivated, or disinterested trainer delivers it. An ideal trainer would be someone with the requisite competencies as a trainer, as well as peer recognition for his or her subject-matter expertise. If the trainer does not have the necessary subject-matter expertise, then it is imperative that this individual should work together with a subject-matter expert in the design phase, so that an effective matching of training content with training design and delivery can take place.[20]

## PREPARING A LESSON PLAN

Program objectives are necessary for pinpointing desired outcomes of a training or HRD program, but these statements alone are insufficient for determining the

■ **FIGURE 5-2**

A GENERAL LESSON PLAN TEMPLATE

Program title:

Objectives of this lesson:

Preparation required:

1. Physical environment

2. Equipment and materials

3. Instructor

4. Trainee(s)

| Time | Major Topics | Instructor Activity | Trainee Activity | Instructional Strategies Intended to Be Achieved |
|------|------|------|------|------|
| | | | | |

SOURCE: From L. Nadler & Z. Nadler (1994). *Designing training programs: The critical events model* (2nd ed.). Houston: Gulf Publishing, 145.

content of the training program, as well as the training methods, techniques, and materials. To translate program objectives into an executable training session, the development of a **lesson plan** is recommended.

A lesson plan is a trainer's guide for the actual delivery of the training content. Creating a lesson plan requires the trainer to determine what is to be covered and how much time to devote to each part of the session. Gilley and Eggland suggest that a lesson plan should specify:

- content to be covered
- sequencing of activities
- selection or design of training media
- selection or development of experiential exercises, or both
- timing and planning of each activity

■ selection of the method of instruction to be used

■ number and type of evaluation items to be used.[21]

Some organizations have program designers whose responsibilities may include defining training objectives and developing lesson plans. Individuals with educational backgrounds in instructional design (usually from colleges of education) are often hired for such positions. The kind of assistance that program designers can provide is particularly important for subject-matter experts who have limited training skills. Some organizations include a section on lesson planning in their train-the-trainer programs.

To assist trainers, we suggest using a standardized lesson plan form. Figure 5–2 presents a general form recommended by Nadler and Nadler. As an alternative, Figure 5-3 presents a condensed version of a completed lesson plan for an experiential team-building training program. As can be seen in this example, the lesson plan serves as a blueprint for conducting the whole weekend training program.

To this point, we have discussed selecting the trainer and preparing the lesson plan. This is a logical sequence, particularly when the trainer is also the one preparing the lesson plan. But sometimes the HRD intervention (including the general lesson plans) is designed before the trainers are selected. This would be most likely to occur in large organizations. Even here, though, the trainer should modify or adapt the general lesson plan to fit each situation in which he or she is asked to present the HRD program.

## SELECTING TRAINING METHODS

Up to this point we have discussed some preliminary steps involved in the design and implementation of a training program. The next step in the training process is to select the appropriate training methods. A 1999 survey conducted by *Training* magazine revealed that, contrary to popular belief, classroom programs were still the most popular instructional method (see Table 5-4). The survey indicated that 90 percent of organizations use the classroom format to deliver at least some of their training.[22] A separate survey of over 500 organizations by ASTD revealed that in 1998 these organizations reported using instructor-led classroom training for 78.4 percent of their training. This was projected to decrease to 64.5 percent by 2001, with the major increase expected for training via learning technologies such as computer-based training, multimedia training, plus training via CD-ROM and company intranets.[23]

One way of classifying training methods is by the degree of activity expected or required of trainees. On one end, lectures and videotapes are generally the least active (or most passive) form of training. At the other extreme, highly experiential methods such as outdoor training, role-playing exercises, games, and simulations demand the greatest amount of activity or action from trainees. Other methods such as computer-based instruction or videoconferencing fall somewhere in between.

■ FIGURE 5-3

A COMPLETED LESSON PLAN
EXPERIENTIAL TEAM-BUILDING RETREAT (RICHARD J. WAGNER, TRAINER)

| TIME | ACTIVITY |
|---|---|
| **Friday Night** | |
| 6–7:30 p.m. | DINNER |
| 7:30–9:00 p.m. | Program introduction and completion of prequestionnaires.<br><br>Initial experiential activity — Silent birthday line-up. Have the group members line up in order of their birthdays (month and day only) without talking.<br><br>Discussion of what happened during the activity and how the group handled the issues it encountered. Presentation of Kolb's experiential learning model (activity, review/discussion, theory development, and generalization), and how this will be used to develop teamwork during the weekend.<br><br>Discussion of the plan for the weekend and some of the goals for the retreat. |
| **Saturday** | |
| 7–8 a.m. | BREAKFAST |
| 8–9 a.m. | Brainstorming session on group goals for the retreat using a flip chart to record the issues. Seek to uncover some of the problems that the group encounters at work, and generate an initial discussion of how working as a team can help deal with these issues.<br><br>Experiential activity — The Marble Pass. Direct the group to move a marble from a starting point to a barrel 40 feet away and then get the marbles into the barrel using a series of 2- to 3-foot-long plastic pipes. The participants may not move the marble backward, and they must work as a group to get this done. |
| 9–10 a.m. | Discussion of how the group members accomplished the task, what problems they encountered, and how they solved these problems. A critical issue will be the discussion of how their problem solving skills might relate to problems encountered at work, and what the team can do to anticipate and solve some of these problems. |
| 10–10:30 a.m. | BREAK |

*continued*

CONTINUED

**■ FIGURE 5-3**

| TIME | ACTIVITY |
|---|---|
| 10:30 a.m.–12:00 p.m. | Experiential activities, working in two groups.<br><br>Blind Polygon. Group members are blindfolded and directed to form a square using a rope.<br><br>Group Juggle. Group members pass a ball around a circle in a pattern, first establishing the pattern, then seeking speed, and then using more than one ball.<br><br>All Aboard. Everyone has to stand on a 2-by-2-foot platform at the same time.<br><br>Have the groups try each of the activities and do their own planning for subsequent activities. |
| 12–1 p.m. | LUNCH |
| 1–2 p.m. | Discussion of the morning activities and what needs to be done to make the afternoon successful. |
| 2–3:30 p.m. | Experiential activities, working in two groups:<br><br>Trolleys. Sort of group skiing, with about six people on the skis at the same time. The group must move everyone about 40 feet using these trolleys.<br><br>Hot Stuff. — Using only some ropes and other provided equipment, the group must transfer water from one can to another in the center of a 10-foot circle without going into the circle.<br><br>Have each group try both activities. |
| 3:30–4 p.m. | BREAK |
| 4–5 p.m. | Review and discussion of the concept of teamwork and how the activities of the day have helped show the group members how effective teams work. |
| 5–7 p.m. | DINNER |
| AFTER DINNER ACTIVITY | NASA Moon Survival, an indoor activity. |

*continued*

CONTINUED

■ FIGURE 5-3

| TIME | ACTIVITY |
|------|----------|
| **Sunday Morning** | |
| 8–9 a.m. | BREAKFAST |
| 9–10 a.m. | Review and discussion of the NASA Moon Survival activity, focusing on how the activity was accomplished using the concepts of teamwork reviewed during the program. |
| 10 a.m.–12 p.m. | Final discussion of teamwork, focusing on specific issues of the organization. The trainer will facilitate this discussion, but the VP will be the leader in developing the issues. |

Training methods can also be grouped into two broad categories: on-the-job training methods (OJT), which typically occur in the employee's normal work setting, and classroom methods, which typically take place away from the job (such as in a conference room or lecture hall). This categorization is not definitive because some training methods have multiple applications. Computer-based training, for example, can be implemented using a computer at an employee's desk or workstation, in a company classroom, or even at an employee's home. We will discuss many of the particular training methods in greater detail in the next chapter (under the topic of implementing training). This placement of training methods in the implementation chapter is admittedly artificial, and was primarily driven by our desire to have more space within the chapter to emphasize the various methods currently in use. We hope it is clear to you that the decision concerning which method or methods to use must be made during the *design* phase of training.

With such an array of training programs available (as seen in Table 5-4), how does an HRD professional go about choosing which approach is most appropriate for maximum learning? Several factors should be considered:

1. **The objectives of the program** This factor is paramount. As will be clear, some methods are more appropriate for achieving particular objectives than others. For example, if the objective is to improve interpersonal skills, then more active methods such as videotaping, role-playing, or behavior modeling would be better choices than the lecture or computer-based training methods.

2. **Time and money available** In an ideal world, we would have all the time and money we need to accomplish our goals. Unfortunately, in many organizations, managers often ask the HRD department to design and

**■ TABLE 5-4**

| Method or Medium | Percent |
|---|---|
| Classroom Programs — Live | 90 |
| Workbooks/Manuals | 74 |
| Videotapes | 69 |
| Public Seminars | 56 |
| Computer-Based Training via CD-ROM | 54 |
| Noncomputerized Self-Study Programs | 39 |
| Role Plays | 37 |
| Audiocassettes | 36 |
| Internet/World Wide Web | 36 |
| Case Studies | 33 |
| Self-Assessment Instruments | 26 |
| Intranet/Internal Computer Network | 24 |
| Games or Simulations (not computer-based) | 23 |
| Videoconferencing (to groups) | 23 |
| Satellite/Broadcast TV | 19 |
| Teleconferencing (audio only) | 14 |
| Outdoor Experiential Programs | 9 |
| Computer-Based Games or Simulations | 9 |
| Desktop Videoconferencing | 6 |
| Virtual Reality | 2 |

SOURCE: From Industry Report 1999 (1999) *Training*, 36 (10), 37–81.

implement programs quickly, while spending as little money as possible. Competing needs may also force HRD professionals to select certain methods because of their low cost. For example, when designing a program to train mechanics to repair a complicated mechanical system, an interactive, computer-based program might be optimal, but because of its cost, the HRD professional may have to settle for a combination of traditional classes (using lecture, discussion, and reference books) and on-the-job training.

3. **Availability of other resources** Some methods require highly trained trainers and specialized equipment and facilities in order to be delivered effectively. Again, trade-offs are likely to be necessary by choosing alternative methods with less demanding resources.

4. **Trainee characteristics and preferences** The issue here focuses on both trainee readiness and the diversity of the target population. Methods such as computer-based training require a fairly high level of literacy. If literacy or fluency is a problem, either a less reading- and writing-intensive method (such as videotape) may be used, or literacy training must be done first. Similarly, because individuals have different learning styles, some training methods may be more appropriate than others. For example, Ronald Sims argues that in designing any program, trainers must pay particular

attention to the principles of learning laid out in Chapter 3, and in particular to the learning styles described by David Kolb.[24]

In the end, the selection of the training method or methods to be used requires that program designers have knowledge of different HRD techniques, and then use sound judgment in their decision making. HRD professionals should investigate all training methods available, and when in doubt, consult experienced colleagues, instructional designers, and consultants.

## PREPARING TRAINING MATERIALS

After the training methods have been selected, the next logical step is to prepare or purchase the training materials, depending upon whether the program is purchased or designed by the organization. If a training program is purchased from an outside vendor, training materials such as books, handouts, and videos will usually be part of the package. Programs designed in-house will require the preparation of materials. If the program is similar to past training programs, those materials may simply need to be modified to fit the current program.

Many kinds of training materials are used, but we will focus our discussion here on program announcements, syllabi or program outlines, training manuals, and textbooks.

### PROGRAM ANNOUNCEMENTS

Program announcements are used to inform the target audience about the training program. The announcement should indicate the purpose of the program, when and where it will be held, and how the employee can qualify to participate in the program. Sufficient lead time should be given to employees so that they can adjust their schedules and process the necessary request forms.

Typically, announcements are sent through supervisory channels, union stewards, company newsletters, an organization's intranet, or mailed individually to employees. Some organizations designate a bulletin board for announcing training opportunities or make use of electronic mail systems. Some organizations (like the Rhode Island State Department of Administration) publish periodic training bulletins dedicated to providing this information.

### PROGRAM OUTLINES

Program outlines (or course syllabi) are documents that communicate the content, goals, and expectations for the program. Typically provided at the beginning of the program, these include such things as course objectives, topics to be covered, materials or tools needed, requirements of each trainee, and a tentative schedule of events.

The program outline can also be used to establish behavioral expectations, including punctuality, attendance, work habits, class participation, and courtesy toward other trainees. Such expectations should be clearly explained. For example, if the training content is sequenced, it will be important for trainees to be present at all sessions. The attendance policy should reflect this requirement and explain that any trainees who are absent may be required to begin a new program from the start.

## TRAINING MANUALS AND TEXTBOOKS

Most trainers rely on a training manual or textbook for the basic instructional material, readings, exercises, and self-tests. Some documents are organized into modules that make it easy to organize the training program into sessions. *Textbooks* provide a broad treatment of the subject, while training manuals are better known for their brevity and hands-on approach. Trainers who decide to use a textbook would normally contact the publisher and determine whether individual modules can be purchased separately, how useful other trainers found the item, and how easily the item can be customized to the needs of the organization.[25] In addition to these factors, the purchase price should be compared with the cost of producing a comparable training manual.

*Training manuals* can be readily produced by an organization, particularly given the availability of desktop publishing software. The production cost would include staff time for curriculum design and writing, cost of equipment, and printing. The availability of desktop publishing software and laser printers makes it much easier to produce a high quality training manual in-house. Even so, unless there is a large demand for the manual, it is usually less expensive in the long run to purchase a commercially produced manual, if one is available.

Before leaving this topic, we would bring to your attention an issue seldom raised in textbooks. It is an infringement of copyright to use materials created by someone else without proper attribution or permission by the author or copyright holder. Unfortunately, this sort of "borrowing" of material from other sources is quite common in work settings, including among HRD professionals and educators. We are aware of a colleague who is both a professor and a consultant. Once a student brought materials from his workplace to show the professor in class — only to find out that the materials had been developed by the professor for another client many years earlier! The student was unaware that his employer did not have permission to use this material. The lesson here is something a parent might say, that is, "Just because everyone is doing it doesn't make it right!" We urge readers to err on the side of caution when making use of material developed by others.

## SCHEDULING THE HRD PROGRAM

The task of scheduling a training or other HRD program may seem relatively simple and straightforward when compared to other decisions made by the trainer, but this is definitely not the case. Organizations can be busy, hectic, and unpredictable, making scheduling HRD and other support activities very difficult. The goal in scheduling an HRD program is to ensure that the participants (both trainer and learners) are available and have their attention focused on the learning task at hand. In this section, we will discuss some of the issues HRD professionals should consider when scheduling their programs. Our discussion to follow applies to scheduling programs that require participants to be in attendance at the time the program will be delivered. In contrast, one of the main advantages of individually oriented delivery methods, such as CD-ROM or self-paced instruction, is that such methods can be done whenever the participants have the time to do them.

### SCHEDULING DURING WORK HOURS

One popular option for program scheduling is to run the program during normal working hours. This timing both avoids outside conflicts (such as commuting and family and personal obligations) and sends a message to employees that learning is an important part of their job. When scheduling a program during normal work hours, the HRD professional should consider factors such as the day of the week, time of day, peak work hours, staff meeting times, and travel requirements.

The *day of the week* becomes an issue because employees often favor some days, such as Monday, Friday, and the days surrounding a holiday, for time off. Employees often try to extend their weekends and holidays, so these days are often avoided (if possible) when scheduling training.

*Time of day* is another factor. Programs scheduled for the start of the workday may face a significant proportion of tardy or tired participants. Scheduling a program for the lunch hour may require building in time for employees to eat during the program, providing lunch, or requiring employees to eat before or after training. Midafternoon programs coincide with the time that many people's circadian rhythms are at a low point, resulting in sluggishness and shorter attention spans. To combat this, the program should include active participation, break periods, or the availability of light snacks and beverages (many trainees appreciate the availability of beverages that include caffeine). In addition, employees attending programs scheduled close to quitting time may be distracted or have to leave early to attend to personal or family demands. Obviously, a program has to be scheduled sometime, but the wise trainer will note these issues and take steps to deal with them as best as possible.

In addition to day of the week and time of day, other working-hour constraints may be unique to particular organizational units or occupational groups. These include peak work hours, staff meeting times, and travel requirements. *Peak work hours* are the times of the day, week, month, or year that departments are the busiest and when scheduling a training program would cause a potential conflict. For example, scheduling a professional development program for accountants and auditors during tax season would prevent most potential participants from attending. Managers and supervisors should also be contacted before scheduling programs to determine if participants have any *staff meetings, travel requirements,* or other special scheduling needs. This information will help the trainer to select the best times and develop contingency plans for any potential conflicts.

**RETURN TO OPENING CASE**

A recent article in *Training* magazine is entitled "Reinventing training at Rockwell Collins." It describes the extensive work that Rockwell Collins has done in overhauling its training efforts. Cliff Purington was hired as manager of learning and development in September 1998 to "change the way the company delivered training to its 14,000 employees."[1] Your instructor has additional information describing what he and the company did, as well as some of the initial outcomes of their efforts.

[1] Fister, S. (2000). Reinventing training at Rockwell Collins. *Training*, April, 64–70.

## SCHEDULING AFTER WORK HOURS

Sometimes, HRD programs are scheduled after work or during the weekend, in order to avoid some of the organizational constraints discussed above. This approach can create other problems. Extending the workday and workweek can cause a hardship for some employees, particularly those who have family obligations or other personal commitments. Even when employees know about a scheduled training program in advance, family problems could arise, causing some trainees to miss important training sessions. Another problem is fatigue. Employees may be physically tired from a day's work and may not be mentally alert. For example, in response to employee requests, a supervisory training program at the Electric Boat Division of General Dynamics was held between midnight and 2:00 a.m. for employees working the second shift (4 p.m. to midnight). The training program was poorly attended, however, and those who did attend experienced fatigue by the second hour of the class. As a result of this experience, the company suspended all future midnight training programs.

Even when after-work and weekend programs do not cause hardships, many employees are reluctant to give up their leisure time. In these situations, some organizations provide inducements, including overtime pay, compensatory time (equal time off), training as a qualification for promotion, and leisure activities to coincide with the training session (e.g., by conducting the training at a resort area).

## REGISTRATION AND ENROLLMENT ISSUES

One practical headache for many training programs is managing the registration process. It must be clear to participants and managers how one should register for training, who is responsible for logistical issues (e.g., travel arrangements, lodging, meals), and what people are to do if they need to cancel or reschedule their training. Fortunately, e-mail and organizational intranets have made this process much easier than it once was. Also, many of the popular Human Resource Information Systems currently available include training registration and tracking modules. Such computer programs and other uses of technology can be a tremendous help to busy HRD professionals as they manage the enrollment process for various HRD programs.

## SUMMARY

This chapter described several important activities related to the design of training and development programs. After an organization identifies a need for training, the next step is to decide whether to purchase the program from an outside vendor or design the program in-house. If the organization decides to stay in-house, the trainer must be selected. If a full-time trainer with content knowledge is available, the decision will be an easy one. If not, then a content specialist may need to be identified and sent to a train-the-trainer program.

The trainer or program development team then has the responsibility for developing training objectives that define the desired outcomes of the training program. This information should be translated into a lesson plan that provides a thorough guide for the training implementation. Well-written program objectives also help in selecting the appropriate training methods and techniques. The three primary methods are on-the-job training (OJT), classroom, and computer-based training. Each method has a number of techniques appropriate for particular situations. The trainer needs to select the best combination of techniques that will maximize trainee learning. Once the trainer designs the program, the next step is to determine the best schedule while avoiding potential conflicts.

## KEY TERMS AND CONCEPTS

classroom training

computer-based training (CBT)

lecture

lesson plan

on-the-job training (OJT)

subject-matter expert (SME)

train-the-trainer programs

training manual

training methods

training program objectives

## QUESTIONS FOR DISCUSSION

1. What are the three essential features of an effective HRD or training program objective? Why is each one so important? Discuss training or classroom experiences that you have had where objectives either did or did not follow the recommendations made by Robert Mager and others.

2. Why are behavioral objectives and lesson plans important to effective HRD interventions? What role should objectives play in the design, implementation, and evaluation of HRD programs?

3. Describe the relative merits of using a trainee's coworkers as a source for selecting a trainer. What should be done to ensure that a coworker is an effective trainer?

4. What are the advantages of holding a training program off-site?

5. How do you feel about attending training sessions or classes scheduled for early in the morning? After lunch? What can a trainer do to maximize the chances that such a session will be effective?

## REFERENCES

1. Mager, R. F. (1984). *Preparing instructional objectives* (2nd ed.). Belmont, CA: Pitman Learning, 3.

2. *Ibid.*

3. Mager, R. F. (1997). *Preparing instructional objectives* (3rd ed.). Atlanta: Center for Effective Performance.

4. *Ibid.*

5. *Ibid.*

6. *Ibid*, 166.

7. *Ibid*, 142.

8. *Ibid*, 25.

9. *Ibid*, adapted from p. 143.

10. Nadler, L., & Nadler, Z. (1994). *Designing training programs: The critical events model* (2nd ed.) Houston: Gulf Publishing.

11. Langdon, D. (1999). Objectives? Get over them. *Training and Development*, February, 54–58.

12. Sims, R. R. (1998). *Reinventing training and development*. Westport, CT: Quorum Books.

13. Carnevale, A. P., Gainer, L. J., Villet, J., & Holland, S. L. (1990). *Training partnerships: Linking employers and providers*. Alexandria, VA: American Society for Training and Development.

14. *Ibid.*

15. *Ibid.*

16. McLagan, P. (1989). *Models for excellence: The conclusions and recommendations of the ASTD training and development competency study*. Alexandria, VA: ASTD.

17. Williams, S.W. (1999). Improving technical training: The effectiveness of technical subject matter experts as trainers. In K. Peter Kuchinke (ed.), Academy of Human Resource Development (vol. 1). Conference Proceedings. Baton Rouge: AHRD, 588–595.

18. Building a winning team with subject matter experts (1997). *Spectrum Online*. http://cted.inel.gov/cted/spectrum/may__1997/gn-sme.html.

19. Dumas, M. A., & Wile, D. E. (1992). The accidental trainer: Helping design instruction. *Personnel Journal*, June, 106–110.

20. Building a winning team with subject matter experts (1997), *supra* note 18.

21. Gilley, J. W., & Eggland, S. A. (1989). *Principles of human resource development*. Reading, MA: Addison-Wesley.

22. Industry Report 1999. *Training*, 36(10), 37–81.

23. 2000 State of the Industry Report (2000). Alexandria, VA: ASTD.

24. Sims (1998), *supra* note 12.

25. McCullough, R. C. (1987). To make or buy. *Training and Development Journal*, 41(1), 25–26.

# 8

# IMPLEMENTING HRD PROGRAMS

## LEARNING OBJECTIVES

*After studying this chapter, the learner will be able to:*

1. Describe the five broad categories of classroom training approaches and the advantages and disadvantages of each approach.

2. Determine when various training techniques are more or less effective in different situations.

3. Develop expertise as a facilitator of a training topic or module.

4. Describe several ways that technology is being used to provide and improve HRD programs.

5. Develop greater expertise in effectively using technology to deliver training content.

6. Understand and explain the activities involved in implementing an HRD program.

The company mission statement reads: "To be the most successful computer company in the world at delivering the best customer experience in the markets we serve." This company was quick to make use of the Internet to sell its computers. In 2000, revenue through its Web site represented about 50 percent of total sales and averaged more than $50 million per day — an increase from $30 million in the prior year. Customer use of the Internet for support services also continued to grow. One-half of all technical support requests and 76 percent of order-status inquiries were handled online. In a three-month period, the company's customer support Web site received 5 million visits.

The company? Dell Computer Corporation. Dell has experienced "hyper-growth" for many years, often adding 200 to 300 new employees per week. How does Dell train new employees and develop new managers amid such rapid growth? Its major response was to create Dell Learning (formerly Dell University) as a major entity within the company.

*Questions: If you were in charge of Dell Learning, what types of training and learning opportunities would you emphasize? Are there particular methods you would expect to emphasize? Why? To what extent would you emphasize technology-based learning? How much control would you encourage or allow trainees in determining what training they receive? Would you seek to involve top management in the training process, and if so, how?*

## INTRODUCTION

As you begin this chapter, do you think the following statements are true or false?

- *The best way to learn any new skill is to learn it on the job.*
- *The lecture method is a very poor method to use for training purposes.*
- *It is relatively easy to come up with questions to stimulate useful group discussion.*
- *Generally, the more "bells and whistles" that you can put in a computer slide presentation, the better.*
- *In most cases, when trainers have trainees discuss a case study, this is little more than a time filler or a chance for the trainer to take a break from lecturing.*
- *Computer-based training has become the dominant form of delivery method across a wide variety of HRD applications.*

*Note: our answers appear in the summary at the end of the chapter.*

This chapter focuses on the third phase of the training process: implementing training and HRD programs. Both assessment and design issues should have been addressed by this point. Figure 6-1 shows where these activities fit within the training and HRD process model.

Proper implementation assumes that an important need for training has been identified and that program objectives have been spelled out. The program objectives should greatly influence the design issues described in Chapter 5, as well as the selection of training methods used to conduct or implement training. In this

**■ FIGURE 6-1**

TRAINING AND **HRD** PROCESS MODEL

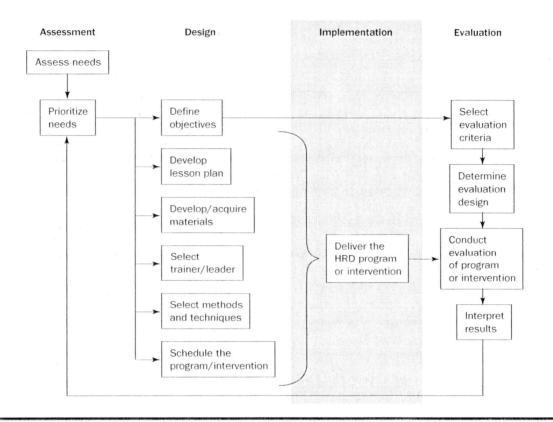

chapter, we will focus in more detail on the array of methods available for conducting training. Some of the most exciting developments in HRD concern the increased use of technology in program implementation. Technological developments will be discussed toward the end of the chapter.

## TRAINING DELIVERY METHODS

Our discussion of learning in Chapter 3 covered differences between expert and novice levels of employee performance. Clearly, training is intended to increase the expertise of trainees in a particular area. When thinking about what training method (or methods) to use, however, it is useful to consider the *current level of expertise* that trainees possess. Figure 6-2 depicts a learning continuum, and suggests that novice trainees generally require more guided or instruction-centered

**■ FIGURE 6-2**

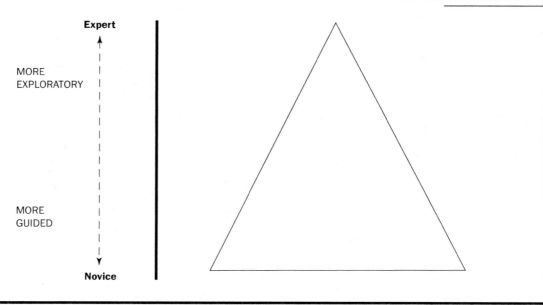

A LEARNING CONTINUUM TO GUIDE IN THE SELECTION
OF APPROPRIATE TRAINING METHODS

Expert

MORE
EXPLORATORY

MORE
GUIDED

Novice

SOURCE: From L. Roger Yin (2000). http://facstaff.uww.edu/yinl/edmedia2000/dlp-ppt/sld018.htm. Adapted by permission.

training methods. In contrast, as trainees' level of expertise increases, the desired or ideal training methods are also likely to shift more toward exploratory or experiential methods.[1] As experiential methods generally require more time to complete than instruction-centered approaches, they are not as commonly used to reach large numbers of individuals (hence, the triangular shape to Figure 6-2). This figure is also consistent with the distinction made in Chapter 3 between declarative and procedural knowledge, that is, in most cases, an individual must first learn *what to do* (declarative knowledge) before they can learn *how to do it* (procedural knowledge). An effective training or HRD program should first identify where trainees fall along this continuum, and then provide assistance for all trainees to "move up" toward an expert level of performance. In many situations, both guided and experiential approaches will be used, for example, when organizations combine the use of lecture, discussion, case studies, behavior modeling, role playing, and games or simulations. Each of these methods of training delivery will be described below. Our first point, though, is that the choice of training method should be guided by both the program objectives (see Chapter 5) and the current level of trainee expertise.

As mentioned in Chapter 5, training methods can be classified by whether they take place on the job versus away from the employee's normal work setting. We

■ **TABLE 6-1**

TRAINING METHODS AND TECHNIQUES

| Methods | Techniques |
| --- | --- |
| On-the-job training | Job instruction training |
| | Job rotation |
| | Coaching |
| | Mentoring |
| Classroom | Lecture |
| | Conference/Discussion |
| | Audiovisual |
| |     static media (e.g., handouts, books) |
| |     dynamic media (e.g., film, video) |
| |     telecommunication (e.g., satellite transmission, Internet) |
| | Experiential techniques |
| |     case study |
| |     business games |
| |     role play |
| |     behavior modeling |
| Self-Paced | Computer-based training |
| |     computer-aided instruction (e.g., multimedia CD-ROM) |
| |     intranet/Internet |
| |     intelligent computer-assisted instruction |

will first discuss on-the-job methods, and then discuss classroom approaches, which typically take place away from the job (such as in a conference room or classroom). Yet a third category of training methods includes those that use a self-paced or individualized approach. For example, computer training can take place on the job (e.g., when an employee works at a computer at his or her desk) or in a computerized classroom. However, much of the recent growth of computer training has used a self-paced approach (e.g., CD-ROM, Web-based, or distance learning) that may be done in a variety of different settings. Table 6-1 lists the on-the-job, classroom, and self-paced training methods that we will discuss in this chapter. Other training methods used for particular audiences (such as mentoring for management development) will be discussed in the appropriate chapters.

## ON-THE-JOB TRAINING (OJT) METHODS

**On-the-job training (OJT)** involves conducting training at a trainee's regular workstation (desk, machine, etc.). This is the most common form of training; most employees receive at least some training and coaching on the job. Virtually any type of one-on-one instruction between coworkers or between the employee and the supervisor can be classified as OJT. On-the-job training has recently been promoted as a means for organizations to deal with the shortage of applicants who possess the skills needed to perform many current jobs.[2] Unfortunately, much on-the-job training is conducted informally, without formal structure, planning, or careful thought. At the extreme, such informal efforts are caricatured with the picture of the busy supervisor telling the new hire to "go sit by Joe."[3] Yet, research indicates that informal OJT "leads to increased error rates, lower productivity, and decreased training efficiency."[4] Why do you suppose that might be?

Structured OJT programs are generally conducted by an assigned trainer who is recognized, rewarded, and trained to provide appropriate instructional techniques. A survey of OJT practices found that 1) supervisors, coworkers, and to a lesser degree, HRD staff members conducted most of the structured OJT programs; 2) a majority of organizations provided train-the-trainer programs for these assigned OJT trainers (see Chapter 5); and 3) top management generally expressed support for structured OJT programs.[5] Formal OJT has two distinct advantages over classroom training. First, OJT facilitates the transfer of learning to the job because the trainee has an immediate opportunity to practice the work tasks on the job. Transfer of learning is enhanced because the learning environment is the same as the performance environment (see our discussion of physical fidelity in Chapter 3). Second, OJT reduces training costs because no training facilities are needed. For example, the Hard Rock Café conducts almost all of its training on the job. Supervisors conduct most training at the start of each new work shift. Job aids are used heavily, and these materials make extensive use of graphics and bullet points, rather than lengthy training manuals. Younger workers are reported to view this approach very favorably, and this is a major source of employees for this restaurant chain.[6]

There are, however, several limitations to OJT. First, the job site may have physical constraints, noise, and other distractions that could inhibit learning. Many of these cannot be changed because of the nature of the job. Second, using expensive equipment for training could result in costly damage or disruption of the production schedule. Third, using OJT while customers are present may inconvenience them and temporarily reduce the quality of service. Fourth, OJT involving heavy equipment or chemicals may threaten the safety of others who are working in close proximity. Precautions should be taken by the trainer to minimize the potential problems from these four areas.

In many cases, OJT is used in conjunction with off-the-job training. For example, KLM Royal Dutch Airlines uses classroom-based training to provide initial customer service training for new flight attendants. Follow-up training is conducted on evaluation flights. Trainees are asked to demonstrate their service delivery skills on the evaluation flights in front of experienced flight attendants.[7] A study of best OJT practices in Great Britain found that OJT was much more likely to be successful when it was operated in a systematic fashion, when there was clear top management support, and when line managers were committed to it. Further, for complex jobs, OJT was more effective when classroom training, OJT, and computer-based training were used in combination.[8]

There are at least four identifiable OJT techniques, including job instruction training (JIT), job rotation, coaching, and mentoring. We will focus on JIT and job rotation now, and discuss coaching and mentoring in later chapters.

## ■ TABLE 6-2

**Step 1: Prepare the Worker.**

a. Put the trainee at ease.
b. Find out what the trainee knows.
c. Motivate.
d. Set up the task.

**Step 2: Present the Task.**

a. Tell.
b. Show.
c. Explain.
d. Demonstrate.

**Step 3: Practice.**

a. Have the trainee perform the task(s).
b. Have the trainee explain the steps.
c. Give feedback on performance.
d. Reinforce correct behavior.

**Step 4: Follow-up.**

a. Have the trainee perform on his or her own.
b. Encourage questioning.
c. Check performance periodically.
d. Gradually taper off training.

SOURCE: From K. N. Wexley & G. P. Latham (1991). *Developing and training human resources in organizations.* Glenview, IL: Scott, Foresman, 109. Adapted by permission.

## JOB INSTRUCTION TRAINING (JIT)

JIT is defined as a sequence of instructional procedures used by the trainer to train employees while they work in their assigned job. It is a form of OJT. The content of a JIT program is distinguished by its simplicity. Table 6-2 details a simple four-step process that helps the trainer to prepare the worker, present the task, allow for practice time, and follow-up. **Preparing the workers** is important because they need to know what to expect. Preparation may include providing employees with a training manual, handouts, or other training or job aids that can be used as references. **Presenting the task** should be carried out in such a way that the trainee understands and can replicate the task. Some trainers demonstrate the task before asking the trainee to repeat the process. **Practice time** is important for the trainee to master a particular set of skills. Finally, the trainer needs to conduct a **follow-up** as a way of ensuring that the trainee is making progress. During this follow-up session, the trainer should apply coaching techniques when appropriate.

For example, Cummins Engine Company combined the JIT approach with the Japanese philosophy of continuous improvement, referred to as Kaizen, in a program they called Just Do It training (JDIT). The JDIT approach begins with instruction on basic principles and then moves to the job where a need for improvement has been identified. The improvement process follows five steps: 1) observe the work processes in action and identify problems; 2) brainstorm possible improvements; 3) analyze each improvement option; 4) implement improvements; and 5) analyze results and make adjustments.[9] The role of the trainer in this approach is to guide the learners and help them to discover potential problems and find solutions on their own. The instructor can then provide feedback and reinforce learning.

The success of JIT depends on the ability of the trainer to adapt his or her own style to the training process. The trainer, particularly if this person is the trainee's coworker or supervisor, should have an opportunity to assess the trainee's needs before beginning the training. If the training material is too difficult or too easy, the OJT trainer should adjust the material or techniques to fit the needs of the trainee.

## JOB ROTATION

So far we have discussed techniques that are intended to develop job-related skills. Job rotation is similar in intent, but with this approach the trainee is generally expected to learn more by observing and doing than by receiving instruction. Rotation, as the term implies, involves a series of assignments to different positions or departments for a specified period of time. During this assignment, the trainee is supervised by a department employee, usually a supervisor, who is responsible for orienting, training, and evaluating the trainee. Throughout the training cycle, the trainee is expected to learn about how each department functions, including some key roles, policies, and procedures. At the end of the cycle, the accumulated evaluations will be used to determine the preparedness of the trainee and if and where the person will be permanently assigned.

Job rotation is frequently used for first-level management training, particularly for new employees. When this technique is used, it is generally assumed that new managers need to develop a working knowledge of the organization before they can be successful managers. Recently, Tyson Foods and the Tribune Company have begun formal job rotation programs for their information technology (IT) workers, with the goal of broadening their skills outside the IT area, and preparing them for future promotions.[10]

## COACHING AND MENTORING

Two other forms of on-the-job training, coaching and mentoring, also involve one-on-one instruction. Coaching typically occurs between an employee and that person's supervisor and focuses on examining employee performance and taking actions to maintain effective performance and correct performance problems. In mentoring, a senior manager is paired with a more junior employee for the purpose of giving support, helping the employee learn the ropes, and preparing the employee for increasing responsibility. These techniques will be discussed in Chapters 10 and 12, respectively.

## CLASSROOM TRAINING APPROACHES

We define classroom training approaches as those conducted outside of the normal work setting. In this sense, a classroom can be any training space away from the work site, such as the company cafeteria or a meeting room. While many organizations capitalize on whatever usable space they have available to conduct training sessions, some larger organizations (including McDonald's, Motorola, Dunkin Donuts, and Pillsbury) maintain facilities that serve as freestanding training centers. These training centers operate as a company college (McDonald's refers to its center as Hamburger U.), with curricula that include courses covering a wide range of skill and content areas. Dell Computer calls their area Dell Learning, to signify that it includes more than simply classroom training.

Conducting training away from the work setting has several advantages over on-the-job training. First, classroom settings permit the use of a variety of training techniques, such as video, lecture, discussion, role playing, and simulation. Second, the environment can be designed or controlled to minimize distractions and create a climate conducive to learning. Third, classroom settings can accommodate larger numbers of trainees than the typical on-the-job setting, allowing for more efficient delivery of training. On the other hand, two potential disadvantages of classroom methods, as a group, include increased costs (such as travel and the rental or purchase and maintenance of rooms and equipment) and dissimilarity to the job setting, making transfer of training more difficult.

Five primary categories of classroom training include:

1. lecture

2. discussion

3. audiovisual media

4. experiential methods

5. self-paced or computer-based training

### THE LECTURE APPROACH

The **lecture** method involves the oral presentation of information by a subject-matter expert to a group of listeners. As we have noted, the lecture remains one of the most popular training techniques. One of the reasons the lecture method is so popular is that it is an efficient way of transmitting factual information to a large audience in a relatively short amount of time. When used in conjunction with visual aids, such as slides, charts, maps, and handouts, the lecture can be an effective way to facilitate the transfer of theories, concepts, procedures, and other factual material.

However, the lecture method has been widely criticized, particularly because it emphasizes one-way communication. It has been suggested that the lecture method perpetuates the traditional authority structure of organizations, thus promoting negative behavior (such as passivity and boredom) and is poorly suited for facilitating transfer of training and individualizing training.[11] Similarly, while a skilled lecturer may effectively communicate conceptual knowledge to trainees who are prepared to receive it, the lecture has little value in facilitating attitudinal and behavioral changes.[12] Trainees must be motivated to learn because when it is used alone, the lecture method does not allow for eliciting audience responses.

A related disadvantage of the lecture method is the lack of sharing of ideas among the trainees. Without dialogue, the trainees may not be able to put things into a common perspective that makes sense to them. Also, many people claim to dislike the lecture method. A survey of training directors showed the lecture was ranked ninth out of nine preferred training methods for acquisition of knowledge.[13] A separate survey reported only 17 percent of respondents (members of a regional ASTD chapter) believed the lecture was an effective training delivery method.[14]

Recent research, however, does not support such a harsh judgment. For example, a meta-analysis found positive learning effects from the lecture method, both when used alone and when used in combination with other methods, such as discussion and role playing.[15] In addition, role playing and lecture methods were found to be equally effective in a skills training course.[16] Could it be that people just don't like to sit through lectures, even though they can and do learn from them?

The results cited above suggest that further research is needed to identify the conditions under which the lecture method is effective as well as ways to improve its effectiveness.[17] At present, two points seem clear. First, it is safe to say that interesting lectures promote greater learning than dull lectures do. Therefore, trainers should make every effort to make their lectures as interesting as possible. Some experienced trainers have argued that younger workers (i.e., those under thirty) are especially likely to tune out lectures that they perceive to be uninteresting or irrelevant.[18] Second, there are likely to be advantages to supplementing the lecture with other methods (including discussion, video, and role playing), particularly when abstract or procedural material is to be presented. These combinations can increase two-way communication and facilitate greater interaction with the material.

### THE DISCUSSION METHOD

The discussion method involves the trainer in two-way communication with the trainees, and the trainees in communication with each other. Because active participation is encouraged, the discussion method offers trainees an opportunity for feedback, clarification, and sharing points of view. Given this dynamic, the discussion technique can overcome some of the limitations of the straight lecture method. A common maxim for discussion facilitators is, "Never do for the group what it is doing for itself." The success of this method is dependent upon the ability of the trainer to initiate and manage class discussion by asking one or more of the following types of questions:

- ■ **Direct questions** can be used to illustrate or produce a very narrow response.

- ■ **Reflective questions** can be used to mirror what someone else has said to make sure the message was received as intended.
- ■ **Open-ended questions** can be used to challenge the trainees to increase their understanding of a specific topic.

Managing discussion goes beyond questioning participants. The trainer must ensure that trainees are reinforced for their responses. The trainer must also act as a gatekeeper, giving everyone an opportunity to express their point of view and not letting the discussion be dominated by a few vocal participants. Managing discussion in large training classes (e.g., thirty or more trainees) can be difficult. Not only are the opportunities for an individual to participate reduced in a large group, some participants may feel intimidated and be reluctant to get involved. Dividing a large class into smaller discussion groups, which can then share their ideas with other groups, can increase the opportunity for discussion.

The discussion method has several limitations. First, a skilled facilitator is needed to manage the discussion process. Skill in facilitating a discussion is not something that one acquires quickly; skilled facilitators have generally practiced extensively and prepared thoroughly before leading a discussion. Second, sufficient time must be available for meaningful discussion to take place. Third, trainees need to have a common reference point for meaningful discussion to occur. Assigning reading material before the discussion session can help overcome this obstacle.

On balance, most trainers and trainees find a well-done discussion to be more interesting and energizing than a traditional lecture. Of course, adequate time, motivation, and resources must be available for this method to work effectively, but then, this is true of any method of delivering training.[19]

## AUDIOVISUAL MEDIA

Both the lecture and discussion methods are limited in their ability to adequately portray dynamic and complex events. Audiovisual methods take advantage of various media to illustrate or demonstrate the training material. Audiovisual media can bring complex events to life by showing and describing details that are often difficult to communicate in other ways. For purposes of this chapter, we will categorize audiovisual methods into three groups: static media, dynamic media, and telecommunications.[20]

*STATIC MEDIA.* Static media typically involve fixed illustrations that use both words and images, for example, printed materials, slides, and overhead transparencies. **Printed materials,** such as handouts, charts, guides, reference books, and textbooks, allow trainees to keep the material, referring to it before, during, and after the training session (some issues involved in selecting and preparing printed materials were discussed in Chapter 5). **Slides** are often used in ways similar to printed materials, but by projecting computer- or camera-generated images onto a screen, they can serve as a common focus for discussion. Slides can also be synchronized with audiotapes to form a standardized presentation. Such a setup can be delivered without using a skilled trainer; at a minimum, someone is

---

**■ TABLE 6-3**

**Preparation**

1. Present one major idea or concept on each slide or transparency.

2. Use only a few key words or phrases (e.g., fewer than six words per line and six lines per slide).

3. Make sure letters and graphics are large and legible (can the participants read it in the back of the room?).

4. Are your slides well designed?

5. Are your slides interesting? Use color, different type styles, and graphics.

6. Are your slides appropriate for the subject?

7. Do your slides add to the presentation?

8. Is current technology being appropriately utilized when making and using the slides?

9. If using PowerPoint (or similar software), do the extras (sound, music, clip art, video clips, special graphics) add to or detract from the presentation?

10. Ensure that the audiovisual or computer equipment is set up and used appropriately.

**Presentation**

11. Have a clear outline for your presentation.

12. Look at the audience, not at the screen.

13. Ensure lighting and seating are appropriate for all to see both the presenter and the screen.

14. Emphasize information by pointing; however, do not point at the screen–point on the transparency, or use a mouse pointer on computer slides.

15. Avoid reading bullet points exactly as they appear on the slide or transparency.

16. Control the pace by progressive disclosure, for example, a cardboard sheet underneath a transparency allows you to see the whole transparency, yet only reveal the points to the audience as you are ready to discuss them.

17. Cover the projector (or make it blank) to emphasize an important verbal point.

18. Use two projectors for increased effect (e.g., when using multiple media).

19. Obtain group involvement by writing on a white board, blank transparency, or flip chart.

---

SOURCES: From J. Kupsch & P. R. Graves (1993). *How to create high impact business presentations.* Lincolnwood, IL: NTC Business Books; S. K. Ellis (1988). *How to survive a training assignment.* Reading, MA: Addison-Wesley; G. Kearsley (1984). *Training and technology.* Reading, MA: Addison-Wesley, 19; M. Eyre (2000). The presenter's toolkit. *Management, 47*:6 (July), 11–12; H. D. Beaver (2000). Visual aids: How much is too much? *ABA Banking Journal, 92*:6 (June), 80.

needed to operate and monitor the equipment (slide projector and tape player). **Overhead transparencies** also allow the trainer to project printed materials or other images on a screen. Transparencies can be more flexible than slides because the trainer can also write on the transparency sheets, turning the screen into a sort of chalkboard. Table 6-3 provides some guidelines for the effective use of computer slides and transparencies to improve training presentations.

Without question, the use of computer-generated slides (such as PowerPoint presentations) has increased dramatically in the past few years. Some go so far as to argue that "the ability to prepare a slide presentation has become an indispensable corporate survival skill."[21] But major efforts to produce fancier and more elaborate slide presentations has also led to a backlash. For example, in April 2000, General Hugh Shelton, chairman of the U.S. Joint Chiefs of Staff, sent out an order to all U.S. military bases stating that all briefings should stick to the point and avoid unnecessary "bells and whistles" in their PowerPoint presentations.[22] It seems that all of the e-mailed briefings were using so much of the military's computer bandwidth that they were slowing down more critical communications between headquarters and the field! Hence, in Table 6-3, we stress (in point 9) that every aspect of a computer-generated slide slow should add value to rather than detract from the overall presentation.

*DYNAMIC MEDIA.*    Techniques that present dynamic sequences of events are considered dynamic media and include audiocassettes and compact discs (CDs), film, videotape, and videodisc. Videos remain one of the most commonly used training techniques. A recent survey found that 69 percent of organizations surveyed use videos for employee training. Audiocassettes are also widely used (by 36 percent of organizations surveyed).[23] Organizations as diverse as Taco Bell and New England Mutual Insurance are taking advantage of the ease with which videotaped training programs can be sent to employees around the country. There are literally thousands of commercially produced films and videos available to HRD professionals through film libraries, professional societies, and retail outlets. Many training vendors emphasize the sale or rental of training videos. In addition, many organizations are able to produce their own videos at relatively low cost. For example, Southwest Airlines produced a 9-minute rap music video that introduces employees to work procedures and all aspects of the company's operations, while at the same time conveying the team spirit and fun-oriented culture that typifies the company. The Travelers, a Hartford-based insurance company, maintains a $20 million education center that produces videos and transmits satellite broadcasts of training programs throughout the company.[24] Entire training programs can be self-contained within a single film or video presentation.

An effective film or video takes advantage of the capabilities of the medium rather than simply reproducing a printed or static presentation. Unfortunately, many videos are indeed little more than reproductions of traditional lectures. Producing an effective training video is not as simple as owning the equipment and having the desire to be "the company's Steven Spielberg." Film and video development involves many activities, including design (like storyboarding), preproduction (including scheduling, casting, crew and equipment selection, prop and set preparation), shooting the film or video, postproduction (including editing and sound mixing), and distribution.[25] The inexperienced HRD professional would be wise to consult a trained professional to produce (or assist in producing) company films and videos.

Some HRD professionals argue that the baby boomers and later generations, who grew up watching films and television, may actually prefer this form of presentation. Yet, one potential limitation of this technique is that trainers may rely too much on the film or video, and focus too little on the training content. Such reliance can lead to complacency among trainees who view the films and videos as entertainment, rather than as opportunities to learn.

Videotape is also used as a visual aid for behavior modeling training by recording actual role plays and then asking group members to critique their experience while they watch the video. For example, a sales training program may include a videotaping segment, so that trainees can observe themselves performing an in-class exercise on how to close a sale. This approach also provides an opportunity for the trainer to reinforce desired behaviors. One potential limitation of this technique is that trainees may feel intimidated by the camera and may even resent the process. To offset this limitation, the trainer must be supportive and create a "safe" environment during the program.

*TELECOMMUNICATION.* The transmission of training programs to different locations via telecommunication is now possible with the advent of satellite, microwave, cable (CATV), and fiber-optic networks. Linking several locations for instructional and conference purposes, known as **instructional television (ITV),** or interactive television, allows entire courses to be televised. For example, colleges and universities are increasingly offering both bachelor's and master's degrees "delivered entirely by cable television and satellite."[26] The National Technological University (NTU) network also offers interactive, satellite-transmitted continuing-education courses to engineers and computer scientists in companies like IBM, General Electric, and Hewlett-Packard.[27]

Telecommunication technology also allows organizations to conduct conferences between remote locations. This technique, known as **teleconferencing,** or **videoconferencing,** is being used by organizations such as JCPenney, IBM, AT&T, Domino's Pizza, and Texas Instruments. JCPenney also sells this service to other organizations.[28] Colleges and universities use teleconferencing to benefit both their students and corporate clients. Teleconferencing helps organizations to reduce trainer, travel, and facility costs, and it increases the availability of training to remote locations.[29] It is estimated that about 23 percent of organizations use video teleconferencing.[30] The North Carolina Office of Day Care Services conducted a study comparing the average cost of traditional classroom training with teleconferencing. It concluded that while teleconferencing cost more for curriculum and materials development, traditional classroom training cost more for trainer, travel, and delivery, but both methods are considered to be equally effective.[31] One issue that merits further research concerns the extent to which teleconferencing affects the interaction between the trainer and trainees.[32]

Computer conferencing is not as widely used as other training techniques. However, given the availability of personal computers and terminals that are being linked into company communication networks (e.g., corporate intranets) and public networks such as the Internet and World Wide Web, its use has grown dramatically since the mid-1990s (see our later discussion on intranet training).

Also, while most organizations use communication networks primarily for business operations, they have an unlimited potential as training vehicles. It has been suggested that computer networks should be used to train adults nationwide, although the start-up cost of hardware and the low level of reading and writing skills may keep some low-income and other potential learners from benefiting from such a system.[33] The rapidly decreasing cost of videoconferencing systems has made this technology increasingly available, even to small- and medium-sized organizations.[34]

Studies have consistently shown that audiovisual training methods like film, television, and videoconferencing are more effective than other methods (primarily lecture).[35] Table 6-4 lists some of the advantages and disadvantages of various audiovisual methods for training.

Given the choices available, HRD professionals must select the most appropriate audiovisual method for each particular HRD program. Kearsley made five primary recommendations concerning media selection:

1. Identify the media attributes required by the conditions, performance, or standards of each instructional objective.

2. Identify student characteristics that suggest or preclude particular media.

3. Identify characteristics of the learning environment that favor or preclude particular media.

4. Identify practical considerations that may determine which media are feasible.

5. Identify economic or organizational factors that may determine which media are feasible.[36]

This list includes both learning-related and practical considerations. In terms of other practical and economic considerations, Rothwell and Kazanas pose several further questions that can guide the proper selection of audiovisual methods:

1. How much time is available to plan and test instruction?

2. What equipment is available to use in designing or delivering instruction, or in doing both?

3. For what media can instructional designers in one organization prepare instruction? Do staff skills lend themselves better to some media than others?

4. How much is an organization willing to spend on the design and development of instruction?[37]

Readers who want to know more about these various audiovisual methods and how to select among them would do well to consult other sources.[38]

## EXPERIENTIAL METHODS

So far, we have discussed training methods that focus primarily on presentation of training content. In many of these methods, such as video and lecture, the learner

**▪ TABLE 6-4**

|  |  | Content |
|---|---|---|
| **Television Broadcast** | **Effective uses:** | Uniform material ensures consistent training |
|  | **Limitations:** | |
| **Videotape** | **Effective uses:** | Can be reviewed in whole or part |
| *Same as television with these differences:* | **Limitations:** | |
| **Tutored Video Instruction** | **Effective uses:** | Subject review with tutor, particularly for students with poor language skills |
| *Same as video-based instruction with these additions:* | **Limitations:** | |
| **Videoconference** | **Effective uses:** | Can use time-sensitive materials; but also many subjects |
|  | **Limitations:** | |
| **Audiographic Conference** | **Effective uses:** | Useful to teach problem solving, also trouble-shooting skills and maintenance procedures |
|  | **Limitations:** | |
| **Computer Conference** | **Effective uses:** | Suitable for wide variety of subjects, including problem solving and discussion |
|  | **Limitations:** | |

SOURCE: From N. P. Eurich (1990). *The learning industry: Education for adult workers.* Lawrenceville, NJ: Princeton University Press, 40. Reprinted by permission.

| Presentation and Participation | Audience and Scheduling | Cost |
|---|---|---|
| Lecture by teacher with other experts<br>Graphics and visuals; informative clips | Unlimited audience; reaches widely scattered employees | |
| Presentation static<br>Passive; no interaction | Time limited to viewing schedule | Costs can be  high for production and broadcast time |
| Stop and replay | Use at any time with television and video-cassette recorder | Cost lowers with reuse and mail distribution |
| | | May be less expensive to produce, but depends on quality |
| Student interaction<br>Encourages discussion | Adaptable for diverse groups of students<br>Permits flexible scheduling | |
| Requires presence of tutor or facilitator and meeting site<br>Group must not be large<br>Not effective for single student | | |
| Lecture or panel discussion<br>Graphics, etc. optional<br>Some interaction allowed via telephone links | Wide distribution | |
| Interaction limited by group size and time element<br>Rather passive | Broadcast time inflexible | Expensive for small group;<br>Requires equipment; if satellite used, receiver sites needed |
| Participants can speak and demonstrate via display screens<br>Complex graphics can be prepared and used interactively | Covers wide geographic area<br>Long-distance telephone data communication | |
| Small number of persons per session is best | Limited by real-time frame | Equipment expensive: student needs telephone-computer hook-up |
| Completely interactive via personal computer and telephone; intense interaction common | Serves geographically dispersed persons<br>Crosses national boundaries<br>There is time to consider response<br>Free of time limitations | |
| No voice or visual contact | Psychological barriers to computer and to working alone<br>May be delay in response | |

is generally assumed to be a passive (or somewhat passive) recipient of information. Experiential learning advocates, such as David Kolb, argue that effective learning requires active engagement on the part of the learner. Keys and Wolfe summarize this point of view as follows:

> Experientialists believe that effective learning is an active experience that challenges the skills, knowledge, and beliefs of participants. This is accomplished by creating a contrived, yet realistic, environment that is both challenging and psychologically safe for the participant to investigate and to employ new concepts, skills, and behaviors. Experiential instructors recognize that learners bring to the learning environment a set of accumulated knowledge and learning methods that are simultaneously functional and/or dysfunctional depending on the learning situation.[39]

Experiential training methods commonly used in organizations include case studies, games and simulations, role playing, and behavior modeling. These methods fall more toward the exploratory level of the learning continuum presented in Figure 6-2. Each of these methods is described below.

*CASE STUDIES.* One way to help trainees learn analytical and problem-solving skills is by presenting a story (called a case) about people in an organization who are facing a problem or decision. Cases may be based on actual events involving real people in an organization, or they can be fictional. Case studies are typically included in college textbooks and courses in management, public administration, law, sociology, and similar subjects. They are increasingly available using video and other media.

While cases vary in complexity and detail, trainees should be given enough information to analyze the situation and recommend their own solutions. In solving the problem, the trainees are generally required to use a rational problem-solving process that includes the following steps:

1. restating important facts
2. drawing inferences from the facts
3. stating the problem or problems
4. developing alternative solutions and then stating the consequences of each
5. determining and supporting a course of action

Cases can be studied by individuals or small groups, and the completed analysis and solutions are typically presented by the trainees to the rest of the class. According to a 1999 survey in *Training* magazine, the case study method is used in about 33 percent of organizations for employee and management training.[40]

Proponents of the case study method argue that this form of problem solving within a management setting offers illustrations of the concepts students are expected to learn and use, improves communication skills, and facilitates the linkage between theory and practice.[41] Proponents also claim that cases allow students to discuss, share, and debate the merits of different inferences, problems, and alternative courses of action. Such insight can help students to develop better analytical skills and improve their ability to integrate new information.[42]

The case study method also has vigorous critics who argue that it can cause groupthink, focuses too much on the past, limits the teaching role of the trainer, reduces the learner's ability to draw generalizations, reinforces passivity on the part of the learner, and promotes the quantity of interaction among students at the expense of the quality of interaction.[43] Andrews and Noel claim that cases often lack realistic complexity and a sense of immediacy, and inhibit development of the ability to collect and distill information.[44] In addition, trainees may get caught up in the details of the situation, at the expense of focusing on the larger issues and concepts they are trying to learn.

In addition, Argyris criticizes case studies from the viewpoint that they may undermine the learning process by not leading trainees to question assumptions and positions taken, and that the case study method may encourage trainees to be dependent on the instructor or facilitator.[45] He feels that trainers should create an atmosphere in which trainees are free to confront themselves and each other without defensiveness, to allow examination of whether the ideas they claim they believe in are consistent with their actions. Berger countered these criticisms by suggesting that Argyris did not adequately define the case method and that methodological flaws undermined his study.[46]

While there appears to be plenty of rhetoric regarding the advantages and disadvantages of the case study method, there is not a large amount of empirical evaluation studies to help us determine the facts.[47] The few studies that do exist offer no clear trend from which to draw conclusions.

To overcome these limitations, the trainer should make expectations clear and provide guidance when needed. In addition, the trainer must effectively guide the discussion portion of the case study to ensure trainees have an opportunity to explore differing assumptions and positions they have taken and the rationale for what constitutes effective responses to the case. The point in discussing cases is not to find the "right" solution, but to be able to provide a reasoned and logical rationale for developing a course of action. Variations in the case method have also been proposed.[48] One such variation, called a living case, has trainees analyze a problem they and their organization are currently facing.[49]

Osigweh encourages potential users of the case study method to match factors such as:

- specific instructional objectives
- objectives of the case approach
- attributes of the particular incident or case (i.e., its content)
- characteristics of the learner
- instructional timing
- general prevailing environment (class size, course level, etc.)
- the teacher's own personal and instructional characteristics[50]

*BUSINESS GAMES AND SIMULATIONS.*   Like the case method, business games are intended to develop or refine problem-solving and decision-making skills. This technique tends to focus primarily on business management decisions (such as maximizing profits). It is estimated that 23 percent of organizations use non-computer-based games or simulations, with 9 percent using computer-based games or simulations.[51]

One example is a business game titled Looking Glass, Inc., developed by the Center for Creative Leadership.[52] The game requires participants to role play decision makers in a fictitious glass manufacturing company and use realistic organizational data to make a variety of decisions. The three-day Looking Glass training program includes one day each for performing the simulation (in which participants operate the company), giving feedback, and practicing the skills emphasized during the feedback sessions.[53] Martin Marietta has used Looking Glass as a diagnostic and feedback tool in its executive development program.[54] The developers of Looking Glass have reported research that shows the activities of trainees in the simulation are similar to those of managers in the field,[55] and suggests that the program is effective, at least in the short term.[56]

Business games, particularly computer simulations of organizations and industries, are widely used in business schools. A review of sixty-one studies reported support for the effectiveness of business games in strategic management courses. Whether these results can be generalized to organizational settings is still an open question.[57]

Another type of simulation used in management development programs and assessments centers is the **in-basket exercise.** The goal of this technique is to assess the trainee's ability to establish priorities, plan, gather relevant information, and make decisions. The sequence of events involved in an in-basket exercise typically includes the following:

1. The trainees are told that they have been promoted to a management position that was suddenly vacated. They are given background information about the organization including personnel, relationships, policies, and union contracts.

2. The trainees then receive the contents of the manager's in-basket. This material includes documents such as telephone messages, notes, memos, letters, and reports.

3. The trainees are then asked to read, organize, prioritize, and make decisions regarding the issues presented by the in-basket material.

4. At the end of the decision period, the trainees' decisions are then evaluated by trained scorers.

The object of this technique is to force the trainees to make decisions in the allotted time period. Since there is usually insufficient time to read each document and respond, the trainees must make quick and accurate decisions. The trainees are evaluated not only on the quality of their decisions but also on their ability to prioritize and to deal effectively with all of the critical documents. Research on the in-basket technique has shown it to be successful both in improving trainee effectiveness[58] and in predicting managerial effectiveness, either alone or in combination with other devices.[59]

One potential limitation of business games and simulations is that while they can be quite complex, these techniques often lack the realistic complexity and information present in real organizations. Factors such as organizational history and politics, social pressures, the risks and consequences of alternatives, and the organization's culture are difficult to replicate in a simulation.[60] This may undermine the extent to which what is learned in the game or simulation will transfer back to the job.

In addition, many games and simulations emphasize the use of quantitative analysis in making business decisions and underplay the importance of interpersonal issues in managerial effectiveness. It has also been argued that the popularity of simulation techniques is based more on circumstantial evidence than on rigorous evaluative research,[61] but because simulations are used in conjunction with other techniques, isolating their effect in research has been difficult.[62]

*ROLE PLAYS.*    A popular training technique, role playing is reportedly used by 37 percent of organizations.[63] In the role-playing technique, trainees are presented with an organizational situation, assigned a role or character in the situation, and asked to act out the role with one or more other trainees. The role play should offer trainees an opportunity for self-discovery and learning. For example, a management development program could include a role-play situation emphasizing interpersonal conflict between a manager and a subordinate. Management trainees would have an opportunity to role play both the manager and the subordinate role, in order to better understand some of the dynamics of this situation, as well as practice interpersonal skills. The value of this technique is enhanced by conducting a feedback session following the role play, in which trainees and the trainer critique the role player's performance. In many organizations, the role-play episode is videotaped, as discussed earlier, which allows for better feedback and self-observation.

While self-discovery and opportunity to practice interpersonal skills are outcomes of role playing, this method does have some limitations. First, as discussed earlier, some trainees may feel intimidated by having to act out a character (and possibly be videotaped doing so). Trainers should take sufficient time in introducing the exercise, explaining the process in detail, and most of all, stressing how participation will help each trainee to better understand and apply different interpersonal skills.

A second limitation of the technique is the extent to which the trainees are able to transfer this learning to their job. Some trainees may perceive this role playing as artificial or as fun and games, but not as a legitimate learning tool. Trainees who do not take this technique seriously may interfere with other trainees' learning. The trainer must manage the process effectively and keep reinforcing the importance of participation.

*BEHAVIOR MODELING.*    Social learning theory (see Chapter 2) suggests that many of our behavior patterns are learned from observing others. This theory forms the basis for behavioral modeling. In organizations, employees learn all kinds of behaviors (some work related and some not), from observing supervisors, managers, union leaders, and coworkers who serve as role models. Under normal conditions, role models can have a tremendous influence on individual behavior.

In this technique, trainees observe a model performing a target behavior correctly (usually on film or video). This is followed by a discussion of the key components of the behavior, practicing the target behavior through role playing, and receiving feedback and reinforcement for the behavior they demonstrate. Behavior modeling is widely used for interpersonal skill training and is a common component of many management training programs.

Research has shown behavior modeling to be an effective training technique and will be described in greater detail in our discussion of management development (Chapter 13).[64]

*OUTDOOR EDUCATION.*   Outdoor-based education, such as ropes courses, have generated significant interest from employers and employees alike, with estimates of over $100 million spent annually on such efforts.[65] This can include work teams being involved with outdoor games, orienteering, or rafting. Frequently, such programs include either low ropes or high ropes elements. A low ropes course typically has limited physical risks, whereas high ropes courses typically have higher perceived risks. Low ropes courses can also be conducted indoors (for an example of such a program, refer to Figure 5-3, the example of a completed lesson plan). Both types of courses usually have a strong focus on group problem solving and team building. While there is evidence that such courses can impact work team functioning and performance, overall, the empirical results to date have been mixed.[66] Those considering use of such programs should make sure that the programs match the objectives set out for training, and that follow-up evaluation is conducted. As Mark Weaver has stated, "Too often, the fun, engaging methodology has outweighed the transfer to workplace issues."[67] Given the current popularity of outdoor education, HRD professionals should ensure that proper assessment and evaluation are included in any such program that is offered.

### SELF-PACED/COMPUTER-BASED TRAINING MEDIA AND METHODS

Computers have had an enormous impact on the delivery of training in organizations.[68] It is estimated that 54 percent of organizations use computer-based training (CBT) via CD-ROM in their training programs, with other multimedia-based efforts certainly pushing the number of computer-based training approaches much higher than this.[69] One of the biggest influences on the growth of CBT is the advent of microcomputers and the rapid increase in their capabilities. In the early days of CBT, one had to have access to terminals connected to a mainframe computer and software that was time-sharing with other business computing needs. PCs are now present in virtually all organizations, and important advances in hardware and software are occurring at a dizzying pace.

The primary advantage CBT has over other methods of training is its interactivity.[70] The interaction between the learner and the computer in many CBT programs mirrors the one-on-one relationship between student and tutor: questions and responses can go back and forth, resulting in immediate feedback. Advanced forms of CBT, like intelligent computer-aided instruction, can even analyze the pattern of a student's responses and errors, draw conclusions, and tailor the lesson the learner receives accordingly. An additional advantage of technology-based training is that it is well suited to "on-demand learners," that is, trainees who need (and increasingly demand) greater control over when and how training is delivered.[71] Three approaches to CBT include computer-aided instruction (CAI), intranet training, and intelligent computer-assisted instruction (ICAI).

*COMPUTER-AIDED INSTRUCTION.* CAI programs can range from electronic workbooks, using the drill-and-practice approach, to compact disc read-only memory (CD-ROM) presentation of a traditional training program. CAI software packages are available at relatively low cost for a wide range of material, from teaching basic skills such as reading and typing, to highly technical scientific, engineering, and machine maintenance topics. CAI programs are available not only as part of business software programs (like the tutorial programs that come with such word-processing packages as Microsoft Word) but also through retail outlets, and some have become software best-sellers. Some organizations custom design software from scratch or modify existing programs to meet their unique needs. For example, Manpower's Skillware program was originally developed by the company (the largest U.S. agency for temporary office workers) but is also used, either as is or with modifications, by some of Manpower's clients, including Xerox and Miller Brewing Company.[72]

Multimedia programs offer an improvement over the more traditional CAI programs because they provide more appealing visual and audio content. The multimedia platform can bring the course to life and make the learning experience more enjoyable. Because audio and video files are very large, most multimedia courses are stored and distributed on a CD-ROM disk. Many companies have replaced instructor-led courses with CD-ROMs. For example, AT&T has replaced its three-day new-employee orientation program with a CD-ROM package that explains how the company is organized, the role and mission of each department, and how the departments relate to one another.[73]

CAI has several advantages over other training methods and techniques, especially considering the **interactive** nature of CAI. Based on the trainee's responses, the computer will present various levels of material until the trainee reaches mastery. A second advantage is CAI's **self-pacing** feature that allows trainees to control the speed of instruction and makes them self-sufficient learners.[74] A third advantage is the **logistics** of CAI that make it more accessible through an internal distribution system (e.g., the HRD department) or downloaded from a central computer or over the Internet to remote sites to eliminate travel and per diem costs.[75] Finally, CAI offers an **instructional management and reporting system** that automatically "tracks student progress and the allocation and use of instructional resources, including terminals, instructors, and classrooms."[76]

The effectiveness of CAI, like other training methods and techniques, can be measured by changes in productivity and profits. Reinhart reported that a four-hour CAI program, which trained sales representatives on selling a piece of computer software, resulted in additional revenues of $4.6 million for Xerox.[77] Another measure of effectiveness is a cost-benefit analysis that compares CAI to other techniques. A financial institution in New York, which was paying trainees while they waited for available classroom training programs, switched to CAI and realized enough savings to offset the development cost of the CAI program.[78] Andersen Consulting realized significant savings in facilities, travel, and payroll costs when it replaced a required six-week instructor-led training program on basic business practices with a CD-ROM program.[79] Research has also shown that trainees using CAI take less time to learn the same amount of material as conventional methods, with no significant difference in test scores.[80]

Some critics worry about the loss of personal interaction between a human trainer and the learner, and suggest that reliance on CBT may restrain the development of interpersonal skills.[81]

CD-ROMs can be purchased off the shelf for less than $100, but they are not particularly effective for material that has to be tailored to an organization's needs. An alternative to purchasing the program is to produce one in-house. Munger reported that it takes about two to ten hours of development time to produce each hour of instruction at an average cost of $5,000 per hour of instruction.[82] CAI may not always be the most appropriate training method. For instance, in training situations that emphasize interpersonal skill building, other techniques (like role playing) may be preferred. Also, traditional training methods might be more suitable for unmotivated trainees who may find it difficult to complete a CAI program without the assistance of a trainer.

*INTERNET- AND INTRANET-BASED TRAINING.* The Internet is one of the fastest-growing technological phenomena the world has ever seen. Today, tens of millions of computers are connected to one another via modems, telephone and cable lines, superconducting (ISDN) transmission lines, and the Internet.[83] There are five distinct levels or uses of internet training (see Table 6-5). **Intranets** are computer networks that use Internet and World Wide Web technology, software tools, and protocols for finding, managing, creating, and distributing information within one organization.[84] A recent survey found that 61 percent of U.S. workers said they would prefer to receive training via computers, the Internet, or television, yet only 26 percent said they currently receive training in this manner.[85] Similarly, in the 2000 State of the Industry Report published by ASTD, less than 9 percent of training is currently being delivered using "learning technologies" (e.g., CBT, CD-ROM, and intranets). However, of this amount, 32.2 percent was conducted via an intranet in 1998, and it is projected that 77.1 percent of technology-based training will be conducted via intranet by 2001.[86] Much technology-based training today is referred to as **e-learning,** for electronic learning, and most of this makes use of either Internet or intranet technology and systems.[87]

Personal computers with a TCP/IP networking protocol make it possible for individuals with different operating systems (such as Windows, Mac, and the various UNIX-based operating systems), to communicate with each other, access information, transmit data, and download data. Current technology also creates a number of safeguards that can limit access to information and ensure privacy. Safeguards include firewalls, encryption, and passwords. Firewalls are "hardware or software that sit between the Internet and your company's private network to form a barrier between your organization and the outside world . . . and which

■ **TABLE 6-5**

| | FIVE LEVELS OF INTERNET TRAINING |
|---|---|
| 1. General Communication | Can be used for communication between trainers and trainees for such things as course announcements, assignments, and questions. Also used for all types of collaborations including threaded discussion groups, forums, and chat sessions between trainees working on joint and group projects. |
| 2. On-line Reference | Using HyperText Markup Language (HTML), the universal programming language of the World Wide Web, trainers can create an entire library of hyperlinked references. A trainee can access all types of training-support materials including product manuals, safety manuals, and technical documents. |
| 3. Needs Assessment, Administration, and Testing | Trainers can conduct a needs assessment (e.g., person analysis), on-line registration, and pretests and posttests, scoring, evaluations, and record keeping. Test results can be sent back quickly and efficiently. |
| 4. Distribution of CBT | Delivering of computer-based training programs can be downloaded as needed any time of the day or night by authorized employees. A File Transfer Protocol, a method for sending computer files over the Internet, can be set up for this purpose. |
| 5. Delivery of Multimedia | Interactive multimedia in real time is now possible with the release of new programming languages. Trainees can now experience interactive lessons complete with sound, animation, and video. |

SOURCE: Adapted from K. Kruse (1997). Five levels of Internet-based training. *Training and Development, 51*(2), 60–61.

keeps track of everyone who tries to access your site."[88] Encryption capability allows individuals to transmit messages through a deciphering mechanism that encodes data when transmitted and then decodes at the destination.

**Intranet-based training (IBT)** uses internal computer networks for training purposes. Through IBT, HRD professionals are able to communicate with learners, conduct needs assessment and other administrative tasks, transmit course materials and other training documents, and administer tests at any time and throughout the organization, whether an employee is in the United States or located overseas. IBT is a powerful delivery system for large international organizations.

IBT has most, if not all, of the features of a multimedia CD-ROM program, plus the capability for users to communicate quickly. With current advances in real-time multimedia technology (e.g., Java, Shockware, and Virtual Reality Modeling Language), IBT is now fully interactive with sound, video, and 3-D imaging, and will compete with disk-based media like CD-ROMs as a primary means of providing training via technology. Companies like Ernst & Young, whose CBT training consisted of over 100 CD-ROMs in 1995, now rely on IBT for distributing and updating CBT.[89]

An innovative development with technology-based training was the development in 1996 of the LearnShare consortium. LearnShare, based in Toledo, Ohio, consisted of seventeen noncompeting organizations, including Owens Corning, 3M, General Motors, Motorola, Northwest Airlines, and Levi Strauss. These organizations agreed to share some of their existing training materials with one another, with a particular focus on building up their online training course offerings. In 1999, 103 programs were available for use by LearnShare member organizations.[90] However, in April 2000, Pensare acquired the distribution rights for LearnShare materials. Interestingly, the model of partnership among the various organizations "has since been overshadowed by new learning collaboration options ushered in by the Web and e-learning advances."[91] It is unclear at this time exactly what will become of the LearnShare partnership.

There are a number of limitations to IBT. Given the multimedia format, which uses large video and audio files, the primary limitation to date has been the network bandwidth — the size of a network's transmittal capacity.[92] However, with the rapid advances in technology (greater bandwidth, and improved abilities to compress data), this limitation is increasingly being overcome. Another limitation has been the use of multiple, potentially incompatible browser software configurations that determined which media types and HyperText Markup Language (HTML) format options were available.[93] Further, different authoring packages (i.e., the programs used to create the training content) have often been incompatible with one another. These limitations are also being overcome, as organizations adopt standard browser software packages, such as Netscape Communicator or Microsoft Internet Explorer, which are capable of accessing format options and multimedia. Recently, the Microsoft Corporation introduced a Learning Resource Interchange Toolkit that uses Extensible Markup Language, or XML. This software has the potential to serve as a universally accepted programming tool that would allow organizations to retrieve and use information from the Internet, regardless of what authoring package was used to create it.[94] On the practical side, online learning has been criticized for pushing the time for learning to the employee's nonwork or off time. That is, the proposed benefit of "anytime, anywhere" learning can in fact mean that trainees are expected to do the training on their own, and often without compensation.[95] Also, many trainees find it difficult to complete self-paced training. This has led the ASTD to commission a study of reasons why some trainees abandon technology-based training after only a few sessions.[96]

*INTELLIGENT COMPUTER-ASSISTED INSTRUCTION.* ICAI goes beyond CAI in terms of flexibility and the ability to qualitatively evaluate learner performance. Whereas a typical CAI program may allow the learner to select from among several levels of presentation (novice, intermediate, etc.), an ICAI program is able to discern the learner's capability from the learner's response patterns and by analyzing the learner's errors. The goal of ICAI systems is to provide learners with an electronic teacher's assistant that can patiently offer advice to individual learners, encourage learner practice, and stimulate learners' curiosity through experimentation. This would potentially make the teacher more available for more creative endeavors, or for helping learners to overcome subtle or difficult problems beyond the capability of ICAI.[97]

While the availability of ICAI programs is limited compared to that of CAI, the potential for ICAI is enormous. Some examples of ICAI programs are the LISP computer language tutor from Carnegie-Mellon University and the Navy's STEAMER program, which allows students to learn to operate and repair a ship's complex steam propulsion system.[98] Expert systems, like Campbell Soup's cooker maintenance program ALDO, which capture the knowledge and experience of experts in a particular field or content area, are also considered ICAI programs.

ICAI programs are based on advances in artificial intelligence, which involves "engineering some aspects of the human thought process" into a computer.[99] Artificial intelligence research is uncovering ways to improve ICAI programs' capability to use natural language to interact with the learner and to understand the learner (by tracking learner responses and learning from them). Given the rate of progress in computer hardware, software, artificial intelligence, and knowledge engineering (designing and organizing information and finding effective ways to present it), it would not be surprising to see ICAI programs become common in training and educational programs in the not-too-distant future.

## IMPLEMENTING THE TRAINING PROGRAM

So, how should the choice of which method or methods to use to deliver training be made? Trainers should make this decision while simultaneously considering the objectives to be achieved, the resources available, and trainee characteristics and expertise (see Chapters 3 through 5). While trends are clearly moving strongly in the direction of technology-based training, this may not be the best solution for every training situation. In this regard, we present to you an interesting response to the "e-learning bandwagon" (see the boxed insert on p. 216).

The primary responsibility for implementing the training program lies, of course, with the trainer. In Chapter 5, we discussed the preparation of training objectives and the lesson plan, as well as issues involved in determining the best schedule. In this chapter, we focused on the selection of training methods. Obviously, at some point, the trainer must pull all of these issues together and put them into practice. Some final thoughts are presented toward this end.

### ARRANGING THE PHYSICAL ENVIRONMENT

An important implementation decision concerns arranging the physical environment. The environment is particularly important to on-the-job training because the trainee must feel comfortable enough to concentrate and learn. If the OJT area has a number of distractions (like noise and phone calls) that may interfere with the training process, for instance, the trainer must find ways to remove or minimize them. Interruptions are another common OJT distraction, particularly when the supervisor is the trainer. Interruptions can be avoided by setting aside certain times of the day or a special location for training that is free from distractions.

---

### LONG LIVE C-LEARNING[1]

All recent surveys and indicators point to the rapid and continuing growth of technology-based training. Such training can be more individualized than group- or classroom-based training, and is often touted as cheaper, given the reduced needs for trainees to travel to the training site, or even to be away from their workplace. However, as we have already pointed out, classroom training remains the dominant form of instructional delivery. Consultant James Farrell argues that there are, in fact, good reasons why classroom training (c-learning) remains popular. Face-to-face instruction has the greatest capacity for "information richness." Information richness has to do with the types of cues that are sent to the receiver of information, for example, when a trainee has the ability to observe the trainer's body language, voice inflection, and nonverbal cues, this can increase the accuracy of the communication that is received. As one moves away from face-to-face communi-

cation, such as with distance learning, computer-based learning, video- and print-based instruction, there is less capacity for rich communication. This may be fine for situations where the knowledge or skills to be taught are relatively straightforward. However, when the skills or procedures to be taught are completely new or different from what has been done in the past, these more complex situations may not be well suited for technology-based learning. Farrell presents the following as a humorous (if extreme) example of where distance learning may not be ideal for attaining certain training objectives:

> You're in a hospital emergency room, and a nurse says you need immediate brain surgery. Two physicians are available, and you must choose. One has undergone traditional one-on-one training with an experienced surgeon. The other has been trained through the hospital's

revolutionary new distance learning program for brain surgeons, which included the completion of a twelve-step CD-ROM course. Which surgeon do you want to operate on you? (p. 44).

Farrell argues that it is important to look at the information processing demands placed on learners. When such demands are high, more face-to-face (or classroom) interaction is likely going to be necessary. While the newer learning technologies can have advantages concerning speed, flexibility, and cost, HRD professionals must make sure that they are appropriate for the given training situation. "Despite the rise in e-learning," Farrell concludes, "it appears that classroom training is here to stay" (p. 46). What do you think?

[1]Farrell, J. N. (2000). Long live C-learning. *Training & Development*, 54(9), September, 43–46.

---

Alternatively, the supervisor can arrange for someone who is not receiving training to handle calls and inquiries during the time established for training.

In a classroom setting, a number of factors should be considered when arranging the physical environment. These include the seating arrangement, comfort, and physical distractions. **Seating** is important because it establishes a spatial relationship between the trainer and the trainees. For example, a classroom with fixed seats in vertical rows limits what the trainer can do in that setting, but this arrangement may be preferred for the lecture technique because it focuses the participants on the lecturer. In a classroom with movable seats, the trainer can arrange the seats to facilitate the program objectives. Arranging the rows on angles (or a chevron shape) or in a semicircle allows the trainees to view one another during a class discussion. This arrangement can encourage interaction and feedback among the participants. In a large class, the seats can be arranged in small groups to facilitate group discussion.

The physical **comfort level** is also important for successful learning. Extremes in room temperature can inhibit learning. A warm, stuffy room can make participants feel tired. A room that is too cold can distract participants and reduce manual dexterity. One of the authors recalls participating in a management development seminar in a room so cold that trainees spent more time focusing on how uncomfortable they were (and consuming hot beverages) than dealing with the training content.

The third factor that should be considered when arranging the physical environment is the potential for **physical distractions,** such as noise, poor lighting, and physical barriers. Noise, including activity outside the classroom, can often be controlled by closing the door or placing a sign stating, "Quiet: Training in session," outside the area. Inappropriate lighting can make it difficult for participants to take notes, read printed material or overheads, or render projected material unviewable. If possible, the trainer should inspect the room in advance to determine whether any physical barriers, such as poles, fixed partitions, and the like, will interfere with the planned activities. If such problems exist, it may be possible to find a more suitable location.

Additional physical factors a trainer may want to consider include wall and floor coverings and colors (carpeted rooms are quieter), the type of chairs, the presence of glare, windows (a view may distract participants), acoustics, and the presence of electrical outlets to run necessary equipment.[100] Also, whenever possible, the screen for overheads or computer slides should be arranged in such a way that it does not block off simultaneous use of the white board or flip chart.

### GETTING STARTED

Having all the elements needed to implement an HRD intervention or program — a viable lesson plan, materials, audiovisual and/or computer equipment on hand, and the physical environment ready — the final step is to do it! It is important for the trainer to get the program off to a good start and maintain it. If multiple sessions are scheduled, the first session sets the tone for the remainder of the program. As we discussed, a trainer can establish clear expectations by preparing a course outline or syllabus that explains the purpose, objectives, topics, and requirements that establish class norms for relevant issues (punctuality, participation, participant interaction, etc.). The course outline should be handed out and explained in detail during the first session and, if needed, restated and reinforced periodically throughout the training program.

In addition to establishing expectations, the trainer should try to determine each trainee's capacity and motivation to learn, if he or she has not already done so before the session. One way to make this determination is to conduct an initial exercise or pretest to assess initial ability. This may be particularly important in one-on-one OJT sessions. Rather than assess participant motivation, it may be more beneficial to include activities that reinforce motivation. Such activities could include asking participants what they'd like to accomplish, illustrating the

**RETURN TO OPENING CASE**[1]

Dell Learning has enjoyed the active support of Michael Dell, the CEO of the company. It has used a variety of means to promote training and learning within the corporation. Your instructor has additional information on Dell Learning and the questions raised in the opening case.

[1]Coné, J. (2000). How Dell does it. *Training & Development, 54*(6), June, 58–70.

benefits of achieving the training objectives, explicitly addressing participants' fears or concerns, or having participants complete a learning contract.

Many training programs include some sort of icebreaker exercise to help participants get to know one another and establish rapport with one another and the trainer. This is important for at least two reasons. First, a benefit of many HRD programs is the opportunity for participants to network and get to know their colleagues in other parts of the organization. Second, in HRD programs, as in any group setting, people generally seek social acceptance. For instance, in classes with one or two minority group members (ethnic, racial, gender, etc.), these indi-

### ▪ TABLE 6-6

#### TIPS FOR TRAINERS

1. Overprepare–know your subject matter inside and out.
2. Get the trainees' attention early (have a "grabber").
3. Focus on the trainees' concerns rather than your own.
4. Ask some initial questions that the trainees can answer, and then continually work for interaction.
5. Listen and acknowledge ideas.
6. Praise people as they learn.
7. Direct questions back to people.
8. Put people at ease.
9. Ask for examples from the trainees' experience.
10. Share your experiences with the trainees.
11. Don't become a slide narrator, i.e., don't let your slides become your presentation.
12. Admit to not knowing an answer–let trainees help you.
13. Avoid disputes and making "right" and "wrong" judgments.
14. Show that you enjoy instructing people.  Have fun!
15. Spend additional time with trainees when necessary.
16. Express confidence in the trainee.
17. Make notes, and follow up on them.
18. Create positive behavior through reinforcement.
19. Use trainees' words when writing on the flip chart or board.
20. Summarize–provide learning points and closure to celebrate what trainees have learned.

SOURCES: From Abernathy, D. J. (1999).  Presentation tips from the pros. *Training & Development*, 53(10), 19-25; Fetteroll, E. C. (1985). 16 tips to increase your effectiveness. *Training & Development Journal, 39*(6), 68-70.

viduals may feel socially isolated, which can affect their ability to perform effectively in that setting. It is important that the trainer be sensitive to the social needs of trainees and respond in ways that enhance their feelings of belonging.

Finally, the trainer should make every effort to build a climate characterized by mutual respect and openness. This in turn will make it easier for trainees to seek help when they need it.

Many skills are involved in effectively running a group meeting, teaching, or facilitating learning. The trainer is encouraged to read about the subject and seek out opportunities to build the trainees' platform and interpersonal skills. One good source for inexperienced trainers is the book *Training and Development Year-book* by Carolyn Nilson.[101] This annual yearbook includes reprints of articles, cases, and other materials concerning HRD. A final section is entitled "The trainer's almanac," and includes a list of conferences, print resources, and a rating of training Web sites. Professional journals like *Training & Development* and *Training* also include frequent articles on effective training skills. In addition, becoming involved in a local ASTD chapter can be very beneficial. In this spirit, we close this chapter with a list of tips offered by Abernathy and Fetteroll to increase training effectiveness (see Table 6-6).[102]

### SUMMARY

This chapter described several important activities related to the implementation of training and development programs. The three primary training methods are OJT, classroom, and self-paced/computer-based training. Each method has a number of techniques appropriate for particular situations. The trainer needs to select the best combination of techniques that will maximize trainee learning. Once the trainer designs and schedules the program, the final step is the actual implementation of the program. This includes arranging the physical environment and getting started on a positive note.

Look again at the true-false questions we presented at the beginning of the chapter. We would categorize each of those questions as false. While there may be *some* truth to each of them, in an absolute sense, we do not think they hold up as accurate statements. It is hoped that our discussion of each topic in this chapter has provided you with our rationale for this.

### KEY TERMS AND CONCEPTS

| | |
|---|---|
| artificial intelligence (AI) | learning climate |
| audiovisual methods | job rotation |
| behavior modeling | job instruction training (JIT) |
| business games | intranet-based training (IBT) |
| case study method | lecture |
| classroom training | on-the-job training (OJT) |
| computer-aided instruction (CAI) | role playing |
| computer-based training (CBT) | simulation |

| discussion method | static media |
|---|---|
| dynamic media | telecommunications |
| expert system | training methods |
| HyperText Markup Language (HTML) | videoconferencing |
| intelligent computer-assisted instruction (ICAI) | |

### QUESTIONS FOR DISCUSSION

1. What experiences have you had with on-the-job training? What can make it function as effectively as possible?

2. Why do you suppose the five categories of classroom training are so popular in HRD? Identify two types of training programs a manager might *not* want to conduct in a classroom format.

3. State and justify your opinion regarding the effectiveness of the lecture method. What can be done to ensure a lecture is effective?

4. Using a training topic (or module) of your choice, what audiovisual methods would be most appropriate in presenting this method to a group of trainees? Why did you pick the method or methods that you did?

5. In what circumstances would learning be promoted through use of the case study method or simulations?

6. What experiences have you had with role playing in training? Under what conditions might a role play be effective? Ineffective?

7. What sorts of skills and knowledge do you think computer-based training methods (such as computer-aided instruction) are well suited for? Poorly suited for?

8. Why is it important for trainers and trainees to establish a rapport with each other before a training session?

### EXERCISE

Consider a training module that you are interested in. Generate at least five questions that could be used to facilitate group or classroom discussion on this topic. Evaluate the extent to which each question is likely to stimulate useful discussion of this training topic.

### REFERENCES

1. Yin, L. R. (2000). Learning continuum. http://facstaff.uww.edu/yinl/edmedia2000/dlp-ppt/sld018.htm.

2. Scott, J. (1999). Employees get OJT. *Memphis Business Journal,* 21(1), May 7, 1–3.

3. Chase, N. (1997). OJT doesn't mean 'sit by Joe.' *Quality, 36* (November), 84.

4. Jacobs, R. L., & Jones, M. J. (1995). *Structured on-the-job training.* San Francisco: Berrett-Koehler, 19.

5. Rothwell, W. J., & Kazanas, H. C. (1994). *Improving on-the-job training.* San Francisco: Jossey-Bass.

6. Knight, J. (2000). The school of hard rocks. *Training,* August, 36–38.

7. Jacobs, R. L., & Jones, M. J. (1997). Teaching tools: When to use on-the-job training. *Security Management, 41*(9), 35–41.

8. Cannell, M. (1997). Practice makes perfect. *People Management, 3*(5), March 6, 26–31.

9. Taylor, D. L., & Ramsey, R. K. (1993). Empowering employees to 'just do it.' *Training & Development, 47*(5), 71–76.

10. Goff, L. (1999). Get promoted. *Computerworld, 33*(35), September 30, 54–55.

11. Korman, A. K. (1971). *Industrial and organizational psychology.* Englewood Cliffs, NJ: Prentice-Hall; The "change-up" in lectures (1997). http://www.indiana.edu/~teaching/changeups.html.

12. Bass, B. M., & Vaughn, J. A. (1966). *Training in industry.* Belmont, WA: Wadsworth.

13. Carroll, S. J., Paine, F. T., & Ivancevich, J. J. (1972). The relative effectiveness of training methods — Expert opinion and research. *Personnel Psychology, 25,* 495–510.

14. Cohen, D. J. (1990). What motivates trainees? *Training and Development Journal, 44*(11), 91–93.

15. Burke, M. J., & Day, R. R. (1986). A cumulative study of the effectiveness of managerial training. *Journal of Applied Psychology, 71,* 232–245.

16. Earley, P. C. (1987). Intercultural training for managers: A comparison of documentary and interpersonal methods. *Academy of Management Journal, 30,* 685–698.

17. The "change-up" in lectures (1997), *supra* note 11.

18. Zemke, R., Raines, C., & Filipczak, B. (1999). Generation gaps in the classroom. *Training,* November, 48–54.

19. Welty, W. M. (1989). Discussion method teaching: How to make it work. *Change,* July/August, 41–49.

20. Kearsley, G. (1984). *Training and technology.* Reading, MA: Addison-Wesley.

21. Nunberg, G. (1999). Slides rule: The trouble with PowerPoint. *Fortune,* December 20, 330–331.

22. Jaffe, G. (2000). What's your point, Lieutenant? Just cut to the pie charts. *Wall Street Journal,* April 26, A1.

23. Industry Report. (1999). *Training, 36*(10), 37–81.

24. Eurich, N. P. (1990). *The learning industry: Education for adult workers.* Lawrenceville, NJ: Princeton University Press.

25. Kearsley (1984), *supra* note 20.

26. Watkins, B. T. (1991). Eighteen Universities join effort to offer bachelor's degrees in management, entirely through cable television. *Chronicle of Higher Education, 38*(5), A18–A19; James, M. L. (1997). Delivering the MBA via the Internet: Where do we begin? *Academy of Educational Leadership Journal, 1,* 41–46.

27. Stackel, L. (1988). National Technological University: Learning by satellite. In J. Casner-Lotto and Associates (eds.), *Successful training strategies.* San Francisco: Jossey-Bass.

28. Eurich (1990), *supra* note 24.

29. Lowenthal, J., & Jankowski, P. (1983). A checklist for selecting the right teleconferencing mode. *Training and Development Journal, 37*(12), 47–50; Bove, R. (1984). Reach out and train someone. *Training and Development Journal, 38*(7), 26.

30. Industry Report (1999), *supra* note 23.

31. Berdiansky, H. (1985). The invisible trainer. *Training and Development Journal, 39*(3), 60–63.

32. Wittock, M. (1986). *The handbook of research on teaching.* New York: Macmillan.

33. Eurich (1990), *supra* note 24.

34. Fister, S. (2000). Tech trends. *Training,* April, 30, 32.

35. Schramm, W. (1962). Learning from instructional television. *Review of Educational Research, 32,* 156–167; Chu, G. C., & Schramm, W. (1967). *Learning from television: What the research says.* Washington, DC: National Association of Educational Broadcasters; Berdiansky, H. (1985). The invisible trainer. *Training and Development Journal, 39*(3), 60–63.

36. Kearsley (1984), *supra* note 20, p. 145.

37. Rothwell, W. J., & Kazanas, H. C. (1992). *Mastering the instructional design process.* San Francisco: Jossey-Bass, 190–191.

38. Kearsley (1984), *supra* note 20; Romiszowski, A. J. (1988). *The selection and use of instructional media* (2nd ed.). New York: Nichols Publishing; Rothwell & Kazanas (1992), *supra* note 37.

39. Keys, B., & Wolfe, J. (1988). Management education and development: Current issues and emerging trends. *Journal of Management, 14,* 205–229, p. 214.

40. Industry Report (1999), *supra* note 23.

41. Osigweh, C. A. B. (1986–1987). The case approach in management training. *Organizational Behavior Teaching Review, 11*(4), 120–133.

42. Barnes, L. B., Christensen, C. R., & Hansen, A. J. (1994). *Teaching and the case method: Text, cases, and readings* (3rd ed.). Boston: Harvard Business School Press; Naumes, W., & Naumes, M. J. (1999). *The art & craft of case writing.* Thousand Oaks, CA: Sage; Wassermann, S. (1994). *Introduction to case method teaching: A guide to the galaxy.* New York: Teachers College Press.

43. Osigweh (1986-1987), *supra* note 41.

44. Andrews, E. S., & Noel, J. L. (1986). Adding life to the case study method. *Training and Development Journal, 40*(2), 28–29.

45. Argyris, C. (1980). Some limitations to the case method: Experiences in a management development program. *Academy of Management Review, 5,* 291–298.

46. Berger, M. A. (1983). In defense of the case method: A reply to Argyris. *Academy of Management Review, 8,* 329–333.

47. Keys & Wolfe (1988), *supra* note 39; Osigweh (1986-1987), *supra* 41.

48. Argyris, C. (1986). Skilled incompetence. *Harvard Business Review, 64*(5), 74–79.

49. Andrews & Noel (1986), *supra* note 44.

50. Osigweh (1986-1987), *supra* note 41, p. 131.

51. *Industry Report (1999). supra* note 23.

52. McCall, M. W., & Lombardo, M. M. (1982). Using simulation for leadership and management research: Through the looking glass. *Management Science, 28,* 533–549.

53. Kaplan, R. E., Lombardo, M. M., & Mazique, M. S. (1985). A mirror for managers: Using simulation to develop management teams. *Journal of Applied Behavioral Science, 21,* 241–253.

54. Thornton, G. C., & Cleveland, J. N. (1990). Developing managerial talent through simulation. *American Psychologist, 45,* 190–199.

55. McCall & Lombardo (1982), *supra* note 52.

56. Kaplan, Lombardo, & Mazique (1985), *supra* note 53.

57. Keys & Wolfe (1988), *supra* note 47.

58. Butler, J. L., & Keys, J. B. (1973). A comparative study of simulation and rational methods of supervisory training in human resource development. In T. B. Green & D. F. Ray (eds.), *Academy of Management Proceedings* (302–305). Boston, MA: Academy of Management.

59. Thornton, G. C., & Byham, W. C. (1982). *Assessment centers and managerial performance.* New York: Academic Press.

60. Thornton, G. C., & Cleveland, J. N. (1990). Developing managerial talent through simulation. *American Psychologist, 45,* 190–199.

61. Wexley, K. N., & Baldwin, T. T. (1986). Management development. *Journal of Management, 12,* 277–294.

62. Keys & Wolfe (1988), *supra* note 47.

63. Industry Report (1999), *supra* note 23.

64. Burke, M. J., & Day, R. R. (1986). A cumulative study of the effectiveness of managerial training. *Journal of Applied Psychology, 71,* 232–245; Werner, J. M., & Crampton, S. M. (1992). The impact of behavior modeling training on measures of learning, behavior, and results: A meta-analytic review. In M. Schnake (ed.), *Proceedings,* Southern Management Association, 279–284.

65. Weaver, M. (1999). Beyond the ropes: Guidelines for selecting experiential training. *Corporate University Review, 7*(1), January/February, 34–37.

66. *Ibid;* Wagner, R. J., & Roland, C. C. (1996). Outdoor-based training: Research findings and recommendations for trainers. *Resources in Education,* June, 7–15.

67. Weaver (1999), *supra* note 65, p. 35.

68. Marquardt, M. J., & Kearsley, G. (1999). *Technology-based learning: Maximizing human performance and corporate success.* Boca Raton, LA: St. Lucie Press.

69. Industry Report (1999). *supra* note 23.

70. Kearsley (1984), *supra* note 20.

71. Hartley, D. E. (2000). *On-demand learning: Training in the new millennium.* Amherst, MA: HRD Press.

72. Hamburg, S. K. (1988). Manpower Temporary Services: Keeping ahead of the competition. In J. Casner-Lotto & Associates (eds.), *Successful training strategies.* San Francisco: Jossey-Bass.

73. Caudron, S. (1996). Wake up to new learning. *Training & Development, 50*(5), 30–35.

74. Ganger, R E. (1990). Computer-based training works. *Personnel Journal, 69*(9), 85–91.

75. Schwade, S. (1985). Is it time to consider computer-based training? *Personnel Administrator, 30*(2), 25–35.

76. Hillelsohn, M. J. (1984). How to think about CBT. *Training and Development Journal, 38*(1), 42–44, p. 43.

77. Reinhart, C. (1989). Developing CBT-The quality way. *Training and Development Journal, 43*(11), 85–89.

78. Ganger (1990), *supra* note 74.

79. Caudron (1996), *supra* note 73.

80. Wexley, K. N. (1984). Personnel training. *Annual Review of Psychology, 35,* 519–551.

81. Foegen, J. H. (1987). Too much negative training. *Business Horizons, 30*(5), 51–53.

82. Munger, P. D. (1996). A guide to high-tech training delivery: Part I. *Training & Development, 50*(12), 55–57.

83. Marquardt & Kearsley (1999), *supra* note 68.

84. Croft, B. (1996). The Intranet: Your newest training tool. *Personnel Journal, 75*(7), 27–28; Curtin, C. (1997). Getting off to a good start on Intranets. *Training & Development, 51*(2), 42–46.

85. Workers praise Internet but bemoan lack of training (2000). *Training, 37*(5), May, 26.

86. 2000 State of the Industry Report (2000). Alexandria, VA: ASTD, p. 18.

87. Hartley, D. (2000). All aboard the e-learning train. *Training & Development, 54*(7), July, 37–42.

88. Glener, D. (1996). The promise of Internet-based training. *Training & Development, 50*(9), September, 57–58.

89. Cohen, S. (1997). Intranets uncovered. *Training & Development, 51*(2), February, 48–50.

90. Anfuso, D. (1999). Trainers prove many heads are better than one: A unique consortium is raising the training function's value. *Workforce, 78*(3), March, 60–65.

91. http://www.learningcircuits.org/may2000/may2000_newsbytes.html.

92. Cohen (1997), *supra* note 89.

93. Curtin, C. (1997). Getting off to a good start on Intranets. *Training & Development, 51*(2), February, 42–46.

94. Dobbs, K. (2000). A step up for standards: Online learning gets compatible. *Training, 37*(5), May, 36, 39.

95. Zielinski, D. (2000). The lie of online learning. *Training, 37*(5), May, 38–40.

96. Zielenski, D. (2000). Can you keep learners online? *Training, 37*(3), March, 64–75.

97. McCalla, G. I., & Greer, J. E. (1987). *The practical use of artificial intelligence in automated tutoring systems: Current status and impediments to progress.* Saskatoon, Canada: University of Saskatchewan, Department of Computational Science. Cited in N. P. Eurich (1990), *The learning industry: Education for adult workers.* Lawrenceville, NJ: Princeton University Press, 74.

98. Eurich (1990), *supra* note 24.

99. *Ibid.,* p. 71.

100. Finkel, C. (1986). Pick a place, but not any place. *Training and Development Journal, 40*(2), February, 51–53.

101. Nilson, C. (2000). *Training & development yearbook 2000.* Paramus, NJ: Prentice-Hall.

102. Abernathy, D. J. (1999). Presentation tips from the pros. *Training & Development, 53*(10), 19–25; Fetteroll, E. C. (1985). Sixteen tips to increase your effectiveness. *Training and Development Journal, 39*(6), June, 68–70.

# 9

# Evaluating HRD Programs

## LEARNING OBJECTIVES

*After reading this chapter, the learner will be able to:*

1. Define *evaluation* and explain its role in HRD.

2. Compare different frameworks for HRD evaluation.

3. Discuss the various types of evaluation information available and compare the methods of data collection.

4. Explain the role of research design in HRD evaluation.

5. Describe the ethical issues involved in conducting HRD evaluation.

6. Identify and explain the choices available for translating evaluation results into dollar terms.

7. Calculate a utility estimate for a target organization.

**OPENING CASE**

In 1992, Dave Palm, the director of training at LensCrafters, got a call suggesting that top executives were looking to improve the company's bottom line, and couldn't find enough tangible evidence that the company's training programs were producing a measurable return on the company's investment. Top management at this optical retailer understood that employee training was important, but it wanted to know what evidence was available to show that there was in fact a payoff to the organization from the money being spent on training. The phone conversation ended with a challenge, "What are you going to do about this?"

*Questions: If you were the director of training in this situation, what types of measures would you like to have available before you respond to top management? That is, what types of evidence do you think that management would find convincing that training was having a positive impact on the organization? Why did you pick the measures that you did? How would you go about collecting the data for the measures you have selected?*

Purcell, A. (2000). 20/ 20 ROI. *Training & Development, 54*(7), July, 28–33.

## INTRODUCTION

In this chapter, we'll deal with some of the following questions:

- *How do you actually evaluate training and HRD interventions?*
- *What measures can be used to evaluate training interventions?*
- *Is there one best model or framework to use to evaluate training?*
- *What important issues should be considered as one prepares to evaluate HRD interventions?*
- *What are the ethical issues involved in evaluating HRD interventions?*
- *To what extent can the value of HRD interventions be expressed in terms of costs and benefits, or dollars and cents?*

In the previous three chapters, we discussed how to identify HRD needs and then design and deliver a program or intervention to satisfy those needs. The training and HRD model (shown in Figure 7-1) illustrates how the evaluation phase relates to the needs assessment, design, and implementation phases in the HRD/training process.

In this chapter, we will discuss how to answer the question upon which HRD evaluation is based: Was the HRD program effective? This is a deceptively simple question, which raises a number of concerns, such as:

- What is meant by effectiveness? Is it the same thing as efficiency?
- How is effectiveness measured?
- What is the purpose of determining effectiveness? That is, what decisions are made after a program is judged effective or ineffective?

As we will see in this chapter, the answers to these questions are far from simple.

**■ FIGURE 7-1**

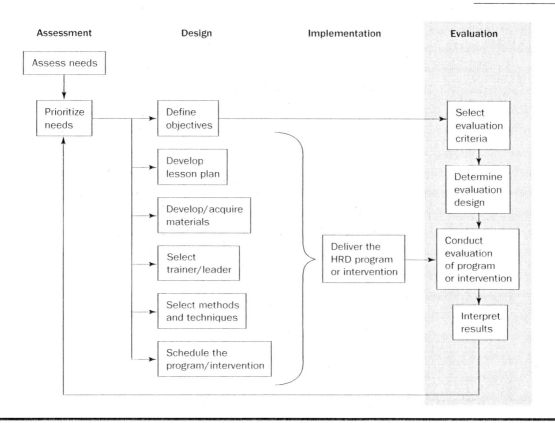

The term **effectiveness** is relative. Typically, effectiveness is determined with respect to the achievement of a goal or a set of goals. HRD effectiveness must be determined with respect to the goals of the program or programs being examined. Therefore, it makes sense to ask the question of effectiveness more specifically. An HRD or training program can be effective in meeting some goals (like staying within budget or increasing a participant's skills) and be ineffective in meeting others (like improving customer satisfaction).

In this chapter we will define HRD evaluation, describe its purposes and the options available for conducting an evaluation of training and other HRD interventions, and discuss how evaluation findings can be communicated.

## THE PURPOSE OF HRD EVALUATION

**HRD evaluation** is defined as "the systematic collection of descriptive and judgmental information necessary to make effective training decisions related to the selection, adoption, value, and modification of various instructional activities."[1] This definition makes several important points. First, when conducting an evaluation, both descriptive and judgmental information may be collected. Descriptive information provides a picture of what is happening or has happened, whereas judgmental information communicates some opinion or belief about what has happened. For example, the statement "25 percent of first-line supervisors attended a budgeting workshop in the last year" contains only descriptive information; it simply states the facts. Similarly, a statement that "20 percent fewer supervisors attended this workshop than in the previous twelve months" also contains descriptive information. However, the statement, "The turnout for the budgeting workshop over the last six months is disappointingly low compared to last year's turnout" provides judgmental information — someone's opinion based on the facts. Both descriptive and judgmental information are needed in an HRD evaluation. Some of the judgments are made by those involved in the program, and others are made by those not involved in the program.

Second, evaluation also involves the systematic collection of information according to a predetermined plan or method to ensure that the information is appropriate and useful. Finally, evaluation is conducted to help managers, employees, and HRD professionals make informed decisions about particular programs and methods. For example, if part of a program is ineffective, it may need to be changed or discarded. Or, if a certain program proves valuable, it may be replicated in other parts of the organization.

Evaluation can serve a number of purposes within the organization. According to Phillips, evaluation can help to do the following:

- determine whether a program is accomplishing its objectives
- identify the strengths and weaknesses of HRD programs, which can lead to changes, as needed
- determine the cost-benefit ratio of an HRD program
- decide who should participate in future HRD programs
- identify which participants benefited the most or least from the program
- reinforce major points to be made to the participants
- gather data to assist in marketing future programs
- determine if the program was appropriate
- establish a database to assist management in making decisions.[2]

Better and more informed decision making, then, is an important benefit of conducting an HRD evaluation. But there are other benefits as well. Zenger and Hargis identified three additional reasons for conducting HRD evaluations:

1. If HRD staff cannot substantiate its contribution to the organization, its funding and programs may be cut during the budgeting process, especially when the organization faces tough times.
2. Evaluation can build credibility with top managers and others in the organization.
3. Senior management often wants to know the benefits of HRD programs.[3]

Building credibility is a key aspect of conducting an evaluation. After all, other functions performed within the organization are evaluated to determine their effectiveness. If the HRD department fails to conform to this norm, it may not be taken seriously within the organization.

Thus, evaluation is a critical step in the HRD process. It is the only way one can know whether an HRD program has fulfilled its objectives.

## How Often Are HRD Programs Evaluated?

Given their importance, one might expect that HRD programs are regularly and carefully evaluated. Unfortunately, this is not the case. A survey of management training and education practices of U.S. companies found that while 92 percent of companies surveyed conduct some form of evaluation for company-sponsored training, 42 percent conduct no evaluation at all for the executive MBA programs they used.[4] In addition, the survey showed that the most commonly used form of evaluation was participant *reaction*, which as we will discuss, is useful for only a few of the decisions that must be made about HRD programs. A more recent survey found the same thing.[5]

The results reported by these surveys are not atypical. The lack of evaluation of HRD programs has been lamented by a number of HRD researchers.[6] Many articles have been written about the importance of conducting evaluations, but more organizations pay lip service to evaluations than actually conduct them.

Why aren't evaluations done more frequently? There are several possibilities. First, those associated with HRD programs may be afraid of criticism and program cuts if the evaluation shows that the program was not effective. Second, conducting an evaluation is not an easy process. It requires time, resources, and expertise that the HRD staff may not have or may not be willing to expend. Third, many factors beyond the program itself (including the economy, equipment, policies and procedures, other HR efforts, and resource availability) can affect whether employee performance improves, thus making it difficult to evaluate the impact of training.

Yet the simple fact is that HRD evaluations can and should be done in organizations to ensure effectiveness and accountability. It is our belief that it is the ethical responsibility of HRD professionals to prove to the organization whether their programs are indeed beneficial.

## The Evaluation of Training and HRD Programs Prior to Purchase

As we discussed in Chapter 5, many HRD and training programs are purchased by organizations from third parties, such as consultants or other vendors. Some practitioners believe that they fulfill their evaluation responsibility in their prepurchase decision. Their logic follows that they wouldn't buy a program they didn't think was going to work, so if they have made a wise purchasing decision (or evaluated the program before buying it), then it isn't necessary to conduct any postprogram evaluation.

Indeed, supervisors and HRD professionals should be wise consumers of programs and equipment used in their HRD efforts. However, it is equally important to judge the effectiveness of the program or device *after* it has been put into place. We have all made personal purchases that have not lived up to expectations, even after careful shopping, and it is unreasonable to assume that HRD and training purchases will be any different.

### EVOLUTION OF EVALUATION EFFORTS

Goldstein suggests that efforts at training evaluation have evolved through the following four stages since the 1960s:

- **Stage 1** focuses on anecdotal reactions from trainers and program participants. Judging from the survey results cited above, it appears many organizations still operate at this level.[7]

- **Stage 2** involves borrowing experimental methodology from academic laboratories to use for program evaluation. Organizational constraints (including time, resources, and the inability to randomly select participants or use control groups that receive no training) make application of these designs difficult, thus discouraging evaluation efforts.

- **Stage 3** creatively matches the appropriate research methodology to existing organizational constraints, thus making program evaluation more practical and feasible.

- **Stage 4** recognizes that the entire training and HRD process affects the organization, and shifts the focus of evaluation from postprogram results to the entire HRD process.[8]

It should be emphasized that it is possible to creatively apply sound research methods to HRD evaluation designs and have useful data for making decisions. Finding ways to perform effective evaluation serves all parties: the organization, the trainer or HRD professional, and the trainees. Before we discuss data collection and research designs, however, we will examine several overall models and frameworks of evaluation.

## MODELS AND FRAMEWORKS OF EVALUATION

A model of evaluation outlines the criteria for and focus of the evaluation effort. Because an HRD program can be examined from a number of perspectives, it is important to specify which perspectives will be considered.

Table 7-1 lists nine frameworks of HRD evaluation that have been suggested.[9] By far, the most widely used evaluation approach to date has been the framework laid out by Donald Kirkpatrick. We will discuss this first. While the different models and frameworks share some features, they also differ in significant ways.

**▪ TABLE 7-1**

| Model/Framework | Training Evaluation Criteria |
|---|---|
| 1. Kirkpatrick (1967, 1987, 1994) | Four levels: Reaction, Learning, Job Behavior, and Results. |
| 2. CIPP (Galvin, 1983) | Four levels: Context, Input, Process, and Product. |
| 3. CIRO (Warr et al., 1970) | Context, Input, Reaction, and Outcome. |
| 4. Brinkerhoff (1987) | Six stages: Goal Setting, Program Design, Program Implementation, Immediate Outcomes, Intermediate or Usage Outcomes, and Impacts and Worth. |
| 5. Systems approach (Bushnell, 1990) | Four sets of activities: Inputs, Process, Outputs, and Outcomes. |
| 6. Kraiger, Ford, & Salas (1993) | A classification scheme that specifies three categories of learning outcomes (cognitive, skill-based, affective) suggested by the literature and proposes evaluation measures appropriate for each category of outcomes. |
| 7. Kaufman & Keller (1994) | Five levels: Enabling and Reaction, Acquisition, Application, Organizational Outputs, and Societal Outcomes. |
| 8. Holton (1996) | Identifies five categories of variables and the relationships among them: Secondary Influences, Motivation Elements, Environmental Elements, Outcomes, Ability/Enabling Elements. |
| 9. Phillips (1996) | Five levels: Reaction and Planned Action, Learning, Applied Learning on the Job, Business Results, Return on Investment. |

## KIRKPATRICK'S EVALUATION FRAMEWORK

The most popular and influential framework for training evaluation was articulated by Kirkpatrick.[10] Kirkpatrick argues that training efforts can be evaluated according to four criteria: reaction, learning, job behavior, and results.

1. **Reaction (Level 1)** Did the trainees like the program and feel it was useful? At this level, the focus is on the trainees' perceptions about the program and its effectiveness. This is useful information. Positive reactions to a training program may make it easier to encourage employees to attend future programs. But if trainees did not like the program or think they didn't learn anything (even if they did), they may discourage others from attending and may be reluctant to use the skills or knowledge obtained in the program. The main limitation of evaluating HRD programs at the reaction level is that this information cannot indicate whether the program met its objectives beyond ensuring participant satisfaction.

2. **Learning (Level 2)** Did the trainees learn what the HRD objectives said they should learn? This is an important criterion, one many in the

organization would expect an effective HRD program to satisfy. Measuring whether someone has learned something in training may involve a quiz or test—clearly a different method from assessing the participants' reaction to the program.

3. **Job Behavior (Level 3)** Does the trainee use what was learned in training back on the job? (Recall our discussion of transfer of training in Chapter 3.) This is also a critical measure of training success. We all know coworkers who have learned how to do something but choose not to. If learning does not transfer to the job, the training effort cannot have an impact on the employee's or organization's effectiveness. Measuring whether training has transferred to the job requires observation of the trainee's on-the-job behavior or viewing organizational records (e.g., reduced customer complaints, a reduction in scrap rate).

4. **Results (Level 4)** Has the training or HRD effort improved the organization's effectiveness? Is the organization more efficient, more profitable, or better able to serve its clients or customers as a result of the training program? Meeting this criterion is considered to be the bottom line as far as most managers are concerned. It is also the most challenging level to assess, given that many things beyond employee performance can affect organizational performance. Typically at this level, economic and operating data (such as sales or waste) are collected and analyzed.

Kirkpatrick's framework provides a useful way of looking at the possible consequences of training and reminds us that HRD efforts often have multiple objectives. It has sometimes been assumed that each succeeding level incorporates the one prior to it, finally culminating in what many people consider to be the ultimate contribution of any organizational activity: improving the organization's effectiveness. However, one of the more enduring (and in our view, depressing) findings about HRD evaluation is the extent to which most organizations do *not* collect information on all four types of evaluation outcomes. For instance, in the 2000 State of the Industry Report (ASTD), a survey of over 500 organizations reported the following: 77 percent collected reaction measures, 36 percent collected learning measures, 15 percent collected behavior measures, and 8 percent collected results measures.[11] Perhaps even more surprising, even the subgroup of organizations that ASTD highlighted as "training investment leaders" reported only slightly higher usage of these measures (80 percent, 43 percent, 16 percent, and 9 percent).[12] It does raise an important question as to why these usage rates are so low, particularly for behavioral and results measures, as these would seem to provide organizations with vital, even invaluable information.

While most discussions about training and HRD evaluation are organized around Kirkpatrick's four levels of criteria, Kirkpatrick's approach has increasingly been the target of criticism and modification. First, some authors point out that the framework evaluates only what happens *after* training, as opposed to the entire training process.[13] A second line of criticism is that what Kirkpatrick proposed would be better described as a *taxonomy* of outcomes, rather than a true model of training outcomes. For example, Holton states that Kirkpatrick failed to specify the causal relationships that exist among elements of the model.[14] Kraiger, Ford, and Salas argue that Kirkpatrick's approach fails to specify what sorts of changes can be expected as a result of learning and what assessment techniques should be used to measure learning at each level.[15] Alliger and Janak question the validity of the assumptions that are implied by the framework (e.g., achieving the outcomes stated in higher levels of the model assumes achievement of outcomes at the lower levels).[16] They suggest that it "may never have been meant to be more than a first, global heuristic for training evaluation" (p. 339). Kirkpatrick has responded to this criticism by stating that "I personally have never called my framework 'a model'" (p. 23), and "I don't care whether my work is called a model or a taxonomy as long as it helps to clarify the meaning of evaluation in simple terms and offers guidelines and suggestions on how to accomplish an evaluation" (pp. 23–24).[17]

## OTHER FRAMEWORKS AND MODELS OF EVALUATION

Training researchers have attempted to expand Kirkpatrick's ideas to develop a model that provides a more complete picture of evaluation and encourages practitioners to do a more thorough job of evaluation. Several authors have suggested modifications to Kirkpatrick's four-level approach that keep the framework essentially intact. These include:

- expanding the reaction level to include assessing the participants' reaction to the training methods and efficiency[18]

- splitting the reaction level to include assessing participants' perceptions of enjoyment, usefulness (utility), and the difficulty of the program[19]

- adding a fifth level (beyond results) to address the societal contribution and outcomes created by an HRD program[20]

- adding a fifth level (beyond results) to specifically address the organization's return on investment.[21]

Galvin, building upon studies in the education field, suggested the CIPP (Context, Input, Process, Product) model.[22] In this model, evaluation focuses on measuring the *context* for training (needs analysis), *inputs* to training (examining the resources available for training, such as budgets and schedules), the *process* of conducting the training program (for feedback to the implementers), and the *product*, or outcome, of training (success in meeting program objectives). Galvin also reported survey results indicating that ASTD members preferred the CIPP model of evaluation to Kirkpatrick's framework.

Similarly, the CIRO (Context, Input, Reaction, Outcome) model was offered by Warr et al.[2] The context, input, and outcome evaluations in this model are essentially the same as the context, input, and product evaluations in CIPP, but CIRO emphasizes trainee **reaction** as a source of information to improve the training program.

Brinkerhoff extends the training evaluation model to six stages:

1. Goal Setting: What is the need?
2. Program Design: What will work to meet the need?
3. Program Implementation: Is it working, with the focus on the implementation of the program?
4. Immediate Outcomes: Did participants learn?
5. Intermediate or Usage Outcomes: Are the participants using what they learned?
6. Impacts and Worth: Did it make a worthwhile difference to the organization?[24]

Brinkerhoff's model suggests a cycle of overlapping steps, with problems identified in one step possibly caused by things occurring in previous steps.

Bushnell suggests a model also based on a systems view of the HRD function (i.e., input — throughput — output), containing four stages:

1. Input: What goes into the training effort? This consists of performance indicators such as trainee qualifications and trainer ability.
2. Process: The planning, design, development, and implementation of the HRD program.
3. Output: Trainee reactions, knowledge or skills gained, and improved job behavior.
4. Outcomes: Effects on the organization, including profits, productivity, and customer satisfaction.[25]

Bushnell states that evaluation measurement can and should occur between each of the stages as well as between the four activities in the process stage to ensure that the program is well designed and meets its objectives.

At least two attempts have been made to develop models or category schemes that incorporate research and theory on learning outcomes and the variables that influence them. In response to a lack of theoretically based training evaluation models, Kraiger, Ford, and Salas used research and theory from a variety of fields to offer a first step toward such a model.[26] Noting that learning outcomes can be of three types (i.e., cognitive, skill-based, and affective), they propose a classification scheme for evaluating learning outcomes in each of these three areas. This scheme (shown in Table 7-2) is quite specific, identifying the types of measures that can be used for learning outcomes in each of the three categories.

Holton suggests a complex model that specifies learning outcomes that are similar to Kirkpatrick's levels (i.e., learning, individual performance, and organizational results).[27] The model also includes individual variables (e.g., motivation to learn, motivation to transfer, ability, job attitudes) and environmental variables (e.g., transfer climate, external events) that influence these outcomes. Although this model has been created in light of recent research and theory, empirical support for this model is still needed.

■ **TABLE 7-2**

A CLASSIFICATION SCHEME FOR LEARNING OUTCOMES
FOR TRAINING EVALUATION

| Category | Learning Construct(s) | Focus of Measurement | Potential Training Evaluation Methods |
|---|---|---|---|
| **Cognitive** | | **Cognitive outcomes** | |
| Verbal knowledge | Declarative knowledge | Amount of knowledge Accuracy of recall | Recognition and recall tests |
| | | Speed, accessibility of knowledge | Power tests Speed tests |
| Knowledge organization | Mental models | Similarity to ideal Interrelationships of elements Hierarchical ordering | Free sorts Structural assessment (e.g. Pathfinder) |
| Cognitive strategies | Self-insight Metacognitive skills | Self-awareness Self-regulation | Probed protocol analysis Self-report Readiness for testing |
| **Skill based** | | **Skill-based outcomes** | |
| Compilation | Composition Proceduralization | Speed of performance Fluidity of performance Error rates Chunking Generalization Discrimination Strengthening | Targeted behavioral observation Hands-on testing Structured situational interviews |
| Automaticity | Automatic processing Tuning | Attentional requirements Available cognitive resources | Secondary task performance Interference problems Embedded measurement |
| **Affective** | | **Affective outcomes** | |
| Attitudinal | Targeted object (e.g., safety awareness) Attitude strength | Attitude direction Attitude strength Accessibility Centrality Conviction | Self-report measures |
| Motivation | Motivational disposition | Mastery versus performance orientations Appropriateness of orientation | Self-report measures |
| | Self-efficacy | Perceived performance capability | Self-report measures |
| | Goal setting | Level of goals Complexity of goal structures Goal commitment | Self-report measures Free recall measures Free sorts |

SOURCE: K. Kraiger, J. K. Ford, & E. Salas (1993). Application of cognitive, skill-based, and affective theories of learning outcomes to new methods of training evaluation. *Journal of Applied Psychology, 78*, 323. Adapted by permission.

## COMPARING EVALUATION FRAMEWORKS

As you might have noticed, all of the evaluation frameworks incorporate Kirkpatrick's four levels of evaluation in one way or another, either as explicit steps in the model or as information collected within the steps. We do not see the expansions offered by Kaufman and Keller, Warr and Bunce, and Phillips as being significant additions, as none are precluded by the framework Kirkpatrick proposed.[28] The only addition that appears to go beyond Kirkpatrick's ideas in any meaningful way is the notion that HRD professionals should be concerned about the impact their programs have on constituencies outside of the organization. Whether that sort of assessment should be routinely included in HRD evaluation would probably depend on how the individual and the management of the organization view their organization's social responsibility. Further, it is likely that those who feel strongly about social responsibility would consider and assess the societal impact of all of their activities, regardless of whether an evaluation model specifies that they should or not. For those who do not, inclusion of such a level is unlikely to lead them to change their point of view.

In addition, some of the alternatives to Kirkpatrick's approach are almost identical. The CIPP and CIRO models differ in only one of the four steps (process and reaction, respectively), and the purpose of the third step in both models is the same (improving program delivery).

The other models differ from Kirkpatrick's in that they bring the earlier phases of the training process, needs assessment, design, and implementation, into the evaluation phase. In fact, the first three stages of Brinkerhoff's model (goal setting, program design, and program implementation) explicitly include these activities.[29]

Simply merging the rest of the training process into the evaluation model may be seen as a modest improvement to Kirkpatrick's approach, as it adds no new understanding to effective training. However, there is some merit in helping managers, supervisors, and HRD professionals realize that evaluation is an ongoing activity, not one that should begin only after the training program has been implemented. Effective HRD involves many decisions, and having accurate, meaningful information available (through evaluation) throughout the training process can improve the decision-making process and enhance the overall effectiveness of the HRD effort.

Overall, we believe that the most serious shortcomings of Kirkpatrick's framework are 1) the lack of explicit causal relationships among the different levels, 2) the lack of specificity in dealing with different types of learning outcomes, and 3) the lack of direction concerning which measures are appropriate to assess which outcome measures. As we have shown in the chapter on learning and HRD (Chapter 3), much has been discovered about the learning process and learning outcomes. We agree with Alliger and Janak that Kirkpatrick's approach provides a useful starting point for thinking about and encouraging HRD evaluation, but it is insufficient as a model to guide HRD evaluation in its current form.[30] It does *not* appear to be the case that there is an inherent hierarchy among the four levels, that is, that trainees must first like the training, then learn something, then perform the desired behaviors, and then produce positive results.[31] For example, in a research project on enhancing the effectiveness of behavior modeling training, a reaction measure was collected immediately after training. Trainees who were told that they needed to use a checklist to track their progress for four weeks after training liked the training significantly *less* than did trainees told to "do their best" to use the principles taught in training. When the same reaction measure was given four week later, however, the trainees who had used the checklists were now more favorable about the training as a whole, whereas those in the "do your best" condition were less favorable toward the training. The means on this measure were now indistinguishable. Furthermore, the trainees who used the checklists demonstrated significantly more retention of the training material four weeks after training, and could demonstrate more of the key behaviors in a spontaneous role-play exercise than could the trainees who had not made use of the checklists.[32] Our point is simply that trainers should not assume positive (or negative) scores on one type of measure will *necessarily* translate into similar scores on measures of a different training outcome.

Therefore, we believe that efforts to incorporate research and theory on learning and learning outcomes are the most useful additions to the literature on models of training evaluation. Although Holton's model may prove to be useful, it requires further development, refinement, and empirical testing.[33] It seems to us that Kraiger, Ford, and Salas's classification scheme represents the most promising new direction for training evaluation since Kirkpatrick's presentation of the four levels of evaluation. It both addresses a specific need (offering conceptually based measurement suggestions to fit various types of learning) and can be used as a foundation on which to build a theory-based model of HRD evaluation.

And yet, we would close this section by suggesting that Kirkpatrick's approach remains a useful way to categorize the criteria that an effective HRD program must satisfy. If possible, information assessing all four levels of criteria should be collected at some point (depending on the question being asked that prompts the evaluation study). It is also important to make informed decisions about all aspects of the HRD program. The proper techniques, including those we discussed in Chapters 4 through 6, along with those we will introduce in this chapter, can ensure that such information is available.

In its simplest form, evaluation should address the question of whether the training program achieved its objectives.[34] Basing training objectives on needs assessment information, and then evaluating those objectives, is the most parsimonious way of summarizing what training evaluation is all about.[35] The process framework that we have emphasized in Chapters 4 through 7 provides a strong platform for systematically approaching HRD efforts (see Figure 7-1). *If* this framework is in place, and is used, then we think that evaluation efforts can focus on some combination of the following points (depending upon the situation). While this is only a modest expansion of Kirkpatrick, it highlights some aspects not fully captured by the "four levels."

1. reaction
   a. affective — How well did trainees like the training? (See the affective measures in Table 7-2.)

| **TABLE 7-3** | |
|---|---|

DATA COLLECTION METHODS FOR HRD EVALUATION

| Method | Description |
|---|---|
| 1. Interview | Conversation with one or more individuals to assess their opinions, observations, and beliefs |
| 2. Questionnaire | A standardized set of questions intended to assess opinions, observations, and beliefs |
| 3. Direct Observation | Observing a task or set of tasks as they are performed and recording what is seen |
| 4. Tests and Simulations | Structured situation to assess an individual's knowledge or proficiency to perform some task or behavior |
| 5. Archival Performance Data | Use of existing information, such as files or reports |

     b. perceived usefulness/utility — What was the perceived usefulness of this training?

2. learning — How much did trainees learn from the training? (See the cognitive measures in Table 7-2.)

3. behavior — What behavior change occurred as a result of training? (See the skill-based measures in Table 7-2.)

4. results

     a. What tangible outcomes or results occurred as a result of training?

     b. What was the return on investment (ROI) for this training? (See ROI and utility sections below.)

     c. What was the contribution of this training program to the community/larger society?

## DATA COLLECTION FOR HRD EVALUATION

By definition, any evaluation effort requires the collection of data to provide decision makers with facts and judgments upon which they can base their decisions. Three important aspects of providing information for HRD evaluation include data collection methods, types of data, and the use of self-report data.

### DATA COLLECTION METHODS

In Chapter 4, we listed some of the data sources and collection methods that can be used to provide information for needs assessments. The same data collection

**■ FIGURE 7-2**

A PARTICIPANT REACTION QUESTIONNAIRE

Title of the session: _____

The purposes of this rapid-feedback evaluation are to find out how you are doing, to find out how we are doing as facilitators of your learning experience, and to get your opinions about the content of the course and the training methods we are using together.

Please circle the number on the 1–5-point scale that best expresses your opinion for each question.

|  | No, waste of time | | It was useful | | Yes, very worthwhile |
|---|---|---|---|---|---|
| 1. Do you think that this session was worthwhile? | 1 | 2 | 3 | 4 | 5 |

|  | Not at all | | It was useful | | Very much |
|---|---|---|---|---|---|
| 2. How much did you personally need this session? | 1 | 2 | 3 | 4 | 5 |

|  | Not at all | | To some degree | | Completely |
|---|---|---|---|---|---|
| 3. To what extent were you able to participate actively in the learning experience? | 1 | 2 | 3 | 4 | 5 |

|  | Poorly | | Well | | Very well |
|---|---|---|---|---|---|
| 4. How well did the trainer(s) do the job? | 1 | 2 | 3 | 4 | 5 |

5. What did you like most about this session?

6. What did you like least, and how could we improve?

7. Do you have any comments or suggestions?

SOURCE: From N. L. Weatherby & M. E. Gorosh (1989). Rapid response with spreadsheets. *Training and Development Journal,* 43(9), 76. Reprinted by permission.

methods and sources are available when conducting training evaluation. Table 7-3 lists some common methods for collecting evaluation data, including interviews, questionnaires, direct observation, tests and simulations, and archival performance data. Additionally, recall the suggestions offered by Kraiger, Ford, and Salas concerning learning outcomes and measures.[36] Questionnaires are most

■ **FIGURE 7-3**

1. **Write simply and clearly, and make the meaning obvious.**
   Good example:     How often does your boss give you feedback on your job performance?
   Bad example:      To what extent do administrative superiors provide information regarding the quality of performance of people on your level?

2. **Ask discrete questions.**
   Good example:     1. The organization's goals are clear.
                     2. My role within the organization is clear.
   Bad example:      The organization's goals and your role within the organization are clear to you.

3. **Provide discrete response options and explain them.**
   Good example:     During the past three months, how often did you receive feedback on your work?

   |  | about | about | about | several |
   | not | every | once/ | every | times a |
   | once | month | week | day or so | day |
   |---|---|---|---|---|
   | 1 | 2 | 3 | 4 | 5 |

   Bad example:      During the past three months, how often did you receive feedback on your work?

   | rarely |  | occasionally |  | frequently |
   |---|---|---|---|---|
   | 1 | 2 | 3 | 4 | 5 |

4. **Limit the number of response options.**
   Good example:     What percent of the time are you generally sure of what the outcomes of your work efforts will be?

   | 0–20% | 21–40% | 41–60% | 61–80% | 81–100% |
   |---|---|---|---|---|
   | 1 | 2 | 3 | 4 | 5 |

   Bad example:      What percent of the time are you generally sure of what the outcomes of your work efforts will be?

   | 0–20 | 21–30 | 31–40 | 41–50 | 51–60 | 61–70 | 71–80 | 81–90 | 91–100 |
   |---|---|---|---|---|---|---|---|---|
   | 1 | 2 | 3 | 4 | 5 | 6 | 7 | 8 | 9 |

5. **Match the response mode to the question.**
   Good example:     To what extent are you generally satisfied with your job?

   | not | a |  | quite | very |
   | at all | little | some | a bit | much |
   |---|---|---|---|---|
   | 1 | 2 | 3 | 4 | 5 |

   Bad example:      Are you generally satisfied with your job?
                     YES     NO

6. **Get all of the important information.**

SOURCE: From J. H. Maher, Jr., & C. E. Kur (1983). Constructing good questionnaires. *Training and Development Journal, 37*(6), 106. Reprinted by permission.

■ **TABLE 7·4**

| Method | Advantages | Limitations |
|---|---|---|
| Interview | Flexible<br>Opportunity for<br>  clarification<br>Depth possible<br>Personal contact | High reactive effects<br>High cost<br>Face-to-face threat potential<br>Labor intensive<br>Trained observers needed |
| Questionnaire | Low cost<br>Honesty increased if<br>  anonymous<br>Anonymity possible<br>Respondent sets pace<br>Variety of options | Possible inaccurate data<br>On-job responding conditions<br>  not controlled<br>Respondents set varying paces<br>Return rate beyond control |
| Direct Observation | Nonthreatening<br>Excellent way to measure<br>  behavior change | Possibly disruptive<br>Reactive effect possible<br>May be unreliable<br>Trained observers needed |
| Written Test | Low purchase cost<br>Readily scored<br>Quickly processed<br>Easily administered<br>Wide sampling possible | May be threatening<br>Possible low relation to job<br>  performance<br>Reliance on norms may distort<br>  individual performance<br>Possible cultural bias |
| Simulation/Performance Test | Reliable<br>Objective<br>Close relation to job<br>  performance | Time consuming<br>Simulation often difficult<br>High development cost |
| Archival Performance Data | Reliable<br>Objective<br>Job-based<br>Easy to review<br>Minimal reactive effects | Lack of knowledge of criteria<br>  for keeping or discarding records<br>Information system discrepancies<br>Indirect<br>Need for conversion to usable form<br>Record prepared for other purposes<br>May be expensive to collect |

SOURCE: From J. J. Phillips (1983). *Handbook of training evaluation and measurement methods.* Houston: Gulf, 92. Adapted by permission.

often used in HRD evaluation because they can be completed and analyzed quickly. Figure 7-2 shows an example of a questionnaire that might be used to gather participant feedback (sometimes called a smile sheet). Some guidelines for writing effective questionnaires are listed in Figure 7-3.

Any or all of these methods are appropriate for collecting evaluation data, depending on their relevance to the questions being asked. For example, if an HRD professional is interested in assessing trainee reactions to a seminar on pension benefits, interviews or questionnaires might be good choices. Alternatively, if management wanted to know whether the seminar affected interest in the company's pension system, the number of inquiries employees make to the HR department about the pension plan could be tracked through direct observation or archival data. Some advantages and disadvantages of using various data collection methods are listed in Table 7-4.

Cheri Ostroff developed an interesting method of data collection targeted at measuring whether trainees use what they have learned back on the job.[37] One problem with using supervisors' observations of job behavior has been the difficulties supervisors often have in recalling specific behaviors that an employee has engaged in. Ostroff's method involves presenting supervisors or others observing employee performance with a scripted situation and asking them to check off which of several behaviors the employee has engaged in or would be most likely to perform.

Ostroff compared this technique to more traditional behavior and performance measures in assessing the effectiveness of a training program for school principals (see Figure 7-4). Only the scripted situation method revealed the significant effects of a training program. Although further research is needed to assess the effectiveness and generalizability of the scripted situation method, Ostroff's findings represent the kind of research that will make data collection and evaluation studies in general more accurate and feasible in organizational settings.

## CHOOSING DATA COLLECTION METHODS

Three vital issues to consider when deciding which data collection method to use are reliability, validity, and practicality. **Reliability** has to do with the consistency of results, and with the freedom from error and bias in a data collection method. A method that has little or no error or bias is highly reliable, whereas the results of a method that has significant error or bias is unreliable and cannot be trusted. Decisions based on unreliable information are likely to be poor ones.

For example, suppose employee leadership skills will be judged by having supervisors watch employees interact with each other in a role-playing exercise. If one of the supervisors assigns consistently harsher scores than the others, that personal bias and error will be reflected in low leadership ability scores for certain employees who might otherwise be considered excellent leaders.

Another issue to consider in selecting a data collection method is validity. **Validity** is concerned with whether the data collection method actually measures what we want it to measure, that is, are we hitting the right target? For example, suppose a trainer decides to use a written test to measure whether trainees have learned the procedure for completing travel expense forms. The test is valid to the extent that the scores on the test indicate whether the employee actually knows how to complete the forms. If the focus of training was on knowing which information to report on the expense form, yet the items on the test focus more on performing calculations, the test scores may be measuring the wrong thing. If this is the case, use of such a test will likely lead to poor decisions.

■ **FIGURE 7-4**

THE SCRIPTED SITUATION DATA COLLECTION METHOD: ITEM FROM
A SCHOOL PRINCIPAL PERFORMANCE SURVEY

The administrator receives a letter from a parent objecting to the content of the science section. The section topic is reproduction. The parent objects to his daughter having exposure to such materials and demands that something be done. The administrator would most likely (check one):

_____ Ask the teacher to provide handouts, materials, and curriculum content for review.

_____ Check the science curriculum for the board-approved approach to reproduction and compare board guidelines to course content.

_____ Ask the head of the science department for his or her own opinion about the teacher's lesson plan.

_____ Check to see if the parent has made similar complaints in the past.

SOURCE: From C. Ostroff (1991). Training effectiveness measures and scoring schemes: A comparison. *Personnel Psychology, 44,* 360. Reprinted by permission.

Reliability and validity are complex issues, and assessing them often requires a knowledge of statistics and measurement concepts, a complete discussion of which is beyond the scope of this book. HRD professionals who are unfamiliar with these concepts should read more about the topic or consult other members of the organization, knowledgeable professors, or consultants who are familiar with these issues.[38]

In addition to being reliable and valid, data collection methods must also be *practical*, given the constraints of the organization. **Practicality** concerns how much time, money, and resources are available for the evaluation method. For example, conducting interviews with all supervisors to assess employee job behavior may take more time than the staff has available. In this case, interviewing a sample of the supervisors or using a questionnaire may be practical alternatives. As we mentioned earlier, realistic and creative trade-offs can ensure that the evaluation effort is carried out and yields useful information.

## TYPES OF DATA

At least three types of data are available for evaluating HRD effectiveness: individual performance, systemwide performance, and economic.[39] Individual performance data emphasize the individual trainee's knowledge and behaviors (Kirkpatrick's Levels 2 and 3). Examples of these kinds of data include an employee's test scores, number of units produced, timeliness of performance, quality of performance, attendance, and attitudes. Systemwide performance data concern the team, the division, or the business unit in which the HRD program was conducted, or potentially could include data concerning the entire organization.

Examples of systemwide data include productivity, rework, scrap, customer and client satisfaction, and timeliness. Economic data report the financial and economic performance of the organization or the unit, that is, the bottom line, and include profits, product liability, avoidance of penalties (such as fines for noncompliance with laws and regulations), and market share. Economic data is what return on investment (ROI) and utility calculations are generally seeking to provide.

A complete evaluation effort is likely to include all three types of data. Different questions demand different kinds of information. For example, Robinson and Robinson list possible data choices to determine whether a sales training program has affected an organization's operations, including ratio of new accounts to old accounts, call-to-close ratio, average sale size, items per order, and add-on sales.[40] These and other data could be tracked for individuals, organizational units, or an entire organization. Another useful source for systemwide performance measures is a recent book by Tesoro and Tootson.[41] Again, the key is to carefully examine the questions being asked or the decisions being made when selecting which data to use.

### THE USE OF SELF-REPORT DATA

**Self-report data,** or data provided directly by individuals involved in the training program, is probably the most commonly used type of data in HR evaluation.[42] Recall that trainee reactions (Kirkpatrick's Level 1) remains the most widely used evaluation measure. Self-reports can offer personality data, attitudes, and perceptions and can provide information to measure the effectiveness of HRD or other programs. For example, the trainer may measure learning (Level 2) by asking trainees to judge how much they knew before training and how much they feel they know after training. Information collected this way, whether through interviews or questionnaires, can be useful and meaningful.

However, Podsakoff and Organ identify two serious problems that can occur when relying on self-report data:

1. **Mono-method bias.** If both reports in a before-and-after evaluation come from the same person at the same time (say, after training), conclusions may be questionable. The respondents may be more concerned about being consistent in their answers than about providing accurate responses.

2. **Socially desirable responses.** Respondents may report what they think the researcher (or boss) wants to hear rather than the truth. For example, employees may be too embarrassed to admit that they learned nothing in a training program.[43]

In addition, there can be what is referred to as a **response shift bias,** in which respondents' perspectives of their skills before training change during the training program and affect their after-training assessment.[44] For example, trainees may discover during training that their pretraining judgment of skill was unrealistically high and adjust their posttraining evaluations accordingly. As a result, the data may show no improvement of skill after training, even though such an improvement may have occurred.

Self-report data can be useful in HRD evaluation, but relying on self-report data alone can be problematic. Depending on the question being asked, direct observation by trained observers (like supervisors), tests, or simulations can often yield better, more conclusive information than self-reports.

## RESEARCH DESIGN

A research design is a plan for conducting an evaluation study. Research design is a complex topic. To inform yourself of all the issues surrounding research design, you could read a whole book just on that topic. Barring that, we would hope that you would read and understand a summary of key points on this topic. However, we also recognize that not every student (or instructor) sees the value of studying this information in the types of courses for which this text is used. So, for the most comprehensive treatment of this topic, we urge you to consult the resources listed in the following endnote.[45] For those who wish to see a thorough, though more condensed form of coverage of research design issues, we provide an appendix to this chapter that goes into much more detail than we do here. We have often found that students are much more interested in this material when they are faced with a project on the job, and they are looking for reference material to help them sort out the appropriate choices for a project they are designing ("What was it you said again was the minimal acceptable design for a training evaluation study?"), and the appendix provides you with some key information that can inform your decisions concerning the most appropriate research design to use for particular situations. At the minimum, however, there are some critical issues that every HRD student should understand. We present these below, and while this is far from a complete treatment of the topic, we hope to convey the importance of research design issues to effective HRD evaluation.

Research design is critical to HRD evaluation. It specifies the expected results of the evaluation study, the methods of data collection, and how the data will be analyzed. Awareness of research design issues and possible research design alternatives can help managers and HRD professionals do a better job of conducting evaluations and critiquing the results of evaluation studies.

When evaluating any training or HRD effort, the researcher or HRD professional would like to have a high level of confidence that any changes observed after the program or intervention were due to that intervention, and not to some other factor (such as changes in the economy, the organization, or the reward structure in place). This is the basic notion of validity, that is, are we confident in the accuracy of our conclusions?

Unfortunately, it still remains quite typical that if outcomes are measured at all, they are only collected *after* the training program has been completed. The basic picture is as follows:

Training provided                    Evaluation measures collected

The trainer would obviously like to see high values on each measure collected, for example, positive reactions, high scores on the learning measures, and positive indications of behavior change and results. But what might be some problems of collecting measures only *after* the training has been completed? For one thing, such a one-shot approach may not be measuring the most important things. Recall our earlier discussions of how evaluation should be tied directly to the objectives determined via the needs assessment process. An evaluation measure that is too broad or generic may not capture real changes that have occurred as a result of training. A second serious drawback of this after-only approach is that one can't be certain that the outcomes attained were due to the training. Simply put, this approach to evaluation doesn't give any indication of trainees' initial skill or knowledge level, that is, where they started from. To have greater confidence that the outcomes observed were brought about by the training (and not some other extraneous factor), the following practices should be included in the research design:

1. **Pretest and posttest** — Including both a pretest and a posttest allows the trainer to see what has changed after the training. If the majority of trainees already knew the material covered in training before they started it, then high scores on the posttest measure of learning become much less impressive.

2. **Control group** — A control group is a group of employees similar to those who receive training, yet who don't receive training at the same time as those who are trained. However, this group receives the same evaluation measures as the group that is trained, and this allows for a comparison of their scores. The ideal scenario is where the training group and the control group have similar scores before training, and then the scores for the training group increase after training, while those of the control group remain constant. This provides fairly strong evidence that the training (and not some other factor) was responsible for the changes on the outcome measures.

Combining these two points creates what can be called the "pretest-posttest with control group" research design. We view this as the minimum acceptable research design for most training and HRD evaluation efforts. There may be times when trainers have to get by with less, but the degree of confidence in one's findings will always be lower if one or both of these factors is missing (though see the Appendix for a reconsideration of "nonexperimental" research designs proposed by Sackett and Mullen).[46]

Two other factors should be included in a strong research design. First, if a control group is used, the trainer should ensure that the training and control groups are as similar as possible. For example, it would be unacceptable if the group receiving training had greater existing knowledge, skills, or abilities than the control group, as this would bias the results that were obtained after training. If the trainer is using existing or intact groups, he or she should use archival data to show that the two groups do not differ in any significant way (e.g., test scores and years of experience). Further, if it is possible, it is advantageous if the trainer randomly assign individuals to the training and control groups. Such **random assignment** further increases the confidence one can have that training brought about the observed changes (and, in this case, not some characteristic that differed between the two groups). It must be pointed out that in many real-life training settings, random assignment is seen as impractical, and is thus not widely used. However, random assignment increases the likelihood of obtaining valid results from one's evaluation efforts. A second factor to consider is the collection of data over time. Such an approach, called a **time series design,** allows the trainer to observe patterns in individual performance. For example, if performance is relatively steady over time, and then shows a clear spike after training, and then remains at this higher level over time, this would again suggest that the result was due to the training, and not some other factor.

A final point to make here has to do with sample size. Researchers and practitioners often get frustrated with one another over this issue, as the number of people providing data for a training evaluation is often lower than what would be recommended for purposes of statistical analysis. That is, there are practical limitations in many training situations that limit the number of people receiving training (or in the control group) to a relatively small number. One study of research on training evaluation found that the median sample size across these studies was 43 people.[47] Yet, having low numbers of trainees is often disastrous for statistical analyses because small sample sizes make it difficult to attain statistically significant results, *even when the training has in fact had an impact.* It is generally recommended that, as a bare minimum, the training and control groups each need at least thirty individuals in them in order to have even a moderate chance of obtaining statistically significant results. However, many researchers would prefer to see this number much higher than this, for example, at least 100 people in each condition (some researchers would go even higher). This is difficult to attain in many situations. One approach is to pool data within an organization (such as collecting data from the same training program offered over time). Also, recent efforts to combine data from different research studies via **meta-analysis** have also helped to determine the impact (or effect size) of various training interventions. For example, in a widely cited meta-analytic study, Burke and Day combined the results from many different studies to find the "average" effectiveness of numerous managerial training methods.[48] The main point, however, is that HRD professionals need to give careful thought to the sample size issue *before* they undertake their training and evaluation efforts. When sample sizes are small, it is much harder to show that the training intervention had a positive impact on desired individual and organizational outcomes.

Another vital topic for training evaluation has to do with ethics. Choices concerning evaluation often force the trainer or researcher to make difficult ethical decisions. These will be discussed next.

## ETHICAL ISSUES CONCERNING EVALUATION RESEARCH

Many of the decisions supervisors and HRD professionals make when conducting HRD evaluations have ethical dimensions. While resolving the paradoxes inherent in ethical dilemmas is no easy task, it is important that these issues be addressed. Actions such as assigning participants to training and control groups, reporting results, and the actual conduct of the evaluation study itself all raise ethical questions. Schmitt and Klimoski have identified four ethical issues relating to HRD evaluation: informed consent, withholding training, the use of deception, and pressure to produce findings.[49] To this list, we add the issue of confidentiality.

### CONFIDENTIALITY

Some evaluation research projects involve asking participants questions about their own or others' job performance. The results of these inquiries may be embarrassing or lead to adverse treatment by others if they are made public. For example, if evaluation of a management development seminar involves asking participants their opinion of their supervisors, supervisors may become angry with participants who report that they don't think the supervisors are doing a good job. Similarly, employees who perform poorly or make mistakes on important outcome measures (like written tests or role-playing exercises) may be ridiculed by other employees.

Wherever possible, steps should be taken to ensure the confidentiality of information collected during an evaluation study. Using code numbers rather than names, collecting only necessary demographic information, reporting group rather than individual results, using encrypted computer files, and securing research materials are all ways to maintain confidentiality. As a result of such efforts, employees may be more willing to participate in the evaluation project.

### INFORMED CONSENT

In many research settings, such as hospitals and academic institutions, evaluation studies are monitored by a review board to ensure that participants are aware that they are participating in a study and know its purpose, what they will be expected to do, and the potential risks and benefits of participating. In addition, participants are asked to sign a form stating that they have been informed of these facts and agree to participate in the study. This is called obtaining the participants' **informed consent.**

Review boards and informed consent are not common in many industrial settings; often the norm in these organizations is that management has control over and responsibility for employees, and that this is viewed as sufficient. We agree with Schmitt and Klimoski that ethical considerations and good management are compatible.[50] Wherever possible, informed consent should be obtained from employees who will participate in the evaluation study. Involving them in this way motivates researchers to treat the employees fairly, and it may actually improve the effectiveness of the training intervention by providing complete information.[51]

### WITHHOLDING TRAINING

Research designs involving control groups require that some employees receive training while others do not. This apparent partiality can be problematic if the training is believed to improve some employees' performance which could lead to organizational benefits like a raise or a promotion, or if the training could increase some employees' well-being, as in health-related programs. If the training is expected to be effective, is it fair to train some employees and not others just for purposes of evaluation?

There are at least three possible resolutions to this dilemma.[52] First, an unbiased procedure, such as a lottery, can be used to assign employees to training groups. Second, employees who are assigned to a control group can be assured that if the training is found to be effective, they will have the option of receiving the training at a later time. Third, the research design can be modified so that both groups are trained, but at different times. One possible design is illustrated below.

| Group 1: | Measure | Training | Measure | Measure |
|----------|---------|----------|---------|---------|
| Group 2: | Measure | Measure | Training | Measure |

In point of fact, when a large number of people are going to be trained in small groups over a period of time, this type of design is quite feasible. Whatever approach is used, dealing with the issue of withholding training is often a matter of practicality, in addition to an ethical matter. It is possible, for example, that employees assigned to a control group may refuse to participate in the study or be less motivated to complete the outcome measures.

## USE OF DECEPTION

In some cases, an investigator may feel that the study will yield better results if employees don't realize they are in an evaluation study, or if they are given some false or misleading information during the study. This is most often the case when the training is conducted as part of a formal research experiment, and less likely with more typical organizational evaluation practices. Nonetheless, we believe this practice is generally unethical and should be used only as a last resort. Employees who are deceived will probably become angry with the management, damaging a trust that is difficult to reestablish. Any benefits of the HRD program are likely to be undermined by the effects on employees who feel that they have been betrayed.

Alternatives to deception should be considered. If deception is used, it should be as minimal as possible, and employees in the study should be informed of the deception and the reasons for it as soon as their participation in the study ends.[53]

## PRESSURE TO PRODUCE POSITIVE RESULTS

HRD professionals and their managers may feel pressure to make certain that the results of their evaluation demonstrate that the program was effective. This may be one reason why rigorous evaluation of HRD programs is not done more often. The HRD people are the ones who design and develop (or purchase), deliver, and evaluate the program. If the evaluation shows the program was not effective, the HRD department may lose funding and support and have their activities curtailed.

Although the possibility exists for "fraud" in the form of doctoring results, reporting partial results, or setting up biased studies, it is unclear how often this occurs in HRD evaluation. Given that reports of evaluation fraud in other areas of organizational life are fairly common, one cannot help but have some concerns about the state of affairs in HRD evaluation.

Professional standards and ethical conduct call for those conducting HRD evaluations to report complete results. That having been said, it is no doubt difficult for many people to face the potential consequences of bad results. This leads to our last major topic in this chapter, namely, how to demonstrate that a training intervention has had a positive impact on important organizational measures.

## ASSESSING THE IMPACT OF HRD PROGRAMS IN DOLLAR TERMS

Following both Kirkpatrick's and Phillips' views on levels of evaluation, one of the more important issues to examine is the effect of the HRD program on the organization's effectiveness. This assessment can be done using a variety of performance indexes, such as productivity and timeliness, but dollars are the most common language understood by managers in most functional areas of an organization. It is important to demonstrate effectiveness on the reaction, learning, and job behavior levels, but HR managers and HRD professionals may be at a disadvantage when their results are compared to those of other divisions that are able to express their results in monetary terms.

One of the goals of translating the effects of training and HRD programs into dollar terms is to make clear that the programs are **investments** and as such will lead to payoffs for the organization in the future. Although many managers and supervisors pay lip service to this idea, they often see HRD and other HR interventions primarily as **costs** — exemplified by the fact that HR programs are often the first programs to be cut when financial and economic pressures force the organization to reduce its expenses.

It has long been argued that HR programs are difficult to assess in financial terms, but the **evaluation of training costs** and **utility analysis** are two practical options to help the HRD professional determine the financial impact of various programs.

### EVALUATION OF TRAINING COSTS

Evaluation of training costs compares the costs incurred in conducting an HRD program to the benefits received by the organization, and can involve two categories of activities: cost-benefit evaluation and cost-effectiveness evaluation.[54] **Cost-benefit analysis** involves comparing the monetary costs of training to the benefits received in nonmonetary terms, like improvements in attitudes, safety, and health. **Cost-effectiveness analysis** focuses on the financial benefits accrued from training, such as increases in quality and profits, and reduction in waste and processing time.[55]

Models, including the model of cost effectiveness offered by Cullen et al., can be very helpful in evaluating the costs of training. This model distinguishes between structured and unstructured training, and it lists possible training costs (e.g., the cost of developing the training, materials, time, and production losses) and benefits (improvements in time to reach job competency, job performance, and work attitudes).

Robinson and Robinson have developed a similar model, dividing training costs into five categories: direct costs, indirect costs, development costs, overhead costs, and compensation for participants (see Table 7-5).[56] These training costs are then compared to benefits as measured by improvements in operational indicators, such as job performance, quality, and work attitudes.

The general strategy for evaluating training costs is to measure cost and benefit indicators in dollar terms (or translate them to dollar terms) and then compare them. For example, a program's **return on investment (ROI)** can be calculated by dividing total results by total costs:

$$\text{Return on investment} = \frac{\text{Results}}{\text{Training Costs}}$$

The greater the ratio of results to costs, the greater the benefit the organization receives by conducting the training program. If the ratio is less than 1, then the training program costs more than it returns to the organization. Such a program either needs to be modified or dropped (of course, at times there may be some noneconomic or legally mandated reason to continue a certain training program; even here, however, if the ROI for this program is negative, some rethinking or reworking of the program is likely in order).

Table 7-6 shows how Robinson and Robinson applied their model to calculate the costs for a training program they conducted at a wood-panel producing plant. Table 7-7 shows how they calculated the results and return on investment for the same plant.[57]

*Issues in Computing and Using ROI Estimates.*    The issues surrounding using ROI estimates as a way to express the contribution of an HRD program have received increasing attention. Two lines of thinking deserve comment. First, some writers have described recommendations and practices for how to compute ROI. For example, Jack Phillips published a three-article series in *Training & Development* that advocated using ROI ratios and offered advice on how HRD practitioners could do this.[58] (Recall that Phillips proposed a modification of Kirkpatrick's four-level evaluation model to include ROI as Level 5.) Phillips also published a very useful book on HRD evaluation.[59] Some of his suggestions focused on research design and data collection issues, while others explain the steps and calculations one would make in arriving at an ROI figure. For example, Phillips offered the following five-step process for collecting the information needed and calculating ROI:

**■ TABLE 7-5**

To calculate the cost of a training program, an HRD professional should consider five categories of expenses.

**Direct costs**

These are costs directly associated with the delivery of the learning activities. They include course materials (reproduced or purchased), instructional aids, equipment rental, travel, food and other refreshments, and the instructor's salary and benefits.

Such costs are so directly tied to the delivery of a particular program that if you canceled the program the day before you planned to conduct it, you would not incur them. (While program materials may have been reproduced or purchased, they would not be consumed, and so they would be available for a future program.)

**Indirect costs**

These costs are incurred in support of learning activities, but cannot be identified with any particular program. Even if the program were canceled at the last minute, such costs could not be recovered.

Examples would be costs for instructor preparation, clerical and administrative support, course materials already sent to participants, and time spent by the training staff in planning the program's implementation. Expenses for marketing the program (e.g., direct-mail costs) would also be considered indirect costs. Marketing may have cost $2,000. If there is insufficient registration and if the program is canceled, the $2,000 cannot be recovered.

**Development costs**

All costs incurred during the development of the program go in this category. Typically, they include the development of videotapes and computer-based instructional programming, design of program materials, piloting of the program, and any necessary redesign. This category also includes the cost of the front-end assessment, or that portion of the assessment directly attributed to the program. In addition, the costs of evaluation and tracking are included.

If a program is to be conducted for a few years, the cost is often amortized over that period. For example, one-third of the development cost may be charged off in the first year of implementation, one-third in the second year, and one-third in the last year. Otherwise, there is a real "bulge" in the budget, because of development costs during the first year.

**Overhead costs**

These costs are not directly related to a training program, but are essential to the smooth operation of the training department.

If you have audiovisual equipment that has been purchased specifically for your department, there is a cost to maintain that equipment. Some portion of that annual cost should be charged to the various training programs. If you have classroom space available to you, there is an overhead cost for supplying heat and lighting. The cost of supporting that space for days when the classroom is used for particular courses should be charged to those programs.

**Compensation for participants**

These costs comprise the salaries and benefits paid to participants for the time they are in a program. If the program is two days long, salaries and benefits for your participants for those two days are costs of the program.

Typically, HRD professionals do not know what individual people earn, but can obtain that information by asking the compensation department to provide a figure for an average salary paid to the various levels of people who will be attending. The average salary is then multiplied by the number of people attending the program, to derive a compensation estimate.

SOURCE: From D. G. Robinson & J. Robinson (1989). Training for impact. *Training and Development Journal*, 43 (8), 39. Reprinted by permission.

**■ TABLE 7-6**

Direct costs: The travel and per diem cost is zero, because training took place adjacent to the plant. There is a cost for classroom space and audiovisual equipment, because these were rented from a local hotel. Refreshments were purchased at the same hotel. Because different supervisors attended the morning and afternoon sessions, lunch was not provided.

**Direct Costs**

| | | |
|---|---|---|
| Outside Instructor | | 0 |
| In-house instructor — 12 days × $125 | $ | 1,500.00 |
| Fringe benefits @ 25% of salary | $ | 375.00 |
| Travel and per diem expenses | | 0 |
| Materials — 56 × $60/participant | $ | 3,360.00 |
| Classroom space and audiovisual equipment — 12 days @ $50 | $ | 600.00 |
| Food, refreshments— $4/day × 3 days × 56 participants | $ | 672.00 |
| **Total direct costs** | $ | 6,507.00 |

Indirect costs: The clerical and administrative costs reflect the amount of clerical time spent on making arrangements for the workshop facilities, sending out notices to all participants, and preparing class rosters and other miscellaneous materials.

**Indirect Costs**

| | | |
|---|---|---|
| Training management | | 0 |
| Clerical/administrative | $ | 750.00 |
| Fringe benefits — 25% of clerical/ administrative salary | $ | 187.00 |
| Postage, shipping, telephone | | 0 |
| Pre- and postlearning materials— $4 × 56 participants | $ | 224.00 |
| **Total indirect costs** (rounded to nearest dollar) | $ | 1,161.00 |

Development costs: These costs represent the purchase of the training program from a vendor. Included are instructional aids, an instructor manual, videotapes, and a licensing fee. The instructor-training costs pertain to the one-week workshop that the instructor attended to become prepared to facilitate the training. Front-end assessment costs were covered by the corporate training budget.

**Development Costs**

| | | |
|---|---|---|
| Fee to purchase program | $ | 3,600.00 |
| Instructor training | | |
| Registration fee | $ | 1,400.00 |
| Travel and lodging | $ | 975.00 |
| Salary | $ | 625.00 |
| Benefits (25 percent of salary) | $ | 156.00 |
| **Total development costs** | $ | 6,756.00 |

Overhead costs: These represent the services that the general organization provides to the training unit. Because figures were not available, we used 10 percent of the direct, indirect, and program development costs.

**Overhead Costs**

| | | |
|---|---|---|
| General organization support | 10 percent of direct, indirect, and development costs | |
| Top management's time | | |
| **Total overhead costs** | $ | 1,443.00 |

Compensation for participants: This figure represents the salaries and benefits paid to all participants while they attended the workshop.

**Compensation for Participants**

Participants' salary and benefits (time away from the job)

| | | |
|---|---|---|
| **Total compensation** | $16,696.00 | |
| **Total training costs** | $32,564.00 | |
| **Cost per participant** | $ | 581.50 |

SOURCE: From D. G. Robinson & J. Robinson (1989). Training for impact. *Training and Development Journal, 43* (8), 40. Reprinted by permission.

■ **TABLE 7-7**

| Operational Results Area | How Measured | Results Before Training | Results After Training | Differences (+ or −) | Expressed in $ |
|---|---|---|---|---|---|
| Quality of panels | % rejected | 2% rejected 1,440 panels per day | 1.5% rejected 1,080 panels per day | .5% 360 panels | $720 per day $172,800 per year |
| Housekeeping | Visual inspection using 20-item checklist | 10 defects (average) | 2 defects (average) | 8 defects | Not measurable in $ |
| Preventable accidents | Number of accidents | 24 per year | 16 per year | 8 per year | |
| | Direct cost of each accident | $144,000 per year | $96,000 per year | $48,000 | $48,000 per year |

Total savings: $220,800.00

$$\text{ROI} = \frac{\text{Return}}{\text{Investment}} = \frac{\text{Operational Results}}{\text{Training Costs}}$$

$$= \frac{\$220,800}{\$32,564} = 6.8$$

SOURCE: From D. G. Robinson & J. Robinson (1989). Training for impact. *Training and Development Journal, 43* (8), 41. Reprinted by permission.

1. Collect Level 4 evaluation data: Ask, Did on-the-job application produce measurable results?
2. Isolate the effects of training from other factors that may have contributed to the results.
3. Convert the results to monetary benefits.
4. Total the costs of training.
5. Compare the monetary benefits with the costs.[60]

Steps 1 and 2 focus on research design issues. With regard to step 3, Phillips advocates collecting both hard and soft data (e.g., units produced and accident costs, employee attitudes and frequency of use of new skills) that demonstrate a program's effectiveness. This step would obviously be part of the evaluation study. Once this collection is done, Phillips provides suggestions concerning how to convert the data to monetary terms (e.g., using historic costs and estimates from various sources). In a similar vein, Parry provides a worksheet that HRD professionals can use to identify and summarize the costs and benefits associated with an HRD program.[61] More recently, Parry provided several helpful worksheets to assist in the calculation of both ROI and cost-benefit estimates.[62]

Phillips also made several suggestions regarding how to increase the credibility of ROI estimates and the cost estimates they are built on.[63] These include using conservative estimates of costs, finding reliable sources for estimates, explaining the assumptions and techniques used to compute costs, and relying on hard data whenever possible. Beyond this, Parry suggests having managers and supervisors calculate training costs.[64] He sees their involvement as a way to remove the potential suspicion that an HRD professional may try to place the data in the most favorable light to his or her own area.

The second line of thinking regarding ROI estimates focuses on whether and when ROI estimates should be used. Recognizing the time and cost involved in creating ROI estimates, Phillips observed that some organizations set targets for how many HRD programs should be evaluated at this level. He cites evaluating 5 percent of an organization's HRD programs at the ROI level as an example of a target that could be used.[65] Willyerd sounds an even more cautionary note on the use of ROI estimates.[66] She points out that some writers (e.g., Kaplan and Norton) question the overreliance on accounting and financial measures in business in general, and instead call for using an approach to performance measurement that balances a number of perspectives (e.g., financial, customer, internal process, and innovation and learning).[67] Willyerd suggests that HRD professionals would be wise to follow Kaplan and Norton's notion of a **balanced scorecard** when presenting the effectiveness of HRD programs, and that they collect and communicate data from each of the four perspectives.[68] Doing this, she argues, avoids the shortcomings of relying strictly on financial measures, while still communicating the impact of the HRD program on all of the organization's strategic dimensions.

We hope this surge of interest in ROI will encourage HRD practitioners to attempt to use ROI estimates as one of the ways they communicate the value of HRD programs. However, we agree with the authors who counsel caution in using these estimates and taking steps to build credibility with management. After all, HRD evaluation is about supporting decisions. Different decisions call for different supporting data, and building credibility can ensure that decision makers will actually heed and use the data provided.

*UTILITY ANALYSIS.*    Usually, the results of an evaluation study express the effect of an HRD program in terms of a change in some aspect of the trainee's performance or behavior. For example, if untrained employees average 22.5 units produced (per day, or per hour) and trained employees average 26 units produced, the gain due to training is 3.5 units per employee. **Utility analysis** provides a way to translate these results into dollar terms. One popular approach to utility analysis is the Brogden-Cronbach-Gleser model.[69] This model computes the gain to the organization in dollar terms, $\Delta U$, or "change in utility", using the following variables:

**N** = Number of trainees

**T** = Length of time the benefits are expected to last

$d_t$ = An effect size, which expresses the true difference of job performance between the trained and untrained groups (expressed in standard deviation units)

$SD_y$ = Dollar value of job performance of untrained employees (expressed in standard deviation units)

**C** = Costs of conducting the training

Wayne Cascio has combined these elements into a formula to compute the dollar value of improved performance due to training.[70] The left side of the equation estimates the benefits of training, while the right side presents the cost. The formula is:

$$\Delta U = (N)(T)(d_t)(SD_y) - C$$

Some of the terms in the equation can be directly measured, such as **N, C,** and $d_t$, but others, such as **T** and $SD_y$, typically must be estimated. More complicated versions of this formula have been developed to account for other factors that may affect the real monetary value of the benefits accrued, such as attrition and decay in the strength of training effects over time.[71]

Cascio also suggests a method for incorporating the results of utility analysis into cost-benefit analysis for training and HRD programs.[72] Drawing upon techniques of capital budgeting, the three phases of Cascio's approach are as follows:

1. Compute the minimum annual benefits required to break even on the program (e.g., how much of a payback must the program generate in order to cover its costs?).
2. Use break-even analysis to determine the minimum effect size **($d_t$)** that will yield the minimum required annual benefit (how much of an improvement in job performance must the trained employees show for the program to generate the payback needed to break even?).
3. Use the results from meta-analytic studies to determine the expected effect size and expected payoff from the program (what is the likely degree of improvement in job performance that the HRD program being proposed has shown in previously conducted research on this program or method?).

The goal of such cost-benefit analyses is to put HRD professionals on a more equal footing with other managers, so they can demonstrate the expected gains of their programs and compare these gains to either the gains from several HRD programs or other potential investments (like the purchase of a new piece of equipment). Although the computational formulas for this approach are somewhat complex, Cascio argues that they can be computerized, thereby requiring only that the HRD manager or professional determine and input the values that correspond to each of the key parameters (like cost, benefits, and effect size).

### EXERCISE: A UTILITY CALCULATION

Assume you work in the HRD function for a large manufacturing facility. Employees have been placed into work teams, and top management is now considering providing additional formal cross-training to team members so that people will be able to do a variety of different tasks within the team. However, the lowest possible cost available for a high quality training program is determined to be $2,000 per employee. In light of this cost, management has asked you to estimate the potential value (utility) of this training program. Initial training will be provided to thirty team members, and their performance will be compared to thirty other employees who have not been trained. To be conservative, you've decided to assume that the effects of training last for one year (though you obviously hope the impact lasts much longer).

Two critical items that you need to calculate a utility estimate are $d_t$ and $SD_y$. After training, you find that the trained employees can now produce an average of 26 units per day, while the untrained employees produce 22.5. To calculate $d_t$, you need to take the difference between these two numbers, and divide this number by the standard deviation in units produced for the trained group. In this case, the standard deviation in units produced turns out to be 5 units per day. The other critical item to determine is $SD_y$. In a manufacturing setting such as this, you can look at actual productivity levels for all employees in this job category and calculate the difference between an employee at the mean or average productivity level and an employee one standard deviation above the mean. From company records, you determine that this number is $10,000.

You now have all the information you need to calculate a utility estimate for this situation. First of all, using the formula above from Cascio, what is the projected benefit to the organization of training these thirty team members? What was the cost? What is the estimated change in utility of this training? How would you present this information to top management, as it considers whether to use this training program for other employees in the organization?

While utility analysis can help to translate the benefits of training programs into dollar terms, many training professionals have concerns about the practicality of such efforts. Further, some researchers have questioned its value due to the nature of the estimates used to determine some of the factors in the formula.[73] Latham reports that economists have not accepted this form of analysis, as it has been developed and refined largely by psychologists.[74] It is also unclear to what extent HR and HRD professionals use utility analysis to communicate the effectiveness of HRD programs. Given that utility analysis is intended to help managers see HRD programs as an investment and to make more informed decisions about HRD programs, it is reasonable to ask whether their decisions are influenced by utility estimates. Research on this question has produced mixed results. On the one hand, Latham and Whyte found that managers are not influenced in the way HR practitioners would hope.[75] They found that including utility analysis information actually *reduced* managers' support for a valid employee selection program. These results led Latham and Whyte to wonder whether managers do in fact make decisions regarding HR programs rationally (a key assumption that underlies the use of dollar information like utility analysis). Similarly, Hazer and Highhouse observed that "the degree to which managers accept the notion that the effectiveness of HR programs can be measured in terms of dollars remains an open question" (p. 110).[76] One the other hand, Morrow, Jarrett, and Rupinski report that having a senior management team that 1) is interested in a serious demonstration that HRD programs are a worthwhile investment and 2) pre-approves the utility model and procedures to be used will lead to acceptance of utility information as legitimate.[77]

We believe that utility analysis (in addition to ROI and cost estimates) presents an opportunity for HRD professionals to provide information to decision makers in dollar terms. However, we agree with authors such as Hazer and Highhouse and Latham that simply providing managers with the dollar estimates generated by utility analysis will not by itself be sufficient to gain acceptance or use.[78] As with ROI estimates, gaining management acceptance appears to be a key consideration. Michael Sturman recently proposed a number of modifications to the equations that are used to calculate utility estimates. He concludes his article by stating that "for a complex decision-making tool to be useful, the users of the decision aid must desire the information it provides and be trained in its use" (p. 297).[79] Commenting on the Whyte and Latham results mentioned above, Sturman continues, "We should not be surprised that an individual untrained with a use of a decision aid fails to adhere to the results of the aid" (p. 297).[80] Toward that end, we provide below a list of recommendations offered by various authors that should increase the chances that management will accept and use utility information:

- Involve senior management in determining the utility model and procedures to be used.
- Train HR professionals and managers in the details of utility analysis.
- Offer an explanation of the components of the utility model.
- Involve management in arriving at estimates.
- Use credible and conservative estimates.
- Admit that the results of utility analysis are often based on fallible but reasonable estimates.
- Use utility analysis to compare alternatives, rather than to justify individual programs.[81]

Finally, it is important to remember that not all decision makers, and not all HRD programs, require justification in dollar terms. We agree with Latham's suggestion that HRD professionals find out from senior managers what they consider when they determine the value of HRD programs and provide management with information in those terms.[82] For some organizations, this may include the dollar value, while in others demonstrating positive improvements in nonmonetary terms may be preferred. A lively debate concerning the inclusion of "values" (other than financial return) in HRD evaluation was presented in *Human Resource Development Quarterly*.[83] Interested readers are encouraged to look further into

## MEASURING ORGANIZATIONAL RESULTS WITHOUT MEASURING ROI[1]

St. Lukes Medical Center is a large healthcare provider in northeastern Pennsylvania. They began a major team-building initiative in the early 1990s and were able to show early on that trainees liked the program, and that behavioral change was taking place. In attempting to demonstrate the value of this training to the organization, Robert Weigand and Richard Wagner considered using utility and ROI formulas similar to those presented in this chapter. They ended up using a simpler approach, which was based on determining what organizational outcomes had changed as a result of the changed behaviors produced by the training initiative. Some of the organizational consequences that they hypothesized (and found) to be impacted by training included:

- changes in turnover rates

- fewer employees needed to staff various shifts and departments

- increased patient return rates (due to satisfaction with the service provided)

- patient recommendations of the medical center to others

It is significant that, in most cases, the medical center was already able to provide the data needed to make such evaluations, that is, no HRD professional or researcher needed to collect new information. Finding tangible changes in the organization is especially critical for a team-building project, where such "soft" skills as listening, delegating, and decision making are emphasized. Using the organization's own measures to capture the value of such training was sufficient in this case to demonstrate the positive impact of training on the organization. While this takes nothing away from efforts to convert such measures into "dollar metrics" (as in ROI or utility analysis), this example suggests that with some common sense and hard work, Level 4 evaluation is doable — and is being done.

[1]Weigand, R. J. & Wagner, R. J. (1999). Results-oriented training evaluation. *The Quality Resource,* 18(4), July/August, 1–5; Wagner, R. J., & Weigand, R. (1998). Evaluating an outdoor-based training program — A search for results: St. Luke's Hospital. In D. L. Kirkpatrick (ed.), *Evaluating training programs: The four levels* (2nd ed.). San Francisco: Berrett-Koehler, 204–220.

these issues, as they again remind us of the ethical issues involved in all evaluation efforts. Finally, we present you with an interesting situation where researchers moved *away from* utility analysis and ROI calculations, and still managed to provide meaningful organizational-level data on the impact of training (see the boxed insert nearby).

## A CLOSING COMMENT ON HRD EVALUATION

HRD professionals should recognize the importance of evaluating HRD programs and the variety of ways evaluation can be conducted. Given the myriad choices and the many constraints placed on HRD efforts, Grove and Ostroff recommend following these six steps:

1. Perform a needs analysis.
2. Develop an explicit evaluation strategy.
3. Insist on specific training objectives.

**RETURN TO OPENING CASE**[1]

The challenge faced by Dave Palm at LensCrafters was to show a clear link between training and the organization's bottom-line financial results. This is what Jack Phillips has referred to as Level 5 evaluation, emphasizing how the monetary value of training exceeds the costs.

Your instructor has additional information on what was done at LensCrafters to meet this challenge to provide evidence for the effectiveness of company training.

[1]Purcell, A. (2000). 20/20 ROI. *Training & Development*, 54(7), July, 28-33.

4. Obtain participant reactions.
5. Develop criterion instruments (to measure valued outcomes).
6. Plan and execute the evaluation study.[84]

Not every program needs to be evaluated to the same extent. New programs and those with high visibility and expense should be evaluated more rigorously and more thoroughly than proven programs and those that are offered less frequently. The key is to have a well-planned evaluation strategy that sets the stage for how and to what extent each program will be evaluated. While those with little evaluation experience may see this task as daunting and burdensome, it remains an essential aspect of human resource development. The challenges now faced by organizations, and the importance of HRD in meeting those challenges, demand serious and sustained evaluation efforts—and results.

### Summary

In this chapter, we introduced the last phase of the training process: HRD evaluation. HRD evaluation is defined as the systematic collection of descriptive and judgmental information necessary to make effective training decisions related to the selection, adoption, value, and modification of various instructional activities. The purposes of HRD evaluation include determining whether the programs have achieved their objectives, building credibility and support for programs, and establishing the value of HRD programs.

We discussed a number of frameworks and models of the evaluation process to emphasize the many options available when evaluating HRD programs. Kirkpatrick's approach, which is the earliest and most popular, proposes four levels of evaluation: participant reaction, learning, behavior, and results. Many of the other frameworks (e.g., CIPP, CIRO, Brinkerhoff, Kaufman and Keller) build upon Kirkpatrick's approach, and expand the focus of evaluation beyond measuring post-program effectiveness, or include elements not explicitly stated by Kirkpatrick, or seek to do both. In addition, two models (Kraiger et al. and Holton) are attempts to create evaluation models that are both theory- and research-based.

Data collection is central to HRD evaluation. Among the types of information that may be collected are individual, systemwide, and economic data. Some of the data collection methods used in HRD evaluation include interviews, surveys, observation, archival data, and tests and simulations.

Options for designing the evaluation study were also presented. The research design provides a plan for conducting the evaluation effort. It spells out the types of information to be collected, how it will be collected, and the data analysis techniques to be used. The design should balance the need for making valid conclusions with practical and ethical concerns. We presented several issues that should be addressed in choosing an appropriate design.

HRD professionals are often asked to justify the allocation of resources. This involves a financial assessment of the impact of HRD programs. This assessment can be done by evaluating training costs using cost-benefit or cost-effectiveness analysis or by translating a trained employee's productivity into dollar terms through utility analysis. More and better efforts are needed at demonstrating the impact of HRD programs on the effectiveness of the organization as a whole.

## KEY TERMS AND CONCEPTS

| | |
|---|---|
| control group | random assignment |
| cost-benefit analysis | reaction criteria |
| cost-effectiveness analysis | research design |
| evaluation | reliability |
| informed consent | results criteria |
| internal validity | return on investment (ROI) |
| job behavior criteria | self-report data |
| learning criteria | statistical power |
| meta-analysis | utility analysis |
| practicality | validity |

## QUESTIONS FOR DISCUSSION

1. Because many HRD professionals agree that HRD evaluation is valuable, why isn't it practiced more frequently by organizations? Identify and describe two reasons why evaluation might not be done. How could the objections raised by these reasons be overcome?

2. Describe the four levels of evaluation that make up Kirkpatrick's model of evaluation. Identify one example of data at each level that might be collected to provide evidence for the effectiveness of a class or training program you have participated in.

3. What do the CIPP and Brinkerhoff models of evaluation add to evaluation that is not included in Kirkpatrick's model? What benefit, if any, is there to viewing evaluation in this way?

4. Suppose you have been asked to design a program intended to train airline flight attendant trainees in emergency evacuation procedures. You are now

designing the evaluation study to show that the flight attendants understand the procedures and use them on the job. Which data collection methods do you think would be the most useful in providing this evidence? How might the type of learning outcome affect your choice of how you measure learning? Support your decision.

5. Identify and describe three potential problems with using self-report measures (e.g., participant questionnaires) in HRD evaluation. How can these problems be minimized?

6. Why is the issue of statistical power important to HRD evaluation? Describe two ways a researcher can increase power while controlling the cost of evaluation.

7. Identify and describe at least three ethical considerations in conducting evaluation research. How do these factors affect the evaluation effort?

8. What is the advantage, if any, to expressing the benefits of conducting HRD programs in dollar terms? Briefly describe the return on investment and utility analysis approaches. What are the limitations to using these approaches? How can they be overcome?

9. Using the information in the appendix, compare and contrast experimental and quasiexperimental research designs. Is one type of design superior to the other? Support your answer.

### REFERENCES

1. Goldstein, I. L. (1980). Training in work organizations. *Annual Review of Psychology, 31,* 229–272, p. 237.

2. Phillips, J. J. (1983). *Handbook of training evaluation and measurement methods.* Houston: Gulf Publishing.

3. Zenger, J. H., & Hargis, K. (1982). Assessment of training results: It's time to take the plunge! *Training and Development Journal, 36*(1), 11–16.

4. Saari, L. M., Johnson, T. R., McLaughlin, S. D., & Zimmerle, D. M. (1988). A survey of management training and education practices in U.S. companies. *Personnel Psychology, 41,* 731–743.

5. *2000 State of the Industry Report* (2000). Alexandria, VA: ASTD.

6. Goldstein (1980), *supra* note 1; Latham, G. P. (1988). Human resource training and development. *Annual Review of Psychology, 39,* 545–582; Wexley, K. N. (1984). Personnel training. *Annual Review of Psychology, 35,* 519–551.

7. Saari et al. (1988), *supra* note 4; *2000 State of the Industry Report* (2000), *supra* note 5.

8. Goldstein (1980), *supra* note 1.

9. Brinkerhoff, R. O. (1987). *Achieving results from training.* San Francisco: Jossey-Bass; Bushnell, D. S. (1990). Input, process, output: A model for evaluating training. *Training and Development Journal, 44*(3), 41–43; Galvin, J. C. (1983). What trainers can learn from educators about evaluating management training. *Training and Development Journal, 37*(8), 52–57; Kirkpatrick, D. L. (1967). Evaluation. In R. L. Craig and L. R. Bittel (eds.), *Training and development handbook* (87–112). New York: McGraw-Hill; Kirkpatrick, D. L. (1987). Evaluation. In R. L. Craig (ed.)

*Training and development handbook* (3rd ed.) (301–319). New York: McGraw-Hill; Kirkpatrick, D. L. (1994). *Evaluating training programs: The four levels.* San Francisco: Berrett-Koehler; Warr, P., Bird, M., & Rackham, N. (1970). *Evaluation of management training.* London: Gower Press.

10. Kirkpatrick (1967, 1987, 1994), *supra* note 9.

11. *2000 State of the Industry Report* (2000), *supra* note 5.

12. *Ibid.*

13. Bushnell (1990), *supra* note 9.

14. Holton, E. F., III (1996). The flawed four-level evaluation model. *Human Resource Development Quarterly, 7,* 5–21.

15. Kraiger, K., Ford, J. K., & Salas, E. (1993). Application of cognitive, skill-based, and affective theories of learning outcomes to new methods of training evaluation. *Journal of Applied Psychology, 78,* 311–328.

16. Alliger, G. M., & Janak, E. A. (1989). Kirkpatrick's levels of training criteria: Thirty years later. *Personnel Psychology, 42,* 331–342.

17. Kirkpatrick, D. L. (1996). Invited reaction: Reaction to Holton article. *Human Resource Development Quarterly, 7,* 23–25.

18. Kaufman, R., & Keller, J. M. (1994). Levels of evaluation: Beyond Kirkpatrick. *Human Resource Development Quarterly, 5,* 371–380.

19. Warr, P., & Bunce, D. (1995). Trainee characteristics and the outcomes of open learning. *Personnel Psychology, 48,* 348–374.

20. Kaufman & Keller (1994), *supra* note 18.

21. Phillips, J. J. (1996). ROI: The search for the best practices. *Training and Development, 50*(2), 43–47.

22. Galvin (1983), *supra* note 9.

23. Warr et al. (1970), *supra* note 9.

24. Brinkerhoff (1987), *supra* note 9.

25. Bushnell (1990), *supra* note 9.

26. Kraiger et al. (1993), *supra* note 15.

27. Holton (1996), *supra* note 14.

28. Kaufman, & Keller (1994), *supra* note 18; Warr & Bunce (1995), *supra* note 19; Phillips (1996), *supra* note 21.

29. Brinkerhoff (1987), *supra* note 9.

30. Alliger & Janak (1989), *supra* note 16; Alliger, G. M., Tannenbaum, S. I., Bennett, W., Jr., Traver, H., & Shotland, A. (1997). A meta-analysis of the relations among training criteria. *Personnel Psychology, 50,* 341–358.

31. Alliger et al. (1997), *supra* note 30.

32. Werner, J. M., O'Leary-Kelly, A. M., Baldwin, T. T., & Wexley, K. N. (1994). Augmenting behavior-modeling training: Testing the effects of pre- and post-training interventions. *Human Resource Development Quarterly, 5*(2), 169–183.

33. Holton (1996), *supra* note 14.

34. Campbell, D., & Graham, M. (1988). *Drugs and alcohol in the workplace: A guide for managers.* New York: Facts on File.

35. *Ibid*; Robinson, D. G., & Robinson, J. (1989). Training for impact. *Training and Development Journal, 43*(8), 34–42.

36. Kraiger, et al. (1993), *supra* note 15.

37. Ostroff, C. (1991). Training effectiveness measures and scoring schemes: A comparison. *Personnel Psychology, 44,* 353–374.

38. Anastasi, A. (1982). *Psychological testing.* New York: Macmillan.; Cook, T. D., & Campbell, D. T. (1979). *Quasi-experimentation: Design and analysis issues for field settings.* Chicago: Rand McNally; Cook, T. D, Campbell, D. T., & Peracchio, L. (1990). Quasi-experimentation. In M. D. Dunnette and L. M. Hough (eds.) *Handbook of industrial and organizational psychology* (2nd ed., vol. 1) (491–576). Palo Alto, CA: Consulting Psychologists Press; Sackett, P. R., & Larson, J. R., Jr. (1990). Research strategies and tactics in industrial and organizational psychology. In M. D. Dunnette and L. M. Hough (eds.) *Handbook of industrial and organizational psychology* (2nd ed., vol. 1) (419–489). Palo Alto, CA: Consulting Psychologists Press; Schmitt, N. W., & Klimoski, R. J. (1991). *Research methods in human resources management.* Cincinnati, OH: South-Western.

39. Phillips (1983), *supra* note 2; Phillips, J. J. (1996). How much is the training worth? *Training and Development, 50*(4), 20–24; Robinson & Robinson (1989), *supra* note 35.

40. Robinson & Robinson (1989), *supra* note 35.

41. Tesoro, F., & Tootson, J. (2000). *Implementing global performance measurement systems: A cookbook approach.* San Francisco: Jossey-Bass/Pfeiffer.

42. Podsakoff, P. M., & Organ, D. W. (1986). Self-reports in organization research: Problems and prospects. *Journal of Management, 12,* 531–544.

43. *Ibid.*

44. Sprangers, M., & Hoogstraten, J. (1989). Pretesting effects in retrospective pretest-posttest designs. *Journal of Applied Psychology, 74,* 265–272.

45. Campbell, D. T., & Stanley, J. C. (1966). *Experimental and quasi-experimental designs for research.* Chicago: Rand McNally; Cook & Campbell (1979), *supra* note 38; Sackett, P. R., & Larson, J. R., Jr. (1990). Research strategies and tactics in industrial and organizational psychology. In M. D. Dunnette and L. M. Hough (eds.) *Handbook of industrial and organizational psychology* (2nd ed., vol. 1) (419–489). Palo Alto, CA: Consulting Psychologists Press; Schmitt & Klimoski (1991), *supra* note 37.

46. Sackett, P. R., & Mullen, E. J. (1993). Beyond formal experimental design: Towards an expanded view of the training evaluation process. *Personnel Psychology, 46,* 613–627.

47. Arvey, R. D., Cole, D. A., Hazucha, J. F., & Hartanto, F. M. (1985). Statistical power of training evaluation designs. *Personnel Psychology, 38,* 493–507.

48. Burke, M. J., & Day, R. R. (1986). A cumulative study of the effectiveness of managerial training. *Journal of Applied Psychology, 71,* 232–245.

49. Schmitt & Klimoski (1991), *supra* note 38.

50. *Ibid.*

51. Hicks, W. D., & Klimoski, R. J. (1987). Entry into training programs and its effects on training outcomes: A field experiment. *Academy of Management Journal, 30,* 542–552.

52. Cook & Campbell (1979), *supra* note 38.

53. Fromkin, H. L., & Streufert, S. (1976). Laboratory experimentation. In M. D. Dunnette (ed.), *Handbook of industrial and organizational psychology* (415–465). New York: Rand McNally.

54. Cascio, W. F. (2000). Costing human resources: The financial impact of behavior in organizations (4th ed.). Cincinnati, OH: South-Western College Publishing.

55. Cullen, J. G., Swazin, S. A., Sisson, G. R., & Swanson, R. A. (1978). Cost effectiveness: A model for assessing the training investment. *Training and Development Journal, 32*(1), 24–29.

56. Robinson & Robinson (1989), *supra* note 35.

57. *Ibid.*

58. Phillips (1996), *supra* note 20; Phillips, J. J. (1996). Was it the training? *Training and Development, 50*(3), 28–32.

59. Phillips, J. J. (1996). *Accountability in human resource management.* Houston: Gulf Publishing.

60. Phillips (1996), *supra* note 39.

61. Parry, S. B. (1996). Measuring training's ROI. *Training & Development, 50*(5), 72–77.

62. Parry, S. B. (2000). *Training for results.* Alexandria, VA: ASTD.

63. Phillips (1996), *supra* note 39.

64. Parry (1996), *supra* note 61.

65. Phillips (1996), *supra* note 21.

66. Willyerd, K. A. (1997). Balancing your evaluation act. *Training, 51*(3), 52–58.

67. Kaplan, R. S., & Norton, D. P. (January-February 1992). The balanced scorecard-Measures that drive performance. *Harvard Business Review,* 71–79.

68. *Ibid.*

69. Brogden, H. E. (1949). When testing pays off. *Personnel Psychology, 2,* 171–185; Cronbach, L. J. (1965). Comments on "A dollar criterion in fixed-treatment employee selection programs" in L. J. Cronbach & G. C. Gleser (eds.), *Psychological tests and personnel decisions* (2nd ed.). Urbana, IL: University of Illinois Press; Schmidt, F. L., Hunter, J. E., & Pearlman, K. (1982). Assessing the impact of personnel programs on workforce productivity. *Personnel Psychology, 35,* 333–347.

70. Cascio (2000), *supra* note 54.

71. Cronshaw, S. F., & Alexander, R. A. (1985). One answer to the demand for accountability: Selection utility as an investment decision. *Organizational Behavior and Human Decision Processes, 35,* 102–118; Cascio, W. F. (1989). Using utility analysis to assess training outcomes. In I. L. Goldstein and Associates, *Training and development in organizations* (63–88). San Francisco: Jossey-Bass; Boudreau, J. W. (1983). Economic considerations in estimating the utility of human resource productivity improvement programs. *Personnel Psychology, 36,* 551–576.

72. Cascio (1989), *supra* note 71.

73. Dreher, G. F., & Sackett, P. R. (eds.) (1983). *Perspectives on employee staffing and selection.* Homewood, IL: Richard D. Irwin.

74. Latham, G. P. (1988). Human resource training and development. *Annual Review of Psychology, 39,* 545–582.

75. Latham, G. P., & Whyte, G. (1994). The futility of utility analysis. *Personnel Psychology, 47,* 31–46; Whyte, G., & Latham, G. P. (1997). The futility of utility analysis revisited: When even an expert fails. *Personnel Psychology, 50,* 601–610.

76. Hazer, J. T., & Highhouse, S. (1997). Factors influencing managers' reactions to utility analysis: Effects of $SD_y$ method, information frame, and focal intervention. *Journal of Applied Psychology, 82,* 104–112.

77. Morrow, C. C., Jarrett, M. Q., & Rupinski, M. T. (1997). An investigation of the effect and economic utility of corporate-wide training. *Personnel Psychology, 50,* 91–119.

78. Hazer & Highhouse (1997), *supra* note 76; Latham (1988), *supra* note 74.

79. Sturman, M. C. (2000). Implications of utility analysis adjustments for estimates of human resource intervention value. *Journal of Management, 26*, 281–299.

80. *Ibid.*

81. Hazer & Highhouse (1997), *supra* note 76; Latham (1988), *supra* note 74; Latham & Whyte (1994), *supra* note 75; Morrow et al. (1997), *supra* note 77; Shultz, K. S. (1996). Utility analysis in public sector personnel management: Issues and keys to implementation. *Public Personnel Management, 25*(3), 369–377; Sturman (2000), *supra* note 79.

82. Latham (1988), *supra* note 74.

83. Parsons, J. G. (1997). Values as a vital supplement to the use of financial analysis in HRD. *Human Resource Development Quarterly, 8*, 5–13; Brinkerhoff, R. O. (1997). Invited reaction: Response to Parsons. *Human Resource Development Quarterly, 8*, 15–21.

84. Grove, D. A., & Ostroff, C. (1991). Program evaluation. In K. N. Wexley (ed.), *Developing human resources*. Wasington, DC: BNA Books.

## Appendix 7-1
## More on Research Design

A research design provides a plan or blueprint for conducting an evaluation study. Research design is a complex topic, and much has been written about it.[1] Our goal in this section is to go beyond our brief coverage in the chapter, and introduce the reader to important issues in research design, and discuss some of the possibilities available when evaluating HRD programs.

Research design is a critical aspect of any evaluation effort. Awareness of research design issues and possible research design alternatives can help a manager or HRD professional conduct effective evaluations, and also critique the results of the evaluation studies done by others.

### Research Design Validity

The validity of a research design depends on the extent to which one can be confident that the conclusions drawn from it are true.[2] Validity of a design is judged on a continuum from high (high confidence that the design yields truthful conclusions) to low (doubtfulness about the design's conclusions).

Research design validity has at least four aspects: internal, external, construct, and statistical conclusion.[3] Typically, the most important of these aspects is internal validity.

**Internal validity** concerns a judgment as to whether conclusions about the relationship between the variables being studied could have been due to some other variable. In the case of HRD evaluation, if an increase in employee performance is observed after an HRD program, we want to assess whether the program was responsible for the change, rather than some other factor such as experience or work rules.

For example, when a sales training program is being evaluated to determine whether it improves sales, one hopes to conclude that any observed increases in sales are a result of the training program. However, other factors could encourage sales, such as economic conditions, the sales territory, or an employee's years of experience in selling. If the evaluation study does not control for these factors (i.e., ensure they don't affect the results), we cannot be sure whether any increases in sales are due to the training program or not. So, if sales after the training program are 15 percent higher than before, but the HRD evaluation did not control or adjust for economic conditions or trainee experience, it will not be clear whether the training or something else caused the increase in sales. Therefore, the study's

■ **TABLE 1**

1. **History**   Unrelated events occurring during the training period that can influence training measurements.
2. **Maturation**   Ongoing processes within the individual, such as aging or gaining job experience, that are a function of the passage of time.
3. **Testing**   The effect of a pretest on posttest performance.
4. **Instrumentation**   The degree to which criterion instruments may measure different attributes of an individual at two different points in time.
5. **Statistical Regression**   Changes in criterion scores resulting from selecting extreme groups on a pretest.
6. **Differential Selection**   Using different procedures for selecting individuals for experimental and control groups.
7. **Experimental Mortality**   Differential loss of respondents from various groups.
8. **Interaction of Differential Selection and Maturation**   Assuming that experimental and control groups were different to begin with, the compounding of the disparity between the groups by maturational changes occurring during the experimental period.
9. **Interaction of Pretest with the Experimental Variable**   During the course of training, something reacting with the pretest in such a way that the pretest affects the trained group more than the untrained group.
10. **Interaction of Differential Selection with Training**   When more than one group is trained, because of differential selection, the groups are not equivalent on the criterion variable to begin with; therefore, they may react differently to the training.
11. **Reactive Effects of the Research Situation**   When the research design itself so changes the trainees' expectations and reactions that results cannot be generalized to future applications of the training.
12. **Multiple Treatment Interference**   Differential residual effects of previous training experiences.

SOURCE: From W. F. Cascio (1991). *Applied Psychology in Personnel Management* (4th ed.) Englewood Cliffs, NJ: Prentice-Hall, 395. Adapted by permission.

internal validity is low, and we cannot be confident that any conclusions based on this study are true.

Cook and Campbell identified a number of factors that can threaten or reduce internal validity if they are not controlled for. Table 1 lists these threats to the internal validity of HRD evaluations.[4]

Any of these factors, if present or not controlled for by the research design, can undermine the results of the study. An HRD professional should always seek to select a research design that will ensure that a valid conclusion can be drawn from it. Many of the conditions present within an organization can make it difficult to ensure a high degree of validity. Concerns over validity and rigor in research design can inhibit people from conducting training evaluation. However, as suggested by Goldstein, creatively matching the research effort to the organizational constraints can ensure that evaluation is done and meaningful conclusions are drawn.[5] Three categories of research designs that we will now discuss are nonexperimental designs, experimental designs, and quasi-experimental designs.

### NONEXPERIMENTAL DESIGNS

A **nonexperimental research design** leaves a great deal of doubt as to whether the HRD program has in fact caused a change in the trainees' skills, knowledge, or performance. Such designs include the case study, relational research, and the one-group pretest-posttest design.[6] Traditional thinking suggests that each of these designs is poorly suited for making conclusive statements about training effectiveness. There are simply too many plausible alternative explanations for any observed changes when using these methods to be able to confidently conclude that an observed change has been caused by an HRD program. However, this thinking assumes that internal validity is always the paramount concern of the evaluation researcher. Yet, as Sackett and Mullen suggest, this is not always the case. We will first describe these designs and then address the issue of their appropriateness for use in HRD evaluation.[7]

*CASE STUDY.*    The **case study research design** involves an intensive, descriptive study of a particular trainee, training group, or organization to determine what has occurred and reactions to it. If diagrammed, this design would look like this:

$$\text{Training} \longrightarrow \text{Posttraining measures and descriptions}$$

The sources of data frequently used in case studies usually include archival data and reports of participants and observers. Because no pretraining information is collected, and there is no untrained comparison group, many threats to internal validity exist. However, a carefully conducted case study can create a record of the training program.

*RELATIONAL RESEARCH.*    **Relational research** involves measuring two or more variables in an attempt to describe or explain their relationship to one another.[8] For example, a manager may distribute a questionnaire to managers who attended an assessment center asking them to rate the value of each of the activities conducted during the program (such as a leaderless group discussion or in-basket exercise). Typically, relational research includes computing correlation coefficients (a numerical index of a relationship between two variables) between the variables measured.

While the pattern of correlations can give an idea of how the variables are related, the conclusions drawn can only be suggestive because measurements are taken at only one point in time. This makes it difficult to assess the direction of the relationships measured. For example, suppose a study shows a strong relationship between attitude toward training and attitude toward one's supervisor. Did one's feeling about the supervisor affect feelings toward the training, or did one's feeling toward training affect feelings toward the supervisor? Correlational data cannot answer such questions.

*ONE-GROUP PRETEST-POSTTEST DESIGN.*    In this design, the trainees are assessed on the variables being observed before training and again after training. That is,

$$\text{Pretest} \longrightarrow \text{Training} \longrightarrow \text{Posttest}$$

This design can help to determine whether the trainees have changed as a result of the training program. For example, if a customer service program is intended to improve the trainees' attitudes toward customers, the tests would measure their attitudes toward customers before and after training. However, if a change is noticed, this design does not show whether the *training program* was the cause of the change. Many factors could threaten its internal validity, such as history, maturation, and instrumentation.

*RECONSIDERATION OF NONEXPERIMENTAL RESEARCH DESIGNS.* As can be seen from the descriptions of the nonexperimental designs, they are highly vulnerable to threats to internal validity. As such, these designs have been seen as poor ways to assess HRD program effectiveness, and most writers caution against using them except as a way to gather details about a program and as the basis for ideas to be investigated in future studies. Given this recommendation against these simple designs and the barriers that many HRD professionals see as preventing them from using more rigorous designs (e.g., no access to control groups or inability to randomly assign participants to groups), it is not terribly surprising that many HRD programs are not evaluated in any serious way.

Recently, however, Sackett and Mullen have called for a reconsideration of the appropriateness of nonexperimental designs in HRD evaluation.[9] They make a case that these designs are appropriate for answering *some* of the questions an HRD professional has about a program and its participants, and they identify some of the considerations and constraints to using these designs. Sackett and Mullen begin their argument by pointing out that HRD professionals conduct evaluations to answer various types of questions, and they argue that the research design to be used should depend on the question being asked. In particular, two types of questions may be of interest:

1. How much change has occurred?
2. Has a particular target level of knowledge, skill, or performance been achieved by trainees?

According to Sackett and Mullen, if the HRD professional must answer the first question (e.g., in order to establish the utility of an HRD program or compare the effectiveness of two HRD programs), then internal validity is the foremost concern, and a research method that can control for threats to internal validity is likely called for. Ordinarily, this would make a nonexperimental design a poor choice. But if the HRD professional wants to answer the second question (which assesses the effectiveness of both the program and the individuals who participated in it), then internal validity is not the foremost concern, and a nonexperimental design may be appropriate.

Being able to answer the question "Has a particular level of performance been achieved?" requires that a clear target level of performance exists and that the organization is interested in establishing the level of performance achieved by each participant. In this case, a one-group posttest-only design (i.e., the case study) or a one-group pretest-posttest design can be used to answer this question. Although one could not conclude whether the performance level was reached *because* of the HRD program, one can confidently state the trainees' level of achievement.

Even in the case where the question "How much change has occurred?" is the focus of evaluation, Sackett and Mullen argue that it is possible to account for some potential threats to internal validity while still using a nonexperimental design. For example, if the HRD professional can obtain knowledge about the events occurring in the organization while the program is being conducted, it may permit an assessment of the extent to which history effects threaten internal validity.

We agree with Sackett and Mullen's arguments in this regard. They provide an excellent example of how creative thinking can expand our view of HRD evaluation and increase the likelihood that HRD practitioners will choose to evaluate their programs.

## EXPERIMENTAL DESIGNS

**Experimental designs** are constructed to show that any effects observed in the study have resulted from training and not from other factors. These designs include two significant factors:

1. a **control group** that does not receive training
2. **random assignment** of participants to the training and control groups

Use of a control group allows the researcher to rule out the effects of factors outside of training (like maturation and history). Usually, the hopes are that the group receiving training improves and the control group does not.

If the training and control groups differ on some important factor, such as experience, prior training, gender, or educational level, then the comparison of the groups is compromised — these factors may be the cause of observed changes. The easiest way to select equivalent control groups is to randomly assign participants to the two groups. Random assignment permits the researcher to assume the groups are equivalent.[10]

Alternatively, a matching strategy could also create equivalent groups, by doing the following:

1. identifying the factors, such as experience or job category, that are likely to affect the groups on the variables being measured
2. measuring potential participants on those factors
3. assigning subjects to balance each group on those factors

For example, if women are found to be better listeners than men, and listening skills may have an effect on learning what is being trained, the proportion of men and women in both the experimental and the control groups should be the same.

Experimental designs include the pretest-posttest with control design, the posttest-only with control design, and the Solomon four-group design.

***PRETEST-POSTTEST WITH CONTROL DESIGN.*** This design allows control for outside influences by including a group that is not trained as a comparison group.

Group 1: Pretest ⟶ Training ⟶ Posttest

Group 2: Pretest ⟶ Posttest

This design allows the researcher to make three comparisons:

1. Are the two groups in fact equivalent before training? This is assessed with the pretest.
2. Did training improve the trainees? This is assessed by comparing Group 1's pretest and posttest scores.
3. Did the untrained group remain unchanged during the course of the study? This is assessed by comparing Group 2's pretest and posttest scores.

If the answer to all three questions is yes, it is safe to conclude that training has had an effect.[11]

***POSTTEST-ONLY WITH CONTROL DESIGN.*** Sometimes, there is not enough time to gather pretest measurements. Also, the use of some pretest procedures may affect the outcome of training. For example, if one is measuring attitudes toward sexual harassment before a workshop about sexual harassment, simply answering questions about the topic may motivate the trainees to seek out more information or be more sensitive to the issue. Therefore, it is possible that changes in attitudes may be the result of the pretraining measure rather than the training. Alternatively, if the same test (such as a test on pricing procedures) is used as both a pretest and a posttest, participants may remember the items, calling the results of the posttest into question.

To resolve these situations and still have the benefit of an untrained comparison group, **a posttest-only with control design** could be used.

Group 1: Training ⟶ Posttest

Group 2: ⟶ Posttest

The effectiveness of this design relies on the assumption that the two groups are equivalent (using a method like random or matched assignment) prior to the study.

***SOLOMON FOUR-GROUP DESIGN.*** Solomon was one of the first researchers to point out how a pretest can affect the results of an evaluation study.[12] His research design therefore uses one experimental group and three different groups to control for the effects of the pretest.

Group 1: Pretest ⟶ Training ⟶ Posttest

Group 2: Pretest ⟶ Posttest

Group 3:    Training ———→ Posttest

Group 4: ——————————→ Posttest

This design is a combination of the two research designs just described. Therefore, it allows the researcher to make strong conclusions about the effectiveness of the HRD program. While it is the most elegant or attractive design from a research standpoint, its main disadvantage is that the number of participants it requires prevents many organizations from being able to use it.

It should be noted that multiple posttest measures can be taken if an experimenter is concerned about whether the effects of training are long lasting or if it may take a while for training to take effect. Multiple measures work best with routine data collection methods that do not affect employee performance, such as personnel (e.g., attendance) or operations data.

Although experimental designs are the most rigorous of the research designs and permit the greatest confidence in conclusions drawn from them, organizational constraints can make it difficult to use them. In many organizations, it is difficult to use random assignment to groups. If employees work in distant locations or if training some employees and not training others will cause friction among employees, using a pure experimental design is not possible.

### QUASI-EXPERIMENTAL DESIGNS

Some people feel that if rigorous adherence to an experimental design cannot be achieved, then evaluation is not worth doing. This is shortsighted. Campbell and Stanley and Cook and Campbell have offered **quasi-experimental designs** as a viable way to conduct evaluations.[13] In these designs, the researcher attempts to control as many threats to validity as possible, while matching evaluation research concerns to organizational constraints. Two quasi-experimental designs include the nonequivalent control group design and the time series design.

*NONEQUIVALENT CONTROL GROUP DESIGN.*    In a nonequivalent control group design, one cannot assume that the two groups—the control group and the group about to receive training—are equivalent. For example, if employees in one location are the trainees and employees at another location make up the control group, any number of factors may lead to nonequivalence, such as years of experience, economic conditions, and equipment.

The threats to validity most likely to affect conclusions from a nonequivalent control group design are selection-maturation interaction, testing-training interaction, and regression effects.[14] The burden for the evaluation researcher is to attempt to discover the factors on which the groups differ and then attempt to control for them, either statistically or in the way the experiment is conducted.

*TIME SERIES DESIGN.*    In the time series design, the researcher takes multiple measures on the variables of interest (e.g., skill operating a lathe) before and after training. This can be done using a training group alone, or with a training and control group.

Simple Time Series Design

Group 1:    $M_1$ $M_2$ $M_3$ $M_4$ $M_5$ $\longrightarrow$ Training $\longrightarrow$ $M_6$ $M_7$ $M_8$ $M_9$ $M_{10}$

Multiple Time Series Design

Group 1:    $M_1$ $M_2$ $M_3$ $M_4$ $M_5$ $\longrightarrow$ Training $\longrightarrow$ $M_6$ $M_7$ $M_8$ $M_9$ $M_{10}$

Group 2:    $M_1$ $M_2$ $M_3$ $M_4$ $M_5$ $\longrightarrow$ $M_6$ $M_7$ $M_8$ $M_9$ $M_{10}$

In the diagrams above, the M indicates the criterion or outcome measure.

Multiple measures allow the researcher to have a better idea of the employee's standing on the criterion both before and after training. The measurements can be graphed to help determine any change in the trends before and after training. If a change is observed, the training program is likely to be the cause.

Time series designs are well suited for handling the validity threat of history, but they may be susceptible to an instrumentation threat if the measurement method can affect employee performance on the criterion measure. As with all quasi-experimental designs, the researchers must be vigilant for possible threats to validity and attempt to control for them.

### STATISTICAL POWER: ENSURING THAT A CHANGE WILL BE DETECTED IF ONE EXISTS

Statistical analysis is the primary way researchers summarize the information collected in a study and is often the basis for drawing conclusions about training effectiveness. This raises the issue of statistical conclusion validity. In general, **statistical conclusion validity** refers to the extent to which the research design and statistical analyses performed can lead to false conclusions.[15] To the extent that the design and analyses are appropriate, one can be confident in the results of the study (keeping in mind the issues of internal, external, and construct validity).

Of particular interest in HRD evaluations is the notion of **statistical power**. In a training evaluation study, statistical power is the probability of concluding there is a difference between the training and control groups (or the scores trainees achieve on a pretest and posttest) *when a difference actually exists.* The higher the power of a design or analysis, the greater the chances of finding a difference; the lower the power, the greater the chances that a true difference between the groups will go undetected.

Clearly, HRD professionals should be aware of statistical power and make sure that they use designs and analyses that have adequate power.[16] Yet, it is unlikely that HRD practitioners consider issues of statistical power when designing evaluation studies. A study investigating the statistical power of studies reported in leading management and applied psychology journals concluded that the power in published research is low.[17] Mone et al. also surveyed study authors and found that researchers did not perceive a strong need for statistical power in their studies. If the academic researchers publishing in leading journals (who are likely more skilled in and aware of research design and methodology issues than the typical HRD practitioner) are using low-power designs and do not perceive a strong need for power, it is probably safe to assume that power is not a significant consideration among HRD practitioners, either. This is a serious oversight. Why go through the time and effort of doing an evaluation if one cannot be confident that the results are true?

One of the best ways to increase statistical power is to increase the number of participants in a study. All things equal, the greater the number of participants in each group, the greater the statistical power will be. However, many organizations do not have this option, given the number of employees available or the cost of including additional participants or both. Arvey et al. reported that the median sample size in training evaluation is 43.[18] Studies with this number of participants have relatively low statistical power (which can be modified somewhat according to the statistical analysis procedure used). This means that in many organizations, reliance on low-power research designs may lead to the mistaken conclusion that training is ineffective.[19]

In discussions of the trade-offs that exist between the four aspects of research design validity, statistical conclusion validity is typically viewed as being less important than internal validity. Yet, several authors have questioned the conventional wisdom. Sackett and Mullen put the issue this way:

> We would like to offer the proposition that statistical conclusion validity needs to take first priority in applied training evaluation research. The question, Is there a difference between trained and untrained groups? needs to be answered before addressing, Can the difference be attributed to the training intervention? What follows from this proposition is that it may be reasonable to trade off internal validity for statistical conclusion validity. (p. 623)[20]

Sackett and Mullen go on to suggest that dividing a limited number of participants equally into a training group and a control group reduces statistical power; yet if no control group were used and the same limited number of participants were all placed into the training group (e.g., as in the nonexperimental one-group pretest-posttest design), statistical power would increase dramatically. This would increase the chances that a difference would be detected, even though it would be difficult to attribute any difference between the groups to the training. Depending on the question the organization wanted to answer, this trade-off may be the preferred course of action. And as mentioned earlier, it may be possible to assess the impact of some of the threats to internal validity using existing knowledge about the participants and the organization.

Yang, Sackett, and Arvey offer a second suggestion for increasing the statistical power of a design: use unequal numbers of participants in the training and control groups.[21] In a paper that addresses the issue of the cost of training evaluation, Yang et al. point out that a trade-off exists between the power of an evaluation design and the cost of implementing the design. Although increasing the number of participants in both the control and training groups equally increases statistical power, it also increases the cost of doing the study, potentially to a prohibitive level. This is because participants in the training group must be trained as well as have their performance assessed. Yang et al. argue that increasing the total number of participants in the study by placing a greater number in the control group keeps the overall cost of the study down, while reaching power levels similar to those using a lower total number of participants divided equally among the two groups. Building on the work of Arvey, Maxwell, and Salas, Yang et al. developed formulas that can be used to identify the optimal ratio of control group size to training group size in an unequal-group-size design.[22]

Yang, Sackett, and Arvey also suggest a third way the sample size could be increased by making another cost-related trade-off: using less expensive, less valid measuring devices (called proxy measures) than one might otherwise use (called the target criterion measure).[23] This trade-off would permit assessing more participants for the same cost, thus increasing power. For example, suppose one was interested in assessing the job-security perceptions of trainees in an evaluation of a career development workshop. Although using a one-item job-security measure would be less valid and less reliable than a lengthier multi-item questionnaire, it would be quicker and less expensive to administer and process. This would allow the researcher to assess more study participants for the same cost, which would increase statistical power. Yang et al. state that as long as one can make the assumption that "any effects of training on the proxy are due to the effects of training on the target (i.e., training target proxy) . . . it is possible to make inferences about the effects of training on the target criterion from a study using the less expensive proxy criterion" (p. 652). They go on to demonstrate the cost savings that could be achieved and offer a series of step-by-step guidelines to help an HRD practitioner figure the cost savings that could be achieved by using a less valid proxy measure.

We find these ideas appealing because they provide some specific suggestions as to how HRD practitioners can take creative steps to conduct meaningful evaluation studies that address important methodological issues. In addition, they represent some concrete ways to move beyond the "experiment or nothing" mind-set that can inhibit practitioners from evaluating HRD programs.

### SELECTING A RESEARCH DESIGN

As we have indicated, there are a number of possible research designs to use when conducting an HRD evaluation study. Therefore, what factors should an HRD professional consider when selecting a design to use for an evaluation study?

Obviously, the validity of the conclusions drawn from the study is an important concern. Without valid conclusions, the evaluation effort is compromised. But other issues besides validity also need to be considered. Schmitt and Klimoski offer four additional criteria: conceptual issues, the costs associated with making a decision error, resources, and the value system and skills of the investigator.[24]

Conceptual issues concern the purpose of the evaluation study and previous research conducted on the training program being evaluated. The design or designs used should permit the investigators to answer the questions they are charged with asking. Recall Sackett and Mullen's arguments regarding matching the design to the questions one must answer.[25] In addition, if previous research indicates that certain factors may affect training effectiveness (like experience or gender), the research design should address these factors.

Second, it is possible that the investigator will make an incorrect conclusion based on the study. The study may show that the training program did not improve job performance, when in fact it did. Or the study may show a high degree of transfer of training, while employees actually apply little of what they learned to their jobs. When selecting a research design, the investigator must consider the costs associated with making an incorrect decision based on the study. If the costs are very high (that is, the organization will spend a large amount of money using the program or will exclude employees from promotions if they do not successfully complete training), validity of the design becomes more important.

Third, certain designs, such as a pretest-posttest design or the Solomon four-group design, use more resources than others. The investigator may have limited time, money, facilities, and subjects for the evaluation effort. Evaluation should be as valid as possible within resource constraints. As we have discussed, it is possible to make cost-related trade-offs to improve various aspects of research design validity.[26]

Fourth, some organization members may be more committed and able to conduct some approaches to evaluation research (e.g., more or less rigorous) than other approaches. The expertise and attitudes of those involved in the evaluation effort should be considered.[27]

All in all, even though research design can be a complicated topic to address, it obviously has a major impact on the success of most evaluation efforts. HRD professionals and others concerned with evaluation ignore research design issues at their own (and their organization's) peril.

## Appendix References

1. Campbell, D. T., & Stanley, J. C. (1966). *Experimental and quasi-experimental designs for research*. Chicago: Rand McNally; Cook, T. D., & Campbell, D. T. (1979). *Quasi-experimentation: Design and analysis issues for field settings*. Chicago: Rand McNally; Sackett, P. R., & Larson, J. R., Jr. (1990). Research strategies and tactics in industrial and organizational psychology. In M. D. Dunnette and L. M. Hough (eds.) *Handbook of industrial and organizational psychology* (2nd ed., vol. 1) (419–489). Palo Alto, CA: Consulting Psychologists Press; Schmitt, N. W., & Klimoski, R. J. (1991). *Research methods in human resources management*. Cincinnati, OH: South-Western.

2. Cook, T. D., & Campbell, D. T. (1976). The design and conduct of quasi-experiments and true experiments in field settings. In M. D. Dunnette (ed.), *Handbook of industrial and organizational psychology* (223–326). New York: Rand McNally.

3. *Ibid*.

4. *Ibid*; Cook & Campbell (1979), *supra* note 1.

5. Goldstein, I. L. (1980). Training in work organizations. *Annual Review of Psychology, 31*, 229–272.

6. Schmitt & Kilmoski (1991), *supra* note 1.

7. Sackett, P. R., & Mullen, E. J. (1993). Beyond formal experimental design: Towards an expanded view of the training evaluation process. *Personnel Psychology, 46,* 613–627.

8. Schmitt & Klimoski (1991), *supra* note 1.

9. Sackett & Mullen (1993), *supra* note 7.

10. Cook & Campbell (1976), *supra* note 2.

11. Schmitt & Klimoski (1991), *supra* note 1.

12. Solomon, R. L. (1949). An extension of the control group design. *Psychological Bulletin, 46,* 137–150.

13. Campbell & Stanley (1966), *supra* note 1; Cook and Campbell (1976), *supra* note 2; Cook and Campbell (1979), *supra* note 1.

14. Cascio, W. F. (1991). *Applied psychology in personnel management* (4th ed.). Englewood Cliffs, NJ: Prentice-Hall.

15. Cook, T. D, Campbell, D. T., & Peracchio, L. (1990). Quasi-experimentation. In M. D. Dunnette and L. M. Hough (eds.) *Handbook of industrial and organizational psychology* (2nd ed., vol. 1) (491–576). Palo Alto, CA: Consulting Psychologists Press.

16. Arvey, R. D., Cole, D. A., Hazucha, J. F., & Hartanto, F. M. (1985). Statistical power of training evaluation designs. *Personnel Psychology, 38,* 493–507.

17. Mone, M. A., Mueller, G. C., & Mauland, W. (1996). The perceptions and usage of statistical power in applied psychology and management research. *Personnel Psychology, 49,* 103–120.

18. Arvey et al. (1985), *supra* note 16.

19. Cascio (1991), *supra* note 14.

20. Sackett & Mullen (1993), *supra* note 7.

21. Yang, H., Sackett, P. R., & Arvey, R. D. (1996). Statistical power and cost in training evaluation: Some new considerations. *Personnel Psychology, 49,* 651–668.

22. Arvey, R. D., Maxwell, S. E., & Salas, E. (1992). The relative power of training designs under different cost configurations. *Journal of Applied Psychology, 77,* 155–160; Yang et al. (1996), *supra* note 21.

23. Yang et al. (1996), *supra* note 21.

24. Schmitt & Klimoski (1991), *supra* note 1.

25. Sackett & Mullen (1993), *supra* note 7.

26. Yang et al. (1996), *supra* note 21.

27. Schmitt & Klimoski (1991), *supra* note 1.

# 10

# SKILLS AND TECHNICAL TRAINING

## LEARNING OBJECTIVES

1. Identify and describe basic workplace competencies.

2. Explain the need for remedial basic skills training programs.

3. Explain the role of apprenticeship programs in today's work environment.

4. Describe a typical technical skills training program.

5. Describe a typical interpersonal skills training program.

6. Understand the professional development and education practices common in many organizations.

**OPENING CASE**

In the 1980s, the auto industry in the United States was criticized by American consumers because it was not competing with the quality, cost, and customer satisfaction achieved by many Japanese auto manufacturers. Japanese manufacturers, led by Toyota, Nissan, and Honda, captured a large share of the U.S. small-car market. The message was clear — if U.S. auto manufacturers did not change the manner in which they produced and sold their products, they would continue to lose market share.

General Motors (GM), the largest U.S. auto manufacturer, decided to challenge the Japanese where they were the strongest — in the small-car market. GM managers felt that if they were going to compete successfully with the Japanese, they could not just make adjustments, but would have to do things entirely differently: create a new division from the ground up using a different management philosophy. Accord-

ingly, in 1983, GM launched the Saturn Corporation, and in 1990, it produced its first vehicles from its plant in Spring Hill, Tennessee. A partnership was formed between General Motors and the United Auto Workers (UAW). This meant that production workers at Spring Hill were members of the UAW, but operated under a different contract than other UAW workers at GM. Saturn's philosophy embraced five core principles, that is, commitment to 1) customer satisfaction, 2) excellence, 3) teamwork, 4) trust and respect for the individual, and 5) continuous improvement. Saturn management felt that the best means of communicating these principles would be comprehensive training programs at all levels and functions within Saturn.

Within the retail and wholesale operations, Saturn management wanted to emphasize the commitment to "customer enthusiasm and teamwork." In order to take a

fresh approach, Saturn management looked outside the organization for a training partner, a vendor with commitment to these principles. They selected Maritz Communications Company. Saturn and Maritz committed approximately 130 training professionals (e.g., designers, writers, and automotive experts) to the task of designing their retail and wholesale operations training program. The Saturn/Maritz team was given the following challenge: "To take an ideal — a belief in a better way to sell cars — and change basic attitudes enough to make it a reality."

*Questions: If you were part of the Saturn training team, what issues would you emphasize in preparing and designing training for salespeople at Saturn dealerships? Would you recommend anything different for managers in both the manufacturing and retail arms of Saturn? How about for production workers at the Spring Hill plant?*

## INTRODUCTION

In this chapter, we will deal with the following types of questions:

- *Is there a literacy problem in the U.S. workplace, and if so, how severe is it?*
- *What types of training are available to individuals through the federal government?*
- *What kinds of apprenticeships are available today?*
- *What issues should trainers attend to when providing computer training?*
- *What makes for an effective training program concerning safety, quality, or team building?*
- *What role can labor unions play in skills and technical training?*

■ *What forms of continuing education and professional development are available to employees after they have received their basic training?*

Organizations have become increasingly dependent on skilled technical and professional employees, and this trend is expected to continue. For example, according to the Bureau of Labor Statistics, the fastest growing occupations between 1994 and 2005 will include those involving professionals and technical and service workers.[1] This trend can be traced to changes in the workplace resulting from such things as technological advances, changing organizational goals, and organizational restructuring. These changes include the need for more cognitive skills (e.g., problem-solving and decision-making skills) and greater interpersonal skills (e.g., teamwork). Whether the changes result from plant modernization, computerization, or other innovations, they have helped create a shift away from jobs requiring low skill levels to jobs demanding higher skill levels.

In this chapter, we will discuss basic workplace competencies and review some of the types of training programs used to improve these competencies. Skills training programs can be categorized in many ways. We've organized our discussion around three categories: basic skills/literacy education, technical training, and interpersonal skills training. **Basic skills/literacy education** refers to training that focuses on upgrading the reading, writing, and computation skills needed to function in most any job. **Technical training** refers to training that involves the process of upgrading a wide range of technical skills (such as computer skills) needed by particular individuals in an organization. **Interpersonal skills training** refers to training that focuses on an individual's relationships with others, including communication and teamwork. As you might imagine, training in all of these areas can be of critical importance to organizations. Table 9-1 lists the categories of skills training programs and the subcategories included within them. We will discuss programs used in each of these categories and subcategories.

## BASIC WORKPLACE COMPETENCIES

As we mentioned in Chapter 1, a major problem facing employers today is the *skills gap* — the difference between the skill requirements of available jobs and the skills possessed by job applicants.[2] The skills gap is the result of at least three factors: 1) the declining skill level achieved by many high school and college graduates; 2) the growing number of racial minorities and non-English-speaking immigrants in the labor market (many of whom are concentrated in the worst-performing schools and school systems in the country); and 3) the increased sophistication of jobs due to increased reliance on information technology.[3] The *declining skills of high school — and even some college — students*, particularly at a time when organizations require increasingly skilled workers, has generated much criticism of public education systems in the United States. A 1999 survey found that 80 percent of employers said that recent high school graduates lacked grammar and spelling skills, and 57 percent of employers said these students couldn't speak English properly.[4] Many employers are finding that graduates

■ **TABLE 9-1**

| Training Category | Subcategories |
|---|---|
| Basic skills/Literacy | Remedial/basic education |
| Technical | Apprenticeship training |
| | Computer training |
| | Technical skills/knowledge training |
| | Safety training |
| | Quality training |
| Interpersonal | Sales training |
| | Customer relations/service training |
| | Team building/training |

with basic skill deficiencies must be given remedial training before they are job-ready. For example, this decline prompted the Los Angeles School District to issue a written warranty with each of its high school diplomas since 1994, stating that if an employer finds a graduate to be deficient in any basic skill, the school will provide remedial training at no cost to the employer.[5] This type of commitment reflects the urgency of the problem and demonstrates how some school administrators are trying to confront the issue.

*It is predicted that racial minorities and non-English-speaking immigrants* will make up approximately a third of total new entrants into the labor force between 1994 and 2005.[6] This change is expected to be gradual. It is also predicted that African-Americans will make up about 11 percent of the labor force, the same as today, by 2020. The number of Hispanic workers will increase from 9 to 14 percent, and the Asian-American representation will increase from 4 to 6 percent, primarily in the South and the West.[7] The ever increasing diversity of the American job market creates unique advantages and challenges for employers. In today's "global society," a dynamic multiethnic and multicultural work environment can foster creativity and innovation in an organization. A large portion of these new workers, however, will be immigrants who lack proficiency in English, and who also may lack basic skills. Thus, two kinds of training may be necessary to get them job-ready — basic skills and basic English-as-a-second-language (ESL). These deficiencies represent a major challenge to potential employers who must rely on these workers.

The *increased sophistication of jobs*, particularly as a result of the information technology explosion, has affected almost every industry. The trend toward increasingly powerful computer hardware and user-friendly computer software systems has led to a proliferation of high technology applications, including robotics (in the manufacturing sector), decision-support systems, electronic-mail systems, and communications networks. Continuous technical training will likely be necessary for those occupations that rely on information technology and are directly affected by the constant changes in hardware and software.

## BASIC SKILLS/LITERACY PROGRAMS

As discussed above, the basic competency skills include reading, writing, and computational skills. While the assessment of these skills is not always standardized, deficiencies in these skills are widely reported. The U.S. Department of Education estimated that almost half of the 191 million adults living in the United States could be classified as functionally illiterate.[8] The former Office of Technology Assessment estimated that between 20 to 30 percent of employees lack basic writing, reading, and computational skills.[9] These estimates reflect the depth of the problem facing employers who attempt to improve operations by introducing more efficient production methods. If employees cannot read or compute at sufficient skill levels, it is extremely difficult to install new equipment that requires operators to read instructions and make decisions.

Worldwide, the greatest number of illiterate adults are in developing nations, especially in rural areas. However, many industrialized nations also face challenges. For example, a 1995 report by the Organization for Economic Cooperation and Development provided the following estimates for adults whose reading proficiency was *below* primary school level:

| | |
|---|---|
| Belgium | 18.6% |
| Canada | 16.6% |
| Germany | 13.8% |
| Ireland | 22.6% |
| Netherlands | 10.4% |
| New Zealand | 18.2% |
| Poland | 42.7% |
| Sweden | 7.2% |
| United Kingdom | 21.6% |
| United States | 20.8%[10] |

When creating a program to address basic skill deficiencies, employers should operationally define each basic skill. Kirsch and Jungeblut provide an example of how to operationally define literacy skills.[11] In their study of literacy among young adults (ages 21 through 25), literacy skills were operationally defined according to three broad categories (p. 64):

1. **Prose literacy** Skills and strategies needed to understand and use information from texts that are frequently found in the home and the community.

■ **TABLE 9-2**

**LITERACY RATES OF ADULTS AGED 21 TO 25 BY RACE**

**Literacy Scale (Mean Score = 305)**

|  | Below 200 | 201–275 | 276–350 | 351+ |
|---|---|---|---|---|
| White | 5% | 17% | 53% | 25% |
| Black | 18 | 43 | 35 | 3 |
| Hispanic | 10 | 33 | 47 | 10 |

SOURCE: Adapted from I. S. Kirsch and A. Jungeblut, "Literacy: Profiles of America's young adults" (1986), National assessment of educational progress. Princeton, NJ: Educational Testing Service, 65–66.

2. **Document literacy** Skills and strategies required to locate and use information contained in nontextual materials that include tables, graphs, charts, indexes, forms, and schedules.

3. **Quantitative literacy** Knowledge and skills needed to apply the arithmetical operations of addition, subtraction, multiplication, and division (either singly or sequentially) in combination with printed materials, as in balancing a checkbook or completing an order form.

The measurement of these skills was accomplished by devising a large number of simulated tasks that were then administered to a nationwide sample. Scores were tabulated on a scale ranging from 0 to 500, with a mean score of 305. Table 9–2 summarizes the results of the study, demonstrating that a significant number of young adults scored below the literacy average, with an even greater number of young minority adults ranking below the average.

## ADDRESSING ILLITERACY IN THE WORKPLACE

Many organizations have recognized illiteracy problems among their workers. It is estimated that over half the U.S. organizations with 1,000 or more employees conduct basic skills programs.[12] Companies like Motorola, Ford, Xerox, Polaroid, and Kodak have already instituted comprehensive basic skills programs.[13] A survey by the American Management Association found that of organizations that have implemented basic skills programs, 70 percent did so in the past decade.[14] The following are examples of some programs.

1. The California State Department of Education assisted nineteen companies by developing a literacy program, involving 600 hours of development time, aimed at improving employee skills for reading work materials, entering required data, making numerical calculations, and using correct technical vocabulary in their speech.[15]

2. Chrysler Corporation invested $5 million in teaching basic skills to 3,000 to 4,000 workers in order to advance them to an eighth-grade level in reading, writing, and math.[16]

3. Federal government agencies have also recognized the literacy problem. For example, the Basic Skills Education Program (BSEP) was developed by the U.S. Army in 1982 to deal with illiteracy issues among the troops. Wilson states that the BSEP "is the largest computer-based basic skills program ever developed . . . containing more than 300 lessons that cover more than 200 basic skills" (p. 38).[17]

## DESIGNING AN IN-HOUSE BASIC SKILLS/LITERACY PROGRAM

The design of basic skills/literacy programs varies widely from organization to organization, but they have at least two common characteristics: 1) an aptitude test and 2) small-group and one-on-one instruction. An *aptitude test* is important for assessing the current ability level of each trainee. For example, a basic skills program developed by the Palo Verde Nuclear Generating Station begins with an assessment of each trainee's learning ability before he or she is assigned to an intensive six-month study skills program.[18] These data are essential for developing an individualized lesson plan that allows the trainer to pinpoint learning objectives and to select the best training methods, techniques, and materials for each trainee.

*Small-group instruction and one-on-one tutoring* are important for supplying feedback to the trainee, as well as for conducting remedial work in any areas of deficiency. Zaslow suggests using supervisors as writing coaches by training them to give feedback to employees on such things as writing techniques.[19] To supplement small-group instruction, some organizations are using self-paced, computer-interactive programs that provide opportunities for employees to practice basic concepts. Many organizations now offer these programs in CD-ROM format or through their intranet. Self-pacing allows a trainee to practice at his or her own rate, without the pressures of a classroom, and to repeat or skip steps or sequences in the program as necessary. Perhaps this is quite obvious, but this approach is best used for trainees who are highly motivated to learn.

The methods used for in-house basic skills training programs also vary. Table 9-3 describes some of the advantages, disadvantages, and costs of different methods. Training manuals, tutorial disks, and videotapes are the least costly methods to use because they do not require a classroom or an instructor, although these methods also have significant disadvantages. The most costly programs are those that are customized, because they require considerable time and expertise to design.

As with most HRD interventions, support from management is an important ingredient of a successful basic skills training program. Yet, that support is not always easy to obtain. A survey of ASTD members regarding organizational support of basic skills programs reported an apparent discrepancy between the attitudes of the majority of HRD professionals and top management toward basic

■ **TABLE 9-3**

| Methods | Advantages | Disadvantages | Cost |
|---|---|---|---|
| Training manual | Reusable and self-paced. | Requires technical orientation. Examples not directly related to organization. Material presented in only one way. | Low |
| Tutorial disks | Same as above. | Same as above. | Low |
| Videotape | Presentation is more personal. Reusable and can stop and start. | Same as above. | Moderate |
| Internal classroom (in-house trainer) | Customer-tailored to meet organization needs. Can adjust presentation to class abilities. Trainer understands organization. | Must have large group to justify cost. In-house trainers may not be effective instructors. | High |
| Internal classroom (consultant) | Customer-tailored to meet organization needs. Can adjust presentation to class abilities. Professional instructor. Consultant not tied to internal politics. | Must have large group to justify cost. Consultant does not have working knowledge of organization. | High |
| Customized external training | Same as above plus fewer interruptions and use of external facilities. Trainees may perceive as a reward. | Same as above. | Very high |
| General courses and seminars | Wide assortment of topics available. Can schedule on an individual basis. | Examples not directly related to organization. | Very high |

SOURCE: Adapted from D. R. Callaghan (1985). "Realistic computer training. *Training and Development, 39* (7), 27–29. Adapted by permission.

skills training.[20] The majority of HRD professionals believed "there is a problem and that many people in the organization are affected," while the majority of top management believed "there is a problem but that few people are affected."[21] This finding suggests that HRD professionals will likely need to inform and educate top management about the extent of the basic skills problem in their own organization if they expect to receive the necessary funding and support for their basic skills programs.

## FEDERAL SUPPORT FOR BASIC SKILLS TRAINING

The federal government has long recognized its role in supporting private training initiatives that are targeted toward the unemployed, displaced, and economically disadvantaged. From 1983 to 2000, the **Job Training and Partnership Act (JTPA)** was the largest federal skills training program. The JTPA had replaced the Comprehensive Employment and Training Act (CETA). The goal of Title IIA of the JTPA was to provide training opportunities to the unemployed, displaced, and economically disadvantaged in order to help them obtain permanent jobs. Beginning July 1, 2000, the JTPA was replaced by the Workforce Investment Act (described more fully below).

Under the JTPA, approximately $4 billion was available every year from the federal government. This money was funneled through 600 individual private industry councils (PICs) to private training institutes and employers in order to fund skills training.[22] The PICs, which are composed of representatives from business, education, community-based agencies, and others, are appointed by local government officials. The role of a PIC is to oversee the distribution of funds and to ensure that state JTPA standards and guidelines are followed.

Most employer-based training programs involve basic skills and job-specific training. While most of the training is conducted on-site in a classroom, JTPA sponsored on-the-job training programs, as long as the employer agreed to hire the trainees once they complete their training. The success of JTPA programs was dependent, in part, on how well these programs were coordinated with the work of other social service agencies. For example, potential trainees could be identified and referred to a training agency by a community-based social agency that served the economically disadvantaged target population. This was the case when the Atlanta Marquis Hotel trained fifty-nine people; thirty-nine were referred by Goodwill Industries, a community-based nonprofit agency, and twenty were referred by the local PIC.[23]

In addition, the JTPA was legislatively tied to the **Worker Adjustment and Retraining Notification (WARN) Act.** The WARN Act requires any employer with 100 or more employees to give sixty-days advance notice of a plant closure to both employees and unions. When plant closings or mass layoffs were imminent, JTPA funds were to be made available to set up "rapid response teams" that would work with unions and companies to administer retraining and worker-displacement programs.[24]

Despite successful JTPA programs, such as that of the Atlanta Marquis, two problems were identified. First, several private institutions and employers received funds fraudulently, that is, some employers used JTPA funds to hire workers whom they would recruit even under normal conditions.[25] Second, while the program was intended to serve a wide target population, JTPA funds provided training programs for only a fraction of the eligible displaced and unemployed workers. This was due in part to the JTPA budget being decreased from $1.4 billion in 1983 to $0.9 billion in 1997 (a 36 percent decrease). The future funding of JTPA-type programs may be affected by the Personal Responsibility and Work Opportunity Reconciliation Act of 1996. A main goal of this act was to move people from welfare to work through a process known as workfare. The act mandates that welfare recipients work a minimum of twenty hours per week (the minimum will be increased to thirty hours by 2002).

The JTPA was one of 150 federal education and training programs that together cost the taxpayers $25 billion a year. According to Judy and D'Amico, these programs were "notoriously ineffective . . . or at least extremely expensive, when their meager results are considered" (p. 133).[26] For example, a federal program attempted to retrain 4,500 laid off garment workers in El Paso, Texas. While the program spent $25 million in almost two years, only 375 trainees were placed in jobs.[27] Beyond these concerns, the U.S. General Accounting Office (GAO) found that the narrow focus of the patchwork of federal education and training programs frustrates and confuses employers, program administrators, and those seeking assistance.[28] The GAO recommended that these programs be overhauled and consolidated to streamline services and make program administrators more accountable.

In response to this, the **Workforce Investment Act (WIA)** was passed in 1998. The goal of this act was to consolidate more than seventy federal education and training programs into block grants that are designed to give states more flexibility in meeting their constituents' education and training needs. The three major funding streams are for youth, adults, and displaced workers (i.e., workers who have lost their jobs through layoffs, downsizing, etc.). The act is designed to give greater control to local boards and the private sector, and to increase the accountability of all training providers for the outcomes of their efforts. While there is optimism about the potential for more positive use of federal training dollars, as this text was written, it is too early to determine what impact this new law is having on federally funded training efforts.[29] Clearly, though, federal funding for basic training will continue; it is imperative that these funds be used as effectively as possible to reach the populations targeted for assistance.

## TECHNICAL TRAINING PROGRAMS

**Technical training,** as discussed earlier, is a generic term that can encompass a wide range of programs. For convenience, we will limit our discussion to five categories of technical training programs: apprenticeship training, computer training, technical skills/knowledge training, safety training, and quality training.

### APPRENTICESHIP TRAINING

**Apprenticeship training** is not a new concept. As discussed in Chapter 1, it began during the Middle Ages as a way of passing on the knowledge of individuals

**■ TABLE 9-4**

POSITIVE OUTCOMES OF A SUCCESSFUL APPRENTICE PROGRAM

1. reduced absenteeism, turnover, and cost of training
2. increased productivity
3. improved community and employee relations
4. facilitated compliance with federal and state Equal Employment Opportunity requirements
5. ensured availability of related technical instruction
6. enhanced problem-solving ability of employees
7. ensured versatility of employees

SOURCE: National Apprenticeship Training Program (1987). Washington, DC: Employment and Training Administration, U.S. Department of Labor.

working in skilled trades and crafts. The primary purpose of these early programs was preservation of the industrial and crafts guilds. Today, the focus of apprenticeship programs is to provide trainees with the skills needed to meet continually changing job requirements. With the challenges of the global economy and the scarcity of skilled employees, it is imperative that apprenticeship programs be more responsive to these needs.

Apprenticeship programs represent a unique partnership between employers, labor unions, schools, and government agencies. In 1988, over 800 different apprenticeship programs in the United States enrolled 335,508 registered apprentices.[30] Of this total, almost one-third of apprenticeships were in carpentry, electricity, and pipe trades. A typical apprenticeship program requires a minimum of 2,000 hours of on-the-job training (OJT) experience.[31] In addition to the OJT experience, all programs require a minimum of 144 hours of classroom training. Classroom training may be given at a local vocational/technical school or community college. For example, the Community College of Rhode Island conducts the classroom portion of the Plastics Process Technician Apprenticeship Program for area employers. The four-year program is broken into 1,050 hours of classroom training and 8,000 hours of OJT training.[32] At the end of the program, the students receive not only certification as journeymen but also an associate's degree in plastics process technology.

The U.S. apprenticeship system is regulated by the Bureau of Apprenticeship and Training (BAT) of the U.S. Department of Labor (DOL). In twenty-seven states, the BAT has delegated its regulatory responsibilities to state apprenticeship councils. For the remaining states, the BAT regulates standards and provides services. BAT claims that a well-planned, properly administered apprenticeship program will result in success. Table 9-4 lists some of these positive outcomes.

The present apprenticeship system does have some problems. The National Center on Education and the Economy issued a report that identified four major concerns: 1) learning is based on time requirements rather than competency, 2) programs are isolated from other education and training institutions, 3) programs are concentrated in traditional blue-collar occupations, and 4) the system has not adjusted to requirements for the period after the initial apprenticeship.[33] In addition, most apprenticeship programs begin after someone has completed high school, that is, they can be considered to be "adult" apprenticeships.

Some of these problems began to be addressed by an initiative called Apprenticeship 2000, started in 1987 by the U.S. Department of Labor. Based on the successes of other countries, like Germany, one purpose of the program was to expand the apprenticeship concept and link it to secondary schools. For example, in 1991, the Wisconsin legislature passed an act that emphasized youth apprenticeships and technical preparation programs. Also in 1991, Oregon redesigned its vocational high school curriculum to allow eleventh-grade students to enter an apprentice-type training program with businesses that guaranteed the students jobs after they graduated.[34] Such efforts are referred to as **school-to-work programs.** The success of the programs in Wisconsin and Oregon prompted other states, such as Rhode Island, New York, North Carolina, and South Carolina, to seek similar reforms. These programs are distinct from more traditional "adult" apprenticeship programs, in that they target high school students, particularly those who are not likely to enroll in four-year colleges.

In response to the success that many states had with school-to-work initiatives, the U.S. Congress enacted the **School-to-Work Opportunities Act** in 1993. The act created a fund through which the federal government made grants available to states to cover the costs of implementing school-to-work programs. For example, Wisconsin received $27 million to support implementation of a variety of school-to-work programs, including youth apprenticeship, over a five-year period.[35] The Wisconsin youth apprenticeship program now offers apprenticeships in twenty-two occupational areas, including engineering, manufacturing, health services, automotive technician, and banking. First-year enrollment in the program was 700 (representing only 1 percent of high school students).[36] It is estimated that nearly 4,000 students will be involved in youth apprenticeships in 2001, with an even higher number of students in co-op education programs.[37]

The success of a school-to-work program depends on the coordinated effort of all participants.[38] Schools should administer vocational assessment tests so that they can properly advise students on which program is best for them. Schools should also ensure that their curriculum sufficiently prepare students in the fundamentals needed to learn advanced skills in the apprenticeship program. Other organizations involved in program administration, such as state government and labor unions, should provide technical support and advice to employers and help coordinate activities to ensure that programs runs smoothly. Finally, employers should ensure that the work assignments provide meaningful learning experiences for each student to build the competencies needed to complete the apprenticeship program.

Benefits to employers from school-to-work programs include access to a trained labor pool, a better public image, and potential eligibility for wage subsidies and tax credits.[39] These benefits should be weighed against the potential costs. The direct costs include wages and benefits paid to students. The indirect costs include the time spent on the programs by HRD professionals and other employees who are responsible for coordinating the program, orienting and training the staff, and training and supervising the students. Despite these costs, given the continuing shortage of skilled workers, school-to-work programs would seem to be a vital element in national efforts to reduce the skills gap.

### COMPUTER TRAINING

Computer skills training has become extremely popular. The Bureau of Labor Statistics (BLS) reported that in 1995, 54.3 percent of employees in companies with fifty or more employees received formal training in computer procedures, programming, and software, making it the top-ranked type of job skills training taken by employees.[40] A 1996 survey by *Training* magazine found that 88 percent of companies conducted computer skills training, and the average company spent 25 percent of its training budget on this form of training.[41] By 2000, estimates had risen to 99 percent of companies conducting computer skills training, with almost 40 percent of all employer-sponsored training devoted to computer skills.[42]

The two basic kinds of computer training are introductory and applications. **Introductory computer training** programs are used to introduce trainees to computer hardware and software. Introductory training programs focus primarily on mastering basic software **tasks,** such as how to navigate the operating system. They do this through the use of manuals and **tutorials** (software programs themselves) that provide hands-on, interactive learning. These courses are designed to help trainees overcome their fear of computers and better understand how computers work.

**Applications training** covers specific software applications available within an organization and instruction on applications development.[43] Unlike introductory courses, which can be offered to an entire organization, applications training is typically provided on an as-needed basis. With the availability of online capabilities via an intranet, employees can access online computer training at any time of the day (or any day of the week — 24/7).

Given the range of options for conducting computer skills training, which approaches do employees prefer? A recent survey revealed that both experienced and less experienced trainees prefer to learn to use software by experimenting or through trial and error.[44] The more traditional training methods, including lectures and seminars, ranked near the bottom of the list of trainee preferences.

Researchers are beginning to explore a number of learning issues involved in computer skills training, such as:

- **Self-Efficacy** — Self-efficacy is an individual's belief that he or she can successfully perform a given behavior (recall our discussion of self-efficacy in Chapter 2). Research has shown that a behavior modeling approach to software training resulted in higher self-efficacy scores and higher scores on an objective measure of computer software mastery than a tutorial approach.[45]

- **Cognitive Playfulness** — Cognitive playfulness includes the spontaneity, imagination, and exploratory approach that a person brings to task performance and learning.[46] Martocchio and Webster found that trainees who scored higher in cognitive playfulness were more likely to exhibit higher learning, positive mood, and satisfaction with feedback.[47] They also found that positive feedback was more beneficial for employees who were lower in cognitive playfulness.

- ■ **Training Format** — There is evidence that the use of behavior modeling for software training is more effective in producing computer skills learning and application than either of the more commonly used self-paced and lecture approaches.[48]

The results of empirical studies like the ones cited above can provide useful guidelines for designing and implementing computer skills training programs. This kind of ongoing research on learning-related issues underscores the need for HRD professionals to keep abreast of developments that could help them improve the design and implementation of computer skills training (and all HRD programs).

## TECHNICAL SKILLS/KNOWLEDGE TRAINING

When organizations introduce new technology (e.g., by modernizing plants or computerizing operations), they typically need to update the skills of the workers who must use it. Organizations often do this through job-specific technical skills/knowledge training programs. One recent survey found that technical skills/knowledge training is conducted by 85 percent of organizations, and new methods/procedures training, by 78 percent.[49] These types of training are often specific to a job, process, or piece of equipment, but can also be more general. For example, a training program used to teach clerical workers how to operate a new telephone system would be classified as job-specific. A training program used to train employees on new policies and procedures pertaining to waste disposal and given to all workers would be classified as general.

There are different levels of technical skills/knowledge training. At the lowest level, the goal is to prepare entry level employees to perform basic functional responsibilities. These programs are similar to basic skills programs and combine classroom instruction with on-the-job training (OJT). As an example, Stanley-Bostitch, Inc., a manufacturer of staples and fasteners, conducts a twenty-eight-week, entry level operator training program of six modules, encompassing basic math, basic measurement skills, blueprint reading, shop practices, basic tooling, and basic machines. The last three modules involve intensive OJT. Successful trainees are expected to operate new, advanced equipment. In a similar situation, IBM assigns entry level clerical workers to a two-week, sixty-eight-hour training program divided into fourteen modules that include automated procedures, time management, problem solving, and stress management.[50]

Beyond apprenticeship training, unions may also help provide training, such as with joint labor-management training programs designed to update union members' skills. For example, the Laborers International Union and the Associated General Contractors (AGC) formed the Laborers-AGC Education and Training Fund. One example of the technical training provided by the Laborers-AGC group was an eighty-hour certificate course in hazardous-waste removal. In 1992, almost

9,000 of 500,000 union members had completed the training qualifying them to be hired to work on hazardous-waste removal projects.[51]

## SAFETY TRAINING

It is estimated that 83 percent of organizations conduct some form of **safety training.**[52] The need for such training has increased dramatically since the passage of the 1970 **Occupational Safety and Health Act (OSHA).** For example, over $40 billion dollars is spent annually in the U.S. on organizational safety and health programs.[53] The act established the **Occupational Safety and Health Administration** (also known as **OSHA**). OSHA (the administration) has four primary areas of responsibility, namely to 1) establish safety standards; 2) conduct safety inspections; 3) grant safety variances for organizations that are unable to comply with standards; and 4) cite organizations where standards are being violated. If an organization is cited for safety violations, safety training may be required to prevent future accidents. OSHA-mandated safety training focuses on safety equipment devices, handling of toxic chemicals, safe work habits, and actions to be taken in case of an accident. For more excessive violations, OSHA has the power to levy fines, shut down an operation, or even prosecute the management (or the owner).

In the first quarter of 2000 alone, OSHA issued nearly eighty citations nationwide totaling nearly $10 million in proposed fines for alleged violations. Of these eighty violations, some forty-four were attributable to "less-than-adequate training." Nearly 55 percent of all violations involved less-than-adequate training as a contributing factor.[54] Further, the impact of inadequate training in an organization can be stated in quantifiable terms. Three of the most common metrics to portray the safety status of a site are

- **Lost Work Day Index (LWDI)** — Number of workdays missed due to personal injury per 100 employees, divided by total number of employees x 100
- **OSHA Recordable Rate** — Number of OSHA Recordables/200,000 hours (the hours that 100 employees work with forty-hour weeks, and fifty-weeks a year)
- **Lost Time Rate** — Number of Lost Time Accidents/200,000 hours

According to OSHA, the national LWDI average is 3.0 workdays missed per 100 employees. The National Safety Council has established a $30,000 daily rate as an average to quantify a missed workday in dollars (based on a Fortune 500 energy company). Using these figures, and calculating the dollar impact of ten lost workdays, the total annualized costs associated with this can be determined to be as follows:

$$10 \text{ lost workdays} \times 3.0 \text{ LWDI} \times \$30,000 \text{ per lost workday} = \$900,000$$

In this hypothetical example, if a solution could be implemented (such as improved safety training) that could reduce lost workdays by even 10 percent, this would result in an annual savings of $90,000.[55] Certainly, greater savings than this are desirable and to be sought after.

■ **TABLE 9-5**

TEN STEPS TOWARD AN EFFECTIVE SAFETY PROGRAM

1. Determine the training objective. All training programs should seek to modify some employee behavior. Determine exactly what you want your employees to be able to do at the end of training.

2. Develop a list of competencies. What must each employee be able to do at a given level of training?

3. Create a trainee profile. Determine who will be undergoing training. Consider their age, gender, education, learning skills, and so on. Knowing your audience helps determine the language you use, making the training easier to follow.

4. Have the training manager determine an outline of the subject matter to be covered based on the competencies and trainee profiles.

5. Expand the outline for completeness and proper sequencing at least once.

6. Develop training based on the outline.

7. Test the training on experts.

8. Test the training on actual trainees to determine usability, understandability, and effectiveness.

9. Correct the training content based on feedback and reviews.

10. Evaluate your testing to make sure all questions are good. A question missed by many students may indicate the question is poorly written, or that the point was not covered well enough in the training.

SOURCE: Ten steps toward an effective safety program (1999). *CEE News, 51* (5), 10.

OSHA regulations were expanded to include hazard communications standards in 1988. These standards supercede right-to-know laws at the state level, and require organizations to 1) establish a written hazard communications policy, 2) replace old state posters with OSHA's posters, 3) establish procedures for obtaining **material safety data sheets (MSDS)** from manufacturers, 4) create notebooks containing MSDS and make them accessible to employees, 5) label hazardous materials and state the effects of such materials, 6) provide orientation for new employees and ongoing training for other employees, and 7) prepare a safety manual.[56]

Even with these regulations in place, injuries and illnesses are still common. For example, in 1989 there were approximately 6.5 million industrial accidents and illnesses on the job.[57] More recently, the Bureau of Labor Statistics reported that the nonfatal occupational injury and illness rate for all industries in 1995 was over 8.1 per 100 employees. Agricultural, landscaping, meat packing, and fishing industries had the highest accident rates. This suggests that organizations still need to work diligently to reinforce safety standards and desired employee work behaviors. Some practical guidelines for safety training are provided in Table 9-5. Other desirable characteristics of an effective safety management program include

1. top management support and reinforcement of safety standards[58]

2. employee involvement in suggesting safer work procedures and the selection of equipment[59]

3. regular and recurring safety training programs that reinforce safety standards and behaviors[60]

4. effective monitoring systems to ensure standards and behaviors are being practiced and to correct any unsafe conditions[61]

Because of OSHA regulations, industries that have historically had the highest incidence of work-related accidents now provide workers with ongoing safety training. The focus of this training is on prevention and emergency procedures. In addition, because of the right-to-know provisions described above, all organizations must orient and train employees on such things as the identification of toxic chemicals and how to use the MSDS system that explains how to neutralize possible negative side effects of chemical exposure.

In addition to OSHA-mandated training, some companies routinely conduct safety training and retraining in order to keep liability insurance premiums to a minimum. Such training can help a company to become "certified" as a safe company. Also, being designated as a safe company can help boost employee morale and make employees feel more secure.

Safety training is particularly important for production workers. They need training in the following areas: 1) recognizing, avoiding, and preventing unsafe conditions in their job and work areas; 2) procedures and rules relating to the use, transport, and storage of dangerous machinery, tools, and substances; 3) rules for the use of protective clothing, systems, and devices for hazardous machinery, tools, and chemicals; and 4) methods of controlling hazards of any type, including the use of a fire extinguisher and other emergency equipment.

Safety training programs should be conducted both in the classroom and on the job site. Classroom training can focus on safety regulations, accident reporting procedures, and other general information. Classroom training typically includes the most common approaches to safety training, that is, live instructors and video presentations, but can also include computer-based interactive training.[62] Computer-based training (CBT) programs can be classified as 1) computer-assisted instruction (CAI), in which the program provides drill and practice; 2) computer-managed instruction (CMI), in which the program evaluates the student's test performance, guides him or her to appropriate instructional resources and tracks progress; and 3) computer-enriched instruction (CEI), in which the computer serves as a simulator or programming device.[63] Research has shown that safety trainees using CBT demonstrate equal or better achievement when compared with those who receive traditional instruction, and do so in less time, regardless of age, type of CBT used, or type of computer used. However, OSHA clearly states that while interactive CBT can be a valuable tool in a training program, its use alone does not meet the intent of most OSHA training requirements. OSHA believes employees must be given the opportunity to ask questions, which requires access to a qualified trainer.[64]

On-site training can focus on actual safety standards and behaviors. **On-site safety observations (OSO)** are a way for organizations to take a proactive approach to improve their safety training efforts. An OSO is a formal, structured approach for conducting a safety needs assessment. Typically, the safety instructor will visit the worksite to gather critical data about workplace conditions, safe work procedures, and to conduct behavioral observations. This information is then used as the basis for developing training programs, better enabling the instructor to craft and tailor materials that are more relevant to trainees in a particular class.[65] Many organizations use behavior modeling as a training technique to reinforce desirable behaviors. As with any form of training, trainee transfer is a critical issue in safety training. Organizations should coordinate and reinforce safety training with other HRM procedures, such as performance evaluation and rewards systems, to motivate employees to put their safety training to use.

The effectiveness of safety training can be assessed by determining whether the safety standards and behaviors are being practiced. OSHA emphasizes evaluating training effectiveness in the short run by using a posttraining test of safety standards and procedures and monitoring behaviors. Long-run effectiveness can be determined by whether incidences of accidents, illness, and death decline.[66] In an effort to help organizations meet the demands of proper safety training, OSHA has developed a **Voluntary Protection Program.** This program encourages organizations to work in conjunction with OSHA to establish workplace safety programs. In return, OSHA provides free (and confidential) consulting services and assists with employee safety training. Participants are then exempted from OSHA inspections concerning the issues raised through the voluntary program.[67]

OSHA has recently changed its focus from a major emphasis on random inspections to an emphasis on a smaller number of highly targeted inspections. As a result, heavier penalties have been levied against fewer, but more serious offenders. Below is a graphical depiction of U.S. OSHA inspections over an eleven-year period:

| Year | # U.S. OSHA Inspections |
|------|-------------------------|
| 1988 | 27,343 |
| 1989 | 52,255 |
| 1990 | 44,821 |
| 1991 | 41,410 |
| 1992 | 42,709 |
| 1993 | 39,921 |
| 1994 | 47,070 |
| 1995 | 26,396 |
| 1996 | 25,850 |
| 1997 | 35,906 |
| 1998 | 3,697[68] |

It is important to note that while management and training professionals are traditionally responsible for training their workers in safety, other effective sources can be used. For example, safety training programs initiated by unions have gained strength and numbers over the past ten years. In addition, successful peer training programs are in place in a number of organizations. Peer trainers have played a major role in safety training, as evidence builds about how effective and credible fellow workers can be in this function.[69]

Ultimately, employee safety hinges on improving both the safety of the working conditions in which employees operate, as well as increasing the amount of safe work behaviors engaged in by employees. Sadly, many workplace accidents are caused by employees acting in an unsafe manner (e.g., removing guards from machines, not wearing required protective gear, or not using equipment in the proper way). OSHA safety rules and regulations, protective gear, and other safety devices can all work to reduce the number of unsafe working conditions faced by employees. However, well-done safety training can be one of the most important elements to ensure that employees have both the skills and the motivation to perform their jobs as safely as possible.

## QUALITY TRAINING

Since the early 1980s, organizations have recognized the value of W. Edwards Deming's theories as a way to increase organizational productivity and quality. Deming's fourteen guiding principles have served as the foundation for many quality improvement initiatives, first in Japan, and later in the United States and elsewhere. One outgrowth of Deming's principles is the concept of total quality management (TQM), defined as a set of principles (and practices) aimed at continually improving organizational effectiveness and efficiency.[70] It is a process designed to empower *all* employees to seek **continous** improvements in quality. For employees, a change to TQM requires them to learn and embrace two fundamental skills: 1) the ability to work effectively with others in a team, and 2) the collection, analysis, and evaluation of quantitative data in decision making.[71] TQM has become a primary vehicle for introducing quality improvement in all kinds of organizations, including nonprofits and those in private industry and government. Depending on the industry, between 60 percent and 90 percent of U.S. companies have adopted some form of TQM.[72] One of the keys to successful TQM programs is **quality training.** The 2000 Industry Report by *Training* estimated that 82 percent of organizations provide training in quality and process improvement.[73]

Since the first-year failure rate of quality management programs is high, it is essential to follow an orderly process in the early stages of any TQM initiative.[74] A critical first step in developing a quality training program is for top management to agree on what quality means to the organization and on a set of metrics for measuring it. Table 9.6 identifies eight primary areas of concern prevalent in organizations that implement TQM.[75] The TQM philosophy argues that this first step should be conducted with input from people throughout the organization, especially frontline workers, and from the customers and clients the organization serves.

Quality can be defined from many perspectives, including product quality, service quality, and customer quality.[76] *Product quality* is defined as the degree to which products achieve or exceed production standards. Indicators of product quality can include things like the number of defects, recalls, and scrap, as well as

■ **TABLE 9-6**

MAJOR AREAS OF CONCERN FOR QUALITY
IMPROVEMENT EFFORTS

- the role of management leadership and quality policy
- training
- process management
- employee relations
- product/service design
- supplier quality management
- the role of the quality department
- quality data and reporting

SOURCE: P. Mandal, A. Howell, & A. S. Sohal (1998). A systemic approach to quality improvements: The interactions between the technical, human and quality systems. *Total Quality Management, 9,* 79–99.

the adherence to design specifications. *Service quality* is how well the organization responds to the customers' needs after the product or service is delivered. It can be viewed as an attitude based on the customer's perceptions of performance.[77] This can be measured by noting things such as service response time, service backlog, and customer satisfaction ratings. *Customer quality* can be defined as the extent to which the organization has met or surpassed overall customer expectations. This can be measured by such things as customer surveys and tracking customer complaints. Customer quality should not be ignored. Even when the product or service is technically perfect, it may fail in the marketplace if it does not meet customer expectations.[78]

It can be advantageous to implement quality training in two phases: quality awareness training and in-depth quality process and skills training. In the first phase, *awareness,* managers are introduced to the concept of quality improvement and how it will change their role. Awareness sessions should be led by a top manager who must demonstrate his or her long-term commitment to change, and make sure that other managers understand their "new" role in this approach, and the kind of support that will be expected from each manager. For example, some organizations, like Rockwell International, ensure that middle management has a vested interest in TQM by linking the program to their reward structure.[79] In turn, these managers are expected to conduct quality awareness sessions in their own units. Some organizations create a new organizational unit that is given direct responsibility for implementing the TQM program, including training programs. In addition, some organizations appoint task groups or "change committees" to oversee the process of organizational change (organizational change processes will be discussed in more detail in Chapter 14).

The next phase of TQM generally involves more *in-depth training* in process skills and quality skills. *Process skills* refer to ways to improve work coordination, solve problems, and resolve conflicts. *Quality skills* refer to the techniques and tools that can be used for tracking quality improvements. There are at least seven

**■ TABLE 9-7**

| Quality Tool | How It Is Used |
|---|---|
| Process Flow Analysis | Used to chart the process or production flow that can lead to reduction of cycle time, cost savings, improvement of service to customers, and increased profitability. |
| Cause-and-Effect Diagram | Can help solve problems by pinpointing their root causes, differentiating between symptoms and causes of problems. Once causes are determined, information obtained can be used to develop an action plan to correct the problem. |
| Run Chart | Used to illustrate trends and results in terms of time and frequency of events. Information can be used for predicting future outcomes given current conditions. |
| Statistical Process Control (SPC) | Helps to determine if a process is stable and predictable, identify common causes of variation, and clarify when employee intervention is needed. |
| Scattergram | Used to determine how two variables are related (or correlated). For example, one variable (number of training days) is positively related to another variable (quality improvements) in any one department or work group. This data can be plotted and shown to management as justification for additional training days. |
| Histogram | Used for displaying data obtained from actual work practices, usually variations in time it takes for different employees to perform a common task. If the data represent even distribution, the majority of the employees would make up the mean (or average) with fewer performing at higher or lower levels. These data are useful for establishing work standards. |
| Pareto Chart | Can be used to assess different tasks or problems in terms of the time needed for performance or resolution. It is similar to a bar chart, which helps the team or the manager to decide on the priority of each event. |

SOURCE: Adapted from C. C. Carter (1992). Seven basic quality tools. *HR Magazine, 37* (1), 81–83.

quality tools (see Table 9-7) that can be used for analyzing causes and effects, problem solving, monitoring results, and recommending courses of action.

Of the quality tools described in Table 9-7, **statistical process control (SPC)** has been most widely applied in various organizational settings (though more heavily in manufacturing than in service organizations). The principle underlying SPC is that most processes demonstrate variations in output and that it is important to determine whether the causes of such a variation are normal or abnormal.[80] SPC focuses on training employees to be able to discern abnormal variations, so that adjustments can be made to the process in order to improve quality. Employees must learn to monitor output using control charts so that they can see variations.

In terms of the outcomes or effectiveness of TQM, there are a number of published evaluation studies of TQM, but only a few isolate the effects of the quality training program. One study, conducted by Motorola, evaluated the company's program using a multiple-group research design.[81] Trainees were assigned to three research groups: 1) those using the entire quality training curriculum (both process skills and quality skills) followed with reinforcement from senior managers; 2) those emphasizing either process or quality skills and followed up by senior managers; and 3) those using one or both methods, with no follow-up. Outcomes for the three groups were as follows: 1) the first yielded a $33 return for every dollar spent on training; 2) the second broke even; and 3) the third had a negative return.[82] These results would indicate that quality training should be comprehensive (covering both process and quality skills), and must be followed up by management.

Other factors often cited as necessary for successful TQM implementation are visionary leadership, upper management commitment and support for the transition to TQM, widespread employee involvement, integrated reward and compensation plans for quality improvements, and a performance evaluation process that is aligned with the nature of a TQM organization.[83]

Of the unsuccessful attempts at TQM initiatives, case studies show that trained employees often fail to transfer their new skills to the workplace for the following reasons: 1) general employee resistance to change; 2) management failure to articulate clear objectives; and 3) few rewards for on-the-job use of new skills.[84] TQM will be discussed further in Chapter 14.

### QUALITY TRAINING AND ISO 9000

A major boost for the quality movement was the establishment of uniform quality standards by the International Standards Organization (ISO). ISO is the international nongovernmental agency that has been established to improve the international exchange of goods and services and to develop international cooperation in intellectual, scientific, technological and economic activity.[85] Prior to ISO, organizations attempting to trade internationally faced different sets of standards for product quality. The primary purpose of ISO was to establish and monitor a set of quality standards that would serve as a common reference point for international trade.[86] The ISO standards have been revised a number of times.

One set of standards, referred to as ISO 9000, is directed at the quality of the processes used in creating a product or service.[87] In addition to the ISO 9000 family of quality process standards, there are presently two offshoots: QS 9000, specifically targeted at the automotive industry; and TL 9000, aimed at reducing the cost of poor quality production within the global telecommunications industry.[88] Since ISO standards are more prevalent and encompassing, our discussion will focus on them.

Companies that comply with ISO 9000 standards are eligible to be officially registered and can use that designation in their trading activities and advertisements. To become ISO-registered (or certified), companies must be able to create and document a systematic program for delivering a product or service. There are three phases to implementing ISO 9000: document writing, implementation of a quality system, and system assessment for effectiveness. The second stage — implementation — takes up about half the time needed for registration, and this is where training takes place.[89] Initially, as U.S. companies became registered, they had a significant advantage over their domestic competition when doing business overseas, particularly in Europe. Today, ISO registration still offers organizations a marketing tool, worldwide recognition, and the ability to demonstrate the company's commitment to quality over competitors who are lacking the ISO designation. However, with almost 100,000 companies having earned this distinction, it is no longer a luxury; ISO has become a necessity for doing business in the international marketplace.

Based on numerous studies covering the ISO registration process, company-wide employee involvement through training is the quickest, most cost-effective way to achieve and maintain certification.[90] One of the ISO 9000 requirements has to do with an organization's quality training practices. Specifically, this requirement 1) focuses on how the organization identifies the training needs of employees who have a direct impact on quality and 2) requires documentation of the training provided. ISO standards require that the organization conduct a job analysis to update job descriptions, including the qualifications needed to perform the work. For example, suppose that an analysis revealed that one of the knowledge requirements (KSAOs) for a particular job was knowledge of statistical process control techniques. The organization must ensure that job incumbents receive the appropriate training and that the training effort is documented.

The ISO monitors compliance by having ISO-certified auditors visit each ISO 9000-registered organization every six to twelve months to review whether the standards are being maintained, including reviewing the organization's training records. Basically, the auditors are checking to make sure that employees are performing a specific task according to the work instructions given. If they are, the employee is deemed to be adequately trained. This holds true for illiterate and handicapped employees as well. If the employee is able to explain the steps of the work instructions, and can demonstrate the necessary skills, the training is deemed adequate.[91] Noncompliance could potentially result in the loss of registration.

HRD professionals in organizations that are ISO 9000 registered (or want to be) must be aware of the ISO 9000 standards and help ensure that their organization is in compliance with them. In many organizations, the HRD professional is responsible for the training element. However, in some organizations, responsibility for ISO 9000 compliance may be given to a "quality assurance" unit, in which case HRD professionals could serve as partners in training-related compliance activities. In any case, it is imperative that HRD professionals take a proactive role in ensuring that training activities meet ISO standards.

For greater detail about ISO 9000, we urge you to seek out further information, including viewing the following Web sites:

http://www.asq.org
http://www.mttc.org/default.htm

http://www.rvarmstrong.com/ISO9000Training.htm
http://qualitymag.com

## INTERPERSONAL SKILLS TRAINING

As discussed before, a number of basic workplace competencies involve skills that are needed to work effectively with other people. These skills, sometimes referred to as "soft" skills, include communication, customer relations, selling, and teamwork. All can be improved through training.

It is estimated that interpersonal skills training is offered by 83 percent of organizations.[92] Interpersonal skills training programs cover a wide range of topics, with the most common ones being team building (67 percent), listening skills (63 percent), and delegation skills (61 percent).

Three trends have increased the need for interpersonal skills training. The first trend is a movement by organizations toward team-based approaches to accomplishing work, which usually involve team training with a strong interpersonal component. Second, graduates from high school and colleges and universities often lack the interpersonal skills that organizations require, and third, many organizations are becoming more multicultural. With changing labor market demographics and the growth of multinational organizations, more and more organizations are developing cultural diversity programs. These courses are intended to change some of the incorrect assumptions, values, and beliefs people have about other cultures, with the desired outcome being the development of more effective crosscultural interpersonal skills. These programs will be discussed in more detail in Chapter 15.

Interpersonal skills training programs offered by organizations vary in content. For example, at Motorola University in Schaumburg, Illinois, employees receive training in such topics as interpersonal communications, parenting, and weight management. Tech Central, a temporary services firm based in Edina, Minnesota, provides training in customer service, conflict resolution, interpersonal relations, and teamwork. At SAS Institute, a software developer in Carey, North Carolina, employees are trained in business ethics, time management, and leadership skills.[93] Finally, Duke Energy, in Charlotte, North Carolina, includes two interpersonal training courses (personal development and relationship development) in its professional development core curriculum.[94] These courses emphasize providing trainees with a better understanding of themselves and the handling of workplace relationships. In this section, we discuss three types of training that can be considered interpersonal skills training: sales training, customer service training, and teamwork training.

### SALES TRAINING

Traditional sales techniques (e.g., the "hard sell") are increasingly being abandoned for more consultative approaches that build trust, solve customers' problems, provide product and service options, and admit limitations.[95] This newer approach is intended to build customer loyalty and improve long-term customer relations.

The key to adopting new sales approaches is sales training. It is estimated that 56 percent of all organizations offer some type of sales training. This figure rises dramatically for the retail and banking industries, reaching levels of 83 percent and 81 percent, respectively.[96] Training varies widely, from traditional sales techniques to the new consultative approaches. Some organizations, following the lead of Saturn Corporation, are overhauling entire retail and wholesale operations through comprehensive sales training programs. For example, at Motorola University, training goes hand in hand with all sales activity. Motorola involves sales managers as part of the "knowledge community" that is used to support their salespeople. These managers are coached on how to question, monitor, and review the efforts of salespeople to ensure that their training is being used. Salespeople must post account plans that are reviewed and revised by sales managers or sales trainers. The idea behind its sales training integration plan is to involve trainers at every step of the process, to measure results as soon after training as possible, and ultimately eliminate the differentiation between training and coaching on the job.[97]

Most organizations, however, are not willing to make such drastic changes. Some supplement sales training with other types of training (e.g., customer service training) that are intended to equip employees with the interpersonal skills needed to be effective. Many organizations also combine sales training with customer relations/service training. A sales training program should be tailored to an organization's needs. In particular, sales training objectives should be operationally defined based on the organization's goals (particularly their marketing goals) and should include input from sales representatives.[98] Listed below are six general objectives of high-performance sales training programs. An organization could use these as the basis to tailor its specific company objectives:

- increased sales productivity
- lower turnover
- enhanced communication within and between all organizational levels
- better morale
- increased self-management of sales teams
- better customer relations

The specific objectives that an organization defines must be clear and must be understood by all employees.[99]

## CUSTOMER RELATIONS/SERVICE TRAINING

The increased emphasis on quality improvement has led organizations to emphasize customer relations and customer service. It is estimated that 74 percent of organizations conduct some form of **customer service training**.[100] In almost any job, customer service skills are important to achieving success, and people skills form the foundation for good customer service. Such skills include interpersonal relations, problem solving, leadership, and teamwork (discussed in the next section). People skills can foster a positive attitude, effective communication, courteous and respectful interaction and the ability to remain calm and in control in difficult situations.[101]

Any employee who interacts with a customer, even if indirectly, represents the organization, and each customer's perception of the quality of that interaction may influence how the organization's products and service are perceived. For example, a survey of over 1,300 retail customers concluded that 1) good service keeps customers coming back, while poor service drives them away, 2) organizations should continuously monitor customers' perceptions of their service, and 3) job skills of customer service employees most likely need to be enhanced through training.[102]

The notion that *good service keeps customers coming back* is the crux of many customer service programs. For example, Guaranteed Eateries in Seattle instituted a customer guarantee program, referred to as "Your Enjoyment Guaranteed," which involved giving free drinks and even entirely free meals if certain service guidelines were not met. The frontline employees were empowered to grant these guarantees. While the program is estimated to cost about $10,000 per month, sales have risen 25 percent and profits have doubled.[103]

*Continuously monitoring customers' perceptions of service* is also critical. An organization must be able to get feedback from its customers to determine if their needs were met. For example, Norand Corporation got "closer to the customer" by instituting a customer feedback system through monthly in-depth telephone surveys that were tabulated and circulated to each sales and service manager.[104] The results of such surveys can be used as part of the needs assessment process.

While customer service training varies considerably across both industries and companies, it has some common components. Stum and Church suggest that it should include four elements:[105]

1. **Introduce customer service training organizationwide.** Organizationwide customer service training can be a key component of a business turnaround. For example, in the 1980s, executives at Scandinavian Airlines Systems (SAS) reversed several years of losses to attain a gross profit of $71 million because, among other things, "they put 27,000 employees through a company-wide (customer service) training program".[106] Most leading service companies place such training on a similar high level of importance by including it in standard employee orientation programs.[107]

2. **Train frontline employees in customer relations skills, including interpersonal skills and operational practices.** This training is necessary for two reasons. First, customer contact employees (e.g., sales associates, customer service representatives, recruiters, secretaries, account executives) must have the skills and abilities to successfully relate to customers. Important interpersonal skills include the ability to listen and speak effectively. Second, the training should reinforce the notion that the long-term health of the organization depends, in part, on frontline employees exceeding customer expectations.[108] This is an important point.

Customer-contact employees must be able to understand each customer's needs so that they can "shape" expectations. To do this, organizations must empower frontline employees to guarantee customer satisfaction, even if this means incurring additional costs.

3. **Train service managers in how to coach employees and how to enforce new customer service standards.** Desatnick suggests that developing a customer-oriented workforce requires the hiring of service managers to train, develop, and motivate employees.[109] Organizations should provide training to service managers to ensure they understand their roles and the need to monitor and reinforce customer service standards. The term **service manager** is used in a wider context here to include any supervisor whose employees interact with customers and other outsiders, from the sales manager to the office manager supervising secretaries who greet and interact with customers and clients.

4. **Provide incentives for supporting and sustaining the new customer service philosophy, including (but not limited to) recognition systems, compensation, and upgrading.** Customer service training should include employee incentives (or disincentives) that serve to reinforce desired behaviors. A wide range of individual and group incentives can be used for this purpose. Historically, organizations have relied on individual incentives, such as commissions, to motivate employees. However, in recent years, more and more organizations are making increasing use of group incentives, such as employee involvement and gain-sharing programs.

Some organizations have highly developed and formalized customer training curricula. For example, Tiffany & Company, a respected jewelry seller, has very high standards concerning what constitutes exceptional customer service. New salespeople must complete six to eight weeks of training before they ever meet with their first customer. All new sales representatives must go through knowledge, skills (customer service is a part of skills training at Tiffany), and product training. They then visit and tour corporate headquarters and the customer service/distribution center for a week of "graduate" coursework. The skills training here consists of telephone skills, presentation skills, and consultative selling. The customer service training process is essential, and allows Tiffany "to uphold the unique tradition and culture" for which it is so widely known.[110] As another example, Fidelity Institutional Retirement Services Company (FIRSCo) created the Service Delivery University (SDU). The SDU is organized into five separate "colleges": Customer Service, Operations Management, Risk Management, Sales and Marketing, and Leadership and Management Development. Associates are required to complete the curriculum in all five colleges. The most critical college is the Customer Service College. Its purpose is "to create a company-wide dialogue about service excellence and how it is best delivered" so that after employees have completed training at the five colleges they will "share a common language of service delivery," which is essential in a heavily regulated industry such as they are in.[111]

▪ **TABLE 9-8**

| Type of Team | Member Roles and Functions | Training Provided |
|---|---|---|
| Quality Circle | Members voluntarily join teams headed by circle leaders, who make quality improvement suggestions to a steering committee that has authority to allocate resources. | Team Building<br>Problem Solving<br>Quality |
| Cross-Functional | Members from different functional areas are assigned to a common work team with common work activities. Members may be required to train others in their specialty. | Team Building<br>Skills Training |
| Semiautonomous | Restructuring of a work team in which members may be given authority to manage and execute some parts of their work tasks. | Team Building<br>Empowerment |
| Self-Managed | Restructuring of a work team in which team members will be able to self-regulate work on their interdependent tasks. Team members may have total control over management and execution of entire tasks. | Team Building<br>Management Skills<br>Empowerment |
| Self-Designed | Creating a new work team in which members will assume total control over the design, membership, role, and tasks of the team. | Team Building<br>Management Skills<br>Organizational Change<br>Empowerment |

SOURCE: Based on information from R. D. Banker, J. M. Field, R. G. Schroeder, and K. K. Sinha (1996). Impact of work teams on manufacturing performance: A longitudinal field study. *Academy of Management Journal, 39* (4), 867–890.

## TEAM BUILDING/TRAINING

Another recent development (partly growing out of the quality improvement movement) is the increasing emphasis on the use of teams as the basic organizational unit. It is estimated that 73 percent of all organizations have some employees working in teams. In those organizations that use teams, 55 percent of employees, on average, work as team members.[112] Team-based structures require that workers be adaptable and able to form and re-form relationships with coworkers quickly and smoothly. Furthermore, the popularity of *team training* is on the rise. According to the American Society for Training and Development, team training is one of the hottest trends in human resources.[113] The 2000 Industry Report estimated that 87 percent of organizations provide team-building training.[114]

A team is defined as a group of "individuals who see themselves and who are seen by others as a social entity, who are embedded in one or more larger social systems (e.g., community, organizations), and who perform tasks that affect others (such as customers or coworkers)."[115] Five common types of work teams are quality circle, cross-functional, semiautonomous, self-managed, and self-designed teams. Table 9-8 provides a description of the team member roles and functions in each type, and gives an example of the kinds of training that team members may receive.

There are at least two sets of team-related skills—task skills and process skills. *Task skills* are skills necessary for accomplishing the work assigned to the group. In a typical organization, employees will likely have the appropriate task-related skills and knowledge, but they must be able to apply those skills in a group setting. In addition, they may need to be cross-trained in skills other members have in order to perform group tasks together. For example, a team of mechanics and technicians that is charged with servicing an airplane will each bring unique and complementary talents to the task. Each member has a specific role to perform, and some roles must be performed in conjunction with other team members. However, to function as a team, members must understand each other's roles and see how they fit together into the overall task. *Process skills* are those skills that primarily have to do with working together as a team and maintaining the team relationships that are essential for teamwork. Interpersonal skills are among the most important process skills, and this includes skills in communication, negotiation, and conflict resolution.

A common form of team training is called **team building.** Team building can be viewed as an effort to unify varied individual energies, direct these energies toward valued goals and outputs, and link these efforts to organizational results.[116] It typically refers to a collection of techniques that are designed to build the trust, cohesiveness, and mutual sense of responsibility that make for an effective team. Most team-building interventions are led by a facilitator (sometimes called a change agent) whose role is to help the team improve its ability to work together effectively, communicate better, improve problem-solving capabilities, and make better decisions. However, teams should not be formed just for the sake of having them. Teams should have a specific purpose, and be formed to accomplish a goal that needs the attention of a diverse group of people within an organization. Organizations should consider forming teams under conditions such as the following:

- A specific goal (or set of goals) needs a multifaceted group of people with complementary talents.

- A specific project is best addressed by cross-functional and multidepartmental coworkers who offer different perspectives.

- Broad-based perspectives are needed to develop and carry out the vision of growing a department or organization.[117]

■ **TABLE 9-9**

FOUR MODELS OF TEAM BUILDING

| Model | Emphasis | Team-member objective |
|---|---|---|
| Goal Setting | Setting objectives and developing individual and team goals | Involved in action planning to identify ways to achieve the goals that have been set |
| Interpersonal Relations | An increase in teamwork skills (mutual supportiveness, communication, sharing ideas) | Develop trust in each other and confidence in the team |
| Problem Solving | Identification of major problems in the team | Become involved in action planning for the solution of problems, as well as implementing and evaluating the solutions |
| Role Clarification | Increased communication among team members regarding their respective roles within the team | Achieve better understanding of their and others' respective roles and duties within the team |

SOURCE: E. Salas, D. Rozell, B. Mullen, & J. E. Driskell (1999). The effect of team building on performance: An integration. *Small Group Research, 30,* 309–329.

Team-based approaches are fairly widespread, and teams have been shown to be an effective organizational intervention.[118] In Table 9-9, four approaches or models for building teams are presented. Under appropriate conditions, each approach can be an effective organizational intervention.[119] There is a growing literature on team effectiveness.[120] However, there remains a limited amount of research concerning the efficacy of *team training* that would help to guide practitioners in designing training systems.[121] HRD professionals should rely on the HRD process framework (i.e., assess, design, implement, evaluate) in designing and delivering team-training programs, be vigilant about new research, and make judicious use of scientific and practical knowledge that is available. Teams will be discussed further (as an intervention to promote organization development) in Chapter 14.

## ROLE OF LABOR UNIONS IN SKILLS AND TECHNICAL TRAINING PROGRAMS

Historically, labor unions have been concerned with promoting the interests of union members, which includes keeping their skills and competencies current. As the demand for higher skilled workers has increased, unions have often taken an active role in providing training for their members, including both developing and sponsoring a wide variety of training programs. Some unions have joined together to establish regional or statewide training centers. Many of these centers receive additional funding from public and private sources. Unions have also sought collaboration with schools and employers to meet the training needs of their members. These efforts are generally referred to as joint training programs.

### JOINT TRAINING PROGRAMS

A joint training program is an extension of the management-labor union relationship in which the goal is to provide meaningful training and personal developmental opportunities for union members. Unlike employer-sponsored HRD programs, which are under an employer's control and are available to a range of employees, joint training programs are administered by both the employer and the union and are usually available only to union members. Joint training programs vary in content. A study of 152 programs revealed that the four most common content areas were 1) safety and health (22 percent), 2) job skills training (17 percent), 3) communication skills (16 percent), and 4) assistance for displaced workers (11 percent).[122]

Most joint training programs comprise individual courses or programs that are fairly simple to administer, but some are large, complex programs. One example of a joint training program is the Alliance for Employee Growth and Development, which was created in 1986 by AT&T, the Communications Workers of America (CWA), and the International Brotherhood of Electrical Workers (IBEW). The alliance is administered by two co-executive directors (one from AT&T and one from CWA) who report to a six-member board of trustees (three from each side).[123] The staff is dispersed among three regional headquarters in New Jersey, Texas, and Georgia. According to Treinen and Ross:

> The backbone of the Alliance organization is the local committees . . . made up of about six persons, three each from the company and unions. It is their job to raise the awareness of the Alliance in the eyes of their work force; to survey the work force to identify training needs; to identify potential vendors of services within the local community; to work for Alliance staff to negotiate contracts with vendors; to monitor training activities for quality and relevant outcomes; and to perform posttraining analysis to ensure that programming is ongoing and fits the needs of the workers themselves.[124]

In the wake of the layoffs that resulted from the divestiture of AT&T in 1984, the first challenge to the alliance was to address the needs of almost 100,000 displaced workers. To deal with this, the alliance established displacement projects, relocation assistance, job placements, and a host of retraining opportunities. In addition to an array of ongoing training and education programs, the alliance developed a comprehensive career and skills assessment process to provide displaced employees with meaningful information to develop individual development plans. Treinen and Ross viewed the alliance's efforts as experimental and an opportunity to try to evaluate ways cooperation can benefit all parties concerned.[125]

The following are other examples of joint partnership programs:

1. In response to concerns about literacy among its members, the Laborers International Union collaborated with the Associated General Contractors to develop a Learn-At-Home video literacy program. The program was completed by 3,000 laborers in a two-year period.[126]

2. In response to the growing need for entry level employment in the service industry, union and casino officials partnered together to offer a two-week training program to provide the skills needed to garner these jobs. The Southern Nevada Joint Management Culinary and Bartenders Training Fund, whose board included both casino and union officials, supported the effort. The center successfully trained more than 2,400 workers.[127]

3. A training trust was set up in Ohio, where the Communications Workers of America Local 4340 partnered with various employers, to help pay for the training and certification of journeyman telecommunications technicians. Both the local union and the employers each pay into the program 12 cents an hour of each member's wages. With this partnership, a person successfully completing the training program is "basically guaranteed" to get hired, as the demand for technicians is high.[128]

These kinds of programs are examples of what can happen when labor unions, employers, state governments, and other institutions collaborate and focus their energies on improving workplace competencies. Joint training programs benefit the participating union members, and they can foster better relationships between union leaders and management.

Joint training programs have a few implications for HRD professionals. First, if union leaders and management have a strong adversarial relationship, HRD professionals may find resistance from either side when proposing programs that are intended to benefit union members. Either side may suggest that these programs should be part of contract negotiations. However, in general, joint programs are best accomplished if they are outside of normal collective bargaining structures. Second, by having union leaders as active partners, HRD professionals should be able to better identify the needs of union members and, as a result, improve the design, implementation, and scheduling of training. Also, program announcements could be disseminated through the union's normal communication channels (e.g., union newsletter). Third, collaborating with unions on a single joint program provides an opportunity for HRD programs to promote other programs to union leaders as well.

## PROFESSIONAL DEVELOPMENT AND EDUCATION

A profession is an occupation that is based on an abstract body of knowledge.[129] Sharma describes the essence of a **profession** this way: a profession is an occupation in which workers "apply in their work a body of knowledge and techniques acquired through training and experience, have a service orientation and distinctive ethics, and have a great deal of autonomy and prestige."[130] Examples of professions include medicine, law, accounting, teaching, and engineering. Professional associations exist in most professions. A **professional association** is a private group that exists to advance and protect the interests of the profession and to offer services to its members (e.g., certification, publications, educational opportunities).

The domain of knowledge that an individual must master in order to be "officially" considered a professional in a given field is typically defined by the professional association (and, in some cases, state governments). In many professions, a credential such as a **license** or **certificate** is required for the individual to practice in that field. Generally speaking, licensing is administered by state governments, whereas certification is administered by professional associations. In both cases, the criteria an individual must typically meet include attainment of a degree, a given level of practical experience, and a passing score on an examination. For example, to earn the *Professional in Human Resources (PHR)* designation, an individual must pass a standardized test (administered by the Human Resource Certification Institute), and have a minimum of two years of exempt-level experience in human resources.

Because effectiveness as a professional is based on applying a body of knowledge, it is critical that professionals keep current with the latest ideas and techniques in their field. Professional associations and licensing agencies typically require license or certificate holders to engage in continuing education to maintain this credential. For example, the American Institute of Certified Public Accountants has adopted a national standard that requires practicing CPAs to attend a minimum of forty hours of mandatory continuing professional education courses per year.[131] Continuing education opportunities are offered by at least three sources—college and universities, professional associations, and the organizations that employ professionals. We will briefly describe each.

## CONTINUING EDUCATION AT COLLEGES AND UNIVERSITIES

Many colleges and universities offer courses to meet the continuing education needs of professionals. Some benefits that can come out of this arrangement are 1) organizations are able to use the expertise available at colleges, 2) organizations can sometimes assist the schools in designing courses that are job specific, 3) organizations can choose instructors, and 4) college credit may be granted, making it possible for employees to obtain a college degree. Whether these benefits are realized depends on the demand for the courses and the flexibility of the academic institution to meet the needs of professionals and organizations.

There are many examples of joint programs between colleges and professional organizations. For instance, the Center for Financial Studies at Fairfield University in Fairfield, Connecticut, developed a cooperative venture with the National Council of Savings Institutions, which offers workshops to area banks and other financial organizations. Companies like NCR, Pacific Bell, and Control Data have developed college-credit courses approved by the American Council on Education Program on Non-collegiate Sponsored Instruction (ACE/PONSI), which uses administrators and faculty from local colleges to evaluate programs.[132] American College offers specialized training for insurance professionals, including those from John Hancock Financial Services.[133]

Some states have experimented with partnership programs. The state of New York began an experiment in 1983 with the Public Employees Federation, a government employees' union, in which public administration courses were designed and offered at area colleges and universities. The uniqueness of this program was that it was tied to the union contract, and thus had greater protection from budget cuts.[134] Similarly, the Governmental Services Center at Kentucky State University provides mandatory training and career management workshops to a full spectrum of public sector employees.[135]

### CONTINUING EDUCATION BY PROFESSIONAL ASSOCIATIONS

The main way professional associations provide continuing education opportunities is by sponsoring conferences, meetings, and workshops for their members. The program for these gatherings typically includes speeches by leading experts, discussion of current issues, and presentation of research findings. One of the primary benefits of these events is the opportunity to meet and share experiences with other professionals.

Another way professional associations try to keep their members current is by publishing journals, magazines, and newsletters that communicate ideas and practices in the field. Increasingly, professional associations are using the World Wide Web to disseminate this information. For example, the Society for Human Resource Management's Web site is a useful site for HRD professionals (http://www.shrm.org).

Some professional associations also offer precertification workshops to help members achieve certification. Precertification programs can be offered at the association's training center or at local colleges. For instance, the insurance industry sponsors two precertification programs leading to the chartered life underwriter (CLU) and chartered financial consultant (ChFC) designations at the American College.[136]

### COMPANY-SPONSORED CONTINUING EDUCATION

Organizations also play an important part in offering continuing education opportunities for the professionals they employ. Some organizations have developed collegelike curricula within their own training centers. At the same time that many organizations are moving toward decentralizing the delivery of training programs, there appears to be a continuing trend toward developing on-site **corporate universities.** It is estimated that 1,000 organizations have developed centralized training curricula, called "university," "college," or "institute of learning," that are based on an academic metaphor.[137] These on-site programs generally include a core curriculum that can be completed in stages so that it can be managed along with employees' jobs. The Service Delivery University at

## NCR OFFERS EDUCATION FOR ALL IN DUNDEE, SCOTLAND[1]

A significant development over the past twenty years has been the emergence of the Automated Teller Machine, or ATM, for obtaining cash and performing other basic banking transactions. U.S.-based NCR has been a leading manufacturer of ATMs, and one of its major manufacturing plants is in Dundee, Scotland. The Dundee plant has won numerous awards for their ATM design and manufacturing.

In the early 1990s, a program entitled Education for All was started at the Dundee facility. The goal was to enhance the plant's capacity to grow through continuous innovation, customer focus, and cost competitiveness. The emphasis at Dundee has been more broadly on employee education, rather than focusing strictly on employee skills. Learning centers were set up in the plant, and links were established with local colleges and universities. Employee self-development and career development were encouraged by this program. NCR paid for any educational courses that were broadly related to the company's business, and gave employees time off work to take such courses.

In 1991, 9 percent of all employees participated in at least one course through Education for All. By 1998, that figure had risen to 20 percent. Courses have included both undergraduate and graduate work in electronics, engineering, and other topics.

NCR Dundee enjoyed strong sales and a high degree of job security for many years. However, in 1998, a decision was announced to lay off 200 of the plant's 1,500 employees, as a portion of their production process was going to be outsourced to other plants.

Judy Pate and her colleagues conducted research in 1999 at the Dundee plant. They surveyed employees who had participated in at least one Education for All course since 1995, and compared these surveys with others taken from a matched sample of employees who had not taken such courses (a control group). As predicted, employees who had used the Education for All program responded that they had used the knowledge and skills learned in their classes to enhance their work performance, that is, that learning transfer had occurred. Another interesting finding was that job satisfaction and organizational commitment were high for both groups. The researchers suggest that the Education for All program had produced a positive effect on employee attitudes— even after a lay-off announcement, and even for employees who had not used the program.

Overall, this case study would suggest that, at least for NCR Dundee, a commitment to employee education had both a direct and an indirect payoff. Employees obviously benefited from this continuing education program, but it would appear that NCR did as well.

[1]Pate, J., Martin, G., Beaumont, P., McGoldrick, J. (2000). Company-based lifelong learning: What's the payoff for employers? *Journal of European Industrial Training*, 24(2/3/4), 149–158.

FIRSCo, discussed earlier, would fit this description. Staffing of these on-site programs varies. Some organizations rely exclusively on employees. Organizations like Motorola hire faculty for their on-site programs, both from among their senior professionals (many of them at retirement age) and from outside experts. This arrangement makes the program organization specific, and enables it to incorporate training in the latest technology. For an interesting example of company-sponsored continuing education, see the boxed inset above, "NCR Offers Education for All in Dundee, Scotland."

Saturn Corporation made a commitment to extensive training for new employees. Topics included technical skills, problem solving, interpersonal skills, teamwork, and continuous improvement techniques. Also, production workers received extensive ongoing training after the initial training efforts were completed.

For employees in the retail side of Saturn, a special program was established, entitled Saturn Training and Partnership (STEP). Your instructor has additional information on what was included in STEP to train employees at the Saturn dealerships.

## HRD DEPARTMENT'S ROLE IN CONTINUING EDUCATION

The HRD department has three distinct roles to play with respect to continuing education — as an enabler, a resource provider, and a monitor. As an *enabler*, the HRD department must establish policies and procedures that foster an effective and equitable distribution of continuing education throughout the organization. As a *resource provider*, the HRD department should consider program support options, including tuition reimbursement, educational leave, paid professional association fees, and compensation of travel expenses to off-site professional development sites. A tuition-reimbursement program is an important part of a professional development program because it increases the chances employees will continue their education. Tuition reimbursement programs are offered by an estimated 95 percent of large organizations.[138] Most programs reimburse educational expenses, including tuition and fees, provided the course is job related and the employee receives a specified grade (e.g., B or better). Many feel that such programs will make employees more valuable to the organization because it is hoped that by attending them the employees will become more creative, innovative, or entrepreneurial.[139]

While not as common, education leaves or sabbaticals offer employees an opportunity to continue their education or conduct research while they continue to receive pay for up to twelve months. Such programs are generally made available after a certain length of employment within the organization. Some organizations also offer these leaves to senior managers so that they can pursue other interests (e.g., teaching, volunteering time in a nonprofit organization, or writing).Usually, the employee must meet certain conditions to qualify for such leave, such as not having other means of support (e.g., another job) while on leave. In addition, return to the former job or organization is mandatory, as well as the production of a detailed report, conducting of seminars, or some other evidence to show that the leave was used productively.

Employers may also pay fees and expenses to allow employees to attend professional meetings and seminars. These sessions provide an opportunity to share ideas and discuss common issues. Such meetings are invaluable to employees who want to remain current in their fields and who want to write and present professional papers. Because of limited resources for such activities, an equitable process of approving these kinds of expenditures must be established. To be equitable, the policy should specify how employees can qualify for programs, provide justification for expenditures, and be approved by management. This policy should be made known throughout the organization.

Finally, the HRD department serves as a *monitor* by ensuring that the professional development process is working as planned. As we have stated many times already, evaluation is a critical part of any HRD effort. For instance, General Foods has a professional development process that requires supervisors to develop skills-assessment and development plans with each subordinate. These are used to organize training and development efforts in critical skill areas. They also allow HRD staff to monitor changes in the skills base of the individual unit or entire department.[140]

## SUMMARY

The need for skilled and technical workers continues to rise. Employers often express concern that many young adults are graduating from schools lacking the skills needed to perform their current jobs. We reviewed three categories of skills and technical training — basic skills, technical, and interpersonal. The level of illiteracy within the workforce has created a demand for basic skills programs. The content of these programs focuses on improving basic competencies, including reading, writing, and computational skills.

Technical training programs include apprenticeships and programs in computers, technical skills/knowledge, safety, and quality. Apprenticeship training, the most formalized employer-based program, involves both on-the-job (OJT) and classroom training. Computer training typically involves either introductory or applications training. Technical skills/knowledge programs are generally job specific and are offered organizationwide. Quality and team-training programs are typically part of a larger quality improvement agenda and may include training needed for the organization to become ISO 9000 registered.

Interpersonal training programs included communication, sales, customer relations, and team building and team training. Many of these programs focus on increasing productivity and improving the quality of products, customer service, and customer relations.

We also reviewed professional development and education programs. In many professions, professional workers are required to participate in continuing education in order to gain or renew a license or certification. Continuing education opportunities are offered by a variety of providers, including colleges and universities, professional associations, and the organizations that employ professional workers.

## KEY TERMS AND CONCEPTS

apprenticeship training
basic skills/literacy education

Occupational Safety and Health
Administration (OSHA)

certification

continuing education

corporate universities

customer service training

interpersonal skills training

ISO 9000

Job Training and Partnership Act
    (JTPA)

license/licensure

material safety data sheets (MSDS)

Occupational Safety and Health Act
    (OSHA)

on-site safety observations (OSO)

professional association

quality training

safety training

school-to-work program

statistical process control (SPC)

team building

team training

technical training

Voluntary Protection Program

Worker Adjustment and Retraining
    Notification (WARN) Act

Workforce Investment Act (WIA)

### QUESTIONS FOR DISCUSSION

1.  Explain why skills training programs are important for the long-term vitality of organizations.

2.  Describe the nature and extent of the literacy problem facing organizations today. How might this problem affect an organization's attempt to introduce new technology (e.g., a computer-aided manufacturing system)? What are the possible solutions?

3.  If you were responsible for designing a basic skills/literacy training program, what approach would you take? How would you determine the effectiveness of this program?

4.  Colleges and universities are primarily service enterprises. What key components would you include in customer service training for college employees, such as security or records office staff, who interact with students?

5.  Identify two ways that advances in information technology have affected organizations today. What are the implications of these advances for HRD professionals in ensuring that workers will be able to make the most of them?

6.  If your organization were contemplating using a team-based approach to increase productivity and reduce cost, what training issues would it be likely to face? How could the organization address these issues?

7.  Explain why continuing education for professionals is important to both organizational and individual success. What kinds of program options would you provide for professionals — such as accountants and dietitians — who need professional certification?

8.  Research and report back on the continuing education offerings (and requirements) in your area of study.

## REFERENCES

1. Judy, R. W., & D'Amico, C. (1997). *Workforce 2020: Work and workers in the 21st century.* Indianapolis: Hudson Institute.

2. Dole, E. (1990). "Ready, set, work,"" says labor secretary. *Training and Development Journal, 44*(5), 17–22.

3. Steck, R. N. (1992). The skills gap and how to deal with it. *D & B Reports, 40*(1), 47–48.

4. Kronholz, J. (1999). High schools get low grades in poll of employers. *Wall Street Journal,* January 8, A4.

5. *Ibid.*

6. Judy & D'Amico (1997), *supra* note 1.

7. *Ibid.*

8. Tyler, K. (1996). Tips for structuring workplace literacy programs. *HR Magazine, 41*(10), 112–116.

9. Stone, N. (1991). Does business have any business in education? *Harvard Business Review, 69*(2), 46–62.

10. Fiske, E. B. (1997). Adults: The forgotten illiterates. *Christian Science Monitor, 89*(129), May 30, 18.

11. Kirsch, I. S., & Jungeblut, A. (1986). *Literacy: Profiles of America's young adults.* National Assessment of Educational Progress. Princeton, NJ: Educational Testing Service.

12. Industry Report. (1996). Who's learning what? *Training, 33*(10), 55–66.

13. Berger, M. A. (1983). In defense of the case method: A reply to Argyris. *Academy of Management Review, 8,* 329–333.

14. Sorohan, E. G. (1995b). High performance skill survey. *Training and Development, 49*(5), 9–10.

15. Kuri, F. (1996). Basics skills training boosts productivity. *HR Magazine, 41*(9), 73–79.

16. Filipczak, B. (1992). What employers teach. *Training, 29*(10), 43–55.

17. Wilson, L. S. (1990). An on-line prescription for basic skills. *Training and Development Journal, 44*(4), 36–41.

18. Carlisle, K. E. (1985). Learning how to learn. *Training and Development Journal, 39*(3), 75–80.

19. Zaslow, R. (1991). Managers as writing coaches. *Training and Development Journal, 45*(7), 61–64.

20. Rothwell, W. J., & Brandenburg, D. C. (1990). *Workplace literacy primer.* Amherst, MA: Human Resource Development Press.

21. *Ibid.,* p. 56.

22. Laabs, J. J. (1996). Leading organizational change. *Personnel Journal, 75*(7), 54–63.

23. *Ibid.*

24. Holley, W. H., Jr., Jennings, K. M., & Wolters, R. S. (2001). *The labor relations process* (7th ed.). Forth Worth, TX: Harcourt College Publishers.

25. *Business Week/Reinventing America* (1992).

26. Judy & D'Amico (1997), *supra* note 1.

27. Templin, N. (2000). Anatomy of a jobs training program that went awry. *Wall Street Journal,* February 11, B1, B4.

28. Pantazis, C. (1996). The state of lifelong learning. *Training and Development, 50*(8), 36–40.

29. Workforce Investment Act of 1998 (http://usworkforce.org/wialaw.txt); Irwin, D. (2000). New era ahead for workforce development. *Inside Tucson Business, 10*(4), April 17, 1–2.

30. Carnevale, A. P., & Johnston, J. W. (1989). *Training America: Strategies for the nation.* Alexandria, VA: American Society for Training and Development.

31. National Apprenticeship Program (1987). Washington, DC: Employment and Training Administration: U.S. Department of Labor.

32. Woodberry, P. (1997, July 15). Personal communication.

33. Carnevale & Johnston (1989), *supra* note 30.

34. *New York Times,* July 10, 1992.

35. Stamps, D. (1996). Will school-to-work work? *Training, 33*(6), 72–81.

36. *Ibid.,* p. 74.

37. Christee, Joyce. (2000, December 28). State of Wisconsin Youth Apprenticeship Director, Personal communication.

38. Jackson, G. B., & Wirt, J. G. (1996). Putting students to work. *Training and Development, 50*(11), 58–60.

39. *Ibid.*

40. Bureau of Labor Statistics (1997). *Employer provided training.* http://stats.bls.gov/news.release/septt0l.htm

41. Industry Report (1996), *supra* note 12.

42. Industry Report-The Tech Emergence (2000). *Training, 37*(10), 87–94.

43. Hall-Sheey, J. (1985). Course design for PC training. *Training and Development Journal, 39*(3), 66–67.

44. Harp, C. (1996). Winging it. *Computerworld, 30*(43), 107–109; Harp, C., Satzinger, J., & Taylor, S. (1997). Many paths to learning software. *Training and Development, 51*(5), 81–84.

45. Gist, M. E., Schwoerer, C., & Rosen, B. (1989). Effects of alternative training methods on self-efficacy and performance in computer software training. *Journal of Applied Psychology, 74,* 884–891.

46. Martocchio, J. J., & Webster, J. (1992). Effects of feedback and cognitive playfulness on performance in microcomputer software training. *Personnel Psychology, 45,* 553–578.

47. *Ibid.*

48. Simon, S. J., & Werner, J. M. (1996). Computer training through behavior modeling, self-paced, and instructional approaches: A field experiment. *Journal of Applied Psychology, 81,* 648–659.

49. Industry Report (1996), *supra* note 12.

50. Henneback, C. (1992). Instant secretaries: Just add training. *Training and Development, 46*(11), 63–65.

51. Goodman, F. F. (1992). A union trains for the future. *Training and Development, 46*(10), 23–29.

52. Industry Report Correction (2000), http://trainingsupersite.com/training/2000/0100/010correction.htm.

53. Hilyer, B., Leviton, L., Overman, L., & Mukherjee, S. (2000). A union-initiated safety training program leads to improved workplace safety. *Labor Studies Journal, 24*(4), 53–66.

54. Franta, B. A. (2000). Bottom-line figures quantify safety training initiatives. *Houston Business Journal, 31*(11), 31.

55. *Ibid.*

56. Rothwell, W. J. (1989). Complying with OSHA. *Training and Development Journal, 43*(5), 52–54.

57. Hackey, M. K. (1991). Injuries and illness in the workplace, 1989. *Monthly Labor Review, 114*(5), 34–36.

58. Thompson, B. L. (1991). OSHA bounces back. *Training, 28*(1), 45–53.

59. Jenkins, J. A. (1990). Self-directed workforce promotes safety. *HR Magazine, 35*(2), 54–56.

60. Rothwell, W. J. (1989). Complying with OSHA. *Training and Development Journal, 43*(5), 52–54.

61. Kimmerling, G. F. (1985). Warning: Workers at risk, train effectively. *Training and Development Journal, 39*(4), 50–55.

62. Ten steps toward an effective safety program (1999). *CEE News, 51*(5), 10.

63. Janicak, C. A. (1999). Computer-based training: Developing programs with the knowledge-based safety training system. *Professional Safety,* June, 34–36.

64. *Ibid.*

65. Flick, J. P., Radomsky, M. C., & Ramani, R. V. (1999). On-site safety observation: The Penn State Approach to site-specific health and safety training. *Professional Safety,* October, 34–38.

66. Kimmerling (1985), *supra* note 61.

67. Hoover, S. K. (1999). OSHA program reflects new focus. *CityBusiness: The Business Journal of the Twin Cities, 17*(16), September 17, 16.

68. *Ibid.*

69. Hilyer et al. (2000), *supra* note 53.

70. Routhieaux, R. L., & Gutek, B. A. (1998). TQM/CQI effectiveness at team and department levels. *Journal of Quality Management, 3,* 39–62.

71. Hartmann, L. C., & Patrickson, M. (1998). Individual decision making: Implications for decision training in TQM. *International Journal of Quality and Reliability Management, 15,* 619–633.

72. Bennett, J. B., Wayne, E. K., & Forst, J. K. (1999). Change, transfer climate, and customer orientation. *Group and Organization Management, 24,* 188–216.

73. Industry Report Correction (2000), *supra* note 52.

74. Hartmann & Patrickson (1998), *supra* note 71.

75. Mandal, P., Howell, A., & Sohal, A. S. (1998). A systemic approach to quality improvements: The interactions between the technical, human and quality systems. *Total Quality Management, 9,* 79–99.

76. Miller, T. O. (1992). A customer's definition of quality. *Journal of Business Strategy, 13*(1), 47.

77. Nowak, L. I., & Washburn, J. H. (1998). Antecedents to client satisfaction in business services. *Journal of Services Marketing, 12,* 441–452.

78. *Ibid.*

79. Vasilash, G. S. (1992). Driving beyond satisfaction at Rockwell Automotive. *Production, 104*(4), 40–43.

80. Mainstone, L. E., & Levi, A. S. (1989). Fundamentals of statistical process control. *Organization Behavior Management, 9*(1), 5–21.

81. Wiggenhorn, W. (1990). Motorola U: When training becomes an education. *Harvard Business Review,* July-August, 71–83.

82. *Ibid.*

83. Routhieaux & Gutek (1998), supra note 70; Kassicieh, S. K., & Yourstone, S. A. (1998). Training, performance evaluation, rewards, and TQM implementation success. *Journal of Quality Management, 3,* 25–38.

84. Bennett et al. (1999), *supra* note 72.

85. Kelley, S. (1998). All types of businesses can benefit from ISO use. *Dallas Business Journal, 22*(16), December 11, B4.

86. Reimann, C. W., & Hertz, H. S. (1996). The Baldrige Award and ISO 9000 registration compared. *Journal for Quality and Participation, 19*(1), 12–19.

87. Elmuti, D. (1996). World class standards for global competition: An overview of ISO 9000. *Industrial Management, 38*(5), 5–9.

88. Another industry gets specific. (1999). *Export Today, 15*(4), 72.

89. Larson, M. (1999). Set up ongoing training. *Quality, 38*(13), 56–57.

90. Geisler, C. D., & Justus, R. (1998). Training: A strategic tool for ISO and QS-9000 implementation. *IIE Solutions, 30*(4), 24–27.

91. Larson (1999), *supra* note 89.

92. Industry Report (1996), *supra* note 12.

93. Oleson, M. (1999). What makes employees stay. *Training and Development, 53*(10), 48–52.

94. Carnevale, A. P., Gainer, L. J., Villet, J., & Holland, S. L. (1990). *Training partnerships: Linking employers and providers.* Alexandria, VA: American Society for Training and Development.

95. Callahan, M. R. (1992). Tending the sales relationship. *Training and Development, 43*(12), 31–55.

96. Industry Report Correction (2000), *supra* note 52; Industry Report (1996), *supra* note 12.

97. Keenan, W., Jr. (2000). Sales training ROI? *Industry Week, 249*(11), June 12, 23.

98. Peterson, R. T. (1990). What makes sales training programs successful? *Training and Development, 44*(8), 59–64.

99. Mescon, M. H., & Mescon, T. S. (1999). Training is lacking in many sales departments. *Orlando Business Journal, 15*(49), April 30, 28–29.

100. Industry Report (1996), *supra* note 12.

101. Evenson, R. (1999). Soft skills, hard sell. *Techniques: Making Education and Career Connections, 74*(3), 29–31.

102. Becker, W. S., & Wellins, R. S. (1990). Customer-service perceptions and reality. *Training and Development Journal, 44*(3), 49–51.

103. Firnstahl, T. W. (1989). My employees are my guarantee. *Harvard Business Review, 67*(4), 28–31.

104. Miller (1992), *supra* note 76.

105. Stum, D. L., & Church, R. P. (1990). Hitting the long ball for the customer. *Training and Development Journal, 44*(3), 45–48.

106. Albrecht, C. (1985). Achieving excellence in service. *Training and Development Journal, 39*(12), 64–67, p. 64.

107. Desatnick, R. L. (1987). Building the customer-oriented work force. *Training and Development Journal, 41*(3), 72–74.

108. Coné, J. (1989). The empowered employee. *Training and Development Journal, 43*(6), 96–98.

109. Desatnick (1987), *supra* note 107.

110. Lorge, S. (1998). A priceless brand. *Sales and Marketing Management, 150*(10), 102–110.

111. McColgan, E. A. (1997). How Fidelity invests in service professionals. *Harvard Business Review,* January-February, 137–143, p. 138.

112. Industry Report (1996), *supra* note 12.

113. *Ibid;* Prager, H. (1999). Cooking up effective training. *Training and Development, 53*(12), 14–15.

114. Industry Report Correction (2000), *supra* note 52.

115. Guzzo, R. A., & Dickson, M. W. (1996). Teams in organizations: Recent research on performance and effectiveness. *Annual Review Psychology, 47,* 307–338, pp. 308–309.

116. De Vany, C. (1999). Championship team-building: Ready, coach? *Journal of Property Management, 64*(2), 92–93.

117. *Ibid.*

118. Banker, R. D., Field, J. M., Schroeder, R. G., Sinha, K. K. (1996). Impact of work teams on manufacturing performance: A longitudinal study. *Academy of Management Journal, 39,* 867–890; Cohen, S. G., & Ledford, G. E., Jr., (1994). The effectiveness of self-managing teams: A quasi-experiment. *Human Relations, 47,* 13–43; Schilder, J. (1992). Work teams boost productivity. *Personnel Journal, 71*(2), 67–71; Musselwhite, E., & Moran, L. (1990). On the road to self-direction. *Journal of Quality and Participation,* 58–63.

119. Salas, E., Rozell, D., Mullen, B., & Driskell, J. E. (1999). The effect of team building on performance: An integration. *Small Group Research, 30,* 309–329.

120. Werner, J. M., & Lester, S. W. (2001). Applying a team effectiveness framework to the performance of student case teams. *Human Resource Development Quarterly, 12,* 385–402.

121. Cannon-Bowers, J. A., Tannenbaum, S. I., Salas, E., & Volpe, C. E. (1995). Defining Competencies and establishing team training requirements. In R. A. Guzzo, E. Salas & Associates (Eds.), *Team effectiveness and decision making in organizations* (333–380). San Francisco: Jossey-Bass; Tannenbaum, S. I., & Yukl, G. (1992). Training and development in work organizations. *Annual Review of Psychology, 43,* 399–441.

122. Hoyman, M., & Ferman, L. A. (1991). Scope and extent of joint training programs. In L. A. Ferman, M. Hoyman, J. Cuthcher-Gershenfeld, & E. J. Savoie, (eds.), Joint partnership programs. Ithaca, NY: ILR Press.

123. Treinen, D. & Ross, K., (1991). The Alliance for Employee Growth and Development, Inc. In L. A. Ferman, M. Hoyman, J. Cuthcher-Gershenfeld, & E. J. Savoie, (Eds.), *Joint Partnership Programs.* Ithaca, NY: ILR Press.

124. *Ibid.*

125. *Ibid.*

126. Goodman (1992), *supra* note 51.

127. Jones, A. (1999). Unions take on the role of training for new jobs. *National Catholic Reporter, 35*(38), September 3, 5.

128. Ettorre, J. (1999). Unions labor to draw more. *Crain's Cleveland Business, 20*(35), August 30, M-10–11.

129. Abbot, J. (1988). The multicultural workforce: New challenges for trainers. *Training and Development Journal, 42*(8), 12–13.

130. Sharma, A. (1997). Professional as agent: Knowledge asymmetry in agency exchange. *Academy of Management Review, 22,* 758–798, quote from p. 763.

131. Walley, E. N. (1996). Is it time to take another look at CPE? *CPA Journal, 66*(2), 26–31.

132. Forsyth, S., & Galloway, S. (1988). Linking college credit with in-house training. *Personnel Administrator, 33*(11), 78–79.

133. Crosson, C. (1990). Hancock enlists American College for courses. *National Underwriter, 94*(12), 7, 36.

134. Faerman, S. R., Quinn, R. E., & Thompson, M. P. (1987). Bridging management practice and theory: New York's public service training program. *Public Administration Review, 47*(4) 310–319.

135. Childress, G. W., & Bugbee, J. A. (1986). Kentucky's across-the-board effort at making HRD work. *Public Personnel Management, 15*(4), 369–376.

136. Crosson (1990), *supra* note 133.

137. Barron, T. (1996). A new wave in training funding. *Training and Development, 50*(8), 28–33.

138. Gutteridge, T. G., Leibowitz, Z. B., & Shore, J. E. (1993). *Organizational career development: Benchmarks for building a world-class workforce.* San Francisco: Jossey-Bass.

139. Toomey, E. L., & Connor, J. M. (1988). Employee sabbaticals: Who benefits and why. *Personnel, 65*(4), 81–84.

140. Courtney, R. S. (1986). A human resources program that helps management and employees prepare for the future. *Personnel, 63*(5), 32–40.

# 11

# MANAGEMENT DEVELOPMENT

## LEARNING OBJECTIVES

1. Define management development and describe the extent to which it is used in U.S. organizations.

2. Describe the approaches that have been taken to describing the managerial job.

3. Explain how management development can be made to be more strategic.

4. Describe the options and trends in management education.

5. Explain how training and on-the-job experiences can be used to develop managers.

6. Describe the components of two approaches frequently used in management development programs: leadership training and behavior modeling training.

7. Discuss the issues involved in designing management development programs.

Imagine yourself among the executives and managers of a large, urban hospital. Your hospital is a private, nonprofit hospital that serves a number of low-income neighborhoods. The long-standing mission of the hospital has been to provide quality service to the community, regardless of an individual's ability to pay. However, recent changes and turmoil in the healthcare industry have raised concerns about your hospital's ability to remain viable and financially solvent. As a top management team, you've decided to maintain your commitment to your existing clients. However, you also wish to attract more clients with the means (or insurance packages) to pay for your services. Add to this situation the fact that you are about to move into a new facility, which includes a new computer system designed to improve the overall efficiency of your hospital. The question has come up about the advisability of offering a management training program. You might address the various changes and challenges in your external environment, for example, with so many other hospitals to choose from, how do you become the preferred healthcare alternative for this "new" population of clients? You're also thinking of ways to improve the internal environment, that is, how you can be more efficient by making the best use of the new technology that will be available in your new facility.

*Questions: If you were part of this top management team, do you think it is a good idea to offer management training at this time? If so, where would you start? What would be your focus? What particular challenges would you expect to face as you moved into this new facility?*

## INTRODUCTION

Do you think the following statements are true or false?

- *It is predicted that there will be fewer managers in the United States by the end of this decade than there are presently.*

- *Researchers have been able to describe the managerial job with a high degree of precision.*

- *The systems model of HRD (assess, design, implement, evaluate) isn't very helpful when it comes to management development.*

- *Management education is a small and decreasing proportion of all the postsecondary educational opportunities that students in the United States are taking.*

- *Corporate universities are only popular among very large organizations.*

- *Behavior modeling training may work fine for entry level training, but it hasn't been found to be very effective for management development efforts.*

For at least the past sixty years, managers have been viewed as a dynamic and important element of business organizations. Given the turbulence in today's environment, an organization must have a high quality, flexible, and adaptive management team if it is to survive and succeed. This is true even for organizations that have chosen to restructure (e.g., with flatter hierarchies and fewer permanent employees) and empower employees to be more a part of organizational decision making. It is managers who are ultimately responsible for making the decision to change their organizations' strategies and structures, and it is managers who must ensure that these new approaches are implemented, modified, and executed in a way that achieves the organizations' goals. While they may do this in a different way than they have in the past (e.g., less command and control, more leading and coaching), managers still play a critical role in organizations' adaptation and success. In essence, using fewer managers in an organization makes it *more* important that each manager is effective.

It should be noted that despite the popular press reports indicating that the number of managers and executives is shrinking, the U.S. Bureau of Labor Statistics has estimated that the category of executive, administrative, and managerial occupations contained approximately 14.8 million people in 1998. Further, this category is expected to show a net gain of 2.4 million jobs between 1998 and 2008, or more than a 16 percent increase. As an occupational group, executives, administrators, and managers are expected to make up 10.5 percent of the total labor force in 2008, which is a slight *increase* from its percentage of the total labor force in 1998.[1]

One way for an organization to increase the chances that its managers will be effective is through management development. While it may have once been believed that the ability to manage (like the ability to lead) was primarily an inborn capability, the current view holds that the KSAs required to be an effective manager can be learned or enhanced.[2]

Management development is one of the most common HRD activities. Although management development has been defined in many ways, we feel that the following definition captures the essence of management development as it can and should be practiced in organizations:

> [A]n organization's conscious effort to provide its managers (and potential managers) with opportunities to learn, grow, and change, in hopes of producing over the long term a cadre of managers with the skills necessary to function effectively in that organization.[3]

This definition makes several key points. First, it suggests that management development should be seen as specific to a particular organization. Although there appear to be roles and competencies that apply to managing in a variety of settings, each organization is unique, and its goal should be to develop individuals to be more effective managers within its own context.[4] Second, management development consists of providing employees with opportunities for learning, growth, and change. While there is no guarantee that particular individuals will take advantage of, or profit from, these opportunities, management development cannot occur unless opportunities are at least provided.[5] Third, management development must be a conscious effort on the part of the organization. Leaving development to chance greatly reduces the likelihood that the organization will achieve the kinds of changes it needs and desires. Fourth, management development (like all HRD activities) should be directly linked to the organization's strategy, that is, it must meet the organization's business needs if it is to be a sound investment and ultimately successful. *Many* current management development programs do not conform to this definition, but we think it can serve as a benchmark to which such programs can and should aspire.

Management development has been described as having three main components: management education, management training, and on-the-job experiences.[6] **Management education** can be defined as "the acquisition of a broad range of conceptual knowledge and skills in formal classroom situations in degree-granting institutions."[7] As we will describe below, the "formal classroom situations" to which the definition refers include a wide range of activities, with the classroom setting increasingly being used to bring together and process the results of outside activities to draw conclusions about what has been learned. **Management training** focuses more on providing specific skills or knowledge that could be immediately applied within an organization and/or to a specific position or set of positions within an organization (e.g., middle managers).[8] **On-the-job experiences** are planned or unplanned opportunities for a manager to gain self-knowledge, enhance existing skills and abilities, or obtain new skills or information within the context of day-to-day activities (e.g., mentoring, coaching, assignment to a task force).

In this chapter, we will discuss a number of management development activities that are used within each of these three components.

### EXTENT OF MANAGEMENT DEVELOPMENT ACTIVITIES

As mentioned earlier, management development is one of the most commonly offered approaches to HRD. In a 2000 survey, 96 percent of organizations provided supervisory skills or management skills development, with 87 percent offering executive development. Strikingly, only 36 percent of all training dollars were spent on nonexempt employees, with the rest going to supervisors, managers, executives, and other exempt-level employees. The total cost of formal training aimed at management was estimated to be $34.5 billion.[9] In an earlier survey, the average number of hours of training individuals in each of these categories received was about thirty-two hours per year, with first-line supervisors receiving slightly more (thirty-five hours).[10]

The most frequently cited reasons for developing managers include broadening the individual and providing knowledge or skills.[11] Few organizations (5 percent in the survey just cited) cited an intent to reward managers as a reason for providing them with developmental opportunities.

### ORGANIZATION OF THE CHAPTER

Management development comprises such a broad range of issues and approaches that it is not realistic to try to cover them all in a single chapter. Rather, we will focus our discussion on the following issues:

1. efforts to describe the managerial job, including *roles* managers must perform and the *competencies* necessary for performing them effectively

2. how to make management development strategic

3. options available for management education

4. options available for management training and using on-the-job experiences for management development

5. a description of two common approaches used to develop managers (leadership training and behavior modeling training for interpersonal skills)

6. the design of management development programs

## DESCRIBING THE MANAGER'S JOB: MANAGEMENT ROLES AND COMPETENCIES

Given the large number of organizations that employ managers, the scrutiny under which managers operate, and the vast literature on management and its subfields, one would expect that we would have a clear idea of what managers do, the KSAs necessary to do those things effectively, and how to identify and develop those KSAs. Unfortunately, little research has been conducted about what managers do, how they learn to do it, and how managers should be developed.[12] Though it is true that popular conceptions of the manager's role and development are available, scientific research has yet to provide a clearly supported and accepted model that can be used to guide management development. Even among the best empirical studies in this area, such as the Management Progress Study conducted over a thirty-year period at AT&T, there are significant limitations (e.g., small sample sizes, analysis of only one organization) that make it difficult to confidently conclude what most or all managers do and how they develop.[13]

The changes that have occurred in organizations in the past decade have only complicated this picture. Many of the research studies from the 1970s and before looked at management in hierarchically structured organizations that operated in relatively stable environments. As we have pointed out many times, organizations have had to respond to environmental challenges to stay competitive, and the structures and strategies they use have changed. The role of management has changed in many organizations as well. It is likely that the established views of the management job may be more relevant for some organizations than others.

This is not to say that what we know from the past is useless and invalid. But we do need to know which aspects from the past are still relevant and descriptive of managing as it exists today. This underscores the need for HRD professionals to identify what the management job is (and needs to be) in their own organization before they can design and deliver management development processes and programs that will meet the needs of their own business and contribute to its competitiveness and effectiveness. In this section of the chapter, we briefly describe several approaches to conceptualizing the management role to suggest a starting point in designing a reasonable management development program. As indicated in the definition of management development presented above, meaningful management development is likely to differ among organizations, considering the context and challenges facing each particular organization. We encourage designers of such programs to begin their efforts by obtaining a clear understanding of the organization (including its external environment, goals, strategic plan, culture, strengths, and weaknesses) and the characteristics of the target population (managers and managers-to-be). The research available on what managers do, how they do it, and how they develop the capabilities to do it can provide a useful base from which to begin the needs assessment process and serve as a source of possible development topics and issues. It is unrealistic, however, to expect such research, no matter how advanced, to provide the blueprint for any particular organization's management development strategy.

### APPROACHES TO UNDERSTANDING THE JOB OF MANAGING

Researchers who have examined the job of managing have done so from at least three perspectives: describing the characteristics of the job as it is typically performed, describing the roles managers serve, and developing process models that show how the various components of managing relate to one another.[14] The **characteristics approach** involves observing the tasks managers perform and grouping them into meaningful categories. McCall, Morrison, and Hannan reviewed the results of a group of observational studies and concluded that ten elements of managing were consistently present.[15] These elements indicate that the management job involves long hours of work, primarily within the organization; high activity levels; fragmented work (e.g., many interruptions); varied activities; primarily oral communication; many contacts; and information gathering. In addition, managers tend *not* to be reflective planners (given the variety of tasks and fragmented nature of the work) and do poorly in accurately estimating how they spend their time.

These observations may be interesting, but they don't provide much assistance in describing specifically what managers do, how they do it, and how they should be developed. A common conclusion from such studies is that important questions about the job remain unanswered (e.g., the relationship of the activities to one another) and that "knowing that the managerial job is varied and complex is not particularly helpful in the identification and/or development process."[16]

A second approach to describing the managerial job is to **identify the roles that managers are typically assigned.** This can be accomplished by using either an observational approach or an empirical approach. The observational approach is typified by Fayol's[17] five management functions (planning, organizing, commanding, coordinating, and controlling) and Mintzberg's[18] managerial roles: interpersonal (figurehead, leader, liaison), informational (monitor, disseminator, spokesperson), and decisional (entrepreneur, disturbance handler, resource allocator, and negotiator). Although these categorizations are extremely popular, they too do not appear to fully and adequately describe what managers do. They also lack specificity and do not adequately describe the interrelations among the various roles.[19]

The empirical approach relies on a descriptive questionnaire (e.g., the Management Position Description Questionnaire) that is completed by managers themselves, and/or by others who work with them.[20] Even this approach has failed to provide practical, meaningful descriptions of the job.[21] Taken together, the observational and empirical approaches to categorizing the managerial role have not proved useful as a definition of the managerial job or as a guide to developing managers.

One way researchers have tried to overcome the limitations of the previous approaches is to develop **process models** that take into account the particularly relevant competencies and constraints involved in performing the management job. Two process models of particular note to the discussion of management development are the integrated competency model[22] and the four-dimensional model.[23]

The **integrated competency model** is based on interviews of over 2,000 managers in twelve organizations that were conducted by the consulting firm McBer and Company. The model focuses on *managerial competencies*, skills and/or personal characteristics that contribute to effective performance, rather than on the roles managers perform.[24] The model identifies twenty-one competencies that are grouped into six categories: human resource management, leadership, goal and action management, directing subordinates, focus on others, and specialized knowledge.[25] Table 13-1 shows the specific competencies included in each cluster. The human resources, leadership, and goal and action clusters are seen as most central to managing. The model also depicts the relationships among the first four clusters, shown in Figure 13-1. "Focus on others" is not shown in the model at the skill level because its key competencies do not exist at that level. "Specialized knowledge" is not shown because it is viewed as having a "pervasive" impact on all the other competencies.

While this model from Richard Boyatzis and colleagues makes other important distinctions (e.g., competencies versus threshold competencies, competencies relevant for various management levels and for public sector and private sector organizations), the main contribution of the model is its attempt to describe the managerial job in terms of the competencies that contribute to performance and the relationships among these competencies. The integrated competency model is one example of a competency-based approach to management development. Competency-based approaches have become extremely popular, not only as the basis for management development programs,[26] but for other training and development programs and HR programs as well.[27]

The integrated competency model itself has been criticized. One weakness is that the model is based on a narrow range of measuring devices, which are not likely to represent or reveal all of the traits, skills, and knowledge needed for managerial performance.[28] In addition, the method by which the competencies were identified has been sharply criticized. The instrument that has been used, called the Behavioral Event Interview (BEI), asks managers to describe three job incidents they felt were effective and three job incidents they felt were ineffective.[29] Barrett and Depinet point out that this method is inappropriate for measuring competencies as Boyatzis describe them.[30] That is, Boyatzis described a competency as "an underlying characteristic of a person in that it may be a

■ **TABLE 13-1**

CLUSTERS AND COMPETENCIES ASSOCIATED WITH
THE INTEGRATED COMPETENCY MODEL

| Cluster | Competencies |
|---------|--------------|
| Human Resource Management | Use of socialized power<br>Positive regard[a]<br>Managing group processes<br>Accurate self-assessment[a] |
| Leadership | Self-confidence<br>Use of oral presentations<br>Conceptualization<br>Logical thought[a] |
| Goal and Action Management | Efficiency orientation<br>Proactivity<br>Concern with impact<br>Diagnostic use of concepts |
| Directing Subordinates | Use of unilateral power[a]<br>Spontaneity[a]<br>Developing others[a] |
| Focus on Others | Perceptual objectivity<br>Self-control<br>Stamina and adaptability<br>Concern with close relationships |
| Specialized Knowledge | Memory<br>Specialized job knowledge[a] |

NOTE: [a]Identified as "threshold competencies," that is, characteristics essential to performing a job, but not causally related to superior job performance.

SOURCE: From L. F. Schoenfeldt and J. A. Steger (1990). Identification and development of managerial talent. In G. R. Ferris and K. M. Rowland (eds.), *Organizational Entry* (p. 210). Greenwich, CT: JAI Press.

motive, trait, skill, aspect of one's self-image or social role, or a body of knowledge he or she uses" (p. 21), and said competencies may be unconscious and that an individual may be "unable to articulate or describe them" (p. 21).[31] Barrett and Depinet also contend that the validation process used to support the model was significantly flawed.

The second process model of the managerial job that can contribute to designing management development efforts is the **four-dimensional model**.[32] Based on various information sources (e.g., managerial diaries, interviews, performance evaluation documents, observation), this model depicts the managerial role as having the following dimensions:

1. Six **functions** — forecasting and planning, training and development, persuasive communication, influence and control, expertise/functional area, and administration

■ **FIGURE 13-1**

AN INTEGRATED MODEL OF MANAGEMENT COMPETENCIES
AT THE SKILL LEVEL

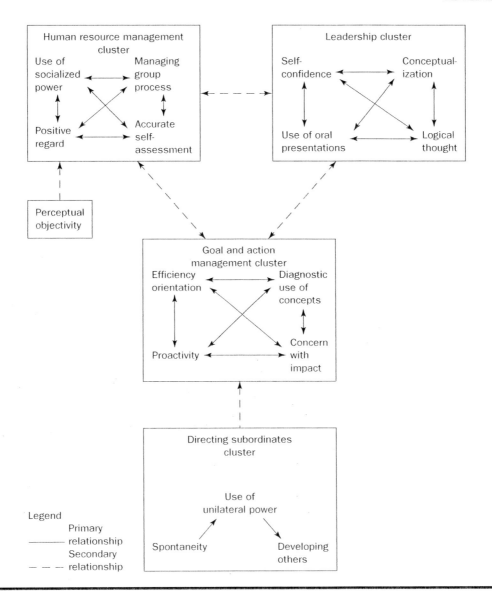

SOURCE: From R. E. Boyatzis (1982). *The competent manager: A model for effective performance*. New York: Wiley, 194. Copyright 1982 by John Wiley and Sons. Reprinted by permission.

2. Four **roles** — innovator, evaluator, motivator, director
3. Five (relational) **targets** — peers, subordinates, superiors, external, and self
4. An unspecified number of managerial **styles** (attributes that describe the image and approach of the manager)—examples include objectivity, personal impact, leadership, energy level, and risk taking

The four-dimensional model states that managers interact with various targets (e.g., subordinates), carrying out an assortment of functions by performing specific roles (i.e., the roles that exist within each of the functions). The way they perform these functions and roles is consistent with their managerial style. For example, in performing the training and development function with a subordinate (the target), the manager may have to direct the subordinate, motivate him or her during training, and evaluate progress (all roles contained within the training and development function). The manager may do this by using a particular style (e.g., objectivity, which involves evaluating and responding to the subordinate in an unbiased manner).

The four-dimensional and integrated competency models include similar skills, roles, and activities and provide a solid basis for describing the managerial job and designing management development programs (see Schoenfeldt and Steger for a discussion of the relationships among the models).[33] Either of these models provides a conceptual basis to begin viewing the role of managers within a specific organization and the competencies managers need to perform effectively. However, it should be emphasized that these models do not have a sizable body of empirical research behind them to support their validity. Just as importantly, these models should not be viewed as substitutes for a thorough needs assessment.

### MANAGERS AS PERSONS: A HOLISTIC VIEW OF THE MANAGER'S JOB

The approaches we have presented to describing the manager's job all have one thing in common: they attempt to describe the manager's job by identifying its elements. This "reductionistic" approach has its risks and limitations, according to authors such as Henry Mintzberg and Peter Vaill.[34] Mintzberg describes the problem as follows:

> If you turn to the formalized literature, you will find all kinds of lists — of tasks or roles or "competencies." But a list is not a model . . . and so the integrated work of managing still gets lost in the process of describing it. And without such a model we can neither understand the job properly nor deal with its many important needs — for design, selection, training, and support. . . . We have been so intent on breaking the job into pieces that we never came to grips with the whole thing.[35]

Vaill raises this concern in light of the turbulent environment in which managers must manage.[36] While he believes that naming the functions that managers must perform can "define the territory that leaders and managers are concerned with" (p. 114), the list-of-functions approach leaves out something essential: the performing of the managerial job. Vaill explains the problem this way:

> The list-of-functions approach forgets that action taking is a concrete process before it is anything else. Furthermore, it is a concrete process performed by a whole person in relation to a whole environment populated by other whole persons (that is, not other lists of functions). This whole process is embedded in time and is subject to the real time of its operation and to all the turbulence and change that surround it, that indeed suffuse it, because the turbulence and change are within action takers as much as they surround them. Simply to name the function to be performed as though it were the action ignores all of this richness of the actual action-taking process, and worst of all, ultimately masks the richness and leads to an empty model of what the action-taking *process* is (emphasis in original).[37]

Vaill uses the metaphor of "managing as a performing art" to show that the job of managing is more than the sum of its competencies, roles, and functions, just as, for example, a jazz band or dance troupe performance is more than the pieces or knowledge and skills that make it up. He has criticized the competency movement, arguing that it is based on a set of assumptions that may not be true, in effect "presuming a world that does not exist, or that is at least quite improbable."[38]

In response to these deficiencies, Mintzberg has developed a model of the manager's job that attempts to bring together what has been learned about managing in a more holistic or integrated way.[39] His goal is to try to develop a model that reflects the richness and variety of styles individuals use in carrying out the managerial job. The model represents the manager's job as a framework of concentric circles, in what he calls a "well-rounded" job. Figure 13-2 shows a diagram of Mintzberg's well-rounded model. The words in the model refer to the seven interrelated roles Mintzberg sees as making up the managerial job: conceiving, scheduling, communicating, controlling, leading, linking, and doing.

At the center of the model is the *person in the job.* The person brings to the job a set of values, experiences, knowledge, competencies, and mental models through which he or she interprets environmental events. These components combine to form the individual's managerial style, which drives how the person carries out the job. The next circle contains, the *frame of the job,* which is the "mental set the incumbent assumes to carry it out" (p.12). The frame includes the person's idea of the purpose of what he or she is trying to accomplish as well as the person's approach to getting the job done. Working within this frame involves the role Mintzberg calls conceiving.

The next circle contains the *agenda of the work.* The agenda is made up of the issues that are of concern to the manager and the schedule (i.e., allocation of time) that the manager uses to accomplish the work. Dealing with the agenda of the work involves the role of scheduling. The frame of the job and agenda of the work are surrounded by the *actual behaviors that managers perform,* both inside and outside of the unit they manage. Mintzberg sees three levels of evoking action: managing through information (which involves the roles of communicating and controlling), managing through people (which involves the roles of linking and leading), and managing through direct action (which involves the role of doing tasks).

Mintzberg's main point is that "while we may be able to separate the components of the job conceptually, I maintain that they cannot be separated behaviorally. . . . it may be useful, even necessary, to delineate the parts for purposes of

■ **FIGURE 13-2**

MINTZBERG'S "WELL ROUNDED" MODEL OF
THE MANAGERIAL JOB

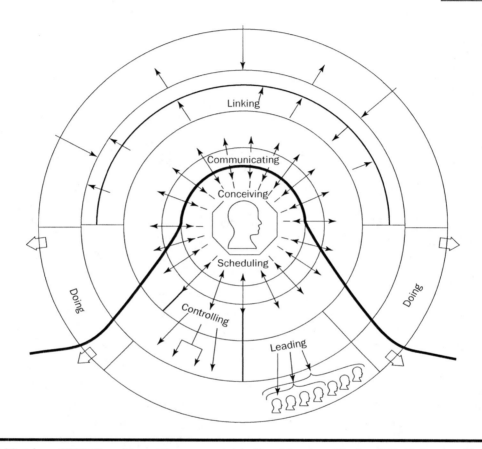

SOURCE: H. Mintzberg, (1994). Rounding out the manager's job, *Sloan Management Review, 36*(1), 23. Reprinted by permission.

design, selection, training and support. But this job cannot be practiced as a set of independent parts" (p. 22). He points out that the manager's job will vary, depending on what is called for by the work and the particular approach or style a manager uses. The manager's style will affect his or her work through the roles he or she favors, the way in which the roles are performed, and the relationship that exists among the roles. Mintzberg states that interviews with managers he has met bear out his ideas of the variety and richness of the managerial job. Like the other approaches to describing the manager's job, Mintzberg's model should be seen as a work-in-progress, awaiting further development and validation through research.

What can HRD professionals take away from the ideas presented by Vaill and Mintzberg? We think the main contribution is that they remind us that 1) managers are people, and 2) the job of managing is a complex, multifaceted, and integrated endeavor. While competency models and lists of KSAs are useful in identifying what it takes to do the job and as focal points for management development processes and programs, HRD professionals must not give in to the temptation of thinking that all management development is only about developing roles and competencies. We need to remember that managers are people who *perform* work, not collections of competencies and KSAs. Some practical implications of this are that HRD professional should:

1. recognize that one of the goals of management development is to develop the whole person, so that he or she can manage effectively within the context of the organization and external environment

2. design programs and processes that go beyond the one-shot event, and include ongoing activities that provide the opportunity to reinforce and refine what has been learned in the context of performing the work

3. build into the programs and practices a recognition of the interrelationships between the "components" of managing so that participants can see and feel how what they are learning can be integrated into the whole of the management job

4. implement programs and processes in a way that recognizes and takes advantage of the values, knowledge, and experiences that participants bring to the management experience

5. consider what the person brings to the job of managing when dealing with learning and transfer of training issues

6. include recognition of these issues when conducting needs assessment and evaluation activities for management development programs

## IMPORTANCE OF NEEDS ASSESSMENT IN DETERMINING MANAGERIAL COMPETENCIES

As we stated in Chapter 4 and elsewhere, needs assessment provides critical information in determining the conditions for training, where training is needed, what kind of training is needed, and who needs training. Given that research on the managerial job has left many unanswered questions, the importance of conducting a thorough needs assessment before designing a management development program is amplified. Despite this, many organizations fail to do a needs assessment. According to a survey of 1,000 organizations by Lise Saari and colleagues, only 27 percent of respondents reported conducting any needs assessment before designing management development programs.[40] This means that many organizations are leaving much to chance and are likely wasting critical resources.

Some organizations are doing a good job of needs assessment for management development and as a result have a clearer idea of the competencies and issues their development programs should address. The experience of New York Telephone can illustrate this approach. After the court-ordered breakup of AT&T, New York Telephone found itself facing competition for the first time in its more than 100 years of existence.[41] As part of a reexamination of the way it conducted business, company officials realized they needed to identify the skills that managers required to respond to a competitive environment.

The human resource department of New York Telephone developed a series of program and policy changes called the Development Partnership, which was designed to help managers improve their abilities (particularly in managing people), perform their nonsupervisory functions better, and aspire to greater responsibility. The partnership focuses on the relationship between a manager and his or her superior, with the individual manager playing the initiating role. The program included three key components: an annual development cycle (in which the manager and superior create a development plan), on-the-job development opportunities (such as task forces and transfers), and managerial accountability for the development of subordinates.

Of particular interest to our discussion is the study New York Telephone conducted to establish its management skills curriculum, a series of courses managers may take as part of achieving their development goals. The study began by having a task force of managers from three levels identify essential, generic management skills. The thirty skills identified by this task force were then included in a questionnaire that asked respondents to rate the importance of each skill in managing effectively in the present and the future. After pilot testing, the questionnaire was mailed to a random sample of over 3,000 managers from various levels. The results of the survey indicated consensus on what were the most important and least important managerial skills. The twenty most important skills were then categorized into six groups (personal, communications, organizing and planning, people and performance management, business, and independent thinking) and used as the basis for identifying the courses to include in the company's management skills curriculum. The final curriculum included some already existing company courses as well as some new ones developed in-house or purchased from vendors. The organization considered the skills study a success in identifying the mix of skills needed for its development program to ensure that New York Telephone would have the quality of management necessary to face future challenges.

New York Telephone's efforts illustrate the value of conducting a thorough investigation of the managerial job and the competencies needed to perform effectively before designing a management development program.

## THE GLOBALLY COMPETENT MANAGER

The advent of the global economy has led some writers to suggest that organizations should create management development programs to produce globally competent managers.[42] Organizations such as Corning Glass, 3M, ITT, and General Electric have incorporated this perspective into their management development programs. We will present three of many possible points of view to serve as examples of how the competencies needed to be an effective global manager have been conceptualized.

Bartlett and Ghoshal take the position that in order to succeed in a global environment, organizations need a network of managers who are specialists in global issues, and that organizations don't need to globalize all managers.[43] They suggest four categories of managers are needed:

1. **Business Managers** — This type of manager plays three roles, serving as "the *strategist* for the organization, the *architect* of its worldwide asset configuration, and the *coordinator* of transactions across national borders" (p. 125).

2. **Country Managers** — This type of manager, who works in the organization's national subsidiaries, also plays three roles, serving as "the *sensor* and interpreter of local opportunities and threats, the *builder* of local resources and capabilities, and the *contributor* to active participation in global strategy" (p. 128).

3. **Functional Managers** — These managers are functional specialists (e.g., in engineering, marketing, human resources) who "*scan* for specialized information worldwide, '*cross-pollinate*' leading-edge knowledge and best practice, and *champion* innovations that may offer transnational opportunities and applications" (p. 130).

4. **Corporate Managers** — These managers serve in corporate headquarters and orchestrate the organization's activities, playing the roles of *leader, talent scout* (i.e., by identifying potential business, country and functional managers), and *developing* promising executives.

Bartlett and Ghoshal illustrate these roles by using case studies of managers at Procter & Gamble, Electrolux, and NEC.[44] They suggest that organizations need to develop management teams capable of performing these functions in concert to achieve the organization's goals. While this categorization of the global manager's role is interesting and provides some sense of how these roles and managers interrelate, further research is needed to determine whether this approach can be a useful basis for developing global managers.

A second point of view is offered by Adler and Bartholomew.[45] These authors identify seven transnational skills that they believe are necessary to managing effectively in a global environment: global perspective, local responsiveness, synergistic learning, transition and adaptation, cross-cultural interaction, collaboration, and foreign experience. They argue that transnationally competent managers need a broader set of skills than traditional international managers, who were developed with a narrower perspective of their role in the global environment. Adler and Bartholomew state that an organization's human resource management strategies must be modified in order to manage and develop such managers, and they conclude from a survey of fifty North American firms that their present HRM strategies are less global than their business strategies.[46] These authors also provide recommendations for how HRM systems can be modified to become more global — for example, they say that developmental activities should prepare managers to work "anywhere in the world with people from all parts of the world" (p. 59).

These two views of the globally competent manager differ in at least two significant ways. First, Bartlett and Ghoshal adopt a role-oriented view, while Adler and Bartholomew focus on the competencies managers need. Second, Adler and Bartholomew suggest that all managers become "globalized," while Bartlett and Ghoshal argue that global management requires a team of managers who perform different functions and roles (and who would require significantly different sets of competencies).[47]

A third point of view on international management competencies is offered by Spreitzer, McCall, and Mahoney.[48] They argue that it is not sufficient to identify competencies based on past successes because managers (international and otherwise) must face future challenges that may require different competencies than those required today. Therefore, Spreitzer and colleagues propose that it is important to include competencies involved in *learning from experience* as a part of the set of competencies used to identify international executive potential and develop effective international managers.

Using existing literature, Spreitzer et al. identified fourteen dimensions that could be used to predict international executive potential. The list includes:

- eight *end-state competency dimensions* — for example, sensitivity to cultural differences, business knowledge, courage to take a stand, bringing out the best in people, acting with integrity, insight, commitment to success, and risk taking
- six *learning-oriented dimensions* — for example, use of feedback, cultural adventurousness, seeking opportunities to learn, openness to criticism, feedback seeking, and flexibility

These authors developed an instrument, called *Prospector,* that could be used to rate managers on each of these dimensions to identify which managers had the greatest potential to be effective international executives. Using over 800 managers from various levels of six international firms in twenty-one countries, Spreitzer et al. established initial evidence of the validity and reliability of the *Prospector* instrument as a way to predict international executive success.

The value of the approach taken by Spreitzer and colleagues is that it 1) gives HRD professionals ideas about what dimensions international management development programs should address, as well as possible ways to select which managers should participate in and most benefit from these activities, 2) reminds HRD professionals to consider future challenges managers may face that may take them beyond the competencies that have been needed in the past, and 3) provides an excellent model for how HRD professionals can take a scientific approach to identifying and generating supporting evidence for the sets of competencies they will use as the basis of management development.

Our purpose in raising these three points of view is not to suggest which is "correct" or would make the better foundation for describing the managerial job and the development of managers (although we believe the method used by

Spreitzer et al. to be the soundest and most worthy of emulation).[49] These models (as well as other ideas about achieving global competency) require further research, testing, and modification. Rather, these approaches illustrate the impact that consideration of the global environment can have on the approach to developing an organization's managers. In addition, they underscore the need to consider an organization's business strategy and the environment in which it operates as a foundation for determining how to develop its managers.

### WHAT COMPETENCIES WILL FUTURE MANAGERS NEED?

Just as Spreitzer et al. included consideration of learning-related dimensions to address competency areas that international managers will need in the future, other researchers are trying to estimate the competencies managers will need to navigate their careers in the 21st century.[50] For example, Allred, Snow, and Miles argue that organizational structure determines the core managerial competencies that are needed, and that new organizational structures will demand new sets of competencies.[51] Based on a survey of managers, HR executives, and recruiters, Allred et al. concluded that five categories of KSAs will be important for managerial careers in this new century: 1) a knowledge-based technical specialty, 2) cross-functional and international experience, 3) collaborative leadership, 4) self-management skills, and 5) personal traits, including integrity, trustworthiness, and flexibility.

While such predictions seem reasonable, they are only predictions. We mention this example not to offer "the answer," but to encourage HRD professionals to at least consider the question. It is important that management development activities prepare managers for the future, not managers who would have succeeded in a past that no longer exists. Guessing and estimates will have to be made, and we believe they will best be made by considering the organization, industry, and trends that will likely affect the businesses that managers will have to manage. Most of all, it means that management development should be seen as a *long-term process*. Management development programs and the development process should not be seen as finished products, but as organic works in progress that are regularly evaluated and modified as trends, strategies, and conditions warrant. This approach is already being used in many organizations, including 3M, General Electric, TRW, and Motorola, to name just a few.[52]

Having explored the nature of the management job and competencies that managing requires, we turn our attention to the issue of making management development strategic and to some of the options organizations use to develop their managers.

## MAKING MANAGEMENT DEVELOPMENT STRATEGIC

We have noted that management development should be tied to the organization's structure and strategy for accomplishing its business goals. Before we describe the various management development practices organizations use, it is useful to examine how these activities can be framed and delivered in a coherent way that ensures that this strategic focus is maintained.

Seibert, Hall, and Kram suggest that three desired linkages should exist between the organization's strategy and its executive and management development activities: 1) the link between the business environment and business strategy, 2) the link between business strategy and the organization's management development strategy, and 3) the link between the management development strategy and management development activities.[53] Based on an examination of management development practices at twenty-two leading organizations, Seibert et al. concluded that these organizations pay attention to the first and last links, but the middle linkage between the business strategy and the management development strategy was weak. They propose that this linkage is weak because the HRD function has focused on itself rather than its customer, has been unable to respond rapidly enough to meet the customer's needs, and has a tendency to see a false dichotomy between developing individuals and conducting business.

Seibert et al. found that some organizations, especially 3M and Motorola, did make this link, by making sure that strategic business issues drove management development, ensuring that HRD professionals provided a timely response to business needs, and by integrating management development as a natural part of doing business. Based on their review of these "best practices," Seibert and colleagues proposed four guiding principles that can help HRD professionals make the necessary strategic links:

1. **Begin by moving out and up to business strategy** — This involves reconceptualizing the HRD professional's role primarily as implementing strategy, and secondarily as a developer of managers. Practical suggestions include becoming intimately familiar with the organization's strategic objectives and business issues, using these as a starting point for identifying management behaviors and competencies, and looking for developmental opportunities within the activities needed to accomplish strategic objectives.

2. **Put job experiences before classroom activities, not vice versa** — This involves using job experiences as the central developmental activity, with classroom activities playing the role of identifying, processing, and sharing the learning that is taking place on the job. This assumes that on-the-job experiences will be actively managed to ensure that learning will take place and strategic needs will be addressed.

3. **Be opportunistic** — Ensure that management development is flexible and open to respond to the business needs and issues the organization is facing and will likely face. This involves moving away from elaborate, rigid programs to programs that can change and are built to be responsive to the organization's changing needs.

4. **Provide support for experience-based learning** — This involves creating a culture that expects, supports, and rewards learning as a part of day-to-day challenges and that reinforces individuals for taking control of their own development as managers.

Another approach to strategic management development is offered by Burack, Hochwarter, and Mathys.[54] Again, using a review of so-called world-class organizations, Burack et al. identified seven themes that they believe are common to strategic management development: 1) a linkage between management development and the business plans and strategies; 2) seamless programs, which cut across hierarchical and functional boundaries; 3) a global orientation and a cross-cultural approach; 4) individual learning focused within organizational learning; 5) a recognition of the organization's culture and ensuring that the management development design fits within and creates or supports the desired culture; 6) a career development focus; and 7) an approach built on empirically determined core competencies.

3M is an example of an organization that has integrated its strategy of global competition into its management development program.[55] An overseas assignment is one element of the developmental process for individuals who are being groomed for senior management positions. These managers are assigned to positions as managing directors for 3M subsidiaries for a period of three to five years. During this time, the individual is responsible for conducting the ordinary business of the subsidiary. Individuals are assigned based on who would benefit most from the experience.

What is unique about 3M's approach to using global assignments is the way the assignments are managed. Specifically, this approach includes the following: 1) international assignments are requirements for promotion to senior positions, so resistance to these assignments disappears; 2) each expatriate has a senior management sponsor (usually the most senior executive in the group the expatriate is leaving) who provides orientation, annual review meetings, and ongoing support; and 3) the assignments are changed as the business strategy and international situations change. For example, changing economic developments in Europe led 3M to change the position the expatriate is assigned to from managing director of a subsidiary to a product manager position on a European management action team to heading up a European business center. The managing director position approach was used in areas of the world for which it still made strategic sense (e.g., Latin America, Asia Pacific, Africa). This kind of flexible approach is a good example of keeping management development responsive to the changing needs of the organization, while making sure development and strategy achievement go hand in hand.[56]

The ideas offered by Seibert et al. and Burack et al. are useful in that they highlight the strategic issues and offer commonalities from the practices being used in respected organizations.[57] They are not time-tested blueprints for success, nor are they supported by empirical evidence (yet). Furthermore, the "best practices" and "leading organizations" approach to identifying principles and actions should be viewed with caution. What is found is determined by who the researchers have chosen to include in their sample and what they were able to discover. As was the case with the organizations profiled in the best-selling book *In Search of Excellence*,[58] not all organizations that meet the criteria for inclusion when the study is done continue to meet the criteria in later years.[59] The environment we live in is too turbulent for any set of principles to hold true in particular organizations for too long.

Finally, the suggestions offered in studies like these should be viewed as suggestions and should not be copied slavishly or unthinkingly.[60] The authors of the studies we cited express such caution in their writing, identify needs for future research to substantiate their suggestions, and remind readers that it is the practitioners' responsibility to ensure that what is done within their organizations should be based on needs assessment and a thorough knowledge of the organization and its environment.

## MANAGEMENT EDUCATION

As defined earlier, management education involves activities designed to help participants gain a broad range of conceptual knowledge and skills in formal classroom situations, most typically from degree-granting institutions. Management education continues to be an extremely popular activity. Enrollments in bachelor's and master's degree programs in the United States grew rapidly during the 1980s and early 1990s.[61] It is estimated that approximately 222,000 bachelor's degrees, 97,000 master's degrees, and over 1,300 doctoral degrees were awarded in business management during the academic year ending in 1997.[62] These figures show a decrease in the number of bachelor's degrees from 1994–1997, but an increase in the number of graduate degrees.[63] Nevertheless, business management remains the most popular bachelor's degree awarded in the U.S., the second most popular master's degree (behind education), and the tenth most popular doctoral degree.[64] Demand for admission to the top American M.B.A. programs remains strong, though there was a drop in applications at many of the top programs in 2000 (e.g., Harvard, the University of Pennsylvania's Wharton School, MIT, Columbia, Michigan, Virginia, Northwestern, and Duke).[65] This interest is despite a price tag of more than $40,000-$50,000 in tuition and fees for two years at most of the top schools, and nearly twice that in lost earnings.[66] The payoff from attending a prestigious school is also sizable, with demand for M.B.A.s from these schools pushing starting salaries to between $75,000 and $150,000 per year in 1997, plus perks.[67] A 2000 survey of fifty top M.B.A. programs found that the median gain in salary for graduates was $29,000 (compared to what they earned before enrolling in their master's degree program). The authors suggested that, on average, graduates recouped their investment, that is, both tuition and forgone salary, in 4.1 years, and this was across the range of more- versus less-expensive programs.[68] Management education activities can be grouped into two categories:

1. bachelor's or master's programs in business administration (B.B.A. or M.B.A.) offered at colleges and universities
2. executive education, which can range from condensed M.B.A. programs to short courses delivered by colleges and universities, consulting firms, private institutes, and professional and industry associations

Each category is discussed below.

## BACHELOR'S OR MASTER'S DEGREE PROGRAMS IN BUSINESS ADMINISTRATION

Traditional management education offered at four-year colleges and universities, leading to a bachelor's or master's degree, generally focuses on management knowledge and general concepts. While there has been some debate as to whether to focus such management education programs on providing primarily conceptual knowledge (e.g., market research techniques, planning and decision models) or developing the skills (e.g., communication, interpersonal) that managers need to be successful, most business school programs seek to provide both. The curricula of many M.B.A. and B.B.A. programs follow the accreditation standards issued by the main accrediting body in management education, the American Assembly of Collegiate Schools of Business (AACSB). The AACSB distinguishes bachelor's and master's education in terms of each one's scope. They see bachelor's education as combining "general education with basic study of business," and master's education as providing a professional general managerial perspective.[69] The AACSB standards are mission-based, in that they provide for flexibility in program content, structure, and delivery based on the institution's mission (e.g., the degree of emphasis on teaching and research).

According to the AACSB curriculum standards, the curricula of both bachelor's and master's programs should provide an understanding of the following issues and how they affect organizations: ethical, global, political, social, technological, legal and regulatory, environmental, and demographic diversity. Bachelor's programs should provide foundational knowledge in accounting, behavioral science, economics, mathematics, and statistics, along with a general education component that makes up at least half of the students' programs. Master's programs should be organized around a core of financial reporting, analysis and markets, domestic and global economic environments, creation of goods and services, and human behavior in organizations. Programs at both levels should provide training in written and oral communication, with master's programs ensuring that graduates have basic quantitative analysis and computer skills.[70]

Business schools were widely criticized as being ineffective during the late 1980s and early 1990s. The criticism prompted a comprehensive review of business school training by the AACSB, which addressed concerns that business schools were not satisfying the needs of organizations in terms of providing students with the education needed to become effective managers.[71] Concerns focused on the lack of cross-functional integration in coursework (e.g., finance, human resource management), perceptions of graduates' levels of "soft" skills (e.g., communication, interpersonal), lack of an international perspective, and a lack of breadth in the students' preparation (i.e., too much focus on business issues at the expense of providing a broad education). Among Porter and McKibbin's recommendations were that business schools should modify their curricula to address these shortcomings and thus become more responsive to making students and organizations more competitive in the current and future environment.[72] These recommendations have far-reaching consequences both in terms of knowledge of subject matter needed by the faculty to develop the content of these programs and the educational techniques needed to deliver them.

Business schools have responded to the challenge. For example, the Wharton School at the University of Pennsylvania became one of the first M.B.A. programs to completely overhaul its curriculum to meet what were perceived to be the realities of doing business in the next century. Rather than offering semester-long courses in separate disciplines, the Wharton program offers courses in four six-week modules that integrate the disciplines to solve problems. The revised program also places a heavy emphasis on the development of "people skills," practical problem solving, and acquiring a global perspective. The curriculum, which was developed with the input of students, faculty, alumni, futurists, CEOs, and corporate recruiters, became both a model to be emulated and a stimulus for program innovations at other schools.[73]

Another example of innovation and change in business schools is the M.B.A. program redesign at the Weatherhead School of Business at Case Western Reserve University in Cleveland, Ohio.[74] Implemented in the fall of 1990, the program was designed to focus on learning outcomes, involve and serve the needs of all stakeholder groups (e.g., students, alumni, potential employers), stimulate students to think about issues in novel ways, expand students' capacity to think and act creatively, and place faculty in the role of managers of learning rather than teachers.[75] The program has six elements:

1. A managerial assessment and development course that provides students with a way to assess and develop the KSAs relevant to their management careers (using a competency-based approach)

2. Development of an individual learning plan

3. Executive Action Teams, which are groups of students who meet regularly with a local executive adviser to integrate learning across courses and from students' experiences

4. Eleven core courses in management and business disciplines (e.g., accounting, finance, human resource, and labor policy)

5. Multidisciplinary perspective courses organized around themes such as managing in a global economy, technology management, and the history of industrial development

6. Advanced elective courses[76]

An evaluation study conducted over a two-year period showed evidence that the outcome-oriented, competency-based program "had a positive impact in helping students to improve their abilities between the time of entry and graduation."[77]

The Wharton and Weatherhead examples show the kinds of vitality and change that have been going on in business schools in recent years. Student input into a wide range of issues, efforts to improve teaching and placement support, and cooperation with business have become commonplace at many business schools.[78] Innovations in teaching have also been implemented. Team-oriented and applied projects and assignments are now widely used. Many business schools use computer and telecommunication technology as a central part of courses, and courses (and even entire programs) taught completely online are becoming increasingly commonplace.[79] The *Journal of Management Education* is a good source of examples, ideas, and issues that management educators are developing and debating to keep business education responsive, relevant, and effective.

It should be noted that degree programs at both the graduate and undergraduate levels should be seen as only one component of a manager's development. It is unreasonable to expect that education at these levels will result in a "whole manager" who has all the KSAs needed to manage effectively. At their best, business programs can provide a valuable foundation for a manager's development and a good way for practicing managers to reflect on their experiences and develop new skills and knowledge. Graduates of such programs should be seen as "works in progress," with the potential to become effective managers with further development and experience.[80]

## EXECUTIVE EDUCATION PROGRAMS

Because of the length of time it can take to complete an M.B.A. program and the crowded lives of many full-time managers, many institutions, both academic and otherwise, have developed a number of alternatives. These alternatives, which can range from condensed M.B.A. programs known as Executive M.B.A.s (E.M.B.A.s), to short courses on given topics and issues, to one-time sessions, can be referred to as **executive education** programs. Executive education has become big business for the universities and institutions that provide it. For example, it is estimated that INSEAD (in Fontainebleu, France), Harvard, and the Center for Creative Leadership earned annual revenues of $37 million, $30.1 million, and $23.5 million, respectively, from executive education programs.[81]

*EXECUTIVE M.B.A. PROGRAMS.*   It is estimated that over 9,500 executives attend E.M.B.A. programs at 102 business schools in North America each year.[82] Most of these programs condense or accelerate the coursework, with courses meeting once a week (typically on weekends). These programs are typically designed to be completed in two years. Students tend to be older, full-time managers from a variety of organizations who have a significant amount of experience as managers.

Commonly perceived advantages of E.M.B.A. programs include the opportunity to interact with managers from other organizations, maximum input of new ideas, high quality of instruction, and the prestige afforded by having a university affiliation. Commonly perceived disadvantages include inadequate exposure to information specific to the organization's needs, the high price, and an insufficient number of instructors within a given program who are effective at teaching adults.[83] In addition, critics have charged that some programs are merely watered-down versions of M.B.A. programs, with poor quality of instruction and lax admission standards, and with the primary goal of generating income for the school.[84]

Are E.M.B.A. programs an effective approach to developing managers? Unfortunately, there is little existing research to answer the question. Evaluations are generally based on anecdotal information. Typical results of the few evaluation studies of E.M.B.A. programs indicate that participants are generally satisfied with their experience, feeling that they have been broadened by their exposure to

**THE PROFESSIONAL FELLOWS PROGRAM AT THE WEATHERHEAD SCHOOL OF MANAGEMENT**[1]

At the Weatherhead School of Management at Case Western Reserve University in Cleveland, Ohio, an innovative approach to executive education has been developed. The program is aimed at midcareer professionals who have little formal management education, but who are entering or already in management positions. Enrollees in this program were designated as "Professional Fellows." It was decided that this would be a nondegree program, rather than an M.B.A.-type program. The program places strong emphasis on self-directed learning. Four distinctive elements make up the Professional Fellows Program, or PFP:

1. An initial course is taken that emphasizes individual assessment and development. Each participant must write up a personal learning plan that will guide his or her studies and personal development over the next five to seven years.

2. Participants take a series of seminars on current challenges in leadership and management.

3. Each participant completes an individualized, intensive study of a particular topic (or topics) through a major research project and via course electives.

4. Participants take part in a "Society of Fellows," which is an active peer network that seeks to facilitate continuous, lifelong learning.

As of 1999, fifty-three people in four classes of fellows had participated in the program. The aspect of the program that was cited as most helpful was the development of the individualized learning plan. In interviews, participants also cited the impact that the program had on their self-confidence. Some of the particular abilities that fellows thought had been most enhanced by their involvement in the program were networking, planning, group management, initiative, and developing others.

The Weatherhead faculty who described this program view it as a successful work in progress. They close their article with three penetrating questions that are worth considering:

a. Can or should this process be expanded to other regions or professional schools?

b. Does the PFP have implications for other forms of management education, for example, E.M.B.A., M.B.A., or undergraduate management education?

c. Can universities view this as a legitimate program, and will faculty involvement in this program be treated as equal in value as involvement in degree-granting programs (M.B.A., undergraduate)?

You might recognize that this program is strongly influenced by the principles of adult learning that we presented in Chapter 3. Given our discussion there, what do you think about applying these principles in a bachelor's or master's program? In your opinion, would it work? Why or why not?

[1]From: Ballou, R., Bowers, D., Boyatzis, R. E., & Kolb, D. A. (1999). Fellowship in lifelong learning: An executive development program for advanced professionals. *Journal of Management Education, 23*, 338–355.

---

new ideas and people, and have gained increased levels of self-confidence.[85] Despite the lack of hard evidence, organizations continue to support such programs.

Most organizations use E.M.B.A. programs as one component of their executive development efforts in addition to other in-house and external activities (e.g., succession planning, short courses).[86] We recommend that organizations interested in using E.M.B.A. programs carefully examine their development needs and investigate the programs they consider using. Discussions with administrators, faculty members, and alumni can yield useful information.

*OTHER APPROACHES TO EXECUTIVE EDUCATION.*     Executive education need not be as comprehensive as an M.B.A. or E.M.B.A. program. Many providers offer courses in a wide range of management topics. These courses generally focus on a particular topic, issue, or skill, and are freestanding (i.e., they do not exist within a degree-oriented curriculum). Before 1980, the dominant external provider of such programs was the American Management Association (AMA), which continues to offer hundreds of courses on a wide range of topics. While other providers did offer courses and programs (e.g., the National Training Laboratories), the AMA nearly held a monopoly on providing such training.[87] The current picture is different in that no single provider dominates the field. In addition to colleges and universities, organizations such as the Center for Creative Leadership, Wilson Learning, industry associations, and a host of consultants offer courses that can be used as part of a total management development program. The boxed insert nearby provides information on an innovative executive education program at the Weatherhead School of Management at Case Western Reserve University.

The intent of many courses is to mix some theory with a great deal of practical relevance in order to provide participants with information and tools that have immediate application to their current jobs. Advances in telecommunications, especially in satellite transmission, videoconferencing, and the Internet, are making long-distance learning a growing part of executive education that could lead to major changes in how executive education is provided. In 1996, it was estimated that 10 percent of all organizations and 22 percent of large organizations used commercial satellite distance learning networks to deliver training.[88] In 2000, it was estimated that 27 percent of all training was delivered outside of the traditional instructor-led classroom (this included distance education, instructorless computer-based training, and other nonclassroom forms of training).[89] A recent special issue in the *Journal of Management Education* was devoted to the topic, "Management education in the information age."[90] Colleges and universities are finding a growing market in beaming lectures and classes conducted by their "star" professors via satellite to remote locations (e.g., alumni clubs, and company classrooms). Two examples of this trend include:

■ a consortium of eight business schools brought together by Westcott Communications, Inc., called the Executive Education Network, which has connections to over 100 classrooms in companies including Kodak, Walt Disney, and Texas Instruments

■ the University of Michigan, which provides live video courses to companies in the United States, Europe, and Asia, in partnership with a consortium headed by British Telecom[91]

Advantages of using such courses offered by external providers include controlling the costs of in-house courses, the specialized expertise of the provider, the design and packaging of such courses, and a practitioner-oriented approach (particularly among courses not offered by universities).[92] In addition, satellite courses can be delivered at the convenience of the client and do not require participants to travel to attend the program.[93] One of the significant disadvantages of such courses is a lack of quality control. Operating in a highly competitive environment, many of these providers are under pressure to stay in business and may reduce their standards to ensure they generate sufficient business in the short term. While market forces will eventually (and ideally) weed out the poor quality programs, this may take time and many clients may purchase poor quality courses in the process.[94] Furthermore, as we discussed in Chapters 5 and 6, the content of the course needs to be matched to the medium used to deliver it. For example, given the current state of technology, satellite transmission may be better suited for knowledge transmission (it is typically a lecture, with all of the associated advantages and disadvantages), while interpersonal skills courses would be better conducted in person.

One potential disadvantage to short courses offered by colleges and universities is a real or perceived lack of relevance and practical orientation. One way some organizations are addressing these concerns is by working with colleges and universities to customize courses that will meet their specific needs. Colleges and universities are increasingly willing to customize courses to fit a particular client's needs. For example, Hoffman-LaRoche, Inc., a New Jersey-based healthcare and pharmaceutical company, convinced the Massachusetts Institute of Technology (MIT) to customize a course that would provide managers with training in strategic management of technology, leadership, and quality.[95] Other similar partnerships exist between Ford Motor Company and the University of Michigan and IBM and Wharton. While this approach may resolve the issues of quality and relevance, it is not inexpensive, with costs per program (e.g., a three- or four-day course) ranging from $50,000 to $80,000.[96] Hequet recommends that organizations interested in such an approach should shop around by discussing their needs with a variety of schools, explaining specifically what they want and finding out what the school can offer (i.e., in terms of times, locations, instructors) and then negotiate to obtain a reasonable price.[97]

Customized or not, short courses offered by external providers are likely to remain a significant part of the management development scene in the future, especially in light of the convenience and variety of the options that are available. One of the best ways an organization can ensure that it purchases courses that will meet its needs is to conduct a thorough needs analysis and evaluate the programs both before and after they are used.

Finally, Vicere suggests the following guidelines be used in designing executive education initiatives, based on his review of several innovative executive education programs:

- Effective executive education is a blend of experience, training, education, and other forms of development and does not rely solely on classroom-based techniques.

- Real-time interaction with real-life business issues is an integral element of effective executive education.

■ Executive education should develop and revitalize both the participant and the organization.

■ Executive education should instill a desire for continuous learning and knowledge creation on the part of both individuals and organizations.

■ Effective executive education efforts should contribute to the development of both the individual talents of leaders and the collective knowledge base of the organization.

■ Executive education should help establish a talent pool of leaders at all levels of the organization.[98]

Regardless of the type of management education provided (bachelor's, M.B.A., E.M.B.A., or other), the challenge facing all management educators today is to ensure the timeliness and "value-added" of what is presented.[99] Joseph Alutto has referred to this as "Just-in-time management education in the 21st century," and this is a useful description of what organizations are seeking from management education.[100] The dynamic social, political, economic, and technological changes occurring today require fundamental changes in the manner in which management education is conducted.[101] We expect major changes in the shape and substance of management education in the coming decade.

## MANAGEMENT TRAINING AND EXPERIENCES

Various surveys indicate that almost 90 percent of organizations provide training and on-the-job experiences as part of their efforts to develop managers.[102] The majority of organizations use a combination of externally provided and internally developed courses and programs to achieve this goal. In this section of the chapter, we focus briefly on company-specific management training approaches. A wide variety of possibilities exist. To illustrate the options in use, we will discuss three approaches: company-designed courses, company academies, "colleges," and corporate universities, and on-the-job experiences.

### COMPANY-DESIGNED COURSES

Organizations frequently design their own courses and seminars as one way to develop their managers. Such courses have the advantage of being tailored to the specific issues, skills, and individual attributes of the organization and its managers. These efforts can range from a specific course focusing on one skill or issue (e.g., evaluating employee performance, budgeting) to a series of interconnected courses (e.g., a two-week-long series of workshops to expose key nonmanagers to all company divisions and products and acquaint them with the challenges the company faces). For example, General Electric (GE) developed a series of courses to prepare managers to compete successfully in a global environment. The program, offered at the company's Crotonville, New York, management development center, is made up of a core curriculum that includes courses offered in a five-stage developmental sequence — Corporate Entry Leadership Conferences, New Manager Development Courses, Advanced Functional Courses, Executive Programs, and Officers' Workshops. This program services employees ranging from new college hires to corporate officers.[103] The courses are tailored to the challenges faced by GE's managers, including the use of GE-specific issues to provide an opportunity for participants to solve problems.

The issues in designing and implementing such courses are the same as for any HRD program. It is particularly important to ensure that such courses fit within an overall framework for developing managers. The idea is to avoid redundancy and help participants see the relevance of the courses to their overall developmental plan. It also helps managers, who are responsible for developing their subordinates, to understand the relationships of the courses the organization offers to the overall development effort. For example, GE makes clear its assumption that 80 percent of development occurs through on-the-job experience, with only 20 percent taking place through formal development (e.g., the Crotonville courses).[104] This perspective makes clear to managers that the bulk of their developmental efforts should be focused on providing subordinates with meaningful developmental experiences on the job.

Some organizations go beyond their own managers as participants in their management development courses. For example, GE invites managers and officials from key overseas customers (and potential customers), such as Aeroflot from Russia and a group of Chinese managers, to attend customized programs alongside GE managers at Crotonville. The purpose of these programs is to develop the skills and talents of the managers involved, form relationships that can lead to greater cooperation and increased business opportunities, and learn the way other organizations and countries conduct business.[105]

### COMPANY ACADEMIES, "COLLEGES," AND CORPORATE UNIVERSITIES

A large number of organizations have concluded that a significant component of their management development strategy should include a company academy or college in which all managers at certain levels are required to complete a specific curriculum. A 2000 report suggested that over 1,600 organizations had their own corporate universities.[106] Organizations that have taken this approach include GE, IBM, McDonald's, Motorola, Intel, Dunkin' Donuts, Holiday Inn, and Xerox. The facilities used for these academies can be quite elaborate (e.g., hundred-acre, landscaped campuses with multiple buildings and residential facilities located away from other company facilities). They have a specific educational mission geared toward the organization's specific needs and preferred ways of doing things. For example, McDonald's, the worldwide fast-food chain, teaches managers its approach to ensuring quality, service, and cleanliness at Hamburger University in Oak Brook, Illinois. The courses at Hamburger University include operational procedures that reinforce the organization's philosophy. Hamburger University uses a wide range of training methods, including lecture and discussion, audiovisuals, and hands-on experiences with equipment.[107]

Xerox Corporation devotes a portion of its over 2,000-acre corporate living, learning, and fitness center in Leesburg, Virginia, to its corporate education center. The center is capable of handling 1,000 students at a time and offers curricula in sales training, service training, and management training. The management training curriculum focuses on teaching participants about the business, their jobs as managers, and about themselves. Faculty for the center is drawn from the company's employees, and course design is performed by a group of professionals (Educational Services) specifically trained in course design that has access to production facilities capable of creating courses using a wide range of technologies (e.g., video, computer-assisted instruction). Members of this group identify needs and develop courses in collaboration with clients, subject-matter experts, and instructors.[108] Another example is Arthur Andersen's Andersen Center, a 645-acre campus that can accommodate 1,700 students, complete with 130 classrooms and 1,000 computer workstations.[109]

While not all company academies are as elaborate as those run by McDonald's, Arthur Andersen, and Xerox, they are an expensive component of management development. Some organizations permit members of outside organizations to use their facilities and attend their courses for a fee when space permits. Critics charge that the standardized curricula at corporate academies can lead to problems (e.g., unresponsiveness to the organization's needs, detachment from the realities of the operating divisions). Eurich suggests, however, that such curricula can be useful if they transmit knowledge and skills that all participants at a particular level should know and that some of the problems that accompany this approach can be mitigated by a "vigilant management and training staff to ensure that a curriculum admits new ideas and responds to change" (p. 167).[110] It should be noted that programs at many corporate universities have kept pace with the changes going on in the rest of HRD and management development, including changing delivery methods and an emphasis on serving the organization's strategic needs.[111] Recent articles describe the latest developments in corporate universities.[112] Interested readers should also peruse the *Corporate University Review*, a journal dedicated to this topic.[113]

## ON-THE-JOB EXPERIENCES

On-the-job experiences play an important role in the development of managers.[114] Organizations also recognize that experience contributes to development (e.g., GE assumes that 80 percent of management development occurs on-the-job),[115] and many organizations use job assignments and experiences as part of their management development efforts. However, despite the importance of on-the-job experience to management development, many organizations leave such development to chance, hoping managers discover the lessons to be learned on their own. In addition, not much is known about how these events influence development and how we can make the most of such experiences.[116] Some observers have noted that

**■ TABLE 13-2**

**Setting and Implementing Agendas**
- Technical/professional skills
- All about the business one is in
- Strategic thinking
- Shouldering full responsibility
- Building and using structure and control systems
- Innovative problem-solving methods

**Handling Relationships**
- Handling political situations
- Getting people to implement solutions
- What executives are like and how to work with them
- Strategies of negotiation
- Dealing with people over whom you have no authority
- Understanding other people's perspectives
- Dealing with conflict
- Directing and motivating subordinates
- Developing other people
- Confronting subordinate performance problems
- Managing former bosses and peers

**Basic Values**
- Recognizing that you can't manage everything all alone
- Sensitivity to the human side of management
- Basic management values

**Executive Temperament**
- Being tough when necessary
- Self-confidence
- Coping with situations beyond your control
- Persevering through adversity
- Coping with ambiguous situations
- Use (and abuse) of power

**Personal Awareness**
- The balance between work and personal life
- Knowing what really excites you about work
- Personal limits and blind spots
- Taking charge of your career
- Recognizing and seizing opportunities

SOURCE: From M. W. McCall, Jr., M. M. Lombardo, and A. M. Morrison (1988). *The lessons of experience: How successful executives develop on the job*, p. 6. Reprinted with the permission of The Free Press, a division of Simon & Schuster, Inc.

**TABLE 13-3**

**Setting the Stage**
- Early work experience
- First supervisory job

**Leading by Persuasion**
- Project/task-force assignments
- Line to staff switches

**Leading on Line**
- Starting from scratch
- Turning a business around
- Managing a larger scope

**When Other People Matter**
- Bosses

**Hardships**
- Personal trauma
- Career setback
- Changing jobs
- Business mistakes
- Subordinate performance problems

SOURCE: From M. W. McCall, Jr., M. M. Lombardo, and A. M. Morrison (1988). *The lessons of experience: How successful executives develop on the job*, p. 10. Reprinted with the permission of The Free Press, a division of Simon & Schuster, Inc.

many on-the-job experiences tend to reinforce old attitudes and behaviors, rather than encourage managers to adopt new ones that can make them more effective.[117]

Clearly, research on the types of events that have developmental potential, the lessons they can teach, and how such lessons can be learned is needed if we are to harness the power of experience. An important step in that direction is a series of studies of the role of experience in executive development conducted at the Center for Creative Leadership (CCL).[118] Researchers from CCL studied 191 successful executives from six major organizations by asking them to describe the key events in their careers and explain what they learned from them. These inquiries yielded over 1,500 lessons executives learned from 616 events. Content analysis of these statements resulted in thirty-two types of lessons that can be grouped into five themes: setting and implementing agendas, handling relationships, basic values, executive temperament, and personal awareness. The developmental events were summarized into five categories: setting the stage, leading by persuasion, leading on the line, when other people matter, and hardships. Table 13-2 lists the themes and the lessons that make up each theme, and Table 13-3 lists the categories of events and types of events that make up each category.

McCall, Lombardo, and Morrison observe that the lessons learned from on-the-job events are hard-won, involving emotion, reflection, and assistance from others to extract the meaning.[119] They conclude that it is management's responsibility (shared with the individual) to be vigilant for opportunities to develop subordinates (e.g., task-force assignments, challenging assignments), and to provide the necessary support, resources, feedback, and time necessary for subordinates to learn from these events. While recognizing that firm conclusions are hard to come by, McCall and colleagues suggest that an effective management development system is one that is characterized by the following:

1. **Opportunism** — taking advantage of opportunities for growth and learning

2. **Individualism** — taking into account the unique attributes of the individuals being developed

3. **Long-term perspective** — taking the view that developing managers is a multiyear process (e.g., 10-20 years)

4. **Encouragement of self-motivation** — encouraging the individuals being developed to be self-motivated

5. **Online approach** — centered on learning on the job

The events approach described by the CCL research is intriguing and presents a variety of useful suggestions for using experiences deliberately to develop managers, although it has its limitations (e.g., the sample studied was composed almost entirely of male, white, middle-aged managers from six large organizations). Nevertheless, we believe this research is a significant step forward in an important area.

One way to make better use of on-the-job experiences for management development would be to have a method to assess the developmental components of jobs. A first step in that direction is the **Developmental Challenge Profile** (DCP).[120] The DCP is a ninety-six-item questionnaire based on the research investigating job features that could be developmental.[121] It contains fifteen scales organized around the following three categories of developmental features:

■ **Job transition** — unfamiliar responsibilities, proving yourself

■ **Task-related characteristics** — which includes nine scales in three areas:

1) creating change — developing new directions, inherited problems, reduction decisions, problems with employees

2) high level of responsibility — high stakes, managing business diversity, job overload, handling external pressure

3) nonauthority relationships — influencing without authority

■ **Obstacles** — adverse business conditions, lack of top management support, lack of personal support, difficult boss

The research done by McCauley et al. during the development of the DCP found that it had high internal consistency and test-retest reliability, and validity evidence supported the relationship of the majority of the scales to "perceptions of the learning of fundamental managerial skills and ways of thinking" (p. 556).

The DCP is still being refined, but McCauley et al. suggest that in addition to being a research tool that can help uncover the developmental process that occurs on the job, it has at least two practical uses for management development: 1) DCP feedback can provide managers with a better understanding of the learning opportunities that are available within their jobs, and 2) the DCP can be used to identify components that can be designed into jobs to improve the opportunities for development.

In addition to the "events" view, there are at least two other approaches to using on-the-job experiences systematically in management development: mentoring and action learning. **Mentoring** was discussed at some length in Chapter 12, so we will not revisit that topic here. **Action learning** is a concept first attributed to British physicist Reg Revans that has become increasingly common in the United States.[122] Originally developed as a way to encourage line managers to provide input to modify operating systems,[123] action learning as it is currently practiced involves having participants select an organizational problem, write a case study describing the problem, and meet with a group of other managers who face similar problems to discuss ways the problem can be dealt with.[124] This idea is sort of a "living case" approach, where instead of analyzing situations that have been resolved in the past, participants deal with ongoing problems and issues. The most widely cited example of action learning (and likely the largest implementation) is the Work-Out program at GE.[125] It is estimated that over 220,000 people have participated in the action-learning Work-Outs.[126]

Among the potential advantages of an action-learning approach is the discovery of a structured way to examine and analyze on-the-job events. Action learning also provides the opportunity to motivate participants to seek additional development (e.g., negotiation skills) that will help them resolve the type of problem discussed. In addition, because participants focus on existing issues, their motivation to learn and seek further development may be stronger. And, in the process, action-learning participants are actually solving problems and implementing solutions, making management development an integral part of strategy implementation and providing the organization tangible benefits beyond development. Most of the writing about action learning has been descriptive and anecdotal rather than empirical, but action learning is clearly a technique that is gaining wide use and enthusiastic reviews.[127] A well-done qualitative research study on action learning in a multinational corporation was conducted by Lyle Yorks and colleagues.[128] Alan Mumford has also provided helpful guidance on the uses and boundaries of action learning.[129]

A key to using on-the-job experiences for developmental purposes is to ensure that time and techniques are provided so that opportunities for learning are not overlooked. Several of the examples we have cited so far in the chapter highlight ways this can be addressed. In addition, Daudelin suggests that building time and methods for reflecting on work experiences into the management development process (and day-to-day work) can be a way to ensure that learning will occur.[130] She describes a number of methods for individual reflection (e.g., journal writing, business writing, assessment instruments, and spontaneous thinking during repetitive activities such as jogging) and reflection with another person or a small group (e.g., performance appraisal discussions, counseling sessions, project review meetings, mentoring, and informal discussions with friends or colleagues).

In summary, organizations can systematically use on-the-job experiences to develop managers in a variety of ways. While there is much research to be done, on-the-job experience should be a significant component of an organization's management development strategy. We recommend that organizations examine the opportunities available to them in this area to determine how they can make the most of experiences in their managers' development.

# EXAMPLES OF APPROACHES USED TO DEVELOP MANAGERS

Many training techniques (see Chapters 5 and 6) and topics are available for conducting management training and development. Training topics include leadership, motivation, interpersonal skills, decision making, cultural and global training, and technical knowledge. We will describe two commonly used management development programs: leadership training and the use of behavior modeling to develop interpersonal and other skills.

## LEADERSHIP TRAINING

Leadership has been one of the most heavily researched and popularly discussed topics in management. There is a widespread belief that leadership skills are essential to effective management, especially for organizations that are trying to implement changes. At any time, dozens of books and popular press articles are available to managers to help them learn how they can become more effective leaders. One of the problems with advice in the popular press on leadership is that it is usually anecdotal, lacks a sound theoretical basis, and is often contradictory.

Leadership training is one of the most commonly offered forms of training, with 89 percent of the organizations surveyed in 2000 offering such training.[131] One widely used approach to leadership training, Leader Match training, has overcome many of the problems connected to many discussions of leadership. The program is based on a theory about what leadership is and how it can be acquired. It has also been the subject of empirical research and is backed by evidence that it can improve one's leadership effectiveness. While Leader Match is not without problems or critics, it does represent a clearheaded, systematic approach to training and development. We will describe the Leader Match program and then discuss how many organizations are using a multifaceted approach to developing leaders that is based on the notion of transformational leadership.

*FIEDLER'S LEADER MATCH PROGRAM.* Leader Match training is based on the notion that effective leadership occurs when there is a match between the leader's style and the situation he or she faces.[132] The theoretical foundation for the program is Fiedler's contingency theory of leadership.[133] Fiedler believes that each person has a particular leadership style, based on his or her needs, that dictates how he or she will act. Because this style is based on the leader's needs, it is very difficult for the leader to change it. According to Fiedler, that style will not be effective in all situations. It is therefore the leader's task to diagnose the situation and either place himself or herself in a situation favorable to his or her style or modify the situation so that it becomes favorable to his or her style.

The **Leader Match** program is a self-administered programmed instruction technique (it is sold as a workbook) designed to help the leader do the following:

1. diagnose his or her leadership style

2. diagnose the situation and categorize it as favorable or unfavorable

3. change the critical elements of the situation so that it will match the leader's style[134]

The program takes about five to twelve hours to complete and can be supplemented by lectures, discussions, and other training media.[135]

Trainees use measuring scales provided in the programmed instruction book to assess their leadership style and situational favorableness. The leader's style is measured by the **Least Preferred Coworker (LPC) scale** shown in Figure 13-3. This instrument requires the leader to describe the person he or she would least like to work with, using a series of bipolar adjectives (e.g., friendly — unfriendly, supportive — hostile). The leader's responses indicate whether the leader has a stronger need for relationships (a high-LPC leader) or for task accomplishment (a low-LPC leader). Fiedler argues that all leaders have both needs, but that one need will be dominant and must be satisfied first. Therefore, relationship-motivated leaders will behave in ways to establish relationships first, and will then focus primarily on task accomplishment. The opposite is true of task-motivated leaders.

Whether the situation is favorable or unfavorable depends on the leader's control over the situation, which is measured by three factors: leader-member relations, task structure, and the leader's position power. The Leader Match book contains measuring scales for each of these dimensions. Contingency theory states that task-motivated leaders are effective in highly favorable and highly unfavorable situations. A highly favorable situation is one that permits a high degree of control (e.g., good relationships with followers, a highly structured task, and adequate power to reward and punish subordinates). An unfavorable situation is one with a low degree of control (e.g., poor relationships with followers, an ambiguous or unstructured task, and inadequate power to reward and punish). The theory further states that relationship-motivated leaders are effective in situations that are moderately favorable (i.e., provide the leader with moderate control).

After the trainee has diagnosed his or her leadership style and the favorableness of the situation he or she manages in, the training program focuses on ways in which the leader can modify the situation to match his or her style. Suggestions are made as to how one can modify leader-member relations, task structure, and position power. For example, to increase position power, the leader can "show [her] subordinates 'who's boss' by exercising fully the powers that the organization provides" or "make sure that information to [her] group gets channeled through [her]."[136]

**■ FIGURE 13-3**

| | 8 | 7 | 6 | 5 | 4 | 3 | 2 | 1 | |
|---|---|---|---|---|---|---|---|---|---|
| Pleasant | 8 | 7 | 6 | 5 | 4 | 3 | 2 | 1 | Unpleasant |
| Friendly | 8 | 7 | 6 | 5 | 4 | 3 | 2 | 1 | Unfriendly |
| Rejecting | 1 | 2 | 3 | 4 | 5 | 6 | 7 | 8 | Accepting |
| Tense | 1 | 2 | 3 | 4 | 5 | 6 | 7 | 8 | Relaxed |
| Distant | 1 | 2 | 3 | 4 | 5 | 6 | 7 | 8 | Close |
| Cold | 1 | 2 | 3 | 4 | 5 | 6 | 7 | 8 | Warm |
| Supportive | 8 | 7 | 6 | 5 | 4 | 3 | 2 | 1 | Hostile |
| Boring | 1 | 2 | 3 | 4 | 5 | 6 | 7 | 8 | Interesting |
| Quarrelsome | 1 | 2 | 3 | 4 | 5 | 6 | 7 | 8 | Harmonious |
| Gloomy | 1 | 2 | 3 | 4 | 5 | 6 | 7 | 8 | Cheerful |
| Open | 8 | 7 | 6 | 5 | 4 | 3 | 2 | 1 | Guarded |
| Backbiting | 1 | 2 | 3 | 4 | 5 | 6 | 7 | 8 | Loyal |
| Untrustworthy | 1 | 2 | 3 | 4 | 5 | 6 | 7 | 8 | Trustworthy |
| Considerate | 8 | 7 | 6 | 5 | 4 | 3 | 2 | 1 | Inconsiderate |
| Nasty | 1 | 2 | 3 | 4 | 5 | 6 | 7 | 8 | Nice |
| Agreeable | 8 | 7 | 6 | 5 | 4 | 3 | 2 | 1 | Disagreeable |
| Insincere | 1 | 2 | 3 | 4 | 5 | 6 | 7 | 8 | Sincere |
| Kind | 8 | 7 | 6 | 5 | 4 | 3 | 2 | 1 | Unkind |

SOURCE: From F. E. Fiedler and M. M. Chemers (1984). *Improving leadership effectiveness: The leader match concept* (2nd ed.). New York: Wiley, 19. Copyright 1984 by John Wiley and Sons. Reprinted by permission.

Both Fiedler's contingency theory and the Leader Match program have been extensively researched.[137] The program has been tested in a variety of settings using working adult leaders, including public health volunteer workers,[138] ROTC military leaders,[139] police and county government middle managers.[140] Overall, there is evidence that Leader Match can improve a leader's effectiveness. Burke and Day, in a meta-analysis of seventy published and unpublished studies of management development programs, concluded that Leader Match is effective when using subjective behavioral criteria (i.e., ratings of changes in on-the-job behavior) and generalized across situations.[141] They recommend the use of Leader Match training based on both the research evidence and cost-effectiveness of the program.

Leader Match and the contingency theory have not been without controversy. Researchers have questioned the soundness of the LPC scale and the linkage between Leader Match and the contingency theory,[142] with rejoinders from Fiedler and his associates.[143] Despite the lack of closure on the controversial aspects of the theory and program, Leader Match and Fiedler's efforts to develop and substantiate a training program based on theory and empirical research are impressive given the tendency in the past for the training and development and HRD fields to rely on fads and testimonials. This approach should be a model for others to emulate.

*TRANSFORMATIONAL LEADERSHIP: THE MISSING PIECE OF THE LEADERSHIP PUZZLE?*   The Leader Match approach to leadership development suffers from the same problems that much of leadership theory does: it seems to be narrowly focused and misses an aspect of leadership that many people see as central. This aspect is the idea that leaders are those who capture our attention, present us with a vision of what could be, inspire us to pursue the vision, and show us the way to get there. These ideas are at the heart of what Bernard Bass refers to as **transformational leadership**.[144] The main elements of transformational leadership include charisma (offering a vision and raising the self-expectations of followers), intellectual stimulation (helping followers change their assumptions and focus on rational solutions), and individualized consideration (e.g., providing coaching and individual development).

Transformational leadership seems to better fit most people's ideas of what "real leaders" do (especially when they are leading an organizational change effort; organizational change will be discussed in Chapter 14). Some evidence suggests that the elements of transformational leadership are related to organizational outcomes.[145] Transformational leadership training is being developed and tested.[146] For example, Barling et al. operationalized transformational leadership training into a one-day group-training session followed by four monthly individual booster sessions.[147] The emphasis was placed on helping participants become more intellectually stimulating (a key transformational leadership element). In the one-day session, participants examined their own views of leadership, received a presentation about transformational and other types of leadership, learned about goal setting, and used role plays to practice goal setting and other leadership behaviors within the context of the organization's mission statement. The booster sessions consisted of goal setting to improve participants' leadership behavior and generating and reviewing action plans. In a two-group pretest-posttest study of managers (total $N = 20$) in a bank branch setting, Barling et al. found that managers in the training group were perceived by their subordinates as higher on all three aspects of transformational leadership. In addition, subordinates of the trained managers showed increased organizational commitment, and some evidence suggested that branches in which the trained managers worked had better financial outcomes.

Research and development on transformational leadership training is in its early stages, but in the past decade, this topic has generated a large amount of research and interest. For example, the summer and fall 1999 issues of *Leadership Quarterly* were devoted entirely to charismatic and transformational leadership theories.[148] Some important criticisms have been made of theory and research in this area,[149] and responses and new directions have been proposed.[150] Such debate and dialogue is healthy. In general, this line of research offers another positive example of taking a theoretically based, scientific approach to leadership development.

*LEADERSHIP DEVELOPMENT: THE STATE OF THE PRACTICE.*    Leadership development in organizations, although not always theory-based, has seen a number of high profile changes driven by organizations' need to compete in a turbulent, uncertain environment. While many examples have appeared in the popular and practitioner literature, we will describe two approaches to give the reader a sense of how practical concerns are driving the state of the practice.

One recent approach in leadership development can be referred to as **leaders developing leaders.** This trend is signified by the direct, frequent involvement of CEOs and senior managers in developing a cadre of leaders within their organizations. For example, at organizations such as Intel, PepsiCo, GE, AlliedSignal, Shell Oil, and the U.S. Navy SEALs, the chief officers see leadership development as one of their primary responsibilities.[151] Cohen and Tichy argue that transformational leadership is the type of leadership that investors are demanding of corporate executives.[152] After investigating best practices in leadership development approaches at a group of top organizations, Cohen and Tichy concluded that the key to these approaches is that leaders must develop leaders. This involves the following ideas on why and how to develop leaders (pp. 60–61):

- Winners are judged by their sustained success.
- Winning companies have leaders at every level.
- The best way to get more leaders is to have leaders develop leaders.
- To develop others, leaders must have a teachable point of view.
- Leaders create stories about the future of their organizations.

Two of these ideas deserve special note: a teachable point of view and storytelling. According to Cohen and Tichy, a teachable point of view focuses on four leadership areas: *ideas* about products, services, and the marketplace, and a real world explanation of the leader's *values*, *edge* (making the tough, go-no go decisions), and *energy* (motivating and energizing others). The teachable point of view must then be articulated in the form of a business-oriented story based on the leader's experience. Cohen and Tichy argue that stories are an engaging, personal way to communicate a leader's vision for the future. The key elements of a leader's story appear to be making a case for change, presenting an idea of where the organization is headed, and showing how the organization will get there.

Cohen and Tichy offer examples of how a leadership development approach based on these ideas was implemented at Shell Oil Company at Shell's Learning Center.[153] The key role for HRD professionals in this approach is to "help leaders craft their teaching approaches. That requires HRD staff to play a different role by collaborating with the leaders and 'driving' the cultural mindset in which teaching and leadership are intertwined" (p. 73).

A second approach to leadership development is the Center for Creative Leadership's LeaderLab.[154] The goal of the program is to prepare and encourage leaders to act more effectively in the leadership situations they face.[155] The program is based on research done at CCL and elsewhere on the nature of leadership and leader development. It lasts six months, beginning with a weeklong session in which participants undergo a range of assessment and feedback exercises (including 360-degree feedback obtained in advance from their superiors, subordinates, and peers) and development of an action plan for leadership improvement. These sessions include working in teams with "change partners," action-oriented exercises, and nontraditional learning activities such as creating pieces of art. A second four-day session occurs three months later, in which the manager's progress and learning over the three months is reviewed, and the action plan is revised accordingly. The revised action plan is then implemented over the remaining three months.[156]

Clearly, these are only two examples of the kinds of approaches organizations are taking to develop leaders. Given the importance many organizations and stakeholders place on leadership, it is critical that HRD professionals design and deliver leadership development approaches that advance their own organization's ability to compete and blend relevant theory and methodology with ongoing efforts at evaluation and modification.

## BEHAVIOR MODELING TRAINING

Behavior modeling training is a popular training technique that has been used primarily to train people to perform manual, interpersonal, and cognitive skills. The technique is based on Bandura's social learning theory, which was applied to supervisory training by Goldstein and Sorcher.[157] The underlying rationale for this form of training is that people can learn by observing other people (models) perform a task, provided they are shown clearly what the components of the behavior are, remember what the behavior is, actually perform the behavior, and are motivated to use what they have learned.[158]

**Behavior modeling** typically involves five steps: modeling, retention, rehearsal, feedback, and transfer of training. During the **modeling phase**, trainees are usually shown a film or videotape in which a model performs the behavior to be learned. The desired behavior is broken into a series of discrete **learning**

**points,** or key behaviors that make up the overall behavior. For example, if supervisors are being trained to handle employee complaints, the film would show a supervisor handling complaints in the desired manner. The learning points for this behavior might include:

1. Listen openly.
2. Do not speak until the employee has had his or her say.
3. Avoid reacting emotionally. (Don't get defensive.)
4. Ask for the employee's expectations about a solution to the problem.
5. Agree on specific steps to be taken and specific deadlines.[159]

In the **retention phase,** trainees perform activities to enhance the memory of what they have observed. These activities include reviewing the learning points, discussing the rationale underlying each point, and talking over the behaviors the model performed to illustrate those points. In the **rehearsal phase,** each trainee role plays the desired behavior with another trainee. For example, each trainee learning how to handle employee complaints would have an opportunity to role play resolving a complaint from another trainee representing the complaining employee. During the **feedback phase,** each trainee receives feedback on his or her performance based on what was done well and what should be improved. Finally, in the **transfer of training phase,** trainees are encouraged to practice the newly learned behavior on the job. In some behavior modeling programs, trainees regroup later to discuss problems and successes in using their newly learned skills.

Two examples of behavior modeling training applied to the mastery of computer software programs were reported by Gist and colleagues, and Simon and Werner.[160] In the Gist et al. study, trainees observed a videotape in which the model illustrated the steps involved in performing each task to be learned. The video also reviewed key learning points and showed trainees the responses to expect from the program on the computer monitor. Following a demonstration of each step, the trainer stopped the videotape to allow trainees to perform it, with the responses from the program on the computer monitor providing feedback as to the correctness of the trainee's performance. In the Simon and Werner study, Navy personnel were trained to use a new computer system using three different approaches: a lecture approach (using PowerPoint slides), a self-paced approach (using individual workbooks), and a behavior modeling approach, where the instructor demonstrated ("modeled") the correct procedures on a computer display viewed by all of the trainees. Both learning and behavioral retention were significantly higher for trainees who received the behavior modeling approach than for those trained using the other two approaches.

Beyond these two studies, growing research evidence supports the effectiveness of behavior modeling training. Although behavior modeling studies conducted during the 1970s[161] were criticized as having flaws that compromised their findings, subsequent research correcting these problems has supported the technique's effectiveness.[162] Burke and Day's meta-analysis of management training also shows that behavior modeling is among the most effective management training techniques for learning and behavioral change.[163] A separate meta-analysis found similar effects for learning and behavioral change, and also sizable effects from behavior modeling interventions on various results measures (from productivity changes to increased free-throw shooting accuracy for a women's basketball team).[164]

One of the reasons that behavior modeling seems to be effective is that it increases a trainee's feelings of self-efficacy, which is one's belief in his or her capacity to perform a particular task (see Chapter 2).[165] Individuals with high self-efficacy tend to perform better than individuals with low self-efficacy.[166]

Research has suggested how behavior modeling works and how it can be improved.[167] For example, a series of studies has demonstrated the importance of learning points in the process. **Learning points** keyed to important behaviors and demonstrated by the model result in greater recall and performance of those behaviors.[168] In addition, research suggests that learning points generated by trainees led to better performance than learning points generated by "experts."[169]

A research study examined two ways such training may be improved: by providing multiple scenarios during training and by exposing trainees to both positive and negative models.[170] Baldwin suggested that providing multiple scenarios may increase the chances trainees would generalize the skills they learn to apply them to other situations. Baldwin also theorized that providing negative models as well as positive models would help trainees not only learn new behaviors but unlearn prior, ineffective behaviors. Baldwin reported two significant findings: 1) that providing both positive and negative models led to greater generalization than using positive models only, but 2) that viewing only positive models led only to greater reproduction of the behavior learned than viewing both positive and negative models.[171] These results suggest that different approaches to using models in behavior modeling training may be needed, depending on the goals of the training (e.g., reproducing a behavior in a particular type of situation or being able to use the behavior in a variety of situations).

Behavior modeling is not without its critics. Parry and Reich argue that the technique can have several weaknesses, including the following:

1. Modeling uses simplistic behavioral models.

2. Trainees may not get explanations of the theory underlying the need for the behaviors being taught. For example, suppose the training session focuses on handling abusive customers. If trainees are told they should let the customer vent his feelings, they should be told why.

3. The classes may be boring because they follow a similar format and have all trainees in a session perform the same role playing.

4. Examples of incorrect behavior are seldom used, even though they provide opportunities for learning.

5. If verbal behavior is being taught, then the use of film or video might interfere by adding extraneous stimuli. Written models may be better for these cases.

6. Many trainees engage in improvisational acting rather than true role playing.

7. While focusing on behaviors rather than underlying attitudes may be effective in the short run, it is important to change attitudes as well. Otherwise, employees will not stick with the newly learned behaviors over the long haul.[172]

Parry and Reich believe the technique can be effective if these limitations are overcome.[173] Rosenbaum replied to Parry and Reich's criticisms, by suggesting, among other things, that the design and delivery of behavior modeling training requires rigorous technique, that models serve as points of reference rather than purporting to show the only way to handle a situation, and that modeling conforms to the tenets of adult learning.[174] This sort of debate is healthy, and combined with research on ways to improve modeling training, can lead to better ways of using behavior modeling to help managers (and others) improve their interpersonal (and other) skills.[175] Pescuric and Byham note that behavior modeling training is also amenable to an interactive, computer-based self-study format.[176] They suggest that classroom-based delivery, the traditional approach to behavior modeling training, is only one of four options that can be used. The other three include classroom training augmented by on-the-job practice under the guidance of a coach; self-study of the principles, model, and application components followed by practice in a classroom setting; and self-study followed by on-the-job practice. Those who wish to use the technique should consult Goldstein and Sorcher[177] and especially the excellent book written by Decker and Nathan for specifics on how to develop a program.[178]

## DESIGNING MANAGEMENT DEVELOPMENT PROGRAMS

While this should not surprise you, management development programs need to be constructed the way any sound HRD program is: through needs assessment, design, implementation, and evaluation. More specifically, the issues discussed in this chapter lead to several recommendations and reminders:

1. Management development must **be tied to the organization's strategic plan** to be responsive to the needs of the organization and those of the individuals being developed.

2. A **thorough needs analysis,** including investigating what managers in the organization do and the skills they need to perform effectively, is essential.

3. **Specific objectives,** both for the overall program and each of its components, (e.g., on-the-job experiences, classroom training) should be established.

4. **Involvement in and commitment of senior management in all phases** of the process, from needs assessment to evaluation, is critical. Simply stated, it is management's responsibility to ensure that the organization has a high quality management team.

**RETURN TO OPENING CASE**

This challenging situation was faced by a large community hospital in New York City. Two management consultants were hired who worked together with executives and human resource professionals at the hospital to design and implement a management training program. This program was first offered to executives, and then to seventeen middle-level hospital managers. A particular focus of the training was on linking the strategic needs of the organization with the individual training needs of participants. Your instructor has additional information on the program and the outcomes obtained by it.

5. A **variety of developmental opportunities,** both formal and on the job, should be used.

6. The program should be designed to ensure that the individuals to be developed are **motivated to participate** in such activities. The day-to-day demands placed on managers at all levels make it easy to put development on the back burner.

7. Action should be taken to **evaluate** the program regularly and **modify and update** it as needs change.

Though this list contains nothing new or startling (especially coming in the thirteenth chapter of this text), many management development programs do not conform to these basic expectations. We present you with the "ideal," realizing full well that reality often falls well short of this. Recently, Ghoshal and colleagues called for a new, more proactive role for managers in organizations and society.[179] In our view, effective management development efforts will be critical for managers to successfully take on this new role. Prescriptions such as those in our list above take on added significance given the environmental turbulance currently facing orgainzation and their managers.

### SUMMARY

Management development is one of the most widely offered and important forms of HRD. It should be deliberate, long-term oriented, specific to the organization, and tied to the organization's strategic plan.

One would expect existing research on the managerial job to provide a clear picture of what managers do, the competencies they need, and how they develop, but there is much we do not yet know. This chapter presented several ways this issue has been addressed and emphasized the importance of careful study by HRD researchers and practitioners to better answer questions about the managerial job when designing management development programs for their own organizations.

Options for management education include college and university degree programs and executive education. In addition, we also explored organizationally based training and experience methods, including courses and programs, corporate academies or universities, and on-the-job experiences.

To illustrate the content of some of the approaches used in management development, we described two common training programs: leadership training and behavior modeling training. Two approaches to leadership development were presented, Leader Match and transformational leadership training. Behavior modeling training involves learning by observing a model perform the behavior in question. Trainees are usually shown a videotape or film of a model performing the behavior. They discuss the components of the behavior, practice the behavior by role playing, and receive constructive feedback on their performance. This form of training has been shown to be effective for both motor and interpersonal skills.

The chapter closed with a list of recommendations for designing an effective management development program.

## KEY TERMS AND CONCEPTS

action learning

behavior modeling

competencies

corporate university

executive M.B.A. programs

four-dimensional model

integrated competency model

Leader Match

Least Preferred Coworker
 (LPC) scale

learning points

management development

management education

on-the-job experiences

transformational leadership

## QUESTIONS FOR DISCUSSION

1. Explain why management development is one of the most common HRD activities found in organizations today.

2. Given the current trends toward empowerment and employing fewer levels of management, how important do you believe management development will be in the next ten years? Support your answer.

3. Why is it important for an HRD practitioner to understand managerial roles and competencies? How are these assessed? How is this information used as a needs assessment in designing a management development program?

4. Efforts to accurately and completely describe the job of managing have met with considerable frustration. Why do you think the job of managing has proved so difficult to pin down? Which of the ideas and models offered so far do you believe to be the most useful in guiding management development? Support your choice.

5. Compare and contrast management education, management training, and on-the-job experiences. How can these be combined in a strategic management development program?

6. Briefly describe the key advantages and disadvantages of the three approaches to management education. Under what conditions would you recommend that an organization send its managers to an executive M.B.A. program?

7. Explain how management education prepares a manager for his or her role. What are the different forms of management education? Can they be substituted by training or on-the-job experiences? Why or why not?

8. Explain the role on-the-job experience plays in a manager's development. Identify two ways an organization can increase the chances that the on-the-job experiences its managers encounter will be developmental experiences.

9. Describe how managing in a global environment can differ from the traditional approach to managing. Describe one way that we can develop managers to be more successful in a global environment.

10. Briefly describe the components of the behavior modeling approach to training. Describe how you would use these components to design a behavior modeling session that trains supervisors to effectively obtain an employee's agreement for improved performance.

## REFERENCES

1. http://stats.bls.gov/news.release/ecopro.t02.htm; see also Judy, R. W., and D'Amico, C. (1997). *Workforce 2020: Work and workers in the 21st century.* Indianapolis: Hudson Institute.

2. Campbell, J. P., Dunnette, M. D., Lawler, E. E., & Weick, K. E., Jr. (1970). *Managerial behavior, performance, and effectiveness.* New York: McGraw-Hill.

3. McCall, M. W., Jr., Lombardo, M. M., & Morrison, A. M. (1988). *The lessons of experience: How successful executives develop on the job.* Lexington, MA: Lexington Books, 147.

4. Schoenfeldt, L. F., & Steger, J. A. (1990). Identification and development of management talent. In G. R. Ferris and K. M. Rowland (eds.), *Organizational entry* (191–251). Greenwich, CT: JAI Press.

5. McCall, Lombardo, & Morrison (1988), *supra* note 3.

6. Keys, B., & Wolfe, J. (1988). Management education and development: Current issues and emerging trends. *Journal of Management, 14,* 205–229; Wexley, K. N., & Baldwin, T. T. (1986). Management development. *Journal of Management, 12,* 277–294.

7. Keys & Wolfe (1988), *supra* note 6, 205.

8. *Ibid;* Wexley & Baldwin (1986), *supra* note 6.

9. Industry Report 2000 (2000). *Training,* 37(10), 45–95.

10. Industry Report. (1996). Who's learning what? *Training,* 33(10), 55–66.

11. Saari, L. M., Johnson, T. R., McLaughlin, S. D., & Zimmerle, D. M. (1988). A survey of management training and education practices in U.S. companies. *Personnel Psychology, 41,* 731–743.

12. Beatty, R. W., Schneier, C. E., & McEvoy, G. M. (1987). Executive development and management succession. *Personnel and Human Resources Management, 5,* 289–322; Schoenfeldt & Steger (1990), *supra* note 4.

13. Bray, D. W., Campbell, R. J., & Grant, D. L. (1974). *Formative years in business: A long-term AT&T study of managerial lives.* New York: Wiley; Howard, A., & Bray, D. W. (1988). *Managerial lives in transition: Advancing age and changing times.* New York: Guilford Press.

14. Schoenfeldt & Steger (1990), *supra* note 4.

15. McCall, M. W., Jr., Morrison, A. M., & Hannan, R. L. (1978). *Studies of managerial work: Results and methods.* (Tech Report No. 14). Greensboro, NC: Center for Creative Leadership.

16. Schoenfeldt & Steger (1990), *supra* note 4, p. 196.

17. Fayol, H. (1949). *General and industrial management.* (C. Storrs, Translator). London: Pitman.

18. Mintzberg, H. (1973). *The nature of managerial work.* New York: Harper and Row; Mintzberg, H. (1975). The manager's job: Folklore and fact. *Harvard Business Review, 53*(4), 49–61.

19. Carroll, S. J., & Gillen, D. J. (1987). Are the classical management functions useful in describing managerial work? *Academy of Management Review, 12,* 38–51.

20. Tornow, W. W., & Pinto, P. R. (1976). The development of a managerial job taxonomy: A system for describing, classifying, and evaluating executive positions. *Journal of Applied Psychology, 61,* 410–418.

21. Schoenfeldt & Steger (1990), *supra* note 4.

22. Boyatzis, R. E. (1982). *The competent manager: A model for effective performance.* New York: Wiley.

23. Manners, G., & Steger, J. A. (1976). Behavioral specifications of the R&D management role. *IEEE Transactions in Engineering Management, 23,* 139–141; Manners, G., & Steger, J. A. (1979). Implications of research in the R&D management role for the selection and training of R&D managers. *R & D Management, 9,* 85–92.

24. Albanese, R. (1988). Competency-based management education. *Journal of Management Development, 8*(2), 66–76.

25. Boyatzis (1982), *supra* note 22.

26. Smith, M. E. (1992). The search for executive skills. *Training and Development, 46*(11), 88–95.

27. McLagan, P. A. (1997). Competencies: The next generation. *Training — Development, 51*(5), 40–47.

28. Schoenfeldt & Steger (1990), *supra* note 4.

29. This is an example of the use of the critical incident technique, which we described in Chapter 4.

30. Barrett, G. V., & Depinet, R. L. (1991). A reconsideration of testing for competence rather than for intelligence. *American Psychologist, 46,* 1012–1024.

31. Boyatzis (1982), *supra* note 22.

32. Schoenfeldt & Steger (1990), *supra* note 4.

33. *Ibid.*

34. Mintzberg, H. (1994), Rounding out the manager's job. *Sloan Management Review, 36*(1), 11–26; Vaill, P. B. (1989). *Managing as a performing art: New ideas for a world of chaotic change.* San Francisco: Jossey-Bass.

35. Mintzberg (1994), *supra* note 34, p. 11.

36. Vaill (1989), *supra* note 34.

37. *Ibid*, 114–115.

38. *Ibid*, 35.

39. Mintzberg (1994), *supra* note 34.

40. Saari et al. (1988), *supra* note 11.

41. Sutton, E. E., & McQuigg-Martinetz, B. (1990). The development partnership: Managing skills for the future. *Training and Development Journal, 44*(4), 63–70.

42. Adler, N. J., & Bartholomew, S. (1992). Managing globally competent people. *The Executive, 6*(3), 52–65; Bartlett, C. A., & Ghoshal, S. (1992). What is a global manager? *Harvard Business Review, 70*(5), 124–132; Bogorya, Y. (1985). Intercultural development for managers involved in international business. *Journal of Management Development, 4*(2), 17–25; Murray, F. T., & Murray, A. H. (1986). SMR forum: Global managers for global business. *Sloan Management Review, 27*(2), 75–80.

43. Bartlett and Ghoshal (1992), *supra* note 42.

44. *Ibid*.

45. Adler and Bartholomew (1992), *supra* note 42.

46. *Ibid*.

47. *Ibid*; Bartlett & Ghosal (1992), *supra* note 42.

48. Spreitzer, G. M., McCall, Jr., M. W., & Mahoney, J. D. (1997). Early identification of international executive potential. *Journal of Applied Psychology, 82*, 6–29.

49. *Ibid*.

50. *Ibid*.

51. Allred, B. B., Snow, C. C., & Miles, R. E. (1996). Characteristics of managerial careers in the 21st century. *Academy of Management Executive, 10*(4), 17–27.

52. Downham, T. A., Noel, J. L., & Prendergast, A. E. (1992). Executive development. *Human Resource Management, 31*, 95–107; Seibert, K. W., Hall, D. T., & Kram, K. E. (1995). Strengthening the weak link in strategic executive development: Integrating individual development and global business strategy. *Human Resource Management, 34*, 549–567.

53. Seibert, Hall, and Kram (1995), *supra* note 52.

54. Burack, E. H., Hochwarter, W., & Mathys, N. J. (1997). The new management development paradigm. *Human Resource Planning, 20*(1), 14–21.

55. Seibert et al. (1995), *supra* note 52.

56. *Ibid*.

57. Seibert et al. (1995), *supra* note 52; Burack et al. (1997), *supra* note 54.

58. Peters, T. J., & Waterman, R. H. (1982). *In search of excellence: Lessons from America's best run companies.* New York: Warner Books.

59. Peters, T. (1996, Dec. 2). The search for excellence continues. *Forbes ASAP*, 239–240.

60. Seibert et al. (1995), *supra* note 52; Burack et al. (1997), *supra* note 54.

61. Porter, L. W., & McKibbin, L. E. (1988). *Management education and development: Drift or thrust into the 21st century?* New York: McGraw-Hill.

62. http://nces.ed.gov/pubs2000/2000174.pdf (Table D).

63. *Chronicle of Higher Education Almanac.* (1996, December 2). The nation: Students, 22.

64. http://nces.ed.gov/pubs2000/2000174.pdf (Table E).

65. Byrne, J. A., Leonhardt, D., Bongiorno, L., & Jespersen, F. (1996, October 21). The best B schools. *Business Week,* 110–122; Leonhardt, D. (2000). Law gains edge on business, and no one knows why. *New York Times,* July 5, C1.

66. Badenhausen, K., Henderson, E., Kump, L., & Stanfl, R. (2000). The bottom line on B-schools. *Forbes, 165*(3), February 7, 100–104.

67. Branch, S. (1997, April 14). MBAs are hot again — and they know it. *Fortune,* 155–157.

68. Badenhausen et al. (2000), *supra* note 66.

69. American Assembly of Collegiate Schools of Business (1996, July 23). Business accreditation standards. <wweb\stand5.html>

70. *Ibid.*

71. Porter & McKibbin (1988), *supra* note 61.

72. *Ibid.*

73. Byrne, J. A. (1991). Wharton rewrites the book on B-schools. *Business Week, 43,* May 13.

74. Boyatzis R. E., Cowen, S. S., & Kolb, D. A. (1995). Management of knowledge: Redesigning the Weatherhead MBA program. In R. E. Boyatzis, S. S. Cowen, D. A. Kolb & associates, *Innovation in professional education: Steps on a journey from teaching to learning* (32–49). San Francisco: Jossey-Bass.

75. *Ibid.*

76. *Ibid.*

77. Boyatzis, R. E., Baker, A., Leonard, D., Rhee, K., & Thompson, L. (1995). Will it make a difference? Assessing a value-added, outcome-oriented, competency-based program. In R. E. Boyatzis, S. S. Cowen, D. A. Kolb & associates, *Innovation in professional education: Steps on a journey from teaching to learning* (167–202). San Francisco: Jossey-Bass, 179.

78. Byrne et al. (1996), *supra* note 65.

79. Phillips, V. (1998). Online universities teach knowledge beyond the books. *HR Magazine, 43*(8), July, 121–128.

80. Linder, J. C., & Smith, H. J. (1992). The complex case of management education. *Harvard Business Review, 70*(5), 16–33.

81. Byrne, J. A. (1995). Virtual B-schools. *Business Week,* October 23, 64–68.

82. Byrne (1991), *supra* note 73.

83. Porter & McKibbin (1988), *supra* note 61.

84. Byrne (1991), *supra* note 73.

85. Andrews, K. R. (1966). *The effectiveness of university management development programs.* Boston: Harvard University; Hollenbeck, G. P. (1991). What did you learn in school? Studies of a university executive program. *Human Resource Planning, 14*(4), 247–260.

86. Fresina, A, J., & Associates. (1988). *Executive education in corporate America.* Palatine, IL: Anthony J. Fresina and Associates.

87. Eurich, N. P. (1990). *The learning industry: Education for adult workers.* Lawrenceville, NJ: Princeton University Press; Porter & McKibbin (1988), *supra* note 61.

88. Industry Report (1996), *supra* note 10.

89. Industry Report 2000 (2000), *supra* note 9.

90. Mainstone, L. E., & Schroeder, D. M. (1999). Management education in the information age. *Journal of Management Education, 23,* 630–634.

91. Byrne (1995), *supra* note 81.

92. Porter & McKibbin (1988), *supra* note 61.

93. Byrne (1995), *supra* note 81.

94. Porter & McKibbin (1988), *supra* note 61.

95. Hequet, M. (1992). Executive education: The custom alternative. *Training, 29*(4), 38–41.

96. *Ibid.*

97. *Ibid.*

98. Vicere, A. A. (1996). Executive education: The leading edge. *Organizational Dynamics, 25*(2), August, 67–81.

99. Weir, D., & Smallman, C. (1998). Managers in the year 2000 and after: A strategy for development. *Management Development, 36*(1), 43–51.

100. Alutto, J. A. (1999). Just-in-time management education in the 21st century. *HR Magazine, 44*(11), 56–57.

101. Bilimoria, D. (2000). Redoing management education's missions and methods. *Journal of Management Education, 24,* 161–166.

102. Lee, C. (1991). Who gets trained in what — 1991. *Training, 28*(10), 47–59; Saari et al., 1988, *supra* note 12.

103. Tichy, N. M. (1989). GE's Crotonville: A staging ground for corporate revolution. *Academy of Management Executive, 3,* 99–107.

104. *Ibid.*

105. Downham et al. (1992), *supra* note 52.

106. Corporate universities open their doors. (2000). *Manager Intelligence Report,* October, 6–8.

107. Eurich (1990), *supra* note 87; Odiorne, G. S., & Rummler, G. A. (1988). *Training and development: A guide for professionals.* Chicago: Commerce Clearing House.

108. Odiorne & Rummler (1988), *supra* note 107.

109. Fulmer, R. M. (1997). The evolving paradigm of leadership development. *Organizational Dynamics, 25*(4), 59–72.

110. Eurich (1990), *supra* note 87, p. 167.

111. Meister, J. C (1993). *Corporate quality universities: Lessons in building a world-class work force.* Burr Ridge, IL: Irwin Professional Publishing.

112. Gerbman, R. V. (2000). Corporate universities 101. *HR Magazine, 45*(2), February, 101–106; Meister, J. C. (1998). Ten steps to creating a corporate university. *Training and Development, 52*(11), November, 38–43; Corporate universities: The new pioneers of management education. (1998). *Harvard Management Update,* October, 5–7.

113. E.g., Densford, L. E. (2000). Motorola University: The next 20 years. *Corporate University Review,* January/February, 15–23.

114. Digman, L. A. (1978). How well-managed organizations develop their executives. *Organizational Dynamics, 7*(2), 63–80; McCall, Lombardo, & Morrison (1988), *supra* note 3;

Zemke, R. (1985). The Honeywell studies: How managers learn to manage. *Training, 22*(8), 46–51.

115. Tichy (1989), *supra* note 103.

116. McCauley, C. D., Ruderman, M. N., Ohlott, P. J., & Morrow, J. E. (1994). Assessing the developmental components of managerial jobs. *Journal of Applied Psychology, 79*, 544–560; Wexley & Baldwin (1986), *supra* note 6.

117. Keys & Wolfe (1988), *supra* note 6.

118. McCall, Lombardo, & Morrison (1988), *supra* note 3.

119. *Ibid.*

120. McCauley, Ruderman, Ohlott, & Morrow (1994), *supra* note 116.

121. *Ibid.*

122. Keys & Wolfe (1988), *supra* note 6; Fulmer (1997), *supra* note 109.

123. Morgan, G., & Ramirez, R. (1983). Action learning: A holographic metaphor for guiding social change. *Human Relations, 37,* 1–28; Revans, R. (1982). What is action learning? *Journal of Management Development, 1*(3), 64–75.

124. Keys & Wolfe, 1988, *supra* note 6.

125. Cohen, E., & Tichy, N. (1997). How leaders develop leaders. *Training and Development, 51*(5), 58–73; Tichy, N., & Sherman, S. (1993). *Control your destiny or someone else will: How Jack Welch is making GE the world's most competitive corporation.* New York: Doubleday; Downham et al. (1992), *supra* note 52.

126. Fulmer (1997), *supra* note 109.

127. Mumford, A. (1987). Action learning (Special Issue). *Journal of Management Development, 6*(2), 1–70.

128. Yorks, L., O'Neil, J., Marsick, V. J., Nilson, G. E., & Kolodny, R. (1996). Boundary management in Action Reflection Learning™ research: Taking the role of a sophisticated barbarian. *Human Resource Development Quarterly, 7,* 313–329; see also the response to this article, Baldwin, T. T. (1996). Invited reaction: Comments on feature article. *Human Resource Development Quarterly, 7,* 331–334.

129. Mumford, A. (1993). *Management development: Strategies for action* (2nd ed.). London: IPM; http://www.free-press.com/journals/gabal/articles/gabal-article-002.htm.

130. Daudelin, M. W. (1996). Learning from experience through reflection. *Organizational Dynamics, 24*(3), 36–48.

131. Industry Report 2000 (2000), *supra* note 9.

132. Fiedler, F. E., & Chemers, M. M. (1984). *Improving leadership effectiveness: The leader match concept* (2nd ed.). New York: Wiley.

133. Fiedler, F. E. (1964). A contingency model of leadership effectiveness. In L. Berkowitz (ed.), *Advances in experimental social psychology* (149–190). New York: Academic Press; Fiedler, F. E. (1967). *A theory of leadership effectiveness.* New York: McGraw-Hill; Fiedler, F. E., & Chemers, M. M. (1974). Leadership and effective management. New York: Scott, Foresman.

134. Fiedler & Chemers (1984), *supra* note 132; Fiedler, F. E., Chemers, M. M., & Mahar, L. (1976). *Improving leadership effectiveness: The leader match concept.* New York: Wiley.

135. Wexley, K. N., & Latham, G. P. (1991). *Developing and training human resources in organizations* (2nd ed.). New York: HarperCollins.

136. Fiedler & Chemers (1984), *supra* note 132, p. 183.

137. Strube, M. J., & Garcia, J. E. (1981). A meta-analytic investigation of Fiedler's contingency theory of leadership effectiveness. *Psychological Bulletin, 93*, 600–603; Burke, M. J., & Day, R. R. (1986). A cumulative study of the effectiveness of managerial training. *Journal of Applied Psychology, 71*, 232–245.

138. Fiedler, F. E., & Mahar, L. (1979). The effectiveness of contingency model training: A review of the validation of Leader Match. *Personnel Psychology, 32*, 45–62.

139. Fiedler, F. E., & Mahar, L. (1979). A field experiment validating contingency model leadership training. *Journal of Applied Psychology, 64*, 247–254.

140. Fiedler & Chemers (1984), *supra* note 132.

141. Burke and Day (1986), *supra* note 137.

142. Schriesheim, C. A., Bannister, B. D., & Money, W. H. (1979). Psychometric properties of the LPC scale: An extension of Rice's review. *Academy of Management Review, 4*, 287–290; Jago, A. G., & Ragan, J. W. (1986). Some assumptions are more troubling than others: Rejoinder to Chemers and Fiedler. *Journal of Applied Psychology, 71*, 564–565; Jago, A. G., & Ragan, J. W. (1986). The trouble with LEADER MATCH is that it doesn't match Fiedler's contingency model. *Journal of Applied Psychology, 71*, 555–559; Kabanoff, B. (1981). The critique of LEADER MATCH and its implications for leadership research. *Personnel Psychology, 34*, 749–764.

143. Rice, R. W. (1978). Construct validity of the Least Preferred Co-worker (LPC) Score. *Psychological Bulletin, 85*, 1199–1237; Rice, R. W. (1979). Reliability and validity of the LPC scale: A reply. *Academy of Management Review, 4*, 291–294; Chemers, M. M., & Fiedler, F. E. (1986). The trouble with assumptions: A reply to Jago and Ragan. *Journal of Applied Psychology, 71*, 560–563.

144. Bass, B. M. (1985). *Leadership and performance beyond expectations*. New York: Basic Books; Bass, B. M. (1990). From transactional to transformational leadership: Learning to share the vision. *Organizational Dynamics, 18*(3), 19–36.

145. Barling, J., Weber, T., & Kelloway, E. K. (1996). Effects of transformational leadership training on attitudinal and financial outcomes: A field experiment. *Journal of Applied Psychology, 81*, 827–832.

146. Popper, M., Landau, O., & Gluskinos, U. M. (1992). The Israeli defense forces: An example of transformational leadership. *Leadership and Organizational Development Journal, 13*(1), 3–8; Barling, Weber, & Kelloway (1996), *supra* note 145.

147. Barling et al. (1996), *supra* note 145.

148. E.g., Conger, J. A. (1999). Charismatic and transformational leadership in organizations: An insider's perspective on these developing streams of research. *Leadership Quarterly, 10*(2), 145–169; Hunt, J. G., & Conger, J. A. (1999). Overview — Charismatic and transformational leadership: Taking stock of the present and future (Part II). *Leadership Quarterly, 10*(3), 331–334.

149. Shamir, B. (1999). An evaluation of conceptual weaknesses in transformational and charismatic leadership theories. *Leadership Quarterly, 10*(2), 285–305; Beyer, J. (1999). Taming and promoting charisma to change organizations. *Leadership Quarterly, 10*(2), 307–330.

150. Shamir, B. (1999). Taming charisma for better understanding and greater usefulness: A response to Beyer. *Leadership Quarterly, 10*(4), 555–562; Mumford, M. D., Zaccaro, S. J., Connelly, M. S., Marks, M. A. (2000). Leadership skills: Conclusions and future directions. *Leadership Quarterly, 11*(1), 155–170.

151. Cohen & Tichy (1997), supra note 125; Sherman, S. (1995, November 27). How tomorrow's best leaders are learning their stuff. *Fortune*, 90–102.

152. Cohen & Tichy (1997), *supra* note 125.

153. *Ibid.*

154. Vicere (1996), supra note 98; Bongiorno, L. (1995). How'm I doing? *Business Week*, October 23, 72–73.

155. Vicere (1996), *supra* note 98.

156. *Ibid.*

157. Goldstein, A. P., & Sorcher, M. (1974). *Changing supervisor behavior.* Elmsford, NY: Pergamon Press.

158. Decker, P. J., & Nathan, B. R. (1985). *Behavior modeling training: Principles and applications.* New York: Praeger.

159. *Ibid*, 145.

160. Gist, M. E., Schwoerer, C., & Rosen, B. (1989). Effects of alternative training methods on self-efficacy and performance in computer software training. *Journal of Applied Psychology, 74*, 884–891; Simon, S. J., & Werner, J. M. (1996). Computer training through behavior modeling, self-paced, and instructional approaches: A field experiment. *Journal of Applied Psychology, 81*, 648–659.

161. Burnaska, R. F. (1976). The effect of behavior-modeling training upon managers' behaviors and employee's perceptions. *Personnel Psychology, 29*, 329–335; Byham, W. C., Adams, D., & Kiggins, A. (1976). Transfer of modeling training to the job. *Personnel Psychology, 29*, 345–349; Moses, J. L., & Ritchie, R. J. (1976). Supervisory relationships training: A behavioral evaluation of a behavior modeling program. *Personnel Psychology, 29*, 337–343; Smith, P. (1976). Management modeling training to improve morale and customer satisfaction. *Personnel Psychology, 29*, 353–359.

162. Gist et al. (1989), *supra* note 160; Latham, G. P., & Saari, L. E. (1979). The application of social learning theory to training supervisors through behavior modeling. *Journal of Applied Psychology, 64*, 239–246; McGehee, W., & Tullar, W. L. (1978). A note on evaluating behavior modification and behavior modeling as industrial training techniques. *Personnel Psychology, 31*, 477–484; Meyer, H. H., & Raich, M. S. (1983). An objective evaluation of a behavior modeling training program. *Personnel Psychology, 36*, 755–761.

163. Burke & Day (1986), *supra* note 137.

164. Werner, J. M., & Crampton, S. M. (1992). The impact of behavior modeling training on learning, behavior, and results criteria: A meta-analytic review. In M. Schnake (ed.), *Proceedings*, Southern Management Association ( 279–284).

165. Bandura, A. (1986). *Social foundations of thought and action.* Englewood Cliffs, NJ: Prentice-Hall.

166. Taylor, M. S., Locke, E. A., Lee, C., & Gist, M. E. (1984). Type A behavior and faculty research productivity: What are the mechanisms? *Organizational Behavior and Human Performance, 34*, 402–418.

167. Decker, P. J. (1983). The effects of rehearsal group size and video feedback in behavior modeling training. *Personnel Psychology, 36*, 763–773; Decker, P. J. (1984). Effects of different symbolic coding stimuli in behavior modeling training. *Personnel Psychology, 37*, 711–720; Latham & Saari, 1979, *supra* note 162.

168. Latham & Saari (1979), supra note 162; Mann, R. B., & Decker, P. J. (1984). The effect of key behavior distinctiveness on generalization and recall in behavior-modeling training. *Academy of Management Journal, 27*, 900–909.

169. Hogan, P. M., Hakel, M. D., & Decker, P. J. (1986). Effects of trainee-generated versus trainer-provided rule codes on generalization in behavior-modeling training. *Journal of Applied Psychology, 71*, 469, 473.

170. Baldwin, T. T. (1992). Effects of alternative modeling strategies on outcomes of interpersonal skills training. *Journal of Applied Psychology, 77*, 147–154.

171. This study also illustrates the importance of evaluating training at different levels, as recommended in Chapter 7.

172. Parry, S. B., & Reich, L. R. (1984). An uneasy look at behavior modeling. *Training and Development Journal, 30*(3) 57–62.

173. *Ibid.*

174. Rosenbaum, B. L. (1984). Back to behavior modeling. *Training and Development Journal, 30*(11), 88–89; Parry and Reich (1984), *supra* note 172.

175. Werner, J. M., O'Leary-Kelly, A. M., Baldwin, T. T., & Wexley, K. N. (1994). Augmenting behavior-modeling training: Testing the effects of pre- and post-training interventions. *Human Resource Development Quarterly, 5*(2), 169–183.

176. Pescuric, A., & Byham, W. C. (1996). The new look of behavior modeling. *Training and Development, 50*(7), 24–30.

177. Goldstein, A. P., & Sorcher, M. (1974). *Changing supervisor behavior.* Elmsford, NY: Pergamon Press.

178. Decker and Nathan (1985), *supra* note 158.

179. Ghoshal, S., Bartlett, C. A., & Moran, P. (1999). A new manifesto for management. *Sloan Management Review, 40*(3), Spring, 9–20.

# 12

# ORGANIZATION DEVELOPMENT AND CHANGE

## LEARNING OBJECTIVES

1. Define organization development (OD).

2. Understand the basic theories and concepts of OD.

3. Describe the planned-change model.

4. Explain the roles of the change agent, manager, and people within the system in developing an intervention strategy.

5. Understand the basic steps involved in designing an implementation strategy.

6. Explain the different types of human processual intervention strategies.

7. Explain the different types of technostructural intervention strategies.

8. Explain the different types of sociotechnical intervention strategies.

9. Explain the different types of organization transformation intervention strategies.

10. Describe the role of HRD practitioners in OD interventions.

████████████████████████████████████████████████████

**OPENING CASE**

Extrusion (a pseudonym) is a Norwegian organization that is seeking to flatten its organizational structure and increase the amount of employee participation in the organization. The new CEO of the company is very enthusiastic about this idea, and has en-

listed the help of a management professor to document the progress and changes that should occur as a result of this major change in the organizational structure.

*Questions: If you were a consultant working on this change project, what*

*issues would you raise* before *the organization switched to a flatter, more participative organizational structure? What issues or problems might this organization face as it seeks to make such a change? What types of things can it do to try to minimize these problems?*

## INTRODUCTION

In this chapter, we will emphasize:

- *HRD interventions that focus on the group or organizational level*
- *theories about how individuals, groups, and organizations successfully deal with change*
- *a model of planned change that integrates individual, group, and organizational-level variables*
- *several HRD efforts that promote transformation of the organization as a whole*
- *a view of organizations as high performance work systems, where all parts are integrated and working together towards common goals*

Change has become a way of life for most organizations. Pressure from increasing competition, globalization, technological developments, and other forces has created an environment that rewards organizations that are capable of identifying trends and issues and responding quickly to them. The element of HRD that can best enable organizations to embrace and manage change is organization development.

### ORGANIZATION DEVELOPMENT (OD) DEFINED

**Organization development (OD)** is a process used to enhance both the effectiveness of an organization and the well-being of its members through planned interventions.[1] This definition makes three key points. First, OD **enhances the effectiveness of the organization.** *Effectiveness,* in this context, is defined as achieving organizational goals and objectives. Second, OD **enhances the well-being of organization members.** The term *well-being* refers to the perceived overall satisfaction each organization member feels toward his or her job and work environment. Generally speaking, "having challenging and meaningful work leads to high work satisfaction and, if rewarded by the organization, to higher satisfaction with rewards as well."[2] Thus, OD is intended to enhance *both* personal and work satisfaction.

Third, OD is used to enhance the effectiveness of organizations and individual well-being through **planned interventions.** Planned interventions refer "to sets of structured activities in which selected organizational units (target groups or individuals) engage with a task or sequence of tasks where the task goals are related directly or indirectly to organizational improvement."[3] Thus, planned interventions, or **intervention strategies,** are the primary means through which organizational improvement and changes take place.

## PLAN OF THE CHAPTER

The purpose of this chapter is to define organizational development theories and concepts. First, we will introduce and discuss a model of planned change. Then, we will discuss the various roles involved in planning and implementing change strategies. Next, we will discuss four types of change strategies and some of the specific techniques used in each. Finally, we will discuss the role of the HRD professional in introducing and managing change.

## ORGANIZATION DEVELOPMENT THEORIES AND CONCEPTS

OD theories have evolved primarily from four academic disciplines — psychology, sociology, anthropology, and management. OD theory can be divided into two categories — change process theory and implementation theory.

## CHANGE PROCESS THEORY

Change process theory tries to explain the dynamics through which organizational improvement and changes take place.[4] The change process was first depicted by Kurt Lewin as occurring in three stages — unfreezing, moving, and refreezing.[5] The *unfreezing* stage involves the process of getting people to accept that change is inevitable, and to stop doing certain things that resist change (e.g., clinging to a current policy, practice, or behavior). The *moving* stage involves getting people to accept the new, desired state (e.g., new policies and practices). The last stage, *refreezing,* involves making the new practices and behaviors a permanent part of the operation or role expectations. Lewin viewed change as deriving from two forces: 1) those internally driven (from a person's own needs) and 2) those imposed or induced by the environment. Environmental forces can be further distinguished as *driving* (pushing for change) or *restraining* (those seeking to maintain the status quo). For change to be environmentally imposed, driving forces must outnumber restraining forces.

■ **TABLE 14-1**

SCHEIN'S THREE-STAGE MODEL OF THE
CHANGE PROCESS

**Stage 1** *Unfreezing* — Creating motivation and readiness to change through:

    a. Disconfirmation or lack of confirmation

    b. Creation of guilt or anxiety

    c. Provision of psychological safety

**Stage 2** *Changing* through cognitive restructuring — Helping the individual to see, judge, feel, and react differently based on a new point of view obtained through:

    a. identifying with a new role model, mentor, and so on

    b. scanning the environment for new relevant information

**Stage 3** *Refreezing* — Helping the individual to integrate the new point of view into:

    a. his or her total personality and self-concept

    b. significant relationships

SOURCE: From E. H. Schein (1987). *Process consultation* (vol. 2). Reading, MA: Addison-Wesley, p. 93.

Edgar Schein further delineated each stage of Lewin's model (see Table 14-1).[6] The emphasis of Schein's change model is on the dynamics of individual change and how a **change agent** must be able to manage these changes. At stage 1 (unfreezing), the change agent motivates the person to accept change by disconfirming his or her attitudes, behaviors, or performance. For example, for an employee to correct poor work habits, he or she must first accept that his or her performance is inappropriate. At stage 2 (changing through cognitive restructuring), the emphasis is on getting the employee to see and do things differently and to actually believe that by changing work habits, his or her performance will improve. Finally, at stage 3 (refreezing), the change agent helps the person to integrate these new behaviors (work habits) into his or her thought patterns. This stage focuses on helping the employee to reconfirm his or her self-concept and reinforce desired performance standards.

Recently, Dent and Goldberg challenged the notion that individuals universally resist change.[7] They argue that,

> People may resist loss of status, loss of pay, or loss of comfort, but these are not the same as resisting change. . . . Employees may resist the unknown, being dictated to, or management ideas that do not seem feasible from the employees' standpoint. However, in our research, we have found few or no instances of employees resisting change (p. 26).[8]

Dent and Goldberg argue that Lewin's notion of resistance to change has been misunderstood, and that the proper focus should be at the *systems* level. That is, work takes place within a system of roles, attitudes, norms, and other factors, and thus, resistance to change should be viewed as an issue or problem for the whole organizational system, rather than focusing on individual employees.[9] This argument is similar to that put forward by proponents of the High Performance Work System concept, which we will cover at the end of this chapter. Dealing with individual-level change is clearly vital, yet this also needs to be understood and handled within the context of changes and forces operating within the organization as a whole.

## IMPLEMENTATION THEORY

Implementation theory focuses on specific intervention strategies that are designed to induce changes. We will briefly discuss some of the underlying theories and concepts of four types of interventions: human processual, technostructural, sociotechnical systems (STS) designs, and large systems. Later in the chapter, we will go into more detail about specific types of OD interventions within each of these categories.

*HUMAN PROCESSUAL INTERVENTION THEORY.*    Human processual theories place a heavy emphasis on the *process* of change, and focus on changing behaviors by modifying individual attitudes, values, problem-solving approaches, and interpersonal styles. The theoretical underpinnings of this approach are drawn from the behavioral sciences (these ideas were discussed in Chapter 2), particularly the need, expectancy, reinforcement, and job-satisfaction theories. The application of these theories to human processual intervention was pioneered in the 1950s by Lewin, in collaboration with others such as Lippitt, White, Likert, and McGregor. Lewin was able to transfer his knowledge of the way planned interventions produce desired behavioral changes in a social setting to organizational settings.[10] Lewin hypothesized that interventions should be directed at the group level rather than at the individual level. He felt that changing an individual's behavior without first changing group norms would be fruitless, because that individual would be viewed as a deviate and pressured to return to his or her former behavior pattern. Lewin's work led to the development of several OD intervention techniques, including survey feedback and force field analysis, which will be discussed later in the chapter.

Chris Argyris, another early pioneer of human processual intervention strategies, postulated that the basic requirements of an intervention activity are valid information, free choice, and internal commitment.[11] To facilitate change, the person involved in the change should have useful information with which to diagnose the situation and then act on that information. Free choice implies that the person involved in the change process has the autonomy, control, and motivation to implement the intervention activity. Internal commitment implies that the person or persons involved in the change process have "ownership" of the strategy and, by implication, "have processed valid information and made an informed free choice."[12] Argyris's early work led to the development of several **team-building** techniques, including process consultation, role clarification, and confrontation meetings. Team building will be discussed later in the chapter.

*TECHNOSTRUCTURAL INTERVENTION THEORY.*    Technostructural theory focuses on improving work content, work method, work flow, performance factors, and relationships among workers.[13] One of the key concepts with this approach is job design. A job has several distinguishing characteristics, including individual tasks or duties, responsibilities, authority, relationships, and skill requirements. Hackman and Oldham hypothesized that certain job characteristics affect employee psychological states, which in turn affect work outcomes and satisfaction.[14] They believe that changing one or more of a job's characteristics — a strategy called **job enrichment** — can induce positive psychological changes resulting in improved performance and satisfaction. Hackman and Oldham's work has been primarily applied to job redesign (job enrichment programs), an intervention tool for increasing job satisfaction and productivity.

Another dimension of technostructural intervention strategies is the level of participation in the change process. Many practitioners readily accept that the design should be "participative" without first understanding the impact of participation on the individual or organization.[15] Statements like "people will participate if given the opportunity" or "people prefer participation to nonparticipation" are too simplistic.[16] One difficulty for practitioners is that participation is still a vaguely defined construct.

*SOCIOTECHNICAL SYSTEMS (STS) DESIGNS.*    Sociotechnical systems (STS) interventions are "directed at the fit between the technological configuration and the social structure of work units . . . [which] results in the rearrangement of relationships among roles or tasks or a sequence of activities to produce self-maintaining, semiautonomous groups."[17] Most of the early research in the 1960s and 1970s focused on *quality of work life* interventions. The projects focused on such things as industrial democratization, participative management, job enrichment, and work rescheduling interventions. The underlying emphasis of these projects was on the efficacy of such interventions on worker satisfaction and productivity.

At the same time that STS designs were being developed, W. E. Deming was pioneering techniques of employee involvement geared toward improving quality. In the early 1950s, Deming introduced these new concepts to U.S. corporations, which were less than receptive to his approaches. Deming was later invited to speak to a group of Japanese industrialists who found his message consistent with their general business philosophy. With the application of Deming's concepts to STS theory, STS interventions theory has begun to focus on "empowering" the worker to assume more lateral responsibility for the work. These innovations include **quality circles, total quality management,** and **self-managed teams.**

*ORGANIZATION TRANSFORMATION CHANGE.*    The theory of organization transformation (OT) change was pioneered by Beckhard, who viewed organizations as complex, human systems, each possessing a unique character, culture, and value system, along with "information and work procedures that must be continually examined, analyzed, and improved if optimum productivity and motivation are to result."[18] His approach is based on the understanding that managers of complex organizations face numerous challenges (see Table 14-2). To meet these

**▪ TABLE 14-2**

CHALLENGES FACING ORGANIZATIONAL LEADERS

1.  changing the shape of the organization

2.  changes in the mission or "reason for being"

3.  changes in ways of doing business

4.  changes in ownership

5.  downsizing

6.  changes in the culture of the organization

SOURCE: From R. Beckhard & R. T. Harris (1987). *Organizational transitions* (2nd ed.). Reading, MA: Addison-Wesley, pp. 2–7.

challenges, organizational leaders must be able to develop a vision guided by beliefs and principles that can be translated into mission and goals. The mission and goals should form the basis for managing the organization, effectively using technology, and distributing rewards. To do this effectively, organizational leaders must understand such things as the nature of culture and what it takes to change it; the significant role of values in an organization's life; the general sociopolitical nature of the world; impacts of currencies and East-West/North-South issues; and, finally, the technology and concepts of managing effective change and of balancing stability and change.[19]

## LIMITATIONS OF RESEARCH SUPPORTING OD THEORIES

As in many areas of HRD, there are limitations in the research that has been conducted to test the underlying theoretical constructs of OD and the effectiveness of OD interventions.[20] These limitations include:

1.  the lack of true experimental designs in most OD research

2.  the lack of resources available to many OD practitioners

3.  the limitations of field research designs

4.  bias by OD evaluators (who are often the designers of the intervention)

5.  simply a "lack of motivation" by the OD evaluator to do the job correctly[21]

In particular, it is difficult to isolate causality in such research. Applying traditional experimental strategies, which attempt to isolate causation, to OD interventions forces researchers to focus on a single intervention episode and overlook the systematic nature of organizations.[22] In addition, most OD research results are measured by changes in attitudes and behaviors. This is a limitation because attitudinal and behavioral changes are considered intervening variables and may have very little to do with the improvements in group and organization performance that OD interventions are ultimately intended to achieve.[23]

One significant methodological development is the application of meta-analysis to OD research. Meta-analysis is a set of analytical techniques that can be used to statistically combine results of studies that are investigating the same variable or intervention, making it easier to draw conclusions from prior research. In addition to examining the effects of change interventions on dependent variables, meta-analysis also makes it possible to examine the effects of moderator variables (e.g., the technology used in the organization, organization types, and the rigor of the research study).[24] Meta-analysis also makes it possible to statistically remove possible effects of things such as reviewer bias.[25] Meta-analytic studies of OD research have made it easier to determine what we can reasonably conclude from prior research.

## MODEL OF PLANNED CHANGE

The lack of fundamental OD research has underscored the need for a universally accepted model of planned change.[26] Because of the lack of a generic model, change process and intervention theories are "recklessly combined and crossed levels of abstraction, levels of analysis, and narrowly defined discipline boundaries."[27] The purpose of this section is to present a model of planned change that attempts to provide a framework for integrating OD theory, research, and practice.

The Porras and Silvers model of planned change provides a useful framework for introducing change within an organizational setting (see Figure 14-1).[28] Specifically, it addresses how planned interventions targeted at specific organization variables with a desired effect on individual change will result in positive organizational outcomes. This model has four distinct parts. First, it distinguishes two types of intervention strategies — OD and **organization transformation** (OT). Porras and Silvers feel that OT should be a separate entity because the underlying theories and concepts are not as well-defined as OD.[29] In comparison, human processual and technostructural theories and concepts have gained widespread acceptance among OD practitioners.

The second part of the model shows the relationship between change interventions and organizational target variables. The model shows two sets of target variables. The first is *vision* variables, which are the underlying organizational values, beliefs, and principles that guide management decisions and provide the foundation for the purpose and mission of the organization. The second type of target variables are identified as *work setting* variables, which are directly related to or influenced by OD interventions and vision variables. Work setting variables include policies, procedures, work rules, job descriptions, formal reporting lines, social factors, and communication patterns. In essence, these form the framework for organization structure.

The third part of the model focuses on the types of individual cognitive change. Porras and Silvers conceptualize cognitive change as the alteration of a person's perception of some existing organizational variable or paradigm.[30] An *organizational paradigm* can be defined as a generally accepted view or belief that is based

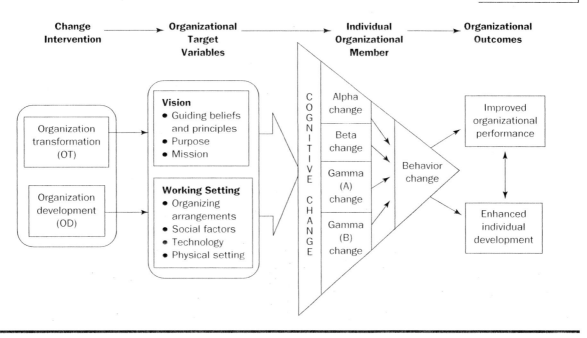

SOURCE: From J. I. Porras & R. C. Silvers (1991). Organization development and transformation. *Annual Review of Psychology, 42*, 53. Copyright 1991 by Annual Reviews. Reprinted by permission.

on unquestioned and unexamined assumptions.[31] Cognitive change can occur at four cognitive levels:

1. *Alpha changes* are possible when individuals perceive a change in the levels of variables (e.g., a perceived improvement in skills) within a paradigm, without altering their configuration (e.g., job design).

2. *Beta changes* are possible when individuals perceive a change in the value of variables (e.g., a change in work standards) within an existing paradigm, without altering their configuration.

3. *Gamma (A) changes* are possible when individuals perceive a change in the configuration of an existing paradigm, without the addition of new variables (e.g., changing the central value of a product-driven paradigm from cost-containment to total quality focus; this results in the reconfiguration of all variables within this paradigm).

4. *Gamma (B) changes* are possible when individuals perceive a replacement of one paradigm with another that contains new variables (e.g., replacing a product-driven paradigm with a customer-responsive paradigm).[32]

As the definitions indicate, each level of cognitive change represents change as an occurrence on a broader scope, from individual to organizational. For example, suppose a shipping clerk attends a training program to improve her reading skill. An alpha change can be said to have occurred if at the end of training she perceives that her reading skill has improved. Further, suppose that the shipping department manager attempts to improve productivity by reducing the standard for effective order processing time from forty-eight hours to twenty-four hours. A beta change can be said to have occurred if the shipping clerks accept this new standard as legitimate. This is so because the employees now define success as processing an order in less than twenty-four hours, as opposed to less than forty-eight hours.

Gamma A and B changes refer to changes occurring at the organization level. Gamma A changes are directed at the manner in which the operation's mission or philosophy is accomplished, but where the core mission would remain intact. For example, if a product-driven organization introduced new cost-containment procedures, without changing its operation philosophy, a gamma A change would have occurred. Alternatively, gamma B changes are directed at the core mission or philosophy. For example, a gamma B change has occurred if the organization redefines itself from being product driven to being customer driven. Unlike a gamma A change, a gamma B change "alters existing behaviors, creates new behaviors, and gives individual employees a totally new way of viewing their work."[33]

Distinguishing the levels of cognitive change has several benefits. First, this can help the change agent to select the kind of intervention strategy that would be appropriate to achieve the desired change. Second, this approach provides a conceptual framework for doing evaluative research on OD interventions. Specifically, the level of change dictates the appropriate research designs and measurement techniques that should be used to assess it. Third, effectiveness can be reported as a change at one or more of the four cognitive levels, making communication of results clearer.

The fourth, and last, part of the model focuses on how individual behavioral changes can lead to two possible outcomes — improved organizational performance and enhanced individual development. Organizational performance, in this context, refers to improvements in efficiency, effectiveness, productivity, and profitability. Enhanced individual development refers to the alteration of behaviors, skills, or both, resulting in such things as improved work habits, increased commitment, and improved performance. These outcomes are consistent with the definition of OD, which referred to enhancing the effectiveness of an organization and the well-being of its members through planned interventions.

## DESIGNING AN INTERVENTION STRATEGY

The model of planned change that we just described is an attempt to provide a framework for integrating OD theory, research, and practice. In this section, we will discuss how OD practitioners go about designing an intervention strategy that targets specific organizational variables. We will first discuss specific roles in the design and implementation phases. Next, we will examine some steps in designing an intervention strategy. Last, we will look at the role of the HRD practitioner in this process.

### SPECIFIC ROLES

There are at least three distinct sets of roles that must be fulfilled when designing and implementing intervention change strategy — the change manager, the change agent, and the roles played by individuals within the system that is being changed.

*ROLE OF CHANGE MANAGER.*    The **change manager** oversees the design of the intervention strategy. This person would have overall responsibility for assessing the need for change, determining the appropriate intervention activities, implementing the strategy, and evaluating the results. Some organizations elect to develop a parallel structure for introducing change — one person responsible for ongoing management functions and another person responsible for managing change. However, using a parallel structure may lead to a situation in which the change manager would not have sufficient power to create the conditions for change, particularly if the functional manager is perceived by others in the organization as not supporting the change process.

Rather than create a parallel structure, most organizations look to the functional manager to assume the additional duties of change manager. When using this approach, it is important that the manager who is selected to be the change manager be at the appropriate organizational level. For example, if a team-building intervention is going to be used in a single department, the change manager should be the department manager. Alternatively, if the target of the intervention were to change the mission of the organization, the appropriate change manager would be the CEO. Managers must understand the nature of planned change as opposed to forced change. Forced change, which uses coercive tactics (e.g., threat of discipline), may produce immediate results, but these changes in behavior may not be permanent. Individuals may react immediately to forced change in order to avoid any aversive consequences. However, when the threats of these consequences are removed, the person may revert to old habits or behaviors. Unfortunately, many managers will continue to use forced change until they learn to balance their short-term needs with the potential for the more permanent long-term benefits of planned change.

Fulfilling the role of the change manager is often difficult. The change manager must pay sufficient attention to the change initiative and see it through to its conclusion. According to one survey, executives attributed the failure of change initiatives to their own inattention to the change efforts.[34] In addition, managers and executives often lack knowledge of the change process and the impact the change has on individuals, and they often lack the skills to manage the human elements of change.[35] These findings suggest that organizations need to do more to prepare executives and other mangers to assume the change management role.

Some organizations have begun to address this need. For example, Corning, Inc., developed a program (referred to as a tool kit), called Exercises for Managing Change, that provides information, activities, handouts, and other resources that help managers and executives to prepare for change, move through the change process, and live with change.[36] Programs like this help change managers to understand their role and encourage them to call on others to assist them in developing and implementing a planned change strategy.

*ROLE OF CHANGE AGENT.*    The **change agent** assists the change manager in designing and implementing change strategy. Among other things, the change agent has primary responsibility for facilitating all of the activities surrounding the design and implementation of the strategy. This person should have knowledge of OD theories, concepts, practices, and research results so that he or she can advise the change manager on implementation issues and the efficacy of different intervention strategies.

The change agent can be an internal staff person (e.g., HRD practitioner) or an external consultant. *Internal change agents* generally are knowledgeable regarding the organization's mission, structural components, technology, internal politics, and social factors. This knowledge can be very important for establishing a trusting relationship with the change manager and members of the system who will undergo the change. However, system members may feel the internal change agent is too close to the existing situation and cannot be objective. In addition, the internal change agent may not possess the specialized knowledge needed for a particular intervention strategy. If this is the case, the organization may decide to hire an external consultant with specialized OD knowledge and skills.

*External change agents* are hired to fulfill a specific function or role for a specified period of time. The external change agent's role is determined by the change manager and is typically outlined in a contract. The contract should specify the exact nature of the work to be performed, the timetable for the work, length of service, method and amount of payment, and some way of evaluating the change agent's performance. Some organizations negotiate a performance clause, which gives the organization the right to evaluate the change agent's efforts at any time and provides that the contract can be terminated if the work is not up to the agreed-upon standards.

Warner Burke described eight roles that a change agent may play (see Table 14-3).[37] Each of these roles represents a different aspect of the relationship between the change agent and the change manager or client. For example, when a change agent assumes the advocate role (i.e., becomes highly directive), he or she is attempting to influence the change manager to select a certain strategy. At the other extreme, when the change agent assumes the role of a reflector (i.e., becomes nondirective), he or she is attempting to clarify information so that the change manager can make the decision. It is not unusual for a change agent to serve in several roles during the same intervention. For example, if during the initial

**▪ TABLE 14-3**

| Role | Definition | When Appropriate |
|---|---|---|
| Advocate | Highly directive role in which the change agent tries to influence the client to use a certain approach | When client is not sure of the approach to take and needs a lot of direction |
| Technical Specialist | Provides specific technical knowledge on special problems | When client seeks direction on a special problem |
| Trainer or Educator | Provides information about OD or different intervention strategies | When client needs training in some aspect of OD |
| Collaborator in Problem Solving | Provides assistance in problem analysis, identifying solutions, and action steps | When client needs assistance in decision making |
| Alternative Identifier | Same as above, but does not collaborate | When client needs assistance in developing a decision-making process |
| Fact Finder | Serves as a research or data collector | When client needs are very specific |
| Process Specialist | Facilitates meetings and group processes | When client's needs are for process consultation |
| Reflector | Helps client to understand situation by reacting to information | When client is not sure of the data and seeks clarification |

SOURCE: From W. W. Burke (1987). *Organization development*. Reading, MA: Addison-Wesley, 146–148.

stages of designing the intervention strategy, the change manager lacks understanding of some of the key concepts of planned change, the change agent may act as a trainer and educator to ensure that these concepts are understood. Having gained sufficient knowledge, the change manager will likely look to the change agent to assume additional roles (e.g., fact finder or process specialist).

In the past decade, a number of consulting firms have promoted the concept of change management. These firms, including McKinsey and Company, Arthur D. Little, and Gemini Consulting, are promoting positive organizational change as well as their roles as external change agents. Some authors have gone so far as to suggest that "change management" will replace the term "organization development" as the heading for organizational-level interventions.[38] This notion has met with vigorous opposition.[39] Whatever the outcome of this current debate, it is clear that external change agents (and consulting firms) are playing a leading role in many ongoing change efforts.

Recently, many intervention strategies have involved various types of team-based interventions. As a result, individuals who serve as change agents are increasingly being called upon to help change managers transform work groups into teams. To do so, they must have several sets of skills. First, the change agent must be able to perform a variety of team-building activities. Second, when working with the team leader (who may be the change manager), the change agent must be able to assist him or her in each of the elements of team development, including facilitating team meetings, managing conflicts, problem solving and decision making, and establishing team roles and expectations. Third, the change agent must have the diagnostic skills needed to understand the culture of the group or system that is targeted for change. Understanding the cultural aspects (e.g., values, norms, beliefs) of the group will enable the change agent to identify important "access leverage points" that can facilitate or impede the implementation of the change strategy.[40] For example, if an organization has a long-standing tradition of celebrating important milestones (e.g., the end of a production run, the completion of a training and education program, or the end of a seasonal sales period), a change agent should identify these customs and traditions and use them to support the change process. If important aspects of the culture are ignored, group members might resist the change. The relationship between culture and change is also important at the individual and organization levels.

*ROLES OF INDIVIDUALS WITHIN A SYSTEM UNDERGOING CHANGE.*   The roles of individuals within the *system*, that is the target of the intervention strategy, are determined by the change manager. The system can be a small work group or the entire organization. Individuals or groups within the system may be asked by the change manager to take on a specific role in the change process. For example, some organizations create a change committee whose role is to work with both the change manager and the change agent in the design and implementation of the intervention strategy. Committees or task forces are important for helping to collect data, develop team skills, and define the emerging tasks and roles within the system.[41] Ideally, these individuals will be energized by their involvement, motivating them to put forth the extra effort needed for committee work.[42]

## DESIGNING THE INTERVENTION STRATEGY

To design an intervention strategy, the change manager, with the help of the change agent and others in the system, must be able to diagnose the existing environment for change, develop and implement a plan of action, and evaluate the results of the intervention to determine if the desired (behavioral) changes have occurred. Each of these steps is discussed below.

*DIAGNOSE THE ENVIRONMENT.*   Diagnosing the environment is an assessment process that focuses on determining the readiness of the target group to accept change. If the group is not ready, resistance will occur and change will likely fail.

■ **FIGURE 14-2**

FORCE FIELD ANALYSIS (INTRODUCING NEW
PRODUCTION STANDARDS)

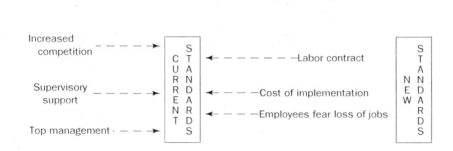

One way to determine readiness to accept change is by conducting force field analysis. Lewin developed **force field analysis** to analyze the driving and restraining forces of change. Figure 14-2 illustrates force field analysis graphically using the example of a company that plans to introduce new production standards. The change manager, change agent, and possibly a change committee or task force would diagnose the environment to determine possible forces both for and against change. These forces are shown as force lines. The length of the lines indicates the relative force — the longer the line, the greater the force. Theoretically, if change is going to take place, the accumulation of forces *for* change would have to exceed the accumulation of forces *against* change. In the example in Figure 14-2, the restraining forces would seem to prevent the introduction of new product standards unless the present situation were modified. Thus, the value of a force field analysis is that it allows the intervention strategists to pinpoint specific support and resistance to a proposed change program. In the example, the change manager must be able to reduce the resistance (e.g., renegotiate the labor contract) or increase the positive forces in favor of change.

*DEVELOP AN ACTION PLAN.* Developing an action plan involves identifying specific target variables and determining the techniques that will be used to bring about change. Identifying specific target variables (e.g., resistance points, existing policies) allows the intervention strategists to better understand the relative complexity of the change program. Using the earlier example of changing production standards, the change manager may view the union, the supervisors, and the production workers as possible resisters to change. The union will have to agree to a change in production standards; supervisors must understand the need to change those standards and why their active support is critical to the outcome; and employees need to know that the change will not affect their job security. The next step is to determine the appropriate intervention techniques for instituting change. In the example, the following techniques may be considered:

1. Schedule a supervisory meeting and follow-up sessions to communicate the critical need for changing standards and impress key employees with the need to actively support the change.

2. Conduct meetings with union officials to determine their interpretation of the labor contract and whether they agree that management has the "right" to change production standards unilaterally. Depending on the results of the meetings, other sessions may be necessary.

3. Conduct an awareness/training session for production-level employees to set forth how the changes in production standards will affect them personally and how those changes will be implemented.

The **action plan** specifies the intervention strategy. Like any other plan, the action plan should specify the objective of each change activity, who will be involved, who is responsible, and when the activity will be completed. Implementation of the action plan involves carrying out each step in the intervention strategy. This may require at least as much energy and commitment of the change manager and change agent as all of the previous steps combined. Too often, people in organizations get bogged down with the planning process and see it as an end in itself, rather than as a means to an end. Thus, when the action plan is prepared, participants may be unwilling to see it through. The role of the change manager, with the assistance of the change agent, is to oversee the implementation of the plan and ensure that all of the steps are followed, that tasks are completed, and that deadlines are met. If there is any delay in carrying out an activity, the change manager should intervene and find out the cause of the delay. The change manager should continually confer with the members of the system to review results, get feedback, and make the appropriate adjustments.

*EVALUATE THE RESULTS OF THE INTERVENTION.*    As indicated by our process model of HRD (first presented in Chapter 1), the results of an OD intervention must be evaluated to determine whether behavior has changed and whether problems have emerged (e.g., new standards may be in place, but the union wants the workers classifications or pay to be upgraded). It is important that members of the system be involved in these steps to determine whether the action plan was effective. Evaluation results should be provided to demonstrate the degree to which the intervention was effective. If other problems are identified, the change manager may want to repeat the action planning process.

## ROLE OF HRD PRACTITIONERS IN THE DESIGN OF OD INTERVENTIONS

HRD practitioners have two primary roles in the design of OD interventions. First, they can serve as change agents. As discussed in Chapter 1, OD competencies are part of the overall competencies of an HRD professional. In planned change situations, particularly those that involve HRD programs and processes as intervention techniques (e.g., behavior modeling training), the HRD practitioner can help the change manager understand the full range of HRD programs and processes and which ones work best under different conditions. In this role, the HRD practitioner can also facilitate some of the change activities (e.g., awareness sessions) that are part of the action plan.

The second role that an HRD practitioner can play in the design and implementation of OD interventions is to serve as the evaluator of intervention strategies. Even in situations where the HRD practitioner was not directly involved in the intervention strategy, he or she could be responsible for designing the evaluative component. Again, it is important that this person possesses the competencies to conduct the needed research and can use the appropriate methodology to evaluate the effects of the change program.

## THE ROLE OF LABOR UNIONS IN OD INTERVENTIONS

OD interventions and labor relations are inextricably linked. While most OD intervention strategies are considered to be a rational process, labor relations are sometimes perceived as irrational and unpredictable, particularly if past relations have been less than satisfactory. If union members generally mistrust management, it is not likely that they will be willing partners in a planned change program. Rather, they may attempt to obstruct the process.

Some OD practitioners would argue that if an organization truly wants to bring about lasting change in a unionized work environment, management must first attempt to make labor relations a more rational process. They must view union leaders as partners in change and emphasize that their commitment to long-term goals for change is as important as that of the top managers. Management and union leaders must share the reality that organizational changes must be made if the organization is to remain a viable entity and prosper. Furthermore, they must be willing to make fundamental changes in accountability and in the ways employees perform their jobs. This kind of arrangement is generally known as a *cooperative agreement*.

Cooperative agreements are usually accomplished within normal contract negotiations. Typically, unions make certain trade-offs as long as they appear to be in the best interest of the membership as a whole. During tough economic times, or when the organization faces financial or market problems, management and union leaders may be more willing to agree on a cooperative arrangement. In such circumstances, the union's priority is to ensure that jobs are saved and that there is no change to the wage structure, and management's priority is to see that business improves. But during stable times, or even boom times, the union may expect something in return for buying into the change.

Team-based approaches that emphasize empowerment (e.g., TQM, semi-autonomous or self-managing team) have come under the scrutiny of unions and the National Labor Relations Board (NLRB). For example, the NLRB cited two companies for engaging in unfair labor practices by dominating or interfering with the formation of a labor organization.[43] The NLRB ruled that if an organization establishes employee committees that have authorization to set wages, hours, and conditions, this can be construed as a labor organization under the law, even if no labor union was present in the organization. The implications of this ruling for a given employer will depend largely on the existing relationship between employees and management (or union and management). If relationships are poor, this could essentially halt any efforts to involve employees (including union members) in most types of employee involvement processes and team-based approaches currently existing in organizations.

## TYPES OF INTERVENTIONS: HUMAN PROCESSUAL

Most of the OD interventions in the 1960s and 1970s were human processual interventions. These interventions are directed at improving interpersonal, intragroup, and intergroup relations. Two of the most common human processual intervention strategies that are still widely used are survey feedback and team building.[44]

### SURVEY FEEDBACK

**Survey feedback** is defined as "the systematic feedback of survey data to groups with the intent of stimulating discussion of problem areas, generating potential solutions, and stimulating motivation for change."[45] The data provide a snapshot of an existing situation, usually measuring some aspect of the group or organization. This data can then be used to compare an organization's current state with some desired state. Ideally, the result of survey feedback sessions is that changes will be attempted to bridge the gap between the current state and desired state.

Survey feedback systems can be implemented in many different ways. For example, Alderfer and Holbrook's peer-intergroup model[46] is one approach that has been used to supply feedback data to superiors and subordinates when relations are strained between them.[47] This approach involves two or more groups and focuses on organizationwide issues only. The groups meet separately to discuss how the data reflect their concerns, and then they join the other groups to share their reactions. Significant concerns are then addressed through the development of action plans.

When using survey feedback as an intervention strategy, it is important for the change manager and change agent to be clear on 1) what organizational variables they are trying to measure; 2) how the survey will be designed and implemented to ensure the data will be reliable and valid; and 3) how best to present the survey results to the intended audience. Many commercially produced (attitude or climate) surveys are available that provide a range of normative items, along with comparative data.[48] Using commercially produced survey instruments can help the change manager address these issues. High quality survey instruments 1) contain items that have been tested and refined to ensure clarity, 2) have undergone reliability studies to demonstrate their accuracy, and 3) permit the user to compare the results of his or her organization with the results of other organizations that have used the instrument.

## TEAM BUILDING

**Team building** is a process used to improve a work group's problem-solving ability and effectiveness.[49] Like individuals, groups experience problems. Groups can become dysfunctional when they experience problems that members cannot resolve or when they are unable to adapt to external changes (e.g., changes in technology). When a group becomes dysfunctional, relationships are strained, conflicts increase among the members, group output declines, and members are more likely to quit. A team-building intervention can be used to address some of these problems.

Even when groups are able to solve problems, management or members of the group (or both) may still feel that the group is not effective. Group effectiveness depends on at least three main elements:

1. the degree to which the group's productive output (its product or service) meets the standards of quantity, quality, and timeliness of the people who receive, review, and/or use the output

2. the degree to which the process of carrying out the work enhances the capability of members to work together interdependently in the future

3. the degree to which the group experience contributes to the growth and personal well-being of team members[50]

If one or more of these elements is missing, it would be possible to increase effectiveness through team building.

Before team building is attempted, several things should occur. First, there should be a preliminary diagnosis of the group's need for team building. Team building works best when there is a "strongly felt need to improve some basic condition or process that is interfering with the achievement of organizational goals."[51] Without a diagnosis of the group's need for team building, it is likely that some members of the group will resist any efforts to bring about change.

Second, a change agent should be selected who is able to use a wide range of OD skills and techniques to facilitate change. This is especially important given the nature of the things OD intervention is intended to change (e.g., attitudes, norms, and habits). One valuable technique for team building is **process consultation** (PC), which is used by change agents to facilitate meetings and encounters with the work group. In this role, the change agent observes group activities and processes, and conducts a feedback session on those observations at the end of the meeting.

Third, the change manager and the change agent should develop a general approach to the team-building sessions. Their roles should be specified clearly, in terms of who is going to facilitate different team-building activities. The approach should also specify the team-building cycle (e.g., action planning steps). Fourth, the change manager and change agent should establish a schedule outlining when these activities take place, including evaluation and follow-up sessions.

### EFFECTIVENESS OF HUMAN PROCESSUAL INTERVENTIONS

There is some evidence that human processual interventions can be effective in bringing about change. Two meta-analyses of the OD literature[52] showed, among other things, that:

1. team building was the most effective human processual intervention for modifying satisfaction and other attitudes[53]
2. team building showed strong effects on productivity measures[54]

A recent meta-analysis found a small, but statistically significant positive effect of team-building interventions on subjective measures of performance; however, the effect on objective measures of performance was nonsignificant.[55] Thus, it still appears to be necessary to urge caution concerning the evidence for the effectiveness of team building on organizational performance.

## TYPES OF INTERVENTIONS: TECHNOSTRUCTURAL

The purpose of technostructural interventions is to 1) improve work content, work method, and relationships among workers[56] and 2) lower costs by replacing inefficient materials, methods, equipment, workflow designs, and costly unnecessary labor with more efficient technology.[57] Given today's competitive climate, many organizations have turned to technostructural interventions to increase worker efficiency and satisfaction. The most common technostructural intervention strategies are job enlargement, job enrichment, and alternative work schedules.[58] We will discuss all three in this section.

### JOB ENLARGEMENT

**Job enlargement** interventions are "attempts to increase satisfaction and performance by consolidating work functions from a 'horizontal slice' of the work unit to provide greater variety and a sense of the whole task."[59] Job enlargement is generally carried out as a normal supervisory practice in most organizations. That is, a supervisor may observe boredom in a worker and diagnose that this person is not being challenged. The supervisor's normal coaching response, given no major obstacles (e.g., restrictions in a collective bargaining agreement), may be to reassign this person to a more challenging job. Thus, some job enlargement interventions are done informally.

Unfortunately, very few published studies isolate the effects of job enlargement from other interventions. One study, conducted by Campion and McClelland, examined whether using job enlargement on clerical jobs would have a desired effect on work outcomes (e.g., employee satisfaction).[60] They concluded that job enlargement had the greatest positive effect on employee satisfaction and customer service but had less effect on alleviating mental overload. Results from meta-analystic studies that compare job enlargement to other technostructural interventions will be presented at the end of this section.

## JOB ENRICHMENT

**Job enrichment** involves varying some aspect of the job in order to increase the potential to motivate workers. Probably the best-developed approach to job enrichment is Hackman and Oldham's **job characteristics model** (JCM). The JCM is based on the premise that jobs have five core dimensions (i.e., skill variety, task identity, task significance, autonomy, and feedback). Hackman and Oldham argue that the core job dimensions affect work outcomes, such as job satisfaction and intrinsic motivation, by determining the extent to which employees experience:

1. **meaningfulness** of the work itself
2. **responsibility** for the work and its outcomes
3. **knowledge of actual results** of the work

Hackman and Oldham developed the *job diagnostic survey* (JDS), a self-report instrument, to measure workers' perception of each core job dimension. The scores on each core job dimension are combined into an overall *motivation potential score* (MPS) that is an indicator of the extent to which the job can be enriched by modifying one or more of the core job dimensions.

The JCM and job enrichment interventions based on it have been the subject of considerable empirical testing and discussion. Overall, researchers have concluded that the model should be refined (e.g., clarifying the relationships among some variables, modifying calculation of the Motivational Potential Score).[61] Further, research suggests that the job characteristics included in the model are significantly related to job satisfaction[62] and to a lesser degree to job performance.[63] These relationships are stronger for individuals who have high growth need strength (i.e., a desire to grow and learn within the job). Taken together, research supports the conclusion that the job characteristics approach to job enrichment can be an effective technostructural intervention.

## ALTERNATIVE WORK SCHEDULES

*ALTERNATIVE WORK SCHEDULES.* (AWS) allow employees to modify their work requirements to satisfy their personal needs. According to a study of 521 corporations, 93 percent of the responding organizations have some type of alternative work schedules.[64] The two most common AWS interventions are the **compressed workweek** and **flextime**.[65]

*COMPRESSED WORKWEEK.* The compressed workweek involves reducing the number of workdays in a week, usually from five to four. Typically, the compressed schedule provides an option to employees to work four ten-hour days, known as the 4/40 schedule. Research on the 4/40 plan seems to show a positive effect on employee attitudes, but its effects on work productivity are mixed.[66]

*FLEXTIME WORK SCHEDULE.* The flextime schedule allows employees some latitude in determining their starting and ending times in a given workday. Employees, particularly those with young children, may find it attractive to have the option of changing their working hours to conform to their family patterns. A substantial number of U.S. families have parents who both work. Further, according to a 1997 study, 19 percent of families are headed by a single parent, and 27 percent of these single parents are men.[67] Although some single parents may be on welfare, a significant majority of workers may have some time restrictions due to their parental responsibilities.

In most flexible work schedule arrangements, each employee must work some standard number of hours per day (e.g., 8 hours), and all employees must be at work during a common core period of the day (usually during the middle of the day). On either side of the core time, usually 4 hours, each employee can decide when to begin and end the workday. A review of research suggests that flextime schedules are positively related to a number of factors, including organizational attachment, attendance, performance, stress, off-job satisfaction, and attitudes.[68] The effects of flextime were strongest on job attitudes (e.g., job satisfaction, satisfaction with work, and satisfaction with supervisor).

### EFFECTIVENESS OF TECHNOSTRUCTURAL INTERVENTIONS

Meta-analyses of technostructural interventions have shown:[69]

1. Alternative work schedules and job redesign had a moderate effect on measures of work output, such as quality and quantity of production.[70]

2. Work rescheduling interventions had a small but significant effect on measures of withdrawal behavior (e.g., absenteeism), whereas work redesign did not have a statistically significant effect on measures of withdrawal behavior.[71]

3. Overall, technostructural interventions had less effect than human processual interventions.[72]

4. Alternative work schedules had a greater effect on attitude than did job design/enlargement or job enrichment.[73]

5. Job enlargement and job enrichment interventions brought about the same amount of overall change (42 percent change), with enrichment having a greater effect on productivity.[74]

It appears, then, that technostructural interventions can lead to changes, but that they are less effective overall than human processual interventions. The general explanation for this difference is that human processual interventions are intended to "affect changes in organizations through the employees rather than through modifications in the work or work environment (technostructural approaches)."[75] Of the three types of technostructural interventions, job design had the greatest effect on productivity, while alternative work schedules had the greatest effect on attitudes. All three types affected managerial/professional employees the most, an important point when considering using these techniques throughout an organization.

# TYPES OF INTERVENTIONS: SOCIOTECHNICAL SYSTEMS

Since the 1970s, organizations have used *sociotechnical systems* (STS) designs as a way to increase productivity and worker satisfaction. Whereas human processual and technostructural interventions focus on interpersonal relationships and job design, STS interventions focus on the *combination* of organizational structural demands (e.g., work flow, task accomplishment, and performance) and social demands (e.g., relationship among workers).[76] This notion was first propounded by Eric Trist of the Tavistock Institute in Great Britain.[77] Today, STS interventions can be viewed as including quality circles, total quality management, and self-directed work teams. Each of these approaches is usually the focal point of a larger change strategy because the factors that determine team effectiveness are linked to the nature and effectiveness of the entire organization.[78] STS interventions have been among the most widely implemented current OD interventions. Research suggests that STS interventions have had a greater effect on productivity than either human processual or technostructural interventions.[79] We will discuss each one and describe the empirical evidence concerning the overall effectiveness of these interventions.

## QUALITY CIRCLES

The **quality circle** (QC) approach is a process of involving employees in meaningful work decisions including, but not limited to, solving job-related problems. While most QC programs are designed to meet an organization's unique needs, there are some common features. First are the QC roles — the steering committee, the facilitator, and the circle leader. The *steering committee*, composed of key managers and staff employees, is responsible for implementing the QC process and making decisions about such things as resource allocation, production or operation changes, and employee assignments. The *facilitator*, selected by the steering committee, has responsibility for training the circle leaders and overseeing the operation of the circles. The facilitator must have OD competencies. *Circle leaders*, usually supervisors, are responsible for such things as calling meetings, encouraging active participation among the members, and preparing the reports for submission to the steering committee.

The second common characteristic of QCs is that participants receive training in group process, diagnosing problems, and problem-solving skills. Group leaders will generally be given additional training in group facilitation. A third common characteristic is that each circle meets on a regular basis to discuss issues like improvement of the work procedures and product quality, working conditions, and facilities. Priority is usually given to problems in the work area of that QC, or under the direct control of the circle leader, or both. While participation is strictly voluntary, the employees are usually given time off to attend meetings. Finally, QCs make recommendations to management about how the issues they investigate can be addressed. They typically do not have the authority to implement the recommendations without management's approval.

The empirical evidence of the overall effectiveness of QCs is mixed. Steel and Lloyd studied the effects of participation in QC programs on several organizational variables.[80] They found the following:

1. There were significant effects on cognitive measures of a sense of competence and interpersonal trust, and on some measures related to properties of the task environment, such as goal congruence (p. 13).

2. QC participants reported significantly greater attachment to the organization as the study progressed (p. 13).

3. The QC process generally produced little overt enhancement in participants' work performance (p. 15).

Park analyzed evaluative data from 154 QC programs in both private and public organizations and found that, overall, QC programs have shown an increase in organizational effectiveness and the empowerment of employees.[81] This conclusion was supported by Botch and Spangle, who found the QC to be a powerful employee development tool, primarily because participants perceived their involvement as a way of getting personal recognition.[82] Others disagree with these findings. They feel that while operating costs did decrease some, no evidence showed that productivity, quality, or attitudes improved where QCs were used.[83]

Even with the mixed reviews of QCs, there seems to be a consensus among researchers that, in order for QC intervention strategies to be effective, they must include 1) comprehensive training for the facilitator, group leaders, and group members; 2) active support from top and middle management; 3) supervisors who possess good communications skills; and 4) inclusion of labor unions (where present).[84]

## TOTAL QUALITY MANAGEMENT

Faced with stiff competition from both domestic and foreign companies, organizations have identified quality as a critical competitive factor. One way to improve quality is to design and implement a popular intervention strategy referred to as the **total quality management program** (TQM).

TQM is defined as a "set of concepts and tools for getting all employees focused on continuous improvement, in the eyes of the customer."[85] Based on the work of Deming, Juran, Crosby, and others, TQM seeks to make every employee responsible for continuous quality improvement. It usually involves a significant change in the way employees do their work.

Most TQM intervention strategies involve five basic components — total commitment from senior management, quality standards and measures, training for employees, communication, and reward, recognition, and celebration. Each of these components is discussed briefly below. Senior management needs to guide the implementation of TQM. For example, Tenant Company, which established a quality program in 1979, found that managers are often isolated and need to be kept informed and involved.[86] A study of the TQM program at Digital Equipment Corporation revealed that the success of the program was dependent on how well management established clear quality goals and related them to business, communicated and reinforced them, and demonstrated behavior consistent with those values.[87]

Quality standards and measures serve as benchmarks for TQM. Organizations that establish clear quality goals must be able to quantify them according to defined standards. TQM emphasizes the role of each manager in terms of reducing cost, particularly nonconformance cost (which accounts for about 20 percent of revenues in most organizations) caused by deviations from performance standards.[88] According to McCormack, supervisors must be able to:

1. specify current performance standards
2. identify where outputs are at variance with standards
3. determine the causes of variances
4. identify and initiate actions to correct causes
5. specify desired performance
6. compare the desired standards to current standards and identify gaps
7. develop alternatives to close the gaps
8. institutionalize new standards[89]

Providing quality training to participants is critical to the overall success of TQM. Therefore, organizations that seek to implement TQM must make a major investment in training. Training should begin with sensitizing managers at all levels to the philosophy and principles of TQM. All managers need training in both TQM awareness and how to implement TQM principles.[90] In addition, employees may need training in statistical process control (SPC) techniques.[91] Also, because the use of problem-solving teams is almost always a part of a TQM intervention, team-building training should be included in quality training.[92]

Rewards, recognition, and celebration are used to keep employees energized and working toward the goals of total quality. Many organizations have linked TQM participation and success to three kinds of rewards: 1) individual monetary, 2) group monetary, and 3) nonmonetary rewards.[93] Individual monetary rewards, the more traditional form of compensation, are still important for linking TQM to a manager's participation and success. However, because individual compensation systems "place a strong emphasis on individual performance, almost always creating a competitive situation among employees," some organizations have abandoned individual rewards such as merit increases.[94] In their place, many organizations are emphasizing gain-sharing programs.

There are several ways an organization can recognize individuals and groups for their contributions. These include awarding of plaques; naming of an employee (or group) of the week, month, or year; and celebrating with recognition luncheons and dinners. The organization can also be recognized for having a successful TQM program. The most prestigious award is the Malcolm Baldrige National Quality Award, which has been instrumental in promoting the concept of TQM. Organizations that want to be recognized must adhere to a nationally accepted set of criteria for evaluating their TQM program. In the public sector, NASA's Quality and Excellence Award is given annually to contractors, subcontractors, and suppliers who consistently improve the quality of their products and services.[95] Most organizations with TQM programs also recognize groups for their successes.

Communication begins with the CEO "going public" with a commitment to TQM and how it will change the direction of the company.[96] In addition, communication should be used to provide performance feedback and reviews. Another component should be a continuous flow of information on product and service quality improvements, so that employees can track their group progress. Many organizations display results on wall charts (or online) for this purpose.

Before considering TQM as an intervention strategy, the change manager should try to solve any preexisting problems that would derail the effort. If employees are dissatisfied with some aspect of the organization, it will be very difficult for them to focus on quality issues. For example, the Wallace Company in Houston, Texas, a recipient of the Baldrige Award in 1990, took the advice of an external change agent and first addressed a problem that irritated employees before launching their now successful TQM program.[97] Another preexisting condition that could delay implementing TQM is organizational **downsizing**, particularly at the management levels. Employees who are in fear of losing their jobs may not be able to focus on TQM principles, unless they see them as a means of saving their jobs.

In addition to extensive applications in industry, many sectors of public service, including government, hospitals, and universities, have introduced TQM. The federal government has established the Federal Quality Institute, which offers quality seminars and in-house consulting to approximately thirty federal agencies.[98] State and local governments have also adopted TQM. For example, the city of Madison, Wisconsin, realized significant budgetary savings through TQM.[99] Hospitals across the United States have been adopting TQM as a means of improving patient care, performance, and market share.[100] In the face of declining budgets and enrollments, universities and colleges are using TQM techniques to help focus on the needs of the market and ways to improve delivery systems. However, to be successful, colleges and universities need the cooperation of their faculty (and their labor unions) to change the tradition of lifelong tenure and peer review of their teaching.[101]

The practitioner literature suggests that there is a high rate of success with TQM, particularly from the organization's perspective. Many companies reported that TQM has led to significant improvements in product quality and service leading to increased market share, profits, and company image. For example, in 1987

Rockwell Tactical Systems was cited by the U.S. Army for having 1,744 quality problems in its Hellfire anti-armor missile production. But by applying TQM principles, it was able to save the existing program and, in 1990, won a new contract for 100 percent production of the missile.[102]

There is also evidence that suggests that TQM has not lived up to expectations. In a survey of organizations that had implemented TQM programs, 70 percent of the respondents indicated that TQM had not yielded benefits in proportion to their investment.[103] In line with this, Hodgetts, Luthans, and Lee state that people who expect improved quality must also expect costs to increase.[104]

Two of the reasons cited for why TQM has not lived up to expectations are the attitudes of top management and lack of visible support for the program.[105] Even in situations with strong management support, lower level employees may be cynical and resist involvement in TQM because they perceive it as a top-down change program conceived by top management.[106]

Successful organizational outcomes of TQM interventions in both the private and public sectors are described in many anecdotal examples in the practitioner literature. But most of the literature measures global outcomes (e.g., improvement in error rates, assembly time, cost savings) and relies on case studies.[107] Unfortunately, little evidence from controlled studies shows the effects on individual productivity and attitudes.[108]

Recently, Yusof and Aspinwall suggested that much of the research and theorizing on TQM has been done in the context of large organizations.[109] They propose a framework for the implementation of TQM in smaller organizations. Given the proliferation of entrepreneurial start-ups in the past decade, the application of TQM principles to smaller businesses is an area worthy of further attention and study by both researchers and practitioners.

### SELF-MANAGING TEAMS

As discussed in Chapter 9, self-managing teams (SMTs) are defined as formal groups in which the group members are interdependent and can have the authority to regulate the team's activities.[110] While most SMTs are designed to meet an organization's specific needs, they have some common characteristics; including the following:

1. There is an interdependent relationship between members of the team.

2. Members have discretion over such things as work assignment, work methods, work schedules, training, and dealing with external customers and suppliers.

3. Team members have a variety of skills that allow them to perform several tasks.

4. The team receives performance feedback.[111]

These characteristics represent a significant change over traditional supervisor-led work teams. In particular, many organizations reduce the numbers of supervisors and middle managers when they implement SMTs. In any case, the organization must establish a new role for the supervisors who remain. Some organizations transform the position of supervisor to team adviser, team facilitator, or coach. In this arrangement, the individual's role is to help train team members and advise on such things as employee selection, budgeting, scheduling, performance evaluation, and discipline.[112]

Organizations typically use SMTs as part of a larger organizational transformation strategy directed at refocusing the organization, increasing employee involvement, increasing productivity, or reducing cost.[113] For example, Corning launched a high performance work system program at its Blacksburg, Virginia, plant using the SMT approach, along with several other intervention activities (e.g., continuous improvement, work process designs).[114]

Education and training are critical components of implementing SMTs. Training should occur at several levels. First, awareness training should be used to introduce the process and explain the benefits to individuals. Second, skills training should be used to provide team members with the skills and competencies they will need to manage their team. These include budgeting and planning, problem solving, and communication. This can be difficult in organizations where the employee education level is low. Third, cross-training is provided by individual team members to other team members who are assigned shared tasks.

It is not clear how many large companies have implemented SMTs. Estimates range from 7 percent to 47 percent.[115] However, because of the visibility SMTs have had in the popular press and practitioner literature, many organizations think that "this is the *only* way to successfully meet the business pressures in the 1990s and on into the 21st century, especially when those pressures demand fuller involvement and utilization of human resources."[116]

The effectiveness of the SMT approach is usually defined in terms of organizational-level performance indicators such as controlling cost and improvements in productivity and quality. Anecdotal evidence of the effectiveness of SMTs includes reports such as:

- At Northern Telecom Canada's repair facility in Morrisville, North Carolina, revenue increased by 63 percent, sales by 26 percent, and earnings by 46 percent in the three years since implementing SMTs.[117]

- At General Electric's plant in Salisbury, North Carolina, part of the workforce of 24,000 was organized into SMTs, resulting in an increase of 250 percent in productivity.[118]

- At Johnsonville Foods in Sheboygan, Wisconsin, employee involvement in decision making increased greatly in 1982, and SMTs were established in 1986. Revenues went from $15 million in 1982 to $130 million in 1990, with productivity increasing over 200 percent during this same period. By 2000, revenues had exceeded $200 million.[119]

Beyond productivity increases, organizations have received other benefits of successful SMT applications. These include better quality products and services, higher employee morale, reduced or flatter management hierarchy, and more responsive organizational structures.[120]

Empirical evidence also appears to suggest that SMTs are effective. A meta-analysis conducted by Beekun found that autonomous work groups (SMTs) were more productive than semi-autonomous and nonautonomous groups.[121] Cohen and Ledford compared traditionally managed teams with self-managed teams over a two-year period and found that self-managed teams were more effective on a variety of indicators, including productivity, quality, safety, customer complaints, and absenteeism.[122]

Other evidence shows that the results of SMTs are not always positive. Wall et al. conducted a long-term field experiment involving autonomous work groups in a manufacturing setting.[123] The intervention involved giving shop floor employees substantially more autonomy in carrying out their daily jobs. The results of the experiment showed positive results on intrinsic job satisfaction, but effects on motivation, organizational commitment, mental health, work performance, and turnover were not very positive.

One possible reason self-managing teams sometimes fail to produce the expected productivity increases is the lack of effective work-team management or supervision.[124] This suggests that organizations that have implemented SMTs may not be committed to changing from a traditional hierarchical structure, or have not developed the proper support mechanisms (e.g., human resource systems, training). Therefore, it is important that other management systems reinforce team structure and team behavior.

## DIFFERENCES BETWEEN TQM AND SMT

Some significant differences exist between a TQM program and an SMT intervention. TQM is a participative process and "participation per se does not always equalize power and may even increase discrepancies."[125] In an SMT approach, each team is empowered with the authority to make decisions affecting the output of that team without the concurrence of a supervisor. Teams used within TQM are usually encouraged to participate in problem solving, but they do not have the authority to implement changes. TQM focuses exclusively on quality, as compared with the SMT, in which quality is one of several goals.

The SMT approach requires significant changes in organizational structure, including accountability systems, policies, procedures, and job descriptions. Changing job descriptions may require collaboration with labor unions and possible changes in the collective bargaining agreement. Alternatively, use of TQM may also require minor structural changes that may need to be reflected in the labor contract.

Another difference between the two is the manner in which employees are trained. Using a TQM approach, the concept of lifelong training may be emphasized, but in reality, employees may only be trained in a limited number of TQM skills (process flow analysis, problem solving, etc.) because teams tend to turn over.

## HRD PROGRAMS AS SOCIOTECHNICAL SYSTEMS INTERVENTION TECHNIQUES

The role HRD professionals play in sociotechnical systems (STS) interventions is similar to their role with respect to human processual and technostructural interventions. That is, they play three specific roles. First, HRD practitioners can be responsible for designing and implementing the training programs needed to make STS work. Second, they meet the less evident, but equally great need to help employees adjust to new roles within the STS design. With so much emphasis on productivity and quality improvement, employees feel considerable pressure to change. HRD practitioners must be able to assist the change manager in correctly diagnosing the system's readiness to accept change and provide help in designing the appropriate change strategy that helps individual employees make the adjustments.

Third, because STS designs also emphasize participation, the HRD practitioner should also assist in determining the appropriate level of employee participation — representative or consultative. *Representative* programs allow employee participation on organizational committees such as advisory committees, employee councils, grievance committees, safety committees, and even boards of directors. Membership on these committees can be determined through appointment, self-selection, or election. If representatives are to be appointed, it is particularly important for the change manager to ensure that appointees understand and communicate the needs and concerns of the employees they represent. *Consultative* programs allow employees to participate directly in job-related issues that affect their daily work life. This is the approach used by most SMTs.

## TYPES OF INTERVENTIONS: ORGANIZATIONAL TRANSFORMATION

Generally speaking, organization transformation (OT) efforts focus on articulating a new vision for the organization, with the purpose of redefining the desired organizational culture, mission, and strategy. In this section, we will discuss four types of OT interventions — cultural change, strategic change, learning organizations, and high performance work systems.

### CULTURAL INTERVENTIONS

**Organizational culture** is defined as a system of learned, shared values, beliefs, and norms that are used to interpret elements in the environment and to guide all kinds of behavior.[126] Organizational culture is not something that is found in a mission statement or a corporate policy manual. Rather, organizational culture is communicated and reinforced through organizational mechanisms like the ones in Table 14-4.

Organizational cultural interventions involve more than simply restating values, beliefs, or norms, and communicating them to individuals. **Cultural changes**

**■ TABLE 14-4**

MECHANISMS THAT SUSTAIN ORGANIZATIONAL CULTURE

1. what managers pay attention to

2. the ways managers react to critical incidents

3. role modeling, coaching, and organizational training programs

4. criteria for allocating rewards and status

5. criteria for recruitment, selection, promotion, and removal from the organization

SOURCE: From R. W. Woodman (1989). Organization change and development: New areas for inquiry and action. *Journal of Management, 15*(2), 217.

involve a complex process of replacing an existing paradigm or way of thinking with another. For example, if an organization wants to become *multicultural* (integrating aspects of other cultures into the fabric of the organization), it must be able to make some fundamental changes to existing organizational paradigms (e.g., valuing cultural differences). The organization will take on a new set of values (as espoused in the vision and mission) that will affect how individual workers relate to others, both in and outside their work setting. This topic will be discussed in more detail in Chapter 15.

## STRATEGIC CHANGES

**Strategic change** is defined as any fundamental change in the organizational purpose or mission requiring systemwide changes (e.g., downsizing). Systemwide changes can be perceived as having three dimensions — size, depth, and pervasiveness.[127] The *size* of the change refers to the number of employees affected by the change. The *depth* of the change refers to the extent to which the change involves limited structural changes or goes to core values of the organization. The *pervasiveness* of the change refers to how many functions and hierarchical levels of the organization will be directly impacted by the change. As the organization moves along any or all of these dimensions, the change process becomes more complex.

Strategic interventions may be necessary when an organization is faced with external pressures to change and adapt. External pressures come from many sources, including the economic, social, legal, and political arenas. Table 14-5 lists some of the more common economic pressures. Organizations unable to create a "dynamic fit" between their own variables and the demands imposed by their environments will face decline and possible elimination.[128] For example, with the cutback in defense spending, many defense-oriented manufacturers have been faced with a reduction in the size and number of defense contracts. In order to adapt to this change, these organizations must consider changing their purpose or mission so that they can convert their manufacturing focus to nonmilitary purposes.

■ **TABLE 14-5**

ECONOMIC PRESSURES ON ORGANIZATIONS

| External Pressures | How Organizations Perceive Pressures |
| --- | --- |
| increasing competition | market imperatives |
| changing stakeholder expectations | new opportunities |
| changing workforce | cultural pressures |
| technological developments | technological imperatives |
| new laws and regulations | legal constraints |
| change in financial markets | economic pressures |

SOURCE: From S. A. Mohrman & A. M. Mohrman (1989). The environment as an agent of change. In A. M. Mohrman, et al. (eds.). *Large scale organizational change* (35–47). San Francisco: Jossey-Bass.

When organization transformation change involves reorganizing parts of the organization, the effects are felt by the employees. For example, during the 1980s over 500 of the largest organizations reorganized their operations, many as a result of mergers and acquisitions, resulting in layoffs and job changes.[129] One such company, General Electric, acquired 338 businesses and sold off 232 — in addition to closing seventy-three plants — between 1980 and 1986. These changes resulted in the loss of tens of thousands of jobs.[130] Beyond the elimination of jobs, **mergers** may require realignment of reporting lines, policies, procedures, allocation processes, and control systems. Depending on the size of the merging organizations, the effects can be very disruptive, particularly to the managers.

**Acquisitions** may be less disruptive than mergers. It is possible that many of the operational components of the acquired organization will remain intact. Some acquisitions involve merging executive offices to establish command and control functions. In most acquisitions, the employees experience many job-related losses that may affect their ability to perform their jobs.[131] These are listed and explained in Table 14-6; the feelings that such losses generate must be addressed as part of the overall change strategy.

An example of a strategic change intervention technique is downsizing of the organization — reducing the number of departments, management levels, and/or overall employees. As stated earlier, most large organizations have announced cutbacks in recent years. Even the few U.S. organizations (e.g., IBM, Digital Equipment Corporation) that have historically avoided layoffs in favor of retraining have made major cutbacks. An anticipated cutback can paralyze some organizations and employees, particularly if employees have a history of continued employment. The effects of a cutback also linger well beyond its implementation among employees who survive the purge. These employees may experience low morale, a decline in productivity, greater distrust of management, and excessive caution.[132]

**▪ TABLE 14-6**

| Feeling | Why? |
| --- | --- |
| 1. Loss of hierarchical status | Often the acquiring company becomes the boss. |
| 2. Loss of knowledge of firm | Procedures and people change. |
| 3. Loss of trusted subordinates | People tend to be shifted around. |
| 4. Loss of network | New connections are formed. |
| 5. Loss of control | Acquiring company usually makes the decisions. |
| 6. Loss of future | No one knows what will happen. |
| 7. Loss of job definition | Most things are in flux for a while. |
| 8. Loss of physical location | Moving is typical in mergers. |
| 9. Loss of friends or peers | Often people leave, are fired, or transfer. |

SOURCE: From J. R. Galosy (1990). The human factors in mergers and acquisitions. *Training and Development Journal, 44,* 90. Copyright 1990, the American Society for Training and Development. All rights reserved. Reprinted by permission.

## BECOMING A LEARNING ORGANIZATION

The earlier success with TQM and continuous improvement programs was the genesis of the learning organization approach. One of the key components of a successful TQM intervention is an emphasis on learning by everyone involved in the process. Managers and employees alike are asked to 1) learn a common language for improvement, 2) learn new tools and techniques, and 3) learn to take the initiative in improving work outcomes. TQM focuses on specific processes and tasks, which sometimes does not lead to the kinds of flexible and adaptive thinking that organizations need to compete in a turbulent environment. Further, the lessons learned are often not shared and applied outside of the specific area in which they are learned. Some organizations have realized that they must be able to develop the capacity to transfer knowledge across the organization by collaborating and sharing expertise and information that is unbounded by status, space, and time. This emphasis on continuous learning, changing, and adapting led to the emergence of a new OT intervention in the 1990s referred to as a **learning organization.**

*DEFINITION AND ORGANIZATION LEARNING LEVELS.*   A learning organization is an organization in which "everyone is engaged in identifying and solving problems, enabling the organization to continuously experiment, improve, and increase its capability."[133] This approach involves a shift in an organizational paradigm — or gamma B change — because employees are expected to continuously learn as they produce. Learning can occur on at least three different levels:

1. *Single-loop learning* emphasizes the identification of problems and then taking corrective action.[134]

2. *Double-loop learning* emphasizes the understanding of basic assumptions and core values that led to a particular problem, and a willingness to change them.[135]

3. *Deuterolearning* is directed at the learning process by improving how the organization performs single- and double-loop learning[136]

Chris Argyris makes the following point about learning:

> If learning is to persist, managers and employees must look inward. In particular, they must learn how the very way they go about defining and solving problems can be a source of problems in its own right. I have coined the terms single-loop and double-loop learning to capture a crucial distinction. To give a simple analogy: A thermostat that automatically turns on the heat whenever the temperature in a room drops below 68 degrees is a good example of single-loop learning. A thermostat that could ask, "Why am I set at 68 degrees?" and then explore whether or not some other temperature might more economically achieve the goal of heating the room would be engaging in double-loop learning (p. 6).[137]

*Single-loop learning* is commonplace in continuous improvement programs, because employees are taught to identify problems and correct them. This type of learning is still important in the day-to-day performance of a learning organization. *Double-loop learning* represents a radical shift in the way employees learn, because it involves changing basic assumptions and core values about how they work. For example, a trainer may become frustrated when he finds out that several training programs were not being well received by trainees. Upon reflection, the trainer might realize that these programs were designed five years ago and have become outdated. Further, the trainer might realize that the practice of HRD staff members relying on their own intuition and knowledge of the organization to determine training needs is not sufficient in these changing times. The trainer then surmises that if the training program is going to be effective in the future, the training design philosophy and approach must be changed and updated. This realization should prompt the trainer to conduct a needs assessment and update the design. *Deuterolearning,* the highest level of learning, is essentially learning to learn. Returning to the example, deuterolearning will have taken place if the trainer encourages other staff members to view all of the organization's training programs as works-in-progress and adopt a mind-set of continually adapting programs to meet the organization's changing needs.

ORGANIZATIONAL DIMENSIONS THAT SUPPORT A LEARNING ORGANIZATION. Researchers and practitioners have an array of notions of what fosters learning in organizations. They've identified at least five different organizational dimensions of a learning organization: structure, information systems, HRM practices, organizational culture, and leadership.

1. **Structure.** One of the key dimensions of a learning organization is the reduction or removal of hierarchical barriers that divide managers and

employees. In place of these barriers, learning organizations have implemented more collaborative structures like self-managed teams and cross-functional teams. Teams provide a natural setting for sharing and disseminating information. If teams develop a learning capacity, they become a microcosm for other teams in the organization. Teams can serve as an incubator for new ideas, because their limited size and focus permit them to mobilize their resources and experiment more efficiently than larger units. New knowledge gained through team learning can be propagated to other teams or individuals, although there is no guarantee this will occur.[138]

2. **Information acquisition, sharing, and retention.** While individuals and teams can learn, solve problems, and create new ideas, the organization will not have learned unless this new knowledge is acquired, stored, and made available to other organizational members, both now and in the future.[139] Indeed, there is a strong and growing interest in the topic of "knowledge management."[140] To create a learning organization, management must institute structures and practices that encourage information sharing and retention. This includes innovative and state-of-the-art information systems. Knowledge can be acquired from both internal and external sources. Internal sources would involve interactions between group members who can think insightfully about complex issues and are able to use their combined potential.[141] For example, General Electric's Corporate Executive Council meets quarterly to share information, ideas, and concerns and to examine best practices both within and outside the industry "to stimulate broad-range thinking."[142] External sources would be unlimited, including organizational reports, industry reports, literature, and events. Knowledge sharing is continuous during all kinds of team interactions. Even if the team members are in different locations around the world, they can still share and communicate electronically.

3. **HRM practices.** A number of human resource management practices are necessary to support a learning organization. For example, performance appraisal and reward systems that reinforce long-term performance and the development and sharing of new skills and knowledge are particularly important.[143] In addition, the HRD function in a learning organization may be radically changed to keep the emphasis on continuous learning. In a learning organization, every employee must take the responsibility for acquiring and transferring knowledge. Formal training programs, developed in advance and delivered according to a preset schedule, are insufficient to address shifting training needs and encourage timely information sharing. Rather, HRD professionals must become learning *facilitators*. Their role should be to assist, consult, and advise teams on how best to approach learning. They must be able to develop new mechanisms for cross-training peers — team members — and new systems for capturing and sharing information.[144] To do this, HRD professionals must be able to think systematically and understand how to foster learning within groups and across the organization.

4. **Organizational culture.** As mentioned earlier, an organization's culture is made up of the shared beliefs, expectations, and behavioral patterns that define the organization's identity to its members. In a learning organization, the organizational culture contains elements that promote learning and knowledge sharing throughout the organization. For example, learning often requires some amount of risk. In a learning organization, risk taking in situations that represent opportunities to learn is not only encouraged, it is expected and rewarded. Mistakes are more likely to be viewed as opportunities to learn, rather than as failures. One of the challenges in becoming a learning organization is to move individuals and groups toward this new set of expectations and norms.[145]

5. **Leadership.** The role of the leader is critical to a learning organization. A leader in a learning organization is viewed by some theorists and practitioners as someone who can move the organization toward the kinds of culture, systems, and practices that are needed to support this philosophy. Peter Senge argues that this kind of leadership is needed not only at the top of a learning organization, but at every level.[146] He advocates three essential types of leaders:

   a) *Executive leaders* are top mangers who must create a vision that embraces organizational learning principles, creates a new culture, and provides support to local line leaders. These individuals are also the transformational leaders who teach, guide, and continually reinforce the organizational vision (see Chapter 13).

   b) *Local line leaders,* or change managers, usually heads of divisions or major departments, provide the impetus for change by experimenting with new learning capabilities that may produce desired results. It is critical that they get actively involved in developing learning linkages throughout their unit to provide access to new information.

   c) The *internal networkers or community builders,* or change agents, are "seed carriers" who assist local line leaders in experimenting with and diffusing new ideas. This is a role that HRD practitioners can fill.

*EFFECTIVENESS OF LEARNING ORGANIZATIONS.*  Many anecdotal examples describe organizations that have become learning organizations, including Motorola, Zytec, and Toyota.[147] However, empirical research demonstrating the effectiveness of learning organization interventions is sparse. One of the problems in the learning organization literature is that theorists and practitioners have projected a wide range of ideas and techniques onto this term. Consequently, it is difficult to design a learning organization intervention and difficult to combine research evidence from different studies. Despite these problems, there still seems to be considerable interest in the learning organization concept.

## HIGH PERFORMANCE WORK SYSTEMS

The high performance work system (HPWS) is another approach that has emerged from the experiences of companies involved in continuous improvement. Today, there is no universal description of what constitutes a high performance workplace. Typically, HPWS are multifaceted, involving different combinations of the intervention strategies discussed earlier. According to Martha Gephart, HPWS intervention strategies have some common characteristics, including "self-managed teams, quality circles, flatter organizational structures, new flexible technologies, innovative compensation schemes, increased training, and continuous improvement."[148] These elements do not exist as separate initiatives. Rather, they are tied together as a *system* with a strategic focus and results-oriented work and management processes. According to Gephart, high performance work systems are organized around eight core principles:

1. They are aligned to an organization's competitive strategy.

2. Clear goals and outcomes are customer driven; individual, team, and organizational goals and outcomes are aligned.

3. Work is organized around processes that create products and services.

4. They include process-oriented tracking and management of results.

5. Organization is by work units that are linked to processes — which enhances ownership, problem solving, and learning.

6. Workplace structures and systems facilitate focus, accountability, cycle time, and responsiveness.

7. They are characterized by collaboration, trust, and mutual support.

8. Strategic change management is key.[149]

A framework for understanding high performance work systems can be seen in Table 14-7.[150] This table shows that an HPWS is argued to have alignment or fit in terms of overall strategy, organizational goals, and internal goals. That is, the organizational structure, management practices, HR systems, and other work practices all need to function together to produce high level outcomes for the organization, its employees, and its customers.

One of the largest U.S. companies that has implemented the HPWS concept is Xerox. It began its transformation in the early 1980s when faced with growing competition from the Japanese. The company began its transformation with the introduction of TQM (referred to as "leadership through quality") in 1984 and the introduction of self-managing teams in 1986. Its strategy began to falter when the company realized that unless other organization systems changed as well, the transformation would not be successful. In particular, team members complained that they were still being evaluated and rewarded as individuals, but they were told to act as a team. This led to a complete refocusing of the organizational design to create a better fit between people, work, information, and technology. Even though the HPWS were still centered on self-managed teams, the company emphasized 1) customer-focused work, 2) clear organizational vision and goals, 3) continuous total process management, 4) accessible information, 5) enriched, motivating work, 6) empowered human resource practices, and 7) flexible and adaptable systems. The return on this significant investment of time and energy was that the company received more than twenty awards for its achievements and the company stock rose dramatically from $29 a share in 1990 to $160 a share in 1996.[151]

■ **TABLE 14-7**

High Performance Work Systems Framework

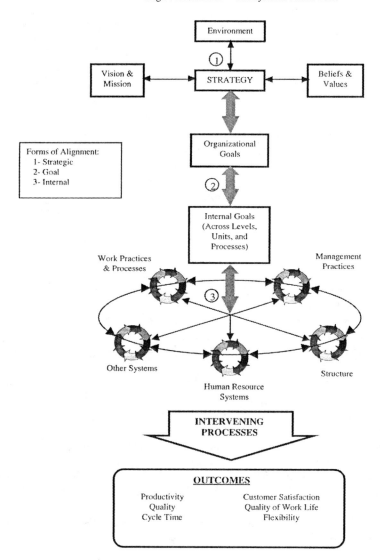

SOURCE: M. E. Van Buren & J. M. Werner, (1996). High performance work systems. *Business and Economic Review, 43*(1), October-December, 15–23. Reprinted by permission.

At Texas Instruments (TI), the introduction of self-managed teams led to some improvement in organizational efficiency and quality, but not as much as management had hoped for.[152] In 1991, a Higher Performing Organizational Development Unit was formed at TI. New initiatives included job enrichment, cross-functional teams, extensive cross-training, and strengthened individual incentives. The TI example emphasizes how the system of the HPWS should enhance the effectiveness of each of its components.

Although research exists about the separate components of an HPWS, as yet little empirical research investigates these systems as a whole. For example, Jeffrey Pfeffer recently amassed considerable evidence for the effectiveness of various high performance work practices, including the use of self-managed teams, extensive employee training, and reduced barriers and status distinctions between management and employees.[153] Further, Edward Lawler and colleagues surveyed Fortune 1000 companies and found that companies with high use of employee involvement and TQM practices had greater return on investment than companies with low use of such practices (14.6 percent vs. 9.0 percent).[154] More recently, Robert Vandenberg and colleagues studied the impact of various "high involvement" practices on the return on equity and employee turnover at forty-nine life insurance companies. One key finding of this study was that the various high involvement practices (e.g., use of teams, incentives, training, and organizational goal clarity) were *collectively* related to organizational effectiveness, and this relationship was positive and statistically significant.[155] We expect further evidence to accumulate concerning the value to organizations of viewing themselves and their work practices as integrated high performance work systems.

### EFFECTIVENESS OF ORGANIZATION TRANSFORMATION CHANGE STRATEGIES

Many anecdotal reports describe successful organization transformation (OT) strategies, but little is known about their effectiveness. The key to successful OT intervention is the articulation of an organizational vision that provides the guiding beliefs and principles (organizational culture), explains the purpose of the organization (mission), and defines how the organization should fulfill its mission (strategy). A survey of executives from twenty countries found that 1) 98 percent perceived that a "strong sense of vision" would be the most important executive trait to be exhibited, 2) the most important executive skill would be "strategy formulation to achieve a vision," and 3) 90 percent perceive a lack of confidence in their own skills and ability to conceive a vision (p. 84).[156] The latter finding is somewhat disconcerting, given the number of organizations that have initiated OT interventions.

In their analysis of successful OT interventions, Trahant and Burke found that the single most determinant predictor of success "is strong committed leadership in the earliest stages of change — hands down."[157] Transformational leaders, as discussed in Chapter 13, emphasize emotional support and inspirational motivation as essential in creating a vision for the organization, hold middle management accountable for changes, and reshape management styles to meet the need of the workers.[158] Transformational leaders must also maintain a long-term view, and not just focus on short-term results, in order to bring about meaningful and lasting change. They must be willing to move from the traditional change mode that looks at isolated programs to one that sees all activities that can be continuously improved.[159]

### ROLE OF HRD PRACTITIONERS IN DESIGN OF OT CHANGE

To say that OT change will have an impact on employees is an understatement. With that in mind, let's take a look at several roles that can be assumed by HRD practitioners. First, they can serve on strategic change committees — not only to give advice on training and development, but also to help strategic planners look at various alternatives and their potential impact on people.[160] This role is key in all OT changes. Second, given the impact of mergers, acquisitions, and downsizing on workers, HRD practitioners must be involved in addressing these issues during the planning stages of such changes. Among other things, management must pay special attention to communicating with employees about the reasons for cutbacks and why they are being made. HRD practitioners can help facilitate awareness sessions. In this role, they can help employees deal with the realities of change. As discussed earlier, the role of the HRD professional needs to be more facilitative in OT interventions like high performance work systems.

Also, the traditional structure of the HRD function, with its separate goals, staff, and space, is generally inappropriate in organizations that implement the HPWS approach. Rather, the HRD function should be reorganized to ensure that training and development activities are integrated with other activities and functions so that learning opportunities are not missed.[161]

Many of the HRD programs and processes discussed in this book can be used as part of an overall change strategy. OD and HRD are closely related. Since the intent of most planned interventions is to ultimately bring about changes in individual behavior, it is difficult to introduce change without using HRD programs and processes. While the relationship between OD and HRD is more apparent at the human processual and technostructural levels, the need for HRD programs and processes is just as critical in organization transformation change interventions. Table 14-8 describes some examples of how HRD programs and processes contained in this text can be used as part of OD interventions.

### WHITHER ORGANIZATION DEVELOPMENT?

Organization development appears to be in a state of flux. As a field of study, it has long been known for its strong emphasis on employee well-being and humanistic values.[162] Yet, current efforts have sought to focus the field of OD more strongly on strategic business issues and on demonstrating its contributions to organizational performance.[163] As one example, TRW was a pioneer in the implementation of organization development techniques in the 1970s. However, by 1984, many line

**# TABLE 14-8**

| Level | Emphasis | HRD Application |
|---|---|---|
| Human processual | Human needs; job satisfaction | Career development; stress management; coaching |
| | Individual differences | Cross-cultural training |
| | Norms and values | Orientation; socialization |
| | Team effectiveness | Team training |
| Technostructural | Job competencies | Skills and technical training |
| Sociotechnical | Self-managed teams | Team training |
| | Total quality management | Quality training |
| Organization transformation | Reorganization (downsizing) | Employee assistance programs; management development |
| | Continuous learning | High performance work systems |

managers at TRW perceived HR and OD practitioners within their organization as having too little concern with business issues and organizational profitability.[164] TRW spent much of the 1980s and 1990s seeking to align HR (and OD) more closely with the strategic goals and direction of the organization. Quite frankly, we are skeptical that OD will be replaced by "change management" as a field of study, as some have advocated.[165] Further, we agree with Burke, who argued that OD must not lose its focus on employee well-being.[166] However, the tension between employee focus and organizational performance will remain. In our view, the holistic approaches (such as high performance work systems) provide the best opportunities to maintain a distinctive focus on both individual and organizational issues. What happens to organization development as a field of study remains to be seen. This much is clear: the need for successful organization development interventions has never been greater.

### SUMMARY

Organization development (OD) is defined as a process used to enhance the effectiveness of an organization and the well-being of its members through planned interventions. OD theory is divided into change process theory and implementation theory. Change process theory tries to explain the dynamics by which individuals, groups, and organizations change. Lewin views change as a three-stage process of unfreezing, transitional action (change), and refreezing. Implementation theory focuses on specific intervention strategies designed to induce changes. We discussed some of the underlying theories and concepts of four different types of interventions: human processual, technostructural, sociotechnical systems (STS) designs, and organization transformations.

**RETURN TO OPENING CASE**[1]

This issue was studied over several years by Professor Bjorn Hennestad of the Norwegian School of Management. Initially, both the CEO and the employees of this organization were very enthusiastic about moving forward with the change to a more participative style of management. After announcing this change, an implementation date was set for five months later. Your instructor has additional information as to what was done in this particular situation.

[1]Adapted from Hennestad, B. W. (2000). Implementing participative mangement: Transition issues from the field. *Journal of Applied Behavioral Science, 36*(3), September, 314-335.

We also introduced a model of planned change that consisted of four interrelated parts: 1) change interventions that alter 2) key targeted organizational variables that then affect 3) individual organizational members and their on-the-job behaviors, resulting in changes in 4) organizational outcomes. The focus of this model is on changing individual behaviors, which ultimately leads to improved organizational outcomes (e.g., performance), as well as individual development.

Three roles must be fulfilled when introducing organizational change — those of manager (client), change agent, and the individuals within the system being changed. The manager's role is to oversee the process. The influences generated within the system to promote change can vary, but the most important is that of members who participate directly in the process. The change agent's role is to consult, advise, and assist the manager in developing appropriate strategies for introducing change. In addition, some organizations hire external change agents (e.g., consultants).

We discussed some basic steps involved in designing a change strategy. In order to design an intervention strategy, the change manager, with the help of the change agent and others in the system, must be able to diagnose the existing environment for change, develop a plan of action, and evaluate the results of the action plan to determine if the desired changes have occurred. HRD professionals have a definite role in this process. Among other things, an HRD professional can help the change manager understand the full range of HRD programs and processes and determine which works best under different conditions.

We described four types of planned interventions — human processual, technostructural, sociotechnical, and organization transformation. Human processual interventions are directed at improving interpersonal, intragroup, and intergroup relations. The most common human processual intervention studies are survey feedback and team building. Technostructural interventions focus on improving the work content, work method, and relationships among workers, and lowering cost by replacing inefficient materials, methods, equipment, workflow designs, and costly unnecessary labor with more efficient technology. Sociotechnical interventions focus more on seeking innovative ways of increasing productivity and worker satisfaction through redesigning workflow structures, work methods, and work content. Organization transformation interventions are used for large-scale strategic, cultural changes, learning organization, and high performance work systems. These approaches are very complex and need to be managed from the top of the organization.

## KEY TERMS AND CONCEPTS

| | |
|---|---|
| action planning | intervention strategy |
| alpha changes | job characteristics model |
| alternative work schedules | job design/enlargement |
| beta changes | job enrichment |
| change agent | organization development |
| change manager | organization transformation |
| client | process consultation |
| cultural change | quality circles |
| downsizing | self-managed teams |
| flextime | sociotechnical systems interventions |
| force field analysis | survey feedback |
| gamma changes | team building |
| high performance work systems | technostructural interventions |
| human processual interventions | total quality management |

## QUESTIONS FOR DISCUSSION

1. Describe how an organization introduces change and how such changes can produce desired effects. Can an organization replicate another organization's procedure and get the same results each time? Why or why not?

2. Why is the role of the manager critical to the success of the intervention? Is it possible to have a successful intervention without the manager's direct involvement? If yes, under what conditions?

3. When are internal change agents more likely to be successful as compared with external change agents? If both are involved in the same intervention, what kinds of problems could arise? How are these problems resolved?

4. What change agent skills are necessary for helping a dysfunctional group become more effective? What if the problems are between the respective managers? What happens if they refuse the help of the change agent?

5. Describe how the skills needed for designing and implementing human processual interventions differ from those needed for technostructural interventions.

6. If you were a manager in a shoe manufacturing plant and you were asked to design and implement self-managed work teams, what kind of

intervention strategy would you use? How would you involve first-line supervision in this process? What kinds of problems would you anticipate?

7. Is organization transformation change a necessity for maintaining an efficient organization? Why or why not? Even though the empirical evidence to support organization transformation change intervention strategies is limited, why do organizations still use this approach? Identify and describe a situation where this approach would not be effective. Support your answer.

## REFERENCES

1. Alderfer, C. P. (1977). Organization development. *Annual Review of Psychology, 28,* 197–223; Beckhard, R. (1969). *Organization development: Strategies and models.* Reading, MA: Addison-Wesley; Beer, M., & Walton, E. (1990). Developing the competitive organization: Interventions and strategies. *American Psychologist, 45,* 154–161; French, W. L., & Bell C. H., Jr. (1990). *Organization development.* Reading, MA: Addison-Wesley; Friedlander, F., & Brown, L. D. (1974). Organization development. *Annual Review of Psychology, 25,* 313–341.

2. Locke, E. A., & Latham, G. P. (1990). *A theory of goal setting and task performance.* Englewood Cliffs, NJ: Prentice-Hall, 16.

3. French & Bell (1990), *supra* note 1, p. 102.

4. Woodman, R. W. (1989). Organization change and development: New areas for inquiry end action. *Journal of Management, 15,* 205–228.

5. Lewin, K. (1958). Group decision and social change. In E. E. Maccoby, T. M. Newcomb, and E. L. Hartley (eds.), *Readings in Social Psychology* (197–211). New York: Holt, Rinehart and Winston.

6. Schein, E. H. (1987). *Process consultation* (vol. 2). Reading, MA: Addison-Wesley.

7. Dent, E. B., & Goldberg, S. G. (1999). Challenging 'resistance to change.' *Journal of Applied Behavioral Science, 35*(1), 25–41.

8. *Ibid.*

9. *Ibid.*

10. Bennis, W. G., Benne, K. D., & Chin, R. (1961). *The planning of change.* New York: Holt, Rinehart and Winston.

11. Argyris, C. (1970). *Intervention theory and method: A behavioral science view.* Reading, MA: Addison-Wesley.

12. *Ibid,* 20.

13. Friedlander & Brown (1974), *supra* note 1.

14. Hackman, J. R., & Oldham, G. R. (1975). Development of the job diagnostic survey. *Journal of Applied Psychology, 60,* 159–170; Hackman, J. R., & Oldham, G. R. (1976). Motivation through the design of work: Test of a theory. *Organizational Behavior and Human Performance, 16,* 250–279; Hackman, J. R., & Oldham, G. R. (1980). *Work redesign.* Reading, MA: Addison-Wesley.

15. Cherns, A. (1987). Principles of sociotechnical design revisited. *Human Relations, 40,* 153–162.

16. Woodman (1989), *supra* note 4.

17. Nicholas, J. M. (1982). The comparative impact of organization development interventions on hard criteria measures. *Academy of Management Review, 7,* 531–542, p. 532.

18. Beckhard (1969), *supra* note 1, p. 3.

19. Beckhard, R. T., & Harris, R. (1987). *Organizational transitions: Managing complex change* (2nd ed.). Reading, MA: Addison-Wesley, 8.

20. Alderfer (1977), *supra* note 1; Beer, M., & Walton, E. (1987). Organization change and development. *Annual Review of Psychology, 38,* 339–367; Bullock, R. J., & Svyantek, D. J. (1987). The impossibility of using random strategies to study the organization development process. *Journal of Applied Behavioral Science, 23,* 255–262; Porras, J. I., & Berg, P. O. (1977). The impact of organization development. *Academy of Management Review, 3,* 249–266.

21. Bullock & Svyantek (1987), *supra* note 20.

22. Beer & Walton (1987), *supra* note 20.

23. Nicholas (1982), *supra* note 17.

24. Neuman, G. A., Edwards, J. E., & Raju, N. S. (1989). Organization development interventions: A meta-analysis of their effects on satisfaction and other attitudes. *Personnel Psychology, 42,* 461–489.

25. Guzzo, R. A., Jette, R. D., & Katzell, R. A. (1985). The effects of psychologically based intervention programs on worker productivity: A meta-analysis. *Personnel Psychology, 38,* 275–291.

26. Bennis et al. (1961), *supra* note 10; Porras, J. I., & Hoffer, S. J. (1986). Common behavior changes in successful organization development efforts. *Journal of Applied Behavioral Science, 22,* 477–494.

27. Woodman (1989), *supra* note 4, p. 206.

28. Porras, J. I., & Silvers, R. C. (1991). Organization development and transformation. *Annual Review of Psychology, 42,* 51–78.

29. *Ibid.*

30. *Ibid.*

31. Golembiewski, R. T., Billingsley, K., & Yeager, S. (1976). Measuring change and persistence in human affairs: Types of change generated by OD designs. *Journal of Applied Behavioral Science, 12,* 133–157; Porras & Silver (1991), *supra* note 28; Thompson, R. C., & Hunt, J. G. (1996). Inside the black box of alpha, beta, and gamma change: Using a cognitive-processing model to assess attitude structure. *Academy of Management Review, 21,* 655–690.

32. Porras & Silvers (1991), *supra* note 28, p. 57.

33. *Ibid*, 58.

34. Laabs, J. J. (1996). Leading organizational change. *Personnel Journal, 75*(7), 54–63.

35. Burke, W. W., Church, A. H., and Waclawski, J. (1993). What do OD practitioners know about managing change. *Leadership and Organization Development Journal, 14*(6), 3–11.

36. Demers, R., Forrer, S. E., Leibowith, Z., and Cahill, C. (1996). Commitment to change. *Training and Development, 50*(8), 22–26.

37. Burke, W. W. (1987). *Organization development.* Reading: Addison-Wesley.

38. Worren, N. A. M., Ruddle, K., & Moore, K. (1999). From organizational development to change management: The emergence of a new profession. *Journal of Applied Behavioral Science, 35*(3), 273–286.

39. Farias, G., & Johnson, H. (2000). Organizational development and change management: Setting the record straight. *Journal of Applied Behavioral Science, 36*(3), 376–379; though see the rejoinder by Worren, N. (2000). Response to Farias and Johnson's commentary. *Journal of Applied Behavioral Science, 36*(3), 380–381.

40. Pearce, C. L., & Osmand, C. P. (1996). Metaphors for change: The ALPs model of change management. *Organizational Dynamics, 24*(3), Winter, 23–35.

41. Beer & Walton (1987), *supra* note 20.

42. Kanter, R. M. (1983). *The change masters: Innovation for productivity in the American corporation.* New York: Simon & Schuster.

43. Hanson, R., Porterfield, R. I., & Ames, K. (1995). Employees empowerment at risk: Effects of recent NLRB ruling. *Academy of Management Executive, 9*(2), 45–54.

44. Friedlander & Brown (1974), *supra* note 1; Guzzo et al. (1985), *supra* note 25; Neuman et al. (1989), *supra* note 24; Nicholas (1982), *supra* note 17; Nicholas, J. M., & Katz, M. (1985). Research methods and reporting practices in organization development: A review and some guidelines. *Academy of Management Review, 10,* 737–749.

45. Nicholas (1982), *supra* note 17.

46. Alderfer (1977), *supra* note 1.

47. Alderfer, C. P., & Holbrook, J. (1973). A new design for survey feedback. *Education Urban Society, 5,* 437–464.

48. Lawler, E. E., III, (1986). *High-involvement management.* San Francisco: Jossey-Bass.

49. Nicholas (1982), *supra* note 17.

50. Hackman, J. R., & Walton, R. E. (1986). Leading groups in organizations. In P. S. Goodman and associates (eds.), *Designing effective work groups* (72–119), 78–79. San Francisco: Jossey-Bass.

51. Dyer, W. G. (1987). *Team building.* Reading, MA: Addison-Wesley, 36.

52. Guzzo et al. (1985), *supra* note 25; Neuman et al. (1989), *supra* note 24.

53. Neuman et al. (1989), *supra* note 24.

54. Guzzo et al. (1985), *supra* note 25.

55. Salas, E., Rozell, D., Mullen, B., & Driskell, J. E. (1999). The effect of team building on performance. *Small Group Research, 30*(3), 309–329.

56. Friedlander & Brown (1974), *supra* note 1.

57. Gerstein, M. S. (1987). *The technology connection.* Reading, MA: Addison-Wesley.

58. Guzzo et al. (1985), *supra* note 25; Neuman et al. (1989), *supra* note 24; Nicholas (1982), *supra* note 17; Nicholas & Katz (1985), *supra* note 44.

59. Nicholas (1982), *supra* note 17.

60. Campion, M. A., & McClelland, C. L. (1991). Interdisciplinary examination of the costs and benefits of enlarged jobs: A job design quasi-experiment. *Journal of Applied Psychology, 76,* 186–198.

61. Fried, Y., & Ferris, G. R. (1987). The validity of the job characteristics model: A review and meta-analysis. *Personnel Psychology, 40,* 287–318.

62. Loher, B. T., Noe, R. A., Moeller, N. L., & Fitzgerald, M. P. (1985). A meta-analysis of the relation of job characteristics to job satisfaction. *Journal of Applied Psychology, 70,* 280–289; Neuman et al. (1989), supra note 24.

63. Fried & Ferris (1987), *supra* note 61.

64. Christensen, K. (1990). Here we go into the "high flex" era. *Across the Board, 27*(7), 22–23.

65. Neuman et al. (1989), *supra* note 24.

66. Dunham, R. B., Pierce, J. L., & Casteneda, M. B. (1987). Alternate work schedules: Two field quasi-experiments. *Personnel Psychology, 40,* 215–242; Neuman et al. (1989), *supra* note 24; Pierce, J. L., Newstron, J. W., Dunham, R. B., & Barber, A. E. (1989). *Alternative work schedules.* Boston: Allyn and Bacon.

67. Bond, J., Galinsky, E., & Swanberg, J. (1998). *The 1997 national study of the changing workforce.* New York: Families and Work Institute.

68. Pierce et al. (1989), *supra* note 66.

69. Nicholas (1982), *supra* note 17; Guzzo et al. (1985), *supra* note 25; Neuman et al. (1989), *supra* note 24.

70. Guzzo et al., *supra* note 25.

71. *Ibid.*

72. Neuman et al. (1989), *supra* note 24.

73. *Ibid.*

74. Nicholas (1982), *supra* note 17.

75. Neuman et al. (1989), *supra* note 24, p. 480.

76. Fagenson, E. A., & Burke, W. W. (1990). The activities of organization-development practitioners at the turn of the decade of the 1990s — A study of their predictions. *Group and Organization Studies, 15*(4), December, 366–380; Guzzo et al. (1985), *supra* note 25; Neuman et al. (1989), *supra* note 24.

77. Fox, W. M. (1995). Sociotechnical system principles and guidelines: Past and present. *Journal of Applied Behavioral Science, 31*(1), 91–105.

78. Guzzo, R. A., & Dickson, M. W. (1996). Teams in organizations: Recent research on performance and effectiveness. *Annual Review of Psychology, 47,* 307–338.

79. Guzzo et al. (1985), *supra* note 25.

80. Steel, R. P., & Lloyd, R. F. (1988). Cognitive, affective, and behavioral outcomes of participation in quality circles: Conceptual and empirical findings. *Journal of Applied Behavioral Sciences, 24,* 1–17.

81. Park, S. (1991). Estimating success rates of quality circle programs: Public and private experiences. *Public Administration Quarterly, 15*(1), 133–146.

82. Botch, K., & Spangle, R. (1990). The effects of quality circles on performance and promotions. *Human Relations, 43,* 573–582.

83. Verney, T., Ackelsberg, R., & Holoviak, S. J. (1989). Participation and worker satisfaction. *Journal for Quality and Participation, 12*(3), 74–77; Townsend, T. M. (1990). Let employees carry the ball. *Personnel Journal, 69*(10), 30–36; Adam, E. E. (1991). Quality circle performance. *Journal of Management, 17,* 25–39.

84. Clark, S. G., & McGee, W. (1988). Evaluation: A method of transition — Our program is great . . . isn't it? *Journal for Quality and Participation, 11* (4), 50–54; Piczak, M. W. (1988). Quality circles come home. *Quality Progress, 21*(12), 37–39; Honeycutt, A. (1989). The key to effective quality circles. *Training and Development Journal, 43*(5), 81–84; Berman, S. J., & Hellweg, S. A. (1989). Perceived supervisor communication competence and supervisor satisfaction as a function of quality circle participation. *Journal of Business Communication, 26*(2) 103–122; Lansing, R. L. (1989). The power of teams. *Supervisory Management, 34*(2), 39–43; Tang, T. L., Tollison, P. S., & Whiteside, H. D. (1989). Quality circle productivity as related to upper-management, attendance, circle initiation, and collar color. *Journal of Management, 15,* 101–113; Steel, R. P., Jennings, K. R., & Lindsey, J. T. (1990). Quality circle problem solving and common cents: Evaluation study findings from a United States federal mint. *Journal of Applied Behavioral Science, 26,* 365–381.

85. Schonberger, R. J. (1992). Total quality management cuts a broad swath through manufacturing and beyond. *Organizational Dynamics, 20*(4), 16–28, p. 17.

86. Hale, R. L. (1989). Tennant Company: Instilling quality from top to bottom. *Management Review, 78*(2), 65.

87. Salemme, T. (1991). Lessons learned from employees about quality improvement efforts. *Tapping the Network Journal, 2*(2), 2–6.

88. McCormack, S. P. (1992). TQM: Getting it right the first time. *Training and Development, 46*(6), 43–46.

89. *Ibid.*

90. Ferketish, B. J., & Hayden, J. W. (1992). HRD and quality: The chicken or the egg? *Training and Development, 46*(1), 38–42; Hackman, J. R., & Wageman, R. (1995). Total quality management: Empirical, conceptual, and practical issues. *Administrative Science Quarterly, 40,* 309–342.

91. Bowen, D. E., & Lawler, E. E., III (1992). Total quality-oriented human resources management. *Organizational Dynamics, 20*(4), 29–41; Tollison, P. (1992). Assessing TQM training needs. *Journal for Quality and Participation, 15*(1), 50–54.

92. Hackman & Wageman (1995), *supra* note 90.

93. Schonberger (1992), *supra* note 85.

94. Bowen & Lawler (1992), *supra* note 91, p. 38.

95. Axland, S. (1991). Two awarded NASA's prize trophy. *Quality Progress, 24*(12), 51–52.

96. Johnson, J. G. (1991). The culture clock: TQM and doing the right thing right at the right time. *Journal for Quality and Participation, 14*(6), 1–14.

97. Altany, D. (1992). Cinderella with a drawl. *Industry Week, 241*(1), 49–51.

98. Reynolds, L. (1992). The Feds join the quality movement. *Management Review, 81*(4), 39–42.

99. Sensenbrenner, J. (1991). Quality for cities. *Nation's Business, 79*(10), 60, 62.

100. McCarthy, G. J. (1991). TQM is key to improving services, but it's not for every hospital. *Health Care Strategic Management, 9*(11), 18–20.

101. McWilliams, G. (1991, October 25). The public sector: A new lesson plan for college. *Business Week,* 144–145.

102. Velocci, A. L., Jr. (1991). TQM makes Rockwell tougher competitor. *Aviation Week and Space Technology, 135*(23), 68–69.

103. Spector, B., & Beer, M. (1994). Beyond TQM programmes. *Journal of Organizational Change Management, 7*(2), 63–70.

104. Hodgetts, R., Luthans, F., & Lee, S. M. (1994). New paradigm organizations: From total quality to learning to world-class. *Organizational Dynamics, 22*(3), Winter, 5–19.

105. Choi, T. Y., & Behling, O. G. (1997). Top managers and TQM success: One more look. *Academy of Management Executive, 11*(1), 37–47; Hackman & Wageman (1995), *supra* note 90.

106. Beer, M. & Eisenstat, R. A. (1996). Developing an organization capable of implementing strategy and learning. *Human Relations, 49*(5), 597–619.

107. Hackman & Wageman (1995), *supra* note 90; Collins, L. K., & Hill, F. M. (1998) Leveraging organizational transformation through incremental and radical approaches to change: Three case studies. *Total Quality Management, 9*(4/5), S30–S34.

108. *Ibid.*

109. Yusof, S. M., & Aspinwall, E. (2000). Total quality management implementation frameworks: Comparison and review. *Total Quality Management, 11*(3), May, 281–294.

110. Cohen, S. G., & Ledford, G. E., Jr., (1994). The effectiveness of self-managing teams: A quasi-experiment. *Human Relations, 47*, 13–43.

111. Wall, T. D., Kemp, N. J., Jackson, P. R., & Clegg, C. W. (1986). Outcomes of autonomous workgroups: A long-term field experiment. *Academy of Management Journal, 29*, 280–304; Goodman, P. S., Devadas, R., & Hughson, T. L. (1988). Groups and productivity: Analyzing the effectiveness of self-managing teams. In J. P. Campbell and R. J. Campbell (eds.), *Productivity in organizations* (295–325). San Francisco: Jossey-Bass; Schilder, J. (1992). Work teams boost productivity. *Personnel Journal, 71*(2), 67–71; Cohen, S. G., Ledford, G. E., Jr., and Spreitzer, G. M., (1996). A predictive model of self-managing work teams effectiveness. *Human Relations, 49*, 643–676; Industry Report. (1996). Who's learning what? *Training, 33*(10), 55–66.

112. Buck, J. T. (1995). The rocky road to team-based management. *Training and Development, 49*(4), 35–38.

113. Guzzo & Dickson (1996), *supra* note 78.

114. Gephart, M. A., Marsick, V. J., Van Buren, M. E., & Spiro, M. S. (1996). Learning organizations come alive. *Training and Development, 50*(12), 35–45.

115. Schilder (1992), *supra* note 111; Cohen et al. (1996), *supra* note 111; Stewart, G. L., & Manz, C. C. (1995). Leadership for self-managing work teams: A typology and integrative model. *Human Relations, 48*, 747–770; Industry Report, 1996, *supra* note 111.

116. Shipper, F., & Manz, C. C. (1992). An alternative road to empowerment. *Organizational Dynamics, 20*(3), 48–61, p. 49.

117. Versteeg, A. (1990). Self-directed work teams yield long-term benefits. *Journal of Business Strategy, 11*(6), 9–12.

118. Schilder (1992), *supra* note 111.

119. Brokaw, L., & Hartman, C. (1990). Managing the journey. *Inc., 12*(11), November, 44–50; Chad Schmidt, personal communication, November 9, 2000.

120. Musselwhite, E., & Moran, L. (1990). On the road to self-direction. *Journal of Quality and Participation*, 58–63.

121. Beekun, R. I. (1989). Assessing the effectiveness of sociotechnical interventions: Antidote or fad? *Human Relations, 42*, 877–897.

122. Cohen & Ledford (1994), *supra* note 110.

123. Wall et al. (1986), *supra* note 111.

124. Stewart, G. L., & Manz, C. C. (1995). Leadership for self-managing work teams: A typology and integrative model. *Human Relations, 48*, 747–770.

125. Kanter (1983), *supra* note 42, p. 258.

126. Geertz, C. (1973). *The interpretation of culture.* New York: Basic Books; Ott, J. S. (1989). *The organizational culture perspective.* Pacific Grove, CA: Brooks/Cole.

127. Ledford, G. E., Mohrman, S. A., Mohrman, A. M., & Lawler, E. E. (1989). The phenomenon of large scale organizational change. In A. M. Mohrman, S. A. Mohrman, G. E. Ledford, T. G. Cummings, and E. E. Lawler (eds.), *Large scale organizational change* (1–32). San Francisco: Jossey-Bass.

128. Lawrence, P. R. (1989). Why organizations change. In A. M. Mohrman, S. A. Mohrman, G. E. Ledford, T. G. Cummings, and E. E. Lawler (eds.), *Large scale organizational change* (48–61). San Francisco: Jossey-Bass.

129. Leana, C. R., & Feldman, D. C. (1990). When mergers force layoffs: Some lessons about managing the human resource problems. *Human Resource Planning, 12*(2), 123–140.

130. *Ibid.*

131. Galosy, J. R. (1990). The human factor in mergers and acquisitions. *Training and Development Journal, 44*(4), 90–95.

132. Rice, D., & Dreilinger, C. (1991). After the downsizing. *Training and Development Journal, 45*(5), 41–44.

133. Daft, R. L. (1997). *Management* (4th ed.) Fort Worth, TX: Dryden Press, 751.

134. Nevis, E. C., DiBella, A. J., & Gould, J. M. (1995). Understanding organizations as learning systems. *Sloan Management Review, 36*(2), 73–85; Hodgetts et al. (1994), *supra* note 104.

135. Argyris, C. (1994). The future of workplace learning and performance. *Training and Development, 48*(5), S36–S47; Senge, P. M. (1990). *The fifth discipline: The art and practice of the learning organization.* New York: Doubleday.

136. Cummings, T. G., & Worley, C. G. (1997). *Organization development and change* (6th ed.). Cincinnati: South-Western College Publishing.

137. Argyris, C. (1991). Teaching smart people how to learn. *Harvard Business Review,* May-June, 5–15, cited in Abernathy, D. J. (1999). *Training and Development, 53*(5), May, 80–84.

138. Senge (1990), *supra* note 135.

139. Gephart et al. (1996) *supra* note 114.

140. Burden, P., MacIntosh, M., Srikantaiah, T. K. (2000). *Knowledge management: The bibliography.* Medford, NJ: Information Today, Inc.; Hicks, S. (2000). Are you ready for knowledge management? *Training and Development, 54*(9), September, 71–72.

141. Senge (1990), *supra* note 135.

142. Gephart et al. (1996) *supra* note 114.

143. Cummings & Worley (1997), *supra* note 136.

144. Gephart et al. (1996) *supra* note 114.

145. *Ibid.*

146. Senge, P. M. (1996). Leading learning organizations. *Training and Development, 50*(12), 36–37.

147. Hodgetts et al. (1994), *supra* note 104.

148. Gephart, M. A. (1995). The road to high performance. *Training and Development, 49*(6), 35–38, p. 30.

149. *Ibid.*, 38.

150. Van Buren, M. E., & Werner, J. M. (1996). High performance work systems. *Business and Economic Review, 43*(1), October-December, 15–23.

151. Gephart, M. A., & Van Buren, M. E. (1996). Building synergy: The power of high performance work systems. *Training and Development, 50*(10), 21–32.

152. Gephart (1995), *supra* note 148.

153. Pfeffer, J. (1998). *The human equation: Building profits by putting people first.* Boston: Harvard Business School Press.

154. Lawler, E. E., III, Mohrman, S. A., & Ledford, G. E., Jr. (1995). *Creating high performance organizations: Practices and results of employee involvement and quality management in Fortune 1000 companies.* San Francisco: Jossey-Bass.

155. Vandenberg, R. J., Richardson, H. A., & Eastman, L. J. (1999). The impact of high involvement work processes on organizational effectiveness: A second-order latent variable approach. *Group and Organization Management, 24*(3), 300–339.

156. Lipton, M (1996). Demystifying the development of organizational vision. *Sloan Management Review, 37*(4), 83–92.

157. Trahant, B., & Burke, W. W. (1996). Traveling through transitions. *Training and Development, 50*(2), 37–41, p. 41.

158. Belasen, A. T., Benke, M., Di Podova, L. N., & Fortunato, M. V. (1996). Downsizing and the hyper-effective manager: The shifting importance of managerial roles during organizational transformation. *Human Resource Management, 35*(1), 87–117.

159. Gill, S. J. (1995). Shifting gears for high performance. *Training and Development, 49*(5), 25–31.

160. Gall, A. L. (1986). What is the role of HRD in a merger? *Training and Development Journal, 40*(4), 18–23.

161. Gill (1995), *supra* note 159.

162. Farias & Johnson (2000), *supra* note 39.

163. Worren et al. (1999), *supra* note 38.

164. Rogers, G. C., & Beer, M. (1996). TRW's Information Services Division: Strategic Human Resource Management. Boston: Harvard Business School Press, Case #9–496–003.

165. Worren et al. (1999), *supra* note 38.

166. Burke, W. W. (1997). The new agenda for organization development. *Organizational Dynamics, 25*, 7–21.

# 13

# LEGAL ISSUES IMPACTING HUMAN RESOURCE MANAGEMENT

## QUESTIONS TO CONSIDER WHILE READING THIS CHAPTER

1. What specific laws and regulations apply to the human resource function?
2. What must the employees do to prove their case of discrimination?
3. What should companies do to remedy a discriminatory situation?
4. What could a company do to prevent a discriminatory practice?

## THE EMERGING ISSUE

Federal, state, and local legislation is often cited by many emerging firms as one of the major barriers to growth. Compliance with legislation covering hiring practices, compensation, employee safety, and labor relations is viewed as a major cost of doing business. For example, when the federal government develops more stringent environmental or ergonomic standards for manufacturing firms, smaller/newer firms suffer because they often lack the capital required to invest in plant redesign, new equipment, and increased employee training. Many owners or managers of smaller firms also lack legal knowledge of discrimination laws and in many cases view these laws as an infringement on their right to run their own business. However, because of the huge expenses related to fighting employee lawsuits or paying government fines, employers in emerging firms must integrate legal compliance into daily management practices.

## CHAPTER OVERVIEW

Legislation and government regulations have done more to spur the development of the human resource function than any other environmental factor. To a great extent the human resource management function has been largely reactive in respect to the legislation. Specifically, requirements for job analysis, test validity, selection, compensation, labor relations, and safety were born out of a particular piece of legislation. This chapter will provide an overview of the four major areas of government legislation, describe in detail equal employment opportunity legislation and requirements (giving special attention to legislation passed in the 1990s), and discuss the legal concepts of employment-at-will and negligent hiring/retention. Also, the concepts of adverse impact and affirmative action will be described.

## THE MAJOR TYPES OF LEGISLATION AND REGULATIONS

The practice of human resource management is heavily influenced by legislation in four areas. These functional areas include equal employment opportunity, compensation, labor relations, and safety. Exhibit 2.1 presents the intent of the legislation

## INTENT OF MAJOR EMPLOYMENT LEGISLATION

### EQUAL EMPLOYMENT OPPORTUNITY

- To prohibit discrimination in employment based on minority/protected group status
- To establish an enforcement agency—The Equal Employment Opportunity Commission (EEOC)
- To encourage government contractor/subcontractor compliance with EEO legislation and regulations

### COMPENSATION AND BENEFITS

- To establish pay equity among protected groups
- To establish pay guidelines for government contractors
- To support the concept of "prevailing wage"
- To provide guidelines regarding minimum wage, overtime, and child labor
- To provide administrative requirements for pension/retirement plans and other employee benefits

### EMPLOYEE SAFETY AND HEALTH

- To provide requirements for establishing a safe workplace
- To establish an enforcement agency—The Occupational Safety and Health Administration

### LABOR RELATIONS

- To protect employee rights to unionize
- To establish bargaining rules for management and labor
- To establish an enforcement agency—The National Labor Relations Board

---

and regulations in these areas. Specifically, compensation laws deal with issues such as minimum wage, overtime, child labor, garnishments, retirement, income projection, paying the prevailing wage in the market for federal contract work, and worker's compensation for work-related accidents. Labor relations laws focus on issues such as union elections and decertifications, unfair labor practices, and plant downsizing notifications or closure. Safety laws focus mainly on employee rights to a safe and healthy work environment, especially in the areas of air quality, safe machine operation and shut down, plant layout, chemical hazards, and blood-borne pathogens. Finally, equal employment opportunity legislation, the main focus of this chapter, addresses illegal discrimination in the areas of recruitment, selection, compensation, training, and labor and employee relations. Protected groups are those individuals who are provided legal protection by the discrimination laws described in the next section of this chapter. The laws and regulations applying to compensation, labor relations, and safety will be discussed in more detail in chapters coming later in this book. Specifically, the impact of legislation and regulations relating to equal employment opportunity will be the focus of the remainder of this chapter.

## EQUAL EMPLOYMENT OPPORTUNITY LEGISLATION AND REGULATIONS

Most equal employment opportunity legislation centers on the concept of illegal discrimination. It is necessary at this point to differentiate illegal discrimination

■ **EXHIBIT 2.2**

**MAJOR LEGISLATION ADDRESSING EMPLOYMENT DISCRIMINATION**

| Source/Law | Intent | Administration/Agency |
|---|---|---|
| U.S. Constitution | | |
| 5th Amendment | Protects against federal violation of "due process" | Federal courts |
| 13th Amendment | Abolishes slavery and "signs" of slavery such as race discrimination | Federal courts |
| 14th Amendment | Protects against state violations of "due process" and ensures equal protection | Federal courts |
| Civil Rights Act, 1866 and 1871 | Establishes the right of all citizens to enforce contracts and to sue for damages | Federal courts |
| Equal Pay Act, 1963 | Prohibits sex discrimination in wages and salary | Equal Employment Opportunity Commission (EEOC) |
| Civil Rights Act, 1964 (Title VII) | Prohibits discrimination in employment on the basis of race, sex, religion, or national origin | EEOC and federal courts |
| Age Discrimination in Employment Act, 1967 (amended 1978 and 1986) | To prohibit discrimination against persons over 40 years of age | EEOC and federal courts |
| Equal Employment Opportunity Act, 1972 | To extend coverage of the 1964 Civil Rights Act to include both public and private sectors, educational institutions, unions, and employment agencies | EEOC and federal courts |
| Pregnancy Discrimination Act, 1978 | Requires employers to treat pregnancy just like any other illness covered by the organization's benefit package | EEOC and federal courts |
| Immigration Reform and Control Act, 1986 | Requires verification of right to work in the United States (I9 form) | Department of Labor |
| Americans with Disabilities Act, 1990 | Prohibits discrimination against handicapped persons | EEOC and Department of Labor |
| Civil Rights Act, 1991 | Refines coverage of existing EEO legislation and allows for jury trials and punitive awards for intentional discrimination | EEOC and Department of Labor |
| Executive Orders 11246, 11375, and 11478 | Prohibits discrimination by contractors or subcontractors of federal agencies and prescribes merit as basis for federal employment policy | Office of Contract Compliance Programs (OFCCP) |

from legal discrimination. By its nature, the human resource function is a discriminatory activity. Decisions have to be made on whom to hire, fire, promote, give pay raises, etc. It is when these decisions are not made according to Equal Employment Opportunity Act requirements that a firm may find it has problems with illegal discrimination. Illegal discrimination can be formally defined as "unfair actions towards members of a protected class."[1] A protected class is a group of individuals who are protected by one or more of the congressional acts described below. The specific laws and Executive Orders are summarized in Exhibit 2.2.

## CONGRESSIONAL ACTS

*Civil Rights Act of 1866 and 1871.* The Civil Rights Act of 1866 prohibits racial discrimination in making and enforcing contracts. In the field of human resource management, this could include hiring and promotion decisions. The Civil Rights Act of 1871 amended the 1866 act and asserts that when acting under coverage of any local, state, or federal government unit, all persons must be given the same rights.[2]

*Equal Pay Act of 1963.* The Equal Pay Act of 1963 (EPA) was passed as an amendment to the Fair Labor Standards Act of 1938 (FLSA). The EPA prohibits gender discrimination in the payment of wages to men and women working in the same jobs in the same company. The law states that two jobs are equal if they require the same skill, effort, and responsibility and are performed under the same working conditions. Exceptions are made when payment is based on a seniority system, a merit system, or any factor other than gender. Another exception is when a system measuring earnings by quality or quantity of production (i.e., piece rates) is used. This act covers private employers engaged in commerce or in the production of goods for commerce who have two or more employees.

Although not supported by a federal law, the theory of comparable worth is often associated with the Equal Pay Act. The difference is that the Equal Pay Act assures equal pay for people doing equal work whereas comparable worth suggests that jobs equal in value to the employer be equal in pay. The problem primarily affects women since they still earn less than 80 percent of the income that men earn. The big controversy concerns why this difference occurs. Four major reasons for this pay discrepancy can be presented. First, some people suggest that females choose occupations that do not compensate them as well as others (e.g., a teacher). Women may be attracted to jobs that pay less in monetary compensation but which offer other intrinsic rewards such as flexible hours or training. Second, females are subject to a "glass ceiling" in some corporations in which very few women are promoted into higher paying positions. Third, differences in pay may be the result of our society's valuing traditionally female-dominated positions less than traditionally male-dominated positions. A common example of this problem is the pay for nurses versus engineers. Fourth, some organizations intentionally discriminate against women. Comparable worth attempts to stop this discrimination.

The justices of the Supreme Court are still inconsistent in their stand on this issue. They believe that making decisions in this area would require an expertise in job evaluations that is found in organizations and not in the Court.

*Title VII of the Civil Rights Act of 1964.* This is one of the major laws regulating how employers select employees. Title VII prohibits employers, unions, and employment agencies from discriminating with regard to any employment decision (i.e., selection, compensation, firing, or other benefits of employment) against an employee on the basis of gender, race, color, religion, or national origin.

In addition, this act created the Equal Employment Opportunity Commission (EEOC). The EEOC was given the power to investigate and challenge any person or company who is allegedly participating in unlawful employment procedures identified in Title VII. The EEOC was originally established to investigate discrimination based on race, color, religion, gender, or national origin. Now, however, they also investigate charges of discrimination based on pay, age, and handicap.

The EEOC is the agency that enforces the Civil Rights Act. When a charge of discrimination is filed, the EEOC first tries to convince the parties to settle the case themselves through conciliation. If this cannot be accomplished, the case is investigated, and the EEOC will issue a statement of "probable cause" or "no probable cause." If a probable cause decision is made and the employer refuses to correct the problem, the EEOC either takes the case to court or issues a "right to sue" notice to the charging party, which allows that individual or group to file an action.

*Age Discrimination in Employment Act of 1967.* The Age Discrimination in Employment Act of 1967 (ADEA) was established to provide equal employment opportunity on the basis of age. The law prohibits discrimination against those aged 40 and above unless the employer can show that age is a bona fide occupational qualification (BFOQ) for the job. An example of age discrimination is when a senior employee is terminated so that a younger employee can be hired for less salary even though the new employee has less knowledge, skill, and ability. An employer must demonstrate that a particular age is "reasonably necessary to the normal operations of the particular business." On January 1, 1987, an amendment to the ADEA took effect, eliminating mandatory retirement at age 70. Organizations covered by the ADEA include private employers with 15 or more employees, labor organizations, employment agencies, and state, local, and federal governments. However, exceptions to the law exist. For example, the act permits mandatory retirement at age 65 for highly compensated executives.

*Equal Employment Opportunity Act of 1972.* The Equal Employment Opportunity Act of 1972 (EEO) was passed as an amendment to strengthen the Civil Rights Act of 1964. The act's primary goal is to provide equal employment opportunities for members of protected groups. The EEO also increased the number of organizations affected by reducing the required number of employees within an organization from 25 to 15.

*Rehabilitation Act of 1973.* This act, amended in 1980, prohibits discrimination against persons with physical or mental disabilities. The act only applies to the federal government and its contractors (those private organizations providing services to the government) and to businesses receiving federal funds. According to the Act, a disability is defined as something that "substantially limits one or more major life functions." Under this act, an employer must make reasonable accommodations for the employee unless the business can show that undue hardship will result from the accommodations. Most components of this act were subsumed under the Americans with Disabilities Act passed in 1990.

*Vietnam Veterans Readjustment Act of 1974.* This act also relates only to the government, government contractors, and businesses receiving federal funds. It protects disabled veterans in seeking employment opportunities. The government contractor is required to list all open job positions with the local state employment agency.

*Pregnancy Discrimination Act of 1978.* The Pregnancy Discrimination Act of 1978 is an amendment of Title VII of the Civil Rights Act. The amendment states that an employer may not discriminate against applicants or employees because of pregnancy, childbirth, abortion, or planned adoption. Disabilities related to pregnancy or childbirth must be treated the same as other types of disabilities or medical conditions. Women cannot be forced to go on leave as long as they are still able to work and are entitled to get their jobs back when they return from their leave of absence. The law also requires that employers may not refuse to give their unmarried employees pregnancy benefits, and they must offer the same benefits to all spouses.

*Immigration Reform and Control Act of 1986.* This act prohibits employers from employing aliens without authorization to work in the United States. An employer is required to verify authorization by asking for a U.S. passport, certificate of U.S. citizenship, certificate of naturalization, resident alien card, birth certificate, social security card, documents authorizing work in the U.S., drivers license, or documentation of personal identity. The employer must believe that the document "reasonably appears on its face to be genuine."[3] If a document's accuracy is questioned, the employer may require additional documentation from the sources listed above.

*Americans with Disabilities Act of 1990.* At least 43 million Americans have a disability. This fact is one reason the Americans with Disabilities Act (ADA) was passed on July 26, 1990. The law covers employers with 15 or more employees. The general premise of the ADA is that "employers may not discriminate against a qualified person with a disability in hiring, advancement, discharge, compensation, training, and other terms, conditions, and privileges or employment." A qualified individual with a disability is defined as "an individual who, with or without reasonable accommodation, can perform the essential functions of the position that he or she desires or holds." Essential functions are job tasks that are fundamental and not marginal.

Seven types of conduct are considered to be discriminatory by the ADA. These discriminatory actions and examples are described below.

- The employer may not limit, segregate, or classify a job applicant in a way that adversely affects employment opportunity or status. Individuals cannot be labeled disabled, and no mention of such disability should be included in an applicant's file.

- Employers cannot involve themselves in any contractual relationship that has the effect of discrimination. For example, an employer cannot refuse a reasonable accommodation by claiming that the lease on the building prohibits any changes to the structure such as ramps or handicap-accessible bathrooms.

- The employer may not utilize standards, criteria, or methods of administration that have the effect of discrimination. An employer cannot refuse to mail application materials and require an applicant to come in person to pick up an application blank, especially because it would cause undue hardship for many disabled people.

- Discrimination is not allowed against an applicant or employee because of their known relationship or association with a person who is disabled. For example, a disabled person's spouse cannot be turned down for a job because he or she might be more likely to utilize family leave (see "Family and Medical Leave Act of 1993" in Chapter 10).

- Employers may not refuse to make "reasonable accommodation" unless they can prove that the accommodation would impose an "undue hardship" on the business. Making some structural changes such as adding elevators or widening doorways may incur an expense that cannot be financed by the company. This may be a particular problem for many smaller firms that operate on very limited capital.

- Qualification standards, employment tests, or other selection criteria that tend to screen out persons with disabilities may not be used. Using techniques such as timed tests may discriminate against a paraplegic individual who has limited use of his or her arms. Accommodating disabled persons by providing additional time may be necessary.

- Retaliation against individuals because of their past charges or participation in an investigation, proceeding, or hearing under the ADA is not permitted. As with any federal discrimination law, an employer cannot terminate, demote, refuse a pay raise, etc., to any party of a discrimination suit.

Medical examinations may be used if all employees are subject to the examination and if information obtained is kept confidential. It is usually recommended that the exam be administered after a tentative hire decision has been made so that there is no temptation to discriminate if a disability is identified. Medical tests may not be utilized to determine whether an individual has a disability or to assess the severity of a known disability. After an individual is hired an employer may only require a medical examination if it is job related.

Individuals protected by the ADA fall into three categories. The first includes any individual who has a physical or mental impairment that substantially limits one or more of the person's major life activities. A physical or mental impairment refers to any physiological disorder or condition, cosmetic disfigurement, anatomical loss affecting a vital body system, or mental or psychological disorder. Examples of major life activities include seeing, hearing, breathing, and learning. These examples categorize an individual as disabled when any one of them is restricted with respect to the conditions, manner, or duration under which it is performed compared with other people. The second category covers persons having a record of such an impairment. This part covers persons who have recovered from a physical or mental impairment, which previously limited them in a major life activity. Finally, an individual regarded or perceived as having such an impairment is also protected. For example, an employee who has complained of a lower back problem for years and had been given job accommodations for it in the past, is perceived to be disabled whether or not medical records exist to support such a disability.

Individuals not protected by the ADA are those currently engaging in the use of illegal drugs. An employer may use a test to detect the use of illegal drugs and may take action (refusal to hire or dismissal) against the employee if the tests result in a positive reading. With regard to rehabilitation programs, drug users are covered if they successfully complete the program.

Others not protected by the ADA are homosexuals, bisexuals, and individuals with behavior disorders. Compulsive gambling, kleptomania, and pyromania are also excluded. Religious entities may give preference to individuals of a particular religion, and the ADA does not prohibit this act.

Two areas that create confusion are health and safety issues and the issues surrounding acquired immunodeficiency syndrome (AIDS). With health and safety issues, the question arises about the extent to which an individual poses a direct threat to the health or safety of others or to property. Determination must be made on a case-by-case basis. The ADA also covers persons infected with human immunodeficiency virus (HIV) or with AIDS. For example, because there is no medical proof suggesting that AIDS can be transmitted through the handling of food, an employer with jobs that require food handling cannot discriminate against those persons.

As stated earlier the ADA requires employers to provide reasonable accommodation to disabled persons unless it would result in an "undue hardship" on the operation of the business. The ADA defines "reasonable accommodation" as "making existing facilities used by employees readily accessible to and usable by disabled persons, job restructuring, part time or modified work schedules, reassignment to a vacant position, acquisition or modification of equipment or devices, appropriate adjustment or modifications of examinations, training materials, or policies, and the provision of qualified readers or interpreters." However, if employers can show that there is "undue hardship" on the business, they may not have to provide the accommodation. Undue hardship is defined as "an action requiring significant difficulty or expense." The determination will be made by the nature and cost of the accommodations in relation to the employer's resources and operations.

To enforce the ADA, a charge must be filed with the EEOC within 180 days of the alleged discriminatory act or within 300 days in states with approved enforcement agencies. The remedies under the ADA are designed to make the individual or class "whole" and to prevent the employer from practicing further discrimination. Relief includes back pay, hiring or reinstatement, and reimbursement of attorneys' fees and costs.

*Civil Rights Act of 1991.*    The Civil Rights Act of 1991 is a major amendment to Title VII. In response to six Supreme Court decisions rendered in the 1980s, which Congress felt adversely affected protection against illegal discrimination, this Act was passed. The major provisions of the Act include the following:

- Puts into law the *Griggs v. Duke Power Company*[4] decision, requiring employers to prove that an employment practice causing disparate treatment was based on business necessity.

- Amends Title VII by allowing proof of an unlawful employment practice to include demonstrating that race, color, religion, gender, or national origin was a motivating factor even though other legal factors also contributed to the decision.[5]

- Expands the scope of Title VII and the ADA to employees working in foreign countries if the company is American owned.

- Broadens the coverage of the Civil Rights act of 1866 to cover cases where the employee was discharged.

- Allows for compensatory and punitive damages in cases of intentional discrimination.

- Prohibits "race norming" of candidate's test scores. Therefore, test scores cannot be adjusted because of a person's protected group status.

- Established a "glass ceiling initiative" for which a special commission was established to study problems relating to the promotion of women to management positions.

## EXECUTIVE ORDERS

*Executive Order 11246 of 1965.*    This order prohibits the federal government from discriminating on the basis of race, color, religion, and natural origin. This includes all agencies, contractors, and subcontractors associated with the federal government.

*Executive Order 11375 of 1966.*    This order prohibits the same organizations mentioned above from discriminating against an employee because of his or her gender.

*Executive Order 11478 of 1969.*    This presidential order requires the federal government to base its employment policies on merit. All government agencies are required to maintain a program of equal employment opportunity. Furthermore, some contractors may be required to have an affirmative action plan on file with the Office of Federal Contract Compliance Programs (OFCCP), the enforcement agency for these Executive Orders.

## EMPLOYEE RIGHTS

Employees also have rights under what is called common law. Common law doctrine is based on court decisions and precedents. Some of the most important human resource issues that have developed through common law include employment-at-will, negligent hiring/retention, and constructive discharge.

*Employment-at-Will.*    Employment-at-will doctrine states that employment is at the will of the employer or the employee and either can sever the relationship at any time. Under a pure interpretation of the at-will doctrine, no notices of separation are necessary. Over the years, the courts have defined exceptions to the employment-at-will doctrine. The first exception is the public policy exception. For example, an employee informs the Environmental Protection Agency (EPA) that his or her firm illegally dumped hazardous chemicals into a local river. The whistle-blower can claim public policy protection because it is in the best interest of the public to be notified of a potential health and environmental concern.

A second exception to employment-at-will includes a written or implied contract. Employees may not be terminated if a contract, either written or implied, has some promise of security. The employer's contractual obligation to provide employment, or at least the compensation from the employment, is based on the duration of the contract. Employers should use caution when writing their employee manuals or handbooks. Although the goal of such handbooks is to provide for consistency in following work rules, no statements should be made that imply that an employee has a job as long as he or she follows the rules.

A third exception is the implied covenant of good faith and fair dealing. This occurs when the employer causes harm without justification. This exception to employment-at-will is more generally applied to longer-term employees who may have earned the right to fairer treatment. This exception is controversial because it significantly narrows the meaning of at-will employment. This implied covenant exception is interpreted very differently from state to state with more liberal states such as California and New York upholding this doctrine more than conservative midwestern states.

A fourth exception to employment-at-will involves a separation that is in violation of an established federal, state, or local law or ordinance. Discrimination law is probably the most common application of this exception. However, another legal exception worth noting is the Workers' Adjustment Retraining and Notification Act (WARN). In general, it states that a company must provide 60 days' notice if it plans to reduce its force by 50 or more employees. Terminated employees must be notified in writing.

*Negligent Hiring/Retention.*   The common law doctrine of negligent hiring and negligent retention holds employers responsible for exercising reasonable care in the hiring of their employees. Reasonable care includes, but is not limited to, activities such as reference checks, criminal background checks, skills testing, and psychological testing. The courts have especially held employers liable for the actions of employees who are in occupations in which they have access to dangerous equipment or their incompetence in operating equipment may cause harm to others.

Negligent retention is similar to negligent hiring. This common law doctrine focuses on the situation in which organizations knowingly retain employees who have a high risk of injuring themselves or others. For example, an employee physically assaults another employee but is only given a suspension instead of termination. If this employee assaults another employee, client, or visitor, the company can be held liable under negligent retention.

*Constructive Discharge.*   The common law doctrine of constructive discharge is based on the behavior of employers when they force employees to resign by creating intolerable working conditions. Intolerable conditions can include job reassignment, changing work hours/shifts, and allowing harassment by other employees. If an employer is proven to have engaged in constructive discharge, the separation is viewed as a termination and the employer can be held liable for any illegal conduct such as employment discrimination. A common occurrence of constructive discharge involves older employees. Employers would often like to bring in younger workers (usually at lower compensation), but they do not want to risk an age discrimination suit, so they try to get older employees to quit by transferring them to jobs the employer knows they cannot handle or to shifts that they do not want. Even if the employee quits because he or she could not handle the changes, the employer still could be held liable for age discrimination because they forced the employee out.

## PROVING ILLEGAL DISCRIMINATION

### ESTABLISHING ADVERSE IMPACT

The process of proving illegal discrimination starts with a plaintiff, the person(s) claiming an unlawful practice, validating that an organization's employment procedures had adverse impact. Formally, the process of determining adverse impact is known as establishing a prima facie ("on the face of it") case of discrimination. Adverse impact occurs when an employment practice has a disproportionate affect on member(s) of one protected group. Adverse impact can be established in one of two ways. The plaintiff can use either a disparate treatment or a disparate impact argument to establish illegal discrimination. Both methods of showing adverse impact are described below.

## DISPARATE IMPACT

The concept of disparate impact was introduced in the *Griggs v. Duke Power Company* (1971) Supreme Court case.[6] In this case, the Supreme Court determined that adverse impact occurs when the same standards are applied to all employees but have different outcomes for certain protected groups. The plaintiff does not have to prove that the employer had intended to illegally discriminate. The *Griggs v. Duke Power Company* case and other court decisions allow three types of data for determining disparate impact. These types of data are comparative statistics, demographic statistics, and concentration statistics.

*Comparative Statistics.* This method for calculating disparate impact compares hiring rates or ratios of protected minority groups to the hiring ratios of the majority group. The decision-making criterion for comparing the two ratios is known as the four-fifths or 80 percent rule of thumb. In other words, if the selection ratio for a protected minority group is less than 80 percent of the majority, adverse impact has occurred. For example, if the selection ratio for males were 60 percent then the selection ratio for females would have to be less than 48 percent $(0.80 \times 0.60)$ for adverse impact to be proven.

*Demographic Statistics.* When demographic statistics are used, comparisons of the firm's workforce to the population at large are conducted. It is important to note that the comparison is made between the workforce and the "relevant labor market," where the relevant labor market consists of all equally qualified individuals. If the firm's employment of protected minorities does not represent a substantial amount of the qualified workforce, then adverse impact may exist. For instance, the relevant labor market in Arizona or Oklahoma would include many more American Indians than that in Pennsylvania or Maryland. Therefore, the requirement for Indians to be represented in firms in Arizona or Oklahoma would be much greater than that in Maryland or Pennsylvania.

*Concentration Statistics.* The third type of data utilized to determine disparate impact is concentration statistics. The intent of this approach is to prove that protected minority groups are restricted to a particular job or level of jobs. Even though an organization may employ representative amounts of minority group members, adverse impact may exist if they are relegated to lower level positions. Some traditional examples of this situation are females in secretarial positions and African Americans and Hispanics in custodial positions. More recent examples include females in lower level sales and managerial positions. To prove discrimination, the plaintiff must identify a specific practice that has caused this result.

These methods for establishing disparate impact are summarized in the *Uniform Guidelines on Employee Selection Procedures.*[7] The Uniform Guidelines on Employee

Selection Procedures were established in 1978 to outline guidelines regarding employment testing and selection. The guidelines prescribed specific requirements for proving the job relatedness of employment practices as well as a specific method for determining whether adverse impact exists.

## DISPARATE TREATMENT

Disparate treatment exists when an employer intentionally illegally discriminates against an individual. Four criteria were established by *McDonnell Douglas Corp. v. Green* (1973).[8] To demonstrate disparate treatment, the plaintiff must show the following:

1. The individual belongs to a protected minority group.
2. The individual applied for a job for which the employer was seeking applicants.
3. Despite being qualified, the individual was rejected.
4. After the individual's rejection, the employer kept looking for people with the applicant's qualifications.

## DEFENSES TO DISCRIMINATION

Once the prima facie case has been established, the burden of proof shifts to the defendant. At this point, the organization accused of illegal employment discrimination has the opportunity to defend itself by proving that its selection procedures were job related, represented a bona fide occupational qualification, or were subject to a seniority system.

*Job Relatedness.* If an employer can show that certain qualifications are necessary to perform a job, then the employer can require an employee to have those qualifications. In other words, as long as a company's selection procedures are related to the employee's ability to perform the job correctly, the company can require these qualifications in its selection of applicants. The process of proving job relatedness is based on determining the validity and reliability of the selection procedure. Validity and reliability are discussed in Chapter 5.

*Bona Fide Occupational Qualifications.* If a company can show that to adequately perform the job in question it is necessary that the employee be of a certain gender, race, color, religion, or national origin, it can use a BFOQ as a defense to the selection procedure. A BFOQ defense is more commonly related to gender or religious requirements than to race, color, or national origin.[9]

*Bona Fide Seniority System.* The use of a seniority system as a defense to an illegal discrimination charge is justified when the intent of the seniority system was not to discriminate.[10] The use of bona fide seniority systems is especially important in layoff situations. Specifically, employers can utilize a "last hired, first fired" defense for layoff decisions.

## AFFIRMATIVE ACTION PROGRAMS

Affirmative action involves an employer taking the steps to recruit, hire, and promote members of protected groups. Although there is some disagreement over just what an affirmative action plan (AAP) should cover, it should consist of the following four parts:

- A utilization analysis showing the percentage of protected groups in the organization.
- An availability analysis showing the availability of protected groups in the community. This information allows demographic statistics to be calculated when adverse impact is determined.
- An identification of problem areas in which protected groups are under-represented or underutilized. Data from the first two parts above can help determine specific problem areas.
- An action plan with specific goals and timetables to deal with the identified problem areas.[11]

The three basic reasons requiring an organization to implement an AAP are being a government contractor, being found guilty of illegal employment discrimination, and starting voluntary implementation. Each cause for an AAP is described below.

### COMPLIANCE WITH EXECUTIVE ORDER 11246

Under Executive Order 11246, employers with federal contracts or subcontracts exceeding $150,000 and whose employment exceeds 50 people must implement an AAP with the four components described above.

### COURT-ORDERED CONSENT DECREE

When found guilty of illegal discrimination, a company may be ordered to comply with an affirmative action program. Under this order a company is required by law to give preferential action to groups that have been discriminated against in selection procedures.[12] This action should bring the discriminated party's representation in the company up to required standards. It should be noted that while a company is under the court-ordered AAP, it cannot be taken to court for reverse discrimination.

### VOLUNTARY AFFIRMATIVE ACTION PLAN

If a company finds, after conducting statistical analysis on its selection procedures, that it has discriminated against a particular group, it might opt to initiate

**LITIGATION-PRONE EMPLOYEES**

The calculated, manipulative, and many times unethical steps that disgruntled employees are sometimes willing to take against their employers for financial benefit seem to be increasing. These activities often result in the employer paying large legal fees, a settlement with the employee to avoid legal fees, or a combination of both. Below are some of the more damaging cases.

Alpha Blouse Corp. (ABC), a 7-year-old apparel maker, hired an elderly woman who claimed that that she just wanted a job "at any wage, just to finish out my time." The woman worked for 10 days and then requested a furlough. The furlough was granted and the woman was told to give the company a call when she was ready to come back. The woman never called ABC, but her lawyer did. The lawyer claimed that the woman had double carpal tunnel syndrome as a result of using the duster at ABC for 10 days and that

she would settle for a mere $20,000 per wrist. Further investigation revealed that the woman had engaged her lawyer *before* applying for work at ABC.

Two managers of a $5 million dollar equipment repair service outside of Philadelphia were accused of criminal actions by an upset employee. The company had calmly been monitoring an employee's behavior as he continued to take unannounced absent periods that were in excess of those acceptable under the company's policy. The worker claimed that he was unexpectedly rendered disabled when his bursitis flared up. After this happened a few times, the company's operating officer drove by the employee's home and saw him outside waxing his car with the arm that was supposedly incapacitated.

When the employee returned to work the following day, the operating officer and supervisor called him into an office to discuss

the situation. To avoiding bothering the clerks outside, they shut the door. The employee then immediately left the room. The next day both of the managers were served with criminal complaints by the sheriff. Among the complaints were assault and battery, stalking, kidnapping, and interfering with the exercise of civil rights. The employee stated, "I was held in a locked room against my will." Furthermore, the employee claimed that, "each time I tried to leave the room the defendant threatened me. . . . The defendant pulled my arm so hard that it injured my shoulder permanently." The outcome of this situation is unknown.

Jay Estes, owner of a new office furniture store in New Jersey called Interior Motives, took great care to follow good employee relations practices carefully. Before an employee was dismissed, Estes would write a performance review and conduct

---

a voluntary AAP. According to *Steelworkers v. Weber* (1979),[13] the Supreme Court ruled that hiring quotas for females were justified due to the past discrimination practices. It is recommended that an employer have a temporary plan (with distinct steps to be taken) that does not unnecessarily ignore the interests of whites or males.

## SEXUAL HARASSMENT

One form of sexual discrimination prohibited by Title VII is sexual harassment. Sexual harassment occurs when a hostile, abusive, or intimidating environment is created and when compensation or advancement opportunities are affected.[14]

an oral review and then repeat the process a second time. He was confident that his decision to dismiss an unproductive manager was justified because the manager had been warned three times within 1 year. The employee turned in his company credit card and left the company. "That's the way to do it," Estes patted himself on the back.

Four weeks later, Interior Motives received its statement from American Express and found that $3,000 more than had been expected had been charged on the card. Because the employee sensed that he was going to be fired, he used the card to eat expensive dinners, rent a fancy car, stay in luxury hotels, and party in nightclubs. Estes took the ex-employee to court, claiming that he "misappropriated funds" by taking a vacation on Interior Motives' tab. The ex-employee claimed that the travel usage of the business credit card was "an implied perk."

A man working for a siding company on the East coast fell from a scaffold due to, according to witnesses, his own carelessness and his disregard for following the scaffold's safety instructions. The incapacitated employee became eligible for medical payments and wages (two-thirds of full pay) for up to 160 months (13.3 years). The employer protested having to shell out $28,000 per year for the employee who, he claimed, was actually malingering and in good physical health. The company president complained that, "he'd hobble into the Industrial Accidents Board with some doctor's statement in hand, and the judge found for him every time." To make things worse, when the company advertised an open management position the disgruntled employee applied. When a person other than he was chosen for the job, he sued the company, claiming discrimination against the handicapped.

Emerging firms face many growth-related obstacles, any one of which can cause a significant level of damage to a company. While new companies do not have the historical experience of having dealt with disgruntled employees, managers should hire experienced HR personnel who do have experience in this field. Although it is unrealistic for a company's management to think that it can eliminate the possibility of experiencing a situation similar to one of those presented above, an experienced HR team will be able to provide a company with the defensive strategy needed to minimize the chances that such a situation will occur.

SOURCE: Mamis, R. A. (1995). "Employees from Hell." *Inc. Magazine,* January: 50–57.

There are two types of sexual harassment: (1) quid pro quo sexual harassment where a supervisor trades sexual activity for advancement opportunities of some sort; and (2) sexual harassment in which an unwelcome hostile environment is created by a supervisor or any other employee.[15] The definition of the second type of harassment was recently broadened by the U.S. Supreme Court when they ruled that the plaintiff no longer had to prove physical or psychological harm. According to Supreme Court Justice Sandra Day O'Connor, "So long as the environment would reasonably be perceived, and is perceived, as hostile or abusive, there is no need for it to be psychologically injurious."

This ruling, coupled with a 53 percent increase in sexual harassment cases filed since the Anita Hill accusations against Supreme Court Justice Clarence Thomas, suggests that this issue will be a front-line topic for many years to come. Two recent court decisions, *Fragher v. Boca Raton*[16] and *Burlington Industries v. Ellerth,*[17]

**HR TOOL KIT**

**FREQUENTLY ASKED QUESTIONS**

**What guidelines should an employer follow when investigating allegations of sexual harassment?**

The employer must take all complaints of sexual harassment seriously, conduct a prompt investigation, and take appropriate action to minimize legal liability. The facts of the complaint should be gathered in an objective and professional manner. When conducting an investigation, follow these guidelines:

- Interview the employee claiming sexual harassment and record all facts, including dates, times, witnesses, etc.
- Interview potential witnesses.
- Interview the accused harasser.
- Investigate conflicting statements.
- Make a final decision. Apply and document appropriate discipline if sexual harassment

has occurred. Consult legal assistance if necessary.

- Follow up with the victim.
- Keep all investigative documents separate from personnel files.

The company should also consider placing a clear sexual harassment policy in its handbook and providing sexual harassment training to every employee in the organization.

**What laws are companies required to comply with when they reach the 15, 20, 50, and 100 employee thresholds?**

The following lists show employment regulations employers are responsible for complying with at certain employee thresholds.

*Employers with at least 1 employee must comply with:*

- Fair Labor Standards Act (FLSA)
- Employee Polygraph Protection Act

- Immigration Reform and Control Act (IRCA)
- Equal Pay Act
- Federal Income Tax Withholding
- Uniformed Services Employment and Re-employment Rights Act of 1994
- Federal Insurance Contribution Act (FICA)
- National Labor Relations Act (NLRA)
- Consumer Credit Protection Act
- Labor Management Relations Act
- Uniform Guidelines for Employment Selection Procedures
- Employment Retirement Income Security Act (ERISA)

*Employers with 11 or more employees must also comply with:*

- Occupational Safety and Health Act (OSHA)

---

helped shape a new foundation for establishing employer liability. In cases dealing with a hostile environment, the employer is liable unless the employer can prove that it exercised care to prevent an occurrence, took quick and immediate corrective action once an occurrence surfaced, and established policies and training programs to prevent the occurrence. The following activities have been suggested to avoid, or at least reduce, liability:

- If you do not already have a written policy against sexual harassment that includes a clearly stated procedure for filing a complaint, get one.
- Once you have a policy and procedure, make sure everyone knows about them.
- Be prepared to investigate every complaint in accordance with your procedures.
- Document every employment decision.[18]

*Employers with 15 or more employees must comply with:*

- Pregnancy Discrimination Act
- Americans with Disabilities Act
- Title VII of Civil Rights Act
- Civil Rights Act of 1964

*Employers with 20 or more employees need to comply with:*

- Age Discrimination in Employment Act
- Consolidated Omnibus Budget Reconciliation Act (COBRA)

*Employers with 50 employees or more need to comply with:*

- Family Medical Leave Act (FMLA)

*Employers with 100 or more employees must comply with:*

- Worker Adjustment Retraining Notification Act (WARN)

And must complete and submit the EEO-1 form to the Equal Employment Opportunity Com-mission (Executive Order 11246 requires that federal contractors with 50 or more employees and $50,000 in government contracts must also file EEO-1 report each year).

**What are my responsibilities as an employer under the Americans with Disabilities Act (ADA)?**

You must know the job and conduct a job analysis to determine the job's essential functions. Be sure to distinguish between the job's essential and nonessential functions. The job analysis provides criteria for determining whether an individual can carry out the essential functions, with or without reasonable accommodation. This information should be utilized to assess job qualifications.

**WEB ADDRESSES**

**http://192.41.4.29/bus.html**
The 'Lectric Law Library offers several articles that should be par-ticularly helpful to HR professionals of small and mid-sized firms. Topics such as hiring and firing, discrimination, privacy rights, sexual harassment, substance abuse, and many others are discussed and documented in this web site.

**www.findlaw.com**
FindLaw.com is an excellent resource for the HR professional. This site allows the user to look up any topic in a search and yield returns of the actual written law, court precedent, and current cases and interpretations. The site also gives topical searches to aide the user in getting started as well as a business section to help put the laws into more practical applications.

**www.ljextra.com/practice/labor employment/labcol.html**
This site, sponsored by the New York Law Publishing Company, offers a wide selection of articles and information related to the legal aspects of human resource management.

## CHAPTER SUMMARY

The legal environment in which the human resource function operates provides a huge challenge to emerging enterprises. Legal issues affect the field of human resource management in at least four areas. These areas are equal employment opportunity, compensation, safety and health, and labor relations. This chapter focused on the specific laws and regulations pertaining to equal employment opportunity and the process by which a discrimination claim is proven and defended. The Civil Rights Act of 1964 serves as the foundation for discrimination laws. This act defined the protected groups covered and established an agency to oversee enforcement. Other laws such as the Equal Pay Act of 1963, Age Discrimination in Employment Act of 1967, Equal Employment Opportunity Act of 1972, Pregnancy Discrimination Act of 1978, Americans with Disabilities Act of 1990, and Civil Rights Act of 1991 further define employment discrimination. Although several of the laws are well established and dealt with effectively by human resource professionals, the recently enacted Americans with Disabilities Act of 1990 and Civil Rights Act of 1991 provide new challenges to the field.

## NOTES

1. Fisher, C. D., Schoenfeldt, L. F., and Shaw, J. B. (1999). *Human Resource Management*, 4th ed. (Boston: Houghton Mifflin Company).

2. Sovereign, K. L. (1994). *Personnel Law* (Englewood Cliffs, NJ: Prentice Hall).

3. Gatewood, R. D., and Feild, H. S. (1998). *Human Resource Selection*, 4th ed. (Fort Worth, TX: Dryden).

4. *Griggs v. Duke Power Co.*, 401 U.S. 424,3 FEP 175 (1971).

5. Fisher et al. (1999).

6. *Griggs v. Duke Power Co.*

7. *Uniform Guidelines on Employee Selection Procedures*, 29 Code of Federal Regulations, Part 1607 (1978).

8. *McDonnell Douglas Corp. v. Green*, 411 U.S. 792 5 FEP 965 (1973).

9. Gatewood and Feild (1998).

10. *Teamsters v. United States*, 431 U.S. 324, 14 FEP 1514 (1977).

11. Fisher et al. (1999).

12. Twomey, D. P. (1994). *Equal Employment Opportunity Law* (Cincinnati: South-Western Publishing Co).

13. *Steelworkers v. Weber*, 443 U.S. 193,20 FEP 1 (1979).

14. *Meritor Savings Bank v. Vinson*, 106 S.Ct. 2399 (1986).

15. *Guidelines on Discrimination Because of Sex*, 29 C.F.R. Sec. 1604.11(a)(1995).

16. *Fragher v. Boca Raton*, No. 97-282 (1998).

17. *Burlington Industries, Inc. v. Ellerth*, No. 97-569 (1998).

18. Sandler, D. (1998). "Sexual harassment rulings: Less than meets the eye." *HRMagazine* October: 136–143.

# 14

# HRD in a Culturally Diverse Environment

## LEARNING OBJECTIVES

1. Understand how the changing demographics of the labor market are changing the cultural fabric of organizations.

2. Describe how organizational culture is being affected by having a greater percentage of women in the workforce, as well as how this has impacted HRD.

3. Describe how having a greater percentage of racial and ethnic minorities in the workforce is impacting organizations, as well as how this will impact HRD.

4. Become familiar with different forms of discrimination, their effects on women and minorities, and how HRD programs and processes can help to reduce these effects.

5. Describe the ways organizations attempt to integrate women and minorities into the organization and the relative success of these efforts.

6. Understand the purpose and methods of cross-cultural training.

████████████████████████████████████████████████████████

**OPENING CASE**

R. R. Donnelley & Sons Co. is the world's third-largest printing company, with fifty-five plants worldwide. It prints magazines such as *TV Guide* and *Time*, and nearly half of the books on the *New York Times* bestseller list.[1] Until 1996, it had primarily emphasized one-time diversity awareness training that focused on stereotypes and prejudices in the workplace.[2] However, the company felt that it needed a broader approach than this, and has given this assignment to its diversity manager.

*Questions: What might be some drawbacks of a one-time-only diver-* *sity training program? If you were the diversity manager, what types of things would you recommend that Donnelley do to change or expand its efforts at diversity training? What would be important to you if you were to go through such a training program? Why?*

[1]http://www.hoovers.com/co/capsule/4/0,2163,11244,00.html
[2]Flynn, G. (1998). The harsh reality of diversity programs *Workforce, 77* (12), 26-33.

## INTRODUCTION

In this chapter, we will address some of the following questions:

- *What is the current status of women and people of color in the U.S. workforce?*
- *Is there a "glass ceiling" that limits the advancement of women and people of color in U.S. organizations?*
- *How do equal employment opportunity, affirmative action, and managing diversity differ?*
- *How effective are diversity training programs employed by organizations?*
- *What can organizations do to better prepare their employees to deal with cross-cultural issues, especially if they are sent to work in another country?*
- *What types of HRD programs can organizations use to develop and promote a culturally diverse workforce?*

In order for organizations to compete successfully in a global economy, they must be able to attract and retain the best employees possible. For most organizations, this means recruiting and hiring a more diverse workforce (especially women and minorities, or "people of color") for roles that they have less typically held — such as management positions. As we have noted before, there has been a gradual increase in the number of women and racial and ethnic minorities (e.g., blacks, Hispanics, and Asians) entering the workforce. This trend is expected to continue at least through the year 2020.[1]

In this chapter, we will emphasize race and gender issues, as these are the most researched forms of diversity to date. However, it is important to consider other forms of diversity as well. For example, Kossek and Lobel suggest that attention also be given to diversity in nationality, language, ability (and disability), religion, lifestyle (including family structure and sexual orientation), and work function and tenure.[2]

■ **TABLE 15-1**

1. Common geographic origin
2. Migratory status
3. Race
4. Language or dialect
5. Religious faith
6. Ties that transcend kinship, neighborhood, and community boundaries
7. Shared traditions, values, and symbols
8. Literature, folklore, music
9. Food preferences
10. Settlement and employment patterns
11. Special interests in regard to politics
12. Institutions that specifically serve and maintain the group
13. An internal perception of distinctness
14. An external perception of distinctness

SOURCE: From S. Thernstrom, A. Orlov, & O. Handlin, (eds.) (1980). *Harvard encyclopedia of American ethnic groups.* Cambridge, MA.

This chapter will focus on the changing labor market and how it is influencing organizations to make changes. First, we will briefly review organizational culture and labor market trends. Next, we will review the different forms of discrimination in the workplace, their impact on women and minorities, and how organizations can eliminate or minimize discrimination. We will then discuss some ways in which organizations have attempted to integrate women and minorities into the workforce, the relative success or failure of these efforts, as well as how they can be improved. Lastly, we will discuss some specific HRD programs and processes used to integrate women and minorities into the workforce or prepare employees for overseas assignments, including orientation, career development, mentoring, sexual harassment training, and cross-cultural training.

## ORGANIZATIONAL CULTURE

Every person exists within a sociopolitical culture. **Culture** can be defined as a set of shared values, beliefs, norms, and artifacts that are used to interpret the environment and as a guide for all kinds of behavior. Each culture is distinguished by a unique set of attributes, which are described in Table 15-1. These attributes help people to differentiate one culture from another. For example, when these attributes are used to describe a nationality (e.g., American), the primary descriptors would be geographic origin, language, and political institutions. These attributes can also describe groupings or subcultures within a larger culture. When describing a subset of the American culture, the descriptors might include race, food preference, religion, employment practices, migratory status, and internal/external distinctness. A visitor to the United States, for example, would notice stark cultural differences between residents of Brainerd, Minnesota, New Orleans, Louisiana, Boston, Massachusetts, and Provo, Utah.

**Organizational culture** was defined in Chapter 14 as a set of shared values, beliefs, norms, artifacts, and patterns of behavior that are used as a frame of reference for the way one looks at, attempts to understand, and works within any organization.[3] Organizations are subsets of larger sociopolitical cultures. Relationships between the larger sociopolitical culture and organizational cultures are referred to as "cultural 'paradigms' that tie together the basic assumptions about humankind, nature, and activities."[4] These assumptions are the building blocks or the roots of an organizational culture. They are often unseen and can be inferred only through artifacts and patterns of behavior.

*Artifacts* are "material and nonmaterial objects and patterns that intentionally or unintentionally communicate information about the organization's technology, beliefs, values, assumptions, and ways of doing things."[5] Material artifacts include documents, physical layout, furnishings, patterns of dress, and so on. Nonmaterial artifacts include organizational stories, ceremonies, and leadership styles. In organizations, leadership style can be influenced by assumptions about gender and race. For example, if a male manager assumes that it is women's nature or role to give family issues priority over work issues, he might be less likely to promote women to higher levels of responsibility. These kinds of beliefs have been prevalent in our society and will be discussed later in this chapter.

*Patterns of behavior* help to reinforce an organization's assumptions, beliefs, and ways of doing things through staff meetings, training programs, filing forms, and other normal organizational practices.[6] For example, if an organization initiates a sexual harassment policy by scheduling a mandatory training program for all employees, it is communicating a high level of importance and value to this responsibility. Conversely, an organization that fails to provide adequate training to curb incidences of sexual harassment — even if it talks about the importance of reaching that goal — will be communicating that it places the issue at a much lower level of importance. Thus, patterns of behavior help to reinforce important assumptions, beliefs, and values.

Both artifacts and patterns of behavior play an important role in the socialization process. As discussed in Chapter 8, socialization is the process whereby new members learn how to function (e.g., learn norms) in a group or organization. In the absence of a prescribed code of conduct, new members typically learn how to behave by observing the artifacts and patterns of behavior in an organization.

The match between the people in an organization and the organizational culture is very important. If an organization employs individuals who make similar assumptions about people and have similar values and beliefs, then there is greater likelihood that they will demonstrate loyalty and commitment to organizational goals. This kind of organization is often referred to as a *monoculture.* Conversely, organizations that employ people from diverse cultures or subcultures, where there may be divergent assumptions, values, and beliefs, may have different experiences. These experiences are not necessarily bad. In fact, a growing number of authors feel that cultural diversity can have many positive outcomes.[7] This diversity, among other things, can bring a richness of perspectives to an organization.

## LABOR MARKET CHANGES AND DISCRIMINATION

The demographic shifts that are occurring in the U.S. population will continue to impact the workforce in the future. Concerning immigration, Steven Camarota writes:

> Partly as a result of reforms of immigration law in the 1960s, the United States is currently experiencing the largest sustained wave of immigration in its history. More than one million legal and illegal immigrants now come to the United States each year. As a result, the foreign-born population has almost tripled in size, from less than 10 million in 1970 to nearly 27 million in 1999.[8]

Examples of other trends include the following predictions:

- The female labor force participation rate will continue to rise from the present 60 percent.
- Blacks will remain at 11 percent of the workforce from 1995 through 2020.
- Hispanics will increase from 9 percent of the workforce in 1995 to 14 percent in 2020.
- Asians will increase from 4 percent of the workforce in 1995 to 6 percent in 2020.[9]

### TREATMENT DISCRIMINATION

Discrimination can occur in various ways. For example, **access discrimination** occurs when an organization places limits on job availability through such things as restricting advertisement and recruitment, rejecting applicants, or offering a lower starting salary.[10] **Treatment discrimination** occurs after a person is hired and takes the form of limiting opportunities (e.g., training, promotion, rewards) or harassing certain individuals because of who they are (e.g., women, members of a racial or ethnic minority). Both types of discrimination are covered under equal employment opportunity laws.

*TREATMENT DISCRIMINATION AGAINST WOMEN IN ORGANIZATIONS.* Over the past century, women have experienced substantial changes in the rights available to them in the workplace. Table 15-2 presents results of a Catalyst study. This

■ **TABLE 15-2**

CHANGES IN THE NUMBER OF WOMEN AT THE TOP OF
FORTUNE 500 COMPANIES, 1995–2000

|  | 1995 | 2000 |
|---|---|---|
| Percent of board of directors who are female: | 9.5% | 11.7% |
| Percent of all corporate officers who are female: | 8.7% | 12.5% |
| Percent of line officers who are female: | 5.3% | 7.3% |
| Percent of top officers who are female: | 1.2% | 4.1% |
| Number of companies where at least 25% of all corporate officers are female: | 25 | 50 |
| Number of CEOs who are female: | 1 | 2 |

SOURCE: *2000 Catalyst census of women corporate officers and top earners* (2000). New York: Catalyst.

depicts both the limited numbers of women in top positions, as well as the advancements women have made, at least in terms of Fortune 500 companies. More broadly, women have made considerable progress moving into formerly male-dominated occupations such as medicine, law, management, advertising and engineering.[11] In 1997, women held 48 percent of the managerial and specialty positions in the U.S.[12] In 1998, women made up 47 percent of the workforce of U.S. organizations with 100 employees or more (who reported employment data to the Equal Employment Opportunity Commission, or EEOC). In these organizations, women held a slight majority (50.9 percent) of all jobs classified as "professional." For the category of "officials and managers," women held 32.7 percent of these jobs.[13] Despite such changes, many concerns over sex-based discrimination remain. For example, in fiscal year 2000, the EEOC received over 25,000 formal charges of alleged sex-based discrimination.[14] This number has remained fairly steady from 1994 to 2000.

Historically, women have faced three kinds of treatment discrimination — promotion (particularly into management), pay, and sexual harassment. Some inroads have been made in terms of *promotion*. Table 15-2 shows that more women are holding top positions in large companies, but women are still extremely underrepresented among senior management positions.[15] In Canada, the number of women holding corporate officer positions (12 percent) is comparable to that in the U.S.; however, in contrast to the United States, women are president or CEO of twelve of the largest 560 Canadian companies, whereas in the U.S. only two women hold those positions in Fortune 500 companies.[16] In February 2001, the two female CEOs of Fortune 500 companies were Carly Fiorina at Hewlett-Packard, and Andrea Jung at Avon Products.[17]

While progress has been made, there is still evidence of *pay* disparity between men and women across most occupational categories.[18] Disparities persist despite the passage of the Equal Pay Act in 1963. In the 1992 Current Population Survey, women were more likely than men to be in the bottom 20 percent of the earnings distribution.[19] Other data from the Current Population Survey compared the median annual earnings for wage and salary earners between the ages of twenty-five and thirty-four. For all workers with a bachelor's degree or higher, the pay disparity has decreased over the past twenty-five years, but has not disappeared. For example, in 1977, males in this category earned 60 percent more than females. In 1987, males earned 38 percent more than females, and in 1997, males earned 22 percent more than females.[20] The discrepancies between males and females were considerably larger for those with lower levels of educational attainment.

Substantial pay disparities also exist between male and female corporate executives. According to an analysis of several surveys, in 1982, women executives earned approximately 68 percent of male executive's pay; by 1992 women executives' average pay had decreased to 57 percent.[21] A survey of salaries at 1,500 larger companies found that the average pay of female executives in 1997 was 73 percent of the salary of male executives. Further, from 1992 to 1997, the percentage of companies with at least one woman among their top five highest paid executives rose from 5.4 percent to 15 percent. However, in this same survey, when bonuses and stock options were included with pay, female executives averaged only 55 percent of what males earned.[22] Many factors contribute to this pay differential, for example, differences in wages across industries, differences in the size of organizations in which male versus female executives work, differences in work experiences, education, and so on. Even when such differences are taken into consideration, wage earnings of men and women still have not reached parity.

*Sexual harassment* is another form of treatment discrimination that occurs most often against women in the workplace. Sexual harassment takes many forms, from unwanted off-color jokes and comments, to outright unwanted sexual propositions and touching, to offers of job rewards in exchange for sexual favors. If an employee's subjection to or rejection of the sexual conduct is used as a basis for an employment decision, this is referred to as quid pro quo sexual harassment.[23] Even if the harassment is not linked directly to an employment decision (such as a cut in pay or loss of a promotion), it can still be illegal harassment if the behavior is found to have created a *hostile work environment.* In 1998, the Supreme Court held that sexual harassment can occur even when there is no tangible job detriment such as a shift to a less desirable job or the denial of a promotion.[24] Some employees choose to endure this kind of treatment for a variety of reasons, including that they need the job, feel powerless to do anything about it, or are not sure of the intent of the perpetrator. The impact of this can be devastating. Some people suffer serious psychological and emotional trauma that can affect their ability to work effectively. Organizations that allow this kind of treatment to go unchecked are essentially sending a message that some of their employees are not valued and are expendable.

Since 1990, several high profile scandals and incidents have raised awareness concerning the widespread problem of sexual harassment. In 1991, the U.S. Navy Tailhook scandal involved the harassment of female enlisted personnel and officers at a social gathering. In 1997, male superior officers at the Army Ordnance Center at Aberdeen, Maryland, sexually harassed female Army trainees. In 1996, the EEOC brought suit against Mitsubishi Motors for widespread sexual harassment at its plant in Normal, Illinois. In 1998, Mitsubishi agreed to pay $34 million to the victims of sexual harassment at the plant, which is the largest settlement ever reached in a sexual harassment case.[25] Incidents such as these have raised publicity and awareness levels about the pervasiveness of the problem. Among other things, organizations and individuals have become more aware of sexual harassment and are beginning to take steps to confront the problem in the workplace. In addition, the passage of the Civil Rights Act of 1991 (which will be discussed later) now allows victims of sexual harassment to sue for compensatory damages for pain and suffering in cases where the "employer acts with malice or reckless indifference to the rights of the individual."[26] One measure of the scope of the problem can be seen in the number of discrimination complaints filed with the EEOC. In fiscal year 2000, 15,836 charges of sexual harassment were filed with the EEOC, an increase of over 50 percent from 1992.[27] Further, women filed 86.4 percent of all charges.

*TREATMENT DISCRIMINATION AGAINST MINORITIES IN ORGANIZATIONS.*    Treatment discrimination against minorities in the workplace is seen primarily in the lack of promotional opportunities and incidents of racial harassment. Similar to the situation for women, the number of formal charges of race discrimination remains high. For example, in fiscal year 2000, the EEOC received almost 29,000 charges of race-based discrimination. From 1992 to 2000, the number of charges has ranged from 26,000 to over 31,000 per year.[28] In terms of *promotional opportunities*, probably the most publicized was the case at Texaco Oil Company. In 1994, a group of Texaco executives were audiotaped by one of the executives discussing a pending civil rights lawsuit by 1,400 black professionals and managers who charged that they were denied promotion because of their race. During this taped conversation, the executives were heard making disparaging racial remarks and innuendos that the black employees belonged at the bottom of the organizational ladder. When the tape was made public, Texaco was forced to take action against the offending executives. Texaco management had to publicly apologize to the black employees and offer them a very attractive ($176 million) out-of-court settlement.[29] Peter Bijur, Texaco's chairman and CEO, stressed in his public comments that bigotry and corporate prejudice are widespread throughout our society.[30] The potential for this kind of public embarrassment may be the best deterrent to acts of discrimination that go on within organizations.

Like women, minorities have entered many nontraditional occupations (e.g., management) and have also had difficulty moving into key executive and policy-making positions. In 1998, blacks made up 13.7 percent of the workforce of organizations reporting employment data to the EEOC. However, blacks constituted only 5.9 percent of the officials and managers, and 6.4 percent of the professionals in these organizations.[31] Similarly, Hispanics made up 9.1 percent of the workforce at these organizations, yet held 3.9 percent of the officials and managers positions and 3.3 percent of the professional positions. In a survey of 400 of the

Fortune 1000 companies, fewer than 9 percent of all managers were minorities, including those who were black, Asian, and Hispanic.[32] A 1995 study of New York firms by the American Management Association found that over half the minority employees were overlooked for promotion (at least some of the time).[33] Powell and Butterfield investigated the effect of race on promotions to top management in a federal agency and found that race did not directly affect promotion decisions, but that other factors (composition of the selection panel and whether panel members had job experience in the hiring department) did have an effect.[34] This suggests that if the hiring panel is composed of all white individuals, a nonwhite candidate may have less chance of being promoted.

In addition, significant differences have been found in career options for white and black employees.[35] Specifically, black employees have "received less favorable assessments of promotability from their supervisors, were likely to have plateaued in their careers, and were more dissatisfied with their careers than whites."[36] Further, the factors affecting the evaluation and development of minorities in organizations have been examined, including bias effects, lost opportunities, and self-limiting behaviors.[37] In terms of development, minorities are affected by such things "as absence of mentors, less interesting or challenging work as a result of being in the out-group, and being left out of the informal social network."[38] This suggests that if organizations are going to attract and retain qualified minorities, they must remove barriers and address the developmental needs of those groups.

*Racial harassment*, a form of treatment discrimination against racial minorities on the job, can take many forms. The more obvious form of racial harassment occurs when a coworker verbally (face-to-face or in writing) or physically attacks a person of color because of racial differences. For example, in 2000, the EEOC reported obtaining a $700,000 settlement from Direct Marketing Services of Arizona. Black employees at the telemarketing firm alleged that they were racially harassed, denied promotions, and paid unequal wages.[39] A more subtle form of racial harassment is when coworkers ostracize an individual by withholding important information and other resources needed to perform the job. The effects of these types of discrimination include the creation of a hostile environment and interference with the targeted person's ability to do his or her job.

## EQUAL EMPLOYMENT OPPORTUNITY

Since the 1960s, the U.S. government and individual states have established many laws and regulations that are intended to protect the civil rights of citizens. One important group of civil rights laws are those mandating **equal employment opportunity** (EEO). EEO is defined as the right to obtain jobs and earn rewards in them regardless of nonjob-related factors. Title VII of the Civil Rights Act of 1964 (the main federal EEO Law) and the amendments and legislation that have followed it make it unlawful for employers to make employment decisions on the basis of race, color, sex, religion, national origin, age, mental or physical handicap, Vietnam-era or disabled veteran status, and pregnancy, unless these factors can be shown to be job related. These laws are directed primarily at employment practices, including access to HRD programs, that have an unfair exclusionary impact on any of the groups specified in the legislation. Essentially, EEO legislation is intended to address illegal discrimination in the workplace, and promote a workplace that is race blind, gender blind, and so on. As such, EEO laws cover all races and both genders. This means that whites and males can allege discrimination under EEO laws in the same manner that minorities and women do, that is, they must argue that they have been discriminated against because of their race or gender. Through Title VII, the U.S. Congress also established the Equal Employment Opportunity Commission (EEOC), which is the federal agency primarily responsible for administering and enforcing EEO laws. Its role is to seek compliance wherever possible and to pursue remedies in civil court only as a last resort.

### THE GLASS CEILING

The rise of women and minorities to management positions, particularly upper-level executive and policy-making positions, has been slow. To many, it has appeared as if an invisible but impenetrable boundary prevented them from advancing to senior management levels. This barrier has been described as the **glass ceiling.** The glass ceiling is defined as subtle attitudes and prejudices that block women and minorities from upward mobility, particularly into management jobs.[40] More specifically, the glass ceiling symbolizes prevailing attitudes about different cultural groups and their general abilities, or the lack thereof, to perform some role or occupation.

The U.S. Department of Labor (DOL) has recognized the glass ceiling. The DOL established the Glass Ceiling Commission, which initiated a study of the effects of the glass ceiling on upward mobility. The goals of the initiative were:

1. to promote a high quality, inclusive, and diverse workforce capable of meeting the challenge of global competition
2. to promote good corporate conduct through an emphasis on corrective and cooperative problem solving
3. to promote equal opportunity, not mandated results
4. to establish a blueprint of procedures to guide the department in conducting future reviews of all management levels of the corporate workforce[41]

The study investigated several companies to determine the extent to which an organization's promotion patterns showed a glass ceiling pattern. Some of the findings were as follows:

1. Neither women nor minorities tended to advance as far as their white male counterparts, although women advanced further than minorities.
2. While most organizations made a concerted effort to identify and develop key (white male) employees, few organizations had taken any ownership for equal employment opportunity and access.

3. The few women and minorities who held executive jobs were in staff positions (e.g., human resources, research, and administration) that were considered outside the corporate mainstream for promotions to senior-level positions

4. While most of these organizations held federal government contracts, most had inadequate equal employment and affirmative action record keeping.

The report also identified some potential barriers to upward mobility. In addition to recruitment practices, the report cited the "lack of opportunity to contribute and participate in corporate developmental experiences."[42] This suggests that organizations should formalize the career development process in order to eliminate glass ceiling effects. A sole reliance on informal mentoring is insufficient to ensure that every qualified person is given an opportunity for advancement. Several recent articles have noted: 1) some "cracks" in the glass ceiling for women,[43] 2) differences in glass ceiling effects for women than for blacks (fewer promotions for blacks than for women),[44] and 3) differences in effects across managerial level in the United States, Sweden, and Australia.[45] This suggests that further research and corporate change efforts are still needed in this area.[46]

## IMPACT OF RECENT IMMIGRATION PATTERNS

One reason for the tremendous growth in the number of minority workers has been the large influx of immigrants since the 1960s. The highest ranking countries of birth for the U.S. foreign-born population are Mexico, the Philippines, China, Hong Kong, Cuba, Vietnam, El Salvador, India, the Dominican Republic, Great Britain, and Korea.[47] For example, Hispanics are the largest foreign-born group, yet are quite diverse, separated by socioeconomic class, national origin, citizenship status, length of residence in the United States, and the degree of assimilation into U.S. culture.[48] Hispanics are predicted to be the largest minority group in the coming decades, growing from 9 percent of the U.S. population in 1990s to an expected 16 percent by 2020.[49] Mexicans currently represent approximately 70 percent of the foreign-born U.S. population. Because many Mexican immigrants have limited education, language skills, and work skills, they are generally relegated to low-skilled jobs. Many illegal immigrants from Mexico are drawn to low-paying, high risk jobs such as those in meatpacking plants, which have one of the highest accident rates in the United States. In the 220 packing plants in Iowa and Nebraska, it is estimated that 25 percent of the workers are illegal aliens.[50] Preparing these workers for higher skilled jobs will mean making a considerable investment in education and training.

The number of Asians, the second-largest immigrant group, doubled in size between 1970 and 1980, from 1.4 million to 3.5 million. Asians are predicted to be the fastest-growing minority group, increasing from 1.6 percent of the U.S. population in the 1980s to a predicted 6.5 percent by 2020.[51] Asians have made considerable advancements in education. For example, while Asian-Americans represented 2 percent of the population in 1986, they represented 12 percent of the freshman class at Harvard that year.[52] Asians, like Hispanics, come from different cultures and religious backgrounds and speak different languages.

The Chinese, who are the largest Asian ethnic group, have been quite successful in gaining professional status. A large number of Chinese immigrants, most of whom were very poor and looking for low-skilled work, entered this country after restrictive immigration laws were lifted in the 1960s. In the intervening years, they have made great strides in assimilating into the American culture. Today, a large proportion of foreign-born and native Chinese hold jobs as small-business owners, managers, professionals, and executives.[53]

The Japanese followed the Chinese in terms of immigration patterns, but not in the same numbers. Today, the growth of Japanese manufacturing industries and Japanese foreign investment in the United States has made Japanese a significant force in U.S. financial markets. As the number of Japanese-owned businesses in the United States has increased, the number of Japanese executives working here has also increased. Asian groups from the southeast region, referred to as the Indochinese, also have grown in size since the end of the Vietnam War. These groups include Laotians, Vietnamese, Cambodians, Thais, and Indonesians.

As we noted earlier, Asians hold very few corporate executive positions, and also face the discrimination and cultural indifference experienced by other racial minorities and women.[54] While Asians have experienced discrimination, sociological studies of discrimination have generally excluded scrutinizing these groups. However, with the tremendous growth in Asian immigration over the past ten years, it is expected that more data will be generated about the impact of these groups on society.

## ADAPTING TO DEMOGRAPHIC CHANGES

Most organizations have recognized the demographic changes that have occurred in the workforce over the past thirty years. In response to the civil rights and feminist movements, as well as the equal employment legislation that began in the 1960s, many organizations established programs to facilitate the recruitment and retention of qualified women and minorities. This inclusion of women and minorities has made organizations more culturally diverse.

**Cultural diversity** is defined as the existence of two or more persons from different cultural groups in any single group or organization. Most organizations are culturally diverse because their employees are from different cultural subgroups (whether gender, race, ethnic origin, etc.). But even if an organization is culturally diverse, it may not be aware of or acknowledge this diversity.

In this section, we will discuss three common approaches to creating a working environment in which all organization members can contribute fully — affirmative action, valuing differences, and managing diversity. In different ways, each approach seeks to extend beyond the legal mandates required by the equal opportunity (EEO) laws discussed earlier.

## AFFIRMATIVE ACTION PROGRAMS

A first effort to go beyond the obligations specified in EEO legislation is **affirmative action.** While organizations that are covered by Title VII are encouraged to practice affirmative action to increase the numbers of women and minorities in their organizations, they are not legally required to do so under Title VII. The purpose of affirmative action programs is "to bring members of underrepresented groups, usually groups that have suffered discrimination, into a higher degree of participation in some beneficial program."[55] The concept of affirmative action was written into law in 1965 as part of Executive Order 11246 (as amended by Order 11375), which was issued by President Johnson. This order requires that certain government agencies and employers (and their subcontractors) who hold federal contracts in excess of $10,000 undertake affirmative action processes to ensure equal employment opportunity. It also established the Office of Federal Contract Compliance Programs (OFCCP), which has the responsibility of overseeing the affirmative action process. According to OFCCP guidelines, organizations should take the following steps to meet affirmative action requirements:

1. Prepare a written policy statement on equal employment opportunity/affirmative action (EEO/AA).
2. Designate an affirmative action officer.
3. Publicize an EEO/AA policy statement.
4. Conduct an analysis of the surrounding labor market to determine if their current labor force is representative.
5. If a protected group is underrepresented in any area within the organization (by department, occupation, etc.), develop goals and timetables in order to achieve parity with the external labor market.
6. Develop specific programs and activities to achieve these goals and timetables.
7. Establish an internal auditing and reporting system of its programs and activities.
8. Develop support for affirmative action, both inside and outside the company.

In essence, affirmative action can sometimes require actions such as preferential recruiting and hiring or placement of certain groups when those groups are underrepresented in an occupation within an organization. This is a very different premise from that used for equal employment opportunity legislation. That is, with EEO, the employer seeks to ignore race and gender as much as possible when making employment decisions. Under affirmative action, the employer is asked to explicitly consider race and gender in such decisions, if women and minorities are not adequately represented in a particular job or job category (compared to their availability in the labor market). The affirmative actions that an employer may engage in often involve HRD programs.

Affirmative action is a volatile topic in the United States. Supporters of affirmative action believe that it is necessary for correcting patterns of discrimination, particularly when an affirmative action plan (AAP) has been ordered by the courts in cases where an organization has been found guilty of long-standing discrimination. For example, this line of reasoning was supported by the U.S. Court of Appeals (Second Circuit) in the case of the *United States v. the National Association for the Advancement of Colored People, Inc.* (1985).[56] This decision upheld an affirmative action decree because the court found the City of Buffalo, New York, was guilty of long-standing discrimination against blacks, women, and Hispanics.

A second justification offered for affirmative action is the belief that because of institutional racism, minorities have been subjected to inferior conditions (e.g., lack of good education) and that they have thus been inhibited in their ability to compete against better-prepared whites. Therefore, preferential treatment can be one way to equalize their chances. This was the reasoning supported in the case of *Weber v. Kaiser Aluminum and Chemicals* (1976).[57] This decision allowed a temporary preference for admitting qualified members of underrepresented groups to jobs and training opportunities when a company could show imbalances in its workforce. In this case, Kaiser had previously negotiated exclusionary terms with a union that barred blacks from accessing the in-house training programs that were required for promotion.[58]

While affirmative action has resulted in some employment gains for women and minorities, particularly in the professional ranks, it has vocal opponents and has created several problems. Critics argue that affirmative action goes beyond providing equal employment opportunity by allowing employers to give preference to members of protected groups at the expense of majority-group members who themselves are not guilty of illegal discrimination. They claim that this preference leads to so-called reverse discrimination against such individuals. Second, it is argued that AAPs have created feelings of animosity toward the individuals and groups that have been perceived to have benefited from them. A third problem with AAPs is that they can **stigmatize** qualified minorities and women who have been hired or promoted based on their achievements. When an AAP is present, some employees may feel that the successes of *all* minority and women candidates are the result of affirmative action alone. This can undermine the self-esteem of people who have worked hard to educate themselves and develop the necessary skills to be successful.

Recent court challenges and legislation on the state level have created uncertainty about the future of affirmative action. First, in 1997, the U.S. Supreme Court agreed to hear a New Jersey case in which affirmative action was given as the reason for retaining an African American teacher while at the same time laying off an equally qualified white teacher (i.e., both had identical amounts of seniority). The case ended up being settled before the Supreme Court heard it, with the white teacher receiving $433,500.[59] Second, the State of California has moved to eliminate race- and gender-based affirmative action from decisions regarding public employment, education, and contracting. The initial step was a decision by the University of California Board of Regents to abolish racial preferences in favor of merit-based admissions and hiring criteria. This was followed by voter approval of Proposition 209 in the 1996 election, which eliminated race- and gender-based AA in decisions regarding public education, contracting, and employment. Civil rights advocates sued for and won a temporary restraining order prohibiting the law's implementation in early 1997, but this restraining order was lifted, and a subsequent request to the U.S. Supreme Court to grant an emergency restraining order was denied. Now that the law has gone into effect, decisions resulting from it will likely lead to further legal challenges. Third, the University of Texas Law School's affirmative action program was declared illegal in 1996, resulting in a significant reduction of minority candidates being admitted to the school in the fall of 1997. Currently, affirmative action has largely been overturned at public universities in Texas, California, and Florida.[60] Taken together, the changes brought about by actions such as these will significantly affect the legality and scope of affirmative action in the current decade.

Advocates of affirmative action have expressed concern about the criticisms leveled at it. For example, R. Roosevelt Thomas, executive director of the American Institute of Managing Diversity, stated that "affirmative action gets blamed for failing to do things it could never do . . . so long as racial and gender equality is something we grant to minorities and women there will be no racial and gender equality."[61] The growing challenge to affirmative action has led some civil rights advocates to propose modifying it as a way to retain what they see as its beneficial effects, while addressing the charges of critics. For example, Deval Patrick, former assistant U.S. attorney general for civil rights, has advocated replacing AA with what he calls affirmative consideration, an approach that supports merit, emphasizes qualifications, and embodies flexibility and the aspirations of an integrated workplace.[62] In summary, it is fair to say that the status of affirmative action remains highly uncertain. As we begin the twenty-first century, race and gender discrimination remain a troubling issue in American society. Government, employers, and citizens are still struggling to find ways to address the basic concerns that these issues raise.

## Valuing Differences and Diversity Training

Barbara Walker, former manager of the International Diversity Program at Digital Equipment Corporation, is credited with coining the phrase **valuing differences** in the 1980s. Her approach was to create an environment in which each person's cultural differences are respected. Valuing differences soon became popularized as **diversity training.** The diversity training movement gained momentum when the Hudson Institute published a report in 1987 that predicted that women and minorities would represent 85 percent of all new entrants in the labor force by the year 2000.[63] This prediction led to a sense of urgency by employers who felt they were ill prepared to handle this kind of change. It also resulted in the proliferation of diversity consultants and programs (e.g., cultural sensitivity training), many of which came with a large price tag.[64]

It is estimated that 47 percent of organizations conducted diversity training in 1996, down 6 percent from 1995.[65] Diversity training programs vary in scope and length. At one extreme are one- to three-day programs for managers that are designed to transform them into culturally sensitive people. Most of these are one-shot programs that have no follow-up to reinforce the issues raised in training. For example, US WEST, a Denver-based telecommunications company, developed a diversity program that includes two kinds of training: 1) a three-day program called Managing a Diverse Workforce for managers and union stewards and 2) a one-day version called The Value of Human Diversity for the remaining 65,000 employees.[66] Other organizations have used a different approach that includes a strategy to foster long-term cultural change. For example, Pacific Gas & Electric (PG&E), a major public utility in California, took a different approach to valuing differences. PG&E's program is built on the assumption that a cadre of internal trainers is needed to cultivate the underpinnings of a multicultural organization. Employees are selected to attend a six-day certification (train-the-trainer) diversity awareness program and, upon graduation, are expected to champion diversity in their day-to-day interactions with others.[67]

*EFFECTIVENESS OF DIVERSITY TRAINING PROGRAMS.*   Some anecdotal evidence suggests that diversity training can at least make individuals aware of cultural distinctions. Three examples illustrate this evidence:

1. A survey of employees who attended diversity training found that 62 percent felt the training was worthwhile in raising awareness of racial and gender differences; however most of the respondents (87 percent of whites and 52 percent of blacks) felt that race relations were good or better in their own organization *before* the training.[68]
2. An organizational evaluation of a diversity-training program at the Federal Aviation Administration (FAA) found that training made a significant difference in raising awareness.[69]
3. The results of a custom-designed diversity-training program at Wisconsin Power and Light Company indicated that employees had been receptive and that the training had improved how they behaved toward others, both internally and externally.[70]

The FAA and Wisconsin Power and Light programs benefited from top management's strong commitment not only to make the program work but also to conduct follow-up activities that would reinforce the changes.

There is growing criticism concerning the value of diversity training. An element of many programs is to highlight ways in which participants are different from one another. A common misgiving about emphasizing differences is that it fails to recognize that people identify with one another because of shared interests, values, goals, and experiences.[71] Another criticism deals with the lack of tangible goals, standards, and outcomes in many programs.[72] Also, the merit of the activities used in some diversity-training programs has been questioned. For example, some participants complain about white male bashing, so-called political correctness, and punishment for insensitivity, and some participants say the workshops are a pointless waste of time.[73] An ironic twist is that the Texaco executives on the tape accused of racist comments used the metaphor "black jelly

**■ TABLE 15-3**

POTENTIAL PROBLEMS WITH MANAGING DIVERSITY TRAINING

| When trainers . . . | When the training program . . . |
|---|---|
| ■ Use their own psychological issues (e.g., trust or group affiliation) as a template for training | ■ Is not integrated into the organization's overall approach to diversity |
| ■ Have their political agenda | ■ Is too brief, too late, or reactive |
| ■ Do not model the philosophy or skills associated with valuing diversity | ■ Is presented as remedial and trainees as people with problems |
| ■ Are chosen because they represent or advocate for a minority group | ■ Does not distinguish the meanings of valuing diversity, EEO, AA, and managing across cultures |
| ■ Are not competent at facilitation and presenting, have poor credibility with trainees, or are known to be insensitive | ■ Does not make a link between stereotyping behavior and personal and organizational effectiveness |
| ■ Force people to reveal their feelings about people | ■ Is based on a philosophy of political correctness |
| ■ Do not respect individual styles of trainees | ■ Is too shallow or too deep |
| ■ Pressure only one group to change | ■ Resource materials are outdated |
| ■ Cover too few issues and do not engage participants individually | ■ Curriculum is not adapted to trainees' needs or not matched with the skills and experience of the trainer |
| | ■ Discussion of certain issues (e.g., reverse discrimination) is not allowed |

SOURCE: From M. Mobley, & T. Payne (1992). Backlash: The challenge to diversity training. *Training and Development Journal,* 43(12), 47. Copyright 1992, the American Society for Training and Development. All rights reserved. Reprinted by permission.

bean," which came directly from a managing diversity workshop in which the colors of jellybeans were used to identify people, rather than as racial or ethnic labels.[74]

The costs of doing diversity training have also been questioned. It is reported that diversity consultants bill an average cost of $2,000 per day (with some demanding four times that amount), and a service such as a "cultural audit" costs as much as $100,000.[75] Flynn estimates that companies spend between $200 million to $300 million per year on diversity training yet, as noted above, lawsuits by women and minorities remain at very high levels.[76] Table 15-3 summarizes some of the potential problems with diversity training.

In a recent review, Ivancevich and Gilbert wrote, "We have not found a single reported program that conducts a rigorous evaluation of diversity training effectiveness" (p. 84).[77] Therefore, more vigorous evaluation of diversity programs is clearly necessary to assess their effectiveness in light of the mounting criticism and the costs. For example, a survey of the factors that lead to diversity program success concluded that success is associated with top-management support, a high strategic priority to diversity relative to other objectives, the presence of positive management beliefs about diversity, large organizations, and presence of a diversity manager.[78] Another criticism of the valuing differences approach is that its primary emphasis is on improving interpersonal relations and not on providing the *skills* needed for working with diverse cultural groups.[79] In order to learn these skills, a managing diversity approach may be needed.

## MANAGING DIVERSITY

Thomas defines **managing diversity** as "a comprehensive managerial process for developing an environment (organizational culture) that works for all employees."[80] This approach goes beyond both affirmative action and valuing diversity because it focuses on building a positive environment for everyone and on full utilization of the total workforce. It does not exclude women or minorities, nor does it exclude whites or males. It is an attempt to create a level playing field for all employees without regard to cultural distinction. Coming to agreement on the definition of diversity can be a very difficult thing, as many experienced trainers will attest.[81] However, one recent article defined it as "the commitment on the part of organizations to recruit, retain, reward, and promote a heterogeneous mix of productive, motivated, and committed workers including people of color, whites, females, and the physically challenged."[82] To do this, the managing diversity approach requires 1) a long-term commitment to change; 2) substantive changes in organizational culture; 3) a modified definition of leadership and management roles; 4) both individual and organizational adaptation; and 5) structural changes.[83]

The *long-term commitment to change*, particularly from top management, is necessary to allow sufficient time and resources to bring about a change in organizational culture. For example, Pillsbury has created the following managing diversity three-year objectives for its division heads:

1. To develop and implement strategic plans for creating more culturally diverse organizations

2. To increase leaders' and managers' knowledge and skills in managing a culturally diverse workplace

3. To attract, motivate, and retain women and people of color[84]

To achieve these objectives, managers must be totally committed to the program. Commitment from key organizational members (top managers, union leaders, etc.) is an important part of managing diversity. How to gain their commitment will be discussed later in this chapter.

A *substantive change in culture* is necessary if an organization expects to change the underlying assumptions, values, and beliefs that have fostered sexist and racist attitudes. Employees must learn to be more understanding of language and cultural differences and be able to identify and reject cultural stereotypes. Most organizations that have developed managing diversity programs rely on education and training programs, much as the valuing differences approach does. For example, organizations like Avon, Apple Computer, and Xerox have made diversity education the cornerstone of their managing diversity programs.

*Modified definitions of leadership and management roles* are needed in order to accommodate the changes in organizational culture. It is important that management roles be redefined not only during the change process but also as part of the managing diversity program. For example, managers may be required to serve as formal mentors to one or more of the women and minorities in their organization. Other organizations may require managers to lead a diversity core group. To ensure that these roles are institutionalized, some organizations have created a new corporate office for managing diversity. This office gives the program high visibility and ensures that all of the managing diversity activities are coordinated.

Managing diversity requires *both individual and organizational adaptation* because as the organizational culture undergoes a redefinition and begins to take on new characteristics, employees must be able to adapt to these changes. How well the organization and its employees adapt is highly dependent on the management and leadership of the change process. Sufficient support systems must be available for people who are not sure about what is expected of them and how to adapt to these new expectations. For example, some employees may feel this program is affirmative action under a new name. Managers must be able to reinforce the point that a managing diversity program favors no subgroup.

*Structural changes* are necessary to accommodate the changes in management and leadership roles and changes in individual expectations. For example, several structural changes within the HRD function may need to be made. These include 1) developing new policies that support the management diversity initiative; 2) changing formal orientation programs to place more emphasis on diversity issues; 3) developing formal career development programs; 4) adding a diversity component to some of the ongoing training programs, particularly management and supervisory training; and 5) developing a diversity resource library for all types of ongoing diversity programs.

*EXAMPLE OF A MANAGEMENT DIVERSITY PROGRAM.*    As noted, managing diversity involves the development of a long-term change strategy, including both structural and cultural changes.

Table 15-4 describes Pillsbury's managing diversity strategy, which has six stages.[85] Stages 1 and 2 are used for developing the context in which the change will take place. The activities include awareness sessions with senior management who need to understand their role in the change process and how to manage diversity. These briefing sessions are followed by team sessions that focus on educating employees about some of the issues that underlie cultural diversity. If necessary, the change agent or agents may review cultural data to illustrate important aspects of the organization's culture (e.g., certain employees feel isolated). The desired outcome of these first two stages is that everyone will feel a shared need to change.

Stages 3 through 5 involve more in-depth education about how diversity can bring added value to the organization. These three-day sessions explore the underlying assumptions that lead to racist and sexist attitudes. The goal is to expand each participant's understanding of cultural differences, the value each

**■ TABLE 15-4**

| Stage | Objectives |
|---|---|
| I. Briefing session, half day — 2 days | a. Review organization's cultural assessment data. |
| | b. Learn basic concepts regarding high performing, culturally diverse organization. |
| | c. Review organization's diversity plan. |
| II. Team session, 2 days | a. Build team skills necessary for addressing cultural diversity. |
| | b. Clarify business rationale for cultural diversity. |
| | c. Understand differences in business style. |
| | d. Understand differences in interpersonal style. |
| III. Added value (race), 3 days | a. Enhance racial interactions and communications. |
| | b. Identify stereotyping (racist) behaviors. |
| | c. Identify and address organizational barriers to contributions of racial minorities. |
| | d. Develop strategies for greater inclusion of racial minorities. |
| IV. Added value (gender), 3 days | a. Enhance gender interactions and communications. |
| | b. Identify stereotyping (sexist) behaviors. |
| | c. Identify and address organizational barriers to women's successful contributions. |
| | d. Develop strategies for greater inclusion of women. |
| V. Added value (style), 3 days | a. Identify the value that differences in style, ethnic/race, gender, and culture bring to the workplace. |
| | b. Practice teamwork that enhances the contribution of each member. |
| VI. Strategic planning, 1-2 days | a. Integrate cultural diversity into the business plan. |
| | b. Develop plans to (1) Expand educational process to the total organization, (2) Enhance the human resource system, and (3) Strengthen recruitment and retention. |

SOURCE: From M. Greenslade (1991). Managing diversity: Lessons from the United States. *Personnel Management* (United Kingdom), 23(12), 30.

person places on cultural differences, and the ways that including a diverse workforce will enhance the organization. The last stage, stage 6, involves integrating the cultural strategy into the organization's business plan. Since the philosophy of managing diversity is predicated on how well managers and other members of an organization view the utilization of people from all cultures, it is essential that the long-term strategy of the organization reflect this philosophy. This strategy also includes any changes in human resource management policies that will be necessary for achieving the long-term strategy, including strengthening the recruitment, hiring, and retention of a diverse workforce.

*EFFECTIVENESS OF MANAGING DIVERSITY PROGRAMS.* While there is growing awareness of the need to address diversity issues, some companies are reluctant to move in this direction. A 1991 Towers/Perrin survey of 645 national companies revealed a widespread acknowledgment (75 percent) of labor market changes, but only 29 percent of those firms have initiated a diversity program.[86] Beyond the fact that a number of organizations (e.g., Armco Steel, Avon, PG&E, and Pillsbury) have achieved some successes, there is very little empirical evidence of the overall effectiveness of their managing diversity programs. PG&E, for example, claims that managing diversity "improves its competitive advantage in recruiting and retaining employees and that it increases productivity, quality, creativity, and morale."[87] Further, a survey of 400 Society for Human Resource Management (SHRM) members found that while there was some criticism (as to communication problems and training costs), almost half of the respondents indicated that managing diversity has created a more tolerant organizational culture.[88] Most of the respondents also indicated that successful programs were the direct result of corporate efforts to open up communication channels and increase sensitivity to cultural and gender differences.[89]

Another problem with managing diversity is the resistance of long-held attitudes to change. Even when organizations bolster their change strategy with diversity education and training programs, there is no guarantee that all employees will place the same value on learning about their own attitudes and about other cultures, particularly if they feel they have nothing in common with members of those cultures. The fact remains that people tend to feel most comfortable among those with whom they have things in common (e.g., cultural attributes).

Furthermore, there is evidence of a backlash among whites, particularly white males. The following reactions to diversity education and training programs have been reported:

1. Deep-seated biases and prejudices that are emerging as a reaction to fast-paced social change
2. A perceived competition for jobs and resources, creating what some people see as a threatening environment
3. Race and gender issues used increasingly as a political football in the workplace
4. Sensationalistic journalism, creating scapegoats and highlighting stereotypes

■ **TABLE 15-5**

| Affirmative Action | Diversity Management |
|---|---|
| 1. Reactive and based on law and moral imperative | Proactive |
| 2. Not linked in any formal manner to team building | Emphasizes building diverse teams |
| 3. Focuses primarily on women and people of color | Inclusive — race ethnicity, age, religion, sexual orientation, and physical limitations all generally considered |
| 4. Emphasis is primarily on employees and not external constituents | Considers diversity in the recruitment pool, in employees, and in the external constituency |

SOURCE: From J. M. Ivancevich, & J. A. Gilbert (2000). Diversity management: Time for a new approach. *Public Personnel Management*, 29(1), 89.

5. The tendency of some people to see the political correctness movement as a direct threat to the First Amendment — which has created a legal and social minefield

6. The tendency of some to feel that a focus on multiculturalism will dissolve the unity of the United States

7. Confusion about such terms as *political correctness, diversity, multiculturalism, pluralism, equal opportunity, and affirmative action*[90]

This perceived backlash should not be ignored in a process of forced change.[91] As discussed in Chapter 14, resistance to change is rooted in personal values, beliefs, and attitudes. To overcome this resistance, we feel that organizations should consider introducing multiculturalism through a planned-change strategy. This would entail making use of theories and interventions such as those discussed in the last chapter. Further, a growing body of work provides guidance concerning how organizations can manage diversity in a way that is strategic, proactive, and more grounded in solid empirical and theoretical research than has typically been true to date. We refer the reader to a number of these writings.[92] As one example, Ivancevich and Gilbert outlined a number of differences between affirmative action and diversity management.[93] These are presented in Table 15-5. Others have also noted the value of a diversity management perspective for the development of self-directed work teams.[94]

## CROSS-CULTURAL EDUCATION AND TRAINING PROGRAMS

Globalization is increasingly being linked to diversity management efforts.[95] The argument is that a multicultural perspective is needed in order for organizations

**▪ TABLE 15-6**

| Question | Potential Areas of Discussion | Examples |
|---|---|---|
| What are some key dissimilarities between people from different cultures? | 1. Physical traits<br>2. System of values<br>3. Language or dialect<br>4. Religion<br>5. Institutions | 1. Sex, age, race<br>2. Work ethic<br>3. Hispanic<br>4. Judaism<br>5. Economic |
| How do these differences come about? | 1. Custom<br>2. Lifestyle<br>3. Shared norms<br>4. Shared experiences<br>5. Communication patterns | 1. Clothing<br>2. Food<br>3. Conforming<br>4. War veteran<br>5. Nonverbal symbols |
| What are the implications when different cultures interact? | 1. Conflict<br><br>2. Stereotyping or ethnocentrism<br><br>3. Sexism or racism | 1. When there is a misunderstanding<br>2. When a group refuses to accept a person from another group<br>3. Discrimination |

SOURCE: From H. Mason & R. S. Spich (1987). *Management: An International Perspective.* Homewood, IL: Irwin.

to successfully compete in the global marketplace. Globalization has also resulted in more U.S. citizens being given expatriate assignments. According to the National Trade Council (NTC), more than 250,000 U.S. citizens are working overseas.[96] To prepare these individuals for their assignments, many organizations are providing cross-cultural training. Most cross-cultural awareness training programs deal with at least four elements:

1. Raising the awareness of cultural differences

2. Focusing on ways attitudes are shaped

3. Providing factual information about each culture

4. Building skills in the areas of language, nonverbal communication, cultural stress management, and adjustment adaptation skills[97]

To *raise the awareness of cultural differences*, some questions that generate discussion need to be asked. Table 15-6 summarizes some sample questions. The discussion should focus on understanding some the assumptions, beliefs, and values people have about other cultures. Without first developing insight into these elements, it will be difficult for people to value cultural differences. For example, people from Japan and some other Asian countries may have difficulty assimilating with the aggressiveness and self-promotion that is common in many U.S. workplaces.[98] Without understanding these differences, Americans may misinterpret the motive of a Japanese manager who is unwilling to confront an American worker who has been overly aggressive toward him.

Programs that *focus on how attitudes are shaped* help people to understand how cultural stereotypes are formed and the destructiveness of cultural bias. Even though people may understand cultural differences, they may not truly understand how assumptions, values, and beliefs underlie sexist and racist attitudes. For example, a male manager may take extra effort to understand gender differences and learn to value women's contributions at the workplace. However, because there are a limited number of female managers, he may assume that most women lack the desire (or ability) to become managers. This assumption may result in his not actively encouraging female subordinates to develop the skills needed to qualify for a management position. This may serve to create a glass ceiling. Without focusing on how these attitudes are developed, it will be difficult to change them.

*Providing factual information about each culture* is necessary to reinforce new assumptions, values, beliefs, and attitudes about different cultures. When people are strongly ethnocentric — that is, feeling that their culture is superior to others — training may be provided, with the goal of reinforcing that every culture has its own unique and valuable experiences, perspectives, and styles of approaching problems. There is empirical evidence suggesting that cultural diversity brings together different experiences, perspectives, and styles that can be used for approaching problems and situations resulting in increased productivity.[99] People need to know what these strengths are and how they can help individual workers and the organization to do a better job.

Programs that *build skills in the areas of language, nonverbal communication, cultural stress management, and adjustment adaptation* address critical interpersonal relations of employees both inside and outside the organization. In order for people to establish effective relations, they must learn how to communicate. Nonverbal communication, including body language (e.g., gestures and handshakes), can be particularly important. Table 15-7 describes how some common forms of body language used by Americans can be misinterpreted by other cultures. Part of the communication training effort should focus on learning to understand cultural differences in body language and other nonverbal communication when dealing with different cultural groups.

It is estimated that 62 percent of U.S. companies offer some form of cross-cultural training, although the average length of this training is less than one day.[100] Given the high cost of much cross-cultural training, it is worth asking whether such programs are effective or not. Fortunately, research on this question has been quite positive.[101] It would appear that well-done cross-cultural training can have beneficial effects on employee adjustment and their performance in international assignments.

## HUMAN RESOURCE DEVELOPMENT PROGRAMS FOR CULTURALLY DIVERSE EMPLOYEES

The changing demographics of the workforce present both opportunities and challenges to HRD professionals. One of the challenges is seeking to eliminate all

■ **TABLE 15-7**

BODY LANGUAGE IN CULTURES WORLDWIDE

■ Acceptable interpersonal distance in various countries is

| | |
|---|---|
| 0 to 18 inches | Middle Eastern males, people from the eastern and southern Mediterranean, and some Hispanic cultures |
| 18 inches to 3 feet | U.S. and Western Europe |
| 3 feet or more | Asians (Japanese the farthest) and many African cultures |

■ It is inappropriate behavior to touch Asians on the head.

■ Acceptable length of eye contact in various countries is

| | |
|---|---|
| 0 to 1 second | Native Americans, East Indians, and Asian cultures (Least is the Cambodian culture, which believes that direct eye contact is flirtatious.) |
| 1 second | U.S. (To continue direct eye contact beyond 1 second can be considered threatening, particularly between Anglo- and African-American persons.) |
| 1 second or more | Middle Eastern, Hispanic, southern European, and French cultures generally advocate very direct eye contact. |

■ Variations of handshakes in various countries are

| | |
|---|---|
| Firm | Americans, Germans |
| Moderate grasp | Hispanics |
| Light | French (not offered to superiors) |
| Soft | British |
| Gentle | Middle Easterners |
| | Asians (For some Asian cultures, though not Koreans, shaking hands is unfamiliar and uncomfortable.) |
| Pointing | Generally poor etiquette in most countries, except in Asian countries where it is considered rude and in poor taste. If pointing is necessary, in Hong Kong you use your middle finger, in Malaysia use the thumb, and in the rest of Asia use the entire hand. |
| Beckoning | The American gesture of using upturned fingers, palm facing the body, is deeply offensive to the Mexicans, Filipinos, and Vietnamese. For example, this gesture in the Philippines is used to beckon prostitutes. |
| Signs of approval | The use of the okay sign, the thumbs-up signal, and the V for "victory" are among the most offensive to other cultures. |
| Signaling no | This can be confusing. In Mexico and the Middle East, a no is indicated by a back-to-forth movement of the index finger. |
| The left hand | Gesturing or handling something with the left hand among Muslims is considered offensive because they consider this the "toilet" hand. |

■ Crossing legs is in poor taste among most Asians and Middle Easterners. The Russians find it distasteful to place the ankle on the knee.

SOURCE: From S. Thiederman (1990). *Bridging cultural barriers for corporate success.* Lexington, MA: Lexington Books, 133–141.

causes of treatment discrimination. HRD professionals can do at least two things. First, they must be willing to confront some of the underlying assumptions, beliefs, and attitudes that foster bigotry and stereotyping that exist within their organization. They can be advocates for people who are victims of discrimination and be willing to fight for institutional justice. Second, HRD professionals should examine their organization's practices in the areas of socialization, orientation, career development, and sexual and racial harassment.

### SOCIALIZATION AND ORIENTATION

In Chapter 8, we defined socialization as the process by which an individual becomes an insider through assimilating the roles, norms, and expectations of the organization. A new employee's initial experiences in an organization are particularly significant in influencing later decisions about career choices and whether to remain in an organization. For example, when learning experiences are designed for new employees, the following issues should be considered:

1. New employees (including women and minorities) may feel isolated when their cultural differences prevent them from obtaining the interesting and challenging work assignments that are needed to learn important job-related skills and to qualify for promotions.[102]
2. Women and minorities may experience additional stresses if they feel they must become "bicultural" in order to be accepted by coworkers in the majority group.[103]
3. Women and minorities are sometimes held to higher standards than other coworkers as they enter nontraditional occupations.[104]

Failure to consider these issues can result in the loss of talented employees, especially females and minorities.

Some organizations have recognized the influences of cultural differences on the socialization process and have taken steps to incorporate them into their orientation and socialization practices. For example, Armco Steel recognized that subtle attitudes and prejudices against women and minorities had a negative effect on their upward mobility. Armco saw how these attitudes and prejudices were manifested during the socialization process. Specifically, they looked for ways in which existing employees could serve as role models during the socialization process.[105] Having role models from one's own race and gender can make it easier for new employees to confront issues like sexism and racism without fearing reprisal from coworkers.

There is disagreement about the value of holding training and orientation programs that are targeted to a segregated audience (e.g., women or minorities only). Some organizations believe that if the goal of managing diversity is to get employees to work together, it is important *not* to segregate women or minorities at any point in their development. However, other organizations see such sessions as important in meeting the special needs of these groups. Organizations like DuPont and GTE provide additional classroom training for newly hired women, but the trend is to avoid the impression of preferential treatment.[106] Morrison and Von Glinow have argued, "Because women and minorities face special situations as tokens, they may need to perfect certain competencies such as conflict resolution."[107] While we agree that it may be beneficial for incoming women and minorities to be given special awareness and training programs to help them make the adjustment and deal with difficult cultural issues, these programs should exist within an overall plan targeted toward all employees to achieve the goal of multiculturalism.

## CAREER DEVELOPMENT

Most career development models and programs (recall our discussion in Chapter 12) do not explicitly deal with the special concerns of a culturally diverse workforce. However, given the continued existence of glass ceiling issues and the failure of affirmative action to fully address inequities in the career advancement of women and minorities, more direct action should be taken in modifying career development systems.

Programs that promote valuing differences and managing diversity can be useful in creating a positive climate for career advancement. Although both of these approaches rely on education and training to change some of the underlying assumptions, values, and beliefs that sustain barriers like the glass ceiling, only the managing diversity approach attempts to integrate these efforts into the organizational strategy. For example, Jim Preston, former CEO of Avon Products, sees managing diversity as a significant part of his organization's business strategy, and states that "if you are going to attract the best . . . people into your organization, you'd better have a culture; you'd better have an environment in which those people feel they can prosper and flourish."[108]

Organizations can modify or create career development policies and programs without using a managing diversity approach. However, if sexist and racist attitudes are prevalent, an organization is less likely to be successful using "traditional" career development techniques to help advance the careers of women and minority employees. A "new" career development program should include specific roles for managers (e.g., serving as mentors or advocates) and a formal role for HRD departments in monitoring the process.

## MENTORING WOMEN AND MINORITIES

As suggested earlier, women and minorities have had difficulties moving into higher level positions. Traditionally, many individuals who successfully reach top management have been assisted by a mentor. In Chapter 12, we defined mentoring as a relationship between a junior and senior member of the organization that contributes to the career development of both members. Some evidence suggests that women perceive barriers to mentoring because they feel that a male mentor might misconstrue their request as a romantic or sexual gesture, are concerned about how others feel about the relationship, and feel that the male mentor would reject them.[109]

In terms of minorities, a study found that the development of minorities in organizations is affected by such things as the "absence of mentors, less interesting or challenging work as a result of being in the outgroup, and being left out of the informal social network."[110] This is supported by research that has examined diversified mentoring relationships (i.e., those made up of a majority member and a minority member) and homogeneous mentorship (i.e., those made up of both minority members or both majority members). The findings show the following relationships:

- Minorities in homogeneous mentoring relationships receive more psychosocial support (e.g., personal support, friendship) than those in diverse mentoring relationships.

- Mentors are also better role models in homogeneous relationships.

- Psychosocial support existed in diverse relationships when both the mentor and the protégé showed the preferred strategy for dealing with (racial) differences.[111]

This research has led Ragins to propose a model that depicts the relationship between mentor functions, protégé outcomes and mentor relationship composition (see Figure 15-1).[112] The model suggests that the dynamics of diversified mentor relationships and their outcomes are different than those of homogeneous mentor relationships. HRD professionals who design and implement mentorship programs should be aware of these possibilities and attempt to construct their programs in a way that maximizes the benefits and minimizes the problems. As we discussed in Chapter 12, even though mentoring has some inherent potential problems, we feel that the benefits outweigh the potential pitfalls, and that mentoring should be part of the career development process.[113]

### SEXUAL AND RACIAL HARASSMENT TRAINING

As suggested earlier, reports of sexual harassment have increased over the past decade. Organizations must take affirmative steps to deal with this problem at the workplace. Recent court decisions make it clear that the burden is on organizations to create a safe environment free from sexual demands or hostile acts.[114] Similar issues exist concerning racial harassment as well.

A number of steps should be taken to implement sexual and racial harassment training. Overall, the HRD process model we discussed in Chapters 4, 5, 6, and 7 provides a framework for the issues that should be addressed in establishing this sort of program. The four steps listed below highlight some of the issues specific to developing and delivering a sexual or racial harassment training program:

1. *Preparation of a Policy and Complaint Procedure.* Make sure the harassment policy is up-to-date and can be understood by all members of the organization. An appropriate policy should include procedures for 1) defining the scope of responsibility, 2) prompt and measured responses to claims of harassment, 3) authority to address the issue, and 4) multiple avenues for filing complaints. Some organizations have employees sign a document indicating that they have read and understood this policy.

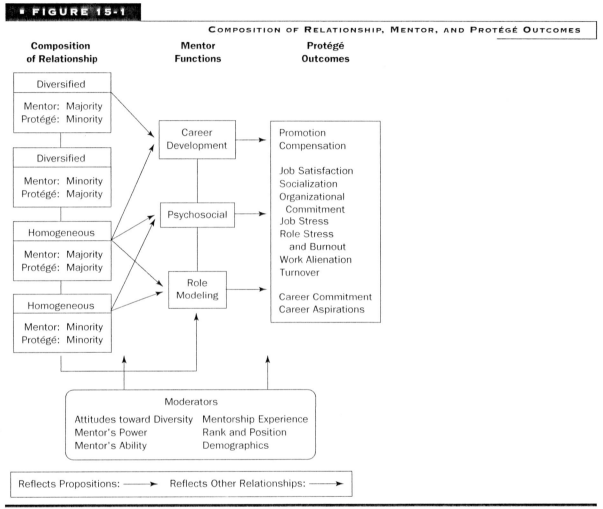

**■ FIGURE 15-1**

COMPOSITION OF RELATIONSHIP, MENTOR, AND PROTÉGÉ OUTCOMES

SOURCE: B.R. Ragins (1997). Diversified mentoring relationships in organizations: A power perspective. *Academy of Management Review, 22* (2), 508. Reprinted by permission.

2. *Assessment of the Organizational Climate.* It is important to determine if the organization is ready to accept the appropriate change, particularly if such training will be mandatory. Also, it is important to survey the employees to see how they feel about harassment issues.[115] The data could be helpful for determining program content. For example, if evidence shows that a number of supervisors try to discourage formal complaints, the program may need to reinforce supervisors' legal responsibilities in this area.

3. *Content of the Training Program.* The program should describe the current laws including interpretation of recent court decisions, review the organization policy and procedures, communicate a set of organizational

standards of conduct, outline responsibilities of supervisors, discuss methods of counseling or referring victims, and address situations where harassment is likely to take place.

4. *Selecting the Trainer or Trainers.* Care must be taken in selecting a trainer who has both expert knowledge of the law and an understanding of the organizational politics. Many organizations seek an outside consultant with legal experience in this area.

In addition, the issue of whether the training should be mandatory should be assessed. As a rule, if there is sufficient evidence of widespread harassment, training should be mandatory. These steps need to be modified in situations with significant resistance to change. If this is the case, organizations often take a more direct approach (e.g., zero tolerance) to ensure that this kind of discrimination is eliminated or at least minimized.

Some organizations advocate zero tolerance, which suggests that all forms of discrimination will not be acceptable. In this situation, policies would probably include strong sanctions against certain kinds of behavior, up to and including dismissal. Even with a strong policy, however, it is recommended that training and education be used as a vehicle for communicating the policy. The Pentagon credits a strong policy, followed up with an aggressive training program, for leading to a reduction in the reported incidences of treatment discrimination in the U.S. military. For example, a Pentagon study completed in May 1995 revealed that the incidence of sexual harassment complaints (as a percentage of all women in the combined services) dropped from 64 percent in 1988 to 55 percent in 1995.[116] The explanation for the drop was not only a zero tolerance philosophy, but also the implementation of an aggressive education program following the Tailhook incident in 1991. However, given the report of widespread sexual harassment at Aberdee Proving Grounds and elsewhere in the Army in 1997, even a zero tolerance philosophy and education program cannot completely eliminate sexual harassment. More stringent measures (e.g., in the military, the possibility of court martial or criminal charges) may be necessary to deter potential harassers.

The long-term effectiveness of these kinds of interventions depends on the continued commitment of top management. As we have stated many times throughout this text, top management sets the climate and the agenda for the organization. Unfortunately, not all CEOs see discrimination (and harassment) as a part of their agenda.[117] Perhaps recent incidents such as those involving Texaco, the U.S. Army, and Mitsubishi Motors, to name a few, will serve as reminders of the potential costs of not taking preventive and proactive actions.

## OTHER HUMAN RESOURCE MANAGEMENT PROGRAMS AND PROCESSES

Many organizations have extended managing diversity programs beyond HRD programs and processes by changing human resource management (HRM) policies and programs to meet the special needs of the new workforce.[118] Through the development of affirmative action and "diversity recruitment" programs, many organizations have been able to develop effective recruitment methods that are more effective in attracting qualified women and minority candidates.[119] A growing number of organizations are holding managers formally accountable for diversity goals, for example, incorporating such goals into their performance evaluation process.[120] Further, the influx of women and minorities into the workforce has led organizations to modify some of their HRM practices to meet the needs of a culturally diverse workforce. For example, some organizations have devised flexible work schedules and child-care programs directed at the growing number of working mothers who are entering or reentering the workforce. IBM, after realizing that 30 percent of its employees had child-care needs and an equal number had elder-care responsibilities, revised its child-care program and established a program for elder care.[121]

Some organizations have responded to the problems of communicating with non-English-speaking employees. A survey of companies in southeastern New England discovered that those organizations that acknowledged problems with non-English-speaking employees identified communication as the major problem. The survey respondents said that using the services of language interpreters and multilingual supervisors was the most effective means of resolving this problem. The language interpreters can help to establish expectations, convey organizational messages, and intervene when there are problems.[122] All of these roles help to support an effective managing diversity policy and program. Hiring multilingual supervisors is probably one of the most effective means of communicating with non-English-speaking employees because they can communicate directly without an interpreter.

## CLOSING COMMENTS

We hope you have gained an appreciation for the complexity of managing a culturally diverse workforce and how HRD programs can be used to achieve this goal. Obviously, no one can provide concrete evidence that organizations that are more diverse will necessarily be more successful in the future than those that are less diverse.[123] However, we are convinced that working toward the goal of reducing the various forms of treatment discrimination is fair and ethical and will ultimately lead to a climate in which all employees can thrive within an organization and contribute to its success. This requires a long-term, integrated effort.[124] Flynn points to the lack of strong positive examples of companies that can be lauded for their diversity efforts. However, companies such as Allstate Insurance have recently gained recognition for their efforts to "make diversity a business strategy."[125] We applaud such efforts, but close with a thought-provoking quote from Erin Kelly and Frank Dobbin:

> Will the weakened version of affirmative action found in current diversity management practices improve the prospects of women and minorities in the future? One recent study shows that diffuse diversity policies and programs are much less effective than are measures that target women and minority groups.[126] Perhaps diversity management will succeed in winning over middle managers because it embraces an economic, rather than political, rationale. But precisely because it is founded on cost-benefit analysis rather than on legal compliance, perhaps diversity management will

**RETURN TO OPENING CASE**

The first thing that R. R. Donnelley did was to change to an ongoing and much more intensive diversity training experience for their managers. Your instructor has additional information concerning what Donnelley did to change its diversity training efforts.

come under the ax of budget-cutters when America faces its next recession. Because it is not required by law, diversity management is not nearly as prevalent today as were the EEO/AA programs that preceded it. But the results of diversity management will have to be examined as the programs evolve.[127]

## Summary

Recent demographic trends suggest that women and minorities will continue to enter the workforce in greater numbers over the next twenty years. Organizations continue to address some of the workplace issues that result from a culturally diverse workforce, with diversity initiatives extending beyond issues of race and gender. A primary concern is treatment discrimination (e.g., promotional barriers, pay, and sexual and racial harassment). There are laws that prohibit treatment discrimination (e.g., Equal Pay Act and civil rights laws), but the law by itself is not sufficient to create a climate of fair treatment.

Historically, organizations have used four ways to integrate the workplace — equal employment opportunity, affirmative action (AA), valuing differences and diversity training, and managing diversity. Equal employment opportunity is a commitment not to discriminate in the workplace, based on various categories protected by law (e.g., race, sex, religion, disability, age). Affirmative action is a federal regulation that places an obligation on public agencies and many other organizations that receive federal grants or contracts. AA has always been highly controversial, and its effectiveness in creating a truly integrated workforce has been modest. Valuing differences or diversity training attempts to deal with the underlying values and attitudes that manifest themselves in sexism and racism. However, because of the proliferation of diversity consultants with unproven methods, diversity training has been widely criticized. The evidence of the effectiveness of this approach is mixed to negative. Managing diversity is a long-term cultural change that seeks to level the playing field for all workers. Despite the appeal of this approach, there is little evidence to date concerning the effectiveness of this approach on the long-term viability of an organization.

As organizations become more global, the need for cross-cultural training has grown. Organizations must prepare employees for overseas assignments by giving them language skills and indoctrinating them in the customs, culture, and laws of the host country.

Managing a culturally diverse workforce may include changes in various HRD and HRM programs and processes. HRD professionals must be able to adapt current socialization, orientation, and career development processes to the needs of the new workforce. HRM professionals should consider adapting other policies (e.g., benefits) in order to meet the special needs of new groups, including such things as day-care services, flextime, interpreters, and multilingual supervisors.

## KEY TERMS AND CONCEPTS

| | |
|---|---|
| access discrimination | glass ceiling |
| affirmative action | managing diversity |
| cross-cultural training | mentoring |
| cultural diversity | racial and sexual harassment |
| diversity training | treatment discrimination |
| equal employment opportunity | valuing differences |
| flexible work schedules | |

## QUESTIONS FOR DISCUSSION

1. Compare and contrast equal employment opportunity, affirmative action, and managing diversity programs. Can they occur simultaneously? Why or why not?

2. What changes, if any, have you personally experienced in the workplace? What needs to be done to ensure that all individuals (including women and minorities) have equal opportunity all of the time?

3. Do you believe it is important to acknowledge, understand, and value differences in your organization? Explain. How are you and your friends from culturally diverse backgrounds different? How are you the same?

4. What kinds of issues would you be faced with if you were given an overseas assignment to Japan? What would you do to prepare? How would this be different if the assignment was in Canada or Mexico?

5. Describe the role of HRD professionals with respect to managing culturally diverse employees. What kinds of HRD programs support this approach?

6. In some organizations, cultural diversity efforts meet with resistance from key managers and employees. Identify at least one reason for this resistance and recommend ways it can be overcome. Support your recommendations.

## REFERENCES

1. Judy, R. W., and D'Amico, C. (1997). *Workforce 2020: Work and workers in the 21st century.* Indianapolis: Hudson Institute.

2. Kossek, E. E., & Lobel, S. A. (eds.) (1996). *Managing diversity: Human resource strategies for transforming the workplace.* Cambridge, MA: Blackwell Publishers.

3. Ott, J. S. (1989). *The organizational culture perspective.* Pacific Grove, CA: Brooks/Cole.

4. Schein, E. H. (1987). *Process consultation* (vol. 2). Reading, MA: Addison-Wesley, 264.

5. Ott (1989), *supra* note 3, p. 24.

6. *Ibid.*

7. Kossek & Lobel (1996), *supra* note 2.

8. Camarota, S. A. (2001). Book review: *Legal U.S. immigration: Influences on gender, age, and skill composition, Industrial and Labor Relations Review, 54*(2), January, 381–382.

9. Judy & D'Amico (1997), *supra* note 1.

10. Ilgen, D. R., & Youtz, M. A. (1986). Factors affecting the evaluation and development of minorities in organizations. *Research in Personnel and Human Resource Management, 4,* 307–337.

11. Martinez, M. (1997). Prepared for the future. *HR Magazine, 42* (4), 80–87; Chaudhuri, A., & Collins, K. (2000). The 2000 salary survey. *Working Woman, 25*(7), July/August, 58–63.

12. Martinez (1997), *supra* note 11.

13. http://www.eeoc.gov/stats/jobpat/tables01.html (2000). Part I: National, and SIC Codes 01–09–243.

14. http://www.eoc.gov/stats/sex.html (2001). Sex-based charges, FY 1992–FY 2000.

15. Morrison, A. M., & Von Glinow, M. A. (1990). Women and minorities in management. *American Psychologist, 45,* 200–208; Hurley, A. E., & Sonnenfeld, J. A. (1995). Organizational growth and employee advancement: Tracking opportunities. In M. London (ed.), *Employee, careers, and job creation.* San Francisco, Jossey-Bass; Blum, T. C.. Fields, D. L., & Goodman, J. S. (1994). Organizational-level determinants of women in management. *Academy of Management Review, 37,* 241–268; Martinez, M. (1997). Prepared for the future: Training women for corporate leadership. *HR Magazine, 42*(4), 8087.

16. Women have little clout in large corporations. (2000). *Worklife, 12*(3), 9.

17. Strauss, G., & Jones, D. (2000). Too-bright spotlight burns female CEOs; Many firms faring poorly now, but women pay dearly. *USA Today,* December 18, B3; Burrows, P. (2001). The radical. *Business Week*(3720), February 19, 70–77; Managers to watch in 2001 (2001). Business Week (3714), January 8, 63–70.

18. Blau, F. D., & Kahn, L. M. (2000). Gender differences in pay. *Journal of Economic Perspectives, 14*(4), Fall, 75–99.

19. Judy & D'Amico (1997), *supra* note 1.

20. http://nces.ed.gov/pubs99/condition99/Indicator-12.html (Table 12–1, Ratio of median annual earnings of all male to al female wage and salary workers ages 25–34, by educational attainment: 1970–1997).

21. Jarratt, J., & Coates, J. F. (1995). Employee development and job creation: Trends, problems, opportunities. In M. London (ed.), *Employees, careers, and job creation.* San Francisco, Jossey-Bass.

22. Koretz, G. (2000). The gender gap in top brass pay. *Business Week* (3708), November 20, p. 32.

23. *Guidelines on discrimination because of sex,* 29 C.F.R. Sec. 1604.11(a) (1995).

24. *Burlington Industries, Inc. v. Ellerth,* No. 97–569 (1998).

25. http://www.eeoc.gov/press/9-6-00.html(2000). Monitors say Mitsubishi in compliance with EEOC consent decree; sexual harassment "firmly under control" at U.S. plant.

26. Zall, M. (1992). What to expect from the Civil Rights Act. *Personnel Journal, 72*(3), 46–50.

27. http://www.eeoc.gov/stats/harass.html. (2001). Sexual harassment charges EEOC and FEPAs combined: FY 1992 — FY 2000.

28. http://www.eeoc.gov/stats/race.html (2001). Race-based charges, FY 1992 — FY 2000.

29. Leo, J. (1997). Jelly bean: The sequel. *U.S. News and World Report, 122*(5), February 10, p. 20.

30. Caudron, S. (1997). Don't make Texaco's $175 million mistake. *Workforce, 76*(3), 58–66.

31. EEOC (2000), *supra* note 13.

32. Morrison & Von Glinow (1990), *supra* note 15.

33. Caudron (1997), *supra* note 30.

34. Powell, G. N., & Butterfield, D. A. (1997). Effect of race on promotions to top management in a federal department. *Academy of Management Journal, 40,* 112–128.

35. Greenhaus, J. H., Parasuraman, S., & Warmley, W. M. (1990). Effects of race on organizational experiences, job performance evaluations, and career outcomes. *Academy of Management Journal, 33,* 64 86.

36. *Ibid,* 80.

37. Ilgen & Youtz (1986), *supra* note 10.

38. *Ibid,* 326.

39. http://www.eeoc.gov/accomplishments-00.html (2001). EEOC accomplishments report for fiscal year 2000.

40. Garland, S. B. (1991). Can the Feds bust through the "glass ceiling?" *Business Week, 33,* April 29; Mize, S. (1992). Shattering the glass ceiling. *Training and Development, 46*(1), 60–62; Morrison & Von Glinow (1990), *supra* note 15; Solomon, C. M. (1990). Careers under glass. *Personnel Journal, 69*(4), 96–105.

41. U.S. Department of Labor (1991). *A report of the glass ceiling initiative* (Publication Number 1992 312–411/64761). Washington, DC: U.S. Government Printing Office, 3.

42. *Ibid,* 21.

43. Solomon, C. M. (2000). Cracks in the glass ceiling. *Workforce,* September, 86–94.

44. Maume, D. J., Jr. (1999). Glass ceilings and glass elevators. *Work and Occupations, 26*(4), 483–509.

45. Baxter, J., & Wright, E. O. (2000). The glass ceiling hypothesis. *Gender and Society, 14*(2), 275–294.

46. Meyerson, D. E., & Fletcher, J. K. (2000). A modest manifesto for shattering the glass ceiling. *Harvard Business Review, 78*(1), January/February, 126–136.

47. U.S. foreign-born population (2001). *World Almanac and Book of Facts 2000, 373.*

48. Heskin, A. D., & Heffner, R. A., (1987). Learning about bilingual, multicultural organizing. *Journal of Applied Behavioral Science, 23,* 525–541.

49. Judy & D'Amico (1997), *supra* note 1.

50. Hedges, S. J., & Hawkins, D. H. (1996). The new jungle. *U.S. News and World Report,* September 23, 34–45.

51. Judy & D'Amico (1997), *supra* note 1.

52. Ramirez, A. (1986). America's super minority. *Fortune,* November 4, 148–164.

53. Hess, B. B., Markson, E. W., & Stein, P. J. (1992). Racial and ethnic minorities: An overview. In P. S. Rothenberg (ed.), *Race, class, and gender in the United States* (96–110). New York: St. Martin's Press.

54. Ramirez (1986), *supra* note 52.

55. Rosenfeld, M. (1991). *Affirmative action and justice.* New Haven: Yale University Press, 42.

56. 779 f. 2d 881 (1985).

57. 415 F. Supp. 761 (1976).

58. Milkovich, G. T., & Boudreau, J. W. (1994). *Human resource management* (7th ed.). Burr Ridge, IL: Richard D. Irwin.

59. Reibstein, L., & Stone, B. (1997). A tactical retreat in a race case. *Newsweek, 130*(22), December 1, 40; Coulter, A. (1997). Why the Piscataway case went thataway. *Human Events, 53*(46), December 5, 5–6.

60. After affirmative action (2000). *New York Times, 149*(51394), May 20, A14.

61. Thomas , R. R., Jr. (1990). From affirmative action to affirming diversity. *Harvard Business Review, 68*(2), 107–117, p. 109.

62. Taylor, R. A. (1996). After Hopwood. *Black Issues in Higher Education, 13*(4), 12.

63. Judy & D'Amico (1997), *supra* note 1.

64. *Ibid.*

65. Industry Report. (1996). Who's learning what? *Training, 33*(10), 55–66.

66. Caudron, S. (1992). U S WEST finds strength in diversity. *Personnel Journal, 71*(3), 40–44.

67. Johnson, R. B., & O'Mara, J. (1992). Shedding new light on diversity training. *Training & Development, 43*(5), 45–52.

68. Lynch, F. R. (1997). *The diversity machine: The drive to change the "white male workplace."* New York: Free Press.

69. Tan, D. L., Morris, L, & Romero, J. (1996). Changes in attitude after diversity training. *Training and Development, 50*(9), 54–55.

70. Mueller, N. (1996). Wisconsin Power and Light's model diversity program. *Training and Development, 50*(3), 57–60.

71. Beekie, R. (1997). Diversity training's big lie. *Training, 34*(2), 122.

72. Paskoff, S. M. (1996). Ending the workplace diversity wars. *Training, 33*(8), 42–47.

73. Nemetz, P. L., & Christensen, S. L. (1996). The challenge of cultural diversity: Harnessing a diversity of views to understand multiculturalism. *Academy of Management Review, 21*(2), 434–462.

74. Leo (1997) *supra* note 29.

75. Judy & D'Amico (1997), *supra* note 1.

76. Flynn, G. (1998). The harsh reality of diversity programs. *Workforce, 77*(12), 26–33.

77. Ivancevich, J. M., & Gilbert, J. A. (2000). Diversity management: Time for a new approach. *Public Personnel Management, 29*(1), 75–92.

78. Rynes, S., & Rosen, B. (1995). A field survey of factors affecting the adoption and perceived success of diversity training. *Personnel Psychology, 48*, 247–271.

79. Galagan, P. A. (1991). Tapping the power of a diverse workforce. *Training and Development Journal, 45*(3), 38–44.

80. Thomas, R. R., Jr. (1991). *Beyond race and gender*. New York: AMACOM, 10.

81. Wellner, A. (2000). How do you spell diversity? *Training, 37*(4), April, 34–36.

82. Ivancevich & Gilbert (2000) *supra* note 77.

83. *Ibid.*

84. Greenslade, M. (1991). Managing diversity: Lessons from the United States. *Personnel Management, 23*(12), 28–33.

85. *Ibid.*

86. Galagan (1991), *supra* note 79.

87. Johnson & O'Mara (1992), *supra* note 67.

88. Rosen, B., & Lovelace, K. (1991). Piecing together the diversity puzzle. *HR Magazine, 36*(6), 78–84.

89. *Ibid.*

90. Mobley, M., & Payne, T. (1992). Backlash: The challenge to diversity training. *Training and Development, 43*(12), 45–52.

91. Karp, H. B., & Sammour, H. Y. (2000). Workforce diversity: Choices in diversity training programs and dealing with resistance to diversity. *College Student Journal, 34*(3), September, 451–458.

92. Jackson, S. A., & associates (1992). *Diversity in the workplace: Human resource initiatives.* New York: Guilford Press; Kossek & Lobel (1996) *supra* note 2; Bond, M. A., & Pyle, J. L. (1998). Diversity dilemmas at work. *Journal of Management Inquiry, 7*(3), 252–269; Ferris, G. R., Arthur, M. M., Berkson, H. M., Kaplan, D. M., Harrell-Cook, G., Frink, D. D. (1998). Toward a social context theory of the human resource management-organization effectiveness relationship. *Human Resource Management Review, 8*(3), 235–264; Dass, P., & Parker, B. (1999). Strategies for managing human resource diversity: From resistance to learning. *Academy of Management Executive, 13*(2), 68–80; Guajardo, S. A. (1999). Workforce diversity: Monitoring employment trends in public organizations. *Public Personnel Management, 28*(1), 63–85; Gilbert, J. A., & Ivancevich, J. M. (2000). Valuing diversity: A tale of two organizations. *Academy of Management Executive, 14*(1), 93–105; Gilbert, J. A. (2000). An empirical examination of resources in a diverse environment. *Public Personnel Management, 29*(2), 175–184.

93. Ivancevich & Gilbert (2000) *supra* note 77.

94. Hickman, G. R., & Creighton-Zollar, A. (1998). Diverse self-directed work teams: Developing strategic initiatives for 21st century organizations. *Public Personnel Management, 27*(2), 187–200.

95. Wentling, R. M., & Palma-Rivas, N. (2000). Current status of diversity initiatives in selected multinational corporations. *Human Resource Development Quarterly, 11*(1), 35–60; Weaver, V. J., & Coker, S. (2001). Globalization and diversity. *Mosaics, 7*(1), January/February, 1–5.

96. Dolanski, S. (1997). Are expats getting lost in the translation? *Workforce, 76*(2), 32–39.

97. Callahan, M. R. (1989). Preparing the new global manager. *Training and Development, 43*(3), 28–32.

98. Cox, T., Jr., (1991). The multicultural organization. *The Executive, 5*(2), 34–47.

99. Gordon, J. (1992). Rethinking diversity. *Training, 29*(1), 23–30.

100. Black, J. S., Gregersen, H. B., Mendenhall, M. E., & Stroh, L. K. (1999). *Globalizing people through international assignments.* Reading, MA: Addison-Wesley.

101. Black, J. S., & Mendenhall, M. (1990). Cross-cultural training effectiveness: A review and theoretical framework for future research. *Academy of Management Review, 15,* 113–136; Deshpande, S. P., & Viswesvaran, C. (1991). Is cross-cultural training of expatriate managers effective: A meta-analysis. Paper presented at the Academy of Management, Miami, FL; Bennett, R., Aston, A., & Colquhoun, T. (2000). Cross-cultural training: A critical step in ensuring the success of international assignments. *Human Resource Management, 39*(2/3), 239–250; Bolino, M. C., & Feldman, D. C. (2000) Increasing the skill utilization of expatriates. *Human Resource Management, 39*(4), 367–379.

102. Kanter, R. M. (1977). *Men and women of the corporation.* New York: Basic Books.

103. Cox, T. H., Lobel, S. A., & McLeod, P. L. (1991). Effects of ethnic group cultural differences on cooperative and competitive behavior on a group task. *Academy of Management Journal, 34,* 827–847.

104. Fernandez, J. P. (1988). Human resources and the extraordinary problems minorities face. In M. London and E. M. Mone (eds.), *Career growth and human resource strategies: The role of the*

*human resource professional in employee development* (227–239). New York: Quorum Books; Solomon (1990), *supra* note 40.

105. Pickard, J. (1991). Steel partners. *Personnel Management, 23*(12), 32.

106. Morrison & Von Glinow (1990), *supra* note 15.

107. *Ibid*, 204.

108. Thomas (1991), *supra* note 80, p. 164.

109. Ragins, B. R., & Cotton, J. L. (1993). Gender and willingness to mentor in organizations. *Journal of Management, 19*, 97–111; Crampton, S. M., & Mishra, J. M. (1999). Women in management. *Public Personnel Management, 28*(1), 87–106.

110. Ilgen & Youtz (1986), *supra* note 10, p. 326.

111. Ragins, B. R. (1997). Diversified mentoring relationships in organizations: A power perspective. *Academy of Management Review, 22*, 482–521; Thomas, 1990, *supra* note 61; Thomas, D. A. (1993). Racial dynamics in cross-race developmental relationships. *Administrative Science Quarterly, 38*, 169–194.

112. Ragins (1997), *supra* note 111.

113. Drazga, B. M. (1998). Mentoring helps break glass ceiling. Denver *Business Journal, 49*(46), July 17, 21A-22A.

114. Segal, J. A. (1998). Sexual harassment prevention: Cement for the glass ceiling? *HR Magazine, 43*(12), November, 129–134.

115. Verespej, M. A. (1997). Zero tolerance. *Industry Week, 246*(1), 24–28.

116. Schafer, S. M. (1996). Sex harassment still embedded in military. *Providence Sunday Journal,* November 10.

117. Verespej (1997), *supra* note 115.

118. Mathews, A. (1999). Diversity: A principle of human resource management. *Public Personnel Management, 27*(2), 175–185.

119. Digh, P. (1999). Getting people in the pool: Diversity recruitment that works. *HR Magazine, 44*(10), 94–98.

120. Digh, P. (1998). The next challenge: Holding people accountable. *HR Magazine, 43*(11), October, 63–68.

121. Sourentian, J. (1989). Four by four. *Training and Development Journal, 43*(11), 21–30.

122. Heskin & Heffner (1987), *supra* note 48.

123. Kuczynski, S. (1999). If diversity, then higher profits? *HR Magazine, 44*(13), December, 66–71; Suttell, S. (1998). Diversity programs a key to companies bottom line. *Crain's Cleveland Business, 19*(26), June 29, 13–14.

124. Adams, M. (1998). Building a rainbow, one stripe at a time. *HR Magazine, 43*(9), August, 72–79; Dobbs, M. F. (1998). Managing diversity: The Department of Energy initiative. *Public Personnel Management, 27*(2), 161–175.

125. Flynn, G. (1998), *supra* note 76; Crockett, J. (1999). Diversity as a business strategy. *Management Review, 88*(5), 62.

126. Konrad, A. M., & Linnehan, F. (1995). Formalized HRM structures: Coordinating equal opportunity or concealing organizational practices? *Academy of Management Journal, 38*, 787–820.

127. Kelly, E., & Dobbin, F. (1998). How affirmative action became diversity management. *American Behavioral Scientist, 41*(7), 960–984.

# *Training and Development*

In order to compete successfully in a global market, more firms are focusing on the role of human resources as a critical part of their core competence and a source of competitive advantage. As Kamoche[1] reminds us: "the human resource refers to the accumulated stock of knowledge, skills, and abilities that the individuals possess, which the firm has built up over time into an identifiable expertise." The question for the multinational firm is how to maintain and leverage its human resources so that suitably trained, internationally oriented personnel are available to support its strategic responses and contribute to its core competencies. An indication of the importance of training and developing staff is the increasing number of multinationals that establish their own "universities," or "schools." Motorola, McDonald's Hamburger, and Disney universities are good examples of these in-house training centers; several European, Japanese, and Korean firms have similar arrangements.

Exhibit 5–1 is a schematic representation of the structure of this chapter. It shows the link between international recruitment and selection (Chapter 3) and training and development activities. As we discussed in Chapter 4, training and development programs are an integral part of an effective performance management system. However, new employees generally undergo some form of training upon selection; for example, you may recall from the account of McDonald's entry into Russia in Chapter 2 that crew members were each given 60 hours of training prior to the opening of the Moscow outlet. In this chapter, we distinguish

**EXHIBIT 5–1**   *International Training and Development*

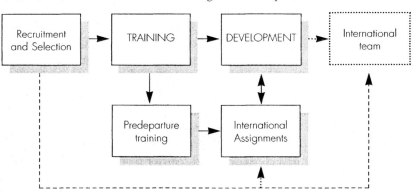

between the terms *training* and *development*. Training aims to improve current work skills and behavior, whereas development aims to increase abilities in relation to some future position or job—usually managerial. We will begin by examining the training approaches and issues for each of the three categories of staff—PCNs, TCNs, and HCNs. Development aspects, especially the impact of international assignments upon career paths within a multinational, will then be addressed.

## EXPATRIATE TRAINING

Most expatriates, whether PCNs or TCNs, are selected from within the multinational's existing operations, though, as indicated by the dotted arrow in Exhibit 5–1, some expatriates may be hired externally. Given that the primary selection criterion is technical ability, it is not surprising to find that most of the literature is devoted to expatriate predeparture training activities that are mainly concerned with developing cultural awareness. Once an employee has been selected for an expatriate position, predeparture training is considered to be the next critical step in attempting to ensure the expatriate's effectiveness and success abroad, particularly where the assignment country is considered culturally tough. Some form of cultural preparation is indicated because, as you may recall from our discussion of expatriate failure in Chapter 3, functional ability alone does not determine success. Effective cultural training also enables individuals to adjust more rapidly to the new culture. As Earley[2] points out, "A major objective of intercultural training is to help people cope with unexpected events in a new culture." For these performance-related reasons, investing resources in training for international assignments can be justified easily.[3]

The limited, predominately U.S.-based, research into this area reveals that a large number of U.S. multinationals have been reluctant to provide even a basic level of predeparture training. Tung[4] asked respondents to indicate the frequency of use of training programs. The results showed that the U.S. multinationals tended to use training programs for expatriates less frequently than the European and Japanese firms (32 percent compared with 69 percent and 57 percent, respectively). According to Ronen[5] this finding was consistent with earlier research.

Our review of extant literature shows that the rate of predeparture training provision has been slow to increase in the intervening years since Tung's 1982 study. A 1984 study of 1,000 U.S. multinationals found that only 25 percent offered extensive predeparture training programs.[6] Another study, conducted in 1989, surveyed U.S. firms regarding relocation programs and found that only 13 percent of respondents indicated that they would offer expatriates a predeparture program.[7] In their 1990 review of U.S. practices, McEnery and DesHarnais[8] estimated that between 50 and 60 percent of U.S. companies operating abroad at that time did not provide any predeparture preparation. The various authors report that, among the various reasons cited by firms for the low use of crosscultural training, top management does not believe predeparture training is necessary or effective.[9] So, while the potential benefits of cultural awareness training are widely acknowledged, such training is not offered by a large number of U.S. multinationals.[10] The emphasis placed by European (including Scandinavian) multinationals on predeparture training, particularly language training, has been found to be stronger than that of U.S. multinationals.[11]

More recently, the 1997–98 Price Waterhouse[12] survey of European firms (including subsidiaries of non–European multinationals) revealed that cultural awareness training remains the most common form of predeparture training, and that it is still offered on a voluntary basis rather than as a mandatory requirement. Only 13 percent of the firms surveyed always provided their expatriates with access to cultural awareness courses, though a further 47 percent now provided briefings for culturally "challenging" postings (compared with 21 percent in their 1995 survey). In the past, regardless of country of origin,[13] firms placed less priority on providing predeparture training for the spouse and family. However, perhaps due to increasing recognition of the interaction between expatriate performance and family adjustment, more multi-nationals are now extending their predeparture training programs to include the spouse or partner and children.

## Components of Effective Predeparture Training Programs

Studies indicate that the essential components of predeparture training programs that contribute to a smooth transition to a foreign post include cultural awareness training, preliminary visits, language instruction, and assistance with practical, day-to-day matters.[14] We will look at each of these in turn.

### Cultural Awareness Programs

It is generally accepted that to be effective the expatriate employee must adapt to and not feel isolated from the host country. A well-designed cultural awareness training program can be extremely beneficial, as it seeks to foster an appreciation of the host-country's culture so that expatriates can behave accordingly, or at least develop appropriate coping patterns. Sieveking, Anchor, and Marston[15] cite the culture of the Middle East to emphasize this point. In that region, emphasis is placed on personal relationships, trust, and respect in business dealings; coupled with this is an overriding emphasis on religion that permeates almost every aspect of life. As discussed in Chapters 3 and 4, without an understanding (or at least an acceptance) of the host-country culture in such a situation, the expatriate is likely to face some difficulties during the international assignment.

The components of cultural awareness programs vary according to country of assignment, duration, purpose of the transfer, and the provider of such programs.[16] As part of her study of expatriate management, Tung[17] identified five categories of predeparture training, based on different learning processes, type of job, country of assignment, and the time available:

- Area studies programs that include environmental briefing and cultural orientation;
- Culture assimilators;
- Language training;
- Sensitivity training; and
- Field experiences.

To understand possible variations in expatriate training, Tung[18] proposed a contingency framework for deciding the nature and level of rigor of training. Two determining factors were the degree of interaction required in the host culture and the similarity between the individual's native culture and the new culture. The related training elements in her framework involved the content of the training and the rigor of the training. Essentially, Tung argued that:

- If the expected interaction between the individual and members of the host culture was low, and the degree of dissimilarity between the individual's native culture and the host culture was low, then training should focus on task- and job-related issues rather than culture-related issues. The level of rigor necessary for effective training should be relatively low.
- If there was a high level of expected interaction with host nationals and a large dissimilarity between the cultures, then training should focus on crosscultural skill development as well as on the new task. The level of rigor for such training should be moderate to high.

Tung's model specifies criteria for making training method decisions—such as degree of expected interaction and cultural similarity. One limitation though is that it does not assist the user to determine which specific training methods to use or what might constitute more or less rigorous training.

Mendenhall and Oddou proposed a model that builds upon Tung's. It was refined subsequently by Mendenhall, Dunbar, and Oddou.[19] They propose three dimensions—training methods, low, medium, and high levels of training rigor, and duration of the training relative to degree of interaction and culture novelty—as useful guidelines for determining an appropriate program. For example, if the expected level of interaction is low and the degree of similarity between the individual's native culture and the host culture is high, the length of the training should probably be less than a week. Methods such as area or cultural briefings via lectures, movies, or books would provide the appropriate level of training rigor.[20] On the other hand, if the individual is going overseas for a period of two to twelve months and is expected to have some interaction with members of the host culture, the level of training rigor should be higher and its length longer (one to four weeks). In addition to the information-giving approaches, training methods such as culture assimilators and roleplays may be appropriate.[21] If the individual is going to a fairly novel and different host culture and the expected degree of inter-action is high, the level of crosscultural training rigor should be high and training should last as long as two months. In addition to the less rigor-ous methods already discussed, sensitivity training, field experiences, and inter-cultural experiential workshops may be appropriate training methods in this situation.

In their literature review, Black and Mendenhall[22] concluded that the Mendenhall, Dunbar, and Oddou model, like that of Tung, is primarily "cultural" in nature, with little integration of the individual's new tasks and the new host culture. Black and Mendenhall proposed what they described as an extensive theoretically based model using Bandura's so-cial learning theory and prior cultural awareness training models. They take three aspects of social learning theory—attention, retention, and reproduction—and show how these are influenced by individual differ-ences in expectations and motivation, and the incentives to apply learned behaviors in the foreign location. This approach recognizes that effective training is only the first step and that the expatriate's willing-ness and ability to act on that training in the new environment is crucial to effective performance. However, their theoretical model and related propositions have yet to be rigorously tested.

An obvious practical limitation of Black and Mendenhall's model is that insufficient time is often given as a reason why multinationals do not provide predeparture training; it would be difficult to develop appropri-ate predeparture training programs in such cases. Other contextual and situational factors—such as cultural toughness, length of assignment, and the nature/type of the job—may have a bearing on the content, method, and processes involved in the cultural awareness training pro-gram. More importantly, monitoring and feedback should be recognized as important components of individual skill development, particularly as adjustment and performance are the desired outcomes of cultural aware-ness training.

Exhibit 5–2 draws together the components of the three models re-viewed above. It stresses the importance of attention paid by the poten-tial expatriate to the behaviors and probable outcomes of a cultural awareness training program, the individual's ability and willingness to retain learned behaviors, and their reproduction as appropriate in the host location. Based on our review of performance management in Chap-ter 4, it seems important that adjustment and performance be linked to the multinational's performance management system. For instance, one could expect that poor performance could be addressed by clarifying

**EXHIBIT 5-2**  *Cultural Awareness Training and Assignment Performance*

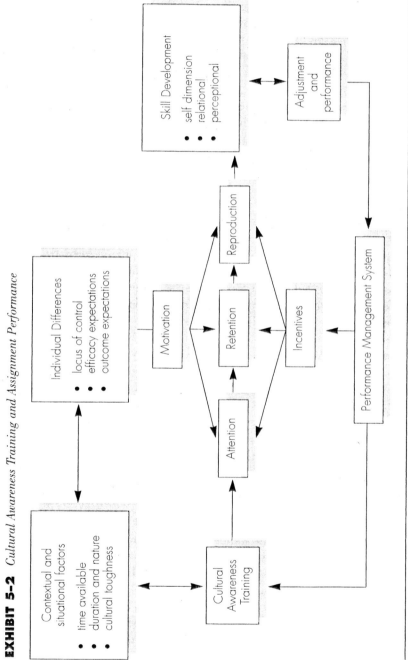

*Source:* Adapted from Tung (1981), Mendenhall, Dunbar, and Oddou (1987), and Black and Mendenhall (1989, 1990, 1991).

incentives for more effective reproduction of the required level of behavior, or by providing additional cultural awareness training. We combine adjustment and performance and link it to the performance management system; Black and Mendenhall have adjustment and performance as separate outcomes, with adjustment leading to performance. We would argue that performance may affect adjustment in some instances.

### *Preliminary Visits*

One useful technique in orienting international employees is to send them on a preliminary trip to the host country. A well-planned overseas trip for the candidate and spouse provides a preview that allows them to assess their suitability for and interest in the assignment. Such a trip also serves to introduce expatriate candidates to the business context in the host location and helps encourage more informed predeparture preparation. When used as part of a predeparture training program, visits to the host location can assist in the initial adjustment process. The 1997–98 Price Waterhouse survey mentioned earlier reports that 53 percent of firms always provided preliminary visits and a further 38 percent indicated such use in certain circumstances. The average length of visit was about a week. The country of assignment was a determining factor; visits were not provided if the country concerned was already known to the expatriate (perhaps from a previous visit either on firm-related business or as a tourist), or was perceived as culturally close (e.g., Zurich to Frankfurt, or New York to Toronto).

Obviously, the couple may reject the assignment on the basis of the preliminary visit. As one firm in the 1997–98 Price Waterhouse survey admits: "We do not provide pre-assignment visits where conditions are so poor that nobody would want to go." Most firms that utilize preliminary visits, though, weigh their cost against premature recall and underperformance risks. A potential problem exists in that the aim of the preliminary visit is often twofold—part selection decision and part predeparture training. The multinational could send mixed signals if it offers the preliminary visit as part of the selection process but the couple find upon arrival in the proposed country of assignment that they are expected to make decisions regarding suitable housing and schools. The couple may interpret such treatment as "accepting the preliminary visit equals accepting the assignment," thus negating its role in the decision-making process. When multinationals use the preliminary visit to allow the couple to make a more informed decision about accepting the overseas assignment, it should be used solely for that purpose. From the couple's perspective, they often find it difficult to reject the assignment in spite of negative impressions gained during the visit when they have been flown to the prospective location at the multinational's expense.

Combined with cultural awareness training, the preliminary visit is a useful component of a predeparture program. Exposure to the expatriate community, if one exists in the proposed host location, can also be a positive outcome of the preliminary visit. Brewster and Pickard[23] found that an expatriate community has an influence on expatriate adjustment. Perhaps the welcome received from, and interaction with, current expatriates may assist in developing a positive attitude to the assignment, confirm acceptance of the assignment, and even provide motivation to reproduce appropriate behaviors retained from cultural awareness training.

### *Language Training*

Language training is a seemingly obvious, desirable component of a predeparture program. However, there are three interrelated aspects related to language ability that need to be recognized.

*1. The Role of English as the Language of World Business.* It is generally accepted that English is the language of world business, though the form of English is more "international English" than that spoken by native speakers of English.[24] Multinationals from English-speaking countries such as the United States, the United Kingdom, and Australia often use this fact as a reason for not considering language ability in the selection process, and for not stressing language training as part of predeparture programs. Such an attitude may lead to the downplaying of the importance of foreign language skills. For example, in a 1989 survey by Columbia University[25] of 1,500 senior executives in twenty countries, participants were asked to rate the importance of a number of attributes "for the CEO of tomorrow." For the attribute "trained in a foreign language" 19 percent of the U.S. respondents gave a rating of very important compared to 64 percent of non-U.S. respondents. Fixman's[26] study of U.S. multinationals' foreign language needs, conducted the same year, found that foreign language skills were seldom included as part of cross-cultural understanding, and that language problems were largely viewed as mechanical and manageable problems that could easily be solved.

However, as Pucik[27] comments, an exclusive reliance on English diminishes the multinational's linguistic capacity. The resultant lack of language competence has strategic and operational implications as it limits the multinational's ability to monitor competitors and process important information. For example, translation services, particularly those external to the firm, cannot make strategic inferences and firm-specific interpretations of language specific data. Fixman[28] raises the question of protecting important technology in international joint venture activities: "It would seem that the less one understands of a partner's language, the less likely one is to detect theft of technology." Perhaps more importantly, as Wright and Wright[29] in their study of British firms point out, to accept English as the *de facto* language of international business gives the advantage to the other person:

> The other speaker controls what is communicated and what is understood. The monolingual English speaker has less room to manoeuvre, no possibility of finding out more that he [or she] is given. His position forces him to be reactive rather than proactive in the relationship. What he says and understands is filtered through the other speaker's competence, over which he has no control.

Disregarding the importance of foreign language skills may reflect a degree of ethnocentrism. A study by Hall and Gudykunst has shown that the lower the level of perceived ethnocentrism in an MNE, the more training it provides in cultural awareness and language training.[30]

Firms are including language training as evidenced by recent surveys, such as the 1997–98 Price Waterhouse survey referred to above. Firms in that survey reported that language training was not only provided where necessary to the expatriate but generally extended to the spouse or partner (81 percent) and children (42 percent). Perhaps as a result of the increased global competitive pressures, and growing awareness of its strategic and operational importance, more U.S. multinationals are requesting that U.S. business schools include foreign languages in their curricula and are giving hiring preference to graduates with foreign language skills. A similar trend is evident in the United Kingdom and in Australia.

### 2. *Host-Country Language Skills and Adjustment.* Clearly, the ability to speak a foreign language can improve the expatriate's effectiveness and negotiating ability. As Baliga and Baker[31] point out, it can improve managers' access to information regarding the host-country's economy, government, and market. Of course, the degree of fluency required may

depend on the level and nature of the position that the expatriate holds in the foreign operation, the amount of interaction with external stakeholders such as government officials, clients, trade officials, as well as with host-country nationals.

The importance of language skills was identified as a critical component in assignment performance in a recent survey of over 400 expatriates conducted by Tung–Arthur Andersen.[32] Respondents indicated that the ability to speak the local language, regardless of how different the culture was to their home country, was as important as cultural awareness in their ability to adapt and perform on assignment. Knowledge of the host-country language can assist expatriates and family members gain access to new social support structures outside of work and the expatriate community.

Language skills, therefore, are important in terms of task performance and cultural adjustment. Its continued omission from predeparture training can be partly explained by the length of time it takes to acquire even a rudimentary level of language competence. Hiring language competent staff to enlarge the "language pool" from which potential expatriates may be drawn is one answer, but its success depends on up-to-date information being kept on all employees, and frequent language auditing to see whether language skills are maintained.[33]

**3. Knowledge of the Corporate Language.** In the literature reviewed, where language skills and fluency are considered, it tends to be in the context of crosscultural communication. Recent work by Marschan, Welch, and Welch[34] highlights what appears to be a somewhat neglected issue—the impact that the adoption of a common corporate language has upon HRM activities within the multinational. As you recall from our discussion on the path to multinational status in Chapter 2, at a certain stage in its internationalization process, multinationals confront control and coordination concerns that force changes upon processes and procedures. Marschan et. al. argue that, for multinationals from non–English-speaking countries, the standardization of information and reporting systems tends to be handled in the language of the parent's country of origin until geographical dispersal makes that problematical. The multinational then adopts (either deliberately or by default) a common company language to facilitate reporting standardization and other control mechanisms, particularly normative control.

As we mention above, English has become the language of international business, and quite often, English becomes the common language within these multinationals. Marschan et. al.[35] suggest that the question of a common corporate language does not consciously arise to the same extent within multinationals from English-speaking countries such as the United States—English is automatically the chosen corporate language. Regardless, the authors argue that language skills become an important aspect. PCNs can find themselves performing as communication conduits between subsidiary and headquarters, due to their ability to speak the corporate language. It also can give added power to their position in the subsidiary as PCNs often have access to information that those not fluent in the corporate language are denied. Marschan et. al. also point out that a PCN fluent in the parent-company language and the language of the host subsidiary can perform a gatekeeping role, whatever the formal position the expatriate may hold. What this line of research suggests is that for multinationals that have adopted a corporate language, predeparture training programs may need to include both language of the host country and the corporate language.

### Practical Assistance

Another component of a predeparture training program is that of providing information that assists in relocation. Practical assistance makes an important contribution toward the adaptation of the expatriate and his or her family to their new environment. Being left to fend for themselves may result in a negative response toward the host-country's culture, and/or contribute to a perceived violation of the psychological contract. Many multinationals now take advantage of relocation specialists to provide this practical assistance. Further language training for the expatriate and family could be provided, particularly if such training was not possible before departure. While local orientation and language programs are normally organized by the personnel staff in the host country, it is important that corporate HRM staff liaize with the sending line manager as well as the HR department in the foreign location to ensure that practical assistance is provided.

### Job-Related Factors

Although the literature reviewed has concentrated almost exclusively on the cultural awareness and adjustment components of predeparture training, it is important that we note that there may be some job-related aspects that need to be addressed in an effective predeparture training program. As we discussed earlier in Chapter 3, expatriates are often used because of a lack of suitably trained staff in the host location. Consequently, expatriates often find themselves training HCNs as their replacements. The obvious question is How are expatriates prepared for this training role? Our review of extant literature indicates that this aspect has yet to be specifically addressed. We do know from the cross-cultural management literature that there are differences in the way people approach tasks and problems, and that this can have an impact on the learning process.[36] The ability to transfer knowledge and skills in a culturally-sensitive manner perhaps should be an integral part of predeparture training programs. A related issue is that an international assignment can be a promotion to a managerial role for which the preparation is effectively the international assignment. We will take up this in our section on career development.

The bulk of this chapter has so far focused on the expatriate, and we have not distinguished between PCNs and TCNs. In theory, all staff should be provided with the necessary level of predeparture training given the demands of the international assignment. Anecdotal evidence does suggest, however, that in some firms predeparture training may not be provided to TCNs—at least to the extent of that available to PCNs. This omission could create perceptions of inequitable treatment in situations where PCNs and TCNs work in the same foreign location. As an Australian working in the Japanese subsidiary of a U.S. multinational remarked, "We were third-class nationals in Japan. The Americans received cultural training about Japan before they left the United States. We were just given our plane tickets."[37]

## HCN Training

There are many issues related to HCN training. Consider the following case. A multinational, as part of its cost leadership strategy, decides to build a production facility in Country X where labor costs are low. It then finds it needs to invest heavily in training local employees, thereby automatically increasing the cost of that labor (the paradox referred to as "the expense of cheap labor"). Not only does the unit cost of labor rise over time, but trained employees may well become attractive to its foreign and local competitors, who simply offer higher wages to lure them away. If this "poaching" of HCNs is successful, the multinational discovers that its competitors reap the training benefits while it receives little return for its investment in human capital. Thus, the level of HCN competence has important training and cost consequences although these may not be initially recognized during country selection.

Mode of operation is another issue related to HCN training. For instance, entering into a joint venture arrangement can lead to unexpected training costs if the local partner regards the joint venture operation as a convenient way of re-deploying surplus employees who may not have the skills required. The multinational has to invest heavily in the training of the joint venture HCNs in order to achieve its strategic objectives for the foreign market, leading to costs perhaps not "factored in" the original market-entry decision. These costs may, however, be offset by intangible factors. For example, in some Chinese joint ventures, training programs are regarded by HCNs as incentives to work for foreigners.[38] Thus the provision of HCN training can help in retaining qualified HCN employees, thereby assisting the multinational to recoup its training costs.

When it comes to HCN training programs, given our understanding of cultural differences, it could be assumed that this is an area that the multinational would automatically delegate to the local operation. To a certain extent, training programs are localized, but there are many cases where multinationals have successfully replicated work practices in their foreign subsidiaries through intensive training programs designed and implemented by headquarters. This is particularly true regarding technical training for operating employees in areas where certain skills and work practices are regarded as strategically essential. Japanese multinationals such as Nissan and Honda have been able to train substantial numbers of HCNs in their U.S., U.K., and European subsidiaries with reasonable success.[39] To save on costs, some multinationals are now using satellite technology to deliver custom-designed training courses from home-country locations.[40]

## International Training of HCNs

HCNs can be transferred into the parent country, into either its headquarters or home-subsidiary operations. There are various motives for HCN staff transfers:

- It facilitates specific firm-based training. You may recall from the GE case presented in Chapter 2, that Tungsram staff were transferred to GE plants in the United States for technical and operative training.

Likewise, the Pepsi-Cola International Management Institute is an umbrella system for the delivery of training programs such as sales force management or production techniques for the manufacturing of Pepsi brands. Part of this approach is the "Designate Program," which brings HCNs to the United States for a minimum of eighteen months of training in the domestic U.S. Pepsi system. Fiat, the Italian automobile manufacturer, uses staff transfers as part of its training program, with HCN recruits spending time at corporate headquarters.

- While technical and managerial training may be the primary goal, there is often a secondary, yet equally important, objective of building a sense of corporate identity. The Swedish telecommunications company, L.M. Ericsson,[41] has two levels of formal management programs. One caters to the top 300 managers in the group, the other to the 1,500 middle managers. While the focus of course content differs for these two programs, there is a common aim to develop informal networks among Ericsson managers throughout the entire global company. As part of its approach, the company established the Ericsson Management Institute. These types of corporate training centers serve as a useful venue for HCNs from various countries to meet and develop personal networks that facilitate informal communication and control (see Exhibit 2–10).

- Particular skills may be required in the subsidiary and the most cost-effective way is to bring certain HCN staff into the parent operations. For example, in the late 1980s when Ford Australia began manufacturing the Capri model—a sports car aimed at the U.S. market—Australian production and engineering employees spent time in Ford's U.S. factories to quickly gain the necessary knowledge required to meet U.S. safety regulations.

- As discussed in Chapter 3, the presence of HCNs may assist in broadening the outlook of parent-company employees. Also, it may be that HCNs have particular knowledge and skills that can be transferred into parent operations. The "importing" by Matsushita of 100 overseas managers a year to work alongside their Japanese counterparts is perhaps an extreme strategy.[42] In Matsushita's case, the necessity of having to use English with the "imported foreigners" improved the parent-company's language base.

In a recent article, Harvey[43] advocates that "inpatriates" (HCNs) need the same predeparture training programs as those designed for expatriate assignments. This is perhaps an obvious point. After all, cultural adjustment is inherent in international staff transfers, regardless of the direction of the transfer—that is, whether it is the PCN moving to a subsidiary, a HCN coming into parent operations, or transferring to another subsidiary. Harvey's suggested model for "inpatriate" predeparture training appears to mirror those proposed for U.S. expatriate cultural-awareness training. In order to design and implement HCN predeparture training, local management, particularly those in the HR department, need to be conscious of the demands of an international assignment—just as we have discussed in terms of corporate/ headquarters HR staff. There perhaps also needs to be recognition and encouragement of this from headquarters, and monitoring to ensure that sufficient subsidiary resources are allocated for such training.

A related aspect is that HCNs require adequate language skills in order to gain the maximum benefit from parent-based training. Lack of language competence may be a major barrier in terms of access to corporate training programs since these are conducted in the parent/ corporate language. As a study[44] of a Finnish multinational—Kone Elevators—found, subsidiary staff who would have benefited from attendance at the corporate training center in Finland were often excluded on the ground of lack of competence in English, the corporate language. Provision of corporate language training may be an important component of HCN training.

## DEVELOPING INTERNATIONAL STAFF AND MULTINATIONAL TEAMS

Foreign assignments have long been recognized as an important mechanism for developing international expertise—for both management and organizational development.[45] As we discussed in Chapter 2, establishing truly global operations means having a team of international managers (PCNs, HCNs, and TCNs) who are available to go anywhere in the world. To develop such teams, many multinationals are conscious that they need to provide international experience to many levels of managers (regardless of nationality) and not just to a small cadre of PCNs. One technique used to develop larger pools of employees with international experience is through short-term development assignments ranging from a few months to several years. However, some very successful multinationals, such as the Swedish-Swiss conglomerate ABB, have carried on the practice of developing a small cadre of international employees rather than internationalizing everyone.

International job rotation, therefore, is one well-established technique for developing multinational teams and international operators. It may be supported by PCN, TCN, and HCN attendance at common training and development programs held either in the parent country, or regional centers, or both. The Global Leadership Program at the University of Michigan is an example of externally provided training programs. For a period of five weeks, teams of American, Japanese, and European executives learn global business skills through action learning. To build crosscultural teams, the program utilizes seminars and lectures, adventure-based exercises, and field trips to investigate business opportunities in countries such as Brazil, China, and India. The overall objective of the Global Leadership Program is to produce individuals with a global perspective.[46] The success of such programs depends on participants being able to apply these skills in their home location and assist in the development of multinational, crossborder, crossfunctional teams.

International meetings in various locations have also become important forums for fostering interaction and personal networks that also may be used later to build global teams.[47] In line with a general trend towards an emphasis on work teams,[48] there is a suggestion in the literature that multinationals would benefit from building on their inherent diversity to foster innovation, organizational learning, and the transfer of knowledge. Fostering a sense of corporate identity and teamwork seems an important aspect of leverage resources and ideas from all parts of the multinational. The following remark from Jack Welch, CEO of GE, reflects this line of thinking:[49]

> The aim in a global business is to get the best ideas from everywhere. Each team puts up its best ideas and processes—constantly. That raises the bar. Our culture is designed around making a hero out of those who translate ideas from one place to another, who help somebody else. They get an award, they get praised and promoted.

## Individual Career Development[50]

The above discussion has been from the multinational's perspective. We now briefly look at the impact that an international assignment has on an individual's career. There is an implicit assumption that an international assignment has *per se* management development potential; perceived career advancement is often a primary motive for accepting such postings. However, there is a paucity of research that demonstrates the link between an international assignment and career advancement. Two exceptions are studies by Feldman and Thomas, and Naumann;[51] while these studies confirm career expectations as motives, the expatriates involved were taken from those currently on assignment. There is a need for research that examines career paths as a direct consequence of international assignments.

It is possible to trace the typical assignment and identify critical decision points that may have career-related outcomes for a particular individual. Exhibit 5–3 attempts to illustrate a sequence that may be common to all expatriates—PCNs as well as HCNs who accept assignments to either the parent operations, or to other subsidiaries (thus becoming TCNs). For ease of discussion, though, we will simply use the term *expatriate* and refer to the sending unit or subsidiary as *parent*.

Exhibit 5–3 follows the stages of expatriation from recruitment and selection to completion of the particular assignment. The numerals are

**EXHIBIT 5–3**   *Expatriate Career Decision Points*

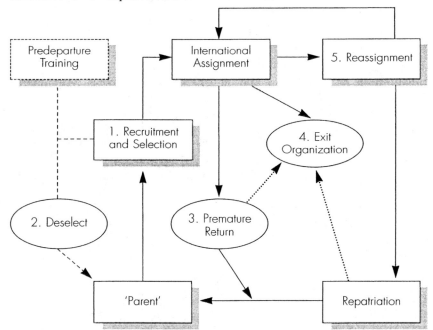

*Source:*   D. Welch, 1997. Expatriation and career development in the changing global workscape, Paper presented at the 23rd Annual EIBA Conference, Stuttgart, December 14–16.

positioned at what have been identified as critical decision points. For example, Decision Point 1 occurs during recruitment and selection for a specific assignment, where the expatriate either applies, or is informally selected, for an international assignment. Further information about the host location during the recruitment and selection process (including predeparture training if that is available), or family considerations, may prompt the potential candidate to withdraw at this point. Hence Decision Point 2 is "deselect." There may be some career considerations as to whether a voluntary withdrawal at the point would have a negative consequence upon the person's future. Such a perception may influence the individual's decision to accept rather than reject the assignment.

As we discussed earlier in terms of adjustment and performance overseas, the expatriate may decide to leave the international assignment (as indicated in Decision Point 3—Premature Return). The individual then is assigned a position back in the "parent" operation. The premature return may or may not have career advancement consequences. Alternatively, as indicated by Decision Point 4, the expatriate may decide to exit the organization—prompted by a perceived violation of the psychological contract, or perhaps as a result of another job offer that is perceived to be better in terms of the person's career. This may be with a domestic firm back in the home country or with another foreign multinational.

Decision Point 5, Reassignment, can be either back into the "parent" organization or the person may accept another overseas assignment. Those who elect to take a consecutive international assignment may, upon subsequent reassignment return to the "parent" operation, or become part of what is often referred to as the international "cadre," or team. As we will discuss in Chapter 7, reassignment (or repatriation) back into the "parent" operation is a common ending to an international assignment and may or may not be to a position that leads to career advancement. There is a suggestion that turnover among repatriates may be as a consequence of a perceived lack of career advancement on the basis of the international experience. Decision Point 4 can be relevant at this stage, as indicated by the dotted arrow connecting "repatriation" with "exit organization."

These decision points are based on the issues we have discussed in the preceding chapters, as well as on the suggestions in the literature regarding the management development potential of international assignments. How individuals react at each point may vary according to the perceived value of the assignment; that is, whether the perceived benefits outweigh the costs in terms of family disruption (including a spouse or partner's career) and the factors that we have identified as important to performance while on an international assignment. Of course, the actual benefits will also depend on the multinational's willingness and ability to utilize the experiences the expatriate has gained during the international assignment. We will return to some of these aspects in Chapter 7.

## SUMMARY

This chapter has concentrated on the issues relating to training and developing PCN, TCN, and HCN staff. We have placed emphasis on expatriate predeparture training mainly because of its emphasis in the relevant literature. Cultural-awareness training does appear to assist in adjustment and performance and should be made available to all categories of staff selected for overseas postings, regardless of duration and location. Predeparture training can also prevent costly mistakes such as that of the highly paid expatriate who brought two miniature bottles of brandy with him into Qatar (a Muslim country in the Middle East). The brandy was discovered by customs, and the expatriate was promptly deported, causing his firm to be "disinvited" and ordered never to return. It is worth noting here that despite the widely recognized value of predeparture training, in the 1997–98 Price Waterhouse survey previously mentioned, only one in ten of the firms measured the success of their programs.

The international assignment emerges as an important way of training international operators, developing the international team, or "cadre," as well as helping to build personal networks to support soft-control mechanisms. In this sense, an international assignment is both training (gaining international experience and competence) and managerial and organizational development. Thus, multinationals must address the growing need for international training and development and deal with controversial questions concerning which employees to train and the overall purpose of the training.

We also have mentioned briefly that mode of operation has an impact on training needs in relation to international joint ventures, and this will be further explored in our final chapter. There has, however, been little reference in the international HRM literature on issues connected with other forms of operation such as exporting, management contracts, and project operations. Again, as mentioned in Chapter 2, this omission is consistent with the preoccupation to date with subsidiary operations. However, analysis of broader training and development issues would provide parameters for corporate HR staff, enabling them to plan training and developmental activities that are congruent with the multinational's often diverse forms of international business operations.

## QUESTIONS

1. What are some of the challenges faced in training expatriate managers?
2. Identify the key aspects of a successful expatriate predeparture training program.
3. What steps can be taken to ensure that trained, skilled HCNs are not lured away by foreign or local competitors?
4. What are the issues and challenges facing multinationals in developing a cadre of global managers?
5. List the key reasons for bringing HCNs into the parent operations for training.
6. Why do some multinationals appear reluctant to provide basic predeparture training?

## FURTHER READING

1. Cyr, D.J., and S. Schneider, 1996. Implications for learning: Human resource management in East-West joint ventures, *Organization Studies*, vol. 17, no. 2, pp. 207–226.
2. Harris, P.R., and R.T. Moran, 1996. *Managing Cultural Differences: Leadership Strategies for a New World Business*, 4th ed. Houston: Gulf.
3. Harvey, M., 1996. Developing leaders rather than managers for the global marketplace, *Human Resource Management Review*, vol. 6, no. 4, pp. 279–304.
4. Kamoche, K., 1997. Knowledge creation and learning in international HRM, *International Journal of Human Resource Management*, vol. 8, no. 2, pp. 213–225.
5. Naumann, E., 1993. Organizational predictors of expatriate job satisfaction, *Journal of International Business Studies*, vol. 24, no. 1, pp. 61–80.

6. Snow, C.C., S.A. Snell, and S.C. Davison, 1996. Use transnational teams to globalize your company, *Organizational Dynamics*, Spring, pp. 50–67.
7. Vance, C., and Y. Paik, 1995. Host-country workforce training in support of the expatriate management assignment, in *Expatriate Management: New Ideas for International Business*, J. Selmer, ed. Westport, CO: Quorum Books.
8. Weiss, J.W., and S. Bloom, 1990. Managing in China: Expatriate experiences and training recommendations, *Business Horizons*, May-June, pp. 23–29.

## ENDNOTES

1. K. Kamoche, 1996. Strategic human resource management with a resource-capability view of the firm, *Journal of Management Studies*, vol. 33, no. 2, p. 216.
2. P.C. Earley, 1987. Intercultural training for managers: A comparison, *Academy of Management Journal*, vol. 30, no. 4, p. 686.
3. S.H. Robock, and K. Simmons, 1989. *International Business and Multinational Enterprises*, 4th ed. Homewood, IL: Richard D. Irwin; Copeland, 1984. Making costs count in international travel, *Personnel Administrator*, vol. 29, no. 7, p. 47.
4. R. Tung, 1982. Selection and training procedures of United States, European, and Japanese multinationals, *California Management Review*, vol. 25, no. 1, pp. 57–71. Tung also asked those respondents who reported no formal training programs to give reasons for omitting these programs. Again, differences were found between the three regions. The U.S. companies cited a trend toward employment of local nationals (45%), the temporary nature of such assignments (28%), the doubtful effectiveness of such training programs (20%), and lack of time (4%). The reasons given by European multinationals were the temporary nature of such assignments (30%), lack of time (30%), a trend toward employment of local nationals (20%), and the doubtful effectiveness of such programs. Responses from the Japanese companies were lack of time (63%) and doubtful effectiveness of such programs (37%).
5. S. Ronen, 1986. *Comparative and Multinational Management*, New York: John Wiley.

6. J.C. Baker, 1984. Foreign language and departure training in U.S. multinational firms, *Personnel Administrator*, July, pp. 68–70.

7. D. Feldman, 1989. Relocation practices, *Personnel*, vol. 66, no. 11, pp. 22–25.

8. J. McEnery, and G. DesHarnais, 1990. Culture shock, *Training and Development Journal*, April, pp. 43–47. Of those multinationals that did provide only brief environmental summaries and some cultural and language preparation, only around half of these programs lasted longer than a week.

9. M. Mendenhall, and G. Oddou, 1985. The dimensions of expatriate acculturation, *Academy of Management Review*, vol. 10, pp. 39–47; H. Schwind, 1985. The state of the art in cross-cultural management training, in *International Human Resource Management Annual*, vol. 1, Robert Doktor, ed. Alexandria, VA: ASTD; and Y. Zeira, 1975. Overlooked personnel problems in multinational corporations, *Columbia Journal of World Business*, vol. 10, no. 2, pp. 96–103.

10. J.S. Black, and M. Mendenhall, 1990. Cross-cultural training effectiveness: A review and a theoretical framework for future research, *Academy of Management Review*, vol. 15, no. 1, pp. 113–136.

11. C. Brewster, 1988. *The Management of Expatriates*, Human Resource Research Centre Monograph Series, no. 2, Bedford, United Kingdom: Cranfield School of Management.

12. Price Waterhouse, 1997–98. *International Assignments: European Policy and Practice*, Price Waterhouse Europe.

13. K. Barham, and M. Devine, 1990. *The Quest for the International Manager: A Survey of Global Human Resource Strategies*, Ashridge Management Research Group, Special Report No. 2098, London: The Economist Intelligence Unit. See also, D. Welch, 1994. Determinants of international human resource management approaches and activities: A suggested framework, *Journal of Management Studies*, vol. 31, no. 2, pp. 139–164; I. Björkman, 1990. Expatriation and repatriation in Finnish companies: A comparison with Swedish and Norwegian practice, Working Paper No. 211, Helsinki: Swedish School of Economics and Business Administration.

14. See, for example, M. Mendenhall, and G. Oddou, 1986. Acculturation profiles of expatriate managers: Implications for cross-cultural training programs, *Columbia Journal of World Business*, Winter, pp. 73–79; R.W. Brislin, *Cross Cultural Encounters*; and D. Landis and R.W. Brislin, *Handbook on Intercultural Training*.

15. N. Sieveking, B. Anchor, and R. Marston, 1981. Selecting and preparing expatriate employees, *Personnel Journal*, March, pp. 197–202. See also N. Sievoking, and R. Marston, 1978. Critical selection and orientation of expatriates, *Personnel Administrator*, April, pp. 20–23.

16. A growing number of websites dealing with these topics appear on the Internet. See, for example: http://www.hbsp.harvard.edu, for a CD-ROM interactive program on managing across different cultures.

17. R. Tung, 1981. Selecting and training of personnel for overseas assignments, *Columbia Journal of World Business*, vol. 16, pp. 68–78.

18. Ibid.

19. Mendenhall, and Oddou, Acculturation profiles of expatriate managers; M. Mendenhall, E. Dunbar, and G. Oddou, 1987. Expatriate selection, training and career-pathing: A review and critique, *Human Resource Management*, vol. 26, pp. 331–345.

20. Earley advocates the use of both documentary and interpersonal methods to prepare managers for intercultural assignments. See P. Earley, 1987. International training for managers: A comparison of documentary and interpersonal methods, *Academy of Management Journal*, vol. 30, pp. 685–698. Baliga and Baker suggest that the expatriate receives training that concentrates on the assigned region's culture, history, politics, economy, religion, and social and business practices. They argue that only with precise knowledge of the varied components of their host culture can the expatriate and family grasp how and why people behave and react as they do (see G. Baliga, and J.C. Baker, 1985. Multinational corporate policies for expatriate managers: Selection, training, and evaluation, *Advanced Management Journal*, Autumn, pp. 31–38).

21. For further information on the use of cultural assimilators, see R.W. Brislin, 1986. A culture general assimilator: Preparation for various types of sojourns, *International Journal of Intercultural Relations*, vol. 10, pp. 215–234; and K. Cushner, 1989. Assessing the impact of a culture general assimilator, *International Journal of Intercultural Relations*, vol. 13, pp. 125–146.

22. J.S. Black, and M. Mendenhall, 1989. A practical but theory-based framework for selecting cross-cultural training methods, *Human Resource Management*, vol. 28, no. 4, pp. 511–539.

23. C. Brewster, and J. Pickard, 1994. Evaluating expatriate training, *International Studies of Management and Organization*, vol. 24, no. 3, pp. 18–35.

24. C. Wright, and S. Wright, 1994. Do languages really matter? The relationship between international business success and a commitment to foreign language use, *Journal of Industrial Affairs*, vol. 3, no. 1, pp. 3–14. These authors suggest that "international English" is perhaps a better term than "poor" or "broken" English.

25. This survey was reported in an article by L.B. Korn, 1989. How the next CEO will be different, *Fortune*, May 22, 1989, pp. 111–113. A similar difference was obtained (United States, 35%; foreign, 70%) in ratings for the attribute "experienced outside home country."

26. C. Fixman, 1990. The foreign language needs of U.S.-based corporations, *Annals, AAPSS*, 511, September, p. 36.

27. V. Pucik, 1985. Strategic human resource management in a multinational firm, in *Strategic Management of Multinational Corporations: The Essentials*, H.V. Wortzel, and L.H. Wortzel, eds. New York: John Wiley.

28. Fixman, The foreign language needs of U.S.-based corporations.

29. Wright and Wright, Do languages really matter?, p. 5.

30. P. Hepner Hall, and W.B. Gudykunst, 1989. The relationship of perceived ethnocentrism in corporate cultures to the selection, training, and success of international employees, *International Journal of Intercultural Relations*, vol. 13, pp. 183–201.

31. Baliga, and Baker, Multinational corporate policies.

32. R.L. Tung, and Arthur Andersen, 1997. *Exploring International Assignees' Viewpoints: A Study of the Expatriation/Repatriation Process.* Chicago IL: Arthur Andersen, International Executive Services.

33. R. Marschan, D. Welch, and L. Welch, 1997. Language: The forgotten factor in multinational management, *European Management Journal*, vol. 15, no. 5, pp. 591–597; see also Fixman, The foreign language needs of U.S.-based corporations.

34. Marschan, Welch, and Welch, Language: The forgotten factor in multinational management.

35. Ibid.

36. See, for example, H. Park, S.D. Hwang, and J.K. Harrison, 1996. Sources and consequences of communication problems in foreign

subsidiaries: The case of United States firms in South Korea, *International Business Review*, vol. 5, no. 1, pp. 79–98; and A. Rao, and K. Hashimoto, 1996. Intercultural influence: A study of Japanese expatriate managers in Canada, *Journal of International Business Studies*, vol. 27, no. 3, pp. 443–466.

37. Interview as part of a study of expatriate management in Australian companies, conducted by D. Welch, 1989.

38. V. Trigo, and E. Khong, 1996. Seeking harmony—training policies in joint ventures China-Guagzhou: An empirical study, Paper presented at the 3rd Workshop in International Business, August, University of Vaasa, Finland.

39. See, for example, S. Beechler, and J.Z. Yang, 1994. The transfer of Japanese-style management to American subsidiaries: Contingencies, constraints, and competencies, *Journal of International Business Studies*, vol. 25, no. 3, pp. 467–491.

40. J.P. Giusti, D.R. Baker, and P.J. Graybash, 1991. Satellites dish out global training, *Personnel Journal*, June, pp. 80–84.

41. Barham and Devine, The quest for the international manager.

42. 1991. The glamour of gaijins, *The Economist*, September 21, p. 78. This example was reproduced in full in the second edition of our textbook.

43. M. Harvey, 1997. "Inpatriation" training: The next challenge for international human resource management, *International Journal of Intercultural Relations*, vol. 21, no. 3, pp. 393–428.

44. Marschan, Welch, and Welch, Language: The forgotten factor in multinational management.

45. D.A. Ondrack, 1985. International transfers of managers in North American and European MNEs, *Journal of International Business Studies*, vol. 16, no. 3, pp. 1–19.

46. J. Main, 1989. How 21 men got global in 35 days, *Fortune*, November 6, pp. 57–60.

47. A number of writers have also made the point that this form of developmental transfer can also function as a coordination and control strategy. See A. Edstrom, and J. Galbraith, 1977. Transfer of managers as a coordination and control strategy in multinational organizations, *Administrative Science Quarterly*, vol. 22, pp. 248–263; and C.K. Prahalad, and Y.L. Doz, 1981. An approach to strategic control in MNCs, *Sloan Management Review*, vol. 22, no. 4, pp. 5–13.

48. See, for example, B.L. Kirkman, and Shapiro, 1997. The impact of cultural values on employee resistance to teams: Toward a model of globalized self-managing work team effectiveness, *Academy of Management Review*, vol. 22, no. 3, pp. 730–757.

49. J. Welch, 1997. Transfer the best ideas from everyone, everywhere, *Financial Times*, October 1, p. 12.

50. This section is based on D. Welch, 1997. Expatriation and career development in the changing global workscape, Paper presented at the 23rd Annual Meeting, EIBA, Stuttgart, December.

51. D.C. Feldman, and D.C. Thomas, 1992. Career issues facing expatriate managers, *Journal of International Business Studies*, vol. 23, no. 2, pp. 271–294; E. Naumann, 1992. A conceptual model of expatriate turnover, *Journal of International Business Studies*, vol. 23, no. 3, pp. 449–531.

# C H A P T E R  16
# Issues, Challenges, and Theoretical Developments in IHRM

In this book we have explored the international HRM issues relating to managing people in a multinational context. To that end, we have focused on the implications that the process of internationalization has for the activities and policies of HRM. Where possible and appropriate, we have endeavored to broaden the discussion of the various topics so that we take account of the fact that there is more to IHRM than expatriation. Despite this objective, there remains an imbalance towards expatriation issues at the expense of the subsidiary perspective. This is mainly due to the increasing volume of expatriate-related literature. As a way of redressing the balance, in this chapter we explore some of the issues and challenges related to host-country staffing through an examination of the HR implications of operating in China and India. These two countries represent huge growth markets, and also are good examples of contrasting societies in which foreign firms attempt to operate. A focus on expatriation also precludes broader strategic issues. We, therefore, include in this chapter a short discussion of key concerns related to ethics and social responsibility—topics, such as bribery, that are receiving increased attention and are somewhat controversial.

While some scholars and practitioners would still regard IHRM as a scientific field in its infancy, there has been considerable progress toward developing theoretical bases. The remainder of this chapter identifies such developments, particularly those that attempt to place specific IHRM activities into the organizational and strategic contexts.

## MANAGING PEOPLE IN AN INTERNATIONAL CONTEXT

This section looks at key HRM aspects of operating in two different countries as a way of illustrating the situations that may confront multinationals attempting to penetrate developing markets. We will trace the impact that recent economic reforms in China and India have had in terms of staffing foreign operations in these two markets. As the more common mode of operation in both cases has been the international joint venture (IJV), it allows us to elaborate on the HRM challenges posed by IJV operations, which were briefly outlined in Chapter 2.

## CHINA*

In late 1978, the Chinese government announced an open-door policy and began economic reforms aimed at moving the country from a centrally planned economy to a market economy. Under its centrally planned economy, industries "were owned and run by the state, and their growth was regulated by planning targets rather than by the profit-maximizing decisions of independent entrepreneurs."[1] Thus, planning was the dominant control mechanism, with the market mechanism in a supplementary role. Industrial enterprises (the Western term *firm* is inappropriate in the communist context) were under the control of relevant government departments.

The past two decades of economic reforms have seen foreign multinationals expand their operations into China—many attracted by the sheer size of its potential market. By the end of 1996, China had absorbed a total foreign direct investment (FDI) of U.S.$171.8 billion with 281,298 projects, and was ranked second to the United States as a global destination for FDI. Of particular interest is the enthusiasm for establishing *foreign invested enterprises (FIEs)*, including foreign joint ventures and

* The authors wish to acknowledge Cherrie Zhu, Monash University, for her contribution to this section.

wholly foreign-owned ventures (FIEs is commonly used as the umbrella term to describe FDI in China). Consequently, employment in FIEs has increased from 550,000 employees in 1986 to 8,820,000 in 1995.[2] FDI has tended to take the form of an international joint venture (IJV) with a state-owned enterprise (SOE) as the local partner, or as a fully owned subsidiary. To a certain extent, foreign ownership is instrumental in protecting FIEs from the various pressures of localization.[3] However, many FIEs in China are either under-performing or failing. As we discuss later in this chapter, the management of people is a critical factor in determining success or failure in international joint ventures. Chinese HRM policies and practices are quite different from those used in developed and market-economy developing countries, and careful consideration of local idiosyncratic practices is required to operate successfully.[4] "The legacy of management 'with Chinese characteristics' still weighs heavily on all firms operating in China."[5] Knowledge of how employees have been managed in the past may help multinationals to understand local managers' difficulty or inertia in accepting nontraditional or Western-style HRM practices. Therefore, we include prior as well as current practices to provide a better appreciation of the effect that the transition to a market economy is having on the four major functions of HRM.[6]

## Staffing[7]

Prior to the reforms, Chinese employees were classified into two groups:

- *Workers:* all blue-collar employees, who were administered by the Ministry of Labor.
- *Cadres:* white-collar staff, managed by the Ministry of Personnel. The broad definition of cadres is "state institution and military 'civil servants' and [its] narrow meaning is persons engaged in 'certain specified leadership work or management work' (e.g., organization cadres and enterprise cadres)."[8]

Since the reforms, the distinction between cadres and workers has gradually become blurred, particularly in foreign-invested and privately owned enterprises. Employees belong to either managerial or nonmanagerial groups. However, the Ministry of Labor and the Ministry of Personnel are still two separate government departments in China.

A centralized labor allocation system determined the staffing levels in Chinese enterprises. Established in the early 1950s, this system was based on the Maoist theory that labor was not a commodity but a national resource, and that the government had a monopoly control of urban jobs. The Ministry of Labor and Ministry of Personnel maintained a tight control over labor allocation by setting quotas for employment at individual enterprises, including annual quotas for new recruits. Local bureaus of labor and personnel assigned workers and staff to a particular job in a work unit—called *danwei* in Chinese. Centralized allocation effectively deprived enterprises of their autonomy to select employees, denied the individual the right to choose his or her employment,[9] and ignored changes in labor supply and demand. However, the centralized allocation system did achieve a high employment rate in urban areas.

Accompanying the centralized labor allocation was the belief in lifelong employment: "the worker's inalienable right to his job and other related benefits."[10] Therefore, over 80 percent of employees in state-owned enterprises (approximately 80 million) enjoyed job security, especially those employed in heavy industries such as mining.[11] The guaranteed continuation of employment, along with various welfare and benefits offered to employees, such as accommodation, medical treatment, child care, and pensions, has been referred to as the *iron rice bowl*. In exchange for job security, employees had little freedom to move to another work unit—that is, they were unable to quit or transfer jobs and were locked into a dependency relationship with their enterprises. Managers were deprived of their right to fire or layoff unqualified employees.[12]

From October 1986, all newly employed workers in the state sector were hired on a contract basis rather than effectively being given permanent employment.[13] By the end of 1996, a labor contract system had become compulsory in both public and private sectors, including the managerial level, thus revoking the long-standing tradition of lifetime employment. In theory, both workers and managers had the freedom to select each other.[14] The new labor contract system has facilitated decentralization of employment practices. Governmental influence has gradually diminished. Enterprises have more autonomy to select their employees, and "two-way selection"—that is, free selection of occupation by individuals and free selection of employees by enterprises—is more common. Two-way selection has been facilitated by the emergence of a labor market with personnel exchange and service centers established by the government to provide job information and relevant services.[15] Western recruitment methods, such as job advertisement and employment tests, are now used, especially by FIEs and privately owned enterprises. As enterprises now have to match production to market demands and be responsible for their own survival, they need to attract and retain competent and motivated employees.

## Performance Appraisal[16]

Prior to the current reforms, performance appraisal for *cadres* was mainly for promotion or transfer, with the main criteria being political loyalty and seniority;[17] the appraisal was usually conducted annually by the personnel department of the cadre's organization. Each cadre was given an appraisal form divided into three parts: self-evaluation, peer-group opinions, and an assessment written by the head of the department in which the cadre worked. Thus, the appraisal method relied heavily on "superior rating subordinate," and lacked specified criteria and other performance measures commonly used in Western market economies.[18]

Performance appraisal for blue-collar *workers* was used less frequently. It was an informal and subjective process, reflected in the emphasis placed on one's *biao-xian*. The term *biao-xian* refers to the "broad and vaguely defined realm of behavior and attitudes subject to leadership evaluation—behavior that indicates underlying attitudes, orientations, and loyalties worthy of reward."[19] A worker's *biao-xian* was usually judged on the basis of subjective impressions of day-to-day job performance and demonstrated cooperation. Consequently, personal relationships with colleagues, especially with the leaders, became the key to getting a good *biao-xian*.[20] Such appraisals were characterized by vagueness, open to individual interpretation, and dominated by political ideology.

As part of the economic reforms, aimed at breaking the iron rice bowl, the government issued a document: "Suggestion for Implementing the Cadre Performance Appraisal System" outlining a performance appraisal scheme for cadres. The new scheme was based on the socialist principle of distribution (i.e., from each according to one's ability and to each according to one's work). It aimed at identifying training needs, as well as distinguishing between high and low performers. More importantly, it held cadres accountable to, as well as for, their subordinates via subordinates' evaluation.[21] New appraisal criteria focused on four broad areas:

- Good moral practice (*de*)—virtue or moral integrity. The cadre is evaluated on whether he or she is in step politically with the Party, and carries out government orders and regulations.

- Adequate competence (*neng*). This covers three main aspects: educational background; ability in leadership, organization, negotiation, planning, forecasting, and decision making; and physical status, which also includes age.
- Positive working attitude (*qing*) refers to diligence and usually assesses attendance at work, discipline, initiative, and sense of responsibility.
- Strong performance record (*jie*) measures the cadre's work effectiveness, including quality and quantity, as well as other contributions made to the organization.[22]

While these criteria have been in practice since the 1980s, some new methods for assessing cadres have been introduced, such as computer-aided panel assessment (*ceping kaohe*) and position-related yearly assessment (*gangwei niandu kaohe*).[23] These methods require both quantitative and qualitative measurement to reduce the subjectivity and informality inherent in the traditional performance appraisal approach.

Performance appraisal has also become more widely used in enterprises at the worker level since 1978. In mid-1990 "The Regulation on Workers' Performance Appraisal" was issued by the Ministry of Labor, which specified the type, content, method, and management of appraisals.[24] Some new approaches have been developed, such as position specification, management by objectives, and internal subcontracting.[25] All aim to break the iron rice bowl by distinguishing high and low performers and linking performance to rewards. For example, position specification usually includes quality control, technical requirements, quantified work loads, tools and machine maintenance, labor discipline, caring for the working environment, team-work cooperation, and safety of production methods.

In their study of performance appraisal in China, Zhu and Dowling[26] found that over 78 percent of employees surveyed (*n* = 440) confirmed that performance appraisal was conducted by their enterprises; however, only 53 percent indicated that a job description existed. Also, whereas the majority of the enterprises surveyed conducted performance appraisal on a yearly basis, the bonus was usually distributed more frequently (either monthly or quarterly). This raises doubt as to whether performance was really being linked to rewards. In addition, other researchers have noted problems with performance assessment in China because of the emphasis given to political considerations, and problems with inconsistent measurement, subjectivity, static rather than forward-looking attitudes, and a lack of communication.[27] Although performance appraisal is primarily used for determining bonus and wages rather than for developmental or communication purposes, it is being used by many Chinese enterprises to weaken the old practice of egalitarianism and to facilitate the abolition of the iron rice bowl.

## Compensation[28]

The compensation system before the reforms was characterized by egalitarianism at both enterprise and individual levels regardless of performance. Enterprises had no right to set up or change any wage scale, let alone to increase (or decrease) their total payroll. A nationally unified wage system was structured by the state in 1956 for both blue- and white-collar employees. Under this system, there were 8 grades for workers, 15 grades for technical personnel, and 25 grades for cadres such as managers and administrative personnel. Usually the highest pay received in an enterprise was only two to three time more than one in the lowest, and the entry level was very low. These minimal wage differentials reflected the strong ideological and political influence upon work enterprises. Wage increases were infrequent, occurring at intervals of several years, and commonly took the form of national unified grade promotions for all employees. Not only was the wage system egalitarian, it also provided numerous benefits to employees, such as insurance, medical coverage, public welfare, nonstaple food, winter heating subsidy, and a home leave travelling allowance. These benefits helped to maintain the iron rice bowl and made the enterprises mini-welfare states.[29]

Reform of the compensation system began at the enterprise level. Enterprises were treated as relatively independent business units, and compensation was linked to performance. The enterprise reform launched in 1984, the Enterprise Law issued in 1988, and related regulations during the 1990s aimed at separating the ownership of an enterprise from its controlling authority so each enterprise had autonomy and incentives.[30] The state-regulated wage system has now been replaced by diversified wage packages with more emphasis on enterprise profitability and individual performance. Since 1985, different systems of wage determination have been introduced, such as floating and structural wage systems.[31] In 1992, the Minister of Labor introduced a new position-and-skills wage system based on the four major working factors emphasized by the International Labor Organization in 1950 (i.e., knowledge and skills required, responsibility assumed, work intensity (load) involved, and working conditions).[32] Enterprises were required to include these four components in their wage packages to override the egalitarianism of the old wage scales. These reforms have tried to quantify each worker's performance and link performance to pay. However, in the absence of job descriptions and performance appraisal, the degree to which performance-related pay was fairly distributed could vary across enterprises.

No matter how diversified wage packages might be, all packages had a bonus as an important part (since the restoration of the bonus after the reforms).[33] As enterprise reform has become more widespread, the distribution of bonuses has been more closely tied to individual performance.[34] How to match compensation with the contributions made by individuals remains a difficult issue and the bonus system is still at an experimental stage. Nonetheless, performance-based compensation has become the trend, and egalitarianism is being replaced by wage differentiation based on individual and enterprise performance.

## Training and Development[35]

Pre-reform employee training was generally divided into two parts:

- *Training for blue-collar workers:* This was primarily in the form of apprenticeships and technical school education that were the major sources of skilled workers.[36] Technical school students would be assigned to an enterprise by the state after completing two to three years of study.
- *Training for cadres:* Training for managers, especially managers who were also members of the Communist Party, was mainly offered by schools run by the Party at central, provincial, and municipal levels, or colleges for cadre education and training. Training priority was usually given to political studies, and this focus is regarded as a major cause of the current shortage of qualified managers in industry. Many cadres, especially managerial staff, lack the knowledge and skills required to change their roles from merely carrying out government orders to assuming full responsibility for the enterprise's performance or deciding on management matters.[37] This shortage has hampered the move to a market economy.

At the *workers'* level, lack of education and training is widespread. A survey covering 20 million industrial employees in 26 provinces and cities was conducted in 1980. It revealed that 8.2 percent of employees were literate or semiliterate, 32 percent had less than 9 years of education, 40.8 percent had completed year 9, 15.9 percent had finished year 12, and only 3.1 percent had a university education.[38] In mid-1980, the state re-introduced apprenticeship programs, which had been abolished during the Cultural Revolution (1966–1976). The traditional post-employment apprenticeships were gradually replaced by pre-employment traineeships and this practice was legitimized in the Labor Law, which became effective in 1995. Reforms introduced in 1990 sought to connect training, examination, job arrangement, and compensation to encourage employees to learn technical skills.[39] These have since been replaced gradually by a vocational qualification verification system. This latest system reflects, to some extent, the government's recognition of the German model of a dual-education system (i.e., liberal education and vocational training). The practice of double certificate (i.e., education certificate and vocational qualification certificate) aims to achieve an outcome similar to the situation in Germany, with young people attaining vocational knowledge and skills. This system has now been widely implemented and has enabled workers to take the training course of their choice and to be more flexible in job selection,[40] and is consistent with the two-way selection system and the position-and-skills wage system discussed above.

Because the lack of adequately trained management had been identified as a major impediment to its reforms, the government established institutions for adult further education for professional and management training.[41] A nationwide program of management training has supported these institutions and the government has collaborated with institutions from several countries, including the United States, United Kingdom, Australia, Canada, Japan, and the European Union nations, to conduct courses, including MBA programs.

In spite of the progress achieved in employee and management training and development many inadequacies and limitations remain. The results from a 1994 survey disclosed that 34 percent of 1,508 respondents had not received any training opportunities in enterprises.[42] Researchers have also found that Chinese enterprises usually only emphasize technical training rather than behavioral training.[43] Many foreign managers may regard training as costly and risky, because they may not receive immediate returns and employees may leave the enterprise after training.[44]

## Implications for Multinationals

By way of conclusion, and to assist in understanding the impact of the transition on HR practices, we pose and answer three questions in relation to managing HCNs in FIEs:

1. *How can foreign firms develop effective HRM strategies to improve the productivity of their workforce in China?* Multinationals need to know the current HRM practices in China. Many practices commonly used in the West are now employed in China. However, foreign firms need to be aware that in China, "the shift from the older practices has only been partial, especially in larger enterprises, whether state-owned enterprises or even Sino-foreign joint ventures."[45] This is mainly because multinationals have a stronger association with government partners in China than in other developing countries, and thus tend to be somewhat locked into maintaining management practices that are a legacy of pre-reform days.[46] Researchers have noted that in some FIEs, the egalitarian pay system is still in practice even though the eight-grade wage structure has been abandoned.[47]

2. *To what extent can foreign multinationals transfer their home-country's HR practices to their subsidiaries in China?* Multinational managers should not assume that identical HR practices can be applied to their Chinese enterprises. Some researchers claim that Western-style HRM practices should be introduced only when a Chinese perspective, and Chinese values and methods, have been incorporated.[48] Take performance appraisal as an example. It has been argued that to increase the effectiveness of appraisal in China, the Western appraisal system, which encourages individual economic performance, should incorporate the Chinese values of satisfying performance, such as harmonious functioning in a work group and fulfillment of individual obligations towards the work unit and colleagues.[49]

3. *What are the future HRM issues for China due to its ongoing economic reforms?*

   *Developing and retaining quality staff.* Chan has noted that "both Western and Chinese management find HRM appropriate as a nonadversarial and consensual management style that succeeds in co-opting the workforce."[50] However, a particular term may have a different connotation or orientation. For example, while the training and development function does exist in China, it is still passive and narrowly defined "in contrast to the Western HRM notion of planning for long-term staff development."[51] Training is more focused on improving current performance deficiencies. There is a lack of career development, particularly as employees tend to change jobs frequently in pursuit of higher wages rather than skills development.[52] The absence of career development plus a high emphasis on material incentives have partly contributed to the problems of high turnover and "disloyalty" observed in many enterprises, including FIEs.[53]

*Compensation.* The change in employee attitudes toward the distribution of bonuses is another identified trend. Traditionally, China has been a collective-oriented society,[54] however, Chinese employees now prefer reward differentials "determined primarily according to individual contributions"[55] and there is greater acceptance of wider reward disparities based on individual performance.[56] With further reforms inevitable in China, a compensation system based on individual performance will become more common and more entrenched.[57]

*Localizing Staffing.* As more foreign multinationals expand their businesses into China, they have sought local management for their operations in order to develop a large corporate presence in China.[58] When hiring Chinese nationals for executive jobs (because of their communication skills, local contacts, and understanding of the domestic market)[59] many multinationals have found that Chinese managers lack decision-making skills and are wary of taking personal initiatives. Along with job-related skills, corporate management training programs are required that provide HRM skills appropriate to the Chinese context and skills for problem-solving in high-pressure situations.[60]

To conclude, it is necessary to remember that China is still undergoing a transition stage, and will continue its economic restructuring and reforms into the next century. The government expects enterprises to become corporate entities and competitors adaptable to the market,[61] so effective HRM practices are needed to develop a competitive workforce.

## INDIA*

With an estimated population of 973.5 million, India is the world's fifth largest economy.[62] It is a heterogeneous country characterized by diverse cultural groups (or subcultures) and a strong social class system (known as the caste system).[63] While the official languages are Hindi and English, there are 14 recognized regional languages. The main religions, as a proportion of the total population, are Hindu (84 percent), Muslim (11 percent), Sikh (2 percent), and Christian (2 percent).[64] In 1997, the country celebrated 50 years of independence from British colonial rule.

Post independence, India pursued a protectionist, import-substitution policy to promote local industries, and this involved restrictions on foreign investment and imports. Foreign firms were "encouraged" to localize, by taking Indian partners and adopting Indian, or hybrid, brand names (such as Lehar-Pepsi or Hero-Honda).[65] However, since 1991, the Indian government has been progressively liberalizing its economy. Foreign firms may now own 100 percent of Indian companies in some sectors, and as much as 74 percent in others. Its large market potential has attracted interest from multinationals from various countries, exposing once protected local firms to foreign competition.

For foreign firms, part of the attraction has been the low cost of Indian labor.[66] However, the competitiveness of India in terms of the availability, qualifications, and skills of its human resources is considered to be one of the lowest in the world.[67] Geissbauer and Siemsen argue that the cost advantage derived from the availability of cheap labor tends to be neutralized by lower productivity.[68] According to the Australian Department of Foreign Affairs and Trade, the low investment of capital employed per worker, combined with a work culture that does not encourage high performance work practices, are mainly responsible for the low level of productivity of the Indian labor force.[69] This adds another dimension to the "expense of cheap labor" paradox we discussed in Chapter 5. However, it is important not to make generalizations. For example, the Indian software industry is highly competitive—Indian firms do not just compete on price, but on the basis of quality, innovation, and technical expertise, and draw on a huge pool of relatively

---

* The authors would like to acknowledge Sharif As-Saber, Massey University, for his contribution to this section.

low-cost, technically-qualified, English-speaking software profession-als.[70] In 1996, 104 firms out of the Fortune 500 outsourced their soft-ware development to India. About 10 percent of Microsoft's 20,000 worldwide workforce is Indian.[71]

The complexity of the Indian business environment has impacted on the method that foreign firms have tended to use to enter and service the Indian market. Even though there is less restriction on the form of opera-tion mode since 1991, when it comes to equity arrangements, foreign multinationals have shown a preference for international joint ventures (IJVs). For those foreign firms not able or willing to invest in equity arrangements, licensing has been a heavily used alternative (see the dis-cussion on mode of operation in Chapter 2).

We discussed briefly the IJV as an example of a strategic alliance in Chapter 2. The motives for entering into an IJV arrangement are many and varied, but a major reason is to spread risks. However, as many firms soon discover, forming an IJV creates a risk in itself and the relevant lit-erature reports a high failure rate.[72] Success seems to depend on an abil-ity to balance "the desire and need to control the venture on the one hand, and the need to maintain harmonious relations with the partner(s) on the other hand."[73] Likewise, the factors attributed to the failure of a joint venture are most frequently human-related—poor decisions, be-havioral errors, or unanticipated staffing events. Interests may be incon-gruent, particularly when one of the parents is the host government. Therefore, an IJV presents a major management challenge, particularly so when a foreign firm has been forced into the IJV by necessity rather than choice—as is often the case in both China and India. It is evident that selecting the right people for key management positions is criti-cal to success, and the harmonization of management styles is also essential.[74]

Of the many reasons for establishing an IJV, two seem particularly relevant for India—dealing with bureaucracy and unfamiliarity and cul-tural distance.

**Dealing with Bureaucracy.** The pervasive corruption encountered by Western firms is attributed to excessive controls and unfulfilled demand for goods and services, leading to India being ranked as the ninth most corrupt country in the world. Indian bureaucracy is said to be parochial and obstructionist—"red tape" is considered one of the most significant problems in conducting business in India.[75] Widespread tax evasion is another feature of the Indian economy.[76]

In the face of such reports, many foreign firms do not want to confront these issues directly. A recent study of Australian firms operating in India found that a major reason for forming IJVs was to entrust the local partner to deal with government officials, other agencies, and the "bureaucracy."[77] Likewise, a study of 26 Norwegian firms in India found that 11 had established IJVs, and only one had a wholly owned subsidiary. The overriding reason for the Norwegian preference for the IJV was to reduce risks by having the local partner deal with "things Indian." As one Norwegian executive commented: "The Indian market is difficult and complex. It's good to have a partner who knows the business and the bureaucracy. A partner who has the right connections."[78]

***Unfamiliarity and Cultural Distance.*** Generally speaking, most Westerners perceive India to be culturally distant and this can lead to a preference for an IJV with a local partner. Hofstede[79] classified India as high on his power-distance dimension (i.e., a society where less powerful members accept the unequal distribution of power). He also ranked India as weak on the uncertainty-avoidance dimension (tolerance for future uncertainty and risk), dominant on the collectivism dimension (emphasis on group orientation), and dominant on the masculine dimension (characterized by, for example, its high level of bureaucracy and the social caste system). One could suggest that high-power distance is one of the major features of the Indian management style. According to Sharma,[80] an average Indian manager represents:

> a plausible picture of the average Indian's resistance for change, his willingness to delegate but unwillingness to accept authority, his fear of taking an independent decision, his possessive attitude towards his inferiors and his abject surrender to his superiors, his strict observance of rituals and his disregard of them in practice, his preaching of high morals against personal immorality, and his near-desperate efforts at maintaining the status quo while talking of change.

The extent of power distance may have a negative correlation with the level of trustworthiness—that is, the higher the power distance, the lower the trust.[81] Ratnam regards perceived trustworthiness as a key HRM problem in the Indian context. He described the scenario as follows:

> Workers consider employers as *Paisa chor* (they swindle and appropriate surpluses from the enterprise). Balance sheets are generally considered to be

excellent pieces of fiction. Employers consider workers as *Kam chor* (mean, lazy people who shun work).[82]

*Labor unrest* is a related feature of the Indian environment that may make an IJV attractive. Two major areas of industrial disputation are wages and working hours.[83] Due to the constant pressure from trade unions, it is often difficult to maintain a part-time and contractual workforce, even though there has been an increase in the number of such arrangements. It has been suggested that, because of the antagonistic nature of trade unions, it is often very difficult to organize an Indian workforce into teams.[84] State intervention is the norm in industrial matters. However, as most trade unions have strong links with political parties and many politicians are current or former union leaders, such interventions tend to be biased towards labor.[85] As a consequence, most multinationals find a local partner very helpful in dealing with situations involving trade unions and labor legislation.

However, the advantages of the local partner can be offset by some of the problems inherent in the IJV as a form of international operation. As we will now explore, HRM plays an important role in assisting foreign firms to achieve their goals for their Indian IJVs.

## *Staffing*

In a complex cultural context like India, it may be more advantageous to use local managers. A study by As-Saber, Dowling, and Liesch[86] found that there was a clear preference for using HCNs in key positions by multinationals operating in India. The authors suggest that a major reason for HCN preference is the belief that the right Indian will know more than an expatriate manager could learn in years on the job. Additional reasons given by the multinationals in their study were:

- Avoids extra costs associated with relocating expatriates;
- Reluctance of many Western managers to live in India;
- Ensures continuity of management as HCNs are likely to stay longer in the position; and
- Creates higher morale among HCNs due to a perceived career path.

Thus, the motives identified in this study for adopting a polycentric approach to staffing Indian IJVs are consistent with those discussed in general terms in Chapter 3. However, the question of control over the IJV remains a concern for multinational firms. In situations of minority equity, control can be obtained through the use of managers who are loyal to the parent company and its organizational ethos. The success of some foreign firms in India may be attributed to effective integration of the local IJV managers into the "global family" as illustrated in the case of Hindustan Lever presented in Exhibit 9–1.

**EXHIBIT 9–1**    *Unilever's Indian Experience*[87]

Unilever, the consumer goods multinational (food, and home and personal care products), was created through the merger in 1929 of the British firm, Lever Brothers, and The Netherlands firm, Margarine Unie. In 1998, it was operating in 90 countries worldwide. It is controlled by two holding companies: Unilever PLC (English) and Unilever N.V. (Netherlands). Its two Chairmen head the seven-member Executive Committee—which includes the Personnel Director—the top decision-making body. Reporting to the Executive Committee is the Executive Council, which includes the heads (Presidents) of the 12 Business Groups based essentially on geographical markets. The Business Groups establish regional strategies and policies. Individual companies in each country report to a business group. Unilever has over 1,000 brands and 13 product categories. It describes itself as an international, multi-focal firm rather than a global multinational—half the products are foods, aimed at local tastes, and it tries to localize as much as possible. The firm currently has an expatriate workforce of 7 percent of total employees, drawn from many countries, including India.

Unilever has been operating in India for over 60 years through a 51 percent local entity, Hindustan Lever. Unilever endeavors to establish a strong sense of corporate identity, referred to as "Unileverization." It has been rather successful in India—to the extent that there is a popular saying: You can take the person out of Hindustan Lever, but you can't take Hindustan Lever out of the person. Values such as thrift and simplicity are advocated from the top. Its current team of 1,200 managers have been drawn from graduates of India's top business schools and developed through its in-house training program. Cultivating its own talent that is familiar with the Indian way of doing business, combined with loyalty to Unilever's worldwide approach to managing, has made Hindustan Lever staff attractive to foreign and local competitors. There has been active poaching of its management staff. In a newspaper interview last year, the Hindustan Lever Chairman was asked about the effects of the arrival of more foreign multinationals in India. He commented that Hindiustan Lever has had to make adjustments: "We have significantly increased our salaries at various levels." Management costs have doubled over the previous four to five years as a percentage of turnover.

### Recruitment and Selection of HCNs

Once hired, it is not easy to dismiss employees under Indian labor law.[88] The Industrial Dispute Act provides strict rules for layoffs and dismissals. Consequently, dismissals and layoffs are difficult, and such actions can be contested through a petition to the government and can lead to a time-consuming process of negotiation.[89] The prolonged dismissal process may be avoided through appropriate selection of staff. One of the attractions of the IJV is the assumption that a more experienced local partner can assist in identifying a suitable workforce. The IJV may perhaps even use the existing human resources (its internal labor market) of the local partner, if this pool of labor is considered to be sufficient in terms of skill and productivity levels.

### Compensation

Since the economic liberalization in the early 1990s, it has become more difficult for foreign multinationals to find and retain high-quality local staff, as the rapid rise in the level of foreign and local investments in India has lead to a shortage of skilled people.[90] This, in turn, is placing pressure on the compensation packages of qualified managers. According to a recent survey, an average Indian manager's annual real-salary increase is one of the highest in the world.[91] Consistent with this report, a recent study found that continuous pay increases, along with a commitment to improve working conditions, are two preconditions to retain experienced staff,[92] particularly in high-growth industries such as telecommunications and computer software development. Pressure is also being brought to bear on the minimum wage level, and this will increase the cost of labor over the longer term. The case of Unilever, outlined in Exhibit 9–1, illustrates how competition for key people can affect even an established subsidiary operation.

### Training and Development

As was discussed in Chapter 5, international business operations places specific demands on effective training and development of PCN, TCN, and HCN staff. The IJV complicates this issue due to potential conflicts in managerial styles and expectations. Training expatriates in negotiation and conflict-resolution skills is advocated to enable them to cope with, and resolve, the unexpected issues and problems inherent in both the Indian context and operating in the joint venture situation.[93]

Despite the availability of cheap labor, as mentioned earlier in this section, low labor productivity is a common complaint among existing manufacturers in India. As a consequence, a multinational may have to provide extensive training programs for its local staff. The introduction of new production equipment and concepts such as just-in-time, quality management, and so on, require additional training. Developing and retaining the workforce so that the multinational has a pool of managerial talent to draw on is also a challenge, as illustrated by the competitive situation now confronting Unilever's Indian operations (Exhibit 9–1).

### Implications for Multinationals

Considering the cultural differences outlined above, it would appear that including local staff and practices is essential in building a performance-based work culture in Indian operations. A skill-based approach may contribute to improved labor productivity and better performance.[94] It is also evident that, as FDI expands, foreign firms are being forced to pay a premium price for quality people. Despite wage and salary increases, it is still cheaper to hire quality HCNs than employing expatriates, with the added advantage that locals are more familiar with the complexities of Indian business culture. However, staff training and development remain as important considerations.

Through this brief overview of two countries undergoing market reforms and liberalization, it has been possible to illustrate the critical role that competent and trained staff play in partly determining the multinational's ability to achieve its strategic goals in these markets. It also reminds us that, as discussed in Chapter 1, having the right people in the right place remains the perennial challenge for firms operating internationally.

## HUMAN RESOURCE ISSUES IN MULTINATIONAL CORPORATE SOCIAL RESPONSIBILITY*

Ethics and the question of corporate social responsibility are complex and the source of much controversy. In this section, we briefly discuss questions often raised about the existence of transcultural standards of moral behavior and the implications for IHR and international managers. Our intention is not to review the literature in international business ethics, but to demonstrate the complexity that surrounds

---

*The authors would like to acknowledge Lorraine Carey, University of Tasmania, for her contribution to this section.

international business conduct, for the multinational, and for expatriates and local staff in subsidiary operations.

In the domestic context, debates about corporate social responsibility have focused on whether a firm should adopt noneconomic goals. Those who argue for a narrow view of corporate social responsibility believe that a firm's only responsibility is to maximize profits for shareholders within the law.[95] Proponents of a broader view of corporate social responsibility argue that firms should adopt the role of a "good citizen" and balance the interests of shareholders with the best interests of society.[96] When business is conducted across national and cultural borders, the debate about corporate social responsibility takes on added layers of complexity.[97] In particular, perplexing questions about the existence of universal ethical standards are raised. This is especially problematic when multinationals operate in host countries with different standards of business practice.[98] The questions of ethical relativity and corporate social responsibility arise not only in the context of different home- and host-country employment practices but also in the central operations and policies of multinationals.

To appreciate the dilemma, take the situation of a multinational assigning a PCN to manage its operations in a host country. Whose standards should prevail? Those of the multinational's parent country or the host country? (This question also arose in Chapter 8 when discussing labor relations.) There are three main responses to this question. The first involves ethical relativism, the second ethical absolutism, and the third, ethical universalism.

For the *ethical relativist*, there are no universal or international rights and wrongs: it all depends on a particular culture's values and beliefs. Thus, if the people of Indonesia tolerate the bribery of their public officials, this is morally no better or worse than the people of Singapore or Denmark who refuse to accept bribery. For the ethical relativist, when in Rome, one should do as the Romans do. While relativism may be appealing to those who fear cultural imperialism, it is a logically and ethically incoherent theory.[99]

Unlike the relativist, the *ethical absolutist* (or imperialist) believes that when in Rome, one should do what one would do at home, regardless of what the Romans do. This view of ethics gives primacy to one's own cultural values. Opponents of this view argue that ethical absolutists are intolerant individuals who confuse respect for local traditions with ethical relativism. It must be noted that while some behaviors are wrong wherever they are practiced (e.g., bribery of government officials), other behaviors may be tolerated in their cultural context (e.g., the practice of routine gift giving between Japanese business people). When PCNs discover too late that the political–legal environment in which their home-country policies were formulated is significantly different from that of the host countries in which they operate, the results can be extreme. Donaldson cites an example of a U.S. expatriate manager in China who followed her firm's policy on employee theft. On catching an employee stealing, she fired the employee and notified the relevant authorities. She was horrified to later learn that the employee had been executed.[100]

In contrast to the ethical relativist, the *ethical universalist* believes there are fundamental principles of right and wrong, which transcend cultural boundaries, and that multinationals must adhere to these fundamental principles. However, unlike the absolutist, the universalist is careful to distinguish between practices that are simply culturally different and those that are morally wrong. The difficulty for managers operating in diverse cultural environments is to identify moral norms, which transcend cultural boundaries, and then, without compromising those norms, recognize and respect diversity where it is morally appropriate to do so.[101] One useful way to determine the ethical dimensions of a proposed project, policy, or behavior is to consider consequences, as well as rights and justice claims, for all stakeholders.

## The Multinational as a Global Citizen

A global world is an interconnected world. It presents a critical challenge to identify common ethical values that underlie cultural, religious, and philosophical differences. While there are important differences between Western and Eastern philosophical traditions, they share four fundamental core human values: good citizenship, respect for human dignity, respect for basic rights, and equity.[102] For example, Donaldson links the Western values of individual liberty and human rights to the Japanese value of living and working together for the common good (*kyosei*) and the Muslim value of the duty to give alms to the poor (*Zakat*).[103] Applications of core human values to specific duties of multinationals include the adoption of adequate workplace and environmental health and safety standards, the payment of basic living wages, equal employment opportunity, refraining from the use of child labor, providing basic employee training and education, and allowing workers to organize and form unions. Many multinationals now place considerable importance on being regarded as good global citizens and have initiated action to address public concerns about the environment and human rights.[104]

However, translating general ethical principles and core values into practice in the international business domain, even allowing for some limited consensus within the international community, is an enormous task in the absence of a supranational legislative authority. A number of mechanisms to facilitate the incorporation of ethical principles into international business behavior have been suggested. Predictably, these have centered on regulation, both self-imposed and government-decreed, the development of international accords, and the use of education and training programs.

## International Accords and Corporate Codes of Conduct

One of the most interesting initiatives in international business self-regulation is the Caux Roundtable Principles for Business Conduct, developed in 1994 by Japanese, European, and North American business leaders meeting in Caux, Switzerland. This is the first international ethics code for business and aims to set a global benchmark against which individual firms can write their own codes and measure the behavior of their executives. The Caux Principles are grounded in two basic ethical ideals: *kyosei* and human dignity. The preamble to the Caux Principles states that:

> The Japanese concept of *kyosei* means living and working together for the common good—enabling cooperation and mutual prosperity to coexist with healthy and fair competition. Human dignity relates to the sacredness or value of each person as an end, not simply as the means to the fulfillment of other's purposes or even majority prescription.[105]

The Caux Principles aim to further the twin values of living and working together and human dignity by promoting free trade, environmental and cultural integrity, and the prevention of bribery and corruption. The Principles have their origin in the Minnesota principles developed by the Minnesota Center for Corporate Responsibility in the United States. Following their adoption in 1994, worldwide endorsements have been sought.

There are a number of international agreements and treaties in place which provide guidelines for managing corporate social responsibility across a wide range of problems in the multinational context. Some of these multilateral compacts were discussed in Chapter 8.[106] Of particular interest to multinationals are the OECD Guidelines for Multinational Enterprises (1976) and the International Labor Office Tripartite Declaration of Principles Concerning Multinational Enterprises and Social Policy (1977). Based on their study of the international codes of conduct of the Organization for Economic Cooperation and Development (OECD), the International Chamber of Commerce (ICC), the International Labor Organization (ILO), and the United Nations, Payne, Raiborn, and Askvik[107] suggest that international standards of ethics should address six major issues:

1. *Organizational relations*—including competition, strategic alliances, and local sourcing;
2. *Economic relations*—including financing, taxation, transfer prices, local reinvestment, equity participation, and fiscal policies;
3. *Employee relations*—including compensation, safety, human rights, nondiscrimination, collective bargaining, whistle blowing, training, and sexual harassment;
4. *Customer relations*—including pricing, quality, and advertising;
5. *Industrial relations*—including technology transfer, research and development, infrastructure development, and organizational stability/longevity; and
6. *Political relations*—including legal compliance, bribery and other corrupt activities, subsidies, tax incentives, environmental protection, and political involvement.[108]

Industries or individual firms can also develop self-regulatory codes. A corporate code of conduct is a public statement of the firm's values and guiding principles. The need for comprehensive and cohesive codes of conduct for firms involved in international business is widely recognized as an important issue. Donaldson reports that 90 percent of all Fortune 500 firms have codes of conduct and 70 percent have statements of vision and values. The percentages in Europe and Asia are lower but increasing rapidly.[109] An example of a U.S. multinational's code of ethics, which is comprehensive in recognizing relationships between the company and its many stakeholders, is Johnson & Johnson's Credo, which, in part, states:

> We are responsible to our employees, the men and women who work with us throughout the world. Everyone must be considered as an individual. We must respect their dignity and recognize their merit. They must have a sense

of security in their jobs. Compensation must be fair and adequate, and working conditions clean, orderly, and safe. We must be mindful of ways to help our employees fulfill their family responsibilities. Employees must feel free to make suggestions and complaints. There must be equal opportunity for employment, development and advancement for those qualified. We must provide competent management, and their actions must be just and ethical. We are responsible to the communities in which we will live and work and to the world community as well. We must be good citizens—support good works and charities and bear our fair share of taxes. We must encourage civic improvements and better health and education. We must maintain in good order the property we are privileged to use, protecting the environment and natural resources.[110]

A common difficulty with codes of conduct is their enforcement. The attitudes of senior management play a crucial role in developing, implementing, and sustaining high ethical standards. Expatriates, line managers, and HR professionals may also play a role in institutionalizing adherence to ethics codes through a range of HR-related activities, including training and the performance–reward system. If self-regulatory mechanisms fail to shape the level of socially responsible behavior required of multinationals by society, then firms can expect legislative measures will be called for to resolve conflicts between themselves and host and home countries. Such is the case with bribery.

## Bribery: A Recurring Problem in International Business

Bribery and corruption top the list of the most frequent ethical problems encountered by international managers.[111] Macken estimates that about U.S.$85 billion is involved in bribes from industrialized countries to developing nations.[112] Bribery involves the payment of agents to do things that are inconsistent with the purpose of their position or office in order to gain an unfair advantage. Bribery can be distinguished from so-called gifts and "facilitating" or "grease," payments. The latter are payments to motivate agents to complete a task they would routinely do in the normal course of their duties. While most people do not openly condone bribery, many argue for a lenient approach based on the view that bribery is necessary to do business. However, it is now generally agreed that bribery undermines public confidence in markets, adds to the cost of products, and may affect the safety and economic well-being of the general public.[113]

For these reasons, there is increased interest in the regulation of bribery. In 1977 the United States enacted the Foreign Corrupt Practices Act (FCPA) to prohibit U.S.-based firms from making bribery payments to foreign government officials. The FCPA also applies to individual U.S. citizens, nationals, and residents. The Act was amended in 1988 to permit "facilitating" payments. In addition, payments to agents violate the Act if it is known that the agent will use those payments to bribe a government official. Sanctions under the Act are severe. Corporate fines can go up to U.S.$2 million and individual penalties to U.S.$100,000 and five years imprisonment. The FCPA mandates record-keeping provisions to help ensure that illegal payments are not disguised as entertainment or business expenses.

The FCPA has been criticized because it places U.S. firms at a competitive disadvantage since European and Japanese firms do not face criminal prosecution for paying bribes to foreign officials.[114] Moreover, nine European countries, as well as Australia and New Zealand, have allowed firms to deduct bribery payments as "business expenses" from their taxable income; on this latter point, it should be noted that most countries require a receipt for such an expense, and receipts for bribes are relatively uncommon. The evidence on the effect of the FCPA is mixed. While some studies report that the Act has had adverse effects, other studies have shown that even though some business may have been lost, the Act has not made U.S. firms less competitive, nor has it caused U.S. exports to decline.[115]

In the absence of adequate international self-regulation to control bribery and corruption, the OECD countries have looked to uniform domestic government regulation to provide a level playing field. At the end of 1997, 34 member countries of the OECD reached formal agreement on an international convention that criminalizes corporate bribery of foreign officials. The *Convention on Combating Bribery of Foreign Public Officials in International Business Transactions* was signed on December 17, 1997. According to the Convention, each member country must introduce and enact its own legislation criminalizing bribery by the end of 1998. Thus it would seem that by the turn of the century the United States will not be alone in legislating against corruption and bribery in the international arena. At the instigation of the United States, the OECD Convention signatories have also been asked to adopt a resolution that prohibits the tax deductibility of bribes, and to rewrite their legislation to bring it into line with the Convention.

Some non-OECD countries have also moved to curtail bribery and corruption. For example, in Malaysia and Singapore several foreign firms caught bribing public officials have been declared ineligible to bid on future government contracts. The debate over payment to foreign officials is likely to continue well into the twenty-first century.

## Implications for the HR Function of the Multinational Firm

Ethical issues are also people issues and thus the issues raised above have direct implications for the HR function. It is recognized that the HR function is responsible for many of the activities that build a sense of corporate identity,[116] such as staff selection and training. As we discussed in Chapter 2 (see Exhibit 2–10), corporate culture is one of the soft control mechanisms, and ethical codes of conduct—along with public statements regarding corporate values—are an important element of such normative control.

To achieve the goal of corporate social responsibility, HR professionals in multinationals may be required to:

- Minimize the exposure of employees to corrupt conduct by assisting in the development, publication, and implementation of appropriate codes of conduct;
- Ensure training programs cover areas of ethical concern—such as bribery, human rights, justice, and the common good—in a manner consistent with the multinational's objectives in this regard;
- Align performance appraisal and compensation systems so that they support the ethical stance taken;
- Be conversant with the type of requests that may be made of staff operating internationally—not just expatriates but also those who visit foreign markets in various capacities—and provide the necessary training so that they have the requisite negotiating skills to handle problem situations that may arise; and
- Ensure that employees understand the difference between corrupt bribery payments, gifts, and allowable facilitation payments. Given the strong positions taken by governments on ethical behavior, it is important that all staff are fully briefed on their responsibilities in this regard.

In conclusion, while people involved in international business activities face many of the same ethical issues as those in domestic business, the issues are made more complex because of the different social, economic, political, cultural, and legal environments in which multinationals operate. Some firms do prepare expatriate managers for the ethical choices they will face in relation to bribery and corruption. However, in their study of 31 U.S. firms, Carlson and Blodgett found that few provided their employees with information about the firm's stand on issues such as child labor, unfair trade practices, pirating of copyrights, and environmental protection.[117] This study indicates that many firms may need to place more emphasis on predeparture training and in-country orientation of expatriates that includes an ethics component covering such basic information. To not do so is likely to increase the risk that difficulties will arise in the operationalization of ethical responsibilities for multinationals.

## Theoretical Developments in International HRM

Various researchers in the IHRM field have been endeavoring to develop a theoretical body of knowledge to provide the necessary robust frameworks and models pertaining to a more mature scientific field of inquiry. Many of these developments have been incorporated into the relevant chapters of this text where appropriate. Reviewing these theoretical contributions, it is possible to identify two streams of inquiry: the micro-level, which has concentrated on HRM activities particularly expatriate management, and the macro-level, which has a more strategic focus. Both streams of research are appropriate and critical to theory development.

Early work in the IHRM field has been dominated by large-scale quantitative studies by U.S. researchers on expatriate management issues in U.S. firms. These have a common approach in using HR managers as the respondents. The work by Tung, Black, Oddou, Mendenhall, Gregersen, and Harvey (reviewed in Chapters 3, 4, 5, and 7) are good examples of such contributions. These studies are important in that the empirical findings identified key issues and challenges in the use of expatriates in staffing subsidiary operations. More significantly, these researchers raised the profile of IHRM as an area of scientific inquiry.

Surveying HR managers is a logical and useful contribution to research and theory building, but it became somewhat inevitable that IHRM, as a scientific field, would need to consider other IHRM phenomena than expatriation management activities. It was also desirous for research to move beyond description—broadening methodological approaches to include inductive as well as deductive research. Some researchers, therefore, are using an inductive, exploratory approach. For example, Welch (see Chapter 2), Monks (Chapter 3), and Tahvanainen (Chapter 4) utilize qualitative case studies. Also, utilizing research methods that allow HR managers' perspectives to be supported by others such as expatriates and partners, as well as archival material and documentation, has yielded additional insights into IHRM activities and issues, and consideration of broader organizational factors. Other researchers have used quantitative methodology to determine linkages between a specific HRM activity and broader organizational strategies. For example, the investigation of Spanish multinationals' expatriate compensation approaches and subsidiary strategies by Bonache and Fernandez; and the study linking the HR function to firm performance by Stroh and Caligiuri.[118]

In a recent review of IHRM research trends, De Cieri and Dowling[119] identify a line of research that has come to be termed *strategic international human resource management (SIHRM)*. It considers the HRM issues and activities that result from, and impact on, the strategic activities and international concerns of multinationals.[120] This line of inquiry parallels that of strategic HRM, which focuses on the link between organizational strategy and performance, and HRM. Its strength, in terms of theory development, is that it draws on various schools in strategic management, rather than solely on domestic human resource management. Thus, institutional theory, resource dependence theory, transaction cost, the behavioral school, and the resource-based view have been drawn on in order to develop a more informed perspective of SIHRM. The theoretical framework derived by Schuler, Dowling, and De Cieri[121] is a good example of such work.

Commenting on the emerging body of research into SIHRM, De Cieri and Dowling remark that, while SIHRM as a distinct area of research has been a useful step, it may be more appropriate to speak of *strategic HRM in multinationals*. This allows a more balanced view to be taken of the similarities and differences between international and domestic HRM. To this end, De Cieri and Dowling propose a revised framework of SHRM in multinational firms, which is shown in Exhibit 9–2.

As depicted in Exhibit 9–2, multinationals operate in the context of worldwide conditions, including the exogenous contexts of industry, nation, region, and interorganizational networks and alliances. The

**EXHIBIT 9-2** *Integrative Framework of Strategic HRM in Multinational Enterprises*

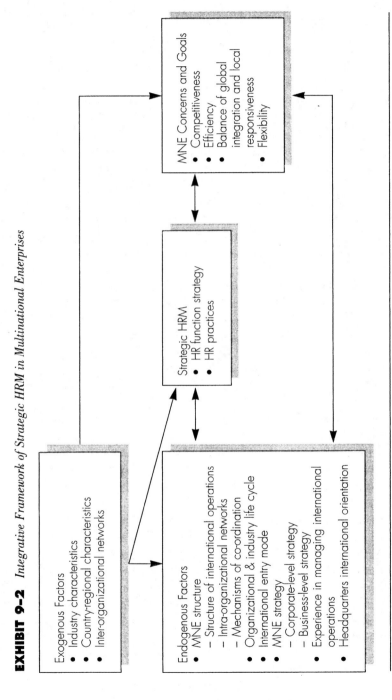

*Source:* H. De Cieri, and P.J. Dowling, 1998. Strategic human resource management in multinational enterprises: Theoretical and empirical developments, unpublished paper. Adapted from: R.S. Schuler, P.J. Dowling, and H. De Cieri, 1993. An integrative framework of strategic international human resource management, *Journal of Management*, vol. 19, pp. 419–459.

economic reforms in China and India, as discussed earlier in this chapter, are strong examples of the impact that the exogenous context has on HR practices. Likewise, the removal of internal trade barriers and integration of national markets in the European Union has brought a new range of interorganizational relationships. The introduction of the European Monetary Union from January 1999 has the potential to hold significant implications for interorganizational relationships. As indicated in their above figure, De Cieri and Dowling, therefore, argue that exogenous factors exert a direct influence on endogenous factors, SHRM strategy and practices, and multinational concerns and goals.

In the above exhibit, endogenous factors are shown in order of most "tangible" to most "intangible." Multinational structure is used as an umbrella term to cover structure of international operations, intraorganizational networks, and mechanisms of co-ordination (such as those outlined in Chapter 2). The life-cycle stage of the firm and the industry in which it operates are important influences for SHRM in multinationals as are international operation modes (although De Cieri and Dowling term these as international entry modes) and levels of firm strategy. Intangible endogenous factors include the multinational's experience in international business and its headquarters' international orientation.

Following developments in the literature, particularly that integrating resource dependence and resource-based perspectives,[122] the authors develop an argument for reciprocal relationships between endogenous factors, SHRM, and multinational concerns and goals, as indicated in Exhibit 9–2. It is also possible to identify reciprocal relationships between strategic issues and SHRM strategy and practices. De Cieri and Dowling refer to several studies that have shown that HR activities such as expatriate management are influenced by both endogenous and exogenous factors. One can see, for example, a similarity between these authors' endogenous factors and the firm-specific variables in the model developed by Welch, reviewed in Chapter 2. Effective SHRM is expected to assist the firm in achieving its goals and objectives. In supporting this position, De Cieri and Dowling refer to the emerging body of SHRM literature that examines the relationships between endogenous characteristics, SHRM strategy and practices, and firm performance or competitive advantage.[123] These authors, however, recognize that some research has suggested that multinationals will gain by utilizing and integrating appropriate SHRM strategy and practices to enhance firm performance,[124] but point out that important questions about the nature of this relationship remain.[125]

Thus, it appears that IHRM research is entering the second phase of theory building. Based on multiple-theory and multiple-method approaches, further work should move the level of analysis from the micro to the more strategic level. Further, the field is increasingly being driven by research outside of the United States. This is evident from the number of studies from scholars from Europe (including the Nordic countries and the United Kingdom), Asia, and the Pacific included in this book. While most research is still single-country, these various studies have identified common IHRM concerns facing firms as they internationalize, regardless of their country of origin. The real challenge is to develop innovative and effective research approaches including the conduct of multi-team, multi-country research that would support the repeated calls for multi-discipline, multi-level, and multi-method theory development. In so doing, scholars may answer some of the methodological criticisms we briefly discuss in the Appendix to this book.

## CONCLUDING REMARKS

Throughout this book, we have endeavored to highlight the challenges faced by firms as they confront human resource management concerns related to international business operations. In the discussion of key aspects pertaining to the management of people in a multinational context, staffing foreign operations remains the critical issue. As we identified, dual-career couples and repatriation are emerging as constraints to the use of expatriates. However, simply switching to host-country nationals is not necessarily the answer. In markets characterized by an acute shortage of skilled staff, it may not be a viable option. More importantly, staff transfers are an important control mechanism. The movement of staff between subsidiaries and into parent-country operations remains an important part of informal control, through the establishment of personal networks and information channels, as well as assisting in knowledge and skills transfer, and the appreciation of global concerns. Thus, despite their cost and other reported disadvantages of their use, staff transfers remain a key mechanism for informal control, and thus expatriate management concerns remain of strategic importance.

However, as we have also stressed throughout this book, IHRM does not equal expatriate management. We pointed out in Chapter 2, for example, that a lot of activity—such as visits to foreign markets for negotiations, foreign intermediary management, and the like—occurs before, and alongside, that of expatriation. Managing people in a multinational context, we argue, is the essence of international human resource management. This requires a broader perspective of what operating internationally involves, and a clear recognition of the range of issues pertaining to all categories of staff operating in different functional, task, and managerial capacities is essential.

## QUESTIONS

1. What are some of the common problems faced by multinationals operating in China and India?
2. Do you agree with the idea of universal ethical principles that transcend national and cultural boundaries or do you wish to develop an argument to defend ethical relativism? Explain your answer and provide examples.
3. What is your view of the recent international initiatives to criminalize foreign bribery? Justify your answer.
4. In what ways might the core ethical values and proposed guidelines for MNEs, identified in this chapter, apply to the HRM problems identified in both India and China?
5. In what way do exogenous and endogenous factors impact on the strategic HR strategy and practices of a multinational firm?

## FURTHER READING

1. Budhwar, P.S., and P.R. Sparrow, 1997. Evaluating levels of strategic integration and devolvement of human resource management in India, *International Journal of Human Resource Management*, vol. 8, no. 4, pp. 476–494.
2. DeGeorge, R.T., 1993. *Competing with Integrity in International Business*, New York: Oxford.
3. Donaldson, T., 1989. *The Ethics of International Business*, New York: Oxford.
4. Lindholm, N., M. Tahvanainen, and I. Björkman, 1998 (forthcoming). Performance appraisal of host country employees: Western MNCs in China, in *International HRM: Contemporary Issues in Europe*, C. Brewster, and H. Harris, eds. London: Routledge.

5. Stroh, L.H., and P.M. Caligiuri, 1998. Strategic human resources: A new source for competitive advantage in the global arena, *International Journal of Human Resource Management*, vol. 9, no. 1, pp. 1–17.
6. Tung, R.L., and V. Worm, 1997. East meets West: Northern European expatriates in China, *Business and the Contemporary World*, vol. 9, no. 1, pp. 137–148.
7. Zhu, C.J., and P.J. Dowling, 1994. The impact of the economic system upon human resource management practices in China, *Human Resource Planning*, vol. 17, no. 4, pp. 1–21.

## ENDNOTES

1. L. Putterman, 1992. Dualism and reform in China, *Economic Development and Cultural Change*, vol. 40, no. 3, p. 468.
2. 1996. *People's Daily*, December 19; T. Walker, and J.Ridding, 1996. Far less of an easy ride, *Financial Times*, May 10, p. 21; and 1996. *China Labor Statistical Yearbook*, Beijing, China: Statistical Publishing House.
3. See Y. Lu, and I. Björkman, 1997. MNC standardization versus localization: HRM practices in China-Western joint ventures. *The International Journal of Human Resource Management*, vol. 8, no. 5, pp. 614–628.
4. P.W. Beamish, 1993. The characteristics of joint ventures in the People's Republic of China. *Journal of International Marketing*, vol. 1, no. 2, pp. 29–48; J. Child, 1994. *Management in China during the Age of Reform*, London: Cambridge University Press; D. Ding, D. Fields, and S. Akhtar, 1997. An empirical study of human resource management policies and practices in foreign-invested enterprises in China: The case of Shenzen Special Economic Zone. *The International Journal of Human Resource Management*, vol. 8, no. 5, pp. 595–613. K. Goodall, and M. Warner, 1997. Human resources in Sino-foreign joint ventures: Selected case studies in Shanghai, compared with Beijing, *The International Journal of Human Resource Management*, vol. 8, no. 5, pp. 567–594; Y. Paik, C.M. Vance, and H.D. Stage, 1996. The extent of divergence in human resource practice across three Chinese national cultures: Hong Kong, Taiwan and Singapore. *Human Resource Management Journal*, vol. 6, no. 2, pp. 20–31.

5. M. Warner, 1996. Management of joint ventures in China, Paper presented at the conference on Cross-cultural Management in China, Baptist University, Hong Kong, August 26–28, p. 5.

6. Although the term *human resource management* has been commonly used in the relevant literature about Chinese management, the Western connotation does not readily apply. Before the reforms, personnel managers administering both workers and cadres at the enterprise level were policy implementers rather than strategic decision makers. In contrast, HRM in the Western context often focuses more on managing organizations than administrative activities. However, the term *human resource management* has become more common in China to show a move away from its traditional personnel and labor administration, and is used in this paper in this broader sense. See for example, J. Child, *Management in China During the Age of Reform*; T.A. Mahoney, and J.R. Deckop, 1986. Evolution of concept and practice in personnel administration/human resource management (PA/HRM), *Yearly Review of Management in the Journal of Management*, vol. 12, no. 2, pp. 223–241.

7. This section is partly based on C.J. Zhu, and P.J. Dowling, 1998. Employment systems and practices in China's industrial sector during and after Mao's regime, Paper presented at the 1998 Annual Meeting of the Academy of Management, San Diego, California.

8. S. Yabuki, 1995. *China's New Political Economy: The Giant Awakes*, S.M. Harner, trans. Oxford: Westview Press.

9. Y.J. Bian, 1994. Guanxi and the allocation of urban jobs in China. *The China Quarterly*, pp. 971–999; M.K. Nyaw, 1995. Human resource management in the People's Republic of China, in *Human Resource Management in the Pacific Rim*, L.F. Moore, and P.D. Jennings, eds. Berlin: Walter de Gruyter.

10. P.N. Lee, 1987. *Industrial Management and Economic Reform in China, 1949–1984*. New York: Oxford University Press.

11. L.J. Yu, and Z.X. Xin, eds. 1994. *Qiye laodong guanlixue jichu (Introduction to enterprise labour management)*, Beijing: China Labor Press. Z.J. Zhang, ed. 1991. *Laodongli guanli yu jiuye (Laborforce management and employment)*, Beijing: China Labour Press. See also, C. Tausky, 1991. Perestroika in the U.S.S.R. and China: Motivational lessons, *Work and Occupations*, vol. 18, no. 1, pp. 94–108.

12. A.G. Walder, 1986. *Communist Neo-traditionalism: Work and Authority in Chinese Industry*. Berkeley: University of California Press; M. Maurer-Fazio, 1995. Labor reform in China: Crossing the river by feeling the stones, *Comparative Economic Studies*, vol. 37, no. 4, pp. 111–123. See also A.H. Chan, 1990. Managerial reforms in Chinese enterprises, in *Advances in Chinese Industrial Studies*, J. Child, and M. Lockett, eds. vol. 1, part A, London: JAI press, pp. 167–177; S. Jackson, 1992. *Chinese Enterprise Management: Reforms in Economic Perspective*, Berlin, New York: Walter de Gruyter; S. Shi, 1995. A new system for utilising human resources. *Laodong Jinji yu Renli Ziyuan Guanli (Labour Economy and Human Resource Management)*, vol. 9, Beijing: China People University Press, pp. 8–10.

13. P. Howard, 1991. Rice bowls and job security: The urban contract labour system. *The Australian Journal of Chinese Affairs*, vol. 25, pp. 93–114; M. Korzec, 1988. Contract labor, the 'right to work' and new labor laws in the People's Republic of China. *Comparative Economic Studies (ASE)*, vol. 30, no. 2, pp. 117–149; C. Riskin, 1987. *China's Political Economy: The Quest for Development Since 1949*. Oxford: Oxford University Press.

14. M. Branine, 1997. Change and continuity in Chinese employment relationships, *New Zealand Journal of Industrial Relations*, vol. 22, no. 1, pp. 77–94; Howard, Rice bowls and job security; M. Warner, 1995. *The Management of Human Resources in Chinese Industry*, London: St. Martin's Press.

15. S.M. Zhao, 1994. Human resource management in China, *Asia Pacific Journal of Human Resources*, vol. 32, no. 2, Winter, pp. 3–12.

16. This part is based on C.J. Zhu, and P.J. Dowling, 1998. Performance appraisal in China, in *International Management in China*, J. Selmer, ed. London: Routledge, in press.

17. T.L. Su, and Q.F. Zhu, eds. 1992. *Ren shi xue dao lun (Fundamentals of personnel)*, Beijing: Beijing Normal College Press; G. Young, 1989. Party reforms, in *China: Modernization in the 1980s*, Cheng, ed. Hong Kong: The Chinese University Press, pp. 61–93.

18. J.P. Burns, 1989. Civil service reform in contemporary China, in *China: Modernisation in the 1980s*, Cheng, ed. Hong Kong: The Chinese University Press, pp. 95–130.

19. Walder, *Communist Neo-traditionalism: Work and Authority in Chinese Industry*, p. 132.

20. D.H. Brown, and M. Branine, 1995. Managing people in China's foreign trade corporations: Some evidence of change, *The International Journal of Human Resource Management*, vol. 6, no. 1, February, pp. 159–175; Walder, *Communist Neo-traditionalism: Work and Authority in Chinese Industry.*

21. Su, and Zhu, *Ren shi xue dao lun (Fundamentals of personnel).*

22. Child, *Management in China During the Age of Reform*; Brown, and Branine, Managing people in China's foreign trade corporations: Some evidence of change; J.P. Burns, 1989. Civil service reform in contemporary China, in *China: Modernisation in the 1980s*, Cheng, ed. Hong Kong: The Chinese University Press, pp. 95–130; S.J. Han, 1992. *Renshi Guanli Xue (Personnel Management)*, Anhui, China: Anhui People's Press; 1986. *Renshi Guanlixue Gaiyao (Introduction to Personnel Management)*, L.K. Zhao, ed. Beijing: China Labor Press.

23. S. Chen, ed. 1990. *Contemporary Labour and Personnel Administration Handbook*, Shanghai, China: People Publishing House; Su, and Zhu, *Ren shi xue dao lun (Fundamentals of personnel).*

24. H.J. Lu, and H.Z. An, 1991. *Xiandai qiye laodong renshi guanli (Personnel and labor administration in contemporary enterprises)*, Beijing: China Labor Press; 1992. *Laodong xinzheng guanli zhishi daquan (Encyclopedia of labor administration)*, J.Z. Xia, ed. Beijing: China Labor Press.

25. S.M. Zhao, 1995. *Zhongguo qiye renli ziyuan guanli (Human resource management in China's enterprises)*, Nanjing, China: Nanjing University Press.

26. Zhu, and Dowling, Performance appraisal in China.

27. Brown, and Branine, Managing people in China's foreign trade corporations: Some evidence of change; J.F. Huang, 1994. *Xiandai qiye zuzhi yu renli ziyuan guanli (Modern enterprise organisation and human resource management)*, Beijing: People's Daily Press; Nyaw, Human resource management in the People's Republic of China.

28. 1998. This section is based on C.J. Zhu, H. De Cieri, and P.J. Dowling, The reform of employee compensation in China's industrial enterprises, Paper presented at the Sixth Conference on International Human Resource Management, June 22–25, Paderborn: Germany.

29. W.H. Li, 1991. *Zhongguo gongzi zhidu (China's wage system)*, Beijing: China Labor Press. See also, L.M. Shore, B.W. Eagle, and M.J.

Jedel, 1993. China-United States joint ventures: A typological model of goal congruence and cultural understanding and their importance for effective human resource management, *International Journal of Human Resource Management*, vol. 4, no. 1, pp. 67–84; 1997. *Gongzi yu gongzi zhengyi chuli shiwu (Wage and wage arbitration)*, X.L. Wang, ed. Beijing: People's Court Press; S.M. Zhao, 1995. *Zhongguo qiye renli ziyuan guanli (Human resource management in China's enterprises)*, Nanjing, China: Nanjing University Press; and Y. Zhu, and I. Campbell, 1996. Economic reform and the challenge of transforming labor regulation in China, *Labour and Industry*, vol. 7, no. 1, p. 33.

30. K. Chen, 1995. *The Chinese Economy in Transition: Micro Changes and Macro Implications*, Singapore: Singapore University Press; Y.C. Xu, 1996. Deepening and widening the economic reform in China: From enterprise reform to macroeconomic stability, *The Journal of Developing Areas*, vol. 30, April, pp. 361–384.

31. S. Jackson, 1988. Management and labour in Chinese industry: A review of the literature, *Labour and Industry*, vol. 1, no. 2, pp. 335–363; A. Takahara, 1992. *The Politics of Wage Policy in Post-Revolutionary China*, London: The Macmillan Press Ltd. The floating wage aimed to link individual wages to enterprise and/or individual performance, and the range of wage fluctuation was usually half or less of the total income. The structural wage was usually composed of four parts: basic pay, post (or job-related) pay, seniority pay (based on the length of service), and bonus. See also, Child, *Management in China During the Age of Reform*; Nyaw, Human resource management in the People's Republic of China.

32. 1992. *Gangwei jineng gongzi shishi wenda (The implementation of post-plus-skills wage system)*, X.Y. Hu, and P. He, eds. Beijing: Wage Research Institute of the Ministry of Labor of China.

33. J.S. Henley, and M.K. Nyaw, 1987. The development of work incentives in Chinese industrial enterprises–material versus nonmaterial incentives, in *Management Reform in China*, M. Warner, ed. London: France Pinter; O. Laaksonen, 1988. *Management in China During and After Mao*, Berlin, New York: Walter de Gruyter; J. Nelson, and J. Reeder, 1985. Labor relations in China, *California Management Review*, vol. 27, no. 4, pp. 13–32; H.S. Tu, and C.A. Jones, 1991. Human resource management issues in Sino-U.S. business ventures, *Akron Business and Economic Review*, vol. 22, no. 4, Winter, pp. 18–28.

34. Ding, Fields, and Akhtar, An empirical study of human resource management policies and practices in foreign-invested enterprises in China: The case of Shenzen Special Economic Zone; Goodall, and Warner, Human resources in Sino-foreign joint ventures: Selected case studies in Shanghai, compared with Beijing; M.H. Zhao, and T. Nichols, 1996. Management control of labor in state-owned enterprises: Cases from the textile industry, *The China Journal*, vol. 36, July, pp. 1–21.

35. This section is based in part on C.J. Zhu, 1997. Human resource development in China during the transition to a new economic system, *Asia Pacific Journal of Human Resources*, vol. 35, no. 3, pp. 19–44.

36. Y.T. Guan, ed. 1990. *Zhiye peixun gailun (An introduction to vocational training)*, Beijing: China's Labor Press; Zhao, Human resource management in China; and Yu, and Xin, *Qiye laodong guanlixue jichu (Introduction to enterprise labour management)*.

37. Su, and Zhu, *Ren shi xue dao lun (Fundamentals of personnel)*; J. Borgonjon, and W.R. Vanhonacker, 1992. Modernizing China's managers, *The China Business Review*, September–October, Special Report, p. 12; A.H. Chan, 1990. Managerial reforms in Chinese enterprises, in *Advances in Chinese Industrial Studies*, J. Child, and M. Lockett, eds. vol. 1, part A, London: JAI Press, pp. 167–177; and Y. Sha, 1987. The role of China's managing directors in the current economic reform, *International Labor Review*, vol. 26, no. 6, pp. 691–701.

38. Yu, and Xin, *Qiye laodong guanlixue jichu (Introduction to enterprise labour management)*.

39. Guan, *Zhiye peixun gailun (An introduction to vocational training)*; Zhao, Human resource management in China.

40. CVQDV (China Vocational Qualification Development and Verification), 1994. *Enhancing China's Vocational Qualification Verification System*, vol. 7, Beijing: Vocational Qualification Verification Centre of the Ministry of Labor.

41. Child, *Management in China During the Age of Reform*; M. Warner, 1993. Human resource management 'with Chinese characteristics,' *International Journal of Human Resource Management*, vol. 4, no. 1, pp. 45–65.

42. Y. Lu, 1994. Cross-century human resource development, *Laodong Jingji yu Renli Ziyuan Guanli (Labor Economy and Human*

*Resource Management)*, vol, 12, Beijing: China People's University, pp. 66–73.

43. M.A. Von Glinow, and M.B. Teagarden, 1990. Contextual determinants of human resource management effectiveness in international cooperative alliances: Evidence from the People's Republic of China, in *International Human Resource Management Review*, A. Nedd, ed. vol. 1, pp. 75–93; C.J. Zhu, 1997. Human resource development in China during the transition to a new economic system, *Asia Pacific Journal of Human Resources*, vol. 35, no. 3, pp. 19–44.

44. Yu, and Xin, *Qiye laodong guanlixue jichu (Introduction to enterprise labour management)*; Zhao, *Zhongguo qiye renli ziyuan guanli (Human resource management in China's enterprises)*.

45. M. Warner, 1997. Management-labour relations in the new Chinese economy, *Human Resource Management Journal*, vol. 7, no. 4, pp. 30–43: 40.

46. Beamish, The characteristics of joint ventures in the People's Republic of China.

47. Goodall, and Warner, 1997. Human resources in Sino-foreign joint ventures: Selected case studies in Shanghai, compared with Beijing.

48. J. Child, 1993. A foreign perspective on the management of people in China, in *Readings in Management, Organisation and Culture in East and Southeast Asia*, P. Blunt, and D. Richards, eds. Darwin: Northern Territory University Press, pp. 213–225; R.J. Fung, 1995. *Organizational Strategies for Cross-Cultural Cooperation: Management of Personnel in International Joint Ventures in Hong Kong and China*, The Netherlands: Eburon Publishers.

49. Fung, ibid.

50. A. Chan, 1995. The emerging patterns of industrial relations in China and the rise of two new labor movements, *China Information*, vol. IX, no. 4, pp. 36–59: 48.

51. Warner, Human resource management 'with Chinese characteristics,' p. 460.

52. Zhu, Human resource development in China.

53. R. Tomlinson, 1997. You get what you pay for, corporate recruiters in China find, *Fortune*, April 28, pp. 218–219.

54. G. Hofstede, 1993. Cultural constraints in management theories, *Academy of Management Executive*, vol. 7, no. 1, pp. 81–94.

55. Y. Zhao, 1995. 'Chinese' motivation theory and application in China: An overview, in *Effective Organizations and Social Values*, H.S.R. Kao, D. Sinha, and S.H. Ng, eds. New Delhi: Sage, p. 127.

56. P. Aiello, 1991. Building a joint venture in China: The case of Chrysler and the Beijing Jeep Corporation, *Journal of General Management*, vol. 17, no. 2, pp. 47–64; Ding, Fields, and Akhtar, An empirical study of human resource management policies and practices in foreign-invested enterprises in China: The case of Shenzen Special Economic Zone; A.G. Walder, 1991. Workers, managers and the state: The reform era and the political crisis of 1989, *China Quarterly*, vol. 127, pp. 247–492.

57. Zhu, De Cieri, and Dowling, The reform of employee compensation in China's industrial enterprises.

58. 1996. *The China Business Review*, July–August, p. 46; S. Melvin, and K. Sylvester, 1997. Shipping out, *The China Business Review*, May–June, pp. 30–34.

59. T.L. Kamis, 1996. Education for the PRC executive, *The China Business Review*, July–August, pp. 36–39.

60. S. Melvin, 1996. Training the troops, *The China Business Review*, March–April, pp. 22–28.

61. *Documents* 1997. Jiang Zemin's report—Hold high the great banner of Deng Xiaoping theory for an all-round advancement of the cause of building socialism with Chinese characteristics into the 21st century, *Beijing Review*, October 6–12, p. 20.

62. According to ranking in terms of purchasing power parity (PPP). See International Institute for Management Development (IMD), 1997. *The World Competitiveness Yearbook 1997*, Lausanne: IMD. The *Financial Times* gave a 1997 estimate of India's population in its June 24, 1997 Supplement on India. The 1991 Census records 846 million. Further statistical information about India can be accessed from the following website: http://www.meadv.gov.in/info/profile/intro.htm.

63. M. Tayeb, 1996. India: A non-tiger of Asia, *International Business Review*, vol. 5, no. 5, pp. 425–445.

64. 1997. *Financial Times*, Supplement on India, June 24, p. 26.

65. 1992. Rao's new dowry, *Far Eastern Economic Review*, February 20, p. 40.

66. Price Waterhouse, 1993. *Doing Business in India*, Calcutta: Price Waterhouse.

67. International Institute for Management Development (IMD), 1997. *The World Competitiveness Yearbook 1997*, Lausanne: IMD.

68. R. Geissbauer, and H. Siemsen, 1996. *Strategies for the Indian Market: Experiences of Indo-German Joint Ventures*, Bombay: Indo-German Chamber of Commerce.

69. Australian Department of Foreign Affairs and Trade, 1995. *Country Economic Brief: India*, Canberra: Department of Foreign Affairs and Trade.

70. 1996. Review of Information Technology, Part II, *Financial Times,* November.

71. 1997. India's software industry, *Financial Times*, Special Report, December.

72. Some U.S. studies, for example, record 50 percent of IJVs failing, while others put the figure as high as 70 percent. Consequently, writers in this area stress the importance of building up a relationship between the partners that will encourage cooperation and trust. See for example, S. Schuler, S.E. Jackson, P.J. Dowling, D.E. Welch, and H. De Cieri, 1991. Formation of an international joint venture: Davidson instrument panel, *Human Resource Planning*, vol. 14, no. 1, pp. 51–60. R.S. Schuler, P.J. Dowling, and H. De Cieri, 1992. The formation of an international joint venture: Marley automotive components, *European Management Journal*, vol. 10, no. 3, pp. 304–309.

73. J-L Schaun, 1988. How to control a joint venture even as a minority partner, *Journal of General Management*, vol. 14, no. 1, p. 5. For a summary of the literature on success factors, see P. Lorange, and G.J.B. Probst, 1987. Joint ventures as self-organizing systems: A key to successful joint venture design and implementation, *Columbia Journal of World Business*, vol. 22, no. 2, pp. 71–77.

74. M.A. Lyles, 1987. Common mistakes of joint venture experienced firms, *Columbia Journal of World Business*, vol. 22, no. 2, p. 80. See also, D. Lei, and J.W. Slocum, 1991. Global strategic alliances: Payoffs and pitfalls, *Organizational Dynamics*, Winter, pp. 44–62; W.F. Cascio, and M.G. Serapio, 1991. Human resource systems in an international alliance: The undoing of a done deal?, *Organizational Dynamics*, Winter, pp. 63–74.

75. 1994. East Asia Analytical Unit, *India's economy at the Midnight Hour: Australia's India Strategy*, Canberra: Department of Foreign Affairs. See also, S. Sen, 1996. Fettered by corruption, *Business India*, November 18–December 1, p. 186; H.B. Rajshekar, and

T. Raman, 1994. Awaiting the deluge, *Business India*, November 7–20, pp. 141–143.

76. D. Khambata, and R. Ajami, 1992. *International Business: Theory and Practice*, New York: Macmillan Publishing Company.

77. S.N. As-Saber, P.J. Dowling, and P.W. Liesch, (forthcoming). The role of human resource management in international joint ventures: A study of Australian-Indian joint ventures, *International Journal of Human Resource Management*.

78. S. Tomassen, L.S. Welch, and G. Benito, 1997. Norwegian companies in India: Operation mode choice, Paper presented at the 23rd Annual Meeting of the European International Business Academy, Stuttgart, December.

79. G. Hofstede, 1980. *Culture's Consequences*, Beverly Hills, CA: Sage Publications.

80. I.J. Sharma, 1994. The culture context of Indian managers, *Management and Labour Studies*, vol. 9, no. 2, pp. 72–80.

81. S. Shane, 1994. The effect of national culture on the choice between licensing and direct foreign investment, *Strategic Management Journal*, vol. 15, no. 8, pp. 627–642.

82. C.S.V. Ratnam, 1995. Economic liberalization and the transformation of industrial relations policies in India, in *Employment Relations in the Growing Asian Economies*, A. Verma, T.A. Kochan, and R.D. Lansbury, eds. London: Routledge.

83. The labor force in India has a reputation for being "militant and obstructionist." See R. Thakur, Restoring India's economic health, *Third World Quarterly*, vol. 14, no. 1, pp. 137–157. See also Ratnam, Economic liberalization and the transformation of industrial relations policies in India; P. Joshi, 1995. Liberalisation ushered problems for workers, *The Pioneer* (Delhi), December 30, p. 3; and Tayeb, India: A non-tiger of Asia.

84. H.C. Jain, and C.S.V. Ratnam, 1994. Affirmative action in employment for the scheduled castes and the scheduled tribes in India, *International Journal of Manpower*, vol. 15, pp. 6–25; and Sharma, The culture context of Indian managers.

85. See Tayeb, India: A non-tiger of Asia; and Ratnam, Economic liberalization and the transformation of industrial relations policies in India; and L. Clarke, and M.A. Von Glinow, 1996. From India to China: A cross-cultural comparative assessment of management practices in Asia, Paper presented at the 13th Pan-Pacific Conference, Chiba, Japan.

86. S.N. As-Saber, P.J. Dowling, and P.W. Liesch, 1997. The role of human resource management in international joint ventures: A study of Australian-Indian joint ventures, *Enhancing Global Business Knowledge Through Business, Government and Academic Community Interface: Surviving Change in the International Business Environment by Developing Dynamic Business Strategies and Policies*, Proceedings of Sixth World Business Congress, International Management Development Association, pp. 21–29. This trend is also observed by R. Jacob, 1992. India: Open for business, *Fortune*, August 10, pp. 20–24; and M. Vicziany, 1993. Australian companies in India: The ingredients for successful entry into the Indian market, in *Australia-India Economic Links: Past, Present and Future*, M. Vicziany, ed. Nedlands, Western Australia: Indian Ocean Centre for Peace Studies, pp. 24–83.

87. This case was prepared by D. Welch and is based on information obtained from Unilever's website, and a report by Miriam Jordan, 1997. Role model for the new multi-nationals, *Financial Times*, India Survey, June 24, *India Business*, p. 19.

88. *The Economist*, 1994. An Indian tiger, April 9, p. 15; and 1994. India's businesses: Blinking in the sunlight, April 9, pp. 76–78.

89. Price Waterhouse, *Doing Business in India*.

90. 1995. On the threshold of a take-off into high economic growth, *Asian Business Review*, June, pp. 22–24.

91. G. Koretz, 1996. Asia's getting the big raises, *Business Week*, November 4, p. 16.

92. S.N. As-Saber, P.W. Liesch, and P.J. Dowling, 1997. Human resource practices in international joint ventures: Preliminary evidence from Australian-Indian joint ventures, *International Business Strategies for Asia-Pacific at the Dawn of the 21st Century*, Asia-Pacific Area Conference Proceedings, Academy of International Business, pp. 121–126.

93. D. Lei, and J.W. Slocum, 1991. Global strategic alliances: Payoffs and pitfalls, *Organizational Dynamics*, Winter, pp. 44–62.

94. P.J. Dowling, S.N. As-Saber, and P.W. Liesch, 1996. International joint ventures as a mechanism for accessing skills sets in culturally different societies: A case for Indo-Australian joint ventures in India, Paper presented at the 16th Annual International Strategic Management Society Conference, Phoenix, U.S.A., November 10–13.

95. Milton Friedman, a Nobel Prize winning economist, strongly endorses this view. See, for example, M. Friedman, 1970. The social responsibility of business is to increase its profits, *New York Times Magazine*, September 13, pp. 32–33, 122, 126.

96. See, for example, R.E. Freeman, 1997. A stakeholder theory of the modern corporation, in *Ethical Theory and Business*, T.L. Beauchamp, and N.E. Bowie, eds. 5th ed. Upper Saddle River, NJ: Prentice Hall, pp. 66–75.

97. The July 1997 special issue of *Business Ethics Quarterly* addresses the growing interconnectedness of ethical issues between international and domestic business. It also reports the proceedings of the First World Congress of Business, Economics and Ethics (1996).

98. For a more complete discussion of the factors impacting upon complexity in international business ethics, see R.T. De George, 1995. *Business Ethics*, 4th ed. Englewood Cliffs, NJ: Prentice Hall, pp. 475–485.

99. For a discussion of ethical relativism, see De George, ibid.

100. T. Donaldson, 1996. Values in tension: Ethics away from home, *Harvard Business Review*, September–October, pp. 48–62.

101. R.M. Green, 1994. *The Ethical Manager*, New York: Macillan, p. 62.

102. A number of comparative studies have found little variation from culture to culture in fundamental ethical beliefs. What differences existed between members of the various cultural groups, appeared to be more a function of differences in their reasoning and decision-making processes rather than core ethical values. See, for example, R. Abrat, D. Nel, and N.S. Higgs, 1992. An examination of the ethical beliefs of managers using selected scenarios in a cross-cultural environment, *Journal of Business Ethics*, vol. 11, pp. 29–35; D. Izraeli, 1988. Ethical beliefs and behavior among managers: A cross-cultural perspective, *Journal of Business Ethics*, vol. 7, pp. 263–271; M. Nyaw, and I. Ng, 1994. A comparative analysis of ethical beliefs: A four country study, *Journal of Business Ethics*, vol. 13, no. 7, pp. 543–556; M.W. Small, 1992. Attitudes towards business ethics held by Western Australian students: A comparative study, *Journal of Business Ethics*, vol. 11, pp. 745–752; J. Tsalikis, and D.J. Fritzsche, 1989. Business ethics: A literature review with a focus on marketing ethics, *Journal of Business Ethics*, vol. 8, pp. 695–743; J. Tsalikis, and O. Nwachukwu, 1989. An in-

vestigation on the ethical beliefs: Differences between Greeks and Americans, *Journal of International Consumer Marketing*, Spring, vol. 1; J. Tsalikis, and O. Nwachukwu, 1991. A comparison of Nigerian to American views of bribery and extortion in international commerce, *Journal of Business Ethics*, vol. 10, pp. 85–98.

103. Donaldson, Values in tension: Ethics away from home.

104. Ironically, the market mechanism itself may yet provide a potent mechanism for multinationals to be good corporate citizens as investors as well as the broader communities of many countries demand greater corporate responsibility than was generally evident during the profligate 1980s. See, for example, D. Spar, 1998. The spotlight and the bottom line, *Foreign Affairs*, vol. 77, no. 2, pp. 7–12.

105. Preamble to the Caux Round Table Principles. Available from *Business Ethics*, 52 S. 10th St., Suite 110, Minneapolis, MN 55403. Reprinted in L.P. Hartman, 1998. *Perspectives in Business Ethics*, Chicago: McGraw-Hill, pp. 723–726. See also web site: www.bath.ac.uk/Centres/Ethical/Papers/caux.htm.

106. A useful description and discussion of multilateral compacts is given by R.A. Buchholz, 1995. *Business Environment and Public Policy Implications for Management*, Upper Saddle River, NJ: Prentice Hall, Chapter 16.

107. D. Payne, C. Raiborn, and J. Askvik, 1997. A global code of business ethics, *Journal of Business Ethics*, vol. 16, no. 16, pp. 1727–1735.

108. For a comprehensive set of guidelines derived from international codes, see W.C. Frederick, 1991. The moral authority of transnational corporate codes, in *Ethical Theory and Business*, T.L. Beuchamp, and N.E. Bowie, eds. pp. 576–588.

109. Donaldson, Values in tension: Ethics away from home.

110. J.R. Boatright, 1997. *Ethics and the Conduct of Business*, 2d ed. Upper Saddle River, NJ: Prentice Hall.

111. See Green, *The Ethical Manager*, p. 290 for a list of practices that pose the most frequent problems for international managers.

112. J. Macken, 1998. Dirty money, *The Australian Financial Review*, March 31, p. 13.

113. An interesting nongovernment lobby group in this field is the Berlin-based *Transparency International (TI)* group, which publishes an annual Corruption Perception Index. For an up-to-

date TI Corruption Index consult the Internet at http://www/gwdg.de/~uwvw/icr.htm.

114. T.L. Carson, 1984. Bribery, extortion, and the foreign corrupt practices act, *Philosophy and Public Affairs*, pp. 66–90.

115. De George, *Business Ethics.*

116. M. Alvesson, and P.O. Berg, 1992. *Corporate Culture and Organizational Symbolism*, Berlin: Walter de Gruyter.

117. Cited in Hartman, *Perspectives in Business Ethics.*

118. J. Bonache, and Z. Fernandez, 1997. Expatriate compensation and its link to the subsidiary strategic role: A theoretical analysis, *Journal of International Human Resource Management*, vol. 8, no. 4, pp. 457–475; L.K. Stroh, and P.M. Caligiuri, 1998. Strategic human resources: A new source for competitive advantage in the global arena, *International Journal of Human Resource Management*, vol. 9, no. 1, pp. 1–17.

119. H. De Cieri, and P.J. Dowling, 1998 (forthcoming). Strategic human resource management in multinational enterprises: Theoretical and empirical developments, in *Research and Theory in SHRM: An Agenda for the 21st Century*, Wright et. al., eds. Greenwich, CT: JAI Press. This section of the chapter draws from the material in this article.

120. R.S. Schuler, P.J. Dowling, and H. De Cieri, 1993. An integrative framework of strategic international human resource management, *Journal of Management*, vol. 19, pp. 419–459.

121. Ibid.

122. S. Taylor, S. Beechler, and N. Napier, 1996. Towards an integrative model of strategic international human resource management, *Academy of Management Review*, vol. 21, pp. 959–985; K. Kamoche, 1997. Knowledge creation and learning in international HRM, *International Journal of Human Resource Management*, vol. 8, pp. 213–222.

123. B. Becker, and B. Gerhart, 1996. The impact of human resource management on organizational performance: Progress and prospects, *Academy of Management Journal*, vol. 39, no. 4, pp. 779–801; L. Dyer, and T. Reeves, 1995. Human resource strategies and firm performance: What do we know and where do we need to go?, *International Journal of Human Resource Management*, vol. 6, pp. 656–670.

124. M. Festing, 1997. International human resource management strategies in multinational corporations: Theoretical assumptions and empirical evidence from German firms, *Management International Review*, vol. 37, no. 1, special issue, pp. 43–63; S.J. Kobrin, 1994. Is there a relationship between a geocentric mind-set and multinational strategy?, *Journal of International Business Studies*, vol. 25, pp. 493–511.

125. P.M. Caligiuri, and L.K. Stroh, 1995. Multinational corporate management strategies and international human resource practices: Bringing IHRM to the bottom line, *International Journal of Human Resource Management*, vol. 6, pp. 494–507; R.B. Peterson, J. Sargent, N.K. Napier, and W.S. Shim, 1996. Corporate expatriate HRM policies, internationalization, and performance in the world's largest MNCs, *Management International Review*, vol. 36, pp. 215–230; P. Sparrow, R.S. Schuler, and S.E. Jackson, 1994. Convergence or divergence: Human resource practices and policies for competitive advantage worldwide, *International Journal of Human Resource Management*, vol. 5, pp. 267–299.

# A P P E N D I X

## PART A: RESEARCH ISSUES

The field of international HRM, like that of international management, has yet to build a rigorous body of theory. For example, Schollhammer[1] noted that much of the field of international management was criticized as being descriptive and lacking in analytical rigor, ad hoc and expedient in research design and planning, self-centered in the sense that existing research literature is frequently ignored, and lacking a sustained research effort to develop case material.

To a certain extent, these criticisms remain valid some 23 years later. There are several reasons for this. First, until recently, the field has tended to be regarded by many management and HRM researchers as a marginal academic area. This attitude is reflected in the relatively small number of stand-alone courses in IHRM on the teaching side, and the lack of visibility of IHRM researchers at international business conferences. One could add that the dominance of economics in the international business field to date, with its focus on foreign direct investment, is a contributing factor here.

A second reason for the lack of international research is cost. International studies are invariably more expensive than domestic studies, and this is a liability for international researchers in a competitive research funding environment.[2] In addition, international research takes more time, involves more travel, and frequently requires the cooperation of host-country organizations, government officials, and researchers. Development of a stream of research is consequently much more difficult.

Third, there are major methodological problems involved in the area of international management and HRM. These problems greatly increase the complexity of doing international research and, as Adler[3] has noted, frequently are impossible to solve with the rigor usually required of within-culture studies by journal editors and reviewers. The major methodological problems in this area are:

- Defining culture;
- The emic–etic distinction;
- Static group comparisons; and
- Translation and stimulus equivalence.

The problems of defining culture and the emic–etic distinction were discussed in Chapter 1. In this appendix, we briefly explore the remaining two problem areas.

## Static Group Comparisons

An enduring issue in international research is that virtually all crosscultural comparisons are based on "static group designs."[4] The difficulty with static group comparisons in international research is that subjects are not randomly assigned from a superordinate population to different levels of a treatment variable. In practice, it is impossible for crosscultural researchers to avoid this methodological problem. Ill-defined notions of culture as an independent variable further compound this difficulty. As Malpass[5] has observed,

> No matter what attribute of culture the investigator prefers to focus upon or to interpret as the causative variable, any other variable correlated with the alleged causative variable could potentially serve in an alternative explanation of a mean difference between two or more local populations.

As a practical solution to this problem, Malpass recommends that investigators attempt to obtain data on as many rival explanations as possible and then demonstrate that they are less plausible (by conducting post hoc statistical analyses, for example) than the investigator's favored interpretation.[6]

## Translation and Stimulus Equivalence

Another issue in international research is that of translation and stimulus equivalence. Researchers need to be aware that problems may arise when translating concepts central to one culture into the language of another culture. Triandis and Brislin[7] note that the problem of translation has received a great deal of attention in the literature[8] and that translation problems should be "a starting point for research rather than a frustrating end to one's aspirations for data collection." Using methods such as the decentering technique,[9] which involves translating from the original to the target language and back again through several iterations, a researcher can test to see if there is any emic coloring of the concepts under investigation. If there are few differences between the original and target translation, then stimulus equivalence has been demonstrated.

Stimulus equivalence problems may also arise on a more subtle level when the researcher and target population speak the same language and national differences are less obvious (in the case, for example, of a U.S. researcher studying Australian managers).

A related point is the need for non-native speakers to translate research findings into English for publication in English language journals. Again, techniques such as decentering are important because the language used during the data collection stage differs from that used at the reporting stage. This applies to within-country as well as across-country studies. It is particularly critical for qualitative data such as that obtained through open-ended items on mail questionnaires and interviews. As with the emic–etic distinction, awareness of possible problems is a precondition for dealing with translation and stimulus equivalence problems.

Different cultures have different attitudes towards mail questionnaires and this may influence a poor response rate. Commenting on the difficulties of conducting large scale, crossnational surveys, Harzing[10] bemoans the paucity of articles that an international business researcher can consult for assistance. She compares this with the wealth of information available about, and congruency of opinion on, conducting mail surveys in a domestic setting. Harzing found, in her study of multinationals operating in 22 countries, that the higher the cultural distance between the country of the researcher (the sender) and the targeted country (the receiver), the lower the response rate. She admits that using English as the language of the questionnaire was probably a contributing factor and speculates that the international orientation of the respondent may have a positive influence on the response rate.

## PART B:  RESOURCES IN INTERNATIONAL HRM

This section contains a short review of major resources that may be helpful for additional material for teaching and research purposes. It is meant only as a starting point and as a way of illustrating the diverse nature of resources now available through electronic databases. We leave it up to the individual to "surf the Net" and explore firms' home pages.

## IHRM-Related Web Sites

http://www.shrm.org/hrlinks/intl.htm
This is the (U.S.) Society for Human Resource Management (SHRM) home page list of International HR web sites.

http://www.shrm.org/docs/IIHR.html
Homepage of the Institute for International HR, a division of the Society for Human Resource Management (SHRM).

This home page is valuable in its details of the *International Human Resource Management Reference Guide*, mentioned later in this Appendix.

http://www.the-hrnet.com/
This is the Web site for Human Resource Professionals worldwide.

http://www.cba.hawaii.edu/aib/
The Academy of International Business home page.

http://www.arthurandersen.com/hcs/globalhr/linkhr.htm
Arthur Andersen–International Executive Services: IHRM Link. A list of Arthur Andersen services related to global HRM and expatriation, and links to other web sites relevant to IHRM. For example, one can obtain details of the results of the R.L Tung–Arthur Andersen survey entitled, A study of the expatriation/repatriation process, referred to in this text, particularly Chapters 3 and 7.

http://www.mcb.co.uk/apmforum/nethome.htm
Produced by MCB publishers, this has more general Asia-Pacific management information.

http://www.ihrim.org/
Home page of the International Association for Human Resource Information Management.

http://www.hrhq.com/index.html
Includes access to a searchable database of 194 articles from *Personnel Journal*.

http://www.ipma-hr.org/
Home page of the International Personnel Management Association (IPMA), a professional association for public personnel professionals, primarily those who work in federal, state, or local government.

The page includes a list of useful HRM sites around the world.

http://www.ipd.co.uk/
Home page of the Institute of Personnel and Development, UK.

http://www.workindex.com/
A search engine (based at Cornell University) targeting work and HR-related web sites.

http://www.euen.co.uk/
The EU Employers' Network and the Personnel Policy Research Unit.

http://www.library.yale.edu/govdocs/euinfor.html
This has links to European Institutions, journal and official European Union texts.

http://www.eurunion.org/
The U.S. site of the European Union.

http://www.ibrc.bschool.ukans.edu/index.htm
The Kansas University International Business Resource Center home page. Aimed at small and medium-sized companies, this web site includes a good list of other web sites.

http://ciber.bus.msu.edu/
The World Wide Web server of the Center for International Business Education and Research (CIBER) at Michigan State University.

http://ciber.centers.purdue.edu/
CIBERWeb, the Internet Hub of the USA's Centers for International Business Education and Research.

http://dylee.keel.econ.ship.edu/intntl/int_home.htm
A list of internet resources for international economics and business.

http://www.webcom.com/one/world/
International business kiosk includes basic information, for example, time zones, voltage, accommodation, car rentals, visa information.

http://www.ita.doc.gov/
This site is produced and maintained by the International Trade Administration, U.S. Department of Commerce.

http://www.windhamint.com/
Windham International's web site provides information about international relocation and expatriate management.

http://www.erc.org/
Employee Relocation Council's web site provides information about international relocation and expatriate management.

http://www.fedworld.gov/
Fedworld information network.

http://www.expatworld.com/
Magazine for expatriates.

http://www.livingabroad.com/
Magazine for expatriates.

http://www.expatforum.com/
Another site aimed at expatriates, with a chat line.

http://www.hbsp.harvard.edu
CD-Rom interactive program on managing across cultures.

http://www.travalang.com/
Online language lessons.

http://www.unicc.org/unctad/en/aboutorg/inbrief.htm
United Nations Centre on Transnational Corporations and International Trade.

http://www.gwdg.de/-uwvw/icr.htm
Transparency International's Corruption Index—ranks over 50 countries on perceived level of corruption.

## Other Resources

The Institute for International Human Resources, a division of the Society for Human Resource Management, produces a *Reference Guide* that is updated regularly. It lists resource organizations, expatriate policies, embassy listings, and web sites. It contains a glossary of terms used in IHRM, classified and alphabetically grouped into six major HRM functional areas: Management Practices, Employment, Training and Development, Employee and External Relations, Compensation and Benefits, and other HRM (such as travel).

*The 1997–98 International Human Resource Management Reference Guide* can be obtained from the SHRM Store, P.O. Box 930, Atlanta, GA 31193. The cost is U.S.$75 per copy (overseas rate U.S.$85 per copy U.S.$/U.S. Bank). Further details can be obtained by visiting the home page listed above.

## ENDNOTES

1. H. Schollhammer, 1975. Current research in international and comparative management issues, *Management International Review*, vol. 15, no. 2–3, pp. 29–40.
2. See N. Adler, 1983. Cross-cultural management research: The ostrich and the trend, *Academy of Management Review*, vol. 8, pp. 226–232.
3. Ibid.
4. See R.S. Bhagat, and S.J. McQuaid, 1982. Role of subjective culture in organizations: A review and directions for future research, *Journal of Applied Psychology*, vol. 67, pp. 653–685; D.T. Campbell, and J. Stanley, 1966. *Experimental and Quasi-Experimental Design for Research*, Chicago: Rand-McNally; and R.S. Malpass, 1977. Theory and method in cross-cultural psychology, *American Psychologist*, vol. 32, pp. 1069–1079.
5. Malpass, Theory and method, p. 1071.
6. See L. Kelly, and R. Worthley, 1981. The role of culture in comparative management: A cross-cultural perspective, *Academy of Management Journal*, vol. 24, pp. 164–173; and P.J. Dowling, and T.W. Nagel, 1986. Nationality and work attitudes: A study of Australian and American business majors, *Journal of Management*, vol. 12, pp. 121–128, for further discussion on this point.
7. H.C. Triandis, and R.W. Brislin, 1984. Cross-cultural psychology, *American Psychologist*, vol. 39, pp. 1006–1016.
8. See R. Brislin, 1976. *Translation: Applications and Research*, New York: Gardner Press, for a review of this literature.
9. O. Werner, and D. Campbell, 1970. Translating, working through interpreters, and the problem of decentering, in *A Handbook of*

*Method in Cultural Anthropology*, R. Naroll, and R. Cohen, eds. New York: Natural History Press.

10. A-V. Harzing, 1997. Response rates in international mail surveys: Results of a 22-country study, *International Business Review*, vol. 6, no. 6, pp. 641–665.